THE BOOK

Volvo 300 Series
Service and Repair Manual

Colin Brown

(715-320-2Y7)

Models covered

All Volvo 340, 343 & 345 models; 1397 cc & 1721 cc
All Volvo 360 models; 1986 cc

Does not cover LPG conversion

ABCDE
FGHIJ

2

© Haynes Publishing 1996

A book in the **Haynes Service and Repair Manual Series**

All rights reserved. No part of this book may be reproduced or transmitted in any form or by any means, electronic or mechanical, including photocopying, recording or by any information storage or retrieval system, without permission in writing from the copyright holder.

ISBN **1 85960 231 2**

British Library Cataloguing in Publication Data
A catalogue record for this book is available from the British Library.

Printed by **J H Haynes & Co. Ltd, Sparkford, Nr Yeovil, Somerset BA22 7JJ**

Haynes Publishing
Sparkford, Nr Yeovil, Somerset BA22 7JJ, England

Haynes North America, Inc
861 Lawrence Drive, Newbury Park, California 91320, USA

Editions Haynes S.A.
147/149, rue Saint Honoré, 75001 PARIS, France

Contents

LIVING WITH YOUR VOLVO

Routine Maintenance

Roadside Repairs

Recommended Lubricants and Fluids

Contents

Introduction to the Volvo 300 Series

The Volvo 343 three-door Hatchback was introduced in the UK in September 1976, being built with traditional Volvo expertise, and incorporating many safety features such as impact bars in the side doors. The first models were available only with the double belt continuously variable (CVT) automatic transmission, which was carried over from the Volvo 66 model. Manual versions became available in September 1978 and were fitted with a rear mounted manual gearbox similar to that fitted to the 240 series.

The 345 five-door Hatchback models were introduced in January 1980.

In 1982 the models were redesignated 340 DL and GL, and at the same time the 360 Series was introduced with a 2 litre engine and transmission torque tube. The top of the range GLE model was introduced in late 1983 and incorporated a boot. It was available with a carburettor or fuel injection engine.

In May 1985 the 360 GLS was redesignated the GL and in August of the same year the 1.7 litre 340 GL and GLE were introduced.

Both 340 and 360 models have received periodic updates to incorporate a number of modern motoring developments; maintaining Volvo's reputation for safety and solid dependability.

Acknowledgements

Thanks are due to Champion Spark Plug who supplied the illustrations showing spark plug conditions. Certain other illustrations are the copyright of AB Volvo, and are used with their permission. The cars used for workshop and photographic purposes were kindly loaned by F W B Saunders of Sherborne, Dorset and the Yeovil Motor Company of Yeovil, Somerset. Thanks are also due to Sykes-Pickavant Limited, who provided some of the workshop tools, and to all those people at Sparkford who helped in the production of this manual.

We take great pride in the accuracy of information given in this manual, but vehicle manufacturers make alterations and design changes during the production run of a particular vehicle of which they do not inform us. No liability can be accepted by the authors or publishers for loss, damage or injury caused by errors in, or omissions from, the information given.

Project vehicles

The vehicles used in the preparation of this manual, and appearing in many of the photographic sequences, were an early Volvo 343, a 360 GLEi, a 360 GLS with B200 engine, and a 340 GL with B172 engine.

Volvo 340 GL Hatchback

Volvo 360 GLE Saloon

Working on your car can be dangerous. This page shows just some of the potential risks and hazards, with the aim of creating a safety-conscious attitude.

General hazards

Scalding

• Don't remove the radiator or expansion tank cap while the engine is hot.
• Engine oil, automatic transmission fluid or power steering fluid may also be dangerously hot if the engine has recently been running.

Burning

• Beware of burns from the exhaust system and from any part of the engine. Brake discs and drums can also be extremely hot immediately after use.

Crushing

• When working under or near a raised vehicle, always supplement the jack with axle stands, or use drive-on ramps. *Never venture under a car which is only supported by a jack.*
• Take care if loosening or tightening high-torque nuts when the vehicle is on stands. Initial loosening and final tightening should be done with the wheels on the ground.

Fire

• Fuel is highly flammable; fuel vapour is explosive.
• Don't let fuel spill onto a hot engine.
• Do not smoke or allow naked lights (including pilot lights) anywhere near a vehicle being worked on. Also beware of creating sparks (electrically or by use of tools).
• Fuel vapour is heavier than air, so don't work on the fuel system with the vehicle over an inspection pit.
• Another cause of fire is an electrical overload or short-circuit. Take care when repairing or modifying the vehicle wiring.
• Keep a fire extinguisher handy, of a type suitable for use on fuel and electrical fires.

Electric shock

• Ignition HT voltage can be dangerous, especially to people with heart problems or a pacemaker. Don't work on or near the ignition system with the engine running or the ignition switched on.

• Mains voltage is also dangerous. Make sure that any mains-operated equipment is correctly earthed. Mains power points should be protected by a residual current device (RCD) circuit breaker.

Fume or gas intoxication

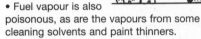

• Exhaust fumes are poisonous; they often contain carbon monoxide, which is rapidly fatal if inhaled. Never run the engine in a confined space such as a garage with the doors shut.
• Fuel vapour is also poisonous, as are the vapours from some cleaning solvents and paint thinners.

Poisonous or irritant substances

• Avoid skin contact with battery acid and with any fuel, fluid or lubricant, especially antifreeze, brake hydraulic fluid and Diesel fuel. Don't syphon them by mouth. If such a substance is swallowed or gets into the eyes, seek medical advice.
• Prolonged contact with used engine oil can cause skin cancer. Wear gloves or use a barrier cream if necessary. Change out of oil-soaked clothes and do not keep oily rags in your pocket.
• Air conditioning refrigerant forms a poisonous gas if exposed to a naked flame (including a cigarette). It can also cause skin burns on contact.

Asbestos

• Asbestos dust can cause cancer if inhaled or swallowed. Asbestos may be found in gaskets and in brake and clutch linings. When dealing with such components it is safest to assume that they contain asbestos.

Special hazards

Hydrofluoric acid

• This extremely corrosive acid is formed when certain types of synthetic rubber, found in some O-rings, oil seals, fuel hoses etc, are exposed to temperatures above 400°C. The rubber changes into a charred or sticky substance containing the acid. *Once formed, the acid remains dangerous for years. If it gets onto the skin, it may be necessary to amputate the limb concerned.*
• When dealing with a vehicle which has suffered a fire, or with components salvaged from such a vehicle, wear protective gloves and discard them after use.

The battery

• Batteries contain sulphuric acid, which attacks clothing, eyes and skin. Take care when topping-up or carrying the battery.
• The hydrogen gas given off by the battery is highly explosive. Never cause a spark or allow a naked light nearby. Be careful when connecting and disconnecting battery chargers or jump leads.

Air bags

• Air bags can cause injury if they go off accidentally. Take care when removing the steering wheel and/or facia. Special storage instructions may apply.

Diesel injection equipment

• Diesel injection pumps supply fuel at very high pressure. Take care when working on the fuel injectors and fuel pipes.

⚠ *Warning: Never expose the hands, face or any other part of the body to injector spray; the fuel can penetrate the skin with potentially fatal results.*

Remember...

DO

• Do use eye protection when using power tools, and when working under the vehicle.
• Do wear gloves or use barrier cream to protect your hands when necessary.
• Do get someone to check periodically that all is well when working alone on the vehicle.
• Do keep loose clothing and long hair well out of the way of moving mechanical parts.
• Do remove rings, wristwatch etc, before working on the vehicle – especially the electrical system.
• Do ensure that any lifting or jacking equipment has a safe working load rating adequate for the job.

DON'T

• Don't attempt to lift a heavy component which may be beyond your capability – get assistance.
• Don't rush to finish a job, or take unverified short cuts.
• Don't use ill-fitting tools which may slip and cause injury.
• Don't leave tools or parts lying around where someone can trip over them. Mop up oil and fuel spills at once.
• Don't allow children or pets to play in or near a vehicle being worked on.

Dimensions

Overall length:
Models up to 1981 .... 165.4 in (4200 mm)
1982 models .... 166.7 in (4235 mm)
Models from 1982 to 1989:
  Hatchback .... 169.3 in (4300 mm)
  Saloon .... 173.8 in (4415 mm)
Models from 1989:
  Hatchback .... 170.2 in (4380 mm)
  Saloon .... 175.3 in (4450 mm)
Overall width .... 65.4 in (1660 mm)
Overall height (unladen):
340 series:
  Up to 1984 .... 56.7 in (1440 mm)
  From 1984 .... 56.3 in (1430 mm)
360 series:
  Carburettor:
  Models up to 1982 .... 57.1 in (1450 mm)
  1982 and 1983 models .... 56.7 in (1440 mm)
  Models from 1984 .... 56.3 in (1430 mm)
  Fuel injection:
  1983 models .... 56.0 in (1423 mm)
  1984 models .... 56.3 in (1430 mm)
  Models from 1985 .... 55.9 in (1420 mm)
Wheelbase:
340 series (except 1.7 litre) .... 94.3 in (2395 mm)
360 series and 1.7 litre .... 94.5 in (2400 mm)
Track (front):
340 series:
  Models up to 1980 .... 53.1 in (1350 mm)
  Models from 1980 .... 53.9 in (1370 mm)
360 series .... 54.3 in (1380 mm)
Track (rear):
340 series:
  Models up to 1980 .... 54.3 in (1380 mm)
  Models from 1980 .... 55.1 in (1400 mm)
360 series .... 55.3 in (1405 mm)
Turning circle (between kerbs):
340 series (except 1.7 litre) .... 30.2 ft (9.20 m)
360 series and 1.7 litre .... 30.7 ft (9.35 m)

Capacities

Engine oil - at oil and filter change:	
1.4 litre models	7.0 pints (4.0 litres)
1.7 litre models	8.8 pints (5.0 litres)
2.0 litre models	7.9 pints (4.5 litres)
Amount required to raise oil level from dipstick MIN to MAX marks:	
1.4 and 2.0 litre models	1.8 pints (1.0 litre)
1.7 litre models	2.6 pints (1.5 litres)
Cooling system (including expansion tank):	
B14 (up to 1989)	9.2 pints (5.2 litres)
B14 (1989 on)	11.5 pints (6.5 litres)
B172	14.1 pints (8.0 litres)
B19:	
Models up to 1982	14.1 pints (8.0 litres)
Models from 1982	12.3 pints (7.0 litres)
B200	12.3 pints (7.0 litres)
Automatic transmission:	
Primary gear case	1.0 pint (0.55 litre)
Secondary gear case	1.8 pints (1.0 litre)
Manual gearbox (total):	
Four-speed:	
Models up to 1984	3.7 pints (2.10 litres)
Models from 1984	4.1 pints (2.35 litres)
Five-speed:	
Plug at rear	4.8 pints (2.70 litres)
Plug at front:	
Models up to 1985	6.2 pints (3.50 litres)
Models from 1985 to 1989	5.3 pints (3.0 litres)
Models from 1989	4.9 pints (2.8 litres)
Final drive unit:	
B14:	
Models up to 1982	2.6 pints (1.45 litres)
Models from 1982	2.4 pints (1.35 litres)
B172	2.4 pints (1.35 litres)
B19 and B200:	
Four-speed	2.6 pints (1.50 litres)
Five-speed	2.4 pints (1.35 litres)
Fuel tank:	
340 Series	9.9 gal (45 litres)
360 Series	12.5 gal (57 litres)

Weights

	3-door	4-door	5-door
Kerb weight:			
B14 automatic:			
Models up to 1984	2160 lb (980 kg)	-	2216 lb (1005 kg)
Models from 1984 to 1986	2152 lb (976 kg)	2072 lb (940 kg)	2196 lb (996 kg)
Models from 1986	2176 lb (987 kg)	-	2229 lb (1011 kg)
B14 manual:			
Models up to 1984	2105 lb (955 kg)	-	2160 lb (980 kg)
Models from 1984 to 1986	2099 lb (952 kg)	2110 lb (957 kg)	2143 lb (972 kg)
Models from 1986	2116 lb (960 kg)	-	2172 lb (985 kg)
B172 . . .2167 lb (983 kg)	2209 lb (1002 kg)		
B19 and B200 (carburettor)	2372 lb (1076 kg)	2370 lb (1075 kg)	2414 lb (1095 kg)
B19 and B200 (fuel injection)	2425 lb (1100 kg)	2410 lb (1093 kg)	2467 lb (1119 kg)
Maximum permissible weight:			
B14 automatic	3197 lb (1450 kg)		
B14 manual	3131 lb (1420 kg)		
B172	3263 lb (1480 kg)		
B19 and B200	3395 lb (1540 kg)		
Trailer weight (maximum):			
B14 automatic	1984 lb (900 kg)		
B14 manual	2205 lb (1000 kg)		
B172	2205 lb (1000 kg)		
B19 and B200	2646 lb (1200 kg)		
Roof rack load (maximum):			
B14 automatic	99 lb (45 kg)		
B14 manual	110 lb (50 kg)		
B172	110 lb (50 kg)		
B19 and B200	132 lb (60 kg)		

For modifications, and information applicable to later models, see Supplement at end of manual

Maintenance is essential for ensuring safety, and desirable for the purpose of getting the best in terms of performance and economy from your car. Over the years the need for periodic lubrication - oiling, greasing and so on - has been drastically reduced, if not totally eliminated. This has unfortunately tended to lead some owners to think that because no such action is required, components either no longer exist, or will last forever. This is certainly not the case; it is essential to carry out regular visual examinations as comprehensively as possible in order to spot any possible defects at an early stage before they develop into major and expensive repairs.

The following Routine Maintenance schedule periods are recommended service intervals only. Where the vehicle is operated under extreme conditions, or used mainly for stop-start type driving, the intervals may need to be reduced.

Every 250 miles (400 km) or weekly - whichever comes first

- ☐ Check engine oil level
- ☐ Check coolant level
- ☐ Check brake fluid level
- ☐ Check tyre pressures
- ☐ Examine tyres for wear, cuts and damage
- ☐ Check and if necessary, top up the water reservoir adding a screen wash
- ☐ Check operation of all lights, horn(s) and other electrical circuits
- ☐ Check battery terminals for security
- ☐ Check battery electrolyte level

Every 6000 miles (10 000 km) or 6 months - whichever comes first

- ☐ Renew engine oil and filter
- ☐ Check valve clearances (B14 models)
- ☐ Check antifreeze concentration
- ☐ Check choke operation (carburettor models)
- ☐ Check CO level and idle speed
- ☐ Check warm start valve (B200K)
- ☐ Renew spark plugs
- ☐ Renew contact breaker points (conventional ignition)
- ☐ Check ignition timing (conventional ignition)
- ☐ Check the pulley gap on the automatic transmission
- ☐ Check gearbox and final drive for leaks
- ☐ Check alternator for cleanliness and security

Every 12 000 miles (20 000 km) or 12 months - whichever comes first

In addition to the 6000 mile service

- ☐ Check engine for leaks and cleanliness
- ☐ Check alternator drivebelt tension (B14, B19 and B200 models)
- ☐ Check coolant hoses for leaks
- ☐ Check exhaust system for leaks and security
- ☐ Check fuel lines for leaks and security
- ☐ Check carburettor dashpot oil level (B19A models)
- ☐ Check fuel filter for blockages (carburettor models)
- ☐ Lubricate the distributor (where applicable)
- ☐ Check clutch for wear and adjustment
- ☐ Lubricate the clutch pedal pivot
- ☐ Check transmission oil/fluid level
- ☐ Check transmission for leaks
- ☐ Check propeller shaft, centre bearing and joint for wear and damage
- ☐ Check the vacuum microswitch (automatic transmission models)
- ☐ Check vacuum servo operation
- ☐ Renew servo air filter
- ☐ Check handbrake adjustment
- ☐ Check pads/shoes for wear
- ☐ Check hydraulic hoses and pipelines for leaks and security
- ☐ Check steering gear for wear, damage and leaks
- ☐ Check suspension for wear, damage and leaks
- ☐ Check all suspension and steering nuts and bolts for tightness
- ☐ Lubricate door, bonnet and boot hinges
- ☐ Check underseal and paintwork for condition
- ☐ Check battery specific gravity

Every 24 000 miles (40 000 km) or 2 years - whichever comes first

In addition to the 12 000 mile service

- ☐ Clean crankcase ventilation system hoses
- ☐ Check valve clearances (B19 and B200 models)
- ☐ Renew coolant
- ☐ Renew air filter
- ☐ Renew fuel filter(s)
- ☐ Renew fluid (automatic models)
- ☐ Check propeller shaft joints for wear
- ☐ Renew brake fluid
- ☐ Check and adjust front wheel bearings

Every 48 000 miles (80 000 km) or 4 years - whichever comes first

In addition to the 24 000 mile service

- ☐ Check valve clearances (B172 models)
- ☐ Renew timing belt (B172, B19 and B200 models)

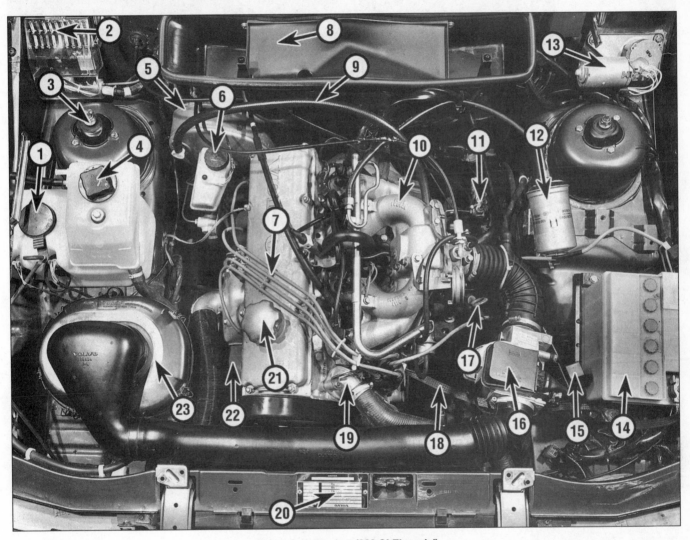

Under-bonnet view (360 GLEi model)

1 Washer reservoir
2 Fusebox
3 Front suspension strut upper mounting
4 Cooling system filler cap
5 Brake servo unit
6 Brake fluid reservoir filler cap
7 Ignition HT leads
8 Heater air inlet
9 Brake servo vacuum hose
10 Inlet manifold
11 Brake pressure-conscious reducing valve
12 Fuel filter (LE-Jetronic)
13 Windscreen wiper motor
14 Battery
15 Fuel injection control relay (LE-Jetronic)
16 Airflow meter (LE-Jetronic)
17 Engine oil dipstick
18 Distributor
19 Thermostat housing
20 Vehicle identification plate
21 Engine oil filler cap
22 Exhaust manifold
23 Air cleaner

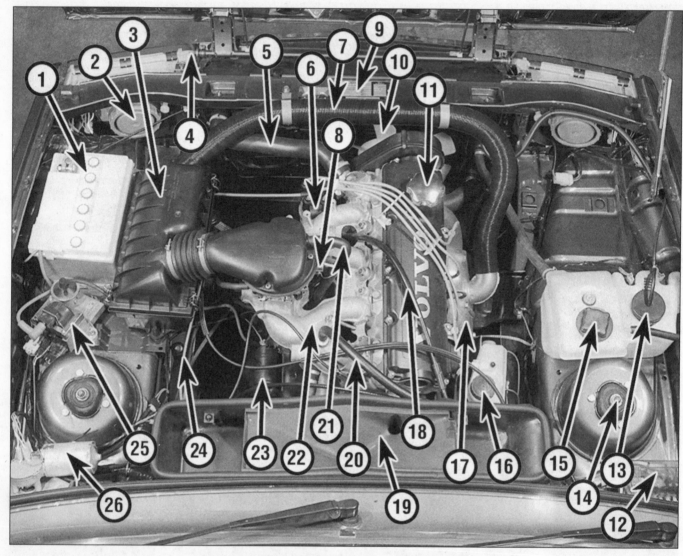

Under-bonnet view (360 GLS with B200 engine)

1 Battery
2 Headlamp rear cover
3 Air cleaner
4 Bonnet hinge
5 Radiator top hose
6 Distributor cap
7 Air cleaner warm air duct
8 Idle solenoid

9 Vehicle identification plate
10 Cooling fan
11 Engine oil filler cap
12 Fusebox and relays
13 Washer reservoir
14 Front suspension strut upper
   mounting

15 Cooling system filler cap and
   expansion tank
16 Brake fluid reservoir filler cap
17 Exhaust manifold and warm
   air shroud
18 Clutch cable
19 Heater intake
20 Brake vacuum servo hose

21 Crankcase ventilation hose
22 Inlet manifold
23 Starter motor
24 Choke cable
25 Renix electronic ignition
   module
26 Windscreen wiper motor

Under-bonnet view (340 GL 1.7 litre)

1 Air intake heating/ventilation	8 Alternator	15 Battery	21 Fusebox
2 Recirculation vacuum valve	9 Drivebelt	16 Fuel pump	22 Distributor
3 Windscreen wiper motor	10 Water pump	17 Carburettor	23 Valve cover
4 Suspension tower	11 Timing belt cover	18 Coolant expansion tank	24 Engine oil filler cap
5 Heater blower motor	12 Crankshaft pulley	19 Brake fluid reservoir	25 Oil filter
6 Renix ignition control unit	13 Thermo-electric cooling fan	20 Brake vacuum servo unit	26 Spark plug HT leads
7 Coolant hose	14 Fuel filter		

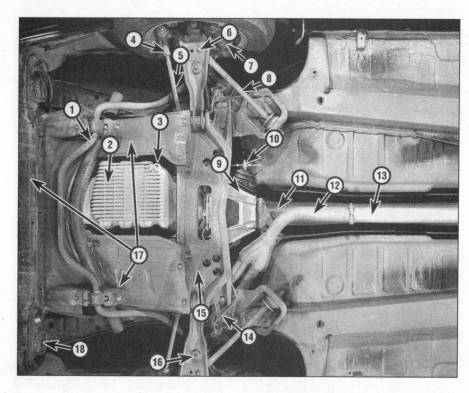

Typical front underbody view (360 GLEi model)

1 Anti-roll bar
2 Engine sump
3 Engine oil drain plug
4 Track rod end
5 Steering rod
6 Lower suspension arm
7 Brake caliper
8 Front radius arm
9 Clutch housing
10 Clutch cable adjusting nut
11 Torque tube and propeller shaft
12 Exhaust downpipe
13 Intermediate exhaust pipe
14 Brake hydraulic line
15 Crossmember
16 Anti-roll bar link
17 Engine splash guards
18 Front foglamp

Typical rear underbody view (360 GLEi model)

1 Torque tube and propeller shaft
2 Intermediate exhaust pipe
3 Gearbox filler plug
4 Rear roadspring
5 Handbrake cable
6 5th gear section of gearbox
7 Transmission mounting
8 Driveshaft
9 De Dion rear axle
10 Brake hydraulic line
11 Rear silencer
12 Rear tailpipe
13 Final drive unit
14 Rear shock absorber lower mounting
15 Fuel tank
16 Main section of gearbox
17 Gearbox drain plug
18 Fuel in-line filter (LE-Jetronic)
19 Crossmember/heat shield with fuel pump (LE-Jetronic)

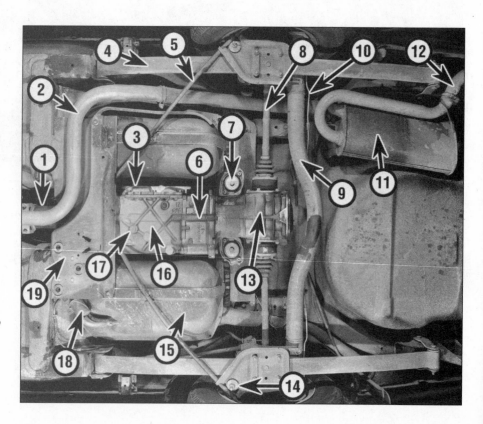

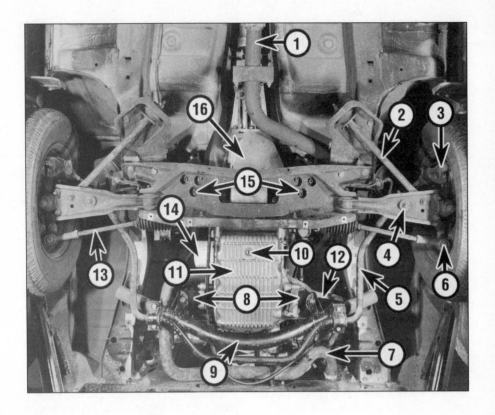

Front underbody view (340 GL 1.7 litre)

1 *Exhaust pipe*
2 *Front radius arm*
3 *Front brake caliper*
4 *Anti-roll bar attachment bolt*
5 *Anti-roll bar*
6 *Track rod end bush*
7 *Coolant hose*
8 *Front engine mountings*
9 *Engine front bearer*
10 *Engine oil drain plug*
11 *Sump*
12 *Engine earth strap*
13 *Track rod*
14 *Oil filter*
15 *Rear engine mounting attachment*
16 *Clutch housing*

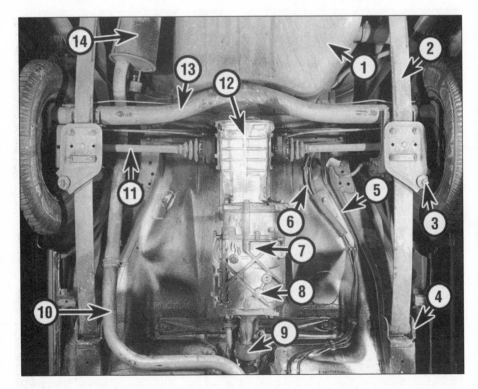

Rear underbody view (340 GL 1.7 litre)

1 *Fuel tank*
2 *Rear suspension road spring*
3 *Shock absorber lower mounting*
4 *Road spring front mounting*
5 *Brake hydraulic lines*
6 *Fuel lines*
7 *Gearbox*
8 *Gearbox drain plug*
9 *Propeller shaft*
10 *Exhaust pipe*
11 *Halfshaft*
12 *Final drive unit*
13 *De Dion rear axle*
14 *Silencer*

Jacking and towing

To change a roadwheel, remove the spare wheel and tool kit from the engine compartment or boot. Check that the handbrake is fully applied, then engage P (automatic transmission) or 1st (manual transmission). Two jacking points are provided on each side of the car. With the car on level ground, open up the jack and slide the lifting pad into the jacking point. Continue to open the jack until it is in contact with the ground. On early models, remove the hub cap or wheel nut caps. Using the brace, unscrew the wheel nuts half a turn. Raise the jack until the wheel is off the ground, then remove the wheel nuts and withdraw the wheel. On late models remove the hub cover.

Fit the spare wheel using a reversal of the removal procedure, but on late models remember to fit the hub cover before fitting the nuts.

When using a trolley jack, position the jack under the four jacking points, the rear engine bearer, or midway along the De Dion rear axle.

Towing eyes are provided below the front and rear bumpers on the right-hand side; do not use these eyes for lifting the car. If being towed, select N (automatic transmission) or neutral (manual transmission) and remember that with the engine stopped, more effort will be required when depressing the footbrake pedal since the servo will be inoperative.

Spare wheel location (340 models)

Spare wheel location (360 models)

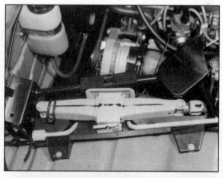

Tool kit with spare wheel removed (340 models)

Jacking up the car (note the early scissor type jack)

Front towing eye

Rear towing eye

Jump starting

Jump starting will get you out of trouble, but you must correct whatever made the battery go flat in the first place. There are three possibilities:

1 *The battery has been drained by repeated attempts to start, or by leaving the lights on.*

2 *The charging system is not working properly (alternator drivebelt slack or broken, alternator wiring fault or alternator itself faulty).*

3 *The battery itself is at fault (electrolyte low, or battery worn out).*

When jump-starting a car using a booster battery, observe the following precautions:

✔ Before connecting the booster battery, make sure that the ignition is switched off.

✔ Ensure that all electrical equipment (lights, heater, wipers, etc) is switched off.

✔ Make sure that the booster battery is the same voltage as the discharged one in the vehicle.

✔ If the battery is being jump-started from the battery in another vehicle, the two vehicles MUST NOT TOUCH each other.

✔ Make sure that the transmission is in neutral (or PARK, in the case of automatic transmission).

1 Connect one end of the red jump lead to the positive (+) terminal of the flat battery

2 Connect the other end of the red lead to the positive (+) terminal of the booster battery.

3 Connect one end of the black jump lead to the negative (-) terminal of the booster battery

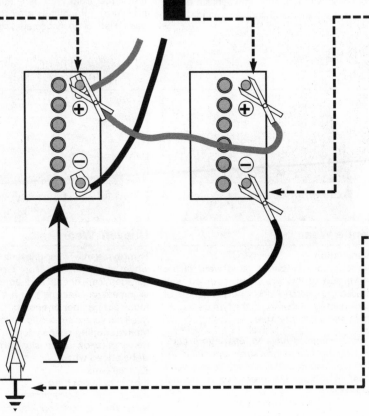

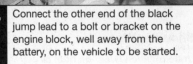

4 Connect the other end of the black jump lead to a bolt or bracket on the engine block, well away from the battery, on the vehicle to be started.

5 Make sure that the jump leads will not come into contact with the fan, drive-belts or other moving parts of the engine.

6 Start the engine using the booster battery, then with the engine running at idle speed, disconnect the jump leads in the reverse order of connection.

Tyre condition and pressure

It is very important that tyres are in good condition, and at the correct pressure - having a tyre failure at any speed is highly dangerous. Tyre wear is influenced by driving style - harsh braking and acceleration, or fast cornering, will all produce more rapid tyre wear. As a general rule, the front tyres wear out faster than the rears. Interchanging the tyres from front to rear ("rotating" the tyres) may result in more even wear. However, if this is completely effective, you may have the expense of replacing all four tyres at once! Remove any nails or stones embedded in the tread before they penetrate the tyre to cause deflation. If removal of a nail does reveal that the tyre has been punctured, refit the nail so that its point of penetration is marked. Then immediately change the wheel, and have the tyre repaired by a tyre dealer.

Regularly check the tyres for damage in the form of cuts or bulges, especially in the sidewalls. Periodically remove the wheels, and clean any dirt or mud from the inside and outside surfaces. Examine the wheel rims for signs of rusting, corrosion or other damage. Light alloy wheels are easily damaged by "kerbing" whilst parking; steel wheels may also become dented or buckled. A new wheel is very often the only way to overcome severe damage.

New tyres should be balanced when they are fitted, but it may become necessary to re-balance them as they wear, or if the balance weights fitted to the wheel rim should fall off. Unbalanced tyres will wear more quickly, as will the steering and suspension components. Wheel imbalance is normally signified by vibration, particularly at a certain speed (typically around 50 mph). If this vibration is felt only through the steering, then it is likely that just the front wheels need balancing. If, however, the vibration is felt through the whole car, the rear wheels could be out of balance. Wheel balancing should be carried out by a tyre dealer or garage.

1 Tread Depth - visual check
The original tyres have tread wear safety bands (B), which will appear when the tread depth reaches approximately 1.6 mm. The band positions are indicated by a triangular mark on the tyre sidewall (A).

2 Tread Depth - manual check
Alternatively, tread wear can be monitored with a simple, inexpensive device known as a tread depth indicator gauge.

3 Tyre Pressure Check
Check the tyre pressures regularly with the tyres cold. Do not adjust the tyre pressures immediately after the vehicle has been used, or an inaccurate setting will result.

Tyre tread wear patterns

Shoulder Wear

Underinflation (wear on both sides)
Under-inflation will cause overheating of the tyre, because the tyre will flex too much, and the tread will not sit correctly on the road surface. This will cause a loss of grip and excessive wear, not to mention the danger of sudden tyre failure due to heat build-up.
Check and adjust pressures

Incorrect wheel camber (wear on one side)
Repair or renew suspension parts

Hard cornering
Reduce speed!

Centre Wear

Overinflation
Over-inflation will cause rapid wear of the centre part of the tyre tread, coupled with reduced grip, harsher ride, and the danger of shock damage occurring in the tyre casing.
Check and adjust pressures

If you sometimes have to inflate your car's tyres to the higher pressures specified for maximum load or sustained high speed, don't forget to reduce the pressures to normal afterwards.

Uneven Wear

Front tyres may wear unevenly as a result of wheel misalignment. Most tyre dealers and garages can check and adjust the wheel alignment (or "tracking") for a modest charge.

Incorrect camber or castor
Repair or renew suspension parts

Malfunctioning suspension
Repair or renew suspension parts

Unbalanced wheel
Balance tyres

Incorrect toe setting
Adjust front wheel alignment

Note: *The feathered edge of the tread which typifies toe wear is best checked by feel.*

Identifying leaks

Puddles on the garage floor or drive, or obvious wetness under the bonnet or underneath the car, suggest a leak that needs investigating. It can sometimes be difficult to decide where the leak is coming from, especially if the engine bay is very dirty already. Leaking oil or fluid can also be blown rearwards by the passage of air under the car, giving a false impression of where the problem lies.

 Warning: Most automotive oils and fluids are poisonous. Wash them off skin, and change out of contaminated clothing, without delay.

HAYNES HiNT *The smell of a fluid leaking from the car may provide a clue to what's leaking. Some fluids are distinctively coloured. It may help to clean the car carefully and to park it over some clean paper overnight as an aid to locating the source of the leak.*

Remember that some leaks may only occur while the engine is running.

Sump oil

Engine oil may leak from the drain plug...

Oil from filter

...or from the base of the oil filter.

Gearbox oil

Gearbox oil can leak from the seals at the inboard ends of the driveshafts.

Antifreeze

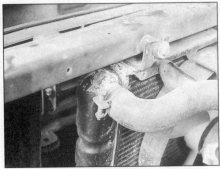

Leaking antifreeze often leaves a crystalline deposit like this.

Brake fluid

A leak occurring at a wheel is almost certainly brake fluid.

Power steering fluid

Power steering fluid may leak from the pipe connectors on the steering rack.

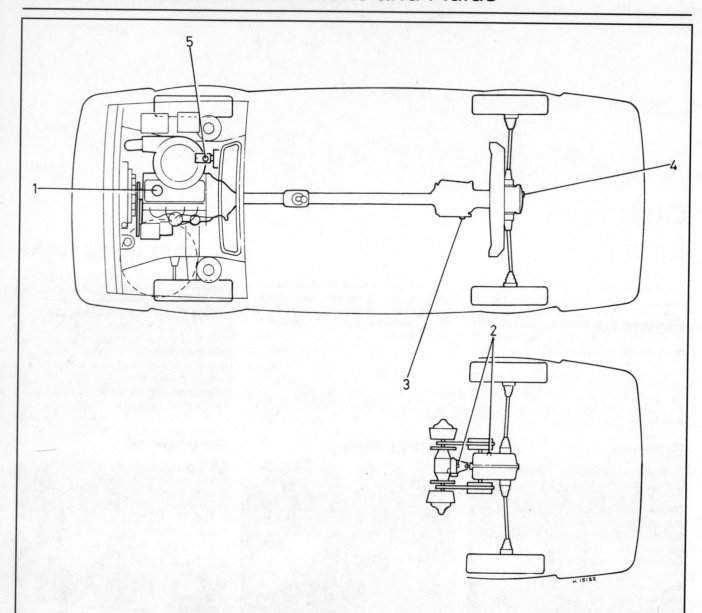

Component or system	Lubricant type/specification
Engine (1)	Multigrade engine oil, viscosity SAE 10W/30 or 15W/40, to API SF
Transmission:	
Automatic (2)	Hypoid gear oil, viscosity SAE 80W/90, to API GL4 or GL5
Manual (3)	ATF type A, suffix A
Final drive (4)	Hypoid gear oil, viscosity SAE 90, to API GL5
Braking system (5)	Hydraulic fluid to DOT 4
Carburettor dashpot (B19A models)	Automatic transmission fluid
Power-assisted steering	ATF type A, suffix A

Chapter 1
Engine

For modifications, and information applicable to later models, see Supplement at end of manual

Contents

Degrees of difficulty

Easy, suitable for novice with little experience	Fairly easy, suitable for beginner with some experience	Fairly difficult, suitable for competent DIY mechanic	Difficult, suitable for experienced DIY mechanic	Very difficult, suitable for expert DIY or professional

Specifications

B 14 engine

General

Type	Four-cylinder, in-line, overhead valve
Displacement	85.25 cu in (1397 cc)
Bore	2.99 in (76 mm)
Stroke	3.03 in (77 mm)
Firing order	1-3-4-2 (No 1 nearest flywheel)
Compression ratio:	
B14.0E	9.5:1
All other engines	9.25:1
Compression pressure (new)	163.6 lbf/in^2 (1128 kPa)
Maximum compression pressure difference between cylinders	7.1 lbf/in^2 (49 kPa)

Cylinder head

Material	Aluminium alloy
Valve seat angle:	
Inlet:	
B14.1E and B14.2E up to chassis No 671999	30°
All other engines	45°
Exhaust	45°
Maximum warp:	
Corner to corner	0.002 in (0.05 mm)
Across width	0.002 in (0.05 mm)
Minimum height after refacing:	
B14.0	2.85 in (72.30 mm)
All other engines	2.84 in (72.05 mm)

Valves

Stem clearance in guide:
Inlet . . . . 0.0004 to 0.0021 in (0.010 to 0.054 mm)
Exhaust . . . . 0.0027 to 0.0033 in (0.069 to 0.084 mm)
Valve spring free length:
Up to chassis No 671999 . . . . 1.661 in (42.2 mm)
From chassis No 672000 . . . . 1.846 in (46.9 mm)

Valve clearances

	Inlet	Exhaust
Cold	0.006 in (0.15 mm)	0.008 in (0.20 mm)
Hot	0.008 in (0.20 mm)	0.010 in (0.25 mm)

Camshaft

Endfloat . . . . 0.002 to 0.004 in (0.05 to 0.10 mm)
Journal diameter . . . . 1.493 to 1.494 in (37.925 to 37.950 mm)
Valve timing (at 0.04 in/1.0 mm valve lift):

	Early camshaft	Late camshaft
Inlet valve opens	4° ATDC	0° 30' ATDC
Inlet valve closes	39° ABDC	36° ABDC
Exhaust valve opens	42° BBDC	44° BBDC
Exhaust valve closes	3° 30' ATDC	0° 30' ATDC

Tappets (camshaft followers)

Clearance in block . . . . 0.0005 to 0.0019 in (0.013 to 0.047 mm)

Cylinder liners and pistons

Liner protrusion above cylinder block (without O-ring seals) . . . . 0.0008 to 0.0035 in (0.02 to 0.09 mm)
Maximum difference in liner height . . . . 0.002 in (0.04 mm)
Piston rings . . . . 2 compression, 1 oil scraper
Piston ring end gap:
Top compression ring . . . . 0.012 to 0.018 in (0.30 to 0.45 mm)
Lower compression ring . . . . 0.010 to 0.016 in (0.25 to 0.40 mm)
Oil scraper:
U-flex type . . . . Nil
Goetze type . . . . 0.010 to 0.016 in (0.25 to 0.40 mm)
Piston ring clearance in groove:
Top compression ring . . . . 0.001 to 0.002 in (0.030 to 0.058 mm)
Lower compression ring . . . . 0.0009 to 0.0020 in (0.024 to 0.050 mm)
Oil scraper:
U-flex type . . . . 0.0010 to 0.0028 in (0.025 to 0.070 mm)
Goetze type . . . . 0.0010 to 0.0020 in (0.025 to 0.052 mm)
Maximum weight difference between any two pistons . . . . 0.07 oz (2.0 g)
Mean piston clearance in liner . . . . 0.002 to 0.003 in (0.045 to 0.065 mm)

Gudgeon pins

Clearance in piston . . . . 0.0002 to 0.0005 in (0.006 to 0.012 mm)
Clearance in connecting rod . . . . Press fit

Connecting rods

Endfloat on crankshaft . . . . 0.012 to 0.022 in (0.31 to 0.57 mm)
Maximum weight difference between any two connecting rods . . . . . . 0.07 oz (2.0 g)

Crankshaft

Endfloat . . . . 0.002 to 0.009 in (0.05 to 0.23 mm)
Main bearing radial clearance . . . . 0.0013 to 0.0029 in (0.032 to 0.074 mm)
Big-end bearing radial clearance . . . . 0.0013 to 0.0026 in (0.032 to 0.065 mm)
Thrust washer thickness:
Standard . . . . 0.110 in (2.80 mm)
Oversize . . . . 0.116 in (2.95 mm)

Lubrication system

Oil type/specification . . . . Multigrade engine oil, viscosity SAE 10W/30 or 15W/40, to API SF
Oil capacity (including filter) . . . . 7.0 pints (4.0 litres)
Oil pump:
Type . . . . Double gear
Gear endfloat . . . . 0.0008 to 0.0034 in (0.020 to 0.086 mm)
Gear radial clearance . . . . 0.004 to 0.009 in (0.095 to 0.222 mm)
Release valve spring free length . . . . 1.811 in (46.0 mm)
Oil pressure at idling . . . . 14.2 to 21.3 lbf/in² (98 to 147 kPa)
Oil filter . . . . Champion C102 or F103*
*Refer to Section 11

1

Torque wrench settings	lbf ft	Nm
Cylinder head:		
Stage 1	20	27
Stage 2	44	60
Main bearing cap bolts	44	60
Big-end bearing nuts	31	42
Flywheel	35	47
Camshaft sprocket bolt	22	30
Crankshaft pulley bolt	55	75
Sump bolts	6	8
Rocker shaft pedestal bolts	12	16
Timing chain tensioner bolts	7	10
Engine mountings:		
Front to engine	19	26
Front to bearer	32	44
Rear to engine	14	19
Rear to bearer	32	44
Oil pump	6	8
Drain plug (oil)	16	22
Oil pressure switch	16	22
Timing cover bolts	7	10
Camshaft flange bolts	7	10

B19 engines

General

Type	Four-cylinder, in-line, single overhead camshaft
Designation:	
Carburettor version	B19A
Fuel injection version	B19E
Displacement	121.19 cu in (1986 cc)
Bore	3.50 in (88.9 mm)
Stroke	3.15 in (80.0 mm)
Firing order	1-3-4-2 (No 1 nearest radiator)
Compression ratio:	
Up to 1982	9.25:1
From 1982	10.0:1
Compression pressure (new):	
Up to 1982	128.0 to 156.5 lbf/in² (883 to 1079 kPa)
From 1982	156.5 to 177.8 lbf/in² (1079 to 1226 kPa)
Maximum compression pressure difference between cylinders	27.8 lbf/in² (192 kPa)

Cylinder head

Material	Aluminium alloy
Valve seat angle	45°
Maximum warp:	
Corner to corner	0.02 in (0.50 mm)
Across width	0.01 in (0.25 mm)
Minimum height after refacing	5.732 in (145.6 mm)

Valves

Stem clearance in guide	0.006 in (0.15 mm)
Valve spring free length	1.772 in (45.0 mm)

Valve clearances (inlet and exhaust)

	Checking	Adjusting
Cold	0.012 to 0.016 in (0.30 to 0.40 mm)	0.014 to 0.016 in (0.35 to 0.40 mm)
Hot	0.014 to 0.018 in (0.35 to 0.45 mm)	0.016 to 0.018 in (0.40 to 0.45 mm)

Camshaft

Endfloat	0.004 to 0.016 in (0.1 to 0.4 mm)
Journal diameter	1.1437 to 1.1445 in (29.050 to 29.070 mm)
Maximum bearing radial clearance	0.006 in (0.15 mm)
Valve timing (at 0.02 in/0.5 mm valve clearance):	
L camshaft	Inlet valve opens 15° BTDC
A camshaft	Inlet valve opens 22° BTDC

Tappets (camshaft followers)
Tappet clearance in head .... 0.001 to 0.003 in (0.030 to 0.075 mm)
Shim clearance in tappet .... 0.0004 to 0.0025 in (0.009 to 0.064 mm)
Shim thicknesses available .... 0.130 to 0.177 in (3.30 to 4.50 mm) in increments of 0.002 in (0.05 mm)

Intermediate shaft
Endfloat .... 0.008 to 0.018 in (0.20 to 0.46 mm)
Journal diameter:
   Front .... 1.8494 to 1.8504 in (46.975 to 47.000 mm)
   Intermediate .... 1.6939 to 1.6949 in (43.025 to 43.050 mm)
   Rear .... 1.6900 to 1.6909 in (42.925 to 42.950 mm)
Maximum bearing radial clearance .... 0.0008 to 0.0030 in (0.020 to 0.075 mm)

Cylinder block
Bore diameter:
   Standard (marked C) .... 3.5000 to 3.5004 in (88.90 to 88.91 mm)
   Standard (marked D) .... 3.5004 to 3.5008 in (88.91 to 88.92 mm)
   Standard (marked E) .... 3.5008 to 3.5012 in (88.92 to 88.93 mm)
   Standard (marked G) .... 3.5016 to 3.5020 in (88.94 to 88.95 mm)
   Oversize 1 .... 3.5153 to 3.5157 in (89.29 to 89.30 mm)
   Oversize 2 .... 3.5303 to 3.5307 in (89.67 to 89.68 mm)

Pistons
Maximum weight difference between 2 pistons .... 0.42 oz (12.0 g)
Piston ring clearance in groove:
   Top compression and lower compression rings .... 0.0016 to 0.0028 in (0.040 to 0.072 mm)
   Oil scraper .... 0.0012 to 0.0024 in (0.030 to 0.062 mm)
Piston ring end gap:
   Top compression ring .... 0.0138 to 0.0256 in (0.35 to 0.65 mm)
   Lower compression ring .... 0.0138 to 0.0217 in (0.35 to 0.55 mm)
   Oil scraper .... 0.0098 to 0.0236 in (0.25 to 0.60 mm)

Gudgeon pins
Diameter:
   Standard .... 0.9449 in (24.00 mm)
   Oversize .... 0.9468 in (24.05 mm)
Clearance in piston .... Push fit
Clearance in connecting rod .... Close running fit

Crankshaft
Maximum out-of-true .... 0.002 in (0.05 mm)
Maximum endfloat .... 0.010 in (0.25 mm)
Main bearing radial clearance .... 0.001 to 0.003 in (0.028 to 0.083 mm)
Main bearing journal:
   Maximum out-of-true .... 0.0028 in (0.07 mm)
   Maximum taper .... 0.0020 in (0.05 mm)
   Diameter (standard) .... 2.4981 to 2.4986 in (63.451 to 63.464 mm)
   Diameter undersizes .... Two, in increments of 0.010 in (0.254 mm)
Big-end bearing journal:
   Maximum out-of-true .... 0.002 in (0.05 mm)
   Maximum taper .... 0.002 in (0.05 in)
   Diameter (standard) .... 2.1255 to 2.1260 in (53.987 to 54.000 mm)
   Diameter undersizes .... Two, in increments of 0.010 in (0.254 mm)

Connecting rods
Big-end bearing:
   Endfloat on crankshaft .... 0.006 to 0.014 in (0.15 to 0.35 mm)
   Radial clearance .... 0.0009 to 0.0028 in (0.024 to 0.070 mm)
Maximum weight difference between 2 connecting rods .... 0.35 oz (10 g)

Flywheel
Maximum axial throw .... 0.002 in (0.05 mm) measured at diameter 5.906 in (150.0 mm)

Lubrication system
Oil type/specification .... Multigrade engine oil, viscosity SAE 10W/30 or 15W/40, to API SF
Oil capacity (including filter) .... 7.9 pints (4.5 litres)
Oil filter .... Champion C102

1

Lubrication system (continued)

Oil pump:

Type	Double gear
Gear endfloat	0.0008 to 0.0047 in (0.02 to 0.12 mm)
Gear radial clearance	0.0008 to 0.0035 in (0.02 to 0.09 mm)
Gear backlash	0.006 to 0.014 in (0.15 to 0.35 mm)
Driveshaft bearing clearance	0.0009 to 0.0019 in (0.024 to 0.049 mm)
Idler shaft bearing clearance	0.0005 to 0.0015 in (0.013 to 0.037 mm)
Relief valve spring free length	1.543 in (39.2 mm)

Torque wrench settings

	lbf ft	Nm
Main bearing caps	81	110
Big-end bearing caps:		
Previously used	47	64
New	52	71
Flywheel	52	71
Camshaft sprocket	37	50
Intermediate shaft sprocket	37	50
Camshaft bearing caps	15	20
Crankshaft sprocket bolt (centre bolt)	122	165
Engine mountings:		
Self-locking	41	56
Other	36	49
Cylinder head bolts:		
Socket head:		
Stage 1	44	60
Stage 2	81	110
Hexagon head:		
Stage 1	15	20
Stage 2	44	60
Stage 3	Tighten a further 90°	Tighten a further 90°

B200 engines

As B19 engines with the following exceptions

General

Designation:

Carburettor version	B200K
Fuel injection version	B200E
Compression ratio:	
B200K 624, B200E 628	10.0:1
B200K 928, B200E 938	9.2:1
Compression pressure (new):	
B200K	128.0 to 156.5 lbf/in² (883 to 1079 kPa)
B200E	156.5 to 177.8 lbf/in² (1079 to 1226 kPa)

Camshaft

Endfloat	0.008 to 0.020 in (0.2 to 0.5 mm)
Valve timing (at 0.028 in/0.7 mm valve clearance):	
L camshaft (B200K)	Inlet valve opens 10° BTDC
A camshaft (B200E)	Inlet valve opens 13° BTDC

Cylinder block

Bore diameter:

Oversize 1	3.5153 in (89.29 mm)
Oversize 2	3.5303 in (89.67 mm)

Pistons

Maximum weight difference between 2 pistons	0.56 oz (16 g)
Piston ring clearance in groove:	
Top compression ring	0.0024 to 0.0036 in (0.060 to 0.092 mm)
Lower compression ring	0.0012 to 0.0024 in (0.030 to 0.062 mm)
Oil scraper	0.0008 to 0.0022 in (0.020 to 0.055 mm)
Piston ring end gap:	
Top compression ring	0.012 to 0.020 in (0.30 to 0.50 mm)
Lower compression ring	0.012 to 0.022 in (0.30 to 0.55 mm)
Oil scraper	0.010 to 0.020 in (0.25 to 0.50 mm)

Gudgeon pins
Diameter:
Standard	0.9055 in (23.00 mm)
Oversize	0.9075 in (23.05 mm)

Crankshaft
Maximum out-of-true	0.001 in (0.025 mm)
Maximum endfloat	0.003 to 0.011 in (0.080 to 0.270 mm)
Main bearing radial clearance	0.0010 to 0.0028 in (0.025 to 0.072 mm)

Main bearing journal:
Maximum out-of-true	0.0002 in (0.005 mm)
Maximum taper	0.0002 in (0.005 mm)
Diameter (standard)	2.1648 to 2.1654 in (54.987 to 55.000 mm)
Diameter undersizes	Two, in increments of 0.0098 in (0.25 mm)

Big-end bearing journal:
Maximum out-of-true	0.0002 in (0.005 mm)
Maximum taper	0.0002 in (0.005 mm)
Diameter (standard)	1.9285 to 1.9293 in (48.984 to 49.005 mm)
Diameter undersizes	Two, in increments of 0.0098 in (0.25 mm)

Connecting rods
Big-end bearing:
Endfloat on crankshaft	0.0059 to 0.0177 in (0.15 to 0.45 mm)
Radial clearance	0.0009 to 0.0026 in (0.023 to 0.067 mm)
Maximum weight difference between 2 connecting rods	0.7 oz (20 g)

Flywheel
Maximum axial throw	0.0008 in (0.02 mm) measured at diameter 3.937 in (100.0 mm)

Lubrication system
Oil pump:
Driveshaft bearing clearance	0.0013 to 0.0028 in (0.032 to 0.070 mm)
Idler shaft bearing clearance	0.0006 to 0.0017 in (0.014 to 0.043 mm)

Torque wrench settings
	lbf ft	Nm
Big-end bearing caps:		
Stage 1	15	20
Stage 2	Tighten a further 90°	Tighten a further 90°
Camshaft sprocket bolt (centre bolt):		
Stage 1	44	60
Stage 2	Tighten a further 60°	Tighten a further 60°

B172 engine

General
Type	Four-cylinder in-line overhead camshaft
Designation	B172K
Bore	3.19 in (81 mm)
Stroke	3.29 in (83.5 mm)
Displacement	105.02 cu in (1721 cc)
Compression ratio	10:1
Firing order	1-3-4-2 (No 1 nearest flywheel)
Compression pressure (new)	128.0 lbf/in^2 (883 kPa)
Maximum compression pressure difference between cylinders	28.0 lbf/in^2 (193 kPa)

Cylinder head
Valve seat angle:
Inlet	30°
Exhaust	45°

Maximum warp:
Corner to corner	0.002 in (0.05 mm)
Across width	0.002 in (0.05 mm)
Height	6.673 ± 0.008 in (169.5 ± 0.2 mm)

Valves
Valve spring free length	1.768 in (44.9 mm)

1

Valve clearances (cold)

	Checking	Adjusting
Inlet	0.006 to 0.010 in (0.15 to 0.25 mm)	0.008 in (0.20 mm)
Exhaust	0.014 to 0.018 in (0.35 to 0.45 mm)	0.016 in (0.40 mm)

Camshaft

Endfloat .... 0.002 to 0.005 in (0.05 to 0.13 mm)
Maximum bearing radial clearance .... 0.002 to 0.006 in (0.05 to 0.15 mm)
Valve timing:
   Inlet (at 0.016 in/0.4 mm valve clearance):
      Valve opens .... 4° BTDC
      Valve closes .... 40° ABDC
   Exhaust (at 0.020 in/0.5 mm valve clearance):
      Valve opens .... 40° BBDC
      Valve closes .... 4° ATDC

Tappets (camshaft followers)

Diameter .... 1.378 in (35.0 mm)
Running clearance .... 0.0010 to 0.0030 in (0.025 to 0.075 mm)
Shim thickness available .... 0.128 to 0.177 in (3.25 to 4.50 mm) in increments of 0.002 in (0.05 mm)

Intermediate shaft

Endfloat .... 0.003 to 0.006 in (0.07 to 0.15 mm)
Bearing bush diameter:
   Inner .... 1.555 in (39.5 mm)
   Outer .... 1.594 in (40.5 mm)

Pistons

Piston ring clearance in groove:
   Top compression ring .... 0.0024 to 0.0035 in (0.060 to 0.090 mm)
   Lower compression ring .... 0.0016 to 0.0028 in (0.040 to 0.070 mm)
   Oil scraper .... 0.0008 to 0.0022 in (0.020 to 0.055 mm)
Piston ring end gap:
   Top compression ring .... 0.012 to 0.018 in (0.30 to 0.45 mm)
   Lower compression ring .... 0.010 to 0.016 in (0.25 to 0.40 mm)
   Oil scraper .... 0.010 to 0.016 in (0.25 to 0.40 mm)

Gudgeon pins

Diameter .... 0.8268 in (21.0 mm)
Clearance in piston .... Close running fit
Clearance in connecting rod .... Press fit

Crankshaft

Maximum endfloat .... 0.0028 to 0.0091 in (0.07 to 0.23 mm)
Main bearing radial clearance .... 0.0004 ± 0.0004 in (0.01 ± 0.01 mm)
Main bearing journal:
   Maximum ovality .... 0.0001 in (0.0025 mm) approx
   Maximum taper .... 0.0002 in (0.0050 mm)
   Diameter (standard) .... 2.1575 ± 0.0002 in (54.800 ± 0.005 mm)
   Diameter undersize .... 2.1476 ± 0.0002 in (54.550 ± 0.005 mm)
Big-end bearing journal:
   Maximum ovality .... 0.0 to 0.0001 in (0.0 to 0.0025 mm)
   Maximum taper .... 0.0002 in (0.005 mm)
   Diameter (standard) .... 1.8898 + 0.0008 in (48.00 + 0.02 mm)
   Diameter undersize .... 1.8799 + 0.0008 in (47.75 + 0.02 mm)

Connecting rods

Big-end bearing:
   Endfloat on crankshaft .... 0.0087 to 0.0157 in (0.22 to 0.40 mm)
   Radial clearance .... 0.0004 ± 0.0004 in (0.01 ± 0.01 mm)

Flywheel

Maximum axial throw .... 0.003 in (0.07 mm) measured at diameter 3.150 in (80 mm)

Lubrication system

Oil type/specification .... Multigrade engine oil, viscosity SAE 10W/30 or 15W/40, to API SF
Oil capacity (including filter) .... 8.8 pints (5.0 litres)
Oil filter .... Champion F103

Torque wrench settings

	lbf ft	Nm
Timing belt tensioner nut	37	50
Idler pulley bolt	21	28
Crankshaft pulley bolt	70	95
Timing belt cover bolts	7	10
Camshaft sprocket bolt	37	50
Camshaft bearing cap bolts (M8)	15	20
Camshaft rear cap bolts (M6)	7	10
Main bearing cap bolts	46	63
Big-end bearing cap bolts	35	48
Intermediate shaft sprocket bolt	37	50
Flywheel bolts	39	53
Inlet and exhaust manifold nuts	15	20
Valve cover nuts	4	5
Oil drain plug in sump	10	13
Engine mounting nuts (front)	38	52
Engine mounting nuts (rear)	35	47
Engine mounting-to-cylinder block bolts	15	20
Sump bolts	10	13
Oil pump retaining bolts	17	23
Oil pump cover bolts	9	12
Water pump housing bolts	9	12
Oil pressure switch	18	25
Cylinder head bolts:		
Stage 1	22	30
Stage 2	52	70
Stage 3 (after 3 minutes wait - see text)	15	20
Stage 4	Tighten a further 123 ± 2°	Tighten a further 123 ± 2°

1

Part A: B14 engine

1 General description

The engine is of four cylinder, in-line overhead valve type. The crankshaft has five main bearings, the centre main bearing incorporating thrust washers which control the crankshaft endfloat. Replaceable wet cylinder liners are fitted. The camshaft is chain driven from the crankshaft and is supported in four bearings. A spring type timing chain tensioner is fitted. The inclined valves are operated by rockers mounted on a rocker shaft. The cylinder head is cast in aluminium alloy.

A semi-closed crankcase ventilation system is employed, and crankcase gases are drawn from the rocker cover via a hose to the air cleaner and inlet manifold.

Lubrication is provided by a gear type oil pump driven from the camshaft and located in the crankcase. Engine oil is fed through an externally mounted full-flow filter to the engine oil gallery, and then to the crankshaft, camshaft, and rocker shaft bearings. A pressure relief valve is incorporated in the oil pump.

The engine has remained basically the same throughout its life apart from minor modifications. The introduction years of the various engines is as follows:

Up to 1979: B14.0E
From 1979 to 1981: B14.1E
From 1981 to 1982: B14.2E
From 1982 to 1984: B14.3E
From 1984: B14.4E

2 Routine maintenance

At the intervals given in the Routine Maintenance Section at the beginning of this manual, carry out the following operations:

Lubrication

1 Check the oil level (photo).
2 Renew the engine oil and filter.

2.1 Topping up engine oil level

Crankcase ventilation system

3 Check the system for blockages, and clean the hoses and valve as necessary.

Valves

4 Check the valve clearances.
5 Tension/renew the timing belt (if applicable).

General

6 Check engine for any leaks, and clean the engine and engine compartment.

3 Major operations possible with engine in car

The following operations can be carried out without having to remove the engine:

a) *Removal and servicing the cylinder head*
b) *Removal of the sump*
c) *Removal of the liner and piston/connecting rod assemblies (through top of block)*
d) *Removal of the timing cover, chain and gears*
e) *Removal of the oil pump*
f) *Renewal of the engine mountings*
g) *Removal of the flywheel*
h) *Renewal of the crankshaft rear oil seal*

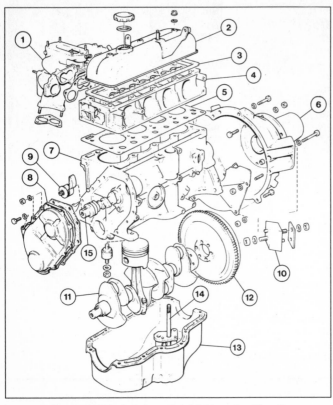

Fig. 1.1 Exploded view of the B14 engine (Sec 1)

1 Inlet and exhaust manifolds
2 Valve cover
3 Gasket
4 Cylinder head
5 Head gasket
6 Clutch housing
7 Cylinder block
8 Timing cover
9 Timing chain tensioner
10 Engine mounting
11 Crankshaft and piston
12 Flywheel
13 Sump
14 Oil pump
15 Camshaft

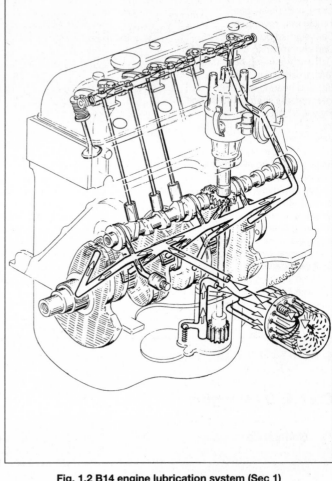

Fig. 1.2 B14 engine lubrication system (Sec 1)

4 Major operations only possible after removal of engine

The following operations can only be carried out after removal of the engine from the car:

a) Removal of the camshaft and followers
b) Renewal of crankshaft main bearings

5 Engine - removal

1 Remove the bonnet as described in Chapter 9.
2 Disconnect the battery negative lead.
3 Remove the spare wheel and drain the cooling system as described in Chapter 2.
4 Drain the engine oil and remove the engine guard panels. From 1985 the panel is one-piece similar to that on B172 engines.

5 Remove the radiator as described in Chapter 2.
6 Detach the exhaust pipe from the manifold and clutch housing mountings and tie it to one side.
7 Unscrew and remove the engine front and rear mounting nuts (photos). From 1985 the front mounting is different, and is shown in Fig. 1.3.
8 Detach the engine earth lead (photo), then

disconnect the leads from the starter motor and vacuum control microswitch when fitted (photo).
9 Detach the vacuum hose(s) and heater hoses and the air filter hose, including the declutching cylinder hose on automatic models.
10 Disconnect the leads from the alternator, oil pressure sender (photo), water temperature sender and coil.

5.7A Front engine mounting (early type)

5.7B Rear engine mounting

5.8A Engine earth strap location (arrowed)

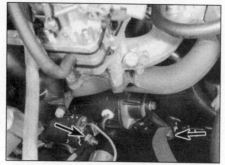

5.8B Engine earth strap and starter leads (arrowed)

5.10 Oil pressure sender switch location

11 Disconnect the throttle and choke cables, then detach the fuel line(s) from the fuel pump and plug them to prevent ingress of dirt.

12 Remove the air filter assembly (Chapter 3).

13 Remove the windscreen washer reservoir.

14 On manual transmission models, loosen the clamp bolt securing the propeller shaft to the clutch shaft. Also disconnect the clutch cable (see Chapter 5).

15 Fit chains or slings securely to the engine and, using a suitable hoist, lift the engine from the mountings, then move it forwards to disengage the propeller shaft splines; make sure that the shaft stays engaged with the transmission.

16 Swing the engine in a clockwise direction (viewed from above), then slowly lift it from the engine compartment, at the same time checking that all connections are detached.

17 Once the engine sump is high enough, pull the hoist forwards and lower the engine onto a workbench.

6 Engine - dismantling (general)

1 It is best to mount the engine on a dismantling stand, but if this is not available, stand the engine on a strong bench, at a comfortable working height. Failing this, it will have to be stripped down on the floor.

2 During the dismantling process, the greatest care should be taken to keep the exposed parts free from dirt. As an aid to achieving this, thoroughly clean down the

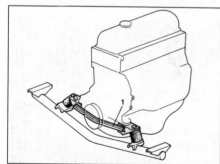

Fig. 1.3 Front engine mounting (1) on B14 engines from 1985 (Sec 5)

outside of the engine, first removing all traces of oil and congealed dirt.

3 A good grease solvent will make the job much easier; after the solvent has been applied and allowed to stand for a time, a vigorous jet of water will wash off the solvent and grease with it. If the dirt is thick and deeply embedded, work the solvent into it with a strong stiff brush.

4 Finally, wipe down the exterior of the engine with a rag, and only then, when it is quite clean, should the dismantling process begin. As the engine is stripped, clean each part in a bath of paraffin.

5 Never immerse parts with oilways in paraffin (eg crankshaft). To clean these parts, wipe down carefully with a petrol-dampened rag. Oilways can be cleaned out with wire. If an air line is available, all parts can be blown dry and the oilways blown through as an added precaution.

6 Re-use of old gaskets is false economy. To avoid the possibility of trouble after the engine has been reassembled, *always use new gaskets throughout.*

> **HAYNES HINT** *Do not throw away the old gaskets, for sometimes it happens that an immediate replacement cannot be found and the old gasket is then very useful as a template. Hang up the gaskets as they are removed.*

7 To strip the engine, it is best to work from the top down. When the stage is reached where the crankshaft must be removed, the engine can be turned on its side and all other work carried out with it in this position.

8 Wherever possible, refit nuts, bolts and washers finger tight from wherever they were removed. This helps to avoid loss and muddle. If they cannot be refitted, arrange them so that it is clear from whence they came.

7 Ancillary components - removal

1 With the engine removed from the car the externally mounted ancillary components should now be removed before dismantling.

2 The following is a suggested sequence of removal; detailed descriptions are to be found in the relevant Chapter of this manual:

a) *Alternator (Chapter 10)*
b) *Clutch assembly (Chapter 5)*
c) *Manifolds and carburettor (Chapter 3)*
d) *Engine mounting rubbers*
e) *Oil filter (see Section 11)*
f) *Distributor and spark plugs (Chapter 4)*
g) *Fuel pump (Chapter 3)*
h) *Water pump and thermostat (Chapter 2)*
i) *Starter motor (Chapter 10)*
j) *Coil (Chapter 4)*

8 Cylinder head - removal

1

Note: *If the cylinder liners are disturbed when removing the cylinder head, it will be necessary to remove the liners (Section 14) for new seals to be fitted*

1 If the head is to be removed with the engine in the car, carry out the following operations:

a) *Disconnect the battery negative terminal. Remove the spare wheel*
b) *Drain the cooling system*
c) *Remove the manifolds complete with carburettor*
d) *Disconnect the spark plug HT leads*
e) *Disconnect the temperature sender lead*
f) *Remove the drivebelt, fan and pulley*
g) *Disconnect all hoses*

2 Unscrew the rocker cover retaining nuts and remove the rocker cover and gasket. Unscrew the retaining nuts and bolts and lift the rocker shaft and rockers from the cylinder head (photo).

8.2 Rocker shaft assembly

8.3 Removing the pushrods

8.6 Removing the cylinder head

Numbering from the front of the cylinder head, exhaust valves are 1-4-5-8 and inlet valves 2-3-6-7.

4 The valve springs and collets should also be kept in their correct sequence as the inlet and exhaust valve components differ.

5 Invert the cylinder head and push the valves out (photo).

6 On models from 1979, prise the special seals from the inlet valve guides.

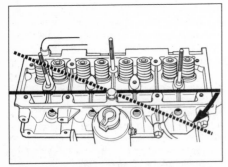

Fig. 1.4 Pivot the cylinder head around No 1 bolt to break the seal (Sec 8)

Fig. 1.5 Cylinder liner retaining clamps - arrowed (Sec 8)

3 Remove the pushrods keeping them in order for refitting in their original positions (photo).

4 Slacken all the cylinder head bolts in the reverse order to that shown in Fig. 1.20. Remove all the bolts except No 1 (nearest the distributor): after the initial slackening, leave this bolt in contact with the cylinder head.

5 Using a copper or wooden mallet, tap the sides of the cylinder head at each end in turn to make it pivot around No 1 bolt (Fig. 1.4). This will break the seal between head, gasket and liners, and so prevent the liners being disturbed.

6 Remove the No 1 bolt. Lift off the cylinder head and recover the gasket (photo). Be careful not to disturb the liners, nor let fragments of gasket enter oilways or water jackets.

7 Note: *the crankshaft must not be rotated with the head removed, otherwise the liners will be displaced.* If it is necessary to turn the engine (eg to clean the piston crowns), use bolts with suitable washers screwed into the top of the block to retain the liners (Fig. 1.5).

9 Cylinder head - dismantling

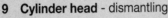
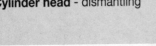

1 Extract the circlip from the end of the rocker shaft, then remove the springs, rocker arms, and pedestals keeping each component in its original fitted sequence.

2 Remove the valves from the cylinder head. Compress each spring in turn with a valve spring compressor until the two halves of the

collets can be removed (photo). Release the compressor and remove the spring, spring retainer, and thrust washer - see Haynes Hint (photo).

3 It is essential that the valves are kept in their correct sequence unless they are so badly worn that they are to be renewed.

9.2A Compressing the valve springs

9.2B Removing a valve spring and retainer

9.5 Removing a valve

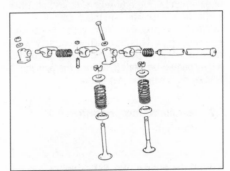

Fig. 1.6 Rocker shaft and valve components (Sec 9)

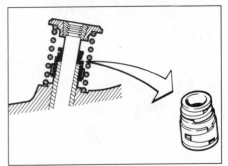

Fig. 1.7 Inlet valve seals fitted to engines from 1979 (Sec 9)

11.1 Oil pump location

11.2 Oil filter location

12.2 Crankshaft pulley and bolt

10 Sump - removal

1 If the sump is to be removed with the engine in the car, carry out the following operations:

a) *Remove the engine splash guards*
b) *Detach the front anti-roll bar from the crossmember*
c) *Disconnect the steering shaft from the*

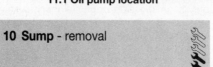

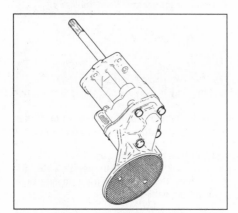

Fig. 1.8 Oil pump (Sec 11)

steering gear, then remove the mounting bolts and pull the steering gear downwards

2 Drain the engine oil.
3 Unscrew and remove all the sump bolts and withdraw the sump from the engine.
4 If the sump is stuck tight, run a blunt knife around the gasket to release it.

11 Oil pump and oil filter - removal

If the oil pump is to be removed with the engine in the car, first remove the sump as described in Section 10.

1 Unscrew and remove the retaining bolts and withdraw the oil pump from the block, at the same time disengaging the shaft from the drivegear (photo).
2 The oil filter is simply removed by unscrewing it; place a small container below it to catch any oil which may be spilled (photo). If difficulty is experienced, use a strap or cord in a tourniquet manner to free it.
3 Discard the filter element.
4 During 1984 the oil filter screw thread was changed from Imperial (3/4 in) to metric (M20).

Make sure that the correct replacement filter is purchased.
5 Some engines produced during the changeover period have an Imperial-to-metric adaptor screwed into the block. If the adaptor unscrews with the filter, remove it from the filter and screw it back into the block using thread locking compound.
6 Fitting a new oil filter is described in Section 36.

12 Timing cover, gears and chain - removal

1 If the timing cover, gears and chain are being removed with the engine in the car, first carry out the following operations:

a) *Remove the radiator (Chapter 2)*
b) *Remove the fan/alternator drivebelt (Chapter 2)*
c) *Remove the sump (Section 10)*

2 Unscrew and remove the crankshaft pulley bolt (photo). To do this use a wide-bladed screwdriver to jam the flywheel gear. If the engine is still in the car, it will first be necessary to remove the starter motor (Chapter 10). Withdraw the crankshaft pulley using two levers if necessary placed behind the pulley at opposite points.
3 Unscrew and remove the timing cover securing bolts and withdraw the cover and its gasket.
4 Using an Allen key, unscrew the retaining bolt and withdraw the timing chain tensioner. Note the fitted position of the spring and pad.

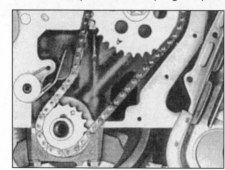

Fig. 1.10 Timing chain and gears, showing timing marks (Sec 12)

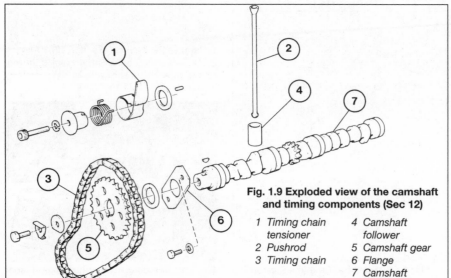

Fig. 1.9 Exploded view of the camshaft and timing components (Sec 12)

1 *Timing chain tensioner*
2 *Pushrod*
3 *Timing chain*
4 *Camshaft follower*
5 *Camshaft gear*
6 *Flange*
7 *Camshaft*

1

13.1 Removing the distributor drivegear

13.2 Removing a camshaft follower

14.3 Removing a big-end bearing cap

14.4 Removing a piston and liner

14 Liners and pistons/ connecting rods - removal

1 If the engine is in the car, carry out the following operations:

a) *Remove the cylinder head (Section 8)*
b) *Remove the sump (Section 10)*

2 Turn the crankshaft so that No 1 crankpin (nearest the flywheel) is at the lowest point of its travel. If the big-end cap and rods are not already numbered, mark them with a centre punch on the side opposite the camshaft (right-hand side when in car). Mark both the cap and rod in relation to the bore it operates in, starting with No 1 at the flywheel end.
3 Unscrew and remove the big-end bearing cap nuts and withdraw the cap complete with bearing shells; keep the shells in their correct sequence if they are to be refitted (photo).
4 Remove the liner clamps if fitted, and withdraw the pistons together with liners from the top of the block (photo); mark the liners using masking tape, so that they may be refitted in their original locations.
5 Remove the pistons from the liners.

15 Flywheel - removal

1 If the engine is in the car, remove the clutch as described in Chapter 5.
2 Lock the flywheel, using a wide-bladed screwdriver on the ring gear. Alternatively, if the sump is removed, place a wooden block between the crankshaft web and the block.
3 Mark the flywheel in relation to the crankshaft, then unscrew the retaining bolts and withdraw the flywheel.

16 Crankshaft rear oil seal - renewal

1 Remove the flywheel (Section 15).
2 Clean the area around the crankshaft rear oil seal, then use a screwdriver to prise it from the block.

5 Turn the engine until the timing marks on the camshaft and crankshaft gears are facing each other, and No 1 (flywheel end) and No 4 pistons are at the top of their cylinders. If the cylinder head is removed the cylinder liners must be held stationary, otherwise they will be displaced and the seals may subsequently leak water. Use bolts with suitable washers, screwed into the top of the block to retain the liners.
6 Bend back the locktab, then unscrew the camshaft gear retaining bolt.
7 Withdraw the camshaft gear and disengage the timing chain from the crankshaft.
8 If the crankshaft gear requires removing, a suitable puller must be used, and care must be taken to avoid damaging the pulley bolt threads. Extract the Woodruff key from the crankshaft once the gear is removed.

13 Camshaft and followers - removal

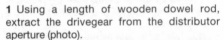

1 Using a length of wooden dowel rod, extract the drivegear from the distributor aperture (photo).
2 Withdraw the camshaft followers (tappets) from the top of the cylinder block, keeping them in order for correct refitting (photo).
3 Unscrew and remove the camshaft flange retaining bolts and carefully withdraw the camshaft, taking care not to damage the four camshaft bearings as the lobes of the cams pass through them.

Fig. 1.11 Removing the camshaft (Sec 13)

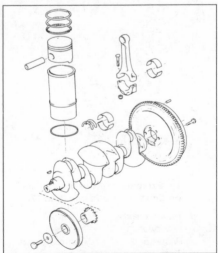

Fig. 1.12 Crankshaft and liner/piston components (Sec 14)

Fig. 1.13 Removing crankshaft rear oil seal (Sec 16)

17.2A A main bearing cap and shell

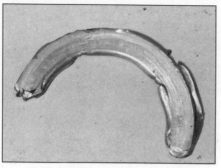

17.2B A badly worn thrust washer

17.4 Removing a main bearing shell

3 Wipe clean the oil seal recess. Dip the new oil seal in clean engine oil and carefully install it over the crankshaft rear journal with the aid of a metal tube of suitable size. Make sure that the open end of the seal faces inwards, and that the outer face of the seal is flush with the block. If the original seal has worn a groove on the journal, refer to Section 29, paragraph 8.

4 Refit the flywheel (Section 30).

17 Crankshaft and main bearings - removal

1 If the main bearing caps are not already numbered, mark them with a centre punch on the side opposite the camshaft (right-hand side when in car). Mark them starting with No 1 at the flywheel end.

2 Unscrew and remove the main bearing bolts and withdraw the caps complete with bearing shells (photo). Note the location of the thrust washers either side of the centre main bearing (photo).

3 Carefully lift out the crankshaft.

4 Extract the bearing shells from the crankcase and mark the bearing caps (photo).

If the original shells are to be refitted, identify them using pieces of masking tape.

5 Remove the crankshaft rear oil seal and discard it.

18 Crankcase ventilation system - description and maintenance

The crankcase ventilation hoses are shown in Figs. 1.14 and 1.15. The hose to the inlet manifold incorporates a calibrated restriction.

When the engine is idling or under partial load conditions, the high depression in the inlet manifold draws the crankcase fumes (diluted by air from the carburettor), through the restriction and into the combustion chambers.

Under full throttle or full load conditions, the crankcase fumes are drawn through the carburettor.

The system ensures that there is always a partial vacuum in the crankcase, and so prevents pressure which could cause oil contamination, fume emission, and oil leakage past seals.

The ventilation system hoses should be removed at the intervals given in the Routine

Maintenance Section at the beginning of this manual and washed clean with a suitable solvent.

19 Examination and renovation - general

With the engine completely stripped, clean all components and examine them for wear. Each part should be checked and, where necessary, renewed or renovated as described in the following Sections.

20 Oil pump - examination and renovation

1

1 Remove the oil pump cover (four bolts) and withdraw the oil pressure relief valve ball, spring and seat (photos).

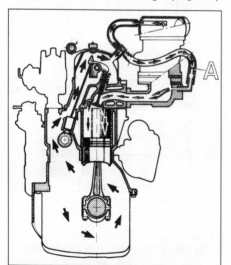

Fig. 1.14 Crankcase ventilation system - idling/partial load conditions (Sec 18)

A Restriction

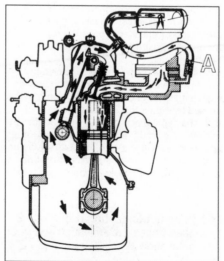

Fig. 1.15 Crankcase ventilation system - full load conditions (Sec 18)

A Restriction

20.1A Removing the oil pump cover

20.1B Oil pressure relief valve seat, ball and spring

20.1C Oil pressure relief valve spring and spring seat

20.4 Checking oil pump gear endfloat

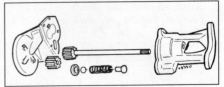

Fig. 1.16 Oil pump components (Sec 20)

2 Lift out the idler gear and drivegear spindle.

3 Clean the components and examine them for wear; renew any that are worn.

4 Install the spindle and gear, then check the end clearance between the gears and the pump body (endfloat). If this is greater than the specified amount the gears must be renewed. Use a straight-edge and feeler gauge to make the check (photo).

5 The oil pressure relief valve is non-adjustable, but it is possible, after high mileages, for the spring to weaken (check free length in Specifications).

6 Refit the cover and tighten the bolts.

21 Crankshaft and main bearings - examination and renovation

1 Examine the bearing surfaces of the crankshaft for scratches or scoring and, using a micrometer, check each journal and crankpin for ovality and taper. Where this is found to be in excess of 0.0001 in (0.0025 mm), the crankshaft will have to be reground and undersize bearings fitted.

2 Your Volvo dealer will decide whether the crankshaft is suitable for regrinding, and will also supply you with the appropriate undersize main and big-end shell bearings.

3 When installed, the bearings should have a running (radial) clearance as given in the Specifications, but these clearances can only be checked by using a proprietary product. However, it is usually assumed that the running clearances will be correct if the reconditioning has been carried out by a reliable company.

4 If the crankshaft bearing surfaces are not worn, check the main and big-end bearing shells for wear and renew them if necessary.

22 Cylinder liners and crankcase - examination and renovation

1 Examine the liners for taper, ovality, scoring and scratches. If a ridge is found at the top of the bore on the thrust side, the bores are worn. The owner will have a good indication of the bore wear prior to dismantling the engine on removing the cylinder head. Excessive oil consumption accompanied by blue smoke from the exhaust is a sure sign of worn bores and piston rings.

2 Measure the bore diameter just under the ridge with a micrometer and compare it with the diameter at the bottom of the bore, which is not subject to wear. If the difference between the two measurements exceeds 0.008 in (0.20 mm) then it will be necessary to fit new piston and liner assemblies.

3 The liners should also be checked for cracking.

4 If the bores are only slightly worn, special oil control rings and pistons can be fitted which will restore compression and stop the engine burning oil. Several different types are available and the manufacturer's instructions concerning their fitting must be followed closely.

5 If new pistons or rings are being fitted to the original bores, it is essential to slightly roughen the hard glaze on the sides of the bores with fine glass paper to enable the new piston rings to bed in properly.

Checking liner protrusion

6 Place the liners in the block without their O-ring seals. Clamp them in position with bolts and washers.

7 Using a straight-edge and feeler blades, or (preferably) a dial test indicator, measure the protrusion of the liners above the top face of the block. Desired values are given in the Specifications.

8 Interchange new liners if necessary to minimise the difference in protrusion between adjacent liners. Excessive protrusion may be caused by dirt on the liner seats.

9 If the specified protrusion cannot be achieved, consult a Volvo dealer or other specialist. New liners or a new block may be required. Excessive or insufficient protrusion will cause the head gasket and/or O-ring seals to fail prematurely.

23 Pistons/connecting rod assemblies - examination and renovation

1 Checking the big-end shell bearings is covered in Section 21.

2 If new pistons are being fitted, removal of each gudgeon pin is best left to a Volvo dealer as it is an interference fit, and a press and installation tool are required to carry out the operation successfully.

3 When correctly assembled, the arrow on the piston crown must face the rear (flywheel end) of the engine with the connecting rods in their normal position (photo).

4 If new piston rings are to be fitted to the original pistons, remove the old rings by expanding them and withdrawing them with a twisting motion. The use of two or three old feeler blades placed at equidistant points between the piston and ring will prevent a ring dropping into an empty groove during removal.

5 Install the new rings by reversing the removal process, but make sure that the following conditions are complied with:

a) The top compression ring must be stepped to avoid the wear ridge which will have formed at the top of the cylinder liner bore

b) The ring gaps and groove clearances are as given in the Specifications

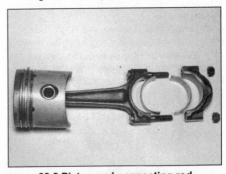

23.3 Piston and connecting rod components

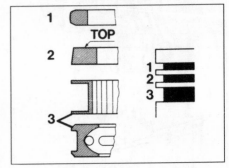

Fig. 1.17 Cross-section of piston rings (Sec 23)

1 Top compression ring
2 Lower compression ring
3 Oil scraper ring (upper U-flex, lower Goetz)

c) *Space the piston ring gaps at equidistant points so that the gaps are not in alignment*

d) *The second compression ring is tapered and must be installed with the mark uppermost*

24 Camshaft and followers - examination and renovation

1 Examine the camshaft bearing surfaces, cam lobes, and gear teeth for wear and scoring.

2 Temporarily fit the sprocket to the front of the camshaft (timing mark facing outwards), and tighten the bolt to the correct torque.

3 Using a feeler gauge, check that the endfloat is within the limits given in the Specifications; if not the flange must be renewed by using a press to remove it and install the new part.

4 Removal of the camshaft bearings is best left in the hands of your Volvo agent or local engineering works.

5 Check the followers for wear, and if evident renew them.

25 Timing gears and chain - examination and renovation

1 Examine the camshaft and crankshaft timing sprockets and renew them if their teeth are 'hooked' in appearance.

2 Examine the chain tensioner. If the rubber pad is worn or hardened it must be renewed.

3 Examine the timing chain. If it has been in operation for a considerable time, or excessive lateral movement is evident on the links, renew it.

26 Flywheel - examination and renovation

1 Examine the surface of the flywheel; if it is scored or damaged it should be renewed or refaced.

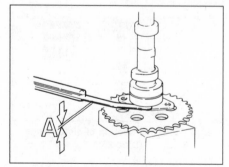

Fig. 1.18 Checking camshaft endfloat (A) with feeler gauges (Sec 24)

2 Using a suitable metal drift, drive the pilot bearing from the flywheel and check it for wear and roughness by spinning it. Renew it if necessary and drive the new bearing into position.

3 Examine the teeth of the flywheel starter ring gear. If they are chipped or worn, the ring must be renewed. To do this, split the ring with a cold chisel and remove it. *Take care to avoid injury from flying fragments.*

4 Heat the new ring to the temperature indicated (usually around 392°F/200°C) in an electric oven, and then quickly fit it to the flywheel so that the chamfered side of the teeth is towards the engine side of the flywheel.

5 Allow the ring to cool naturally without quenching.

27 Cylinder head - decarbonising, valve grinding and renovation

1 This operation will normally only be required at comparatively high mileages, due to the improvements in fuel and oil quality, and modern engine design in recent years. However, if a lack of power is noticed or pinking occurs, but the engine is otherwise in a good tuned condition, it will be necessary to decarbonise the head and grind in the valves.

2 With the cylinder head removed, use a blunt scraper to remove all traces of carbon from the combustion spaces and ports. Use a wire brush to clean the flat surface of the head, then wipe it with a paraffin-soaked rag. Clean the oilways and water channels with a test tube brush or similar item.

3 Similarly clean the cylinder block upper face, but if the engine is still in the car be careful not to allow carbon to fall into the cylinder liner bores. Clean the tops of the pistons with them at the top of their strokes, but first mask the oilways and waterways to prevent contaminating them. It is a good idea to press a little grease into the gap between the pistons and liner bores to prevent carbon entering; wipe the grease and carbon away when the cleaning is finished. To prevent the build-up of carbon on the piston crowns they can be polished with a metal polish.

Fig. 1.19 Pressing off the camshaft flange (Sec 24)

4 Check the cylinder head for distortion using a straight-edge and feeler gauge. If warping in excess of the specified amount has occurred, the head will have to be resurfaced by a specialist engineering works.

5 Examine the heads of the valves for pitting and burning, especially the heads of the exhaust valves. Also examine the valve seatings. If there are only slight marks on both faces, grinding the seats and valves together with coarse then fine grinding paste will be sufficient.

6 Where excessive pitting has occurred, the valves must be renewed, and the seats recut as necessary by a specialist engineering works.

7 To grind in the valves, smear a trace of coarse grinding paste on the valve face and, using a suction grinding tool, grind the valve head onto the valve seat using a semi-rotary action, occasionally lifting the valve from the seat. When a dull matt finish is produced on both surfaces evenly, wipe off the paste and repeat the process using fine paste. When an even light matt ring is produced on the valve and seat the grinding operation is finished.

 HAYNES HiNT *A light spring placed beneath the valve head will greatly assist this grinding-in operation.*

8 Clean away every trace of grinding paste and, if available, use an air line to blow out the ports and valve guides.

9 If the valve guides are worn (indicated by a side-to-side rocking motion of the valve) oversize valve guides should be fitted by a specialist engineering works.

10 Check the free length of the valve springs; if they are shorter than the dimension given in the Specifications renew them as a set.

11 Examine the rocker shaft and rockers for wear, and renew them as necessary. Make sure that the bearing pads on the rocker arms do not show signs of deterioration.

28 Engine reassembly - general

1 To ensure maximum life from a rebuilt engine, not only must everything be correctly assembled, but each component must be spotlessly clean. All the oilways must also be clean and unobstructed.

2 Spring and lockwashers must always be fitted where indicated and all bearing and working surfaces must be thoroughly lubricated during reassembly.

3 Before starting reassembly, renew any damaged bolts or studs and obtain a set of gaskets, crankshaft front and rear oil seals, and a new oil filter element.

4 Wherever possible tighten all nuts and bolts to the specified torque settings using an accurate torque wrench.

1

29.2 Centre main bearing and thrust washer location

29.3 Crankshaft lowered into crankcase

29.5 Tightening main bearing cap bolts

29 Crankshaft and main bearings - installation

1 Clean the backs of the bearing shells and the bearing recesses in both the crankcase and the caps.

2 The bearing shells with the oil holes are fitted in the cylinder block, and the shells without the oil holes in the bearing caps. Fit the thrust washers to the centre bearing in the crankcase, using grease to hold them in position (photo).

3 Oil the bearings liberally, then carefully lower the crankshaft into position (photo).

4 The thrust washers on the centre main bearing cap are positioned using grease to hold them in place, while the bearing cap is being installed. Ensure that the thrust washers are fitted with the lubrication grooves facing the crankshaft webs.

5 Install the remaining main bearing caps matching the identification marks, and tighten the retaining bolts evenly to the specified torque (photo).

6 Turn the crankshaft and check that it rotates smoothly.

7 Check the crankshaft endfloat using a dial gauge or feeler gauge (photo); if new thrust washers have been fitted the endfloat should be in accordance with the Specifications; if the original washers have been refitted and the endfloat is excessive, new thrust washers must be fitted (they are obtainable in a number of oversizes).

8 Smear the rear oil seal with engine oil on its inner and outer surfaces and carefully install it over the crankshaft rear journal with the aid of a metal tube; make sure that the open end of the seal faces inwards, and that the outer face of the seal is flush with the block (photo). Volvo use a special drift for fitting the oil seal to the correct depth. If the surface of the crankshaft is scored where the old oil seal has rubbed against it, then the new seal should be fitted 0.039 to 0.059 in (1.0 to 1.5 mm) less deep. To do this it is obvious that the special drift must be used.

29.7 Checking crankshaft endfloat

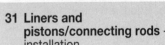

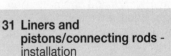

30 Flywheel - installation

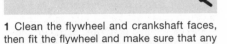

1 Clean the flywheel and crankshaft faces, then fit the flywheel and make sure that any previously made marks are aligned.

2 Smear the threads of the retaining bolts with a liquid locking agent, then tighten them to the specified torque, while restraining the flywheel with a wide-bladed screwdriver inserted into the teeth of the ring gear (photo).

3 If the engine is already in the car, refit the clutch as described in Chapter 5.

Note: *B14 models with the Renix electronic ignition system have a modified flywheel which has an extra ring gear with 40 teeth spaced around its circumference, in order that the electronic sensor can determine both engine speed and TDC. Be sure to use the correct flywheel.*

30.2 Tightening flywheel retaining bolts

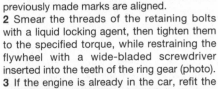

29.8 Installing crankshaft rear oil seal

31 Liners and pistons/connecting rods - installation

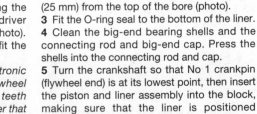

1 Lubricate the cylinder liner bores and the piston rings with engine oil.

2 Fit a piston ring compressor to No 1 piston, and with the liner inverted on the bench, install it into the liner to a position about 1 in (25 mm) from the top of the bore (photo).

3 Fit the O-ring seal to the bottom of the liner.

4 Clean the big-end bearing shells and the connecting rod and big-end cap. Press the shells into the connecting rod and cap.

5 Turn the crankshaft so that No 1 crankpin (flywheel end) is at its lowest point, then insert the piston and liner assembly into the block, making sure that the liner is positioned correctly and that the arrow on the piston crown is facing the flywheel end of the engine.

6 Clamp the liner in position, then lubricate the crankpin with engine oil.

31.2 Fitting a piston to a liner

31.9 Tightening a big-end cap nut

33.3 Checking timing mark alignment with a steel rule

33.4 Tensioning the chain will move the timing marks slightly

7 Using the handle of a hammer, tap the piston down the liner, at the same time guiding the connecting rod onto the crankpin. Make sure that the bearing shell does not become displaced.

8 Install the big-end bearing cap complete with bearing shell, making sure that the matching marks on the rod and cap are in alignment and are on the correct side of the engine. This will be automatic, providing the piston has been assembled to the connecting rod correctly and the arrows on the piston crown are pointing towards the flywheel end of the engine.

9 Fit the big-end nuts and tighten them to the specified torque (photo).

10 Turn the crankshaft to check that the bearings are free, then repeat the foregoing operations on the remaining three piston/liner assemblies.

11 If the engine is already in the car, refit the sump (Section 34) and cylinder head (Section 35).

32 Camshaft and followers - installation

1 Lubricate the camshaft bearings with engine oil and carefully insert the camshaft from the front of the cylinder block.

2 Install the flange retaining bolts and tighten to the specified torque, then check that the camshaft rotates smoothly.

3 Lubricate the followers and insert them into the cylinder block; if the original followers are being installed, make sure that they are replaced in their correct locations.

33 Timing covers, gear and chain - installation

1 If the crankshaft sprocket has been removed, locate the Woodruff key and tap the gear back into position, making sure that the timing mark is to the front. Turn the crankshaft until No 1 piston is at the top of its cylinder.

2 Temporarily locate the camshaft sprocket on the camshaft and turn both gears until the

timing marks are facing each other, and coincide with an imaginary line joining the crankshaft and camshaft centres, then remove the camshaft gear.

3 Fit the timing chain to the camshaft gear, then offer the timing chain to the crankshaft gear, keeping the camshaft gear over its location and the timing marks in alignment (photo).

4 Locate the timing chain over the crankshaft gear and fit the camshaft gear to the camshaft. Check that the timing marks are still aligned. **Note:** *Tensioning the chain will displace the timing marks from the centreline (photo).*

5 Install the camshaft gear bolt with a new lockplate, tighten it to the specified torque, and bend the tabs over the bolt head to lock it.

6 Fit the chain tensioner and locate the spring ends in the block and on the pad plate. Tighten the retaining bolt using an Allen key.

7 Remove the timing cover oil seal and drive in a new one using a piece of tubing as a drift. Apply engine oil to the seal lips and then install the timing cover, using a new gasket. Tighten the bolts only finger tight at this stage.

8 Fit the crankshaft pulley and tighten two opposite timing cover bolts. Remove the pulley and tighten all the timing cover bolts to the specified torque.

9 Fit the crankshaft pulley again and tighten the securing bolt to the specified torque.

10 If the engine is already in the car, refit the sump (Section 34) drivebelt (Chapter 2), and radiator (Chapter 2).

34 Oil pump and sump - installation

1 Install the oil pump onto the cylinder block and tighten the retaining bolts to the specified torque; note that there is no gasket between the pump and the cylinder block.

2 Locate the rubber strips in the timing cover and the rear main bearing cap grooves.

3 Grease the cork gaskets sparingly and locate them on the cylinder block, making sure that the ends cover the lips of the rubber strips.

4 Apply a sealing compound to the sump flange, then install it onto the cylinder block and tighten the retaining bolts in diagonal sequence to the specified torque.

5 If the engine is already in the car, reverse the preliminary procedure given in Section 10.

35 Cylinder head - reassembly and installation

1 On models from 1979, press the special seals onto the inlet valve guides. On all models, install the valves in their original sequence or, if new ones have been purchased, to the seats to which they have been ground, after having lubricated their stems.

2 Working on the first valve, fit the thrust washer to the cylinder head, followed by the valve spring and retainer. Note that the spring should be fitted with the end where the coils are closest towards the cylinder head.

3 Compress the valve spring and locate the split collets in the recess in the valve stem. Note that the collets are different for the inlet and exhaust valves (photo), the latter type having two curved collars. Release the compressor, then repeat the procedure on the remaining valves.

4 With all the valves installed, place the cylinder head flat on the bench and, using a hammer and interposed block of wood, tap the end of each valve stem to settle the components.

5 Oil the rocker shaft, then reassemble the

35.3 Exhaust (left) and inlet (right) valve spring collets

35.6 Cylinder head gasket mark

springs, rocker arms and pedestals in the reverse order to removal, and finally fit the circlip. Check that the bolt holes in the pedestals are aligned with the recesses in the rocker shaft.

6 Remove the cylinder liner clamps, if fitted, and make sure that the faces of the cylinder head and the cylinder block are perfectly clean. Lay a new gasket on the cylinder block with the words HAUT-TOP uppermost (photo). Do not use any kind of jointing compound.

7 Lower the cylinder head into position, insert the cylinder head bolts, and tighten them to the specified torque in the sequence shown in Fig. 1.20 (photo), and in two stages as given in the Specifications.

8 Install the pushrods in their original locations.

9 Lower the rocker shaft assembly onto the cylinder head; making sure that the adjusting ball-ends locate in the pushrods. Install the spring washers (convex side uppermost), nuts, and bolts and tighten them to the specified torque.

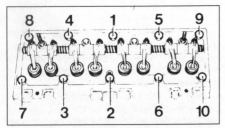

Fig. 1.20 Cylinder head bolt tightening sequence (Sec 35)

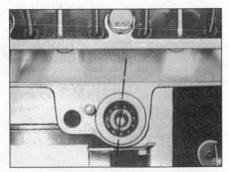

Fig. 1.21 Correct alignment of the distributor drivegear with No 1 piston at TDC compression (Sec 35)

35.7 Tightening the cylinder head bolts

10 Adjust the valve clearances, as described in Section 38, to the specified cold setting.

11 Using a ring spanner on the crankshaft pulley bolt, turn the crankshaft until No 1 piston (flywheel end) is at the top of its compression stroke. This position can be established by placing a finger over No 1 plug hole and rotating the crankshaft until compression can be felt; continue turning the crankshaft until the piston reaches the top of its stroke. Use a screwdriver through the plug hole to feel the movement of the piston, but be careful not to damage the piston crown or plug threads in the cylinder head.

12 Without moving the crankshaft, lower the distributor drivegear into mesh with the camshaft so that it assumes the position shown in Fig. 1.21. The larger segment of the drivegear must face the flywheel end of the engine.

13 Install the rocker cover with a new gasket and tighten the retaining nuts.

14 If the cylinder head is being installed with the engine in the car, reverse the preliminary procedure in Section 8, with reference to Chapter 2 for adjusting the drivebelt and refilling the cooling system. See Section 39 for the procedure for starting the engine and retightening the cylinder head bolts.

36 Ancillary components - installation

This is a reversal of the removal sequence given in Section 7 of this Chapter, but in addition the oil filter should be renewed.

To fit the new oil filter element, first clean the mating surfaces of the cylinder block and oil filter, then smear a thin film of engine oil on the filter sealing ring. Screw in the filter element until it touches the block, then tighten it a further one half turn *by hand.*

37 Engine - installation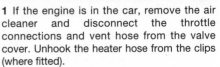

This is a reversal of the removal operations described in Section 5 but the following additional points should be noted:

a) *Grease the clutch output splines before engaging it with the propeller shaft*

b) *Adjust the throttle and choke cables as described in Chapter 3*
c) *Vent the cooling system as described in Chapter 2*
d) *Refill the engine with oil*
e) *On manual transmission models, adjust the clutch cable as described in Chapter 5*

38 Valve clearances - adjustment

1 If the engine is in the car, remove the air cleaner and disconnect the throttle connections and vent hose from the valve cover. Unhook the heater hose from the clips (where fitted).

2 Unscrew the nuts and remove the valve cover and gasket. Note the location of the fuel pipe clip on the rear nut.

3 Number the valves 1 to 8 from the front or rear of the engine then, using a ring spanner on the crankshaft pulley bolt, turn the engine in a clockwise direction until No 8 valve is fully open (ie spring compressed).

4 Insert a feeler blade of the correct thickness for an exhaust valve (see Specifications) between the end of No 1 valve stem and the rocker arm. The blade should be a firm sliding fit. If adjustment is necessary, slacken the locknut and turn the adjuster screw until the clearance is correct. Hold the adjuster screw stationary and tighten the locknut (photo). Recheck the adjustment, then repeat the procedure on the remaining valves in the following sequence:

Valve open	Valve to adjust
No 8 ex	No 1 ex
No 6 in	No 3 in
No 4 ex	No 5 ex
No 7 in	No 2 in
No 1 ex	No 8 ex
No 3 in	No 6 in
No 5 ex	No 4 ex
No 2 in	No 7 in

5 Refit the valve cover and gasket.

6 If the engine is in the car, refit the throttle connections, vent hose, heater hose (where fitted), and air cleaner.

38.4 Adjusting the valve clearances

39 Engine - adjustment after overhaul

1 Check that everything has been reconnected and that no loose rags or tools have been left within the engine compartment.
2 Turn the engine slow running screw in about half-a-turn to increase the engine idling speed (see Chapter 3). This will be necessary due to the tightness of the new engine components.

3 Pull the choke fully out and, with neutral selected, start the engine. This may take a little longer than usual as the fuel pump and carburettor bowl will be initially empty.
4 As soon as the engine starts, push the choke in until the engine runs at a fast tickover. Visually check the engine for leaks, particularly checking the water hoses, oil filter, and fuel hose unions.
5 Run the car on the road until the engine reaches its normal operating temperature.
6 Stop the engine and allow it to cool for approximately 2 1/2 hours. Remove the valve cover, then, referring to Fig. 1.20, loosen bolt 1 approximately 90° and retighten it to the specified second stage torque. Repeat the procedure on the remaining cylinder head bolts in the correct sequence. Refit the valve cover.
7 Start the engine and adjust the idling speed as described in Chapter 3.
8 Where new internal components have been installed, the engine speed should be restricted for the first 500 miles (800 km). At this mileage the engine oil should be renewed, the cylinder head bolts checked for correct torque, and the valve clearances readjusted.

Part B: B19 and B200 engines

40 General description and routine maintenance

The B19A and B19E engines were introduced in 1981 and were fitted to what are now called the 360 models. Both are four-cylinder, 1986 cc units; the A designating the carburettor version and the E the fuel injected version. In 1985, the B19 series engines were replaced by the B200K (carburettor version), and B200E (fuel injected version). Both types of engine are basically the same, the B200 series having minor modifications over the B19.

The engine is of four-cylinder, in-line type with a single overhead camshaft. The camshaft incorporates five main bearings with endfloat controlled by flanged main bearing shells on the rear main bearing. The cylinder head is of crossflow design.

The camshaft is driven by a toothed belt from the crankshaft, and the belt also drives the intermediate shaft. The camshaft is supported in five bearings.

The intermediate shaft is located on the left-hand side of the engine and incorporates three bearings. It drives the distributor, oil pump and, on carburettor engines, the fuel pump.

The cylinder block is of cast iron, and the cylinder head of aluminium alloy.

The vertical valves are operated by tappets (camshaft followers) running direct in the cylinder head and incorporating shims in contact with the camshaft. Valve stem oil seals are fitted to the inlet valve guides.

Lubrication is by means of a double gear oil pump located in the crankcase and driven by the intermediate shaft. The pump draws oil from the sump and forces it through a full-flow filter to the crankshaft, camshaft and intermediate shaft. The filter incorporates a bypass valve which opens if the filter becomes blocked. The pump incorporates a pressure relief valve to prevent excessive pressure.

The crankcase ventilation system consists of an oil separator on the cylinder block with a hose connected to the air inlet system (photo).

The engine mountings on early models are of the rubber cushion type, however as from 1984 they are hydraulic and filled with glycol.

Note: *The main Sections of this Part relate specifically to the B19 engine. Where any major differences in procedures for B200 engines occur, they will be pointed out in the text.*

Routine maintenance

Refer to Section 2.

41 Major operations possible with engine in car

The following operations can be carried out without having to remove the engine from the car:
a) *Removal and servicing of the cylinder head*
b) *Removal of the camshaft*
c) *Removal of the sump*
d) *Removal of the oil pump*
e) *Removal of the pistons and connecting rods*
f) *Removal of the timing belt*
g) *Removal of the intermediate shaft after removal of the radiator*
h) *Renewal of the engine mountings*
i) *Removal of the clutch and flywheel*
j) *Renewal of crankshaft, camshaft and intermediate shaft oil seals*

42 Major operations possible only after engine removal

The following operations can only be carried out after removal of the engine from the car:
a) *Removal of the crankshaft*
b) *Renewal of the crankshaft main bearings*

43 Engine - removal

1 Disconnect the battery negative lead. Remove the drivebelt and cooling fan, with reference to Chapter 2.
2 Unbolt the front exhaust bracket from the front pipe, clutch housing and exhaust manifold.
3 Remove the radiator, and unbolt the air inlet ducting from the front crossmember.
4 Unbolt and remove the cooling fan shroud.
5 Disconnect the following wiring:

Voltage regulator connector
Earth lead from valve cover (photo)
Engine wiring harness connector
Coil HT lead from the centre of the distributor cap

6 Unbolt the earth lead from the left-hand side of the cylinder block.
7 Disconnect the wiring from the starter motor.

40.1 Crankcase ventilation oil separator on the cylinder block

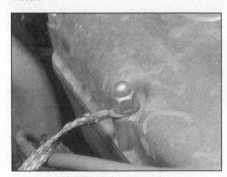

43.5 Earth lead location on the valve cover

1

43.28 Bottom view of an engine mounting

45.1 Top view of an engine mounting

8 Disconnect the heater supply and return hoses.

9 Disconnect the inlet hose from the carburettor or throttle valve housing (fuel injection models).

10 Disconnect the crankcase ventilation hose from the cylinder block.

11 Disconnect the brake servo from the inlet manifold.

12 On carburettor models disconnect the supply hose from the fuel pump, and also disconnect the throttle and choke cables.

13 On fuel injection models loosen the union nut and disconnect the fuel filter hose from the injection pressure manifold. Also disconnect the throttle cable.

 HAYNES HiNT *Cover the exposed fuel hose apertures with tape to prevent the ingress of dirt.*

14 If necessary, remove the air cleaner assembly to provide more working room.

15 Apply the handbrake, then jack up the front of the car and support it on axle stands.

16 Remove the engine splash guards.

17 Unbolt the front cover from the clutch housing.

18 Disconnect the clutch cable from the release arm and clutch housing.

19 Unbolt the bracket from the front of the exhaust system.

20 Unscrew the nuts and pull the exhaust downpipe from the exhaust manifold. Tie the downpipe to one side. Remove the gasket.

21 Remove the starter motor, with reference to Chapter 10.

22 Unscrew and remove the lower bolts securing the clutch housing to the engine.

23 Unscrew the engine shock absorber lower mounting nut from the front crossmember.

24 Unbolt and remove the front crossmember.

25 Lower the front of the car to the ground.

26 Attach a suitable hoist to the engine and take the weight of the unit.

27 Unscrew the engine mounting lower nuts.

28 Unbolt the engine mounting arms from the cylinder block and withdraw them from the mountings (photo).

29 Using a trolley jack and block of wood, support the front end of the torque tube.

30 Unscrew and remove the upper bolts securing the clutch housing to the engine.

31 Move the engine forwards until the clutch

is clear of the shaft and housing, then lift the engine from the engine compartment; taking care not to damage components on the bulkhead and sidepanels. Once the engine is high enough, pull the hoist forwards and lower the engine onto a workbench.

44 Engine - dismantling (general)

Refer to Section 6.

45 Ancillary components - removal

1 With the engine removed from the car the externally mounted ancillary components should now be removed before dismantling begins. The removal sequence need not necessarily follow the order given:

46.2 Engine oil drain plug

46.5 Oil filter

a) Inlet and exhaust manifolds (Chapter 3)
b) Fuel pump (carburettor engine) (Chapter 3)
c) Fuel injection components (Chapter 3)
d) Alternator and bracket (Chapter 10)
e) Engine mountings from the body, if necessary (photo)

46 Engine - dismantling

1 Disconnect the ignition setting sender (17 mm open ring spanner) where applicable.

2 Unbolt the dipstick tube from the block and remove it from the sump. Drain the engine oil (photo).

3 Remove the pulley from the water pump.

4 Disconnect the lead and remove the oil pressure sensor (photo).

5 Remove the oil filter (photo).

6 Remove the distributor (photo).

7 Remove the cover protecting the timing gears.

8 Remove the coolant pipe to the heater element and remove the water pump. Remove the thermostat housing, the thermostat and the lifting eye (photos).

9 Slacken the belt tensioner nut and slacken the belt by pushing the roller back against the spring. Lock the spring by inserting a 3 mm pin (eg drill) in the hole on the thrust pin. Remove the toothed drivebelt.

10 Remove the retaining nut and washer and pull off the belt tensioner roller.

11 Restrain the camshaft from turning (a bar in one of the holes) and remove the camshaft

46.4 Oil pressure sensor

46.6 Removing the distributor

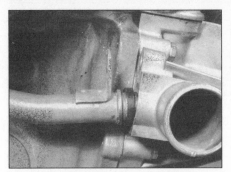

46.8A Removing the heater pipe from the water pump

46.8B Thermostat housing and lifting eye

46.13 Removing the crankshaft gear

46.15 Timing belt rear guard and bolt

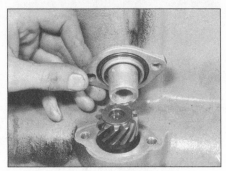

46.16 Removing the cover and oil pump pinion

46.18A Removing the clutch

46.18B Pilot bearing and circlip

46.19 Removing the flywheel bolts

46.21 Removing the oil pump

gear retaining nut. The gearwheel and guide plates can be pulled off by hand.

12 Remove the six bolts securing the crankshaft pulley and lift off the pulley. Remove the centre bolt from the front of the crankshaft and remove the front hub.

13 Remove the crankshaft gear and guide plate. Use a puller, if necessary (photo).

14 Remove the retaining bolt and gearwheel from the intermediate shaft.

15 Remove the cable harness and the rear part of the belt guard. Remove the front sealing flange and press out the seals (photo).

16 Remove the oil pump pinion cover and lift out the oil pump pinion. Pull out the intermediate shaft, taking care that the shaft gear does not damage the bearing bushing in the engine block (photo).

17 Remove the valve cover and gasket. Remove the cylinder head bolts, in the reverse order to Fig. 1.34 using an Allen key, and lift off the head.

18 Unscrew the bolts holding the clutch assembly to the flywheel a little at a time, keeping them in step to avoid risk of distorting the clutch cover. Mark the clutch assembly and flywheel to identify position for replacement and remove the clutch assembly. Remove the circlip retaining the pilot bearing and remove the washer and bearing (photos).

19 Restrain the flywheel from turning and remove the eight retaining bolts. Remove the flywheel taking care not to push in the ignition setting sender, if Renix ignition is fitted.

20 Remove the reinforcing bracket. Remove the rear sealing flange and press out the seal.

21 Remove the sump. Remove the oil pump and the O-ring seals from the block and also from the pipe, if fitted (photo),

22 Check the marking on the connecting rods and caps, and mark the pistons accordingly, so that they can be identified regarding their respective cylinders when being refitted. The five main bearing caps are

marked 1 to 5 with No 1 at the front. When removing bearing shells, mark them too, so that they can be refitted in the same location if they are not being renewed.

23 Remove the pistons and connecting rods by removing the bearing caps and shells and pushing the connecting rods through the cylinders and steadying the pistons as they emerge. Take care not to scratch or damage the pistons as they are removed.

24 Remove the main bearing caps and lift out the crankshaft. Remove the bearing shells from the engine block and caps (photos),

47 Cylinder head and camshaft
- dismantling

1 Remove the spark plugs and, on the fuel injection engine, the injectors.

2 Check the marking on the camshaft bearing

46.24A Lifting out the crankshaft

46.24B Removing the main bearing shells

47.3 Removing the tappets

47.5A Compressing the valve springs with home made tools

47.5B Removing the valve springs

caps, they are numbered 1 to 5 from the front. Slacken off the cap retaining nuts, evenly and in rotation till the tension is off the camshaft, then remove the bearing caps and the camshaft. Remove the front seal and the half-moon shaped rubber seal at the rear of the cylinder head.

3 Lift out the valve tappets (camshaft followers) and adjuster washers and remove the rubber rings. Identify the tappets to their location so that they can be fitted in the same position on reassembly (photo).

4 Clean the oil and grease off the cylinder head and remove the carbon from the combustion chambers and valve heads with a scraper or a rotary wire brush.

5 Using a suitable valve spring compressing tool, compress the spring until the collets are free from their recess, remove the collets, release the pressure on the spring, lift off the upper spring retainer, the spring and the lower spring retainer. Push the valve through the valve guide and remove it. If the valve seems a tight fit in the guide, this may be because the upper part of the stem has carbon on it. Give it a clean in this case. Remove the valve stem seals from the inlet valve guides (photos).

6 Keep the valves lined up in the order you remove them and place them with their springs and retainers, together with their tappets (camshaft followers).

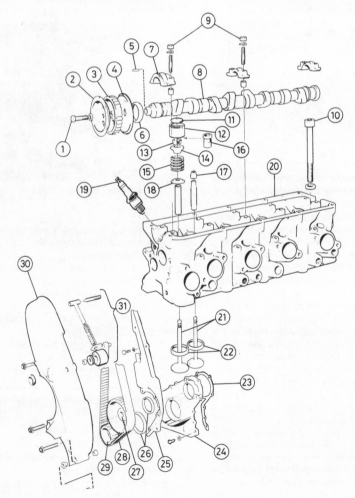

Fig. 1.22 Cylinder head and timing components (Sec 47)

1 Bolt	16 Rubber ring
2 Outer guide plate	17 Inlet valve stem oil seal
3 Camshaft gear	18 Seat
4 Inner guide plate	19 Spark plug
5 Key	20 Cylinder head
6 Oil seal	21 Valves
7 Bearing cap	22 Valve seats
8 Camshaft	23 Gasket
9 Nuts	24 Front sealing flange
10 Head bolt	25 Belt guard (rear)
11 Adjuster washer	26 Oil seals
(pressure pad)	27 Intermediate shaft gear
12 Tappet	28 Timing belt
13 Collets	29 Crankshaft gear
14 Retainer	30 Belt guard (front)
15 Spring	31 Tensioner

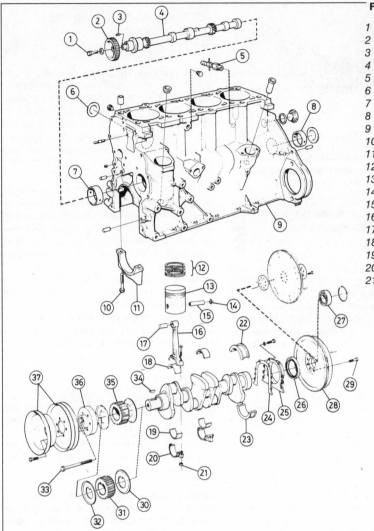

Fig. 1.23 Cylinder block and crankshaft components (Sec 47)

1 Bolt	22 Rear main bearing upper shell
2 Intermediate shaft gear	
3 Key	23 Rear main bearing lower shell
4 Intermediate shaft	
5 Drain plug	24 Gasket
6 Core plug	25 Rear sealing flange
7 Front bearing	26 Oil seal
8 Rear bearing	27 Pilot bearing
9 Cylinder block	28 Flywheel
10 Bolt	29 Bolt
11 Main bearing cap	30 Inner guide plate
12 Piston rings	31 Crankshaft gear (later models)
13 Piston	
14 Circlip	32 Outer guide plate
15 Gudgeon pin	33 Bolt
16 Connecting rod	34 Key
17 Small end bearing	35 Crankshaft gear (early models)
18 Big-end bearing upper shell	
19 Big-end bearing lower shell	36 Hub
20 Big-end bearing cap	37 Pulleys
21 Nut	

Note: *On B200 engines there is a plastic seal at the rear end of the cylinder head. The seal can be removed by prising it out with a screwdriver, and refitted using a flat drift of suitable size. The seal should be fitted flush with the surface of the cylinder head.*

48 Examination and renovation - general

With the engine now completely stripped, clean all the components and examine them for wear. Each part should be checked and, where necessary, renewed or renovated, as described in the following Sections.

49 Oil pump - examination and renovation

1 Unscrew the bolts and separate the cover and strainer from the main body of the oil pump, then remove the guide, spring and plunger. Check that the gears are marked for position then remove them.

2 Clean the components in paraffin and wipe dry. Use an air line to clean the internal oilways.

3 Examine the gears and housing for damage. Check the cover for wear. Fit the gears and check the backlash, this should be

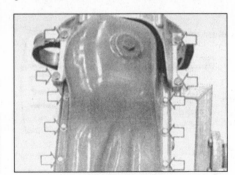

Fig. 1.24 Sump and reinforcing bracket bolts - arrowed (Sec 49)

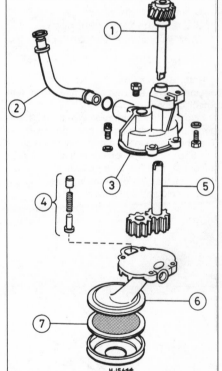

Fig. 1.25 Exploded view of the oil pump (Sec 49)

1 Pinion	5 Gears
2 Delivery pipe	6 Cover
3 Body	7 Strainer
4 Pressure relief valve	

1

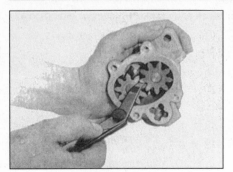

Fig. 1.26 Checking the oil pump gear backlash (Sec 49)

Fig. 1.27 Checking the oil pump gear endfloat (Sec 49)

as specified. Check the endfloat as shown in Fig. 1.27, this should also be as specified. Check for wear by fitting the drivegear; the gear should rotate freely without side play. If wear is apparent the pump will have to be renewed.

4 Check that the free length of the pressure relief spring is as given in the Specifications, and renew it if necessary.

5 Reassemble the oil pump in reverse order and finally prime it by lowering the pick-up in clean engine oil and turning the gears by inserting the pinion and rotating it clockwise. Renew the sealing rings at each end of the delivery pipe.

50 Crankshaft and bearings - examination and renovation

Refer to Section 21. Note that these engines have different wear tolerances (see Specifications).

Inspect the bearing shells for signs of general wear, scoring, pitting and scratches. The shells should be a matt grey in colour. If any trace of copper colour is noticed, it is an indication that the bearings are badly worn, because the white metal is plated onto a copper coloured underlay.

51 Pistons and piston rings - examination and renovation

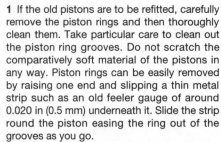

1 If the old pistons are to be refitted, carefully remove the piston rings and then thoroughly clean them. Take particular care to clean out the piston ring grooves. Do not scratch the comparatively soft material of the pistons in any way. Piston rings can be easily removed by raising one end and slipping a thin metal strip such as an old feeler gauge of around 0.020 in (0.5 mm) underneath it. Slide the strip round the piston easing the ring out of the grooves as you go.

2 If new rings are to be fitted to the old pistons, then the top ring should be stepped so as to clear the ridge left above the previous top ring. If a normal but oversize new ring is fitted it will hit the ridge and break, because the new ring will not have worn in the same way as the old.

3 Before fitting the rings on the pistons, put them in the cylinder bore at a point below the bottom limit of their travel and check their gap with reference to the Specifications. To keep the rings square in the bore for measurement, line them up with a piston in the bore.

4 Check the fit of the piston rings in the grooves by rolling them around the outside of the grooves and inserting a feeler blade.

5 When refitting the piston rings make sure that they are located in the correct grooves, as shown in Fig. 1.29, and locate the gaps at 120° intervals.

52 Gudgeon pins - examination and renovation

1 The gudgeon pins are retained in the pistons by circlips and can easily be pushed out of the pistons when these are removed. When you separate the connecting rod from the piston, mark the connecting rod so that you can refit it the same way round. There is no need to mark the piston as this has a small slot (which must always face forwards when the piston is in the engine) on the top (photo).

2 The fit of the gudgeon pin in the connecting rod should be such that it can be pushed out with light thumb pressure, but should have no noticeable looseness. It should fit in the piston so that you can push it through by hand, against light resistance. If the gudgeon pin hole in the piston is worn, an over-sized gudgeon pin must be fitted. In this case the holes must be reamed out in line to the correct measurement.

3 If the bush in the connecting rod is worn, it can be pressed out and a new bush pressed in. The new bush must be reamed to the correct fit.

53 Intermediate shaft - examination and renovation

1 Examine the pinions for the distributor and oil pump for chipping or damage. Check the fuel pump operating cam for wear.

2 Fit the shaft in its bearings in the engine block. If there is noticeable play between the intermediate shaft and its bearings, they will have to be renewed, but this is a highly specialised job, involving the reaming of three bearings in line - a task for a specialist.

54 Cylinder bores and crankcase - examination and renovation

1 The procedure is basically identical to that given in Section 22, however the liners cannot

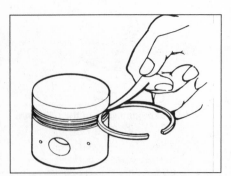

Fig. 1.28 Checking the piston ring clearance (Sec 51)

Fig. 1.29 Cross-section of the piston rings (Sec 51)

52.1 The slot in the piston crown must face the front of the engine

be removed on this engine. If the bores are worn excessively they must be rebored to an oversize dimension, by a specialist engineering firm.

55 Camshaft and tappets - examination and renovation

1 If there should be noticeable play between the camshaft and its bearings, or if the bearings are damaged then the cylinder head will have to be renewed as the bearings are machined in the head. If very light scratches are present on the camshaft these can be removed by gently rubbing down with a very fine grade emery cloth or oil stone. The greatest care must be taken to keep the cam profiles smooth.

2 Examine the tappets (camshaft followers) for scoring or damage. Place them in the cylinder head and check that they move easily but have no noticeable side play.

3 Check the condition of the adjuster washers; if they show signs of wear they must be renewed.

56 Cylinder head - decarbonising, valve grinding and renovation

The procedure is described in Section 27, but the information on the rocker shaft does not apply. Use the Specifications for the B19 or B200 engine as applicable.

57 Flywheel - examination and renovation

1 Examine the surface of the flywheel; if it is scored or damaged it should be renewed or refaced.

2 Examine the teeth of the starter ring gear and renew the gear if they are chipped or badly worn. To do this, drill the ring then split it with a cold chisel, and withdraw the ring.

3 Heat the new ring to 446°F (230°C) in an oven, then quickly fit it to the flywheel (inner chamfered edge first).

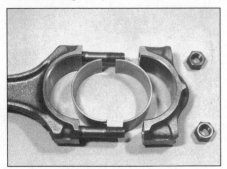

60.1A Big-end bearing components

59.3 Rear main bearing shell

4 Allow the ring to cool naturally without quenching.

Note: *Since 1984 the flywheel has been modified in order that the Renix electronic ignition system can function. Be sure to utilise the correct flywheel.*

58 Engine reassembly - general

Refer to Section 28.

59 Crankshaft - refitting

1 Make sure that the crankcase is thoroughly clean and that all the oilways are clear. Inject oil into the oilways at several points with a forcefeed oil can or plastic bottle: this will have the two-fold benefit of checking that the oilways are clear and getting oil into them before you start assembly. Do the same with the crankshaft - it is important to get as much oil as possible into the crankshaft oilways.

2 Remove every trace of protective grease from new bearing shells.

3 Wipe the seats of the main bearing shells in the crankcase clean and fit the appropriate shells in them. The rear shell incorporates thrust flanges. Note that the bearing shells have tabs on them which fit into grooves in the casing, so they can only be fitted the one way. If the old bearings are being refitted be sure to place them in their original positions (photo).

60.1B Marking on connecting rod and cap

59.8 Tightening the main bearing cap bolts

4 Oil the shells generously and place the crankshaft on top of them - be sure that it is the right way round.

5 Wipe the bearing cap housings and fit their shells into them, keeping an eye of the order if necessary.

6 Oil the bearing surfaces of the crankshaft generously and fit the bearing caps over them, ensuring that they locate properly. The mating surfaces must be spotlessly clean or the caps will not seat correctly. As each cap is fitted, put a new pair of fixing bolts through the holes and screw them up finger tight. Be sure the caps are fitted in their right order and the right way round.

7 When all the caps are fitted and the nuts finger tight, check that the crankshaft rotates freely without any suggestion of high spots. If it does not, there is something wrong; do not go any further in the assembly until the case has been found. The most likely cause is dirt on one of the bearing shells.

8 Tighten the bolts evenly to the specified torque and check that the crankshaft rotates freely (photo).

9 Using a feeler blade between the crankshaft web and the rear main bearing shell flange, check that the endfloat is as given in the Specifications.

60 Pistons and connecting rods - refitting

1 With the pistons and connecting rods reassembled, check that the marks are as shown in Fig. 1.30 (photo).

2 Oil the cylinder bores and the pistons.

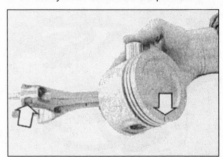

Fig. 1.30 Correct relation of the connecting rod and piston - arrows (Sec 60)

1

60.4 Using a piston ring compressor to fit the pistons

60.5A Fit the big-end bearing caps . . .

60.5B . . . and tighten the nuts

3 Wipe the recesses in the connecting rods and big-end caps and fit the shells with the locating tabs engaged with the corresponding grooves.

4 Insert the pistons into the cylinders from the top, using a device like the one shown in the photograph to clamp the rings (photo). If you haven't got the correct tool it is a very simple matter to make a substitute. We have used a large worm drive clip with success. Whatever you use, make sure that you do not scratch the piston. Gently tap the piston through the piston ring compressor into the cylinder. Ensure that each piston is the correct one for the bore and that the front of the piston (with the slot) faces forwards. As the piston is fitted, lubricate the crankpin and guide the connecting rod onto it.

5 Fit the big-end bearing cap and tighten the nuts evenly to the specified torque (photo). Check that the crankshaft turns freely.

6 Repeat the procedure on the other pistons.

Additional note for B200 engines

The big-end bearing bolts on B200 engines may be re-used provided their length does not exceed 2.185 in (55.5 mm).

61 Oil pump - refitting

Fit new sealing rings on both ends of the delivery pipe. Make sure the pipe is located properly in the crankcase and the pump. Fit the pump retaining bolts.

62 Rear sealing flange - refitting

1 Press a new seal into the sealing flange.
2 Clean the surface of the block, and using a smear of grease, stick the new gasket in place on the block.
3 Grease the rubber lip on the sealing ring and opposite surface on the crankshaft with mineral grease.
4 Fit the sealing flange, taking great care that the rubber lip is not damaged by the edge of the crankshaft or twisted so that the spring jumps out of its position (photo).
5 Trim off the projecting parts of the gasket with a knife (photo).

63 Intermediate shaft and front sealing flange - refitting

1 Oil the intermediate shaft journals. Fit the shaft in the block taking care that the gears do not damage the bearing bushes in the block (photo).
2 Press new oil seals into the front sealing flange.
3 Clean the joint faces of the block and sealing flange, and fit a new gasket and the front sealing flange (photo).
4 Cut off the projecting parts of the gasket and fit the rear part of the belt guard and the cable harness (photo).

62.4 Fitting the rear sealing flange

62.5 Trimming the rear sealing flange gasket

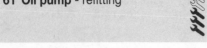

63.1 Fitting the intermediate shaft

63.3 Fitting the front sealing flange

63.4 Fitting the timing belt rear guard

64 Sump - removal and refitting

1 If the sump is to be removed with the engine in the car, first carry out the following:

a) *Apply the handbrake, then jack up the front of the car and support on axle stands*
b) *Remove the engine splash guards*
c) *Remove the oil level dipstick and pull the dipstick tube away from the sump*
d) *Unscrew the engine shock absorber lower mounting nut from the crossmember*
e) *Unbolt and remove the front crossmember*
f) *Drain the engine oil into a container*
g) *Unbolt and remove the sump. Remove the gasket*

2 If the engine is removed from the car, the removal of the sump is described as part of engine dismantling (Section 46).
3 Ensure that the sump is really clean and that all traces of the old gasket have been removed from the flanges of the sump and the crankcase. Fit the new gasket to the crankcase with the writing downwards and the mark facing the starter location.
4 Fit the sump and tighten the bolts evenly.
5 If the engine is in the car, reverse the remaining removal procedures.

65 Water pump - refitting

The water pump is simply screwed to the cylinder block, a gasket being required even though there is no water outlet from the pump into the side of the block. A sealing ring is placed in the groove at the top of the pump and will be compressed by the cylinder head when it is fitted (photos).

Fitting the water pump when the head is removed, as we are doing here, is somewhat simpler than fitting it with the head in position because you have to push the pump up against the head, ensuring that the ring is properly located, as you put in the bolts. This will have to be done, of course, if the pump has been removed for some reason when the head has not been taken off.

66 Flywheel and clutch - refitting

1 Turn the crankshaft so that No 1 cylinder is at TDC (top-dead-centre).
2 Position the flywheel on the crankshaft so that pin (A) is approximately 15° from the horizontal position and pointing away from the starter motor mounting, as shown in Fig. 1.31. Note that there are two pins (A) and (B).
3 Fit the retaining bolts and tighten them to the specified torque (photo).

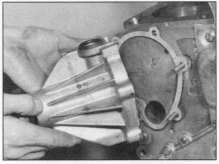

65.1A Fitting the water pump

65.1B O-ring in the top of the water pump

66.3 Tightening the flywheel bolts

66.5 Marking on the friction plate

4 Fit the pilot bearing (packed with grease), the retaining washer and circlip. Fit the reinforcing bracket.
5 Refit the clutch friction plate and pressure plate assembly and lightly secure it in position with its securing bolts (photo).
6 Carefully line up the friction plate with the pilot bearing. This is ideally done by using the shaft from the clutch housing, if it is available, otherwise use a mandrel with a diameter the same as the friction plate hub and having a spigot on the end which fits in the pilot bearing.
7 When the clutch friction plate is correctly aligned, tighten the clutch assembly bolts in stages in a diagonal and progressive manner.

Additional note for engines with Renix electronic ignition

8 To ensure correct ignition timing on engines fitted with Renix electronic ignition, the flywheel must be fitted as follows.

9 Rotate the crankshaft so that No 1 cylinder is at TDC by lining up the timing mark on the crankshaft pulley with the zero degree mark on the timing scale.
10 Offer up the flywheel to the crankshaft so that the first hole after one of the two wider spaced gaps between the holes is positioned at 30 degrees to the vertical centre line of the engine (see Fig. 1.32).
11 Fit and tighten the flywheel retaining bolts as described for conventional ignition models,

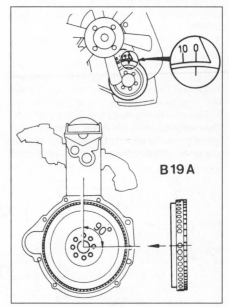

Fig. 1.32 Aligning the modified flywheel for Renix ignition (Sec 66)

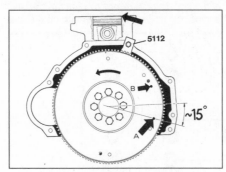

Fig. 1.31 Correct location of the flywheel on the crankshaft (Sec 66)

A Pin   B Pin

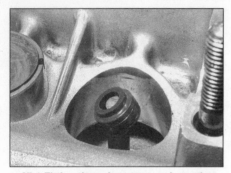

67.1 Fitting the valve stem seals on the inlet valve guides

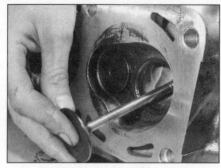

67.2A Inserting an inlet valve

67.2B Valve spring collets fitted in position

67.2C Rubber ring fitted above the collets

Fig. 1.33 Fitting the shim in the tappet

then check the flywheel is correctly fitted as follows.

12 Rotate the engine 90 degrees from the TDC position, at which point the first hole after a wide space should be located directly below the Renix speed sensor opening.

67 Cylinder head and camshaft - reassembly

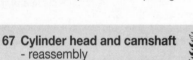

1 Fit new valve stem seals on the inlet valve guides (photo).

2 Unless parts have been renewed, refit the valves, springs and tappets (camshaft followers) in the positions from which they were removed. Oil the valve stems before inserting them in the valve guides (photo). Over each valve fit the lower spring retainer, the valve spring and the upper spring retainer. Using a valve spring compressing tool,

compress the spring and fit the collets in the recess in the valve stem and release the compression tool. Fit the rubber ring (photos).

3 Oil the bearing seats for the camshaft, the bearing caps, the camshaft and the tappets (camshaft followers). Fit the tappets and the adjuster shims (Fig. 1.33).

4 Place the camshaft in the cylinder head with the front dowel upwards.

5 Coat the face of the front cap that mates with the cylinder head with a sealing compound. Fit the caps, with the markings aligned as previously noted, and the retaining nuts. Screw down the nuts in an even and progressive manner to compress the valve springs without putting uneven stress on the camshaft. Tighten the nuts to the specified torque, then check the camshaft endfloat.

6 Before refitting the camshaft seal apply mineral grease to the rubber lip of the seal and the corresponding surface on the camshaft. Take care not to damage the seal against the edge of the camshaft. Fit the seal

so that a new wear surface is obtained against the camshaft.

7 Fit the rear guide plate, the gearwheel with the slot on the gear located on the pin on the camshaft end, then the front guide plate, washer and retaining bolt. Restrain the gearwheel from turning and torque tighten the bolt to the specified torque.

8 Fit the spark plugs and, on the fuel injection engine, the injectors (using new O-ring seals).

68 Cylinder head and camshaft - refitting

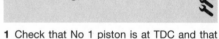

1 Check that No 1 piston is at TDC and that the camshaft lobes for No 1 cylinder are both pointing obliquely upwards.

2 Check that both cylinder block and cylinder head mating faces are perfectly clean. Also ensure that all foreign matter is removed from the cylinder head bolt holes in both the head and block, using compressed air. This is particularly important, since one of the bolt holes in the head (No 3 in the tightening sequence - see Fig. 1.34) forms part of an oil feed passage to the camshaft. Always use a new cylinder head gasket, since the old gasket will be compressed, and incapable of giving a good seal. Do not use grease or gasket cement on the gasket.

3 Place the gasket on the cylinder block the right way up and carefully aligned with the bolt holes in the block.

4 Place the cylinder head in position, being careful to align the bolt holes accurately (photo). Clean the head bolts thoroughly, in

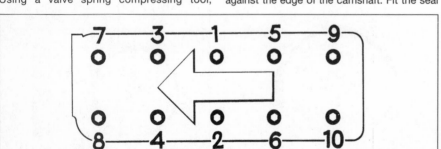

Fig. 1.34 Cylinder head bolt tightening sequence (Sec 68)
Fig. 1.35 Cylinder head bolt with

68.4 Fitting the cylinder head

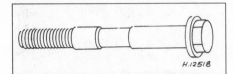

recessed section (Sec 68)
Fig. 1.36 Tightening the crankshaft front

hub centre bolt (Sec 69)
Fig. 1.37 Timing belt and gear alignment

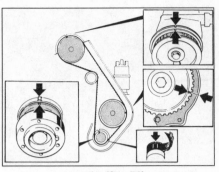

marks (Sec 70)
Fig. 1.38 Using Volvo tool 5022 to depress

particular the bolt which is No 3 in the tightening sequence (see Fig. 1.34), then fit them.

5 Tighten the cylinder head bolts, in the specified stages, in the numerical sequence shown in Fig. 1.34. Tighten the bolts to the specified torque.

Additional note for B200 engines

6 On B200 engines the cylinder head bolts incorporate a recessed centre section. If this section shows any sign of necking or distortion of any one bolt, then the cylinder head bolts should be renewed as a set.

7 The cylinder head bolts should be renewed in any case after they have been used five times.

---

69 Crankshaft and intermediate shaft gears - refitting

Fit the gearwheel on the intermediate shaft, and restraining the shaft from turning, fit the retaining bolt and tighten to the specified torque (photo).

Fit the guide plate on the crankshaft, the gear, the front hub and the centre bolt. Tighten the centre bolt to the specified torque while restraining the crankshaft from turning by blocking the flywheel. Where applicable the keyway bevel on the gear must face the cylinder block.

---

70 Timing belt - removal and refitting

1 If the timing belt is to be removed with the engine in the car, first carry out the following operations.

a) *Refer to the relevant Chapter/Section and remove the carburettor preheating hose or air intake pipe, viscous cooling fan and the drivebelt(s)*

b) *Remove the upper timing belt cover, then rotate the engine until the mark on the crankshaft pulley lines up with the TDC mark on the lower cover*

c) *On B200K engines, remove the two clips for the preheating hose then (on all types) remove the bolts and withdraw the shroud*

d) *Remove the six bolts from the crankshaft pulley wheel, remove the pulley, then remove the bolts from and withdraw the lower cover*

e) *Slacken the timing belt tensioner and remove the belt*

2 If the engine is removed from the car, the removal of the timing belt is described as part of engine dismantling (Section 46).

3 Fit the belt tensioner and retaining nut. Tighten the nut and remove the pin (fitted at disassembly) compressing the spring.

4 Rotate the crankshaft to where the timing marks coincide (Fig. 1.37).

5 Rotate the intermediate shaft to where the marks coincide (Fig. 1.37).

6 Place the valve cover in position and rotate the camshaft to where the marks coincide (Fig. 1.37).

7 Fit the toothed belt on the crankshaft gear. Ensure that the belt is in good condition and clean, with no trace of oil or grease. New belts have a colour marking. Set the double lines on the belt against the crankshaft mark, the next

line should then be opposite the intermediate shaft mark and the other mark opposite the camshaft mark (photo).

8 Stretch the belt and fit it on the camshaft gear and belt tensioner. Do not use any tools for this as they might damage the belt.

9 Slacken the tensioner retaining nut, so that the spring tensions the belt and then re-tighten the nut (photo).

10 Rotate the engine clockwise and then check that the belt marks are correctly aligned. Retension the belt and tighten the nut.

11 Fit the pulley on the crankshaft front hub and tighten the bolts.

12 Fit the belt guard casing.

13 If the engine is in the car, reverse the remaining removal procedures.

---

71 Valve clearances - adjustment

1 Lift off the valve cover and turn the engine to the firing position for No 1 cylinder (both cams on No 1 cylinder pointing obliquely upwards at equal angles, and the ignition mark on crankshaft pulley at 0°). Always turn the crankshaft with the centre bolt.

2 Measure the valve clearance with a feeler gauge (photo). Compare the measured clearance with the value given in the Specifications. Only adjust a clearance if it is outside the checking tolerance.

1

69.1 Fitting the intermediate shaft gearwheel

70.7 Timing belt marks

70.9 Timing belt tensioner

71.2 Checking the valve clearances

71.6 Using a metal bar to keep the tappets depressed when changing the shims

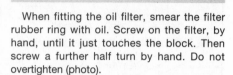

74 Oil filter - refitting

When fitting the oil filter, smear the filter rubber ring with oil. Screw on the filter, by hand, until it just touches the block. Then screw a further half turn by hand. Do not overtighten (photo).

71.7A Fitting the valve cover gasket

71.7B Ignition setting indicator

75 Ancillary components - refitting

1 The procedure is a reversal of the removal procedure.
2 Fit the thermostat housing, inlet and exhaust manifolds together with the lifting brackets. When fitting the exhaust manifold always use new gaskets and position them with the marking UT facing outwards. Centre the manifold round to No 1 cylinder lower stud and fit washers so that the marking UT/OUT faces outwards. Fit the lifting bracket at No 3 cylinder. Tighten the nuts (photo).
3 When fitting the alternator, tension the belt, as described in Chapter 2.
4 When fitting the cold start valve (fuel injection engines) don't forget to connect the earth lead at one of the retaining screws.
5 When fitting the water pump to heater pipe always fit new rubber seals.

3 To adjust the clearance, turn the tappet so that the slots are at right-angles to the camshaft. Position the Volvo tool 5022 as shown in Fig. 1.38 and depress the tappets (camshaft followers) so that the shim can be removed.
4 Remove the shim and fit another shim of the correct thickness to obtain the specified clearance. Shims are available in different thicknesses. The thickness of the shim is marked on one side; always fit the shim with the marked face downwards. Oil the shim before fitting it. Remove the tappet depressing tool.
5 Rotate the engine to No 3 cylinder firing position and proceed as for No 1 cylinder, then to No 4 cylinder and No 2 cylinder.
6 If the Volvo tappet depressing tool is not available the tappet can be depressed by turning the engine till the cam depresses the tappet, then fitting a wedge to hold the tappet down while you turn the camshaft to the

checking position and lift out the shim, as shown in photograph (photo).
7 Fit the halfmoon-shaped rubber seal at the rear of the cylinder head. Place the gasket in position. Oil the camshaft and fit the valve cover. Attach the ignition setting indicator (where applicable - Renix ignition) to the valve cover with one of the nuts (photos).

72 Distributor - refitting

Refer to Chapter 4.

73 Fuel pump (carburettor engine) - refitting

Refer to Chapter 3.

76 Engine - refitting

Refitting is a reversal of removal, but before tightening the engine mounting nuts measure the distance from the crankshaft pulley to the mounting holes or underbody members on each side. The right-hand side dimension should be 0.040 to 0.120 in (1.0 to 3.0 mm) more than the left-hand side dimension (see Fig. 1.39). Adjust the clutch cable, as described in Chapter 5. Fill the engine with oil, and the cooling system with coolant.

the tappets (Sec 71)
Fig. 1.39 Engine alignment dimensions

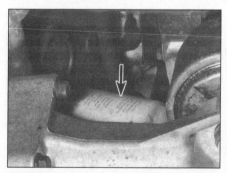

74.1 Bottom view of the oil filter (arrowed)

75.2 Exhaust manifold showing lifting eye location

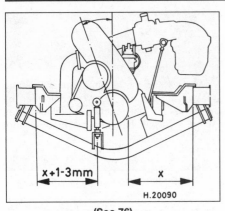

(Sec 76)
Fig. 1.40 Cutaway view of the B172 engine

77 Engine - adjustment after major overhaul

Refer to Section 39.

Where socket-head cylinder head bolts are fitted, retighten them to the final torque given in the Specifications using the method described in Section 39. Where hexagon head cylinder head bolts are fitted there is no need to retighten them.

Part C: B172 engine

78 General description and routine maintenance

The B172K is a four-cylinder, in-line petrol engine with overhead camshaft. The cylinder head is light alloy, the camshaft running in five bearings machined in the head. The camshaft is driven from the crankshaft by a toothed belt, and operates the valves directly, there being no pushrods. Valve clearances are set by shims which are set in the tappet head.

The fuel pump and distributor are located on the cylinder head and are driven by the camshaft.

The cylinder block is of cast iron, the crankshaft running in five main bearings lined with horizontally split white metal bearings. The cylinder bores are machined directly in the block, and cannot be renewed. Part of the water pump, which is driven by the alternator drivebelt, is machined in the engine block. The crankshaft front oil seal is located in a housing which is then bolted to the block. The rear oil seal is more conventional. The oil pump, which is bolted to the bottom of the block, is driven by an intermediate shaft which is driven by the toothed belt.

The pistons and connecting rods are of light alloy and are of a special design known as 'bowl in piston' or 'Heron head'. This simply means that the combustion chambers are in the bowl of the piston and not in the cylinder head. This design is more efficient than conventional combustion chambers.

Routine maintenance

Refer to Section 2.

79 Major operations possible with engine in car

The following operations can be carried out without having to remove the engine:

a) *Removal and refitting of the timing belt*
b) *Removal and refitting of the camshaft*
c) *Removal and refitting of the cylinder head*
d) *Removal and refitting of the sump*
e) *Removal and refitting of the oil pump*
f) *Removal and refitting of the connecting rod and piston assemblies*
g) *Removal and refitting of the intermediate shaft*
h) *Removal and refitting of the engine mountings*
i) *Removal and refitting of the flywheel*
j) *Removal and refitting of the crankshaft rear oil seal*

80 Major operations requiring engine removal

The following operation can only be carried out after removal of the engine from the car:
Removal and refitting of the crankshaft and main bearings

81 Engine - removal

General note on engine removal

The engine is removed complete with the clutch housing. Two lifting eyes are provided, bolted to the engine; make sure that the sling and lifting gantry you intend to use are in good condition and capable of lifting the weight of the engine. Before starting work, check on the

(Sec 78)
1 *Distributor*

2 *Camshaft*
3 *Timing belt*
4 *Belt cover*
5 *Idler pulley*
6 *Alternator*
7 *Tensioning sprocket*
8 *Drivebelt*
9 *Water pump*
10 *Intermediate shaft*
11 *Oil pump*
Fig. 1.41 Typical

1

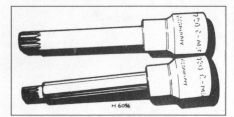

**splined socket bits
(Sec 81)**

availability of spare parts and gasket overhaul sets, normally obtainable from your Volvo dealer. Socket-headed, multi-point bolts are used extensively in the construction of the engine, and a set of suitable wrenches are essential. Where reference is made to removing ancillary components, refer to the relevant Chapter of the manual.

1 Remove the battery (Chapter 10).

2 Remove the bonnet (Chapter 9).

3 Remove the engine splash guard and drain the coolant by disconnecting the lower radiator hose. Drain the engine oil.

4 Release the exhaust mounting bracket on the clutch housing, and remove the clamp securing the exhaust downpipe to the exhaust manifold (Chapter 2).

5 Disconnect the propeller shaft (Chapter 6).

6 Disconnect the clutch cable (Chapter 5).

7 Disconnect the engine earth strap (photo).

8 Remove the nuts from the front and rear engine mountings.

9 Disconnect the water pipe bracket.

10 Remove the two lower bolts from the thermo electric cooling fan.

11 Remove the air filter housing assembly and air intake hoses (Chapter 3).

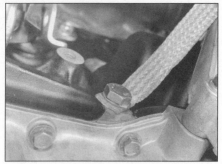

81.7 Engine earth strap bolt on the cylinder block

12 Disconnect the coolant hose from the thermostat housing and release the pipe from the bracket.

13 Disconnect the two heater hoses from the engine and tie them back out of the way (photo).

14 Disconnect the fuel inlet and return hoses from the fuel pump (Chapter 3).

15 Disconnect the accelerator and choke control cables (Chapter 3).

16 Remove the two upper bolts from the thermo electric cooling fan, disconnect the electrical connector, and remove the fan and support bracket assembly (Chapter 2).

17 Disconnect the brake servo vacuum hose from the servo (photo).

18 Release the cables from the cable bracket on the starter motor (photo).

19 Disconnect the coolant hose to the expansion tank at the T-piece.

20 Disconnect the following electrical connections.

81.13 Engine heater hose connections

The starter motor (Chapter 10)
The temperature transmitter in the cylinder head (photo)
The idle solenoid on the carburettor (Chapter 3)
The alternator (Chapter 10)
The oil pressure switch on the cylinder block (photo)
The connector on the ignition control unit which connects with the speed sensor (photo)
The HT connector on the ignition control unit (photo)

21 Assemble the lifting equipment over the engine, connect a suitable sling to the engine lifting eyes, and prepare a place on the bench for the engine. If required, the weight of the engine can be reduced further by removing ancillary components such as the alternator, the carburettor and exhaust manifold. The engine must be lifted out at an angle, with the front higher than the rear. Make a final check to ensure that all disconnections have been made.

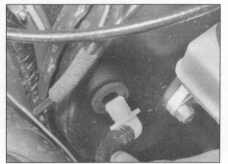

81.17 Brake servo hose connection

81.18 Starter motor cable bracket (arrowed)

81.20A Temperature transmitter . . .

81.20B . . . oil pressure transmitter . . .

81.20C . . . speed sensor . . .

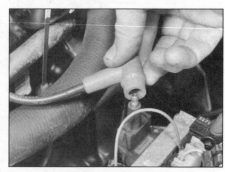

81.20D . . . and HT lead

81.22 Lifting out the engine

83.2A Removing a clutch housing bolt

83.2B Coolant transfer pipe front . . .

83.2C . . . and rear connection with bracket

83.2D Removing the accelerator quadrant bracket . . .

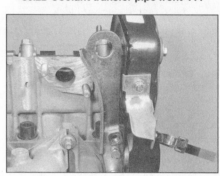

83.2E . . . and the front lifting eye

 HAYNES HiNT *To avoid damaging the fuel filter, it may be advantageous to remove the screw from the filter on the front frame and tie it back out of the way.*

22 Take the weight of the engine on the lifting gear and, as lifting progresses, ensure the engine mountings are released. Prevent the engine from swinging forward into the radiator. It may be necessary to turn the engine to one side to remove it, especially if the alternator is still in position (photo).

23 Once the engine is clear of the engine bay, transfer it to the work bench and lower it onto suitable wooden blocks to support it in an upright position.

82 Engine dismantling - general

Refer to the notes in Section 6.

83 Ancillary components - removal

1 With the engine removed from the car, the externally mounted components may now be removed from the engine, before dismantling.
2 The following is a suggested sequence of removal, detailed descriptions being given in the relevant Chapter/Section of this manual.

a) Alternator and drivebelt (Chapter 10)
b) Clutch assembly, but see note on timing marks in Section 84 (photo)
c) Inlet and exhaust manifold, complete with carburettor (Chapter 3)
d) Engine mounting pads
e) Oil filter (Section 126)
f) Spark plugs, and distributor cap and rotor arm (Chapter 4)
g) Fuel pump (Chapter 3)
h) Water pump and thermostat housing (Chapter 2)
i) Coolant transfer pipe (photos)
j) Ancillary support brackets (photos)

84 Timing belt - removal and examination

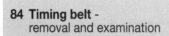

1 If work is being done with the engine in the car, first disconnect the battery negative (-)

84.3A Align flywheel mark with clutch housing TDC mark, as shown . . .

terminal, then remove the alternator/water pump drivebelt (Chapter 2).
2 Prise the rubber plug out of the inspection aperture in the top of the clutch housing, then remove the spark plugs (Chapter 4); use clean rag to seal the plug holes against dirt entry etc.
3 Using a spanner on the crankshaft pulley bolt and rotating the crankshaft clockwise (seen from the front of the car), turn the engine until No 1 cylinder (flywheel end) is at Top Dead Centre (TDC) on the compression stroke. This is found when the flywheel timing mark is aligned with the clutch housing TDC mark and then removing the oil filler cap to check that No 4 cylinder's valves are open (cam lobes pointing diagonally downwards); if the lobes point upwards, turn the engine forwards one full turn until the flywheel mark re-aligns. Note that if the clutch housing has been removed, the flywheel mark should be aligned instead with the raised casting on the cylinder block (photos).
4 Unscrew the plug from the left-hand rear

84.3B . . . or with cylinder block raised casting (arrowed)

84.4A Unscrew plug (arrowed) from left-hand rear of cylinder block . . .

84.4B . . . and insert 8 mm metal rod to lock crankshaft at TDC

84.5 Removing the timing belt cover

end of the cylinder block, next to the base of the dipstick tube, and insert a metal rod 8 mm in diameter (eg, a drill bit or a bolt) into the hole to engage with the TDC-locating slot in the crankshaft's web; move the crankshaft back and forth to ensure that it is locked (photos). Check that the flywheel mark is aligned **exactly** with the fixed TDC mark, to ensure that the rod is engaged in the slot rather than in one of the crankshaft's balancing holes.

5 Unscrew its four retaining bolts and withdraw the timing belt cover (photo).

6 Lock the crankshaft, either by selecting first or reverse gear and applying the brakes or by using a screwdriver as described in Section 94, as appropriate. With the crankshaft locked, unscrew the crankshaft pulley bolt and withdraw the pulley. **Note:** *Do not rely on the metal TDC-locating rod to hold the crankshaft while the pulley bolt is slackened (and tightened); it may shear - use only the appropriate locking method recommended.*

7 With the crankshaft still located at TDC by the metal rod, check (for reference only) that the camshaft sprocket timing mark aligns with the notch in its backing plate and that the notch in the crankshaft sprocket's inboard guide perimeter is in the 6 o'clock position (see photos 121.5A, 121.5B and 121.5C); ignore any marks on the intermediate shaft sprocket. While the bands marked across the belt can be ignored at this stage, check for arrows indicating the belt's normal running direction; if none can be found and the belt is to be re-used, make your own.

8 Slacken the tensioner locknut and move the tensioner to release belt tension, then retighten the nut (photo). Slip the belt off the sprockets, starting at the intermediate shaft.

9 Check the belt for any signs of uneven wear, splitting, cracks (especially at the roots of the belt teeth) or oil contamination and renew it if there is the slightest doubt about its condition; it must be renewed as a matter of course at the interval specified in Routine Maintenance. Check the sprockets for signs of wear or damage and ensure that the tensioner and idler pulleys rotate smoothly on their bearings; renew any worn or damaged component.

85 Cylinder head - removal

The procedure given here is with the engine removed from the car. If the cylinder head is being removed with the engine *in situ* carry out the following operations:

a) *Drain the cooling system*
b) *Disconnect the battery*
c) *Remove the alternator drivebelt*
d) *Remove the inlet and exhaust manifold, complete with carburettor*
e) *Remove fuel pump from the cylinder head (there is no need to disconnect any fuel hoses)*
f) *Remove the distributor cap and rotor arm*
g) *Disconnect the coolant hoses*
h) *Disconnect the crankcase ventilation hoses*

i) *Disconnect the lead to the coolant temperature sensor*
j) *Disconnect the spark plug leads*

1 Remove the timing belt, as described in Section 84.

2 Remove the cylinder head bolts using the reverse sequence to that given in Fig. 1.52 (photo).

3 Tap gently round the cylinder head using a plastic mallet to break the seal, then lift the cylinder head from the block, and place it on the bench (the cylinder head cannot be removed using a twisting motion because of the locating dowels).

86 Camshaft and tappets - removal

1 If the engine is in the car, first carry out the following operations:

a) *Remove the timing belt*
b) *Remove the distributor cap*
c) *Remove the camshaft cover*
d) *Remove the fuel pump*

2 Undo the bolt securing the camshaft sprocket to the camshaft and withdraw the socket. The camshaft may be prevented from turning during this operation by holding it between the cam lobes using grips or, preferably, by wrapping an old timing belt around the sprocket, clamping the belt tight and holding securely. With the sprocket removed, check whether the locating

84.8 Timing belt tensioner (arrowed)

85.2 Removing a cylinder head bolt

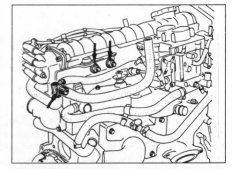

Fig. 1.42 Crankshaft ventilation hoses and bracket location on cylinder head (Sec 85)

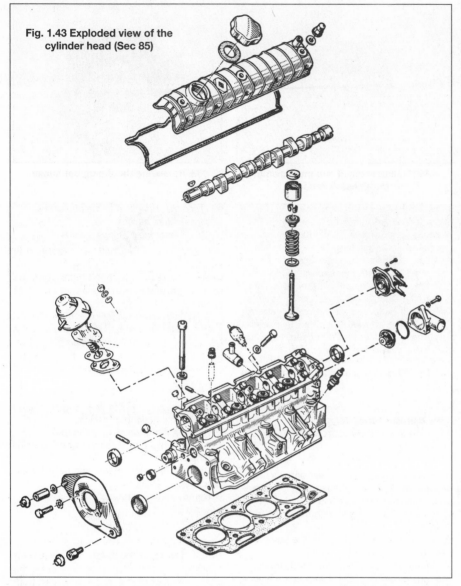

Fig. 1.43 Exploded view of the cylinder head (Sec 85)

86.2 Camshaft sprocket Woodruff key and channel (arrowed)

86.3A Removing the backing plate . . .

86.3B . . . and bolts

Woodruff key is likely to drop out of its camshaft groove and if it is, remove it and store it safely (photo).

3 Undo the bolts securing the metal sprocket backing plate to the cylinder head and remove the plate (photos).

4 Number the camshaft bearing caps 1 to 5 with No 1 nearest the flywheel, and also mark them with an arrow pointing towards the flywheel, to indicate their fitted direction.

5 Progressively slacken all the camshaft bearing cap retaining bolts and, when all are

slack, remove them from the caps (photo).

6 Lift off the five bearing caps and then remove the camshaft, at complete with oil seals, from the cylinder head (photo).

7 Withdraw the tappet buckets, complete with shims, from their bores in the head. Lay the

86.5 Slacken the camshaft cap bolts

86.6 Removing the camshaft

86.7A Remove the tappet buckets

86.7B Underside of a shim showing thickness number

86.7C Underside of a tappet bucket

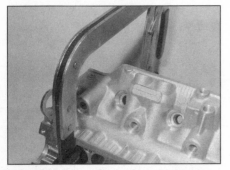

87.1A Using a valve spring compressor

87.1B Withdrawing a collet with a magnet

87.1C Valve and components

buckets on a sheet of cardboard numbered 1 to 8 with No 1 at the flywheel end. It is a good idea to write the shim thickness size on the card alongside each bucket in case the shims are accidentally knocked off their buckets and mixed up. The size is stamped on the shim bottom face (photos).

87 Cylinder head - dismantling

1 Using a valve spring compressor, compress each valve spring in turn until the split collets can be removed. Release the compressor and lift off the cap, spring and spring seat (photos).
2 If, when the valve spring compressor is screwed down, the valve spring cap refuses to free and expose the split collets, gently tap the top of the tool, directly over the cap with a light hammer. This will free the cap.
3 Withdraw the oil seal off the top of the valve guide, and then remove the valve through the combustion chamber.
4 It is essential that the valves are kept in their correct sequence unless they are so badly worn that they are to be renewed. If they are going to be kept and used again, place them in a sheet of card having eight holes numbered 1 to 8 corresponding to the relative fitted positions of the valves. Note that No 1 valve is nearest to the flywheel end of the engine.
5 If required the thermostat can be removed, as described in Chapter 2.

88 Sump - removal (engine removed from car)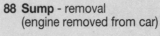

1 Turn the cylinder block over onto its face (it is assumed that the cylinder head is removed as part of an engine overhaul).
2 Remove the bolts securing the sump to the block.
3 Use a plastic mallet to tap the sump free, and remove the sump.
4 Clean all sealing compound from the mating surface of the sump and cylinder block, and inspect the surfaces for signs of damage.
5 Light scoring or scratches can be removed by polishing with fine emery cloth, but anything more serious will mean the renewal of components if sealing compound will not stop leakage.

89 Sump - removal (engine in car)

1 Drain the engine oil and remove the engine splash guard.
2 Position lifting gear over the engine and attach a sling to the front lifting eye.
3 Remove the nuts from the front engine mounting brackets and raise the front of the engine as far as it will go.
4 Refer to Chapter 8 and release the steering

gear housing from the rear engine bearer, then pull the steering gear clear.
5 Remove the flywheel guard (photo).
6 Remove the four retaining bolts from the engine crossmember.
7 Remove the right-hand engine mounting bracket.
8 Remove the sump, as described in Section 88.

90 Oil pump - removal

With the sump removed, as described in Section 88 or 89, remove the four retaining bolts from the pump, and remove the pump from the bottom of the block (photo).

89.5 The flywheel guard plate

90.1 Oil pump retaining bolts (arrowed)

91.1 Removing the pump cover bolts

91.3 Component parts of the oil pump

91 Oil pump -
examination and renovation

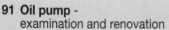

1 Undo the retaining bolts and lift off the pump cover (photo).
2 Withdraw the idler gear and the drivegear and shaft.
3 Extract the retaining clip and remove the oil pressure relief valve spring retainer, spring, spring seat and plunger (photo).
4 Clean the components and carefully examine the gears, pump body and relief valve plunger for any scoring or wear. Renew the pump if these conditions are apparent.
5 If the components appear serviceable, reassemble the components in the order of removal, fill the pump with oil and refit the cover (photos).

91.5A Insert the gears . . .

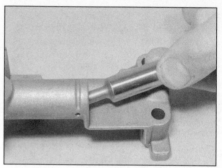

91.5B . . . and pressure relief valve

92 Crankshaft front plate -
removal

1 If the engine is still in the car, first remove the timing belt and the sump.
2 Use a puller, or two suitable levers, to remove the crankshaft sprocket; note its locating Woodruff key and store it with the sprocket.
3 Undo the bolts securing the front plate to the cylinder block and remove the plate (photo). The two bolts arrowed in the photo do not have to be removed.
4 Note the two locating dowels in the lower bolt holes.

92.3 Front plate securing bolts (do not remove the bolts arrowed)

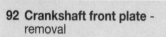

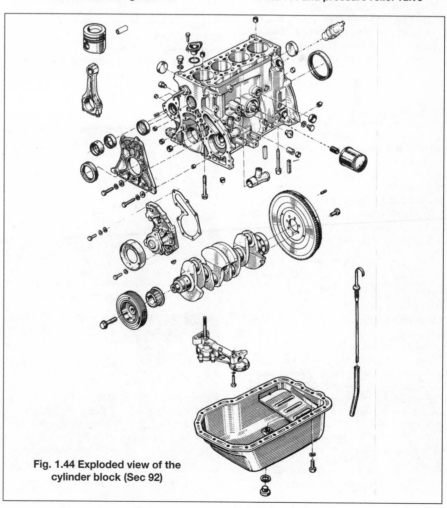

Fig. 1.44 Exploded view of the cylinder block (Sec 92)

1

93.3A Removing a big-end cap nut . . .

93.3B . . . lifting off the cap

93.4 Withdrawing a piston from the cylinder

93 Pistons and connecting rods
- removal

1 If the engine is in the car, first carry out the following operations:

a) *Remove the oil pump*
b) *Remove the cylinder head (not necessary if only the big-end bearings are to be removed)*
c) *Remove the sump. The procedure for removal of the sump is given in Section 89. This requires the engine to be lifted by means of the front engine lifting eye. The engine must then be supported from underneath in order to remove the cylinder head (which would mean removal of the lifting gear). It would appear more appropriate, therefore, to remove the engine if piston/connecting rod removal is envisaged*

2 Rotate the crankshaft so that No 1 big-end cap (nearest the flywheel) is at the lowest point of its travel. Using a centre punch, number the cap and rod on the intermediate shaft side to indicate the cylinder to which they are fitted.
3 Undo and remove the big-end bearing cap bolts (photo) and withdraw the cap, complete with shell bearing from the connecting rod (photo). If only the bearing shells are being attended to, push the connecting rod up and off the crankpin then remove the upper bearing shell. Keep the bearing shells and cap together in their correct sequence if they are to be refitted.

4 Push the connecting rod up and withdraw the piston and connecting rod assembly from the top of the cylinder block (photo).
5 Now repeat these operations on the remaining three piston and connecting rod assemblies.

94 Flywheel - removal

1 If the engine is *in situ*, remove the propeller shaft, clutch housing and clutch assembly.
2 Prevent the flywheel from turning by screwing a bolt into the clutch housing bolt threads, then jamming the flywheel with a wide-bladed screwdriver.
3 Remove the flywheel retaining bolts (photo), and lift off the flywheel.

94.3 Removing the flywheel bolts

95.3 Lifting out the crankshaft

95 Crankshaft and main bearings - removal

1 Identification numbers should be cast onto the base of each main bearing cap, but if not, number the cap and crankcase using a centre punch, as was done for the connecting rods and caps.
2 Undo and remove the main bearing cap retaining bolts, noting that a hexagonal socket bit will be needed for No 1 main bearing cap bolts (photo). Withdraw the caps and the bearing shell lower halves.
3 Carefully lift the crankshaft from the crankcase (photo).
4 Remove the thrust washers from each side of No 2 main bearing (photo), then remove the bearing shell upper halves from the crankcase. Place each shell with its respective bearing cap (photos).

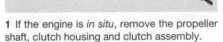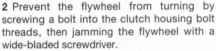

95.2 Undoing No 1 main bearing cap

95.4A Remove the thrust washers (arrowed) . . .

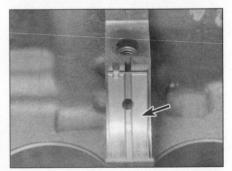

95.4B . . . and the bearing shells (arrowed)

96.4 Crankshaft rear oil seal correctly fitted

97.6 Fitting the front crankshaft oil seal

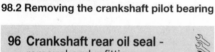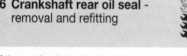

98.2 Removing the crankshaft pilot bearing

98.3 Tapping home the pilot bearing

96 Crankshaft rear oil seal - removal and refitting

If the engine is *in situ*, it will be necessary to remove the propeller shaft, clutch housing and clutch assembly.

1 Remove the flywheel as described in Section 94.
2 Prise out the old seal using a screwdriver, being careful not to score the seal bearing surfaces on the crankshaft or the cylinder block.
3 Coat the new seal with grease.
4 Fit the new seal, using a large mandrel of suitable diameter to drive the seal into its housing, until it is flush with the flange on the cylinder block (photo).

97 Crankshaft front oil seal - removal and refitting

1 If the engine is *in situ,* remove the alternator drivebelt and the toothed timing belt.
2 Remove the crankshaft pulley wheel.
3 Remove the crankshaft sprocket (both these operations are described in Section 92).
4 If the sprocket is stuck use a puller to remove it from the shaft, and do not lose the Woodruff key.
5 Prise out the old oil seal with a screwdriver, being careful not to score the oil seal bearing faces on the crankshaft or the cylinder block. Clean both bearing surfaces.

6 Coat the new seal with grease, then press it home using a socket of suitable size (photo). If the engine front plate has been removed, the oil seal could be fitted in the plate before the plate is refitted.

99.2A Front left-hand engine bearer . . .

99.2C Rear left engine bearer . . .

98 Crankshaft rear pilot bearing - removal and refitting

1 If the engine is *in situ*, it will be necessary to remove the propeller shaft, clutch housing and clutch assembly.
2 Using a thin-bladed internal puller, withdraw the pilot bearing from the crankshaft (photo).
3 Using a drift of suitable size, tap the new bearing into the crankshaft until it bottoms in the recess (photo).

99 Engine mountings - general

1 The engine is supported on four cast alloy mountings, two at the front and two at the rear.
2 The mountings are bolted to the cylinder block, and to the front engine cross bearer and the rear engine bearer (photos).
3 Interposed between the mountings and the bearers are rubber blocks which absorb vibration and prevent it being transmitted to the car.
4 When disconnecting the engine mountings for engine removal, undo the nut securing the rubber blocks to the engine bearers. The cast alloy mountings may be removed after the engine has been lifted out.
5 Inspect the rubber blocks for deterioration and contamination by oil and grease, which will affect their performance, and renew them as required.

99.2B . . . and the right-hand engine bearer

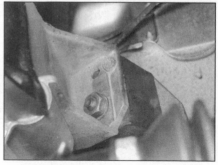

99.2D . . . and the right engine bearer

1

100.2 Crankcase ventilation oil separator

101.2 Removing the bolt from the intermediate shaft sprocket

101.3 Tapping home a new oil seal

101.4 Remove the four bolts (arrowed)

101.5 Guide plate and bolts (arrowed)

101.6 Withdraw the intermediate shaft

100 Crankcase ventilation system - general description

1 The crankcase has a positive ventilation system, which means that the crankcase fumes do not escape directly to atmosphere but are drawn back into the inlet manifold, where they are burnt and passed on through the exhaust system.
2 An oil separator is fitted to the top of the crankcase (photo), and the fumes are drawn through the separator, then via a hose to either the air filter assembly or the inlet manifold. This depends upon engine condition. At idle and low engine speeds the fumes go to the inlet manifold, and at wide throttle openings to the air filter.
3 This control is achieved by a calibrated orifice, which senses the inlet manifold depression, and directs the fumes as necessary.
4 The oil separator is bonded into the cylinder block. Should renewal be required, consult your Volvo dealer.

101 Intermediate shaft - removal, inspection and refitting

1 If the engine is *in situ* first remove the timing belt and the engine splash guard.
2 Prevent the intermediate shaft from turning by using a C-spanner on the sprocket and undo the centre bolt (photo).
3 Remove the sprocket using a two legged puller if it is stuck. The oil seal can be removed and refitted in this condition by prising it out with a sharp instrument, then liberally oiling a new seal and tapping it home with a suitable-sized socket (photo).
4 Remove the four bolts from the cover (photo), remove the cover.
5 Remove the two bolts from the guide plate (photo), and remove the plate.
6 Withdraw the intermediate shaft (photo).
7 Remove the two bolts from the plastic seal housing at the top of the housing and lift out the seal housing (photo).

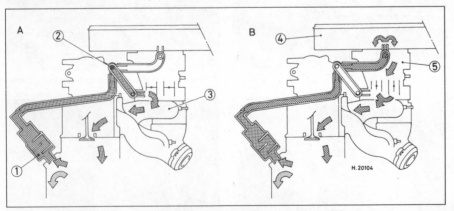

Fig. 1.45 Crankcase ventilation system (Sec 100)

A High inlet manifold depression
B Low inlet manifold depression
1 Oil separator
2 Calibrated orifice

3 Inlet manifold
4 Air filter
5 Carburettor

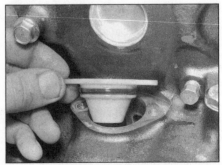

101.7 Lift out the seal housing . . .

101.8 . . . and the driveshaft

101.9 Component parts of the intermediate shaft

101.10 Bearing liners in the cylinder block

101.11 Refitting the cover

101.12 Tightening the sprocket bolt

8 Withdraw the oil pump driveshaft, using a magnet, or screw a bolt into the threaded end (photo).
9 Wash the component parts (photo) in petrol and inspect them for wear, cracking or chipped gear teeth.
10 If the white metal bearing liners in the cylinder block appear worn, then consult your Volvo dealer who will advise on renewal (photo).
11 Refitting is a reversal of removal, coating all parts liberally with clean engine oil. Use new oil seal on the plastic seal housing and a proprietary sealing compound on the mating surface of the cover plate (photo).
12 Tighten all bolts to their specified torque, do not forget the Woodruff key in the end of the shaft and prevent the shaft turning by using a C-spanner while doing up the sprocket bolt (photo).

102 Examination and renovation - general

With the engine completely stripped, clean all the components and examine them for wear. Each part should be checked and, where necessary, renewed or renovated, as described in the following Sections. Renew main and big-end bearing shells as a matter of course unless you know that they have had little wear and are in perfect condition.

103 Crankshaft and main bearings - examination and renovation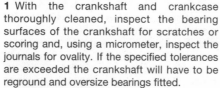

1 With the crankshaft and crankcase thoroughly cleaned, inspect the bearing surfaces of the crankshaft for scratches or scoring and, using a micrometer, inspect the journals for ovality. If the specified tolerances are exceeded the crankshaft will have to be reground and oversize bearings fitted.
2 Crankshaft regrinding is best dealt with by your Volvo dealer, who will also supply the new bearings for both the main and big-end bearings.
3 Temporarily lay the crankshaft in place in the cylinder block, fit the thrust washers to either side of No 2 main bearing and then check the endfloat, using either a dial test indicator or feeler gauge (photos). If the

tolerance is exceeded, then larger thrust washers will have to be obtained and fitted to bring the endfloat within that specified.

104 Cylinder block and crankcase - examination and renovation

1 The cylinder bores must be examined for taper, ovality, scoring and scratches. Start by examining the top of the bores; if these are worn, a slight ridge will be found which marks the top of the piston ring travel. If the wear is excessive, the engine will have had a high oil consumption rate accompanied by blue smoke from the exhaust.
2 If available, use an inside dial gauge to measure the bore diameter just below the ridge and compare it with the diameter at the bottom of the bore which is not subject to wear. If the difference is more than 0.006 in (0.152 mm), the cylinders will normally require boring with new oversize pistons fitted.
3 However, provided the cylinder bore wear does not exceed 0.008 in (0.203 mm), special oil control rings and pistons can be fitted to restore compression and stop oil burning.
4 If new piston rings are being fitted to old bores, it is essential to roughen the bore walls slightly with fine glasspaper to enable the new piston rings to bed in properly.
5 Thoroughly examine the crankcase and cylinder blocks for cracks and damage and use a piece of wire to probe all oilways and waterways to ensure they are unobstructed.

103.3A Using a dial test indicator . . .

103.3B . . . and a feeler gauge to check endfloat

105.3 Marks on the piston crown

105 Pistons and connecting rod assemblies - examination and renovation

1 The general procedure to be followed is the same as that described in Sections 23 and 51, using the Specifications for the B172 engine, and the additional notes given here.

2 The pistons marked with the figures 1, 2 or 3, or the letters A, B or C are for cylinder bore of 3.19 in (81.00 mm); and with 4, 5 or 6, or U, V or W for cylinder bore of 3.20 in (81.25 mm). The home mechanic should not be too involved with these markings, as the dealer or engineering firm which carries out the reboring will supply the correct oversize pistons and piston rings.

3 The arrow on the piston head (photo) should face toward the flywheel end of the engine, as should the location dowels on the connecting rod which are set to one side.

106 Camshaft and tappets - examination and renovation

1 Examine the camshaft journals and cam lobes for wear, ridges, pitting and scoring.

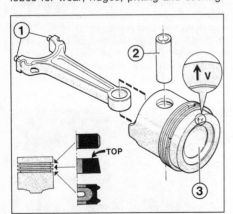
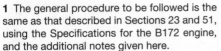

Fig. 1.46 Exploded view of the piston and connecting rod (Sec 105)

1 Connecting rod location dowels
2 Gudgeon pin
3 Bowl in piston crown
Inset shows piston ring profiles

Renew the camshaft if any of these conditions are evident.

2 Remove the oil seals from each end of the camshaft, grease the new oil seals and slide them onto the camshaft, closed face outwards. If the camshaft is not being refitted immediately, store the camshaft in such a way that the oil seals are not bearing any weight.

3 Inspect the camshaft caps and the bearing surfaces in the cylinder head for wear, scratching, scoring and pitting. If serious signs of these conditions are evident, consult your Volvo dealer, as the bearings are machined directly in the cylinder head and cannot be rebored.

4 Inspect the tappet buckets for scoring, pitting etc, and the shims for wear ridges. Some scuffing is normal and acceptable.

107 Crankshaft front plate - examination and renovation

Check the front plate for signs of distortion or damage to the threads. If serviceable, clean off all traces of sealant and tap out the oil seal using a tube of suitable diameter.

108 Flywheel - examination and renovation

Examine the flywheel for scoring of the clutch face and for chipping of the ring gear teeth. If the clutch face is scored, the flywheel may be machined until flat, but renewal is preferable. If the ring gear is worn or damaged it may be renewed separately, but this job is best left to a Volvo dealer or engineering works. The temperature to which the new ring gear must be heated for installation is critical, and if not done accurately the hardness of the teeth will be destroyed.

109 Cylinder head - decarbonising and examination

Refer to Section 56 which gives the general procedure to be followed; using the Specifications for the B172 engine.

The cylinder head cannot be resurfaced as the reduced height could cause the valves to hit the pistons.

110 Engine reassembly - general

Refer to Section 28.

---

111 Crankshaft and main bearings - refitting

1 Before fitting the crankshaft or main bearings it is necessary to determine the correct thickness of side seals to be fitted to No 1 main bearing cap. To do this, place the bearing cap in position without any seals and secure it with the two retaining bolts. Locate a twist drill, dowel rod or other suitable implement which will just fit in the side seal groove. Now measure the implement and this dimension is the side seal groove size. If the dimension is less than or equal to 0.197 in (5 mm), a 0.201 in (5.10 mm) thick side seal is needed. If the dimension is more than 0.197 in (5 mm), a 0.209 in (5.3 mm) thick side seal is required. Having determined the side seal size and obtained the necessary seals, proceed as follows:

2 Clean the backs of the bearing shells and the bearing recesses in both the cylinder block and main bearing caps.

3 Press the bearing shells without oil holes into the caps, ensuring that the tag on the shell engages in the notch in the cap.

4 Press the bearing shells with the oil holes into the recesses in the cylinder block (photo).

5 If the original bearing shells are being refitted, these must be placed in their original locations.

6 Using a little grease, stick the thrust washers to each side of No 2 main bearing, so that the oilway grooves on each thrust washer face outwards (photo).

7 Lubricate the lips of a new crankshaft rear

111.4 Oiling a bearing shell after fitting

111.6 Fitting a thrust washer

111.7 Crankshaft rear seal in position

111.9A Oil the journals . . .

111.9B . . . before fitting the caps

oil seal and carefully slip it over the crankshaft journal. Do this carefully as the seal lips are very delicate. Ensure that the open side of the seal faces the engine (photo).

8 Liberally lubricate each bearing shell in the cylinder block and lower the crankshaft into position.

9 Fit all the bearing caps, with the exception of No 1, in their numbered or previously noted locations so that the bearing shell locating notches in the cap and block are both on the same side (photos). Fit the retaining bolts and tighten them hand tight at this stage.

10 Ensure the grooves in No 1 main bearing cap and their mating surfaces on the crankcase are perfectly clean and dry.

11 Install the cap into the bearing recess in the crankcase so that it is approximately 0.4 in (10.0 mm) from the bottom of the recess (ie, not quite fully home).

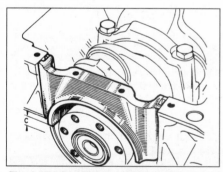

Fig. 1.47 Initial fitting of No 1 main bearing cap before application of gasket cement (Sec 111)

C = 0.4 in (10.0 mm) approximately

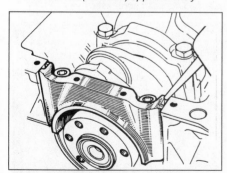

Fig. 1.48 Applying gasket cement to No 1 main bearing cap side grooves (Sec 111)

12 Apply liquid gasket cement (obtainable from your Volvo dealer) to the side grooves ensuring it is fed right down the grooves and onto the crankcase mating surface.

13 Fit and tighten the cap bolts to the specified torque and then remove any excess gasket cement.

14 Position the oil seal so that its face is flush with the bearing cap and block, then tighten all the retaining bolts to the specified torque. Check that the crankshaft is free to turn.

15 Check the crankshaft endfloat using feeler gauges inserted between the thrust washers and the side of the bearing journal. If new thrust washers have been fitted the endfloat should be in accordance with the dimension given in the Specifications. If the original washers have been refitted and the endfloat is excessive, new thrust washers must be obtained. These are available in a number of oversizes.

112 Pistons and connecting rods - refitting

1 Clean the backs of the bearing shells and the recesses in the connecting rods and big-end caps. If new shells are being fitted, ensure that all traces of the protective grease are cleaned off using paraffin.

2 Press the big-end bearing shells into the connecting rods and caps in their correct positions and oil them liberally.

3 Fit a ring compressor to No 1 piston then insert the piston and connecting rod into No 1

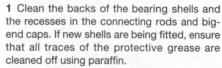

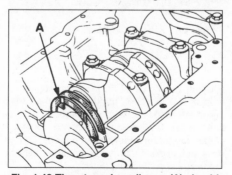

Fig. 1.49 Thrust washer oilways (A) should face outwards (Sec 111)

cylinder. With No 1 crankpin at its lowest point, drive the piston carefully into the cylinder with the wooden handle of a hammer and at the same time guide the connecting rod onto the crankpin (photo). Make sure that the V mark on the piston crown, or arrow, is facing the flywheel end of the engine.

4 Fit the big-end bearing cap in its previously noted position then tighten the nuts to the specified torque.

5 Check that the crankshaft turns freely.

6 Repeat the procedure given in paragraphs 3 to 5 for No 4 piston and connecting rod, then turn the crankshaft through half a turn and repeat the procedure on No 2 and No 3 pistons.

7 If the engine is in the car, refit the oil pump, sump and cylinder head.

113 Crankshaft front plate - refitting

1 Apply a bead of CAF 4/60 THIXO paste to the mating surface of the front plate (photo).

2 If the oil seal has already been fitted to the plate, liberally oil the lips of the seal, then fit the plate to the cylinder block. **Note**: *The crescent-shaped hollow at the bottom of the plate is an oilway and should not be blocked with sealing compound.*

3 Tighten the retaining bolts, using a diagonal sequence.

4 If the oil seal has not been fitted, fit it now, following the procedure given in Section 97.

5 If the two bolts either side of the crankshaft

112.3 Using a piston ring compressor to fit the piston

1

113.1 Fitting the front plate . . .

113.6 . . . and the crankshaft sprocket

114.1 Fitting the oil pump

115.2A Apply sealant to the sump face . . .

115.2B . . . and tighten the bolts

116.2 Use thread locking compound on the flywheel bolts

have been removed, apply sealant to their threads before refitting them.
6 Refit the crankshaft sprocket, not forgetting the Woodruff key (photo).

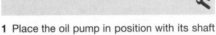

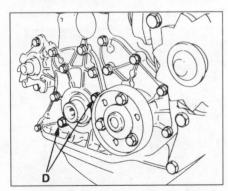

Fig. 1.50 Apply sealant to the front plate; keeping the oilway (C) clear (Sec 113)

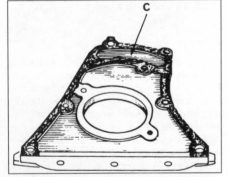

Fig. 1.51 Apply sealant to the threads of the two bolts (D) (Sec 113)

114 Oil pump - refitting

1 Place the oil pump in position with its shaft engaged with the drivegear (photo).
2 Refit the bolts and tighten them securely.
3 If the engine is in the car, refit the sump.

115 Sump - refitting

Ensure that the mating faces of the sump and crankcase are clean and dry.

Apply a bead of CAF 4/60 THIXO paste to the sump face and place the sump in position. Refit the retaining bolts and tighten them progressively in a diagonal sequence (photos).

116 Flywheel - refitting

1 Clean the flywheel and crankshaft faces then fit the flywheel, making sure that any previously made marks are aligned.
2 Apply a few drops of thread locking compound to the retaining bolt threads, fit the bolts and tighten them in a diagonal sequence to the specified torque (photo).
3 The flywheel will only go on one way as the bolt holes are asymmetrical.

Note: *To avoid danger of the valve hitting the pistons, the flywheel should only be fitted before the cylinder head is fitted, or after the timing belt has been installed.*

117 Cylinder block - ancillary reassembly checks

1 With the sump refitted, check that the oil drain plug is in position, with a new washer fitted under the head.
2 Turn the engine upright and support it on wooden blocks.
3 If not already fitted, the intermediate shaft should be installed.
4 If removed, refit the engine mountings and the alternator mounting bracket (photo).
5 Refit the water pump, referring to Chapter 2.
6 Refit the camshaft tensioner (photo) and, if not already done, the crankshaft and intermediate shaft sprockets.

117.4 Alternator mounting bracket

117.6 Fitting the timing belt tensioner

117.7 Oil pressure switch

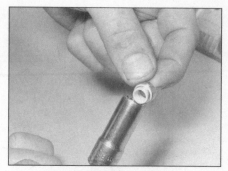
118.1A Using a socket . . .

118.1B . . . to fit the seals (arrowed)

118.2 Fitting a valve . . .

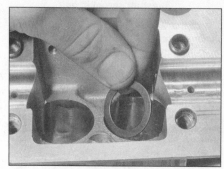
118.3A . . . valve spring seat . . .

7 Refit the oil pressure switch (photo) using a new washer.
8 Refer to Section 126 and refit the oil filter.

118 Cylinder head - reassembly

1 Using a suitable tube fit new oil seals to each of the valve guides (photos).
2 Lubricate the stems of the valves and insert them into their original locations. If new valves are being fitted, insert them into the locations to which they have been ground (photo).
3 Working on the first valve, fit the spring seat to the cylinder head followed by the valve spring and cap (photos).
4 Compress the valve spring and locate the split collets in the recess in the valve stem. Release the compressor then repeat the procedure on the remaining valves.
5 With all the valves installed, lay the cylinder

head on one side and tap each valve stem with a plastic mallet to settle the components.
6 If the cylinder head has been removed with the engine in the car, refit the tappets (camshaft followers) and camshaft, the fuel pump, fuel filter and manifolds, and the thermostat.

119 Camshaft and tappets - refitting

1 Lubricate the tappet buckets and insert them into their respective locations as noted during removal. Make sure that each bucket has its correct tappet shim in place on its upper face.
2 Lubricate the camshaft bearings (photo) then lay the camshaft in position. Position the oil seals so that they are flush with the cylinder head faces and refit the bearing caps. Ensure that the caps are fitted facing the

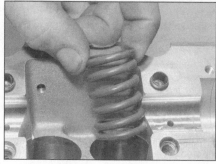
118.3B . . . and spring

same way as noted during removal and in their original locations (photo).
3 Apply a thread locking compound to the bearing cap retaining bolts, refit the bolts and progressively tighten them to the specified torque (photo).
4 Refit the camshaft sprocket backing plate to the cylinder head and secure with the bolts.

119.2A Oil the bearings . . .

119.2B . . . before fitting the camshaft and caps . . .

119.3 . . . and tightening the bolts

1

119.5 Tightening the camshaft sprocket bolt

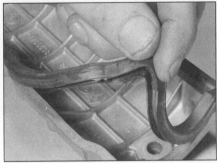

119.6A Fit a new seal . . .

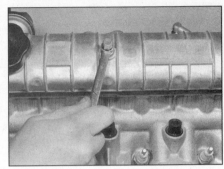

119.6B . . . before fitting the cover

5 With the Woodruff key in its groove, fit the camshaft sprocket and retaining bolt. Prevent the camshaft turning using the same method as for removal and tighten the sprocket retaining bolt to the specified torque (photo).

6 If the engine is in the car, refit the fuel pump, timing belt and distributor cap, then check the valve clearances before refitting the camshaft cover (photos).

120 Cylinder head - refitting

1 Ensure that the mating faces of the cylinder block and head are spotlessly clean, that the retaining bolt threads are also clean and dry and that they screw easily in and out of their locations.

2 Turn the crankshaft as necessary to bring No 1 piston to the TDC position. Retain the crankshaft in this position using a metal rod in the TDC locating hole in the cylinder block.

3 Place a new gasket on the block face and located over the studs. Do not use any jointing compound on the gasket (photo).

4 Turn the camshaft sprocket until the mark on its outer face is aligned with the mark on the sprocket backing plate.

5 Lower the cylinder head into position on the block and engage the dowels (photo).

6 Lightly lubricate the cylinder head retaining bolt threads and under the bolt heads with clean engine oil and screw in the bolts finger tight.

7 Tighten the retaining bolts in the sequence shown in Fig. 1.52 to the 1st tightening setting given in the Specifications. Now repeat the sequence, but this time to the 2nd tightening setting.

8 Wait 3 minutes then loosen all the bolts completely. Tighten them again this time to the 3rd tightening setting, still in the correct sequence.

9 The final tightening is done using an angular measurement. To do this, draw two lines at 123° to each other on a sheet of card and punch a hole for the socket bit at the point where the lines intersect. Starting with bolt No 1, engage the socket through the card and into the bolt head. Position the first line on the

card under, and directly in line with the socket extension bar. Hold the card, and in one movement tighten the bolt until the extension bar is aligned with the second line on the card. Repeat this procedure for the remaining bolts in the correct sequence (photo).

10 Refit the timing belt and check the valve clearances. If the engine is in the car, refit the controls, cables and services using the reverse of the removal procedure described in Section 85, but bearing in mind the following points:

a) Tighten the exhaust front section-to-manifold retaining bolts

b) Adjust the choke and accelerator cables, as described in Chapter 3

c) Adjust the drivebelt tension, as described in Chapter 2

d) Refill the cooling system, as described in Chapter 2

120.3 Place a new gasket on the block face

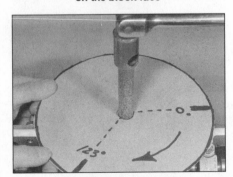

120.9 Using a card template for angular tightening

121 Timing belt - refitting

Note: With the timing belt removed, do not move the camshaft or crankshaft more than is necessary to line up the timing marks, or the valves may strike the pistons.

1 Check that the crankshaft is at TDC position for No 1 cylinder and that the crankshaft is locked in this position using the metal rod through the hole in the crankcase.

2 Check that the camshaft sprocket timing mark is aligned with the notch in its backing plate and that the notch in the crankshaft sprocket's inboard guide perimeter is in the 6 o'clock position; ignore any marks on the intermediate shaft sprocket. Ensure that the tensioner is secured in the fully-slack position.

120.5 Fitting the cylinder head

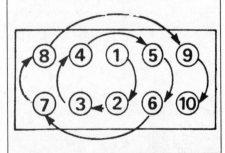

Fig. 1.52 Cylinder head bolt tightening sequence (Sec 120)

121.5A Align the first band on the belt with the crankshaft sprocket notch . . .

121.5B . . . the second band on the belt is aligned with the camshaft sprocket mark

121.5C The arrows indicating the belt's normal running direction

3 The timing belt should have two bands marked across it, and two arrows (showing the belt's normal running direction) along it at some point. The belt is to be fitted so that each of the two bands is aligned exactly with the corresponding sprocket mark; the two arrows will then usually be midway between the intermediate shaft sprocket and the idler pulley.

4 Aligning the bands on their respective sprocket marks and ensuring that the arrows point the correct way, fit the belt in the following sequence. Start at the crankshaft sprocket, then slip it over the intermediate shaft sprocket, the tensioner pulley, the camshaft sprocket and finally the idler pulley.

5 Temporarily tension the belt by slackening its locknut and turning the tensioner pulley anti-clockwise; as a rough guide to the correct tension, it should just be possible to twist the belt through 90° using only a finger and thumb placed approximately midway between the intermediate shaft sprocket and the idler pulley. Tighten the tensioner locknut and check that both timing marks are still aligned (photos).

6 Remove the TDC-locating rod.

7 Refit the crankshaft pulley and retaining bolt. Lock the crankshaft by the method used on removal and tighten the pulley bolt to its specified torque wrench setting.

8 Using a spanner applied to the crankshaft pulley bolt, turn the engine forwards (clockwise) through two full turns, then return it to No 1 cylinder being at TDC on the compression stroke and re-insert the TDC-locating rod (Section 84, paragraphs 3 and 4).

9 Check that the sprocket timing marks are still aligned exactly; ignore the location of the belt bands - these serve only as a guide on belt installation. If the sprocket timing marks are not in exact alignment when the belt is correctly tensioned, the belt must be removed and refitted until the setting is correct.

10 The belt's tension must now be set correctly. Volvo specify the use of a special tool for this task, a tension gauge available as either Part Number 5197 or Part Number 998 8500; if neither of these is available the following procedure will provide a setting adequate for the engine to be started and the car to be driven to a Volvo dealer so that the

belt tension can be set by a trained mechanic using the correct equipment. **Note:** *If the belt slips or breaks in service, extensive damage may result. Use of the appropriate tension gauge is recommended.*

11 To tension the belt without the special tool, either use the belt-twist method outlined in paragraph 5 above, or tighten the belt until it deflects by 0.3 in (7.5 mm) when moderate pressure is applied midway between the intermediate shaft sprocket and the idler pulley.

12 When the belt tension is correct, hold the tensioner pulley and tighten the tensioner locknut to its specified torque wrench setting. If the belt's setting was altered significantly, repeat the procedure given in paragraphs 8 and 9 above. Remove the TDC-locating rod and refit its plug.

13 Refit the timing belt cover, the spark plugs and the rubber plug to the clutch housing aperture. Refit the alternator/water pump drivebelt and tension it (Chapter 2), then reconnect the battery.

14 Do not forget, where applicable, to have the timing belt tension checked as soon as possible using the correct tool.

122 Ancillary components - refitting

Refit all ancillary components removed after engine removal (see Section 83).

123 Engine - refitting

Refitting the engine is a reversal of the removal procedure in Section 81, but bear in mind the following points:

a) *Tighten all attachment bolts/nuts to their specified torque*
b) *Refill the cooling system (Chapter 2)*
c) *Fill the engine with the recommended oil*
d) *Adjust the choke and accelerator cables (Chapter 3)*
e) *If not already done, check and adjust the valve clearances as described in Section 124*

f) *Check and adjust the clutch cable (Chapter 5)*

124 Valve clearances - checking and adjustment

1 The valve clearances should be checked and adjusted as necessary at the intervals given in the Routine Maintenance Section at the beginning of this manual.

2 The valve clearances are checked with the engine cold.

3 Remove the air filter housing and the valve cover.

4 Turn the engine by means of a socket spanner on the crankshaft pulley nut until the peak of the cam lobe for number 1 valve (nearest the flywheel) is facing upward, and not in contact with the tappet.

5 Check the clearance between the cam and the shim in the tappet head, which should be as given in the Specifications.

6 Adjustment is made by replacing the existing shim with a thicker or thinner shim as necessary to bring the clearance within limits.

7 To remove a shim the tappet should be turned so that the slot in the tappet head is facing slightly inward.

8 Volvo produce a special tool for depressing the tappet to remove the shim, but if this is not available, the tappets (camshaft followers) may be depressed using a wide-bladed screwdriver. This is a delicate operation as the screwdriver must only bear on the edge of the tappet so that the shim can be removed, and will probably need two people to do it.

9 Before depressing the tappet, make sure the cylinder being worked on is not at TDC or the valve may strike the piston.

10 Depress the tappet by whatever method is decided upon (photo) and prise out the shim. The shim thickness is stamped on the bottom of the shim, enabling the thickness of the replacement shim to be calculated.

11 Fit the new shim by the same method as removal, having coated it with clean engine oil and with the number facing inward toward the tappet. Recheck the valve clearance.

12 Repeat the operation on the other seven valves. The valves are numbered 1 to 8 from

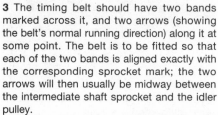

124.10 Prising out a shim from the tappet

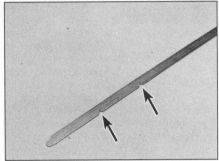

125.4 High and low level dipstick marks (arrowed)

125.6 Removing the oil drain plug

the flywheel end of the engine; numbers 1, 3, 6 and 8 are exhaust valves, and 2, 4, 5 and 7 inlet valves.

13 On completion, refit the valve cover, using a new gasket, and the air filter housing.

125 Engine oil - renewal

1 The engine oil should be renewed at the intervals given in the Routine Maintenance Section at the beginning of this manual.

2 The oil level should also be checked, again at the intervals shown in the Routine Maintenance Section.

3 The oil level is checked when the engine is cold, and with the car on level ground.

4 Remove the oil dipstick from the dipstick tube on the left-hand side of the engine, wipe the dipstick clean with a rag or tissue, then insert the dipstick back in the dipstick tube as far as it will go. Remove the dipstick and check the oil level which should be seen on the bottom of the dipstick (photo).

5 The oil level should be maintained between the two indentations on the dipstick.

6 To renew the engine oil, which is best done with the engine warm to aid drainage, remove the drain plug from the bottom of the sump and allow the oil to drain into a suitable container (photo).

7 Fit a new washer to the drain plug, and refit it to the sump, tightening it to the specified torque.

8 Refill the engine with new engine oil (refer to the Specifications for quantity), through the filler on the valve cover at the top of the engine (photo).

126 Oil filter - removal and refitting

1 The oil filter is situated on the right-hand side of the cylinder block.

2 The filter should be renewed at the intervals given in the Routine Maintenance Section at the beginning of this manual, and is usually in conjunction with an oil change.

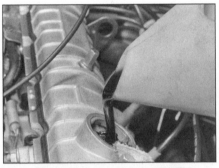

125.8 Filling the engine with oil

3 Remove the filter with the air of a strap wrench if it is tight, unscrewing the filter from its housing.

4 Apply some grease to the sealing ring of the new filter, then screw it back into the housing, using only hand pressure (photo).

126.4 Fitting an oil filter

5 If the filter is renewed without renewing the engine oil, then approximately 0.9 pints (0.5 litre) of engine oil should be added to the engine, to allow for filter content.

6 On completion, run the engine to operating temperature and check for leaks.

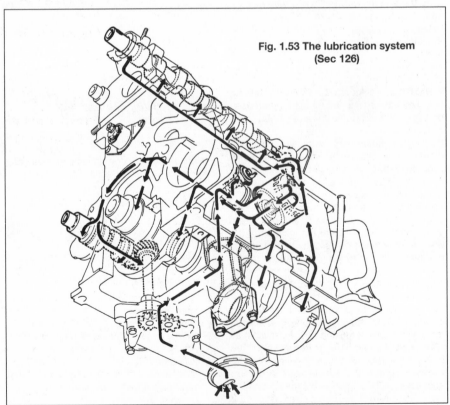

Fig. 1.53 The lubrication system (Sec 126)

127 Compression test

1 If it is suspected that the cylinder bores, piston rings or valves and valve guides are worn, then a compression test may confirm the presence of one or all of the above conditions. Particular emphasis should be placed on the difference of compression pressure between cylinders, rather than on individual pressure.

2 Carry out a compression check as follows and in conjunction with the compression tester manufacturer's instructions:

3 Disconnect the spark plug leads and remove the spark plugs.

4 The engine should be at normal operating temperature.

5 Place the compression tester into No 1 cylinder spark plug hole, and have someone spin the engine on the starter using wide open throttle. Record the pressure while pressing down firmly on the tester, repeat on the other cylinders. Compression pressures should be as given in the Specifications.

6 Note that the condition of the battery, carbon deposits in the engine and different testers can influence the test.

7 On completion, refit the spark plugs and HT leads.

Fault finding - engine

Engine fails to start

- ☐ Discharged battery
- ☐ Loose battery connection
- ☐ Loose or broken ignition leads
- ☐ Moisture on spark plugs, distributor cap, or HT leads
- ☐ Incorrect spark plug gaps
- ☐ Cracked distributor cap or rotor
- ☐ Other ignition system fault
- ☐ Dirt or water in carburettor (if applicable)
- ☐ Empty fuel tank
- ☐ Faulty fuel pump
- ☐ Other fuel system fault
- ☐ Faulty starter motor
- ☐ Low cylinder compressions

Engine idles erratically

- ☐ Inlet manifold air leak
- ☐ Leaking cylinder head gasket
- ☐ Worn rocker arms, timing chain or belt, gears or sprockets
- ☐ Worn camshaft lobes
- ☐ Faulty fuel pump
- ☐ Incorrect valve clearances
- ☐ Loose crankcase ventilation hoses
- ☐ Carburettor adjustment incorrect (if applicable)
- ☐ Uneven cylinder compressions

Engine misfires

- ☐ Spark plugs worn or incorrectly gapped
- ☐ Dirt or water in carburettor (if applicable)
- ☐ Carburettor adjustment incorrect (if applicable)
- ☐ Burnt out valve
- ☐ Leaking cylinder head gasket
- ☐ Distributor cap cracked
- ☐ Incorrect valve clearances
- ☐ Uneven cylinder compressions
- ☐ Worn carburettor (if applicable)

Engine stalls

- ☐ Carburettor adjustment incorrect (if applicable)
- ☐ Inlet manifold air leak
- ☐ Ignition timing incorrect

Excessive oil consumption

- ☐ Worn pistons, cylinder bores or piston rings
- ☐ Valve guides and valve stem seals worn
- ☐ Oil leaking from rocker cover, camshaft cover, engine gaskets or oil seals

Engine backfires

- ☐ Carburettor adjustment incorrect (if applicable)
- ☐ Ignition timing incorrect
- ☐ Incorrect valve clearances
- ☐ Inlet manifold air leak
- ☐ Sticking valve

Engine runs on

- ☐ Excess carbon build-up causing ignition
- ☐ Idle speed too high
- ☐ Faulty idle cut-off solenoid

1

Notes

Chapter 2
Cooling system

Contents

Degrees of difficulty

Easy, suitable for novice with little experience	Fairly easy, suitable for beginner with some experience	Fairly difficult, suitable for competent DIY mechanic	Difficult, suitable for experienced DIY mechanic	Very difficult, suitable for expert DIY or professional

Specifications

System type .... Sealed, with expansion tank, thermostat, water pump and either fixed fan, viscous coupling or thermo-electric fan, depending on model

Thermostat
Type .... Wax
Opening temperature:
  B14 .... 187 to 192°F (86 to 89°C) or 192 to 198°F (89 to 92°C)
  B172 .... 192°F (89°C)
  B19 .... 196 to 199°F (91 to 93°C)
  B200 .... 187 to 190°F (86 to 88°C) or 196 to 199°F (91 to 93°C)
Fully open temperature:
  B14 .... 212°F (100°C) or 221°F (105°C)
  B172 .... 214°F (101°C)
  B19 .... 216°F (102°C)
  B200 .... 207°F (97°C) or 216°F (102°C)

Radiator
Type .... Twin core

Expansion tank
Pressure cap opens:
  B200 .... 9.4 to 12.3 lbf/in² (65 to 85 kPa)
  All other models .... 10.9 lbf/in² (75 kPa)

Coolant capacity
B14:
  Up to 1980 .... 9.7 pints (5.5 litre)
  From 1980 .... 9.2 pints (5.2 litre)
B172 .... 14.1 pints (8.0 litre)
B19:
  Up to 1982 .... 14.1 pints (8.0 litre)
  From 1982 .... 12.3 pints (7.0 litre)
B200 .... 12.3 pints (7.0 litre)

Torque wrench settings

	lbf ft	Nm
B14 models		
Thermal switch in radiator	13	18
Water pump cover	6	8
Water pump backing plate	6	8
Water pump body on cylinder head	6	8
Radiator mounting bolts	15	20
Water pump pulley	15	21
Water pump pulley with extra fan	11	15
B19 and B200 models (where different to above)		
Viscous coupling, bolts and nuts	7	9
Thermostat housing	7	10
B172 models (where different to above)		
Water pump bolts	9	12
Thermostat housing	7	9
Temperature sender in cylinder head	15	20

1 General description

The cooling system consists of a front-mounted radiator, fan, thermostat and water pump. System pressure is controlled by a valve in the expansion tank cap.

The fan and water pump are driven by a V-belt from the crankshaft pulley, this belt also driving the alternator. Auxiliary circuits provide hot water to the car interior heater and carburettor heating flange.

The water pump draws cooled water from the bottom of the radiator and pumps it through the internal waterways of the cylinder head and cylinder block to cool the internal components of the engine. When the engine is cold the thermostat remains closed and the water cannot pass through the radiator, but is channelled back through the engine. This allows for a quick warm-up of the engine and, as soon as the temperature of the water reaches the temperature of the thermostat operating level, the thermostat will open and allow water to pass through the radiator. The water is then cooled under the action of the airflow through the radiator, which is enhanced by the action of the fan. Thus the engine temperature is maintained at its optimum level.

A thermo-electric sensor in the cylinder head relays the coolant temperature to a gauge in the instrument panel.

The expansion tank allows the coolant to expand when heated and also ensures that the system remains full at all times.

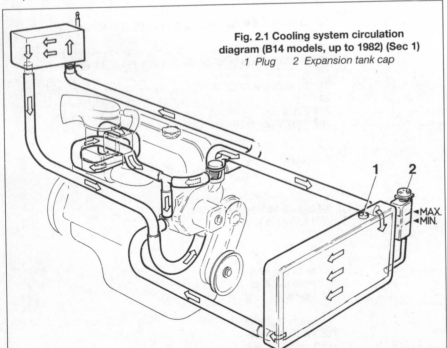

Fig. 2.1 Cooling system circulation diagram (B14 models, up to 1982) (Sec 1)
1 Plug   2 Expansion tank cap

2 Routine maintenance

At the intervals specified in the Routine Maintenance Section at the beginning of this manual, carry out the following operations:

Coolant

1 Check the coolant level and top up as necessary. If frequent topping-up is necessary, check the system for leaks (Sections 4 and 5).
2 The coolant should be changed every two years in the autumn. This is because the corrosion protection additives begin to lose their effectiveness after this time (Sections 3, 4 and 5).

General

3 Periodically check all coolant hoses for deterioration and leaks, renewing any hoses as necessary. This is especially prudent at the onset of winter.

3 Cooling system - draining and flushing

1 It is preferable to drain the cooling system when the engine has cooled. If this is not possible, place a rag over the expansion tank cap and turn it in an anti-clockwise direction slowly. Allow the pressure to escape from the system, then continue turning the cap and remove it (photo).
2 If the coolant is to be retained for further use, place a suitable container beneath the radiator bottom hose.
3 Disconnect the bottom hose, remove the plug from the top of the radiator, and move the heater controls to the maximum heat position.
4 Unscrew the cylinder block drain plug(s) located on the right-hand side beneath the

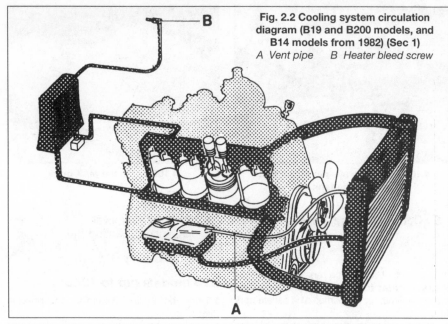

Fig. 2.2 Cooling system circulation diagram (B19 and B200 models, and B14 models from 1982) (Sec 1)
A Vent pipe   B Heater bleed screw

exhaust manifold (early models only) and on the front below the water pump (photo). B172 models have no drain plug on the cylinder block and the radiator bottom hose must be disconnected. This can also be done on other models to speed up the draining process.

5 If the coolant appears to be rusty or a dark brown colour, the radiator and cylinder block waterways should be flushed clean using a hose pipe inserted into the top of the radiator or top radiator hose. **Note**: *Make sure the cylinder block has cooled down or the introduction of cold water into the block could cause cracking.*

6 If, after a reasonable period the water still does not run clear, the radiator can be flushed with a good proprietary cleaning system. The regular renewal of the antifreeze mixture will eliminate the need for vigorous flushing.

7 Refill the system as described in Section 4.

4 Cooling system - filling

B14 models (up to 1982)

1 Refit and tighten the cylinder block drain plug(s) and reconnect the bottom hose to the radiator. Check that the heater controls are in the maximum heat position.

2 Pour coolant of the specified mixture (see next Section) into the radiator until the level is at the bottom of the plug aperture.

3 Fill the expansion tank with coolant to the maximum mark, then refit the plastic cap.

4 Start the engine and run it at a fast idling speed until it is at the normal operating temperature with the thermostat open.

5 With the engine idling, loosen the vent screw (where fitted) on the three-way union at the front of the engine and allow any trapped air to escape. Tighten the screw when no more air bubbles emerge.

6 Connect a length of plastic tubing from the heater vent screw (photo) to the radiator plug aperture. With the engine running at a fast idling speed, loosen the screw and allow any trapped air to escape. Tighten the screw when no more air bubbles emerge. Remove the tubing.

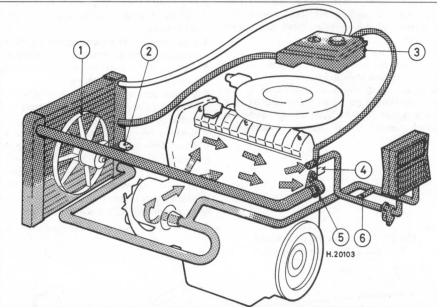

Fig. 2.3 Cooling system circulation diagram (B17 models) (Sec 1)
1 Fan   2 Switch   3 Expansion tank   4 Sender   5 Thermostat   6 Bypass

3.1 Removing the filler cap from the expansion tank

3.4 Cylinder block drain plug below the water pump (arrowed)

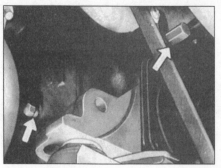

Fig. 2.4 Cylinder block drain plug locations (early B14 models) (Sec 3)

4.6 Heater vent screw location (early models)

4.10A Filling the system through the expansion tank . . .

4.10B . . . to the MAX mark

7 Stop the engine and fill the radiator to the top of the plug aperture, then refit and tighten the plug.

8 Remove the filler cap and top up the expansion tank to the maximum level mark. Refit the cap.

B14 (from 1982), B172, B19 and B200 models

9 These models incorporate a self-bleeding expansion tank and there is no filler plug in the radiator. Draining is otherwise as for early models.

10 Fill the system to the maximum mark on the expansion tank (photos), run the engine until it reaches normal operating temperature, when the thermostat should open. Watch the expansion tank and, when the coolant flowing into the tank is free from air, stop the engine and allow it to cool before topping-up to the maximum mark.

6.6 Radiator-to-expansion tank hose (arrowed)

6.9 Radiator upper mounting bolt (arrowed) (B14 models up to 1983)

---

5 Coolant mixture - renewal

1 The coolant should be renewed every two years in order to retain the antifreeze and corrosion inhibitor properties at a satisfactory level.

2 Before adding fresh mixture, check all hose connections and preferably check the tightness of the cylinder head bolts (See Chapter 1).

3 Mix the correct quantity of coolant in a separate container, then fill the cooling system as described in Section 4.

4 When using Volvo coolant type C the mixture should be 1 part Volvo coolant to 2 parts water. If other types of antifreeze are being used, follow the manufacturer's instructions.

---

6 Radiator - removal, inspection, cleaning and refitting

B14 models (up to 1983)

1 Drain the cooling system as described in Section 3.

2 Disconnect the battery negative terminal.

3 Remove the spare wheel from the engine compartment.

4 Remove the screws and washers securing the bottom of the fan housing to the radiator.

5 Remove the radiator lower mounting bolts, washers, sleeves and rubbers.

6 Disconnect the expansion tank hose from the right-hand side of the radiator (photo), and from the bottom clip.

7 Remove the screws and washers securing the top of the fan housing to the radiator and hang the housing over the fan.

8 Disconnect the top hose from the radiator.

9 Remove the radiator upper mounting bolt, washers, and rubbers while supporting the radiator (photo). Lift the radiator from the

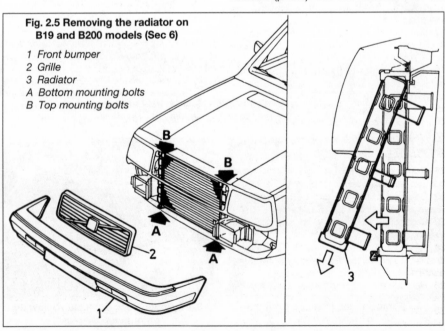

Fig. 2.5 Removing the radiator on B19 and B200 models (Sec 6)

1 *Front bumper*
2 *Grille*
3 *Radiator*
A *Bottom mounting bolts*
B *Top mounting bolts*

6.22 Radiator bottom and vent hoses on B19 and B200 models (arrowed)

6.24A Radiator bottom mounting bolt and bracket on B19 and B200 models

6.24B Top mounting bracket and retaining bolts on B172 models

engine compartment, being careful not to damage the matrix on the fan blades. Do not allow any coolant to drop onto the bodywork, as the paintwork may be damaged.

10 If necessary, remove the screws and clamp and withdraw the expansion tank.

11 Radiator repair is best entrusted to a specialist, but minor leaks may be repaired with a proprietary product.

12 Clean the radiator matrix. Remove any flies or leaves with a soft brush or with a hose.

13 Flush the radiator as described in Section 3. Examine the hoses and clips for deterioration, renewing them as necessary.

14 Refitting is a reversal of removal, but the following additional points should be noted:

a) Tighten all hoses making sure that the clips are positioned correctly

b) Check the expansion tank filler cap for damage or deterioration and renew it if necessary

B14 models (from 1983)

15 Disconnect the leads from the thermal switch.

16 Remove the lower retaining bolts from the radiator and the bottom screws securing the fan assembly.

17 Disconnect the radiator bottom hose, the two expansion tank hoses and the upper radiator hose.

18 Release the radiator top mounting, remove the top screws and place the fan on the front crossmember.

19 Lift the radiator up and out of position.

20 Refer to the paragraphs on earlier models for cleaning and repair.

B172, B19 and B200 models

21 Remove the radiator grille and front bumper, as described in Chapter 9.

22 Disconnect the top and bottom radiator hoses and the small vent hose (photo).

23 Disconnect the leads to the thermal switch (if fitted).

24 Remove the bottom radiator bolts and bracket, then the top left-hand bolt, then the right-hand bolts and brackets (photos).

25 Remove the radiator forwards, pulling the lower edge out and then down.

26 Cleaning and repair is as described for B14 models.

27 Refitting is a reversal of removal, but apply Vaseline to the rubber mounting blocks.

7 Thermostat - removal, testing and refitting

B14 models

1 A faulty thermostat can cause overheating or slow engine warm-up, and can also affect the performance of the heater.

2 Drain the cooling system as described in Section 3 but only drain off enough coolant to bring the level below the top of the water pump.

3 Loosen the clip and disconnect the top hose from the water pump.

4 Loosen the clip retaining the thermostat in the hose, then withdraw the thermostat (photo).

5 To test whether the unit is serviceable, suspend the thermostat by a piece of string in a pan of cold water and heat the water. Use a thermometer to check the opening temperature, which should be in accordance with the information given in the Specifications.

6 Remove the thermostat from the water and allow it to cool; when completely cooled the valve must be firmly shut.

7 Refitting is a reversal of removal, but make sure that the clip is fitted over the thermostat to prevent it from moving. Refill the cooling system as described in Section 4.

7.4 Thermostat location in radiator hose on early B14 models

B19 and B200 models

8 The action of the thermostat is shown in Fig. 2.7. Note the definite change-over action when the coolant is allowed to flow through the main hose which is connected from the top of the thermostat casing to the radiator: the circulation path to the water pump is closed up by the tongue on the bottom of the thermostat. For proper operation of the system, therefore, you should be careful not to bend or twist this tongue when removing or fitting the thermostat.

9 To replace a faulty thermostat, lower the level of the coolant in the engine by partially draining the system through the tap on the cylinder block. Collect the coolant in a clean container for using again.

10 Remove the nuts securing the thermostat housing and lifting eye. Lift off the housing and remove the thermostat (photo).

11 Clean off the contact faces of the head and the housing, fit a new thermostat, in the identical position, and a new gasket. Refit the housing and the lifting eye. Refill the system through the expansion tank.

B172 models

12 The thermostat is fitted in a housing mounted at the rear end of the cylinder block (photo).

13 Remove the hose, undo the three housing bolts and remove the housing and thermostat.

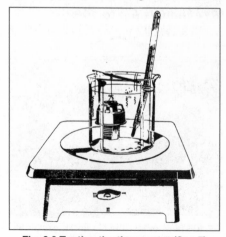

Fig. 2.6 Testing the thermostat (Sec 7)

2

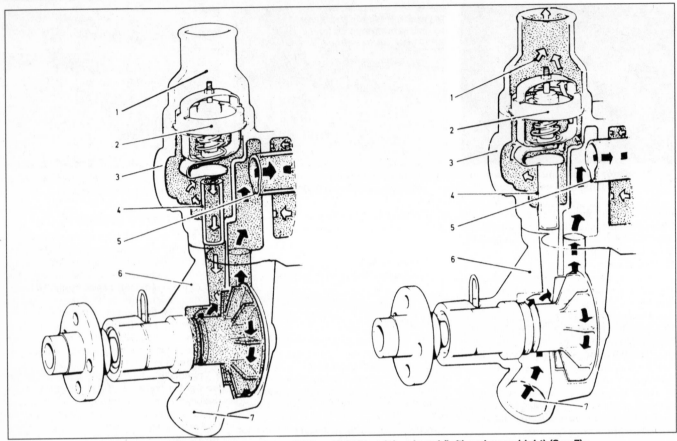

Fig. 2.7 Operation of the thermostat on B19 and B200 models: closed (left) and open (right) (Sec 7)

1 *To radiator (top)*	4 *Bypass*	7 *From radiator (bottom)*
2 *Thermostat*	5 *Distribution pipe*	A *Tongue open*
3 *Cylinder head*	6 *Water pump*	B *Tongue closed*

14 On refitting, ensure that rubber seal around the thermostat is in good condition, renewing it as necessary (photo).

---

8 Water pump - removal and refitting

B14 models (up to 1982)

1 Disconnect the battery negative terminal, and drain the cooling system.

2 Remove the radiator as described in Section 6, and remove the fan housing.

3 Loosen the alternator retaining and adjusting bolts and push the alternator towards the engine; the drivebelt can now be removed from the water pump pulley.

4 Unscrew and remove the fan retaining bolts and withdraw the fan and pulley from the water pump flange. Note the location of the spacer ring. **Note:** *Early fan-to-pulley bolts were fitted with lock washers and plain washer under the bolt head. Later bolts, which are*

shorter, are fitted with a wave washer under the head. The longer bolts used previously should not be fitted with only a wave washer because the bolts could foul the water pump housing.

5 Loosen the clips and remove the hoses from the water pump (photo).

6 If it is only required to renew the water pump cover, unscrew and remove the cover retaining bolts evenly in diagonal sequence and carefully pull the cover assembly away from the base housing. Remove the gasket.

7.10 Thermostat housing and thermostat on B19 and B200 models

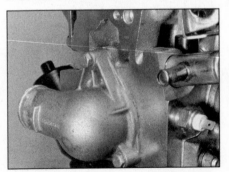

7.12 Thermostat housing on B172 models

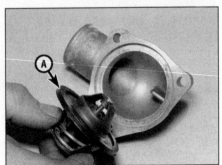

7.14 Fitting the thermostat to the housing on B172 models. Sealing ring A

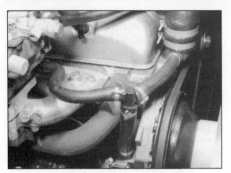

8.5 Water pump and hoses on early B14 models

8.7 Water pump unit on early B14 models

7 If the complete water pump is being removed, unscrew and remove the bolts shown in Fig. 2.10 and lift the unit away from the cylinder head (photo).

8 Remove all traces of gasket from the water pump and/or cylinder head, being careful not to damage the contact surfaces.

9 Refitting is a reversal of removal, but the following points should be noted:

a) *Always fit new gaskets*

b) *Tighten all nuts and bolts to the correct torque wrench settings and in diagonal sequence where possible*

c) *Where hose clips requiring a special tool are fitted, replace them with the worm drive type*

d) *Adjust the drivebelt tension (Section 9)*

e) *Fill the cooling system with reference to Section 4*

f) *Run the engine and check for leaks when completed*

Fig. 2.8 Radiator and water pump components (early B14 models) (Sec 8)

1 *Thermostat*
2 *Gasket*
3 *Water pump housing*
4 *Gasket*
5 *Water pump*
6 *Bottom hose*
7 *Top hose*
8 *Pulley*
9 *Fan*
10 *Expansion tank*
11 *Radiator*

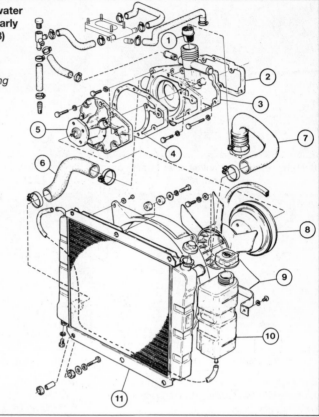

B14 models (from 1982)

10 The procedure is similar to that described for earlier models except that the water pump is of different design.

11 The gasket between the pump housing and the backing plate should be fitted dry, and the backing plate bolts should not be tightened to their specified torque until after the pump housing has been fitted to the engine block.

B19 and B200 models

12 Remove the radiator (see Section 6).

13 Loosen the alternator mounting and adjustment bolts, push the alternator towards the engine and remove the drivebelts.

14 Unbolt the fan and pulley, and remove the timing belt outer cover.

15 Unscrew the engine shock absorber top mounting bolt, also unbolt the bracket top mounting bolts, remove the bushes and move the bracket to one side.

16 Disconnect the radiator hose and the return water pipe. Remove the bolts securing the pump and remove the pump.

17 Remove the residue of the old gasket on the cylinder block mating surface and also clean the rubber ring contact surface on the cylinder head. Fit a new rubber sealing ring on the new pump, ensure you fit the correct ring. Varying heights of rings are available to allow for different thickness of cylinder head gaskets.

18 Fit a new gasket against the cylinder block, use a smear of grease to hold it in position. Press the pump upwards against the cylinder head and fit the retaining bolts. Fit a

Fig. 2.9 Water pump cover retaining bolts - arrowed (early B14 models) (Sec 8)

Fig. 2.10 Water pump-to-cylinder block retaining bolts - arrowed (early B14 models) (Sec 8)

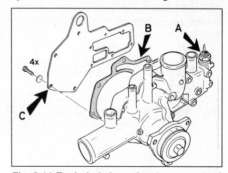

Fig. 2.11 Exploded view of water pump and backing plate (late B14 models) (Sec 8)
A Sender   B Gasket   C Backing plate

8.22 Preventing the pulley from turning on B172 models

8.23 Removing the pump-to-cylinder block bolts on B172 models

8.25A Fit the new gasket dry . . .

8.25B . . . and then the pump housing

new rubber ring on the water return pipe, fit the pipe and the retaining bolts. Connect the lower radiator hose.

19 The remaining refitting procedure is a reversal of removal. Tension the drivebelts with reference to Section 9.

B172 models

20 Disconnect the battery positive lead, remove the engine splash guard from beneath the engine and drain the cooling system by disconnecting the bottom radiator hose.

21 Slacken the alternator adjusting bolts, push the alternator in toward the engine and remove the water pump/alternator drivebelt.

22 Insert a suitable tool through one of the holes in the water pump drive pulley to prevent it turning while removing the pulley retaining bolts (photo).

23 Remove the pulley, then undo the bolts securing the pump housing to the engine block (photo).

24 The water pump is a sealed unit and cannot be repaired, so if it is unserviceable it should be renewed.

25 Clean the joint faces of the cylinder block and the pump, fit a new gasket (dry) (photo), fit the pump (photo) and tighten the retaining bolts to their specified torque.

26 The remaining refitting sequence is a reversal of removal.

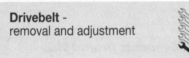

9 Drivebelt -
removal and adjustment

B14 models

1 To renew the drivebelt, first loosen the

9.3 Checking drivebelt tension - B14 models

9.6 Alternator adjustment bolt on B172 models

alternator retaining and adjusting bolts, move the unit towards the engine and remove the belt from the crankshaft, alternator, and fan pulleys. Finally lift it over the fan blades.

2 Installation is a reversal of removal, but the tension should be adjusted as follows. **Note**: *Incorrect fanbelt tension can cause premature wear of the alternator and water pump bearings, or insufficient charging and cooling.*

3 The correct tension is measured by depressing the upper run of the belt with firm thumb pressure at a midway point (photo); the belt should move 0.4 in (10 mm).

4 To adjust the tension, first loosen the alternator retaining and adjusting bolts. Move the unit in or out as necessary to achieve the correct tension, then tighten the bolts. Take care when using a lever on the alternator, and only apply it to the pulley end housing.

B19 and B200 models

5 The procedure is as given for B14 models, but two drivebelts are fitted (photo).

B172 models

6 Loosen the alternator mounting bolts then slacken the alternator adjustment bolt (photo) sufficiently for the belt to be removed.

7 The belt should be renewed if the grooves in the belt are worn or cut, if there is an excessive amount of rubber deposits in the bottom of the grooves, if the textile backing in the belt is visible at any point, or if the belt has become contaminated with oil or grease.

8 Before refitting a used belt, thoroughly clean the belt grooves.

9 Fit the belt over the crankshaft pulley, water pump pully and alternator pulley (photo).

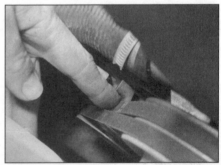

9.5 B19 and B200 models have two belts

9.9 Poly drivebelt fitted around the pulleys on B172 models

10.3A Water temperature sender on B14 models . . .

10.3B . . . and B172 models

11.5 Radiator hose lower retaining clip and bracket

10 Tension the belt by screwing down on the alternator adjustment bolt until the belt can just be turned through 90 degrees using moderate thumb and finger pressure midway along the longest run. If the belt is too tight it will be heard to hum when the engine is running. Belt tension should be set with the engine cold. **Note**: *A special tool is available from Volvo for setting the belt.*
11 On completion of tensioning the belt, tighten the alternator mounting bolts.

10 Water temperature sender - removal, testing and refitting

1 The water temperature sender is a semiconductor whose electrical resistance varies with temperature. Variations in resistance cause a varying current to pass through the sender to the gauge, which indicates water temperature.
2 The sender could be tested by removing it from the cylinder head and placing its probe in hot water (with the leads still connected) and observing the temperature gauge.
3 To remove the sender, disconnect the electrical leads, then unscrew the sender from the cylinder block (photos).
4 Refitting is a reversal of removal, but use a new sealing washer under the sender, and if a substantial amount of coolant has been lost, fill and bleed the system as described in Section 4.

11 Thermo-electric cooling fan and thermal time switch - removal and refitting

1 A thermal-electric cooling fan controlled by a thermal time switch is fitted to all B172 models, and to B14 models from 1983.
2 The fan is mounted in a frame which is bolted to the rear of the radiator. The thermal time switch is screwed into the radiator, the fan motor and time switch being connected electrically.
3 Normally the fan remains off until the temperature reaches a preset figure when the thermal time switch, in response to changes of resistance caused by the rising temperature of the coolant, switches the fan motor on, thereby increasing the airflow through the radiator and the cooling effect of the air.
4 To remove the fan, first disconnect the leads to the time switch.
5 Remove the four bolts securing the fan frame to the radiator (it may be necessary on some models to release the lower coolant hose in order to gain access to the frame bolts (photo), but this can be done without disconnecting the hose and losing coolant).
6 Lift the fan and frame out of the engine bay.
7 The fan can be removed from the motor driveshaft by removing the circlip. The motor is held to the frame by bolts (photo).
8 The time switch simply unscrews from the radiator, and can be tested using a similar method to that described for the water

temperature sender in Section 10. Use a new sealing washer under the head when refitting.
9 Refitting of the fan is a reversal of removal.

12 Viscous coupling cooling fan (B19 and B200) - removal and refitting

1 B19 models produced from 1984 and all B200 models are equipped with a temperature-sensitive coupling cooling fan.
2 The viscous coupling is fitted between the fan and water pump pulley, removal and refitting being self-evident with reference to Fig. 2.14 (photo).

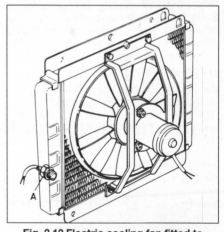

Fig. 2.12 Electric cooling fan fitted to B14 models from 1984 (Sec 11)
A Thermo-switch

11.7 Cooling fan-to-frame retaining nuts (arrowed)

12.2 Viscous coupling cooling fan fitted to B19 and B200 models

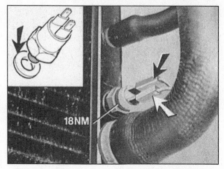

Fig. 2.13 Thermo-switch electrical leads and sealing washer (arrowed) (Sec 11)

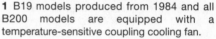

2

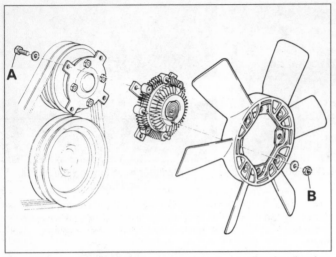

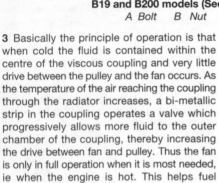

Fig. 2.14 Components of the viscous coupling cooling fan fitted to B19 and B200 models (Sec 12)

A Bolt   B Nut

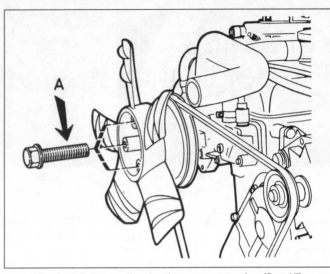

Fig. 2.15 Extra cooling fan for caravan towing (Sec 15)

A Three bolts

3 Basically the principle of operation is that when cold the fluid is contained within the centre of the viscous coupling and very little drive between the pulley and the fan occurs. As the temperature of the air reaching the coupling through the radiator increases, a bi-metallic strip in the coupling operates a valve which progressively allows more fluid to the outer chamber of the coupling, thereby increasing the drive between fan and pulley. Thus the fan is only in full operation when it is most needed, ie when the engine is hot. This helps fuel consumption by reducing engine load, and also results in quieter engine running.

4 The viscous coupling cooling unit is a sealed unit and cannot be repaired, and should be renewed if it is suspected of malfunction.

13 Extra cooling fan for caravan towing - certain models only

The manufacturers strongly recommend the fitting of an extra cooling fan if the vehicle is to be used for caravan towing, especially in mountainous country.

This extra cooling fan is fitted on to the water pump pulley as shown in Fig. 2.15, and is only applicable to certain models, therefore the advice of your Volvo dealer should be sought if this situation is applicable.

Fault finding - cooling system

Overheating

- [ ] Low coolant level
- [ ] Faulty thermostat
- [ ] Loose drivebelt
- [ ] Clogged radiator matrix
- [ ] Incorrect ignition timing
- [ ] Clogged cooling system
- [ ] Blown cylinder head gasket
- [ ] Faulty expansion tank filler cap
- [ ] Incorrect carburettor mixture setting
- [ ] Faulty fan thermo-switch

Cool running or slow warm-up

- [ ] Faulty thermostat

Coolant loss

- [ ] Faulty expansion tank filler cap
- [ ] Cracked hose
- [ ] Blown cylinder head gasket
- [ ] Worn water pump
- [ ] Leaking radiator

Chapter 3
Fuel and exhaust systems

For modifications, and information applicable to later models, see Supplement at end of manual

Contents

Degrees of difficulty

Easy, suitable for novice with little experience	**Fairly easy,** suitable for beginner with some experience	**Fairly difficult,** suitable for competent DIY mechanic	**Difficult,** suitable for experienced DIY mechanic	**Very difficult,** suitable for expert DIY or professional

3

Specifications

B14 models

General

Fuel tank capacity:	
Total	9.9 gal (45 litre)
Reserve	1.1 gal (5 litre)
Fuel pump:	
Type	Mechanical
Delivery pressure	2.32 to 3.77 lbf/in² (16 to 26 kPa)
Fuel octane rating	96 RON

Air cleaner element
Champion W109 (1976 to 1980) or Champion W146 (1981-on)

Weber carburettor

Type	Twin barrel, downdraught
Code	Weber 32 DIR
Idling speed:	
B14.0	750 rpm
B14.1/2/3/4:	
Manual transmission	900 ± 50 rpm
Automatic transmission	800 ± 50 rpm
CO content at idle:	
B14.0	1.5 to 4.0%
B14.1/2/3/4	1.5 to 3.0%

Weber carburettor (continued)

Settings (up to 1982):

93-100 and 95-100

	First stage	Second stage
Venturi	24	24
Main jet (fuel)	110 to 115	132 to 135
Main jet (air)	135 to 155	155 to 175
Emulsion tube	F20	F6
Idle jet (fuel)	42 to 48	47 to 53
Idle jet (air)	125 to 145	65 to 75
Accelerator pump jet	60	-
Mechanical choke valve opening	3.5 to 4.5 mm	3.5 to 4.5 mm
Pneumatic choke valve opening	5.5 to 6.5 mm	5.5 to 6.5 mm
Throttle valve opening (with full choke)	0.85 to 0.95 mm	
Float needle	1.75 mm	
Float height (with gasket)	7 mm	

All other carburettors

	First stage	Second stage
Venturi	23	24
Main jet (fuel)	125 to 130[1]	117 to 123
Main jet (air)	170 to 190	125 to 145
Emulsion tube	F53	F6
Idle jet (fuel)	44 to 50	55 to 65[2]
Idle jet (air)	105 to 125	-
Accelerator pump jet	50	-
Mechanical choke valve opening	3.5 to 4.5 mm	3.5 to 4.5 mm
Pneumatic choke valve opening	4.0 to 5.0[3] mm	4.0 to 5.0[3] mm
Throttle valve opening (with full choke)	0.85 to 0.95 mm	
Float needle	1.75 mm	
Float height (with gasket)	7 mm	

[1] Carburettor 84-100: 127 to 133
[2] Carburettors 74-100, 83-100 and 85-100:0
[3] Carburettor 85-100:5.5 to 6.5 mm

Settings (from 1982):

93-101 and 95-101

	First stage	Second stage
Venturi	24	24
Main jet (fuel)	110 to 115	132 to 135
Main jet (air)	145 to 165[4]	Emulsion tube
Emulsion tube	F20	F6
Idle jet (fuel)	47 to 53	0
Idle jet (air)	125 to 145	65 to 75
Accelerator pump jet	45	45
Mechanical choke valve opening	3.5 to 4.5 mm	3.5 to 4.5 mm
Pneumatic choke valve opening	5.5 to 6.5 mm	5.5 to 6.5 mm
Throttle valve opening (with full choke)	0.85 to 0.95 mm	-
Float needle	1.75 mm	
Float height (with gasket)	7 mm	

[4] Carburettor 95-101: 135 to 155

104-100, 105-100, 109 (with fuel cut-off) and 110 (without fuel cut-off)

	First stage	Second stage
Venturi	23	24
Main jet (fuel)	120 to 125[5]	135 to 140
Main jet (air)	180 to 200	180 to 200
Emulsion tube	F20	F20
Idle jet (fuel)	47 to 53	47 to 53
Idle jet (air)	130 to 140	65 to 75
Accelerator pump jet	45	45
Mechanical choke valve opening	3.5 to 4.5 mm	-
Pneumatic choke valve opening	5.5 to 6.5 mm	-
Throttle valve opening (with full choke)	0.85 to 0.95 mm	-
Float needle	1.75 mm	
Float height (with gasket)	7 mm	

[5] Carburettors 105-100 and 110: 122 to 127

Weber carburettor (continued)

Settings (from 1982):

100 and 110	First stage	Second stage
Venturi	23	24
Main jet (fuel)	115 to 120	135 to 140
Main jet (air)	185 to 195	185 to 195
Emulsion tube	F20	F20
Idle jet (fuel)	50	50
Idle jet (air)	135	70
Accelerator pump jet	45	-
Mechanical choke valve opening	3.5 to 4.5 mm	-
Pneumatic choke valve opening	5.5 to 6.5 mm	
Throttle valve opening (with full choke)	-	-
Float needle	1.75 mm	
Float height (with gasket)	7 mm	

Solex carburettor

Type	Single barrel downdraught
Code	32-SEIA REN
Idling speed:	
Manual transmission	900 ± 150 rpm
Automatic transmission	800 ± 50 rpm
CO content at idle:	1.5 to 3.0%

Settings:

796	
Venturi	24 asymmetrical
Main jet (fuel)	125.5 to 130.5
Main jet (air)	150 to 160
Emulsion tube	X16
Idle jet	42 to 48
Accelerator pump jet	35
Mechanical choke valve opening	4.0 to 5.0 mm
Throttle valve opening (with full choke)	0.8 mm
Float needle	1.5 mm
Float height	22.7 mm
Float chamber ventilation valve opening	3.0 to 4.0 mm

814 and 828	
Venturi	24 symmetrical
Main jet (fuel)	120 to 125
Main jet (air)	160 to 170
Emulsion tube	X17
Idle jet	40 to 46
Accelerator pump jet	35
Mechanical choke valve opening	4.0 to 5.0 mm
Throttle valve opening (with full choke)	0.8 mm
Float needle	1.5 mm
Float height	22.7[6] mm
Float chamber ventilation valve opening	3.0 to 4.0 mm

[6] *Carburettor 828: 22.5 mm*

B172 models

General

Fuel tank capacity:	
Total	9.9 gal (45 litre)
Reserve	1.1 gal (5 litre)
Fuel pump:	
Type	Sofabex M8736
Delivery pressure	2.32 to 4.06 lbf/in^2 (16 to 28 kPa)
Fuel octane rating	98 RON

Air cleaner element . . . . Champion W146

3

Solex carburettor

Type	....	Twin barrel, downdraught
Code	....	28-34 CISAC Z-10
Idling speed	....	900 ± 50 rpm
CO content at idle	....	0.5 to 2.0%

Settings:	**First stage**	**Second stage**
Venturi	20	26
Main jet (fuel)	95	120
Main jet (air)	185	145
Emulsion tube	22761	22762
Idle jet (fuel)	40	40
Idle jet (air)	160	70
Accelerator pump jet	-	46
Accelerator pump bearing	202	
Pneumatic choke valve opening	3.5 mm	
Throttle valve opening (with full choke)	2.0 mm	
Float needle	1.8 mm	
Float weight	6g	
Float height (with gasket)	33.8 mm	
Float chamber ventilation valve opening	2.0 to 3.0 mm	

B19A carburettor models

General

Fuel tank capacity:		
Total	....	12.5 gal (57 litre)
Reserve	....	1.1 gal (5 litre)
Fuel pump:		
Type	....	Mechanical
Delivery pressure	....	2.18 to 3.92 lf/in^2 (15 to to 27 kPa)
Fuel octane rating	....	98 RON
Air cleaner element	....	Champion U531

Zenith carburettor

Type	....	Single barrel, side draught
Code	....	175 CD -2SE
Idling speed	....	900 ± 50 rpm
CO content at idle:		
Engines 568, 854, 902, 906, 982 and 984	....	1.5 to 3.0%
Engines 552, 566, 658 and 660	....	1.0 to 2.5%
Settings:		
Damper piston endplay	....	1.0 to 1.8 mm
Metering needle	....	B1FG (B2BG)
Fast idle speed	....	1250 to 1350 rpm (with headlights on)
Needle valve	....	2 mm
Float level:		
High point	....	15 to 17 mm
Low point	....	9 to 13 mm
Throttle lever clearance	....	0.5 mm
Temperature compensator	....	60L
Thermostatic air valve control range	....	68 to 86°F (20 to 30°C)
Dashpot oil type/specification	....	Automatic transmission fluid

B200K carburettor models

General

Fuel tank capacity:		
Total	....	12.5 gal (57 litre)
Reserve	....	1.1 gal (5 litre)
Fuel pump:		
Type	....	Mechanical
Delivery pressure	....	2.18 to 3.92 lf/in^2 (15 to 27 kPa)
Fuel octane rating	....	98 RON
Air cleaner element	....	Champion U531

Solex carburettor

Type . . . . Twin barrel, downdraught
Code . . . . 34-34 CISAC
Idling speed . . . . 900 rpm
CO content at idle . . . . 1.0 to 2.5%

Settings:	First stage	Second stage
Venturi	15	27
Main jet (fuel)	120	115
Main jet (air)	145	130
Emulsion tube	ZN	ZC
Idle jet (fuel)	41	60
Idle jet (air)	100	100
Accelerator pump jet	60	
Float needle	21 mm	
Float height (with gasket)	33.8 mm	

B19E and B200E fuel injection models

General

Fuel tank capacity:
  Total . . . . 12.5 gal (57 litre)
  Reserve . . . . 1.1 gal (5 litre)
Fuel pump:
  Type . . . . Electric
  Current rating 6.5A
Delivery capacity . . . . 211 pints/hour (120 litre/hour) at 68°F (20°C)
Fuel octane rating . . . . 98 RON

Bosch LE-Jetronic fuel injection

Idling speed . . . . 900 ± 50 rpm
  C0 content at idle . . . . 0.5 to 2.0%
Auxiliary air valve:
  Resistance . . . . 40 to 60 ohm
  Fully open at . . . . -22°F (-30°C)
  Fully closed at . . . . 158°F (70°C)
Cold start injector:
  Injector time . . . . 7 secs at -4°F (-20°C) to 0 secs at 95°F (35°C)
Injectors:
  Resistance . . . . 15 to 17.5 ohm at 68°F (20°C) 17 to 19 ohm at 176°F (80°C)
Injection pressure:
  Line . . . . 35.6 lbf/in^2 (245 kPa)
  Residual . . . . 32.7 to 34.1 lbf/in^2 (226 to 235 kPa)
Thermostatic air valve control range . . . . 77 to 95°F (25 to 35°C)

All models

Torque wrench settings

	lbf ft	Nm
Inlet manifold to exhaust manifold:		
Bolt	7 to 13	10 to 18
Screw	11 to 15	15 to 20
Nut	11 to 15	15 to 20
Manifolds to cylinder head:		
B172 models	13	18
All other models	11 to 15	15 to 20
Carburettor	11 to 15	15 to 20
Fuel pump:		
B14:		
Old type	11 to 15	15 to 20
New type	7	10
B19 and B200	15	20

3

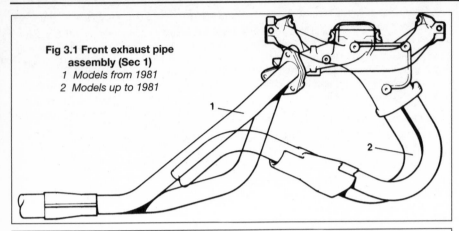

Fig 3.1 Front exhaust pipe assembly (Sec 1)
1 Models from 1981
2 Models up to 1981

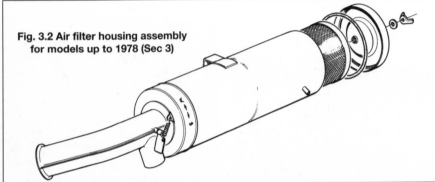

Fig. 3.2 Air filter housing assembly for models up to 1978 (Sec 3)

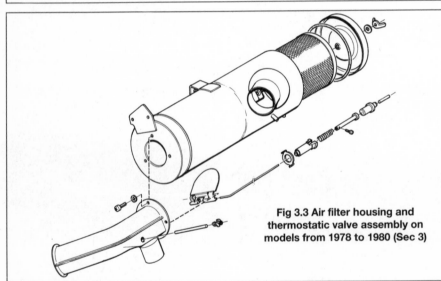

Fig 3.3 Air filter housing and thermostatic valve assembly on models from 1978 to 1980 (Sec 3)

1 General description

The fuel system consists of a rear-mounted fuel tank, a fuel pump (mechanical or electric), and a carburettor or fuel injection system.

An air filtration system is fitted to all models, incorporating a disposable paper element. On early models the selection of cool or hot air to the intake system is manual, but as from 1978 this is controlled by a thermo-statically controlled valve.

The exhaust system is in three sections - the front downpipe, intermediate section and silencer, and the rear section and resonator/tailpipe. On early models the exhaust manifold outlet faces forward, and the exhaust pipe curves toward the rear, but as from 1981 the manifold outlet faces the rear and the front pipe has no curve.

Before working on any part of the fuel system, take every precaution, and do read the Safety First section at the beginning of this manual.

Before any overhaul work is commenced, make sure that parts for renovation are available. Most dealers stock carburettor repair kits which contain all the seals, gaskets, etc which are required.

It should be noted that, up to and including model year 1986, no engine model is equipped for operation on unleaded fuel. The recommended fuel octane rating should be used. All 1987 models will run on leaded and unleaded fuel.

2 Routine maintenance

At the intervals laid down in the Routine Maintenance Section at the beginning of this manual, carry out the following operations:

Air filter

1 Renew the element.

Carburettor

2 Check dashpot oil level (B19A models).
3 Check choke operation and fast idle speed.

Fuel filter

4 Check for blockage/renew filter(s).

Exhaust

5 Check for leaks, condition and security.

General

6 Check CO level and idle speed.
7 Check fuel lines for leaks.

3 Air filter and filter housing assembly - removal and refitting

B14 models (up to 1981)

1 To renew the filter, lift the windscreen wash reservoir and disconnect the supply hose. (On early models this entails removing the filler cap.)
2 Identify all breather and vacuum hoses for reconnection and then disconnect them.
3 Disconnect the hot and cold air intake hoses.
4 Remove the bolts securing the filter assembly to the support bracket and withdraw the assembly.

Fig. 3.4 Air filter housing mounting bolts on models up to 1981 (Sec 3)

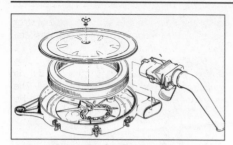

Fig. 3.5 Air filter housing assembly for models from 1981 (Sec 3)

5 Remove the wing nut from the rear cover and remove the cover and air filter.

6 Refit in the reverse order, ensuring the O-ring seal is correctly located under the rear cover.

B14 models (from 1981, Weber carburettor)

7 Remove the air filter housing centre nut, remove the lid and lift out the filter (photo).

8 To remove the complete housing, remove the three bolts securing the housing to the carburettor (there may be a further bolt fitted to an external bracket on the side of the housing), lift the housing and disconnect the breather hoses before removing the housing completely.

9 Refitting is a reversal of removal.

B14 models (from 1981, Solex carburettor)

10 The procedure is much the same as for the Weber carburettor, but there are only two bolts securing the housing to the carburettor. On automatic models, disconnect the hose to the electromagnetic valve. If work is to be carried out on the carburettor, then also remove the air filter bracket which is bolted to the carburettor.

11 Refitting is a reversal of removal, but ensure the arrows line up (photo).

B19 and B200 models

12 Release the clips and lift off the cover (photos). If necessary, disconnect the air inlet hose (photo).

13 To remove the complete housing, pull the housing upward from its rubber mountings. Some of the rubber mountings may come away with the housing. Refit them in their original position.

14 Refitting is a reversal of removal.

B172 models

15 To renew the air filter undo the clips (photo), remove the nut from the centre of the air cleaner lid (photo), remove the lid and lift out the air filter (photo).

16 Refit in the reverse order.

17 To remove the complete air cleaner assembly, first remove the filter (paragraph 15).

18 Remove the cold and hot air intake hose (photos).

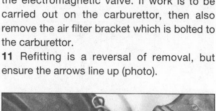

3.7 Removing the air filter on B14 models (from 1981)

3.11 Air filter housing lid alignment marks

3.12A An air filter lid retaining clip on B19 models

3

3.12B Removing the air filter on B200K models

3.12C Air filter on B19 models

3.12D Inlet hose to the carburettor on B200K models

3.15A Undoing an air filter clip . . .

3.15B . . . removing the nut . . .

3.15C . . . and lifting out the filter

3.18A Disconnecting the cold . . .

3.18B . . . and hot air hoses

3.19 Air filter housing retaining nuts (arrowed)

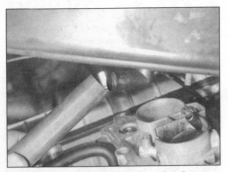

3.20 Disconnecting the breather hose

3.21 Removing the screw on the thermostatic air valve

19 Remove the three nuts securing the air cleaner assembly to the carburettor (photo).
20 Lift the housing and disconnect the breather hoses underneath (photo) before lifting the assembly away.
21 The thermostatic air control valve can be removed from the housing by undoing the screw (photo).
22 The procedure for testing the thermostatic valve is given in Section 4.
23 Refitting the air cleaner assembly is a reversal of removal.

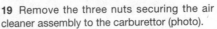

4   Air filter thermostatic valve - description and testing

1 Models up to 1978 are fitted with a manually controlled air flap which can be set to a summer or winter position. On models from

1978 the flap is thermostatically controlled (photos), but as from 1981 it is not adjustable.
2 Cold air is drawn into the air filter at engine compartment temperature while hot air is drawn through a hose from the area of the exhaust manifold (photo).
3 The thermostatic valve is located at the air filter end of the air cleaner and is activated by the temperature of the air entering the carburettor. When the temperature of the air is below 15°C (1978 models) or 20°C (1979 and 1980 models) the cold air supply is closed, and when the temperature is above 25°C (1978 models) or 35°C (1979 and 1980 models) the hot air supply is closed. The air flap is automatically regulated between these two limits, and the air entering the engine is therefore maintained at a suitable temperature.
4 To test the thermostatic valve, first remove the air filter element as described in Section 3.

4.1A Thermostatic air valve housing on models from 1981

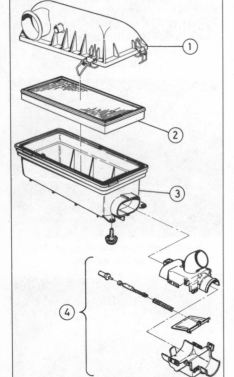

Fig. 3.6 Components of the air filter assembly on B19A and B200K models (Sec 3)

1 Cover   3 Housing
2 Filter   4 Thermostatic valve

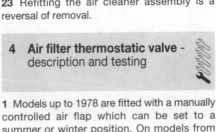

4.1B View of the housing showing the thermostat

4.2 Hot air collector plate on exhaust manifold (models from 1981)

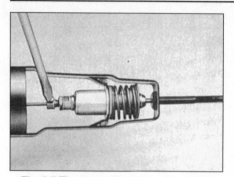

Fig. 3.7 Thermostatic valve adjustment screw on models up to 1981 (Sec 4)

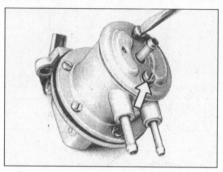

Fig. 3.8 Removing the fuel pump cover (B14 models) (Sec 5)

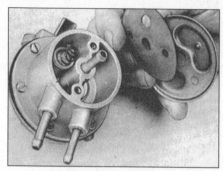

Fig. 3.9 Fuel pump filter and spring (B14 models) (Sec 5)

5 Check the position of the air flap after removing the assembly from the air cleaner.

6 Using a thermometer and air heater such as a hair dryer, heat the air around the thermostat; when the temperature reaches 25°C (1978 models) or 35°C (1979 and 1980 models) the air flap should close the hot air supply completely. Cool the air and check that the cold air supply is closed at 15°C (1978 models) or 20°C (1979 and 1980 models).

7 If adjustment is required, loosen the locking screw and reposition the air flap as necessary.

8 If the thermostat is proved faulty, remove it, together with the spring and spacers, and renew it.

9 Reassembly of the air filter is a reversal of dismantling.

5 Fuel pump (carburettor models) - removal, refitting and overhaul

1 Several different types of fuel pump are fitted to different models, but all follow the same general principle of operation and the servicing procedures given here cover all types (photos).

2 The fuel pump can be tested by disconnecting the outlet pipe at the carburettor, disconnecting the coil HT lead and spinning the engine on the starter motor.

3 If strong regular spurts of fuel emerge from the outlet pipe it can be assumed the pump is serviceable, if not then the pump should be renewed. The delivery pressure of the pump

can be checked by fitting a pressure gauge to the outlet pipe via a T-piece and running the engine. Refer to the Specifications for pump pressure.

4 To remove the pump, disconnect the inlet, outlet and return pipelines (where fitted).

5 Remove the nuts securing the pump to the cylinder block and withdraw the pump and insulating flange.

6 Some oil will escape when the flange is removed and this should be mopped up and all mating surfaces cleaned of gasket material.

7 Where an oil leak has been present from the flange, a steel flange should be fitted on B14 models and an aluminium flange on B19 models.

8 The filter, which is situated inside the pump, can be renewed by removing the top cover, then the inner cover (see Fig. 3.8). **Note**: *The fuel pump fitted to B172 models is a sealed unit and cannot be dismantled, but should be*

renewed as a complete unit if it proves faulty (photos). Also on B172 models, there is an in-line filter, mounted in the engine bay on the front valance (photo). This should be renewed at the intervals given in the Routine Maintenance Section. It should also be checked as in paragraph 11.

9 Refitting the pump is a reversal of removal, but use new gaskets either side of the insulating flange.

10 If it is found by test that the fuel pressure is too high, on B14 models the fitting of extra gaskets under the flange will lower the pressure, on other models the pump should be renewed.

11 If the pressure is too low, first check that the filter is not blocked, or fuel pipelines kinked, before renewing the pump.

12 The fuel pipelines are connected by either worm drive type clips or the one-piece types which are crimped together after fitting.

5.1A Fuel pump showing outlet pipe (top) and inlet and return pipes

5.1B Removing the fuel pump on B19A and B200K models

5.8A Removing the fuel pump retaining nuts on B172 models . . .

5.8B . . . withdrawing the pump

5.8C Fuel filter on B172 models

3

5.13 Refitting one-piece hose clips

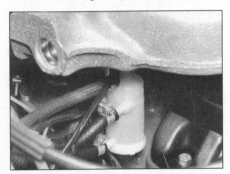

5.14 Fuel pressure regulator
fitted to the B200K model

13 When using this type, remember to fit the clip over the pipe before fitting the pipe (photo).

14 B200K models are fitted with a fuel pressure regulator (photo). If fuel pressure problems occur, then change the regulator before the pump.

6 Fuel tank -
removal and refitting

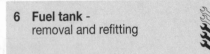

B14 models

1 Jack up the rear of the car and support it adequately on axle stands.

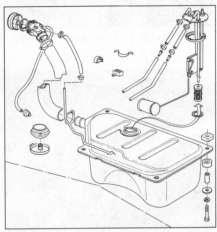

Fig. 3.11 Fuel tank components on models
up to 1982 (B14 models) (Sec 6)

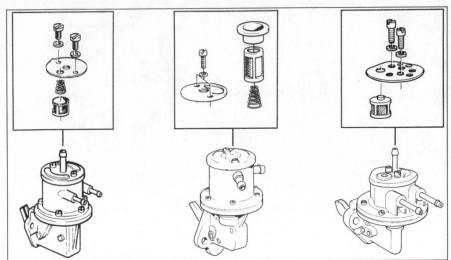

Fig. 3.10 Comparison of the different fuel pumps and filters (Sec 5)

2 Remove the filler cap and syphon out any fuel left in the tank with a suitable hose.

Models up to 1979

3 Open the tailgate and remove the parcel shelf.

4 Push the rear seat forwards and remove the right-hand side central panel.

5 Remove the tail light interior cover on the right-hand side.

6 Detach the right-hand side hinge from the rear seat backrest.

7 Disconnect the battery negative terminal.

8 Disconnect the leads from the luggage compartment interior light.

9 Remove the right-hand side rear panel.

All models up to 1982

10 Disconnect the fuel tank vent hose at the tank end. As from 1979 models, the hose is attached to the fuel tank flange by clips.

11 Move the floor mat to one side and remove the transmitter cover.

12 Disconnect the leads from the transmitter unit, then detach the supply and return hoses.

13 Disconnect the fuel filler hose at the tank end. On models from 1979, disconnect the overflow hose from the fuel tank (photo).

14 Unscrew the mounting bolts and lower the fuel tank to the ground. Remove the rubber mountings and transmitter unit as necessary.

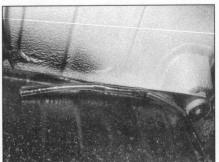

6.13 Fuel tank overflow hose
clipped to fuel tank

15 A leak in the fuel tank should be repaired by specialists, or alternatively a new tank fitted; *never be tempted to solder or weld a leaking fuel tank.*

16 If the tank is contaminated with sediment or water, it can be swilled out using several changes of fuel, but if any vigorous shaking is required to dislodge accumulations of dirt or rust, the tank transmitter unit should be removed as described in Section 7.

17 Refitting is a reversal of removal.

Models from 1982

18 As from 1982 an expansion tank has been added to the filler system. This is as described for B172 models. When fitting a new tank, it may be found that the filler hoses are too long. They should be cut to the required length.

B19 models

19 The fuel tank on these models is formed in a saddle type shape so that it can straddle the transmission unit. The bottom part of each tank section is connected by a pipe. The tank is removed as follows.

20 Remove the gearbox and final drive, as described in Chapter 6.

21 Disconnect the hose from the bottom of each tank section and drain the fuel into a suitable container. Also disconnect the filler hose in the luggage compartment (photo).

6.21 Fuel tank filler hoses in the luggage
area on B19 models

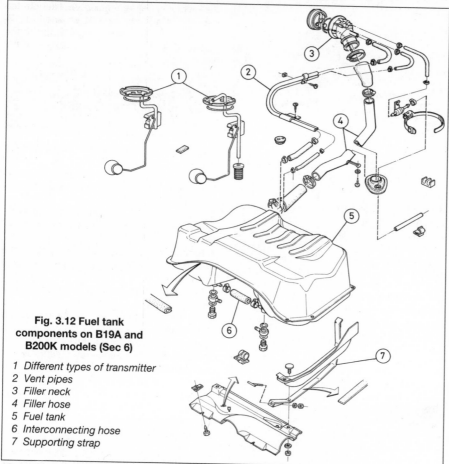

Fig. 3.12 Fuel tank components on B19A and B200K models (Sec 6)

1 Different types of transmitter
2 Vent pipes
3 Filler neck
4 Filler hose
5 Fuel tank
6 Interconnecting hose
7 Supporting strap

30 Lower the fuel tank and remove it from under the car. Remove the transmitter unit.

31 A leak in the fuel tank should be repaired by specialists, or alternatively a new tank fitted; *never be tempted to solder or weld a leaking fuel tank*. If the tank is contaminated with sediment or water, it can be swilled out using several changes of fuel.

32 Refitting is a reversal of removal.

B172 models (and B14 models with expansion tank)

33 There is no drain plug and any fuel in the tank should be siphoned out through the filler neck.

34 Gain access to the top of the tank by referring to the procedure for B14 models, then remove the tank transmitter cover and disconnect the fuel hoses and electrical connection.

35 Disconnect the fuel filler and overflow hoses from the tank.

36 Disconnect the vent hose and pull the hose from the clips holding it to the tank.

37 Remove the four retaining bolts and lower the tank to the ground.

38 Follow the tank repair and cleaning procedure as described earlier for B14 models.

39 Refit in the reverse order to removal.

40 To remove the expansion tank, first make a note of each hose connection, preferably tying an identification label to each one before disconnecting the hoses (photo). Ensure there is no fuel in the tank or the filler pipe before carrying out this operation.

41 Disconnect the check valve from the expansion tank.

42 Remove the self-tapping screws and withdraw the expansion tank.

22 Lift the rear seat cushion, then prise out the rubber cover and disconnect the wiring from the fuel tank transmitter unit. Disconnect the hose and tie it to one side, if applicable.

23 Pull the handbrake cables from the clips on the fuel tank straps (photo).

24 On fuel injection models, unscrew the nuts and lower the crossmember. Note the location of the hoses then disconnect them from the tank.

25 Unbolt the heat shield from the left-hand side of the tank.

26 On carburettor models unbolt and remove the crossmember. Note the location of the hoses then disconnect them from the tank.

27 Unclip the hose from the front of the tank.

28 Support the fuel tank with a trolley jack and length of wood, then unscrew the nuts from the front of the straps.

29 Unhook the rear ends of the straps.

6.23 Handbrake cable clip on the bottom of the fuel tank

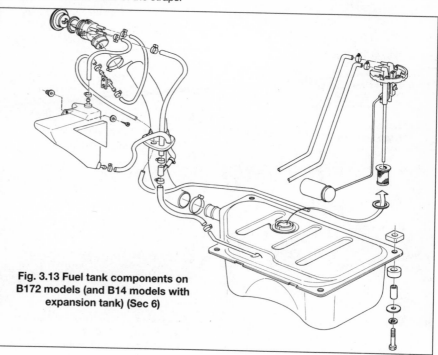

Fig. 3.13 Fuel tank components on B172 models (and B14 models with expansion tank) (Sec 6)

6.40 Fuel tank filler hoses and expansion tank (B172 model shown)

43 The filler cap assembly can be removed by depressing the lugs which secure the assembly to the side panel and withdrawing the unit to the outside of the car.

44 Refit in the reverse order, but when fitting the check valve the arrow on the valve body should point toward the discharge end.

7 Fuel tank transmitter unit - removal and refitting

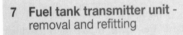

1 The procedure is similar on all models.
2 Refer to Chapter 9 and remove the rear seat squab on Saloon versions. On hatchback models, simply remove the carpeting from the luggage area.
3 Remove the screws from the cover and lift it away (photos).

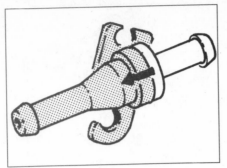

Fig. 3.14 Showing the arrow on the check valve (Sec 6)

4 Disconnect the fuel hoses and electrical connections (photo).
5 The transmitter is secured to the top of the tank by a spring clip on early B14 models. On other models the unit has to be turned anticlockwise to release it, using the lugs provided and a suitable peg spanner, or large bar. Remove the transmitter unit.
6 Check the float is sound, and clean the contacts of the float electrical connections.
7 Wash out the filter in clean petrol (it is a push-fit on the suction pipe).
8 Renew any items which show signs of being defective. (On later models it may only be possible to renew the complete transmitter unit.)
9 Refit in the reverse order, using new seals and hose clips.
10 Where problems of rough engine running have been encountered due to sediment in

the fuel tank, before refitting the filter cut the end of the suction pipe at an angle of 45 degrees. Push the filter completely on to the pipe so that the end contacts the base of the filter.

8 Accelerator pedal (all models) - removal and refitting

1 Disconnect the accelerator cable from the pedal.
2 Remove the clip or nut securing the pedal to the pivot pin, remove the pin and withdraw the pedal.
3 Check the pivot pin and bushing for wear, and renew any parts which show signs of wear.
4 Refit in the reverse order, applying a little grease to the pivot pin, then adjust the pedal as follows.
5 Depress the accelerator pedal down fully against its stop.
6 Set the adjusting bolt to the dimension shown in Fig. 3.19 between the bolt end and the bulkhead, then tighten the locknut.
7 Check that the accelerator cable is not pulling the pedal out of true adjustment.

7.3A Fuel tank transmitter cover

7.3B The cover removed (360 GLE model shown)

7.4 Disconnect the fuel hoses and electrical leads

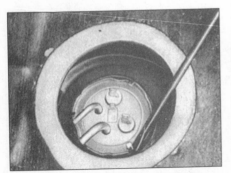

Fig. 3.15 Removing the fuel tank transmitter retaining ring (Sec 7)

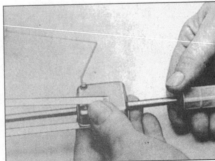

Fig. 3.16 Removing the filter from the tank transmitter unit (Sec 7)

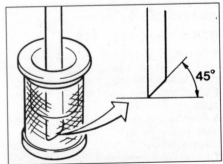

Fig. 3.17 Cutting the suction pipe to an angle of 45 degrees (Sec 7)

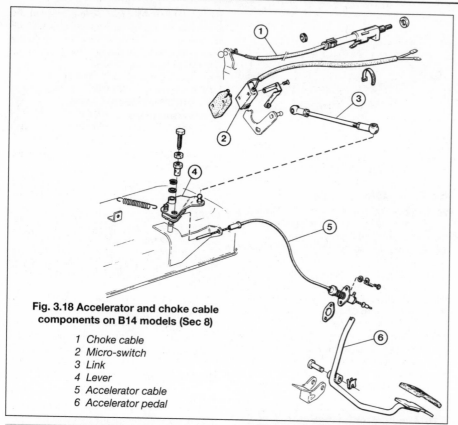

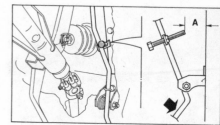

Fig. 3.19 Accelerator pedal adjuster (Sec 8)
B14 models: A = 1.4 in (35.5 mm)
All other models: A = 1.2 in (30.5 mm)

b) *On automatic versions, check that the kickdown comes into operation in the fully open position*

B14 models from 1981

10 The procedure is similar to that described for up to 1981 models except that the cable should be withdrawn into the engine compartment.

B19 and B200 models

11 Release the accelerator cable from the spring roller (B19 and B200E) (photo) or the plastic cam on B200K models.
12 The remaining removal procedure is as described for B14 models.
13 Refit in the reverse order, then carry out the following adjustment checks:

B19A models

14 Disconnect the link rod from the carburettor (photo).
15 Adjust the accelerator cable so that the roller is just touching the stop.

Fig. 3.18 Accelerator and choke cable components on B14 models (Sec 8)

1 *Choke cable*
2 *Micro-switch*
3 *Link*
4 *Lever*
5 *Accelerator cable*
6 *Accelerator pedal*

9 Accelerator cable - removal and refitting

General servicing notes applicable to all models

1 Periodically check that the cable is free to move inside its outer sheath. Lubricate the exposed ends of the inner cable with grease and work the cable in and out of the outer sheath to allow the grease to penetrate as far as possible.
2 Check the exposed ends of the cable for kinks, which could cause sticking, and for fraying. Renew the cable as necessary.
3 Check that the cable is lying in a straight run, with no excessively sharp bends, and that it is routed clear of other components which could cause jamming or wear.

B14 models up to 1981

4 Disconnect the accelerator cable from the lever bracket on the engine by undoing the clamp bolt and releasing the grommet (photo).
5 Disconnect the cable at the accelerator pedal end.
6 Remove the screws from the bulkhead plate where the cable passes through the bulkhead (photo).
7 On automatic models, disconnect the kickdown electrical lead.
8 Withdraw the cable inwards, into the car.

9 Refitting is a reversal of this procedure, but carry out the following adjustment checks:
a) *Check the throttle butterfly rests on its stops in released and fully open positions*

9.4 Accelerator cable and lever bracket on a B14 model

9.6 Accelerator bulkhead plate

9.11 Spring roller and cable end on B19E and B200E models

9.14 Link rod between spring roller and carburettor

3

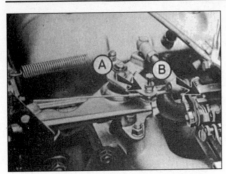

Fig. 3.20 Accelerator cable end fitting on B14 models (Sec 9)
A Clamp bolt
B Throttle butterfly stop

16 Fit the link rod and adjust its length so that the cam is just touching the flange on the throttle butterfly spindle.

B200K models

17 Fit the accelerator cable to the plastic cam and fiy the retaining clip to the adjuster (photo).
18 Turn the adjuster so that the plastic cam is resting on its stop and the cable is tension-free. **Note:** The choke knob must be pushed fully in during this operation.

B19E and B200E models

19 The procedure is similar to that for B200K models except that with the cable adjusted so that it is just tension-free the cable drum should be against its stop.

9.17 Choke cable (1) and accelerator cable (2) on B200K models

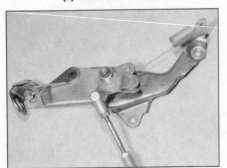

10.1A Accelerator linkage and lever bracket on B172 models

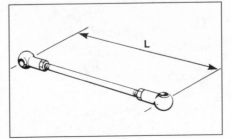

Fig. 3.21 Setting dimension of linkage control rod (Sec 10)

B172 models

20 Remove the panel from under the facia, and remove the split pin securing the cable to the accelerator pedal (photo).
21 Remove the screws from the bulkhead bracket.
22 Disconnect the cable from the lever bracket on the engine and feed the cable through the bulkhead from the engine bay side.
23 Refit in the reverse order, then adjust the pedal as described in Section 8.
24 On completion check that the throttle butterfly rests against its stops in both fully open and released positions (photo), and that the accelerator pedal rests against its stop, with the accelerator cable lightly tensioned.

10 Accelerator linkage control rods - adjustment

1 The control rods connect the accelerator

9.20 Accelerator cable-to-pedal connection on B172 models

10.1B Connecting the link rod ball end

B14.0E up to engine No 32248:
L = 7.8 to 7.9 in (198 to 200 mm)
B14.0E from engine No 32249:
L = 7.5 to 7.6 in (190 to 192 mm)
B14.0S up to engine No 9420:
L = 7.8 to 7.9 in (198 to 200 mm)
B14.0S from engine No 9421:
L = 7.5 to 7.6 in (190 to 192 mm)
B14.1E from engine No 10022:
L = 7.2 to 7.3 in (184 to 186 mm)
B14.1S: L = 7.2 to 7.3 in (184 to 186 mm)
B172: L = 3.6in (91 mm)
B19: see Section 9

lever to the carburettor, being a push-fit onto the ball-studs (photo).
2 Adjust the control rods by loosening the locknuts at each end then turning the rod in or out to obtain the dimensions in Fig. 3.21.
3 On completion, tighten the locknuts and check the accelerator cable and pedal for correct adjustment.

11 Choke cable - removal and refitting

B14 models

1 Loosen the pin clamps and detach the inner and outer cable from the carburettor (photo).
2 Loosen the clamp and remove the cable from the valve cover bracket.
3 Unscrew the choke knob, then remove the ignition key and detach the lower steering column cap.

9.24 Throttle butterfly stop (arrowed) on B172 models (carburettor removed)

11.1 Carburettor choke cable end fitting on B14 models

11.12 Fitting the choke cable to choke lever spigot

11.13 Choke cable retaining clip

4 Disconnect the choke warning lamp wiring.
5 Unscrew the nut and detach the cable from the ignition switch bracket.
6 Withdraw the choke cable from inside the car by pulling it through the bulkhead.
7 Refitting is a reversal of removal, but make sure that the bulkhead grommet is in good condition. Before tightening the pin clamp adjust the inner cable to provide 0.0625 in (1.59 mm) free play.

B19A and B200K models

8 Remove/refit the cable as described above, then adjust as follows.

9 Insert the inner cable as far as the bend in the lever and secure it in this position.
10 Push in both the choke knob and the lever on the carburettor, then secure the outer cable. On the B200K engine make sure that the choke lever on the carburettor is correctly located in the plastic groove, otherwise the choke valve will not fully return to the idling position.

B172 models

11 The procedure is similar to that described for B14 models - on completion adjust the cable as follows.

12 Fit the cable to the choke lever spigot (photo).
13 Push back on the cable and sheath to lightly tension the cable then fit the retaining clip (photo).
14 Check that the choke operating lever contacts both stops.

12 Weber and Solex 32-SEIA REN carburettors - general description

Up until 1982, B14 engines were fitted with different versions of the Weber 32 DIR carburettor. From 1982, when the economy B14.3E engine was introduced, it was fitted with a Solex 32-SEIA REN 796 carburettor, which was changed again in 1983 for a modified version of the same carburettor. The new 53kW B14.4E engine, introduced in 1984, had a Weber 32 DIR 104-100 or 105-100 fitted.

Weber 32 DIR carburettor

The Weber 32 DIR is a twin barrel downdraught type of carburettor, with fixed metering jets and a manually operated choke. A hot spot is fitted to the bottom of the

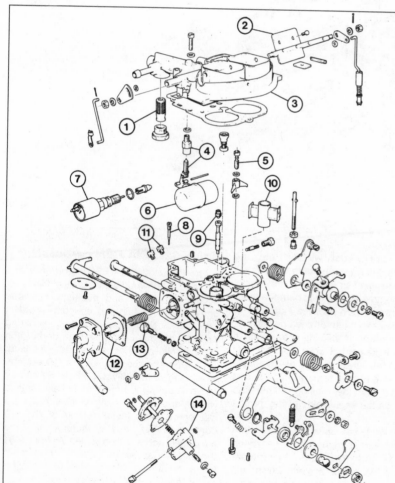

Fig. 3.22 Exploded view of the Weber carburettor fitted to models up to 1979 (Sec 12)

1 Filter
2 Choke valve
3 Upper cover
4 Needle valve
5 Accelerator pump injector
6 Float
7 Idle solenoid
8 Pump discharge blanking needle
9 Air correction jet and emulsion tube
10 Venturi
11 Main jets
12 Accelerator pump
13 Volume control screw
14 Choke control unit

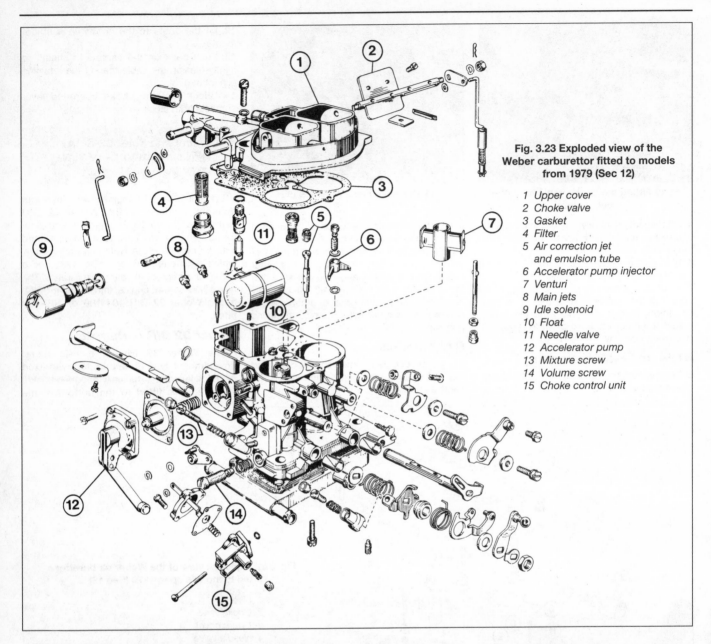

Fig. 3.23 Exploded view of the Weber carburettor fitted to models from 1979 (Sec 12)

1 Upper cover
2 Choke valve
3 Gasket
4 Filter
5 Air correction jet and emulsion tube
6 Accelerator pump injector
7 Venturi
8 Main jets
9 Idle solenoid
10 Float
11 Needle valve
12 Accelerator pump
13 Mixture screw
14 Volume screw
15 Choke control unit

carburettor and is heated by the engine cooling system. Its function is to heat the air entering the engine, and it is separated from the carburettor and manifold by insulating flanges.

When the engine is idling, fuel flows from the primary well, through the pilot jet to the idling control screw. Air is supplied through the air jet, and the electrically controlled pilot jet stops the supply of fuel into the idling circuit when it is de-energised; this prevents any tendency for the engine to run-on. At increased engine speed the bypass bores of the idling circuit are opened and the primary venturi provides increased amounts of fuel and air through the primary venturi.

After the primary throttle valve has opened a predetermined amount, further movement of

the accelerator pedal will operate the secondary throttle valve and both venturis will then supply fuel and air mixture to the engine. A diaphragm type accelerator pump is fitted to the carburettor and supplies extra fuel to both venturis when the throttle is opened.

The carburettor is also equipped with a pneumatic choke control which automatically opens the choke valves as soon as the engine starts. The unit is of diaphragm type and is operated by the depression within the carburettor on the engine side of the throttle valves.

As from 1984, the constant CO system used on the earlier carburettors has been discontinued, and 1986 models incorporate an automatic fuel cut-off system, which cuts off the fuel supply during overrun conditions.

Solex 32-SEIA REN carburettor

The Solex 32-SEIA REN carburettor is a single barrel downdraught type with fixed jets, accelerator pump and manually operated choke. It has a full load enrichment valve, operated by diaphragm, which opens during periods of low inlet manifold depression pressure when the engine is under full load. The carburettor has a constant CO system, which allows the idling speed to be altered approximately 400 rpm from its basic setting without appreciably changing the exhaust gas CO percentage. Initial setting of the CO content is set at the factory, and the adjustment screw is then sealed. As from 1984 the engine depression outlet is taken from below the throttle valve in order to connect it to the computerised ignition system.

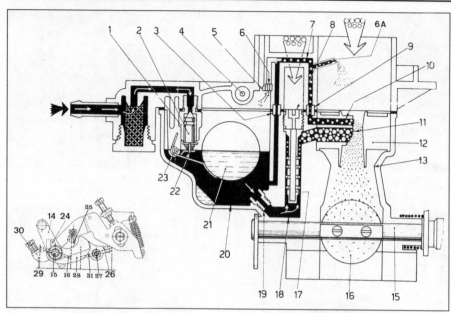

Fig. 3.24 Cross-sectional view of the Weber carburettor (Sec 12)

1 Needle valve housing	11 Main fuel supply	22 Float arm
2 Needle valve	12 Venturi	23 Float pivot
3 Calibrated jet	13 Body	24 Engine lug
4 Vent	14 Throttle operating lever	25 Lug
5 Vent passage	15 Throttle valve spindle	26 Lever
6 Calibrated jet	16 Throttle valve	27 Pivot
6A Calibrated jet	17 Emulsion tube	28 Lever
7 Venturi passage	18 Mixing chamber	29 Lever
8 Air correction jet	19 Main jet	30 Volume control screw
9 Calibrated jet	20 Float chamber	31 Throttle valve
10 Auxiliary fuel supply	21 Float	

13 Weber carburettor - idling adjustment

1 Note that in order to adjust the carburettor correctly, the ignition timing should be correct and the air cleaner should be on the correct setting (manual operation) or functioning correctly (automatic thermostatic operation).
2 Connect a tachometer to the engine.
3 With the engine cold, pull the choke control fully out and start the engine; the engine speed should be between 1800 and 2000 rpm. If the engine speed is incorrect the

carburettor will have to be removed, and adjusted as described in Section 15.
4 Run the engine until it reaches normal operating temperature, then check the engine idling speed, which should be as given in the Specifications. If necessary adjust the idling speed screw. Note that, as from late 1978 models, tamperproof plugs are fitted to the throttle stop screw and mixture screw, and a bypass idle volume screw is fitted as extra. Normally it will only be necessary to adjust the bypass volume screw to adjust the idling speed (photo). However, if it is required to adjust the mixture, the plugs can be removed provided local legislation permits this action.

Fig. 3.25 Idle mixture (1) and speed (2) adjusting screw locations on the Weber 32 DIR 104-100 carburettor (Sec 13)

5 If the engine refuses to idle evenly, or if the CO content when using a CO meter is not as given in Specifications, adjust the mixture screw as follows. With the engine at normal operating temperature, turn the mixture screw in either direction until the point is reached where the engine speed is highest. If necessary, adjust the idling speed on the idling speed (throttle stop) screw. **Note:** *From carburettor model number 32 DIR 104-100, the constant CO idling system has been discontinued. Idle speed adjustment is as described for the Solex 32-SEIA REN carburettor with reference to Fig. 3.25.*

14 Weber carburettor - removal and refitting

1 Remove the air cleaner assembly as described in Section 3. On models from 1981, remove the air filter element, then unscrew the nuts and lift the air cleaner body from the carburettor (photos).
2 On up to 1981 models, disconnect the crankcase breather hose and detach the air supply pipe from the carburettor.
3 Disconnect the choke cable and throttle control rod from the carburettor, then detach the fuel supply and vent hoses (photos). On automatic transmission models disconnect the vacuum hose (photo).

3

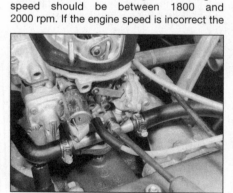

13.4 Adjusting the carburettor bypass volume screw

14.1A Removing the air cleaner-to-carburettor nuts (models from 1981)

14.1B Air cleaner mounting (models from 1981)

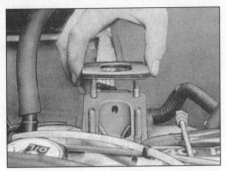

Fig. 3.26 Removing the carburettor insulating flange (Sec 14)

14.3A Choke cable and throttle control rod locations

14.3B Disconnecting the throttle control rod

14.3C Disconnecting the carburettor fuel supply hose

14.3D Disconnecting the crankcase ventilation hose

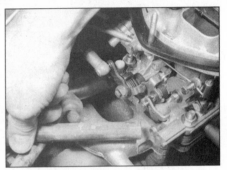

14.3E Disconnecting automatic transmission vacuum hose

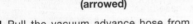

14.4 Vacuum advance hose location (arrowed)

14.5 Disconnecting lead from fuel cut-off solenoid

4 Pull the vacuum advance hose from the carburettor (photo).
5 Disconnect the lead to the electrically controlled fuel cut-off solenoid (photo).
6 On early models unscrew the two retaining screws and remove the vacuum control microswitch.
7 Drain the cooling system as described in Chapter 2, then detach the hoses from the carburettor hot spot.
8 Unscrew and remove the four carburettor retaining nuts evenly, and withdraw the carburettor from the manifold.
9 Lift the insulating flange from the manifold and clean the mating faces of the carburettor and manifold.
10 Refitting is a reversal of removal, but the following additional points should be noted:

a) Always fit a new gasket on both sides of the insulating flange
b) Adjust the throttle rod so that there is a little free play with the throttle in the closed position. Check that with the accelerator pedal fully depressed, the throttle lever on the carburettor is fully open
c) Adjust the choke cable so that the operating lever is in the fully released position with the control knob pushed fully in. Check that the choke valve plates are in the closed position with the control knob pulled fully out
d) After fitting the microswitch adjust it as described in Chapter 6 (early models only)
e) Fill the cooling system, referring to Chapter 2 as necessary
f) Make sure that the rubber seal is correctly located to the air supply pipe
g) On manual transmission models manufactured from March 1980, make sure that the rubber plug fitted to the insulating flange is in good condition

15 Weber carburettors - dismantling and reassembly

1 Clean the exterior of the carburettor before dismantling.
2 From the bottom of the carburettor, unscrew the retaining screws and remove the hot spot and insulating flange.
3 Clean away any remains of gasket from the insulating flange, hot spot, and carburettor faces. **Note:** *the second stage throttle valve screw must not be adjusted as it is set during manufacture.*
4 Unscrew the hexagon bolt at the fuel inlet and remove the gauze filter.
5 Prise the spring clip from the pneumatic choke control rod and disconnect it from the lever. Lift the nylon bush and detach the mechanical choke rod from the lever.

Fig. 3.27 Removing the filter from the fuel inlet union (Sec 15)

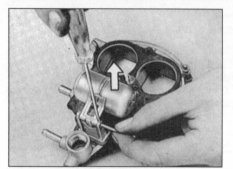

Fig. 3.28 Extracting the float pivot pin (Sec 15)

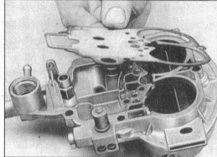

Fig. 3.29 Removing the carburettor cover gasket (Sec 15)

Fig. 3.30 Dismantling the accelerator pump (Sec 15)

Fig. 3.31 Removing the idle jet cut-off solenoid (Sec 15)

Fig. 3.32 Removing the air correction jets and emulsion tubes (Sec 15)

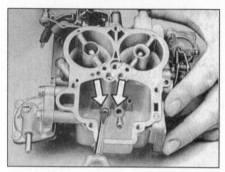

Fig. 3.33 Removing the main jets (Sec 15)

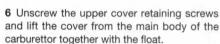

Fig. 3.34 Choke control diaphragm unit components (Sec 15)

Fig. 3.35 Securing the float pivot pin (Sec 15)

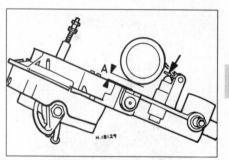

Fig. 3.36 Checking the float level dimension (A) showing point of adjustment - arrowed (Sec 15)

3

6 Unscrew the upper cover retaining screws and lift the cover from the main body of the carburettor together with the float.
7 Extract the pivot pin and withdraw the float and needle valve, then unhook the needle valve from the float.
8 Remove the gasket from the upper cover.
9 Extract the spring clips and remove both choke control rods and washers from the cover, noting their locations.
10 Unscrew the screws and remove the accelerator pump cover, diaphragm, and spring.
11 Slacken the Allen screw, then remove the electrically controlled pilot jet. Note the seal fitted to later models.
12 Unscrew and remove the pilot jet (early models), both air correction jets, the two main jets, the pump injector, and emulsion tubes.
13 Unscrew and remove the volume control screw and seal (early models) or bypass idle volume screw (later models).
14 Unscrew the choke control diaphragm unit retaining screws, remove the circlip and washer, and withdraw the diaphragm unit from the main body.
15 Dismantle the choke control diaphragm unit by removing the three screws and withdrawing the diaphragm and spring. Mark

the two halves of the unit to ensure correct reassembly.
16 Slide both venturis from the choke tubes, but be very careful to mark them in relation to their correct locations.
17 Clean all components and renew any that are worn. Obtain new gaskets, diaphragms, etc in the form of a repair kit.
18 Check the float for leakage by shaking it vigorously and listening for any fuel which may have entered it. Renew it if it is faulty.
19 Start reassembly by installing the two main jets in the bottom of the float chamber.
20 Fit the two emulsion tubes and air correction jets.
21 Fit the pump injector seals and tighten the assembly into the carburettor main body.
22 Install the venturis into the choke tubes, making sure that they are each located in the correct stage.
23 Assemble the choke control diaphragm unit and tighten the three screws, then fit it to

the carburettor main body together with a new O-ring seal.
24 Install the pilot jet (early models).
25 Screw the electrically controlled pilot jet into the main body and lock it in position by tightening the Allen screw.
26 Fit the spring and seal into the volume control screw (early models) then screw it into the side of the main body. Fit the bypass idle volume screw (later models).
27 Assemble the accelerator pump with a new diaphragm and gasket, then tighten the retaining screws evenly in diagonal sequence.
28 Locate a new gasket on the upper cover, then install the needle valve and float. When the pivot pin is correctly located, use a pair of pliers to close the split pillar and lock the pin.
29 Invert the upper cover and measure the distance between the gasket and the float; this should be 0.28 in (7.0 mm). Adjust the float arm if necessary.
30 Tighten the filter into the upper cover.

Fig. 3.37 Air filter bracket bolts (arrowed) on Solex 32-SEIA REN carburettor (Sec 16)

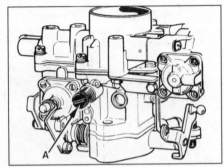

Fig. 3.38 Idle speed adjusting screw (A) on Solex 32-SEIA REN carburettor (Sec 17)

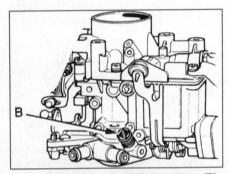

Fig. 3.39 Idle mixture adjusting screw (B) on Solex 32-SEIA REN carburettor (Sec 17)

31 Lower the upper cover onto the main body and tighten the retaining screws evenly in diagonal sequence.
32 Connect the two choke control rods and secure with the spring clip.
33 Locate the hot spot insulating flange with a new gasket on each side, then install the hot spot and tighten the retaining screws to the carburettor.
34 With the carburettor assembled, use a suitable size drill to check that the clearance between the choke valves and choke wall when the choke is operated is as specified; if not, bend the choke control rod as necessary, or fit a different shim.
35 Check the pneumatic choke control by operating the choke until the valve plates are about to move, then fully press in the vacuum chamber rod; the clearance as checked in paragraph 34 should now be different (see Specifications). If not remove the pneumatic

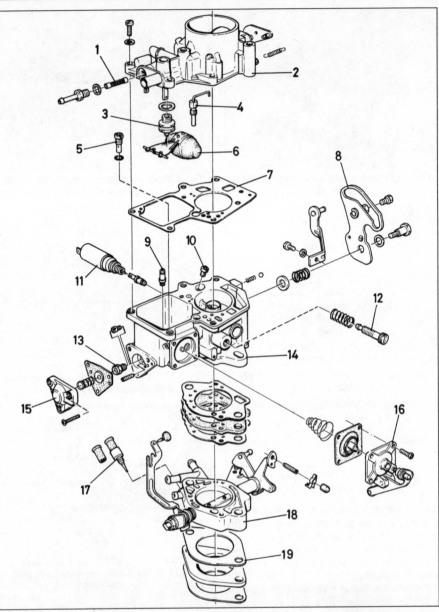

Fig. 3.40 Exploded view of the Solex 32-SEIA REN carburettor (Sec 18)

1 Filter	8 Choke lever	13 Full-load delivery valve
2 Cover	9 Accelerator pump	14 Main body
3 Needle valve	non-return valve	15 Full-load enrichment cover
4 Accelerator pump injector	10 Air correction jet and	16 Accelerator pump cover
5 Main jet	emulsion tube	17 Idle mixture screw
6 Float	11 Idle solenoid	18 Throttle valve housing
7 Gasket	12 Idle speed screw	19 Gasket

control screw plug and turn the adjusting screw as necessary.
36 Fully operate the choke and check that the first stage throttle valve is open by the specified amount measured with a suitable drill; if not, adjust the screw on the control rod.
37 Check that the vent valve closes as soon as the throttle lever is operated; if not, adjust the operating rod as necessary.

Weber 32 DIR 104-100 upwards

38 These carburettors do not have the constant CO idling system, and the internal jet arrangement differs from earlier Weber models.
39 The idle and CO% are set by turning the mixture and throttle stop screws (refer to Fig. 3.25) in or out until the desired idling speed and CO content are obtained in much the same way as described for the Solex 32-SEIA REN carburettor.

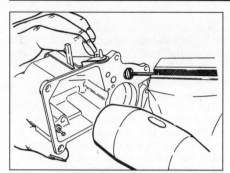

Fig. 3.41 Extracting the air correction jet (Sec 18)

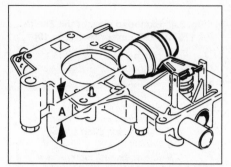

Fig. 3.42 Float level dimension (A) on the Solex 32-SEIA REN carburettor (Sec 18)

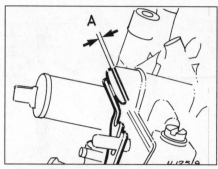

Fig. 3.43 Ventilation valve opening (A) on Solex 32-SEIA REN carburettor (Sec 18)

40 The idling solenoid on models from 1986 is similar to that described for the Solex 34-34 CISAC carburettor in Section 24.

16 Solex 32-SEIA REN carburettors - removal and refitting

The procedure is similar to that described for Weber carburettors in Section 14, but the air filter bracket should be removed and the crankcase ventilation hose disconnected.

17 Solex 32-SEIA REN carburettors - idle speed adjustment

1 Start the engine and allow it to reach normal operating temperature.
2 Connect a tachometer and exhaust gas analyser to the engine.
3 Check that the engine idling speed is as given in the Specifications. If not, turn the adjusting screw (Fig. 3.38) as necessary.
4 Check the CO content at idling is as given in the Specifications. If not, remove the tamperproof seal, where fitted, and turn the mixture screw (Fig. 3.39) as necessary.

Fig. 3.44 Choke valve opening adjustment points (Sec 18)

1 Choke lever
2 Adjusting screw
A Gap, measured with drill

18 Solex 32-SEIA REN carburettor - dismantling and reassembly

1 Clean the exterior of the carburettor.
2 Unbolt the choke lever and recover the ball and spring.
3 Unscrew the fuel supply tube and remove the copper washer and filter.
4 Remove the screws and lift off the cover. Remove the gasket.
5 Drive out the pivot pin and remove the float.
6 Unscrew and remove the needle valve and washer.
7 Remove the screws and withdraw the accelerator pump cover, together with the diaphragm and spring.
8 Pull the accelerator pump injector from the carburettor body.
9 Unscrew and remove the accelerator pump non-return valve and the idle solenoid.
10 Remove the screws and withdraw the full-load enrichment cover, spring and diaphragm.
11 Unscrew and remove the full-load delivery valve, calibrated screw, and the main jet, together with its sleeve.
12 Unscrew and remove the air correction jet, then screw an M4 bolt into the emulsion tube and extract the emulsion tube using the method shown in Fig. 3.41. Take care not to damage the carburettor body.
13 If necessary, remove the idle speed and mixture screws, and the throttle valve housing. The auxiliary venturi can be removed by lightly tapping it from the bottom of the carburettor.
14 Clean all the components and check them for wear and damage. Use an air line or tyre pump to blow through the jets and internal passages. Check that the delivery ball is free in the accelerator pump valve. Check the float for leakage by immersing it in warm water and checking for air bubbles.
15 Reassemble the carburettor in the reverse order of dismantling using new gaskets and washers. If the idle speed and mixture screws were removed, fully tighten them, then back off 4 turns for the idle speed screw and 2 1/2 turns for the mixture screw. Locate the emulsion tube with the slot facing the auxiliary

venturi. When fitting the accelerator pump injector make sure that it is not touching the auxiliary venturi.
16 Check the float level by inverting the cover and measuring the distance from the centre of the float to the cover (gasket removed). If the distance is not as given in the Specifications bend the float arm.
17 When fitting the choke lever, either use locking fluid on the original bolt or fit a new self-locking bolt. Apply a little grease to the choke lever cam.
18 Adjust the accelerator pump stroke as follows. With the throttle valve in the idling position and the accelerator pump roller touching the cam, turn the adjustment screw until it touches the plunger then tighten it a further half turn.
19 Adjust the float chamber ventilation arm as follows. With the throttle valve in the idling position measure the ventilation valve opening (A in Fig. 3.43). If the dimension is not as given in the Specifications bend the bottom of the lever as necessary.
20 Adjust the full choke valve opening as follows. With the choke lever in the shut position use a twist drill or feeler blade to check the throttle valve opening. If it is not as given in the Specifications turn the adjustment screw as necessary.
21 Note: *If high fuel consumption is a problem on models up to 1983, Volvo produce a special kit for fitting to the carburettor which should reduce the problem.*
22 The idle solenoid can be tested by connecting it to a 12 volt supply and checking that the needle pulls in when the supply is switched on. If not, the solenoid should be renewed.

19 Zenith 175 CD-2SE carburettor - general description

The Zenith 175 CD-2SE carburettor is a constant depression, side draught pattern, with separate cold start device. The fuel metering needle is tapered and fixed to the air valve and diaphragm, the underside of which is open to atmosphere and the upper side connected to the depression caused in the

3

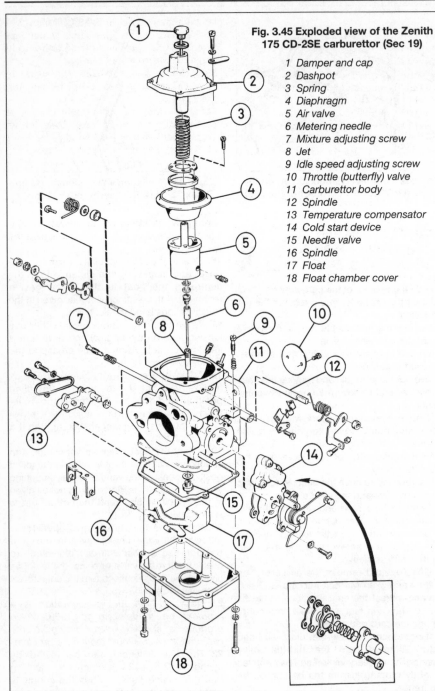

Fig. 3.45 Exploded view of the Zenith 175 CD-2SE carburettor (Sec 19)

1 Damper and cap
2 Dashpot
3 Spring
4 Diaphragm
5 Air valve
6 Metering needle
7 Mixture adjusting screw
8 Jet
9 Idle speed adjusting screw
10 Throttle (butterfly) valve
11 Carburettor body
12 Spindle
13 Temperature compensator
14 Cold start device
15 Needle valve
16 Spindle
17 Float
18 Float chamber cover

20 Zenith 175 CD-2SE carburettor - idle speed adjustment

1 Run the engine to normal operating temperature then stop it and connect a tachometer and exhaust gas analyser. Make sure that the dashpot damper is topped up with the correct oil, as described in Section 21.

2 Start the engine and check that it runs at the specified idling speed - if not turn the idle adjustment screw as necessary.

3 Increase the engine speed to 1500 rpm, then let it idle again and lightly tap the dashpot to ensure that the air valve is settled.

4 Check the CO content and if necessary turn the mixture screw located by the temperature compensator. If there is insufficient adjustment on the screw, it will be necessary to adjust the metering needle height using a special tool inserted in the top of the air valve. Turning the tool clockwise enrichens the mixture and increases the CO percentage, and *vice versa*. Note that the air valve must be held stationary, otherwise the diaphragm may be damaged, also note that before adjusting the needle, the mixture screw must be fully tightened. Top up the damper before checking the CO content again.

5 With the engine cold, pull out the choke control knob until the mark on the choke lever is aligned with the fast idle adjustment bolt. Start the engine and check that the engine runs at the specified fast idle speed. If not turn the adjustment bolt as necessary.

Fig. 3.46 Idle adjustment screw (A) on the Zenith 175 CD-2SE carburettor (Sec 20)

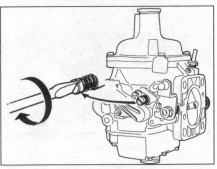

Fig. 3.47 Mixture screw on the Zenith 175 CD-2SE carburettor (Sec 20)

inlet manifold when the engine is running. This causes the needle, via the air valve and diaphragm, to be drawn out of the fixed jet in the carburettor throat, allowing fuel to be sucked into the inlet manifold where it is mixed with air to form a combustible mixture. The cold start device is a simple plate valve with progressive size holes allowing more fuel into the inlet manifold, coincidental with increased throttle opening.

The carburettor fitted to the B19A engine is designed to reduce the emission of harmful exhaust gases. The carburettor is fitted with a temperature compensator which acts as an air valve during periods of high under-bonnet or fuel temperature levels. A hot-start valve is fitted to offset the effects of accumulations of fuel vapour which occur in the carburettor intake during periods of high under-bonnet temperatures. This vapour originates from the carburettor float chamber and makes it difficult to start the engine in hot conditions. The valve discharges the fumes to atmosphere under throttle closed conditions and deflects them into the air cleaner where they are drawn into the engine as soon as the engine starts running.

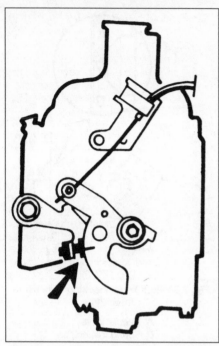

Fig. 3.48 Fast idle mark on the choke lever aligned with the adjustment bolt (Sec 20)

21 Zenith 175 CD-2SE carburettor - removal and refitting

1 Disconnect the air inlet duct at the carburettor.
2 Disconnect the throttle and choke cables.
3 Disconnect all hoses and the throttle control rod.
4 Unscrew the nuts and withdraw the carburettor from the inlet manifold.
5 Refitting is a reversal of removal, but clean the mating faces and use a new gasket. Finally adjust the accelerator and choke cables. If necessary the throttle control rod should be adjusted so that there is 0.5 mm (0.020 in) clearance, shown in Fig. 3.49. Remove the damper cap and check that the oil level is such that resistance is felt when the bottom of the cap is 18.0 mm (0.71 in) from the top of the dashpot.

Fig. 3.51 Temperature compensator with cover removed, showing screw to loosen when centralising valve (Sec 22)

22 Zenith 175 CD-2SE carburettor - dismantling and reassembly

1 Clean the exterior of the carburettor.
2 Unbolt the inlet duct adaptor.
3 Unscrew and remove the damper.
4 Mark the dashpot in relation to the main body then remove the screws, lift off the dashpot, and remove the spring and air valve with diaphragm. Pour the oil from the air valve.
5 Remove the screws and withdraw the float chamber cover and gasket.
6 Push out the pin and remove the float.
7 Unscrew the needle valve and remove the washer. Remove the small filter from the needle valve.
8 Remove the screws and withdraw the temperature compensator and O-ring.
9 Unscrew the mixture screw, noting how many turns are required to remove it.
10 Remove the screws and withdraw the cold start device, together with the intermediate flange and air metering slide valve. Remove the gasket.
11 Note the position of the return springs, then unscrew the nuts and remove the levers and springs from the throttle butterfly spindle. *Do not alter the setting of the throttle stop screw*. Prise out the spindle seals with a small screwdriver.
12 To check the temperature compensator, remove the screws and take off the cover. At

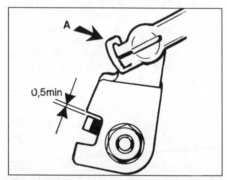

Fig. 3.49 Adjust the throttle control rod (A) on the Zenith 175 CD-2SE carburettor to give the clearance indicated (Sec 21)

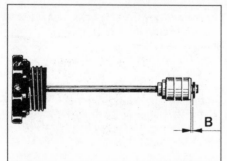

Fig. 3.52 Damper piston clearance (Sec 22)
B = 0.039 to 0.071 in (1.0 to 1.8 mm)

temperatures above 79°F (26°C) it should be possible to depress the valve under light pressure, and the valve should return to its original position without sticking.
13 If necessary, centralise the valve by loosening the cross-head screw furthest from the valve.
14 Check that the valve starts to open at 68°F (20°C) and, if necessary, adjust the cross-head screw nearest the valve.
15 Renew the complete valve if it is worn or coated with a deposit which would cause it to stick. Refit the cover if it is to be re-used.
16 Check the cold start device for excessive wear and smooth movement. Renew it if necessary.
17 Remove the cross-head screws and withdraw the air valve housing from the cold start device, followed by the return spring, intermediate flange, diaphragm and gaskets. Recover the spacers. Check the diaphragm for damage and renew it if necessary.
18 Check the damper piston for damage and make sure that the clearance is as given in Fig. 3.52.
19 Check that the throttle butterfly moves freely. If the butterfly is damaged renew it, but note that it must be fitted so that it bears the same relation to the spindle, and it must be centralised before tightening and staking the screws.
20 Check the air valve and diaphragm for wear and damage. If the diaphragm is renewed, make sure that the lug engages the cut-out in the valve.

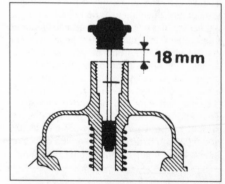

Fig. 3.50 Oil level checking dimension on the Zenith 175 CD-2SE carburettor (Sec 21)

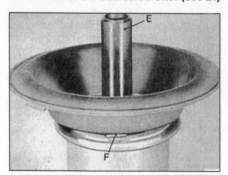

Fig. 3.53 Air valve (E) and diaphragm locating lug (F) (Sec 22)

3

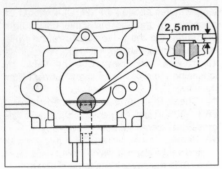

Fig. 3.54 Cross-section of fuel jet, showing correct height (Sec 22)

21 Check the fuel jet and metering needle for wear. The fuel jet height must be as shown in Fig. 3.54. Special tools are required to renew the fuel jet although careful use of suitable drifts may be possible.

22 To renew the metering needle, remove the guide screw from the air valve then, using the special tool 5159, turn the adjusting screw anti-clockwise until the needle is released. Fit the new needle so that its base is flush with the bottom of the air valve.

23 Check the needle valve for wear and renew it if necessary.

24 Clean all the components, then reassemble them in the reverse order of dismantling using new gaskets and seals. Check the float level by holding the carburettor (float chamber cover removed) so that the float hangs down with the float arm just touching the spring-loaded pin without actually depressing the pin. If the dimensions are not as shown in Fig. 3.56 bend the arm as necessary. If a new throttle butterfly has been fitted, check the basic setting as follows, but do not alter the setting of the throttle stop screw. Disconnect the cold start lever and move the butterfly to the closed position. Measure dimension A in Fig. 3.57 then refit the cold start lever and measure dimension B. The difference between the two dimensions should be between 0.7 and 0.9 mm (0.028 and 0.035 in). If necessary bend the cold start device lever where it contacts the stop screw.

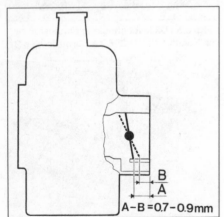

Fig. 3.57 Throttle butterfly setting dimensions (Sec 22)

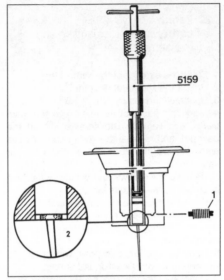

Fig. 3.55 Special tool for adjusting and removing the metering needle (Sec 22)

1 Guide screw
2 Initial setting for the metering needle

23 Solex 34-34 CISAC carburettor - general description

The Solex 34-34 CISAC carburettor is used on the B200K engine which replaced the B19A engine in 1985.

It is a twin barrel downdraught design incorporating a preheating system. The throttle valves operate progressively, the second stage only opening after the first valve has opened by 75%. However, the second stage valve is locked in the closed position while the choke is in use.

24 Solex 34-34 CISAC carburettor - idle speed and CO adjustment

1 On carburettors up to 1986 with a constant CO system and a fuel cut-off solenoid, idle adjustments are made on the screw shown in the photograph (photo).

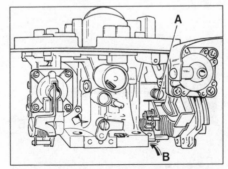

Fig. 3.58 Throttle stop screw (A) and mixture screw (B) - later carburettors (Sec 24)

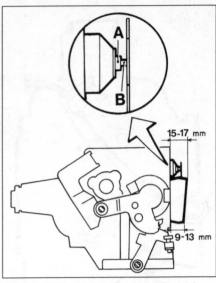

Fig. 3.56 Float level checking dimension (Sec 22)

A Needle Valve
B Spring loaded pin

2 On later carburettors, the constant CO system was discontinued and idle adjustments are made on the throttle stop screw as shown in Fig. 3.58. Note that this applies only to carburettors which still have the fuel cut-off solenoid.

3 The engine should be at normal operating temperature, and the cooling fan should be off.

4 Connect a tachometer to the engine for idle speed adjustment and, if the CO content is being checked, connect an exhaust gas analyser also.

5 With the engine idling, check the idle speed against that given in the Specifications and adjust as necessary according to paragraphs 1 or 2 above.

6 Similarly check the CO level and adjust on the screw, first removing the tamperproof plug.

7 Switch off the engine and remove the test equipment.

24.1 Adjusting the idle speed of the Solex 34-34 CISAC carburettor

25.2 Disconnecting the fuel inlet hose on the Solex 34-34 CISAC carburettor

25.3 Disconnecting idle solenoid (arrowed) on the Solex 34-34 CISAC carburettor

25.5 Carburettor-to-inlet manifold nuts (arrowed) on Solex 34-34 CISAC carburettor

26.2A Solex 34.34 CISAC carburettor cover screws (arrowed)

26.2B View of the underside of the Solex 34-34 CISAC carburettor

26.2C Solex 34-34 CISAC carburettor with cover removed

25 Solex 34-34 CISAC carburettor - removal and refitting

1 Disconnect the crankcase breather hose and the air intake duct and remove the air intake cap.
2 Disconnect the fuel inlet hose (photo).
3 Disconnect the idle solenoid (photo).
4 Disconnect the accelerator and choke cables.
5 Remove the nuts securing the carburettor to the inlet manifold and lift off the carburettor (photo).
6 Refit in the reverse order, but make sure the carburettor flange and gasket are in good condition, and the O-ring seal is refitted under the air intake cap.

26 Solex 34-34 CISAC carburettor - dismantling and reassembly

1 Dismantling should be limited to cleaning the jets.
2 Note how the choke lever locates against the throttle lever fast idle cam, then remove the screws and lift off the cover (photos). Take care not to break the gasket.
3 Unscrew and remove the emulsion tubes and main jets.
4 Remove the screws and withdraw the cover, spring and diaphragm, then unscrew and remove the idle jets (photo).

5 Unscrew and remove the idle solenoid and washer.
6 Clean all the components and check them for wear and damage. Clean any sediment from the bottom of the float chambers. Use an air line or tyre pump to blow through the jets and internal passages. Check the floats for leakage by immersing them in warm water and checking for air bubbles. Check the idle solenoid by connecting a 12 volt supply - if the needle does not move, the solenoid must be renewed.
7 Reassemble the carburettor in the reverse order of dismantling using new gaskets and washers. Check the float level before fitting the cover as follows. Hold the cover so that the float arm is resting on the spring-tensioned ball in the end of the needle valve, but without depressing the ball. Measure the distance from the gasket to the peak of one float (photo). If the dimension is not as given in

the Specifications bend the tab on the arm as necessary.
8 The idle solenoid can be checked *in situ* by switching on the ignition, ensuring the choke is pushed fully in, then disconnecting the idle solenoid lead. If a distinct click is heard, the solenoid is serviceable. If no click is heard, check that fuse number 10 is intact before renewing the solenoid.
9 If after renewal of the solenoid there is still a problem, then the electronic control unit is suspect, and should be tested by your Volvo dealer.
10 **Note**: *To improve hot start conditions, later carburettors have a modified float chamber ventilation valve fitted. This modification can be successfully carried out by the home mechanic as follows (if the modification has already been done there should be a white paint mark on the valve body).*

3

26.4 The idle jets are beneath this cover (arrowed) on Solex 34-34 CISAC carburettor

26.7 Checking the float height on the Solex 34-34 CISAC carburettor

27.1 In-line fuel filter on the B200K engine

11 Remove the carburettor cover then remove the ventilation valve from the cover. Remove the nut from the base of the valve, then pull off the rubber bellows, spindle and spring.

12 Either obtain a new spring, or shorten the existing spring by cutting it to 0.906 in (23 mm).

13 Refit the valve in the reverse order, the largest opening in the rubber bellows facing toward the carburettor, and the cut end of the spring facing downward. Use a new gasket under the valve.

14 On completion mark the valve body with a dab of white paint then adjust the valve as follows.

15 Close the throttle butterfly valve.

16 Fully open the choke.

17 Move the adjusting nut up or down the threaded shank to give a clearance of 0.004 to 0.020 in (0.1 to 0.5 mm) between the nut and the operating arm.

27 Fuel filter (B200K engine) - renewal

1 An in-line fuel filter is fitted between the fuel pump and the carburettor (photo).

2 The filter should be renewed at the intervals given in the Routine Maintenance Section at the beginning of this manual.

3 To remove the filter, undo the clips from the fuel line and pull the filter from the hoses.

4 Fit a new filter, making sure the flow direction arrow faces toward the carburettor, and that the clips are tightened fully.

28 Solex 28-34 CISAC carburettor - general description

The Solex 28-34 CISAC carburettor fitted to the B172 engine is a twin barrel, downdraught carburettor, mounted directly on the inlet manifold. The carburettor base is heated or cooled according to prevailing conditions, and the design of the carburettor is such that optimum fuel flow is obtained over extreme temperature variations. The throttle butterfly valve in the second stage venturi opens later than that in the first, giving improved fuel

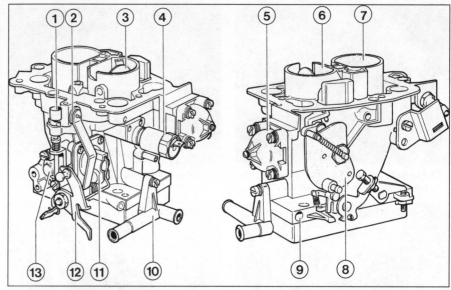

Fig. 3.59 View of the components of the Solex 28-34 CISAC carburettor (Sec 28)

1 Idle adusting screw
2 Float chamber ventilation
3 Choke butterfly
4 Idle solenoid
5 Pneumatic choke mechanism
6 First stage venturi
7 Second stage venturi
8 Choke lever
9 Mixture adjusting screw
10 Preheating pipes
11 Accelerator pump
12 Throttle lever
13 Full load enrichment valve

consumption. The carburettor is fitted with an idle solenoid which cuts off the fuel supply when the ignition is turned off. To aid cold starting a manual choke, operated by cable, is fitted.

29 Solex 28-34 CISAC carburettor - idle speed and CO adjustment

1 Connect a tachometer and exhaust gas analyser to the engine.

2 Start the engine and allow it to reach normal operating temperature.

3 During the adjustment checks, all electrical consumers should be switched off, including the thermally switched radiator fan.

4 Check the idling speed is as given in the Specifications. Adjust using a thin screwdriver inserted through the hole in the air filter

housing (photo) which allows access to the idle screw.

5 Check the CO content is within the limits given in the Specifications. Adjust with the screw (see paragraph 16 of Section 31); on completion fit a new tamperproof plug.

30 Solex 28-34 CISAC carburettor - removal and refitting

1 Remove the air filter assembly as described in Section 3.

2 Disconnect the throttle operating rod and the choke cable.

3 Disconnect the vacuum hose to the Renix ignition unit.

4 Remove the screw from the bracket and pull away the preheating hose (there is no need to disconnect the hoses) (photo).

29.4 Adjusting the idle speed through the hole in the air filter housing on the Solex 28-34 CISAC carburettor

30.4 Removing the hoses from the preheating flange on the Solex 28-34 CISAC carburettor

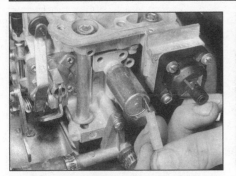

30.7 Disconnecting the idle solenoid on the Solex 28-34 CISAC carburettor . . .

30.8 . . . removing the gasket . . .

30.9 . . . and the carburettor bolts (arrowed)

5 Pull off the crankcase breather hose.
6 Disconnect the fuel supply hose.
7 Disconnect the electrical lead to the idle solenoid (photo).
8 Remove the gasket from the top of the carburettor (photo).

30.10 Remove the heat transfer flange

9 Undo and remove the four bolts securing the carburettor to the inlet manifold (photo).
10 Lift the carburettor from the inlet manifold, then remove the special heat transfer flange (photo).
11 Refitting is a reversal of removal.

31 Solex 28-34 CISAC carburettor - dismantling and reassembly

1 Invert the carburettor and remove the insulating flange from the base by removing its retaining screw.
2 Thoroughly clean the exterior of the carburettor in clean petrol and then dry it, preferably using an air line.
3 Remove the cover bolt from the fuel inlet flange, remove the filter and wash the filter in clean fuel (photos).
4 Remove the five retaining screws and carefully lift off the cover (photo).
5 Carefully knock the pin from the float hinge brackets, remove the float and the cover gasket (photo).
6 Check the float assembly for leaks by weighing the float (photo) and checking it against the Specifications. If the float is too heavy it must be suspected of being punctured, and renewed.
7 Remove the needle valve (photo) and check that the needle is free to move.
8 On refitting the float, check the float height with the cover inverted and the float resting lightly against the needle valve. Float height is the distance from the float cover with gasket in place, to the highest point of the float (photo).
9 Adjust the height by bending the tongue - B in Fig. 3.60.
10 Remove the idle solenoid and check its operation by connecting it to a 12 volt supply,

3

31.3A Remove the cover bolt . . .

31.3B . . . and take out the filter

31.4 Remove the five cover retaining screws (arrowed)

31.5 Knock out the pin from the float pivot brackets

31.6 Float assembly

31.7 Remove the needle valve (arrowed)

31.8 Measuring the float height (A)

31.11 Full load enrichment assembly screws (arrowed)

31.12 The pneumatic choke cover (arrowed)

31.13 Float chamber ventilation valve

31.15 The accelerator pump injector (A) and air jets (B)

31.16 Tamperproof plug covering the mixture screw (arrowed)

switching on and seeing whether the needle is drawn in. If not the solenoid is defective and should be renewed.

11 Remove the three screws from the pneumatic full load enrichment assembly (photo) and recover the spring, diaphragm and idle speed adjusting rod. Check the diaphragm for splits and renew if evident.

12 Remove the cover from the pneumatic choke (photo) and recover the spring, then unhook the diaphragm operating rod. Check the diaphragm for splits and renew if evident.

13 Remove the nut from the end of the throttle butterfly spindle, remove the lever assembly and the float chamber ventilation

31.18A Using a twist drill to measure the gap

valve (photo). Check that the face of the rubber valve is sound and in good condition, renewing as necessary.

14 Remove the cover from the accelerator pump, recover the spring and diaphragm and inspect the diaphragm as described previously.

15 Carefully lever out the accelerator pump injector and fuel feed pipe, then unscrew the air jets (photo), which will give access to the main fuel jets which can be removed using a long thin screwdriver.

16 Remove the mixture control screw from the base flange of the carburettor. This will be hidden under a tamperproof plug which should be removed using a sharp instrument (photo).

17 If necessary, the auxiliary venturis may be pulled up out of the carburettor body by carefully using pliers.

18 Reassembly is a reversal of removal, bearing in mind the following points:

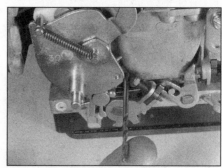

31.18B Measuring the throttle butterfly-to-choke flap clearance

a) The auxiliary venturis must be located with their bores opposite the bores in the carburettor body. The first stage venturi has an interrupted bridge

b) The mixture screw should be screwed in lightly to its full extent, then backed off 1 1/2 to 2 turns. Do not refit the seal until after the mixture has been set

c) Use a new O-ring seal under the head of the accelerator pump injector, and the idle solenoid

d) Check the pneumatic choke setting by turning the cam anti-clockwise against its stop then press the lever of the diaphragm down as far as it will go. In this condition the choke flap opening should be as given in the Specifications. Adjustment is provided for by the screw in the lever. The gap can be measured by using a twist drill of the relevant size (photo).

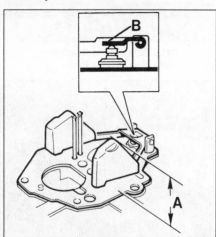

Fig. 3.60 Float height (A) and tongue (B) (Sec 31)

e) Check the relation of the throttle butterfly to the choke flap by fully opening the choke flap and measuring the gap between the lever cam and the head of the adjusting screw (photo). Turn the screw in or out to obtain the specified gap

f) The float chamber ventilation valve should close as soon as the throttle is opened. With the throttle closed the valve should open by the amount in the Specifications

32 Bosch LE-Jetronic fuel injection system - general description

The fuel injection system used on Volvo 300 models is the LE-Jetronic system developed by Bosch. This system is fully electronically controlled, and delivers the correct amount of fuel to the right cylinder at the desired time. This is known as intermittent injection.

The volume of air entering the engine is measured by an airflow meter, which, along with other information such as throttle position, engine temperature, engine speed, etc, is fed to the electronic control unit (ECU), which then computes the length of time and when the fuel injectors should be open. Fuel is fed to the injectors by an electric pump, and the fuel pressure is controlled by a fuel pressure regulator.

33 Fuel injection system - safety precautions

As the system incorporates semiconductor components, the following precautions must be heeded at all times to avoid damage and failure. Ensure the battery is connected correctly, but disconnect the lead when charging the battery. Remove the ECU if ambient temperatures are likely to exceed 76°F (80°C) (when drying paint). Do not disconnect or connect the system wiring with the ignition switched on. Disconnect the wiring from the ECU before carrying out a compression test as this will prevent fuel being injected. Remove the ECU before using electric welding equipment on the car. Never interchange the fuel pump wires.

34 Fuel injection system - idle speed adjustment

1 First adjust the throttle butterfly switch. Loosen the two bolts then turn the switch clockwise. Now turn it slowly anti-clockwise until the internal contacts are heard to click; tighten the bolts with the switch in this position.

2 Run the engine to normal operating temperature then connect a tachometer and check that the idle speed is as given in the Specifications. If not, turn the knurled adjustment screw at the bottom of the throttle housing as necessary (photo).

3 Connect an exhaust gas analyser and allow the engine to idle. If the CO content is not as given in the Specifications prise the seal from

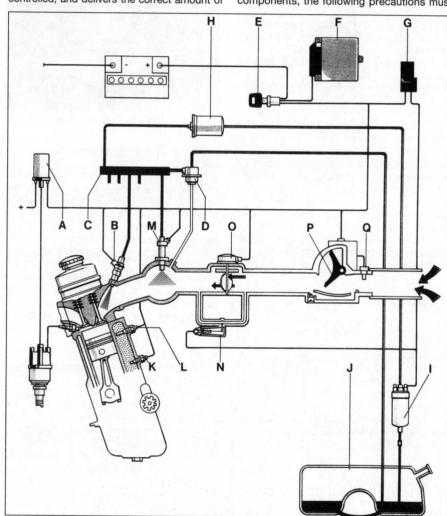

Fig. 3.61 Schematic diagram of the Bosch LE-Jetronic fuel injection system (Sec 32)

A Ignition coil
B Fuel injectors (four)
C Fuel injection manifold
D Line pressure regulator
E Ignition switch
F Electronic control unit

G Control relay
H Fuel filter (in engine bay)
I Fuel pump with mesh filter
J Fuel tank
K Coolant temperature sensor
L Thermal time switch

M Cold start injector
N Auxiliary air valve
O Throttle/butterfly switch
P Air volume meter
Q Induction air temperature sensor

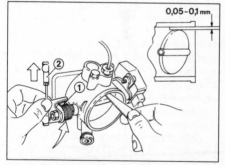

Fig. 3.62 Adjusting the LE-Jetronic throttle butterfly (Sec 34)

1 Adjusting screw
2 Throttle control rod

34.2 Idle speed adjustment screw on the throttle housing (B19E engine)

3

34.3 Prising the seal from the airflow meter to adjust the CO content

35.1A Disconnecting the plug from the auxiliary air valve

35.1B LE-Jetronic control relay

the airflow meter and use a screwdriver to turn the adjustment screw as necessary (photo). Turning the screw clockwise enrichens the mixture and increases the CO content, and *vice versa*. Fit a new seal after making the adjustment.

4 If after making the previous adjustments the engine does not idle correctly, and the ignition, valve clearances and compressions are in order, check the throttle butterfly spindle for wear then check the butterfly adjustment as follows. Remove the inlet duct, open the throttle and insert a 0.05 mm (0.002 in) feeler gauge between the edge of the butterfly and the housing then close the throttle. The feeler gauge should move without lifting the butterfly. Now repeat the test using a 0.1 mm (0.004 in) feeler gauge and check that the gauge is held firm. If necessary turn the adjustment screw on the throttle housing.

35 Fuel injection system - complete check

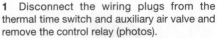

1 Disconnect the wiring plugs from the thermal time switch and auxiliary air valve and remove the control relay (photos).

2 Check that all hoses are secure and not damaged, also check the injector seals.

3 Check the control relay wiring. Connect a test lamp from the battery + terminal to terminal 31; it should light, proving that the earth is in order. Connect the test lamp from the battery - terminal to each of the terminals shown in Fig. 3.64. Terminal 30 should light at all times, terminal 15 with the ignition on, terminal 50 when starting, and terminal 1 should flash when starting.

4 Check the cold start injector by disconnecting the auxiliary air valve hose, then disconnect the thermal time switch plug and connect the terminal W in the plug to earth. Spin the engine in the starter and check that the cold start injector is spraying fuel by

35.5 Auxiliary air valve

looking in the hose aperture on the inlet manifold.

5 Check the auxiliary air valve (photo). The valve should be half open at 68°F (20°C) fully open at -22°F (-30°C), and fully closed at 158°F (70°C). Tap the housing gently if it does not operate initially, otherwise renew it. Bridge terminals 30 and 87 and check that the valve fully closes after approximately 5 minutes at 68°F (20°C).

6 Check the fuel pressure. Depressurize the system by temporarily loosening the outlet hose from the fuel filter. Connect a pressure gauge to the cold start injector by inserting a T-piece into the fuel line between the filter and the fuel injection manifold.

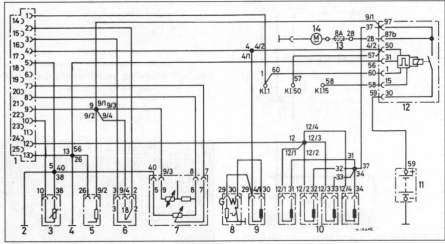

Fig. 3.63 Wiring diagram for the LE-Jetronic fuel injection system (Sec 35)

1 ECU connector	6 Throttle butterfly switch
2 Earthing point	7 Airflow meter
3 Temperature sensor	8 Thermal time switch
4 Output stage earthing point	9 Cold start injector
5 Auxiliary air valve	10 Injectors

11 Battery
12 Control relay
13 Fuse for fuel pump
14 Fuel pump

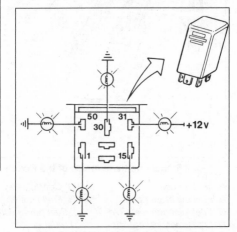

Fig. 3.64 LE-Jetronic control relay terminals (Sec 35)

35.7 Pressure regulator, showing vacuum connection (arrowed)

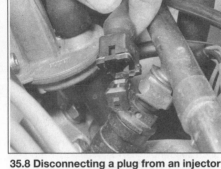

35.8 Disconnecting a plug from an injector

35.10 Disconnecting the throttle butterfly switch connector

35.14 Disconnecting the airflow meter connector

7 Bridge terminals 30 and 87b and check that the line pressure rises to the specified level. Connect a vacuum gauge and pump to the vacuum connection on the pressure regulator, then apply vacuum and check that the sum of the vacuum and pressure gauge readings equals the line pressure (photo). Remove the vacuum gauge. Disconnect the bridging wire and check that the line pressure drops immediately by 1.4 to 2.8 lbf/in² (9.81 to 19.6 kPa).

8 Connect a voltmeter to one of the injectors as shown in Fig. 3.65 (photo). Start the engine and check that 1.0 volt is registered with a cold engine. During the warm-up period the reading should drop fairly quickly to 0.6 volt then gradually to 0.4 volt. Check that all the injectors are operating by listening at the handle end of a screwdriver held against each injector in turn. A clicking noise should be heard.

9 With the engine at operating temperature, slowly increase the speed to 3000 rpm and check that the voltage now reads between 0.9 and 1.0 volt. Let the engine idle then raise it quickly again to 3000 rpm - initially a reading near 2.0 volt should occur then it should return to 0.9 to 1.0 volt. Reduce the engine speed quickly to idling from 2500.

10 Disconnect the throttle butterfly switch connector and bridge terminals 3 and 18 (photo). The reading should be approximately 0.1 volt.

11 Remove the cap from the ECU located in the left-hand side of the console. **Note:** *When carrying out resistance checks on the ECU always use the holes on the side of the connector. The terminals are numbered on the side of the connector.*

12 Using an ohmmeter, check that terminals 5 and 13 are correctly earthed (ie 0 ohm to earth point). Using a test lamp between terminals 4 and 9 and earth, check that the lamp lights when the starter is operated. Using an ohmmeter check the throttle butterfly switch by connecting the meter between terminals 2 and 9 on the ECU - with the accelerator pedal released the reading should be 0 ohm, but with it slightly depressed the reading should be infinity. Between terminals 3 and 9 the reading should be infinity with the pedal released and 0 ohm with it fully depressed.

13 Connect the ohmmeter between terminals 9 and 12 on the ECU to test the total resistance of the injectors which should be between 4 and 5 ohm. Individual injectors should have the specified resistance. Check the airflow meter resistance by connecting between terminals 5 and 8 (100 to 200 ohm), and 5 and 7 (100 ohm). Check the coolant temperature sensor resistance by connecting between terminals 5 and 10. The resistance should be 2 to 3 kohm at 68°F (20°C).

14 To check the airflow meter, disconnect the supply hose, unplug the connector and remove the control relay (photo). Connect the ohmmeter between terminal 87 on the relay socket and terminal 9 on the meter connector - the reading should be 0 ohm. Connect between terminals 5 and 7 on the connector and move the airflow meter arm to and fro - the resistance should vary between 100 and 1000 ohm.

15 Between terminals 8 and E, which are the terminals of the fixed resistor, the resistance should be approximately 150 ohm, and between 9 and E, the terminals of the airflow temperature transmitter, 50 ohm at 68°F (20°C).

16 If current is not available for any of the foregoing tests, refer to the wiring diagrams to check the remaining circuit.

36 Fuel pump (fuel injection models) - removal and refitting

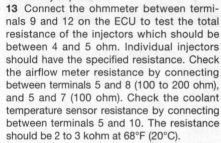
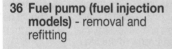

1 The fuel pump is located underneath the car, just behind the transmission unit (photo).
2 Remove the heat shield, secured by bolts and self-tapping screws.
3 Pull off the baseplate held by rubber mountings to the support plate.

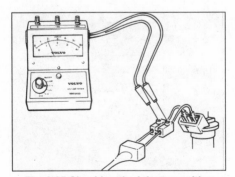

Fig. 3.65 Checking the injectors with a voltmeter (Sec 35)

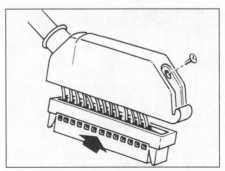

Fig. 3.66 Electronic control unit multi-plug connection (Sec 35)

36.1 Fuel pump and filter location under the vehicle

37.1 Fuel filter located in the engine bay

4 Disconnect the electrical connections.
5 Clamp the fuel hoses at both ends of the pump, undo the unions and disconnect both hoses.
6 Release the two mounting clips and remove the pump.
7 Refit in the reverse order, ensuring the electrical leads are connected properly, and that the flow direction of the pump is correctly orientated.
8 Check the pump for correct operation (refer to Section 35).

37 Fuel filter (fuel injection models) - renewal

1 There are two fuel filters on fuel injection systems, one is located by the fuel pump under the car (see photo 36.1), the other is located in the engine bay on the fuel inlet hose before the injection manifold (photo).
2 The routine maintenance procedures regarding servicing of the fuel filter refers to both filters.
3 To remove a filter, pinch off the hoses both sides of the filter, undo the hose clips (if these are plastic compression types, they should be cut through and renewed), pull the hoses from the filter and remove the filter.
4 The filter should be inspected at the recommended intervals, and renewed if clogged, and renewed anyway at the longer indicated interval.
5 Refit in the reverse order, making sure the arrow on the filter body faces in the direction of flow.

38 Electronic Control Unit (ECU) - removal and refitting

1 Disconnect the battery negative lead.
2 Remove the two side panels from the centre console.
3 Remove the multi-plug connector from the ECU by pushing in the locking tab and pulling the connector free.
4 Remove the radio, and then remove the ECU securing screws (on early models) accessible through the radio aperture and the holes in the tunnel console. On later models the ECU is fixed with a snap lock fitting.
5 Refit in the reverse order.

39 Inlet and exhaust manifold - removal and refitting

B14 models up to 1982

1 Disconnect the battery negative terminal.
2 Detach the filler cap or supply tube, then remove the windscreen washer reservoir.
3 Remove the carburettor.
4 Detach the vacuum hoses from the inlet manifold as applicable.
5 Detach the heating and crankcase ventilation hoses.
6 Remove the engine guard plates.
7 Unscrew the exhaust pipe-to-manifold nuts (photo), detach the mounting at the starter motor and pull the exhaust from the manifold.
8 Unscrew and remove the manifold retaining nuts and washers, withdraw the heatshield (early models) or hose (later models), and lift the manifold assembly from the engine.
9 Thoroughly clean the cylinder head and manifold faces and examine the manifolds for damage and deterioration.
10 Refitting is a reversal of removal, but the following additional points should be noted:

a) Always fit a new gasket
b) Tighten all nuts to the correct specified torque. Make sure the components are tightened in this sequence: manifold to cylinder head, exhaust pipe to manifold, exhaust mounting to clutch housing

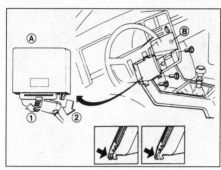

Fig. 3.67 Electronic control unit location (Sec 38)

1 Locking tab
2 Connector
A ECU

B Radio/blanking
plate

c) Adjust the carburettor
d) Adjust the vacuum control microswitch when fitted, as described in Chapter 6

B14.3E models from 1982

11 The inlet and exhaust manifold are a single casting and not two separate castings as on previous B14 engines, but the removal and refitting procedure is similar.

B19 and B200 models

12 To remove the inlet manifold first remove the carburettor or fuel injection equipment, as applicable. Disconnect all hoses and wiring, then unscrew the nuts and withdraw the inlet manifold from the cylinder head (photos). Remove the gasket. Clean the mating faces and fit a new gasket. Refitting is a reversal of removal, but fit a new carburettor flange gasket where applicable.
13 To remove the exhaust manifold disconnect the hot air duct and unbolt the shroud (photo). Unbolt the downpipe then unscrew the nuts and withdraw the exhaust manifold from the cylinder head, noting the location of the lifting eyes (photo). Remove the gaskets. Clean the mating faces and fit new gaskets. Refitting is a reversal of removal, but fit a new downpipe gasket.

B172 models

14 The procedure is similar to that described for other models (photo).

39.7 Front exhaust pipe-to-manifold joint (B14 models)

39.12A Removing the inlet manifold on the B19A and B200K engines

39.12B The inlet manifold fitted to the B19E and B200E engines

39.13A Exhaust manifold hot air shroud

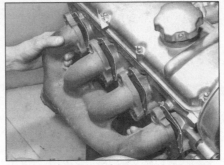

39.13B Removing the exhaust manifold

39.14 Inlet and exhaust manifold on B172 engines

15 Remember the two nuts accessible from underneath (photo).
16 On these models the inlet and exhaust manifolds can be separated after removal of the three bolts (photo).

40 Exhaust system -
removal and refitting

B14 models up to 1985

1 Jack up the front and rear of the car and support it adequately on axle stands. Alternatively position the car over an inspection pit.
2 If the retaining nuts are rusted, apply penetrating oil to them to facilitate removal.
3 Loosen the rear-to-central section clamps, detach the rear section mounting rubbers (photos) and withdraw the rear section from the centre section.

39.15 The two nuts accessible from underneath

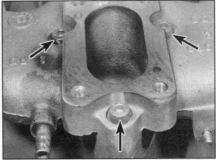

39.16 Separate the manifolds by removing the three bolts (arrowed)

40.3A Rear exhaust section rear mounting

40.3B Rear exhaust section front mounting

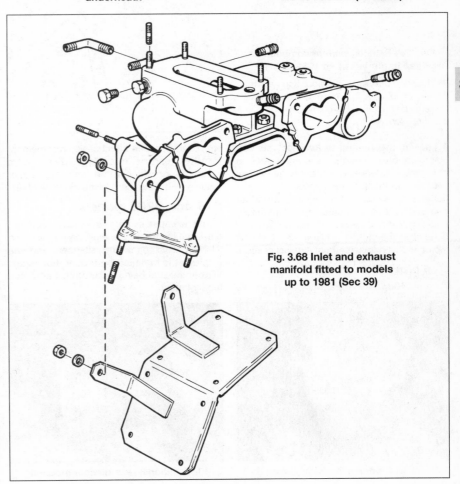

Fig. 3.68 Inlet and exhaust manifold fitted to models up to 1981 (Sec 39)

3

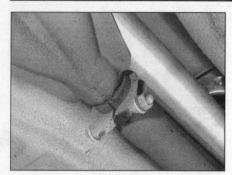

40.4 Central section-to-front exhaust pipe connection

40.8A Front exhaust mounting on the torque tube (B19 and B200 models)

Fig. 3.69 Exhaust system components fitted to models up to 1981 (Sec 40)

1 Mounting bracket	5 Mounting rubber
2 Downpipe	6 Rear silencer
3 Heat shield	(resonator)
4 Front silencer	

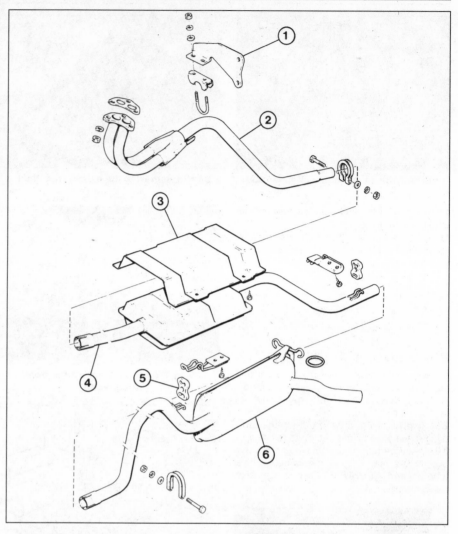

4 Loosen the central-to-foremost section clamp (photo), detach the central section mounting rubbers and withdraw the central section from the foremost section.

5 Detach the right-hand engine guard plate and unscrew the exhaust pipe-to-manifold retaining nuts.

6 Remove the mounting clamp at the starter motor and withdraw the front exhaust section.

B14 models from 1985

7 From 1985 an extra support point is employed between the chassis crossmember for the gearbox mounting. These extra mounting points can be fitted to earlier models by bolting them to the crossmember.

B19 and B200 models

8 The exhaust system is in four sections, these are the front downpipe, centre pipe and silencer, rear pipe and silencer, and the tailpipe. It is mounted on rubber mountings, the central one being secured to the torque tube (photos).

B172 models

9 The exhaust system is similar to that on B200 models, but there is no torque tube mounting, the centre section being supported as described in paragraph 8 (photos).

All models

10 Refitting the exhaust system is a reversal of removal, ensuring there is a clearance between neighbouring components.

40.8B Central exhaust mounting

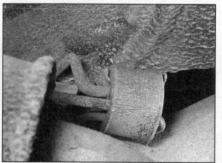

40.8C Exhaust rear silencer mounting

40.8D Exhaust tailpipe joint and mounting

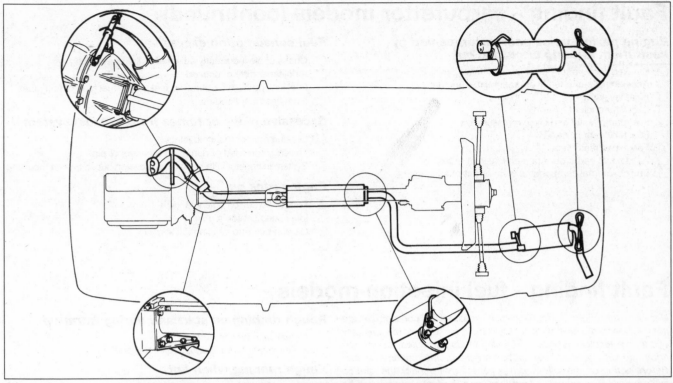

Fig. 3.70 Exhaust system components on B172, B19 and B200 models (Sec 40)

40.9A Exhaust manifold-to-downpipe connection on B172 models

40.9B Centre support bracket on B172 models

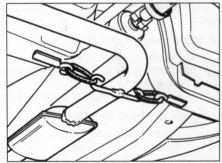

Fig. 3.71 Extra support point on B14 models from 1985 (Sec 40)

Fault finding - carburettor models

Unsatisfactory engine performance and excessive fuel consumption are not necessarily the fault of the carburettor. In fact they more commonly occur as a result of ignition and timing faults particularly on models equipped with conventional contact breaker point ignition systems. Before acting on the following it is necessary to check the ignition system first. Even though a fault may lie in the fuel system it will be difficult to trace unless the ignition system is correct. The faults below, therefore, assume that this has been attended to first (where appropriate).

Engine difficult to start when cold

☐ Choke cable incorrectly adjusted
☐ Choke flap not closing
☐ Insufficient fuel in float chamber

Engine difficult to start when hot

☐ Choke cable incorrectly adjusted
☐ Air cleaner element dirty or choked
☐ Insufficient fuel in float chamber
☐ Float chamber flooding

Engine will not idle or idles erratically

☐ Air cleaner dirty or choked
☐ Choke cable incorrectly adjusted
☐ Carburettor idling adjustments incorrectly set
☐ Blocked carburettor jets or internal passages
☐ Disconnected, perished or leaking crankcase ventilation hoses
☐ Air leaks at carburettor or manifold joint faces
☐ Generally worn carburettor
☐ Engine internal defect

Fault finding - carburettor models (continued)

Engine performance poor accompanied by hesitation, missing or cutting out

☐ Blocked carburettor jets or internal passages
☐ Accelerator pump faulty or diaphragm punctured
☐ Float level low
☐ Fuel filter choked
☐ Fuel pump faulty or delivery pressure low
☐ Fuel tank vent blocked
☐ Fuel pipes restricted
☐ Air leaks at carburettor or manifold joint faces
☐ Engine internal components worn or out of adjustment

Fuel consumption excessive

☐ Choke cable incorrectly adjusted or linkage sticking
☐ Air cleaner dirty or choked
☐ Fuel leaking from carburettor, fuel pump, fuel tank or fuel pipes
☐ Float chamber flooding

Excessive noise or fumes from exhaust system

☐ Leaking pipe or manifold joints
☐ Leaking, corroded or damaged silencers or pipe
☐ System in contact with body or suspension due to broken mounting

Engine runs on

☐ Faulty idle/cut-off solenoid valve
☐ Idle speed set too high
☐ Carbon build-up causing ignition

Fault finding - fuel injection models

Unsatisfactory engine performance and excessive fuel consumption are not necessarily the fault of the fuel system. In fact they more commonly occur as a result of ignition and timing faults particularly on models equipped with conventional contact breaker point ignition systems. Before acting on the following it is necessary to check the ignition system first. Even though a fault may lie in the fuel system it will be difficult to trace unless the ignition system is correct. The faults below, therefore, assume that this has been attended to first (where appropriate).

Engine does not start

☐ Air leak on induction system
☐ Fuel pump not working or set at incorrect pressure
☐ Cold start injector failure
☐ Air flow meter or coolant temperature sensor not working

Engine difficult to start when cold

☐ Cold start injector failure
☐ Auxiliary air valve malfunction

Engine difficult to start when hot

☐ Cold start injector leaking
☐ Residual pressure too low
☐ Incorrect fuel pressure

Engine difficult to start hot and cold

☐ Air leak in induction system
☐ Incorrect fuel pressure
☐ Airflow meter malfunction

Rough running on start and during warm-up

☐ Air leak in induction system
☐ Airflow meter or auxiliary air valve malfunction

Rough running when hot

☐ Incorrect fuel pressure
☐ Air leak in induction system

Rough running hot and cold

☐ Air leak in induction system
☐ Incorrect fuel pressure
☐ One or more injectors not working
☐ CO content incorrect
☐ Airflow meter malfunction

Rough running accompanied by high fuel consumption

☐ Cold start injector leaking
☐ Incorrect fuel pressure
☐ Other fuel leakage
☐ CO content incorrect
☐ Airflow meter malfunction

Engine lacks power and has low top speed

☐ Throttle linkage/butterfly incorrectly adjusted
☐ Line pressure incorrect
☐ CO content incorrect

Rough running at idle

☐ Engine not running on all cylinders
☐ Air leak in induction system
☐ Airflow meter sticking
☐ Throttle butterfly switch defective
☐ Injectors leaking, or have bad spray pattern

Chapter 4
Ignition system

Contents

Degrees of difficulty

Easy, suitable for novice with little experience	**Fairly easy,** suitable for beginner with some experience	**Fairly difficult,** suitable for competent DIY mechanic	**Difficult,** suitable for experienced DIY mechanic	**Very difficult,** suitable for expert DIY or professional

Specifications

Part A: Conventional ignition system

Type .... 12V battery and coil, mechanical contact breaker points

Distributor

Make:
  B14 .... Ducellier, AC Delco or SEV
  B19 .... Bosch
Direction of rotation .... Clockwise
Contact breaker gap:
  B14 .... 0.016 to 0.020 in (0.4 to 0.5 mm)
  B19 .... 0.016 in (0.4 mm)
Dwell angle:
  B14:
    AC Delco distributor .... 50° ± 3°
    All other distributors .... 57° ± 3°
  B19 .... 62° ± 3°
Firing order:
  B14 .... 1 - 3 - 4 - 2 (No 1 cylinder nearest flywheel)
  B19 .... 1 - 3 - 4 - 2 (No 1 cylinder nearest radiator)

Ignition timing

Static or dynamic at idle (vacuum hose disconnected):
  B14.0E/S .... 3° ± 1° BTDC
  B14.1/2/3S .... 6° ± 1° BTDC
  B14.1/2E .... 6° ± 1° BTDC
  B14.3E .... 10° ±1° BTDC
  B19A 984 .... 10° ± 2° BTDC
  B19A 552/566 .... 7° ± 2° BTDC

Spark plugs

	Type	Electrode gap
B14.0 (1976 to September 1978)	Champion L87YCC	0.032 in (0.8 mm)
	Champion L87YC	0.024 in (0.6 mm)
B14.1/2/3 (September 1978 on)	Champion N9YCC	0.032 in (0.8 mm)
	Champion N9YC	0.024 in (0.6 mm)
B19A	Champion RN9YCC	0.032 in (0.8 mm)
	Champion RN9YC	0.028 in (0.7 mm)

HT leads

B14 models (1976 to 1982)	Champion LS 21, boxed set
B14 models (1983-on)	Champion LS 01, boxed set
B19 models	Not available

Torque wrench settings

	lbf ft	Nm
Spark plugs:		
B14	13	18
B19	18	25

Part B: Electronic (breakerless) ignition system

Type

....	12V battery and coil, breakerless Hall effect distributor

Distributor

Make	Bosch
Direction of rotation	Clockwise
Dwell angle	62° ± 3°
Firing order	1 - 3 - 4 - 2 (No 1 cylinder nearest radiator)

Ignition timing

Dynamic at idle (vacuum hose disconnected):	
B19E	10° ± 2° BTDC

Spark plugs

	Type	Electrode gap
B19E	Champion RN7YCC	0.032 in (0.8 mm)
	Champion RN7YC	0.028 in (0.7 mm)

Torque wrench setting

	lbf ft	Nm
Spark plugs	18	25

Part C: Electronic (Renix) ignition system

Type

....	12V battery, fully electronic computerised system

Distributor

Make:	
B14	Ducellier
B172	Ducellier
B19	Bosch
B200	Bosch
Direction of rotation	Clockwise
Firing order:	
B14 and B172	1 - 3 - 4 - 2 (No 1 cylinder nearest flywheel)
B19 and B200	1 - 3 - 4 - 2 (No 1 cylinder nearest radiator)

Ignition timing

Dynamic at idle (vacuum hose disconnected):	
B14.3E	10° ± 2° BTDC
B14.4E	6° ± 2° BTDC
B14.4S	6° ± 2° BTDC
B172	6° BTDC
B19A	15° ± 2° BTDC
B200E	12° ± 2° BTDC
B200K	15° ± 2° BTDC

Spark plugs

		Type	Electrode gap
B14.4	....	Champion RN9YCC	0.032 in (0.8 mm)
		Champion RN9YC	0.028 in (0.7 mm)
B172	....	Champion RN7YCC	0.032 in (0.8 mm)
		Champion RN7YC	0.028 in (0.7 mm)
B19A	....	Champion RN9YCC	0.032 in (0.8 mm)
		Champion RN9YC	0.028 in (0.7 mm)
B200E	....	Champion RN7YCC	0.032 in (0.8 mm)
		Champion RN7YC	0.028 in (0.7 mm)
B200K	....	Champion RN9YCC	0.032 in (0.8 mm)
		Champion RN9YC	0.028 in (0.7 mm)

HT leads

B14	....	Champion LS 01, boxed set
B17 1985-on	....	Champion LS 20, boxed set

Torque wrench settings

Spark plugs:		lbf ft	Nm
B14	....	13	18
All other engines (except B172)	....	18	25
B172	....	22	30

Part A: Conventional ignition system

1 General description

The ignition system is conventional and comprises a 12 volt battery, coil, distributor and spark plugs. The distributor is driven by a skew gear on the camshaft. Correct running of the engine depends on a spark occurring at the spark plugs at exactly the right moment in relation to engine speed and load.

The ignition system is divided into two circuits, the low tension (LT) circuit, and the high tension (HT) circuit.

The low tension (sometimes known as the primary) circuit consists of the battery, lead to the ignition switch, lead from the ignition switch to the low tension or primary coil windings (terminal +), and the lead from the low tension coil windings (terminal -) to the contact breaker points and condenser in the distributor.

The high tension (or secondary) circuit consists of the high tension or secondary coil windings, the HT lead from the centre of the coil to the centre terminal of the distributor cap, the rotor arm, spark plug leads and spark plugs.

The system functions in the following manner. Low tension voltage in the coil produces an electromagnetic field around the secondary windings. When the contact breaker points separate, the collapse of the magnetic field induces a much higher voltage in the secondary windings which is fed via the distributor cap and carbon brush to the rotor arm. The rotor arm turns at half engine speed and releases the HT current to each of the four segments in the distributor cap as required. The current finally reaches the spark plug electrodes and the spark is produced.

The ignition advance is controlled both mechanically and by a vacuum operated system. The mechanical control comprises weights which move out from the distributor shaft under centrifugal force as the engine speed rises, and the distributor cam is thus rotated and the spark advanced. The weights are held in position by light springs, and it is the tension of these springs which controls the amount of advance.

The vacuum control consists of a diaphragm, one side of which is connected via a small pipe to the carburettor and the other side to the contact breaker plate. Depression in the inlet manifold and carburettor (which varies with engine speed and throttle opening) causes the diaphragm to move, thus advancing or retarding the spark.

The contact points on Ducellier distributors are of the self-cleaning type where the action of the vacuum advance moves the points in relation to each other, thus ensuring that the electrical contact occurs over a wide area of the contact points.

On B14 and B19A engines up to 1984, the conventional ignition system incorporates a ballast resistor which effectively increases the voltage available at the spark plugs during starting. On the B14 engine the resistor is of the thermistor type - initially the resistance is low so that full current flows, but this current causes a rise in temperature of the thermistor which increases the resistance and reduces the current for normal running. In the B19 engine a conventional ballast resistor is located in the circuit between the battery and the ignition coil - during starting a resistance-free circuit is supplied to the coil via the starter motor.

4

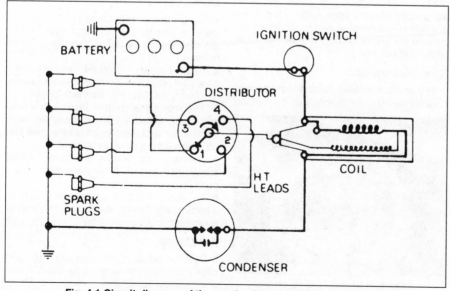

Fig. 4.1 Circuit diagram of the mechanical ignition system (Sec 1)

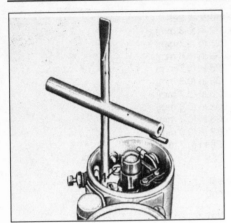

Fig. 4.2 Adjusting the contact breaker gap
on the Ducellier distributor using the
special tool (Sec 3)

1 Fixed contact securing screw

2 Routine maintenance

At the intervals laid down in the Routine
Maintenance Section at the beginning of this
manual, carry out the following operations:

Distributor

1 Renew the contact breaker points
(Section 4).
2 Check the contact breaker points dwell
angle (Section 3).
3 Lubricate the distributor (Section 3).

Spark plugs (Section 10)

4 Renew the spark plugs.

Ignition timing (Section 8)

5 Check the ignition timing.

3 Contact breaker points -
adjustment and lubrication

*Ducellier, AC Delco
and Bosch distributors*

1 To check the contact breaker gap, first

**3.4 Checking the contact breaker
points gap (Ducellier)**

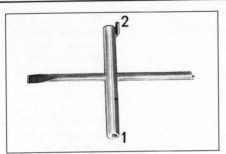

Fig. 4.3 Ducellier distributor
adjustment tool (Sec 3)

1 Vacuum cam adjustment
2 Vacuum toothed segment adjustment

remove the distributor cap by unclipping the
two springs, or removing the two screws.
2 Pull off the rotor arm.
3 Turn the crankshaft pulley bolt with a
spanner, until the heel of the movable contact
breaker is on the high point of the cam.
4 Insert a feeler gauge between the two
contact breaker points (photo) and check that
the gap is as given in the Specifications. If
adjustment is required, loosen the baseplate
securing screw and move the contact breaker
points until the correct feeler gauge blade is a
sliding fit between the points. Tighten the
screw and recheck the adjustment. If
available, use the special adjustment tool for
the Ducellier distributor (see Fig. 4.2)
obtainable from motor accessory shops.
5 Periodically, inject two or three drops of the
engine oil through the hole in the distributor
baseplate to lubricate the advance
mechanism.
6 Lubricate the cam with a thin film of lithium
based grease and apply one or two drops of
engine oil to the felt pad at the top of the
distributor shaft.
7 Refit the rotor and distributor cap.
8 Where a dwell meter is available, check the
contact points gap and dwell angle in
accordance with the Specifications and make
any final adjustments as previously described.
Reduce the points gap to increase the dwell
angle, and vice versa.

SEV distributor

*SEV distributors have cassette type contact
breaker points. The points gap cannot be*

**4.2 Contact breaker points on the
Ducellier distributor**

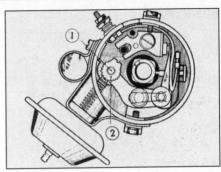

Fig. 4.4 Ducellier distributor contact points
showing cam (1) and segment (2)
locations (Sec 3)

*adjusted on these distributors. Adjust the
dwell angle as follows:*
9 Slide the plastic cover on the side of the
distributor to one side to uncover the
adjusting bolt.
10 Insert a 3 mm Allen key into the adjusting
bolt head.
11 Connect up a dwell angle meter to the
distributor in accordance with the
manufacturer's instructions, then start the
engine and allow it to idle.
12 Using the Allen key, adjust the dwell angle
to the specified value by turning the key
clockwise to increase, and anti-clockwise to
decrease, the angle.
13 On completion stop the engine, remove
the Allen key and refit the plastic cover.

Lubrication

14 Lubrication for the SEV distributor is as
given previously for the other distributors.

4 Contact breaker points -
renovation and renewal

Ducellier

1 Remove the distributor cap and rotor, and
prise the contact breaker points apart. If they
are discoloured or pitted, remove them as
follows.
2 Slide the spring clip off the moving contact
pivot post and carefully lift the contact breaker
arm and spring from the baseplate (photo).
3 Disconnect the ignition low tension lead
from the distributor, then unscrew the inner
terminal nut until the contact breaker lead can
be released from the inner terminal.
4 Unscrew and remove the fixed contact
retaining screw and lift the screw and contact
point from the baseplate.
5 Do not disturb the vacuum advance
serrated cam setting as this requires special
equipment to adjust correctly.

AC Delco

6 Remove the distributor cap and rotor, and
prise the contact breaker points apart. If they
are discoloured or pitted, remove them as
follows.

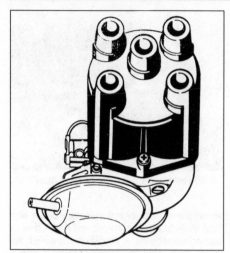

Fig. 4.5 AC Delco distributor cap (Sec 4)

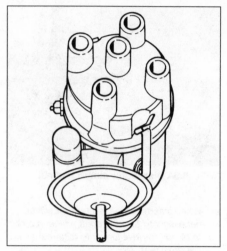

Fig. 4.6 Ducellier distributor cap (Sec 4)

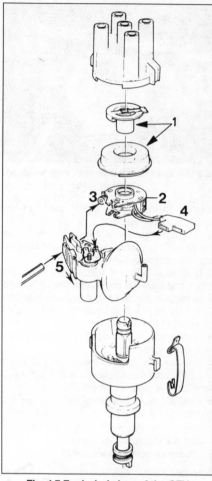

Fig. 4.7 Exploded view of the SEV distributor (Sec 4)

1 Rotor and condensation cover
2 Cassette points
3 Adjusting bolt
4 Connector
5 Plastic cover

7 Press the terminal end of the moving contact spring towards the centre of the distributor to release it from the terminal post insulator. Lift the moving contact point from its pivot post.

8 Prise the condenser and LT supply leads from the terminal post insulator, and remove the fixed contact retaining screw. Take care not to lose the small washer.

9 Lift the fixed contact from the pivot post and extract the square insulator by pressing the two ears together.

Bosch

10 Remove the distributor cap and rotor, and prise the contact breaker points apart. If they are discoloured or pitted, remove them as follows.

11 Remove the screw holding the points to the baseplate, disconnect the lead and lift the points from the distributor.

Ducellier, AC Delco and Bosch

12 Where only small pips or craters appear on the contact point surfaces, these may be removed by using an oilstone, but care should be taken to retain the original contour of the points. If the contact points are badly worn, they must be renewed.

13 Refitting is a reversal of removal but the following additional points should be noted:

a) *Thoroughly clean the contact points*
b) *Lubricate the moving contact pivot post with a little engine oil*
c) *Clean the baseplate with a fuel-moistened cloth to prevent the points being contaminated*
d) *Adjust the points gap as described in Section 3*

SEV

14 Remove the distributor cap, rotor arm and condensation cap.

15 Lift the vacuum unit assembly upward, then remove the contact breaker points cassette and unplug the connector.

16 The condenser can now be removed by disconnecting the earth cable and sliding the capacitor upward.

17 Lightly coat the lobes of the distributor driveshaft with grease.

18 Refit the condenser if this was removed and connect the earth lead.

19 Plug in the connector of the cassette points and fit the cassette to the vacuum unit.

20 Refit the vacuum unit to the distributor, fit the condensation cap, rotor arm and distributor cap.

21 Adjust the dwell angle as described in Section 3.

5 Condenser -
testing, removal and refitting

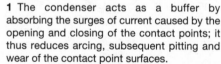

1 The condenser acts as a buffer by absorbing the surges of current caused by the opening and closing of the contact points; it thus reduces arcing, subsequent pitting and wear of the contact point surfaces.

2 Failure of the condenser will automatically affect the complete ignition circuit as the points will be prevented from functioning correctly.

Ducellier and AC Delco

3 One simple way to test the condenser is to switch on the ignition with the contact points closed, then separate them with a screwdriver blade. If this action is accompanied by a strong blue flash, a faulty condenser is indicated. Difficult starting, misfiring and discoloured points are other indications of a faulty condenser.

4 To remove the condenser on the Ducellier distributor, unscrew and remove the nut and detach the ignition lead from the distributor terminal. Remove the inner nut and condenser lead. Remove the retaining screw and washers and withdraw the condenser.

5 To remove the condenser on the AC Delco distributor, remove the moving contact as described in Section 4, disconnect the lead from the terminal post insulator, and remove the condenser retaining screw, noting that the earth lead is fitted beneath the screw. Withdraw the condenser.

6 Refitting is a reversal of removal.

SEV

7 Removal and refitting of the condenser is covered in Section 4.

Bosch

8 Disconnect the electrical leads and remove the screw securing the condenser to the side of the distributor. Refit in the reverse order to removal.

6 Distributor -
removal and refitting

1 Before removing the distributor it is helpful to mark the distributor housing position

4

6.3 Ducellier distributor with cap removed, showing rotor

6.5A Distributor clamp and nut

6.5B Removing the distributor (Ducellier)

relative to the engine block; use a centre punch or touch-up paint.

2 Turn the engine until the timing marks (see Section 8) are aligned, with No 1 piston at the top of its compression stroke.

3 Disconnect the HT leads from the spark plugs and from the centre terminal of the coil, then remove the distributor cap and note that the rotor is pointing towards the No 1 HT segment of the cap (photo).

4 Disconnect the LT ignition lead from the distributor terminal.

5 Unscrew and remove the nut and withdraw the distributor clamp plate; the distributor can now be lifted from its recess (photos).

6 Refitting is a reversal of removal but the following additional points should be noted:

a) When inserting the distributor it will be necessary to turn the shaft a little in order to bring the drive lugs into alignment with the drivegear

b) Adjust the ignition timing (see Section 8)

c) Any difficulty encountered in refitting the distributor correctly, or timing the ignition, may be due to incorrect installation of the drivegear (see Chapter 1)

7 Distributor - dismantling and reassembly

1 The distributor is designed to operate without the need for major dismantling, and

when wear does eventually take place at a high mileage it is recommended that a new or reconditioned unit is obtained. However, for those who wish to dismantle and repair a faulty or worn distributor, the following points are given as a guide.

2 Check that spare parts are available before starting work.

3 On the Ducellier distributor note the position of the serrated cam in relation to the vacuum diaphragm spring connection as this affects the vacuum advance characteristics. If necessary, the distributor should be taken to a suitably equipped garage or auto electrician to have the setting checked.

4 The mainshaft on most distributors can be removed after driving out the drive dog retaining pin.

5 Where possible mark items in relation to each other to ensure correct reassembly, in particular the drive dog and mainshaft.

8 Ignition timing - adjustment

Note: *Up until 1982 the ignition timing marks on the flywheel signify 0, 3 and 6 degrees. After 1982 they signify 0, 6 and 10 degrees.*

B14 models

One of two methods may be used to check the ignition timing; with a test bulb or with a stroboscopic timing light. Of these two methods the stroboscopic timing light is the more accurate.

Test bulb

1 Connect a 12 volt test lamp and leads between a good earth and the distributor LT terminal.

2 Rotate the crankshaft with a spanner on the pulley bolt in the normal direction of rotation, until No 1 piston (furthest from radiator) starts its compression stroke; this can be ascertained by removing No 1 spark plug and feeling the compression being generated with the finger.

3 Disconnect the HT lead from the coil.

4 Continue turning the crankshaft until the correct timing marks are in alignment. The timing marks are on the flywheel periphery,

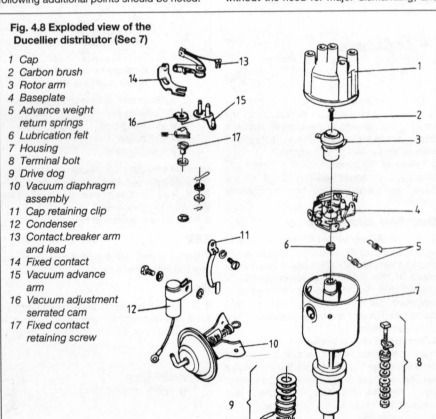

Fig. 4.8 Exploded view of the Ducellier distributor (Sec 7)

1 Cap
2 Carbon brush
3 Rotor arm
4 Baseplate
5 Advance weight return springs
6 Lubrication felt
7 Housing
8 Terminal bolt
9 Drive dog
10 Vacuum diaphragm assembly
11 Cap retaining clip
12 Condenser
13 Contact breaker arm and lead
14 Fixed contact
15 Vacuum advance arm
16 Vacuum adjustment serrated cam
17 Fixed contact retaining screw

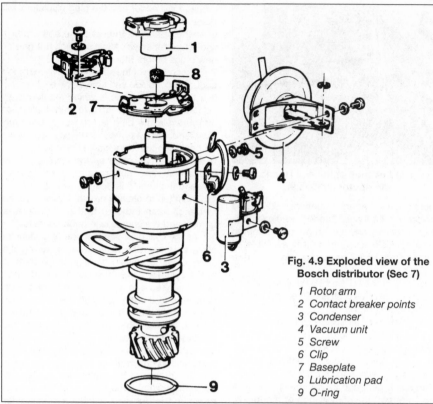

Fig. 4.9 Exploded view of the
Bosch distributor (Sec 7)

1 Rotor arm
2 Contact breaker points
3 Condenser
4 Vacuum unit
5 Screw
6 Clip
7 Baseplate
8 Lubrication pad
9 O-ring

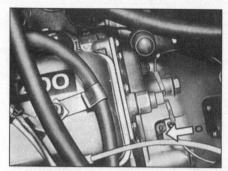

Fig. 4.10 Flywheel timing mark visible
through clutch housing aperture (Sec 8)

16 A similar check can be made on the vacuum advance by refitting the vacuum pipe and observing the additional advance.

17 When completed, remove the timing light and ensure that the spark plug and vacuum pipe connections are secure.

B19 models

18 The ignition timing procedure is similar to that described for B14 models, but note that No 1 cylinder is nearest the radiator.

19 There are timing marks on the front of the engine as well as on the flywheel (photo). These can be viewed from the left-hand side of the engine after removing the ducting from the top of the radiator.

20 On some engines an ignition timing indicator is fitted for use in conjunction with test equipment which only a Volvo dealer will have, therefore it is suggested that the strobe light method of timing be used. The timing indicator is not fitted to later models (photo).

and should be aligned with the cutaway on the clutch housing at the rear of the engine (photo). Refer to Specifications for the correct timing applicable to each model. On later models it is marked on the HT lead (photo).

5 Loosen the distributor clamp and switch on the ignition.

6 If the test lamp is on, turn the distributor slightly clockwise until it goes out.

7 Turn the distributor anti-clockwise until the test lamp *just* lights up then tighten the clamp.

8 Test the setting by turning the engine a complete turn and noting when the lamp glows.

9 Switch off the ignition, remove the test lamp, and refit the HT lead to the coil.

Stroboscopic timing light

10 Disconnect the vacuum pipe from the distributor and plug its end with a pencil or similar object.

11 To make subsequent operations easier, it is advisable to mark the timing marks with chalk or white paint.

12 Connect the timing light in accordance with the manufacturer's instructions (usually interposed between the end of No 1 spark plug HT lead and No 1 spark plug terminal).

13 Start the engine and make sure that the idling speed is as specified (Chapter 3).

14 Point the timing light at the timing marks, and they will appear to be stationary. The correct marks should be in alignment, but if this is not the case, loosen the distributor clamp and turn it one way or the other until the setting is correct. Tighten the clamp and check the adjustment again.

15 With the timing light still connected, a check can be made on the operation of the advance mechanism by momentarily increasing the engine speed. The flywheel mark will advance in relation to the fixed point if the mechanism is working correctly.

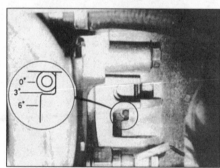

8.4A Flywheel timing marks

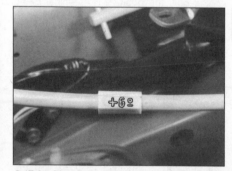

8.4B Ignition timing reference - later models

8.19 Ignition timing marks on the front of
the B19 engine

8.20 Ignition setting indicator on
early B19 engines

4

9.1 Coil location on later models

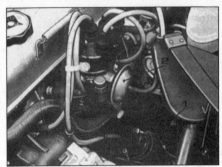

Fig. 4.11 Location of the coil (1) and the distributor (2) (Sec 9)

9 Coil - description

On early models the coil is bolted to the left-hand side of the cylinder block below the distributor. On later models it is bolted to the left-hand bulkhead (photo).

Accurate testing of the coil requires specialised equipment and is therefore best left to an auto-electrician. Alternatively, if it is thought to be faulty, a new coil should be fitted and a comparison made with the original unit.

Besides periodically cleaning the coil there is little that can be done in the way of maintenance. Make sure the low tension (LT) leads are connected to their correct terminals; failure to do this can result in a 60% loss of efficiency. The LT wire from the distributor must be connected to the negative (-) terminal on the coil, the positive (+) terminal being connected to the ignition switch lead.

10 Spark plugs and HT leads - general

1 The correct functioning of the spark plugs is vital for the correct running and efficiency of the engine. It is essential that the plugs fitted are appropriate for the engine, and the suitable type is specified at the beginning of this chapter. If this type is used and the engine is in good condition, the spark plugs should not need attention between scheduled replacement intervals. Spark plug cleaning is rarely necessary and should not be attempted unless specialised equipment is available as damage can easily be caused to the firing ends.

2 Disconnect the HT leads by pulling them off the spark plug. Pull on the rubber cap, not on the lead itself (photo).

3 Use a brush or air line to clean around the spark plug recess (photo).

4 Use a long reach socket to remove each plug in turn. Where access is difficult, use an extension bar with a universal joint (photo).

5 The spark plug gap is of prime importance as, if incorrect, the combustion of the fuel/air mixture within the engine will be seriously impaired. The gap should be measured with a feeler gauge, and if adjustment is necessary, the outer electrode must be bent accordingly. Never bend the centre electrode otherwise

damage will occur and the plug insulation will break down (photo).

6 At the specified intervals the spark plugs should be renewed. Always check the gap of new plugs before fitting them.

7 The condition of the spark plugs will tell much about the condition and tune of the engine.

8 If the insulator nose is white in colour with no deposits, a weak mixture is indicated, or alternatively the plug is too hot (a hot plug transfers heat away from the electrode slowly - a cold plug transfers it away quickly).

9 Black soot deposits on the insulator nose indicate a rich mixture and, if oil is also present, the engine is likely to be well worn.

10 Light tan to greyish brown deposits on the insulator nose indicate that the mixture is correct and the engine is in good condition.

11 As the cylinder head is made of aluminium alloy, care must be taken when installing the spark plugs to prevent damage to the threads in the cylinder head (see Haynes Hint). It is recommended that a little engine oil or grease is applied to the threads, and the spark plugs are screwed in as far as possible with the fingers. Finally tighten the spark plugs to the specified torque (photo).

12 Wipe the HT leads occasionally with a rag and always connect them in the correct order.

13 The interior of the distributor cap should be periodically wiped clean and the carbon brush on the Ducellier distributor checked for freedom of movement; it should return to its original position after being depressed into the cap against the spring. At the same time check that the HT leads are fully entered into the distributor cap terminals.

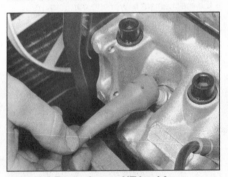

10.2 Removing an HT lead from a spark plug

10.3 Brushing out the spark plug recess

10.4 Removing the spark plug

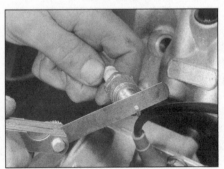

10.5 Checking the electrode gap with feeler gauges

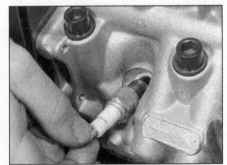

10.11 Fitting a spark plug

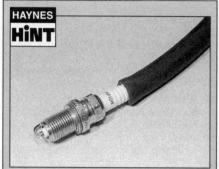

HAYNES HINT

It is very often difficult to insert spark plugs into their holes without cross-threading them. To avoid this possibility, fit a short length of 5/16 inch internal diameter rubber hose over the end of the spark plug. The flexible hose acts as a universal joint to help align the plug with the plug hole. Should the plug begin to cross-thread, the hose will slip on the spark plug, preventing thread damage to the cylinder head.

11 Ignition system - fault finding

By far the majority of breakdown and running troubles are caused by faults in the ignition system, either in the low tension or high tension circuits.

There are two main symptoms indicating ignition faults. Either the engine will not start or fire, or the engine is difficult to start and misfires. If it is a regular misfire, ie the engine is running on only two or three cylinders, the fault is almost sure to be in the secondary or high tension circuit. If the misfiring is intermittent, the fault could be in either the high or low tension circuits. If the car stops suddenly, or will not start at all, it is likely that the fault is in the low tension circuit. Loss of power and overheating, apart from faulty carburation settings, are normally due to faults in the distributor or to incorrect ignition timing.

12 Fault finding - engine fails to start

1 If the engine fails to start and the car was running normally when it was last used, first check that there is fuel in the petrol tank. If the engine turns over normally on the starter motor and the battery is evidently well charged, then the fault may be in either the high or low tension circuits. First check the HT circuit. If the battery is known to be fully charged, the ignition light comes on, and the starter motor fails to turn the engine, check the tightness of the leads on the battery terminals and also the

secureness of the earth lead to its connection to the body. It is quite common for the leads to have worked loose even if they look and feel secure. If one of the battery terminal posts gets very hot when trying to work the starter motor this is a sure indication of a faulty connection to that terminal.

2 One of the commonest reasons for bad starting is wet or damp spark plug leads and distributor. Remove the distributor cap. If condensation is visible internally, dry the cap with a rag and also wipe over the leads. Refit the cap. A moisture dispersant can be very effective in these situations.

3 If the engine still fails to start, check that the current is reaching the plugs by disconnecting each plug lead in turn at the spark plug end, and holding the end of the cable about 3/16 inch (5 mm) away from the cylinder block. Spin the engine on the starter motor.

4 Sparking between the end of the cable and the block should be fairly strong with a good, regular blue spark. (Hold the lead with rubber to avoid electric shocks.) If current is reaching the plugs then remove them and clean and regap them. The engine should now start.

5 If there is no spark at the plug leads, take off the HT lead from the centre of the distributor cap and hold it to the block as before. Spin the engine on the starter once more. A rapid succession of blue sparks between the end of the lead and the block indicates that the coil is in order and that the distributor cap is cracked, the rotor arm faulty, or the carbon brush in the top of the distributor cap is not making good contact with the rotor arm. Possibly, the points are in bad condition. Renew them as described in Section 4.

6 If there are no sparks from the end of the lead from the coil, check the connections at the coil end of the lead. If it is in order start checking the low tension circuit.

7 Use a 12V voltmeter or a 12V bulb and two lengths of wire. With the ignition switched on and the points open, test between the low tension wire to the coil (if it is marked SW or +) and earth. No reading indicates a break in the supply from the ignition switch. Check the connections at the switch to see if any are loose. Refit them and the engine should run. A reading shows a faulty coil or condenser, or broken lead between the coil and the distributor.

8 Take the condenser wire off the points assembly, and with the points open test between the moving point and earth. If there is now a reading then the fault is in the condenser. Fit a new one as described in this Chapter, Section 5, and the fault should clear.

9 With no reading from the moving point to earth, take a reading between earth and the CB or negative (-) terminal of the coil. A reading here shows a broken wire which will need to be renewed between the coil and distributor. No reading confirms that the coil has failed and must be renewed, after which the engine will run once more. Remember to

refit the condenser wire to the points assembly. For these tests it is sufficient to separate the points with a piece of dry paper while testing with the points open.

13 Fault finding - engine misfires

1 If the engine misfires regularly, run it at fast idling speed. Pull off each of the plug caps in turn and listen to the note of the engine. Hold the plug cap in a dry cloth or with a rubber glove as additional protection against a shock from the HT supply.

2 No difference in engine running will be noticed when the lead from the defective circuit is removed. Removing the lead from one of the good cylinders will accentuate the misfire.

3 Remove the plug lead from the end of the defective plug and hold it about 3/16 inch (5 mm) away from the block. Restart the engine. If the sparking is fairly strong and regular the fault must lie in the spark plug.

4 The plug may be loose, the insulation may be cracked, or the electrodes may have burnt away, giving too wide a gap for the spark to jump. Worse still, one of the electrodes may have broken off.

5 If there is no spark at the end of the plug lead, or if it is weak and intermittent, check the ignition lead from the distributor to the plug. If the insulation is cracked or perished, renew the lead. Check the connections at the distributor cap.

6 If there is still no spark, examine the distributor cap carefully for tracking. This can be recognised by a very thin black line running between two or more electrodes, or between an electrode and some other part of the distributor. These lines are paths which now conduct electricity across the cap thus letting it run to earth. The only answer is a new distributor cap.

7 Apart from the ignition timing being incorrect, other causes of misfiring have already been dealt with under the section dealing with the failure of the engine to start. To recap these are that:

a) *The coil may be faulty giving an intermittent misfire*

b) *There may be a damaged wire or loose connection in the low tension circuit*

c) *The condenser may be short circuiting*

d) *There may be a mechanical fault in the distributor (broken driving spindle or contact breaker spring)*

8 If the ignition timing is too far retarded, it should be noted that the engine will tend to overheat, and there will be quite a noticeable drop in power. If the engine is overheating and the power is down, and the ignition timing is correct, then the carburettor should be checked, as it is likely that this is where the fault lies.

4

Part B: Electronic (breakerless) ignition system

14 General description

The breakerless electronic ignition system fitted to B19E fuel injection engines is of the Hall Inductive Capacitor type, where a Hall transmitter replaces the contact breaker points and a control unit is used for switching the coil primary circuit. The transmitter consists of a slotted rotor and permanent magnet, both in the distributor, and as the engine turns, electrical impulses are produced which are used in the control unit to switch the primary circuit (photos).

⚠️ *Warning: High tension voltages produced by electronic ignition systems can be very much higher than in normal systems. Extra care and precautions should be taken when working on these systems. If HT current is allowed to jump across a gap of more then 0.80 in (20 mm) (such as when checking for a spark between an HT lead and the cylinder head) permanent damage can be caused to the control unit. Care should also be taken to ensure that sparks do not arc across the control unit housing.*

14.1A Distributor location on the B19E engine

14.1B The Hall effect slotted rotor in the distributor on B19E engines

15 Routine maintenance

At the intervals laid down in the Routine Maintenance Section at the beginning of this manual, carry out the following operations:

Spark plugs (Section 10)

Renew the spark plugs.

Ignition timing (Section 16)

Check the ignition timing.

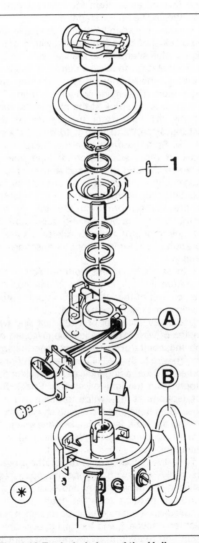

Fig. 4.12 Exploded view of the Hall sensor on the electronic distributor fitted to B19E engines (Sec 16)

1 *Locking key*
A *Hall transmitter*
B *Vacuum governor*
* *Timing mark*

16 Servicing and overhaul

General note: *As there are no moving contacts there is no contact breaker gap to set, neither can the ignition timing be set by the static method, described in Section 8. Ignition timing should be set using the strobe method.*

Distributor - removal and refitting

1 Remove the distributor cap and disconnect the wiring.
2 Disconnect the vacuum hose and low tension lead.
3 Remove the rotor arm, withdraw the condensation cover, then temporarily refit the rotor arm.
4 Turn the engine until the rotor arm is aligned with the line on the distributor rim.
5 Mark the distributor body in relation to the cylinder block, so that it is refitted in the same position.
6 Remove the screw securing the distributor to the cylinder block and withdraw the distributor.
7 Refit in the reverse order, on completion adjusting the ignition timing as described in paragraph 9.

Distributor - overhaul

8 An exploded view of the distributor appears in Fig. 4.12. Remove the parts in the sequence shown, being careful not to lose the locking key (1). On reassembly, ensure that the Hall transmitter (A) engages correctly with the spindle of the vacuum governor.

Ignition timing

9 As described earlier, the ignition timing can only be set using the strobe method (Section 8). If the timing should need adjusting, loosen the distributor securing screw and turn the distributor in its housing, either clockwise or anti-clockwise to bring the timing marks on the flywheel into alignment. Tighten the screw on completion.

17 Coil, spark plugs and HT leads - general

Refer to Sections 9 and 10 (photo).

18 Fault finding - electronic (breakerless) ignition

1 The B19E ignition system consists of three components, as indicated in Fig. 4.13.
2 If the engine refuses to start, remove the

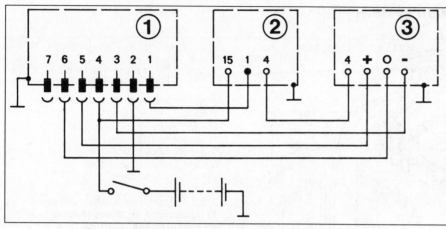

Fig. 4.13 Wiring diagram of the electronic ignition system fitted to the B19E engines (Sec 18)

1 Control unit   2 Ignition coil   3 Distributor

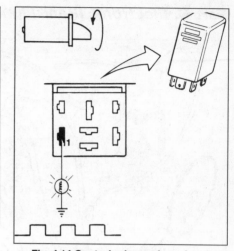

Fig. 4.14 Control relay and number 1 terminal (Sec 18)

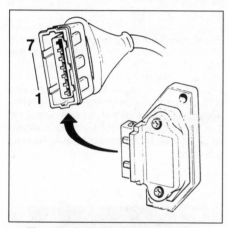

Fig. 4.15 Control unit and multi-plug connector (Sec 18)

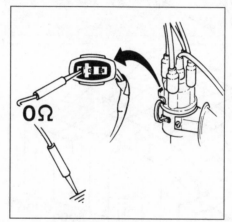

Fig. 4.16 Connector and terminal at distributor (Sec 18)

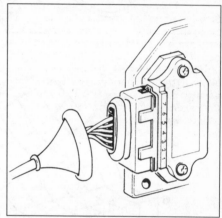

Fig. 4.17 Connector at control unit with rubber boot pulled away (Sec 18)

4

17.1 Ignition coil on the B19E engine

control relay from the fuel injection system and connect a voltmeter between terminal 1 of the connector and a good earth.

3 Attempt to restart the engine. If a response is seen on the voltmeter, the fault lies in the fuel injection system. If the voltmeter shows no response, the fault is in the ignition system. Remove the voltmeter and refit the relay.

4 Remove the connector from the control unit and connect an ohmmeter between terminal 2 of the connector and a good earth. There should be no resistance, in which case proceed to the next paragraph. If there is resistance, the fault lies somewhere in the cable.

5 Measure the resistance between terminals 1 and 4 which should be 0.7 to 0.8 ohms. If the resistance is not as specified, the ignition coil is defective. If the resistance shows infinity, the cable and/or the coil is defective.

6 Connect a voltmeter between terminal 1 and earth, and then between terminal 4 and earth. With the ignition switched on, a reading of 12 volts should be recorded on both terminals. If there is no reading then the cable is faulty.

7 Using an ohmmeter, measure the resistance between terminal 1 of the connector and the HT terminal on the ignition coil. The resistance should be 7.7 kilo-ohms. If different, the coil is defective and if infinity is recorded then the cable and/or the coil is defective.

8 Refit the connector to the control unit and disconnect the cable from the distributor, then using the ohmmeter measure the resistance between earth and the terminal on the distributor as shown in Fig. 4.16. The resistance should be zero ohm. If infinity is recorded the fault lies in the cable or contacts, or the control unit is defective.

9 Refit the connector and pull the rubber boot away from the control unit connector. Connect a voltmeter between terminal 5 (reached from the rear of the connector) and earth. Switch on the ignition and the voltage should be 11.5 volts. If different the control unit is defective and should be renewed.

10 Connect the voltmeter between terminal 6 and earth in the same way as above. Remove the distributor cap and then, using a spanner on the crankshaft pulley, slowly turn the engine. Each time a flange of the rotor passes the Hall transmitter, 8 volts should be recorded on the voltmeter. When a gap in the rotor passes the transmitter the voltage should virtually disappear. If this is not so the Hall transmitter is defective.

Part C: Electronic (Renix) ignition system

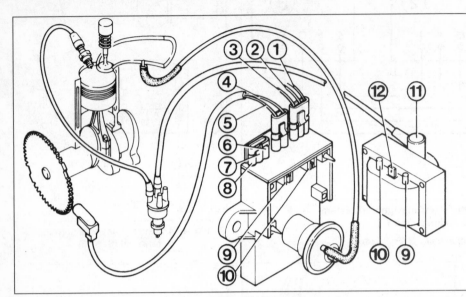

Fig. 4.18 Renix electronic ignition system (Sec 19)

1 Rev counter wire
2 Earth
3 Supply wire
4 Sensor module (red)
5 Sensor module (white)
6 Earth (certain models only)
7 Earth (certain models only)
8 Not used
9 and 10 Ignition coil, primary winding
11 Ignition coil, secondary winding
12 Radio interference suppression

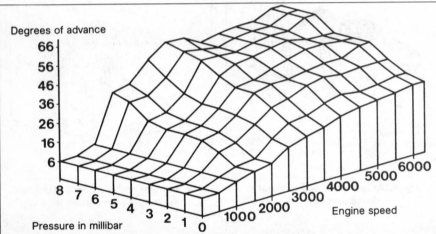

Fig. 4.19 Renix ignition timing chart (Sec 19)

plug, via the distributor in the conventional way. The function of the centrifugal and vacuum advance mechanisms, as well as the contact breaker points normally associated with a distributor, are all catered for by the computer module, so that the sole purpose of the distributor is to direct the the HT voltage from the coil to the appropriate spark plug (photos).

19 General description

The Renix fully electronic computerised ignition system is fitted to all carburettor models from 1984. It is also fitted to B200E fuel injection models.

The system consists of three main components, namely the computer module which incorporates an ignition coil and a vacuum advance unit, the distributor which directs the HT voltage received from the coil to the appropriate spark plug, and an angular position sensor which determines the position and speed of the crankshaft by sensing special magnetic segments in the flywheel.

The computer module receives information on crankshaft position relative to TDC and also engine speed from the angular position sensor, and receives information on engine

load from the vacuum advance unit. From these constantly changing variables, the computer calculates the precise instant at which HT voltage should be supplied and triggers the coil accordingly. The voltage then passes from the coil to the appropriate spark

19.1A Distributor location at rear of cylinder head on B172 engines

19.1B Angular sensor on clutch bellhousing (arrowed)

19.1C Control unit (B14/19 shown)

23.2 Distributor cap retaining screws on the B172 engine (arrowed)

23.3 Removing the rotor from the camshaft on B172 engines

23.4A Distributor with cap removed on B14/19 engines . . .

20 Routine maintenance

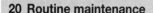

The only components of the electronic ignition system which require periodic maintenance are the distributor cap, HT leads and spark plugs. These should be treated in the same way as on a conventional system and reference should be made to Section 10.

On this system dwell angle and ignition timing are a function of the computer module and there is no provision for adjustment. It is possible to check the ignition timing using a stroboscopic timing light, but this should only be necessary as part of a fault finding procedure, as any deviation from the specified setting would indicate a possible fault in the computer module.

21 Spark plugs and HT leads - general

Refer to Section 10.

22 Electronic ignition system - precautions

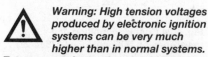

Warning: High tension voltages produced by electronic ignition systems can be very much higher than in normal systems. Extra care and attention should be taken when working on these systems. If HT current is allowed to jump across a gap of more than 0.80 in (20 mm) (such as when checking for a spark between an HT lead and the cylinder head - see Section 27 paragraph 11), permanent damage can be caused to the control unit. Care should also be taken to ensure that sparks do not arc across the control unit.

Due to the sophisticated nature of the electronic ignition system the following precautions must be observed to prevent damage to the components and reduce the risk of personal injury.

23.4B . . . and with the rotor and condensation cover removed

1 Ensure the ignition is switched off before disconnecting any of the ignition wiring.
2 Ensure that the ignition is switched off before connecting or disconnecting any ignition test equipment such as a timing light.
3 Do not connect a suppression condenser or test lamp to the ignition coil negative terminal.
4 Do not connect any test appliance or stroboscopic timing light requiring a 12 volt supply to the ignition coil positive terminal.
5 Do not allow an HT lead to short out or spark against the computer module body.

23 Distributor - removal and refitting

1 On B172 models the distributor is driven directly from the camshaft and is mounted on the rear of the cylinder head.
2 To remove the distributor cap, remove the three screws (photo) and withdraw the cap.
3 The rotor arm is fitted directly to the camshaft and pulls off (photo).
4 On other models the procedure is similar to that for conventional models (photos), described in Section 6.
5 Refitting is a reversal of removal.

24 Ignition timing - checking and adjustment

It is not possible to adjust the ignition timing with the Renix system, but the timing can be

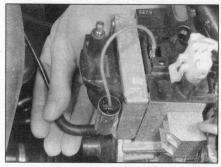

24.1 Vacuum hose connection on the control unit (B172 shown)

checked using the strobe light method described in Section 8. The vacuum hose from the control unit should be disconnected and plugged during the check (photo).

25 Control unit - removal and refitting

1 The control unit is located as shown in Fig. 4.20 on B14 and B19 models, and on B172 models it is bolted to the left-hand chassis member in the engine bay (as viewed from the driver's seat).
2 To remove the unit, disconnect the multi-plugs, the ignition coil lead and the vacuum hose.
3 Remove the two bolts securing the unit and lift it from the engine bay.

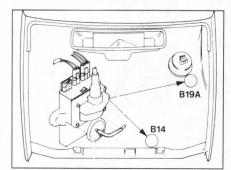

Fig. 4.20 Location of the control unit on B14 and B19 models (Sec 25)

4

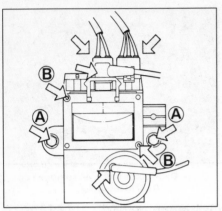

Fig. 4.21 Control unit securing bolts (A) and the coil-to-control unit bolts (B) (Sec 25)

4 The ignition coil can be removed from the control unit by removing the two bolts.

5 Refitting is a reversal of removal. *Caution: Do not try to remove the vacuum unit from the control unit, or internal wires connecting it to the circuitry will be damaged.*

26 Angular position sensor - removal and refitting

1 Disconnect the battery negative terminal.
2 Disconnect the smaller of the two multi-plugs on the control unit.
3 Remove the two bolts securing the sensor to the top of the clutch bellhousing, and lift the sensor clear. Note that the bolts are of the shouldered type and should not be replaced by ordinary bolts.
4 Refitting is a reversal of removal.

27 Fault finding - Renix ignition system

1 First check that the wiring and connectors are securely fitted and not damaged. Also check that the spark plugs and distributor rotor arm are in good condition.
2 If the engine will not start, follow paragraphs 3 to 11.
3 Disconnect plug A (Fig. 4.22) from the

ignition control unit and connect a voltmeter between terminal 3 and earth. Switch on the ignition and spin the engine on the starter. A minimum of 9.5 volts should be registered.
4 Switch off the ignition and connect an ohmmeter between terminal 2 and earth. Zero ohm should be registered,
5 Disconnect plug B (Fig. 4.23) and connect the ohmmeter between terminals 4 and 5. The resistance of the sensor module should be 220 ± 60 ohm. If not, renew the sensor.
6 Disconnect the HT lead then unbolt the ignition coil using an Allen key. Check that the coil terminals are clean, then use the ohmmeter to check that the resistance between terminals 3 and 9 is zero ohm. If higher, renew the control unit.
7 Reconnect plugs A and B then connect a 12 volt test lamp (4 watt minimum) between terminals 9 and 10 on the control unit. Spin the engine on the starter motor and check that the test lamp flashes. If not, renew the control unit.
8 Using the ohmmeter, check the ignition coil secondary winding resistance between terminals 9 and 11. Renew the coil if the resistance is not 4000 ± 1500 ohm.
9 Check the ignition coil primary winding resistance between terminals 9 and 10. Renew the coil if the resistance is not 0.6 ± 0.2 ohm.
10 Refit the ignition coil and HT lead.
11 Disconnect the coil HT lead from the distributor cap and hold it approximately 20 mm (0.8 in) from the cylinder head with **well insulated pliers**. Spin the engine on the starter and check that there are strong HT sparks. If not, renew the control unit.

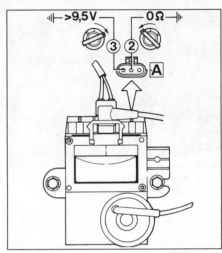

Fig. 4.22 Checking plug A supply on the control unit (Sec 27)

12 If the engine is difficult to start, or runs erratically, follow paragraphs 13 to 15.
13 Carry out the procedure in paragraphs 3, 4 and 5, then reconnect plugs A and B.
14 Connect a tachometer to the engine then disconnect the vacuum hose from the diaphragm unit. Run the engine at 2500 rpm and check that when the hose is reconnected the engine speed increases. If not, renew the control unit complete with diaphragm unit. Switch off the engine.
15 Check the ignition timing, as described in Section 24 and if not as given in Specifications, renew the control unit.

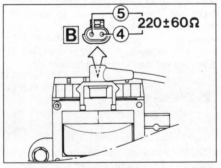

Fig. 4.23 Checking plug B (sensor module) resistance (Sec 27)

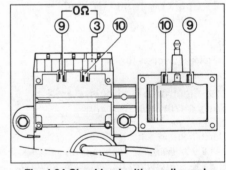

Fig. 4.24 Checking ignition coil supply resistance on the control unit (Sec 27)

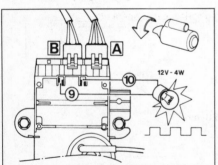

Fig. 4.25 Using a test lamp to check the control unit (Sec 27)

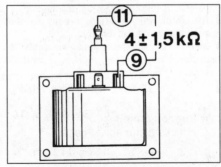

Fig. 4.26 Checking the ignition coil secondary winding resistance (Sec 27)

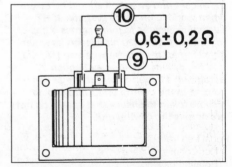

Fig. 4.27 Checking the coil primary winding resistance (Sec 27)

Chapter 5
Clutch

Contents

Degrees of difficulty

Easy, suitable for novice with little experience	Fairly easy, suitable for beginner with some experience	Fairly difficult, suitable for competent DIY mechanic	Difficult, suitable for experienced DIY mechanic	Very difficult, suitable for expert DIY or professional

Specifications

Part A: Automatic transmission models

General

Type	Centrifugal, single dry plate
Clutch plate diameter	7.15 in (181.6 mm)
Minimum clutch plate lining thickness	0.04 in (1.0 mm)
Engagement speed	1050 to 1150 rpm at zero torque
Declutching servo fork clearance	0.04 to 0.06 in (1.0 to 1.5 mm)

Torque wrench settings

	lbf ft	Nm
Clutch cover bolts	15	20
Clutch housing bolts	33	45
Bearing housing nuts	18	24

Part B: Manual transmission models

General

Type	Single dry plate, diaphragm spring, cable operated
Clutch plate diameter:	
B14 and B172	7.48 in (190 mm)
B19 and B200	8.47 in (215 mm)
Thrust bearing type:	
Models up to 1981	Self-centring, non-rotating
Models from 1981	Self-centring, rotating
Release fork clearance:	
Non-rotating bearing	0.118 to 0.197 in (3.0 to 5.0 mm)
Rotating bearing	Nil
Pedal free travel:	
Non-rotating bearing	0.55 in (14.0 mm)
Rotating bearing	Nil
Pedal height (models with rotating bearing):	
All models	5.9 ± 0.04 in (150 ± 10 mm)

5

Torque wrench settings

	lbf ft	Nm
Clutch cover bolts	17	23
Clutch housing bolts:		
B14 and B172	33	45
B19 and B200	44	60
Bearing housing nuts (B14 and B172)	18	24
Propeller shaft (B14 and B172)	27	37
Torque tube to clutch housing (B19 and B200)	35	47
Clutch pedal pivot pin	7	10

Part A: Automatic transmission models

1 General description

The clutch is of centrifugal type, incorporating three rollers which act as centrifugal weights to engage the clutch. The clutch plate is located between the flywheel and clutch cover pressure plate, and when the engine speed is increased from idling, the rollers move outwards and force the pressure plate against the friction plate.

A declutching servo mechanism is attached to the clutch housing (photo). This effectively raises the engagement speed of the clutch to allow the transmission selector lever to be moved to positions R or D. The servo is operated by a microswitch in the selector lever, which activates a vacuum valve connected to the engine inlet manifold; the servo is also operative with the lever in positions N and P regardless of whether the lever is being moved. With the selector lever in position R or D without being held, clutch engagement occurs at the normal lower engine speed.

2 Clutch - removal and refitting

1 Disconnect the negative lead from the battery.
2 Unscrew the two top bolts from the clutch housing and remove the drain hose from the heater air intake unit.
3 Jack up the front of the car and support it on axle stands.
4 Unscrew and remove the nuts and washers, and remove the front exhaust clamp from the exhaust pipe.
5 Remove the engine splash guards.
6 Remove the starter motor (see Chapter 10), and, on early models, move the exhaust bracket forwards.
7 Remove the screws and withdraw the heat shield (if fitted) from above the silencer.
8 Spray the clutch and pinion shafts with a penetrating oil, then push the propeller shaft to the rear as far as it will go and detach it from the clutch shaft. Slide it forwards, remove it from the transmission pinion shaft, and withdraw the propeller shaft from the car.
9 Pull the vacuum hose from the clutch servo unit.
10 Unscrew the nuts and bolts and remove the guard plate from the front of the clutch housing.
11 Using a trolley jack and a block of wood, support the engine beneath the sump.
12 Unscrew and remove the nuts and bolts

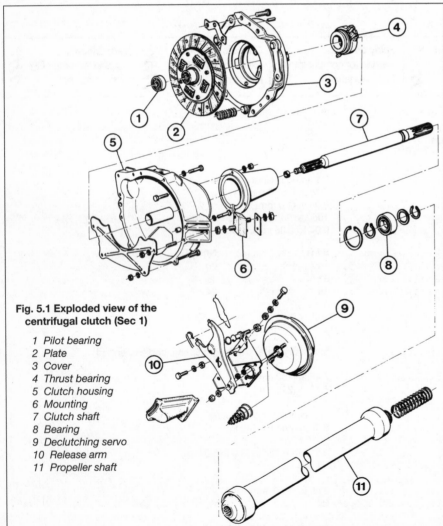

Fig. 5.1 Exploded view of the centrifugal clutch (Sec 1)

1 Pilot bearing
2 Plate
3 Cover
4 Thrust bearing
5 Clutch housing
6 Mounting
7 Clutch shaft
8 Bearing
9 Declutching servo
10 Release arm
11 Propeller shaft

1.1 Declutching servo on an automatic transmission model

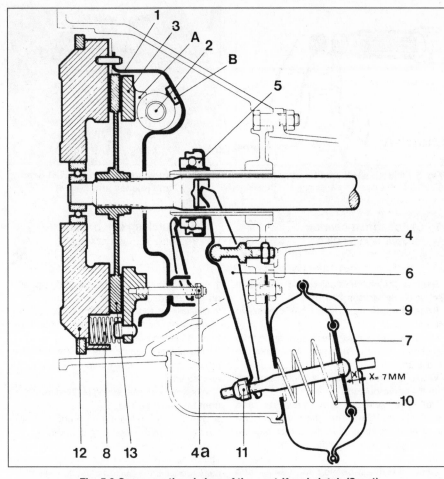

Fig. 5.2 Cross-sectional view of the centrifugal clutch (Sec 1)

1 Cover	5 Thrust bearing	11 Adjusting nut
2 Centrifugal weight spindle and cylinder	6 Release arm	12 Flywheel
3 Pressure plate	7 Declutching servo	13 Clutch plate
4 Thrust fingers	8 Return spring	A Spindle contact surface
4a Support post	9 Diaphragm	B Cylinder contact surface
	10 Spring	

the same time, note the location and amount of shims fitted beneath the cover, and the location of the three return springs.

16 Clean the surfaces of the flywheel and pressure plate, and examine them for excessive scoring. If evident, the pressure plate and/or flywheel should be renewed, although in the case of the flywheel it may be possible to have it refaced by a competent engineering firm.

17 Renew the clutch plate if the linings are worn down to or near the rivets, or if the plate and damper springs show signs of general wear and distortion. Also check the linings for oil contamination.

18 If the pressure plate release levers are in need of adjustment (noticeable by a difference in height in their retracted position), they must be adjusted by a Volvo garage or clutch specialist using a special fixture.

19 Check the pilot bearing in the centre of the flywheel for wear by turning the inner track. If necessary, remove the flywheel and renew the bearing as described in Chapter 1.

20 Check the thrust bearing in the clutch housing for wear and if necessary renew it as described in Section 4.

21 Refitting the clutch is a reversal of removal, but the following additional points should be noted:

a) *The clutch plate must be fitted with the extended side towards the clutch cover*

b) *It is not necessary to centralise the clutch plate as the pressure plate is not in contact with it*

c) *After fitting a new clutch plate, shims to the thickness of 0.118 in (3 mm) should be fitted at the three locations beneath the clutch cover. With the cover bolts fully tightened, this will provide a clearance of 0.004 to 0.012 in (0.1 to 0.3 mm) between the flywheel and clutch plate lining. Check the clearance at three points with a feeler blade, and if necessary change the thickness of shims*

d) *Apply a small amount of brake grease to the splines on the clutch shaft to ensure free movement of the clutch plate*

e) *Adjust the release fork and clutch servo as described in Section 5*

f) *Tighten the exhaust clamp nuts before the starter motor bolts*

retaining both rear engine mountings and withdraw them. An Allen key will be required for the bolts. Note the location of the locking plate on the left-hand mounting.

13 Unscrew the remaining clutch housing bolts and withdraw it from the rear of the engine.

14 Hold the flywheel stationary by inserting a wide-bladed screwdriver into engagement with the starter ring gear. Mark the clutch cover and flywheel in relation to each other.

15 Using an Allen key, unscrew the clutch cover retaining bolts and withdraw the assembly, together with the clutch plate. At

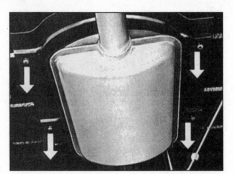

Fig. 5.3 Removing the exhaust heat shield (Sec 2)

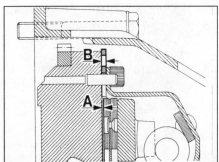

Fig. 5.4 Cross-sectional view of the clutch plate clearance (A) and shim (B) (Sec 2)

Fig. 5.5 Checking the clutch plate clearance (Sec 2)

Fig. 5.6 Removing the clutch shaft and bearing housing (Sec 3)

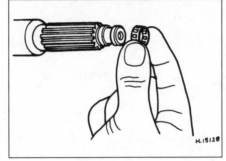

Fig. 5.7 Clutch shaft split bearing (Sec 3)

Fig. 5.8 Removing the clutch thrust bearing and release arm (Sec 4)

3 Clutch shaft and bearing - removal and refitting

1 Remove the clutch housing as described in Section 2, paragraphs 1 to 13.
2 Unscrew the nuts and washers, and separate the bearing housing and clutch shaft from the clutch housing.
3 Using circlip pliers, extract the large circlip from the rear of the bearing housing.
4 Heat the bearing housing with a gas blowtorch, then support the housing and drive out the shaft and bearing using a soft-headed mallet.
5 Using circlip pliers, extract the two circlips and lockring (where fitted) from the clutch shaft, then mount the bearing on a vice and drive out the shaft; alternatively use a suitable puller to remove the bearing.
6 Refitting is a reversal of removal, but the following additional points should be noted:

a) *Lubricate the bearing housing bore to facilitate fitting the bearing, or alternatively heat the housing*
b) *Tighten the bearing housing nuts to the correct torque wrench setting*
c) *Always renew the split bearing on the front of the clutch shaft*
d) *Refer to Section 2 when refitting the clutch housing*

4 Clutch thrust bearing - removal and refitting

1 Remove the clutch housing as described in Section 2, paragraphs 1 to 13.
2 Prise the plastic cover from the servo bracket.
3 Unscrew and remove the release arm/servo adjusting nut and washer and disconnect the release arm.
4 Where an external spring is fitted, remove it from the servo pullrod.
5 Pull the release arm outwards and disengage the clips from the pivot pin and thrust bearing, then slide the thrust bearing from the guide tube and withdraw the release arm.
6 Check the thrust bearing and release arm for wear and renew them as necessary. Similarly check the pivot pin and nylon cap if fitted.
7 Refitting is a reversal of removal, but lubricate sparingly the guide tube and contact areas of the release arm with a molybdenum disulphide based grease, and make sure that the release arm spring clip is located behind the nylon cap (where fitted). Before fitting the plastic cover, adjust the clutch servo/release arm as described in Section 5.

5 Declutching servo - removal, refitting and adjustment

1 Jack up the front of the car and support it on axle stands. Apply the handbrake.
2 Disconnect the vacuum hose from the rear of the servo unit, and prise the plastic cover from the servo bracket.
3 Unscrew and remove the release arm/servo adjusting nut and washer and disconnect the release arm.
4 Where an external spring is fitted, remove it from the servo pullrod.
5 Unscrew the retaining nuts and withdraw the servo from the mounting bracket.
6 Refitting is a reversal of removal, but before fitting the plastic cover (and vacuum hose on early models), the pullrod must be adjusted.

Servo with internal spring (up to chassis No HC 314541)

7 Loosen the adjusting nut until there is free play, indicating that the internal diaphragm is touching the cover.
8 Using a length of dowel rod, or preferably vernier calipers, measure the distance from the diaphragm rod to the outer edge of the entry tube.
9 Tighten the self-locking adjusting nut until the dimension in paragraph 8 has been increased by 0.28 in (7 mm) - see Fig. 5.12.

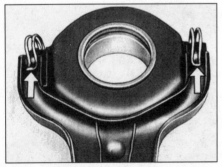

Fig. 5.9 Correct fitted position of thrust bearing clips - arrowed (Sec 4)

Fig. 5.10 Correct fitted position of the release arm clip (arrowed) (Sec 4)

Fig. 5.11 Removing the declutching servo - clutch housing removed for clarity (Sec 5)

Servo with external spring (from chassis No HC 314542)

10 Turn the self-locking adjusting nut until the clearance between the release arm and the clutch housing (see Fig. 5.13) is between 0.040 and 0.060 in (1 and 1.5 mm)

Part B: Manual transmission models

6 General description

The clutch is of single dry plate type with a diaphragm spring. Actuation is by means of a cable through a pendant-mounted pedal.

The clutch plate is sandwiched between the flywheel and clutch cover pressure plate, and is also free to slide along the splined clutch shaft.

With the clutch pedal in the released position, the diaphragm spring forces the pressure plate against the clutch friction plate, which in turn is forced against the flywheel. Drive is then transmitted from the flywheel, through the clutch, to the clutch shaft and propeller shaft.

When the clutch pedal is depressed, the cable moves the release arm, and the thrust bearing is forced against the centre of the diaphragm spring. The spring releases the pressure plate from the clutch friction plate, which now moves fractionally away from the flywheel. There is now no drive through the clutch.

7 Routine maintenance

At the intervals laid down in the Routine Maintenance Section at the beginning of this manual carry out the following maintenance tasks:

General

Check and adjust the clutch free play as described in Section 8.

Periodically lubricate the clutch pedal pivot point with engine oil.

8 Clutch - adjustment

Models up to 1981

1 With the clutch pedal in the released position, the thrust bearing must be clear of the diaphragm spring. The adjustment

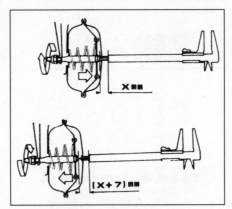

Fig. 5.12 Adjusting the declutching servo with internal spring - see text (Sec 5)

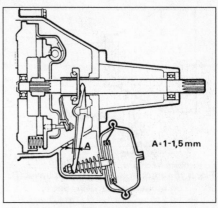

Fig. 5.13 Adjusting the declutching servo with external spring - see text (Sec 5)

A = 1-1,5 mm

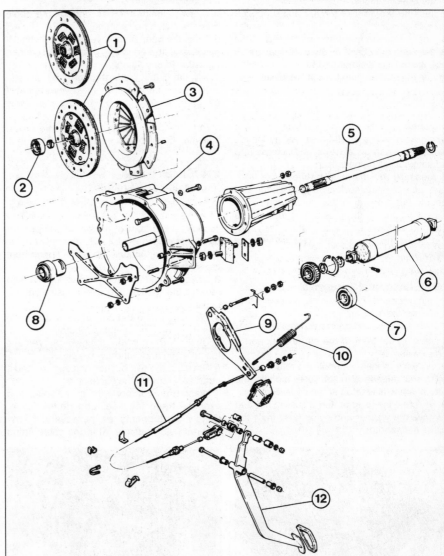

Fig. 5.14 Exploded view of the clutch - B14 models, manual (Sec 6)

1 Plate	5 Clutch shaft	9 Release arm
2 Pilot bearing	6 Propeller shaft	10 Spring
3 Pressure plate (cover)	7 Bearing	11 Clutch cable
4 Clutch housing	8 Thrust bearing	12 Clutch pedal

5

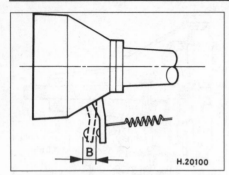

Fig. 5.15 Clutch release arm free travel (B) on models up to 1981 (Sec 8)

B = 0.118 to 0.197 in (3.0 to 5.0 mm)

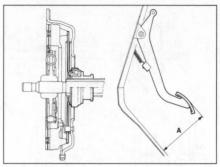

Fig. 5.16 Clutch pedal height (A) on models from 1981 (Sec 8)

A = 5.9 + 0.4 in (150 +10 mm)

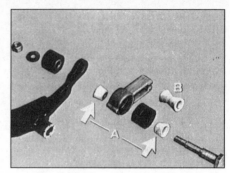

Fig. 5.17 Alternative clutch pedal nylon bushes - see text (Sec 10)

procedure determines the clearance as given in the Specifications.

2 Jack up the front of the car and support it on axle stands.

3 Check that the free travel of the end of the release arm is as given in the Specifications. If not, loosen the locknut and turn the adjusting nut as necessary, then tighten the locknut.

Models from 1981

4 The clutch thrust bearing has been modified and is now in contact with the diaphragm spring at all times. As the linings wear, the clutch pedal height will increase and adjustment will be necessary.

5 Measure the distance between the floor mat and the top surface of the pedal and check that it is within the limits given in the Specifications. If not, jack up the front of the car and support it on axle stands, then turn the adjusting nut on the release arm as necessary.

9 Clutch cable - renewal

1 Jack up the front of the car and support it on axle stands.

2 On early models, unhook the return spring from the release arm (on later models the return spring is located at the pedal end).

3 Unscrew the locknut and adjusting nut and remove the washer and nylon bush from the cable end (photo).

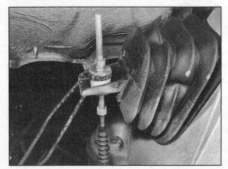

9.3 Clutch cable showing adjusting nut and locknut

4 Pull the clutch cable from the release arm and clutch housing.

5 Working inside the car, unhook the cable from the clutch pedal fitting.

6 Open the bonnet, remove the spare wheel if necessary, and undo any plastic ties securing the cable to any fittings.

7 Pull the clutch cable through the bulkhead and remove it from the engine compartment (if the grommet from the bulkhead comes away with the cable, transfer it to the new cable).

8 Refit the new cable in the reverse order; adjusting the clutch as described in Section 8.

10 Clutch pedal - removal and refitting

1 Jack up the front of the car and support it on axle stands.

2 Where fitted, unhook the return spring from the release lever.

3 Unscrew the locknut and adjusting nut, and remove the washer and nylon bush from the cable end.

4 Working inside the car, unhook the cable from the clutch pedal fitting (photo).

5 Unscrew the nut from the pivot pin, remove the pivot pin and withdraw the pedal.

6 Drive out the two bushes and spacer, and if necessary remove the cable fitting.

7 Wash the components in paraffin and examine them for wear and deterioration. Renew components as necessary. If the tapered nylon bushes (A) in the cable fitting

10.4 Clutch cable fitting at the pedal end (arrowed)

require renewal, a single bush (B) (see Fig. 5.17) can be fitted.

8 Refitting is a reversal of removal, but lubricate all bearing surfaces with a molybdenum disulphide grease, and adjust the clutch as described in Section 8.

11 Clutch - removal and refitting

B14 models

1 Disconnect the negative lead from the battery.

2 Unscrew the two top bolts from the clutch housing and remove the drain hose from the heater air intake unit.

3 Jack up the front of the car and support it on axle stands.

4 Unscrew and remove the nuts and washers, and remove the front exhaust clamp from the exhaust pipe.

5 Remove the engine splash guards.

6 Remove the starter motor (see Chapter 10) and, on early models, move the exhaust bracket forwards.

7 If necessary, unbolt the anti-roll bar front mountings with reference to Chapter 8.

8 Where necessary, detach the exhaust front downpipe from the manifold (see Chapter 3).

9 Where fitted, unhook the return spring from the release arm, then unscrew the locknut and adjusting nut and remove the washer and nylon bush from the clutch cable end.

10 Pull the clutch cable from the release arm and clutch housing.

11 Unscrew the nuts and bolts and remove the cover plate from the front of the clutch housing.

12 Using an Allen key, unscrew the clamp bolts securing the propeller shaft to the clutch shaft and gearbox input shaft.

13 Loosen the transmission front cross-member mounting nuts in order to lower the front of the transmission, then slide the propeller shaft from the clutch shaft and gearbox input shaft.

14 Using a trolley jack and a block of wood, support the engine beneath the sump.

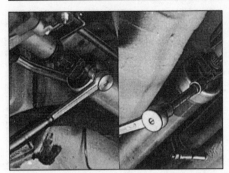

Fig. 5.18 Loosening the propeller shaft clamp bolts (Sec 11)

Fig. 5.19 Transmission front crossmember mounting nuts - arrowed (Sec 11)

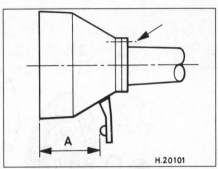

Fig. 5.20 Release arm adjustment dimension A (Sec 11)
Chassis No up to 788921 A = 5.55 to 5.63 in (141 to 143 mm)
Chassis No from 788922 A = 5.71 to 5.79 in (145 to 147 mm)

15 Unscrew and remove the nuts and bolts retaining both rear engine mountings and withdraw them. An Allen key will be required for the bolts. Note the location of the locking plate on the left-hand mounting.
16 Unscrew the remaining clutch housing bolts and withdraw it from the rear of the engine.
17 Mark the clutch cover and flywheel in relation to each other.
18 Hold the flywheel stationary by inserting a wide-bladed screwdriver into engagement with the starter ring gear, then unscrew the clutch cover bolts a turn at a time until the pressure of the diaphragm spring is relieved.
19 Remove the bolts then lift away the pressure plate/cover assembly and clutch plate from the face of the flywheel.
20 Clean the surfaces of the flywheel and pressure plate, and examine them for excessive scoring. If evident, the pressure plate and/or flywheel should be renewed, although in the case of the flywheel it may be possible to have it refaced by a competent engineering firm.
21 Renew the clutch plate if the linings are worn down to or near the rivets, of if they are contaminated with oil. Also check the plate for general wear or distortion. Where the clutch plate has four damper springs, the red spring must be loose, but the three plain springs may be loose or firmly fixed. Where the clutch plate has six damper springs, the red and blue springs must be firm, but the four green springs may be loose or firmly fixed.
22 Check the pilot bearing in the centre of the flywheel for wear, and renew it if necessary. If a ball-bearing type is fitted, renew it by removing the flywheel as described in Chapter 1. If a needle bearing type is fitted, use a hooked instrument to remove it and tap the new bearing into position with a soft-faced hammer.
23 Check the thrust bearing in the clutch housing for wear, and if necessary renew it as described in Section 12.
24 When refitting the clutch, it is necessary to centralise the clutch plate. To do this, either obtain a tool from a tool hire agent, or alternatively make up a suitable length of dowelling to fit in the pilot bearing and clutch plate.

25 Locate the clutch plate against the flywheel making sure that it is the correct way round with the flywheel side facing the flywheel.
26 Insert the centralising tool through the plate and into the pilot bearing.
27 Fit the pressure plate assembly onto the flywheel and over the locating dowels. Insert the retaining bolts finger tight.
28 Check that the guide tool is central, then tighten the bolts a turn at a time in diagonal sequence to the specified torque, while holding the flywheel stationary as described in paragraph 18.
29 Remove the centralising tool and refit the clutch housing using a reversal of the procedure described in paragraphs 1 to 16, but noting the following points:
a) *Apply a small amount of brake grease to the splines on the clutch shaft to ensure free movement of the clutch plate*
b) *Tighten the exhaust clamp nuts before the starter motor bolts*
c) *After tightening the clutch housing bolts. and before fitting the clutch cable, move the release arm forwards until it just touches the diaphragm spring. Measure dimension A (Fig. 5.20) and check that it is as specified. If not, loosen the locknut adjust the position of the ballpin, and tighten the locknut*
d) *After fitting the cable, adjust the clutch as described in Section 8*
e) *Where the exhaust front downpipe has been disconnected, always fit a new gasket*
f) *On models produced from chassis No 788922, the method of attaching the clutch housing to the engine is different, as a modified housing is used. On the right-hand side there is a long bolt with a nut at its other end. This bolt must be fitted to the housing before offering the housing to the engine as it is too long to be fitted afterwards*

B19 and B200 models

30 Carry out operations 1 to 3 as for B14 models.
31 Jack up the rear of the car and, on B19 models from chassis No EC 810500, slacken the top bolt of the rear spring shackle and

remove the bottom bolt from both leaf spring-to-shackle attachment points. This allows the rear axle to be lowered sufficiently to allow the final drive unit to be moved rearward (see later text).
32 Remove the engine splash guards.
33 Disconnect the clutch cable from the release arm and housing (see Section 9).
34 Remove the complete exhaust system (refer to Chapter 3).
35 Remove the starter motor as described in Chapter 10.
36 Remove the lower clutch housing-to-engine bolts.
37 Remove the bolts from the front cover on the clutch housing and remove the cover sideways.
38 Remove the gearchange support rod from the clutch housing and torque tube.
39 Remove the heat shield from beneath the fuel tank. On fuel injection models leave the hoses connected to the pump.
40 Disconnect the gearchange rod from the transmission and also unclip the handbrake cables from beneath the fuel tank.
41 Unclip the brake hydraulic line from the rear axle and pull it behind the axle.
42 If fitted, remove the transmission shock absorber from the underbody. On later models the shock absorber has been discontinued.
43 Support the transmission and final drive unit on a trolley jack then unbolt the two transmission mountings.
44 While supporting the clutch housing, pull it from the engine at the same time guiding the transmission assembly backwards. Once the clutch propeller shaft is clear of the clutch, lower the clutch housing, if necessary placing a block of wood between the final drive unit and the underbody to prevent damage.
45 The remaining procedure is as described in paragraphs 17 to 28.
46 It is possible to fit the clutch without using a centralising tool on these models as follows: Locate the pressure plate and clutch plate on the splined shaft in the clutch housing, then lift the housing onto the rear of the engine and

5

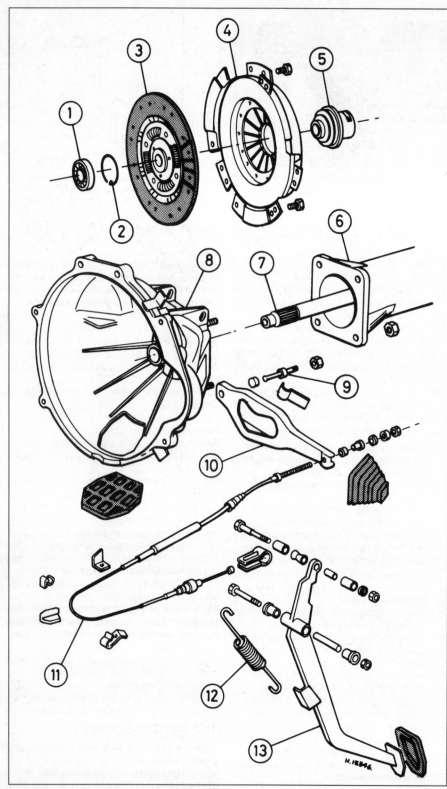

Fig. 5.21 Exploded view of the clutch - B19 and B200 models, manual (Sec 11)

1 Pilot (spigot) bearing
2 Circlip
3 Clutch plate
4 Pressure plate
5 Thrust bearing
6 Torque tube
7 Clutch/propeller shaft
8 Clutch housing
9 Ball pin
10 Release arm
11 Clutch cable
12 Return spring
13 Clutch pedal
Note. LHD model shown

11.46 Clutch cover plate access hole showing clutch bolt (arrowed)

fit the bolts to the pressure plate through the access hole provided (photo).

47 Refitting is a reversal of removal, but make sure that the gearchange support rod is not trapped between the clutch housing and the underbody.

48 On completion adjust the clutch as described in Section 8.

B172 models

49 The procedure is similar to that described for B14 models with the following differences:

50 It is not necessary to remove the drain hose from the air inlet unit.

51 The two bolts at the top of the clutch housing cannot be removed until the engine mountings have been removed and the engine lowered slightly.

52 Disconnect the electrical lead to the timing sensor at the control unit.

53 If the starter motor bolts are difficult to remove, release the mounting bracket on the engine block.

54 Disconnect the exhaust downpipe from the manifold.

55 Remove the bolts from the clutch housing and remove the housing, then remove the clutch as described for B14 models.

12 Clutch thrust bearing - removal and refitting

1 Remove the clutch housing as described in Section 11.

2 On B19 and B200 models, remove the nuts securing the clutch housing to the torque tube, supporting the torque tube on an axle stand. **Note:** *The nuts securing the torque tube to the clutch housing should be renewed once removed.*

3 Prise the rubber grommet from the housing.

4 Pull the release arm from the pivot pin and withdraw the arm, complete with thrust bearing, from the housing.

5 Unclip the bearing from the release arm.

6 Check all parts for wear and renew them as necessary. If the guide sleeve in the housing is worn, press the old bush off the sleeve, and the new one on, until the new bush is flush.

7 Refitting is a reversal of removal, but

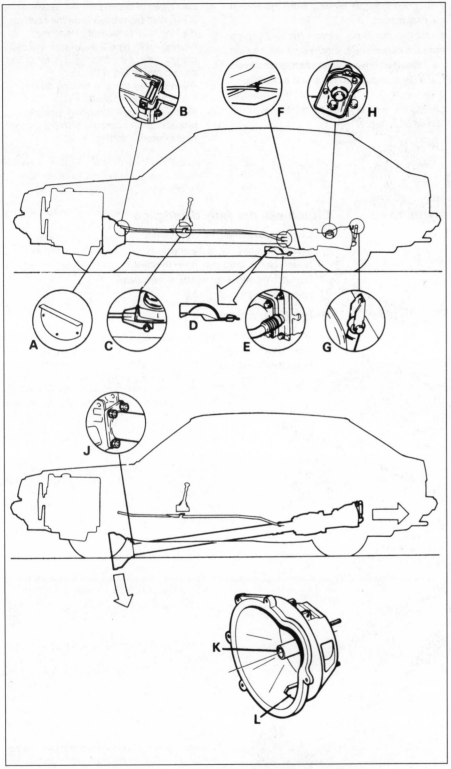

Fig. 5.22 Clutch removal on B19 and B200 models (Sec 11)

A Front cover
B Gearchange support rod (front)
C Gearchange support rod (rear)
D Heat shield
E Gearchange connection to transmission
F Handbrake cable clips

G Transmission shock absorber mounting
H Transmission mountings
J Torque tube-to-clutch housing nuts
K Guide sleeve
L Access hole

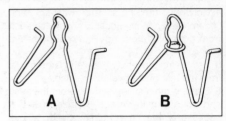

Fig. 5.23 Alternative types of release arm-
to-ball pin spring clip (Sec 12)

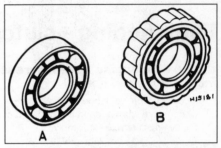

Fig. 5.24 Alternative types of clutch shaft
bearing (Sec 13)

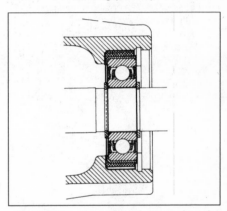

Fig. 5.25 Cross-section of serrated track
clutch shaft bearing (Sec 13)

lubricate the sleeve, ball pin, and bearing
surfaces of the release arm with graphited
grease.
8 On completion of refitting, adjust the
release arm as described in Section 11 and
the clutch as described in Section 8.

13 Clutch shaft and bearing -
removal and refitting

B14 and B172 models

1 Jack up the front of the car and support it
on axle stands.
2 Using an Allen key, unscrew the clamp
bolts securing the propeller shaft to the clutch
shaft and gearbox input shaft.
3 Loosen the transmission front
crossmember mounting nuts in order to lower
the front of the transmission, then slide the
propeller shaft from the clutch shaft and
gearbox input shaft.

4 Unscrew the nuts and washers and separate the bearing housing and clutch shaft from the clutch housing. Remove the return spring.

5 Using circlip pliers, extract the large circlip from the rear of the bearing housing.

6 Support the housing and drive out the shaft and bearing using a soft-headed mallet. If necessary heat the housing with a gas blowtorch.

7 Remove the split bearing from the end of the clutch shaft.

8 Using circlip pliers, extract the two circlips from the clutch shaft, then mount the bearing on a vice and drive out the shaft; alternatively use a suitable puller to remove the bearing.

9 Refitting is a reversal of the removal procedure, but the following additional points should be noted:

a) Two types of bearing are in use (see Fig. 5.24). With type A, lubricate the bearing housing bore to facilitate fitting the bearing - with type B make sure that the correct side of the bearing is entered first by referring to Fig. 5.25

b) Always renew the split bearing on the front of the clutch shaft

c) Tighten the bearing housing nuts and propeller shaft clamp bolts to the correct torque wrench setting

Fault finding - clutch

Clutch slip (engine speed increases with no increase in road speed)

- [ ] Incorrect cable adjustment (manual)
- [ ] Clutch plate worn or contaminated with oil or grease
- [ ] Faulty pressure plate assembly

Clutch judder

- [ ] Clutch plate hinges contaminated with oil or grease
- [ ] Loose or broken engine mountings
- [ ] Clutch plate distorted
- [ ] Worn flywheel pilot bearing
- [ ] Clutch shaft splines worn

Clutch will not fully disengage

- [ ] Clutch plate sticking on clutch shaft
- [ ] Clutch plate sticking to flywheel
- [ ] Seized clutch shaft bearing in flywheel
- [ ] Declutching servo out of adjustment (auto)
- [ ] Idling speed too high (auto)

Noise from clutch

- [ ] Worn clutch plate linings
- [ ] Worn pilot bearing
- [ ] Worn thrust bearing

Chapter 6
Transmission and final drive

Contents

Degrees of difficulty

Easy, suitable for novice with little experience	**Fairly easy,** suitable for beginner with some experience	**Fairly difficult,** suitable for competent DIY mechanic	**Difficult,** suitable for experienced DIY mechanic	**Very difficult,** suitable for expert DIY or professional

Specifications

Automatic transmission

Type . . . . Automatic, continuously variable with two drivebelts and a centrifugal control system

Lubrication

Type/specification:
 Gear case . . . . Hypoid gear oil, viscosity SAE 80W/90, to API GL4 or GL5
 Sliding pulley halves . . . . ATF type A/A or F, or Dexron type
Oil capacity:
 Gear case:
  Primary transmission unit . . . . 1.0 pint (0.55 litre)
  Secondary transmission unit . . . . 1.8 pint (1.00 litre)
 Sliding pulley halves:
  Primary transmission unit . . . . 0.18 pint (0.100 litre)
  Secondary transmission unit . . . . 0.13 pint (0.075 litre)

Primary transmission unit

Reduction ratio 1.53: 1

Secondary transmission unit

Reduction ratio 4.51: 1
Gap between pulley halves:
 New belts . . . . 0.06 to 0.08 in (1.5 to 2.0 mm)
 Minimum permissible . . . . 0.06 in (1.5 mm)

6

Total transmission reduction ratio
Secondary pulley gap 0.06 in (1.5 mm):
    Maximum 14.15: 1
    Minimum 4.00: 1

Microswitch cut-in speed
Models up to 1978 .... 2400 to 2600 rpm

Vacuum control unit set speed
Models up to 1978 .... 1776 to 1812 rpm

Torque wrench settings

	lbf ft	Nm
Primary transmission unit		
Rear cover nuts	10	14
Bearing housing nuts	10	14
Pinion shaft nut	46	62
Forward drivegear nut	118	160
Cross-shaft nuts	86	117
Level plug	31	42
Drain plug	31	42
Locknut (for adjustment of locking sleeve shaft)	22	30
Secondary transmission		
Gear shaft nuts	140	190
Gear case nuts	13	17
Level plug	31	42
Drain plug	31	42
Driveshaft-to-drive flange bolts	25	34
Mounting nuts	19	26
Drive flange-to-transmission bolts	18	24

Manual transmission

Type:
M45R 4-speed
M47R 5-speed

Ratios (4 and 5-speed)
1st 3.71:1
2nd 2.16:1
3rd 1.37:1
4th 1.00:1
5th 0.83:1
Reverse 3.68:1

Clearances
Reverse gear-to-gear lever .... 0.004 to 0.098 in (0.1 to 2.50 mm)
Input shaft endfloat .... 0.0004 to 0.0079 in (0.01 to 0.20 mm)
Countershaft endfloat (M45R) .... 0.001 to 0.004 in (0.025 to 0.100 mm)
Mainshaft endfloat .... 0.0004 to 0.0079 in (0.01 to 0.20 mm)

Lubrication
Type/specification .... ATF type A, suffix A

Oil capacity (total)
4-speed - up to 1984 .... 3.7 pints (2.10 litre)
4-speed - from 1984 .... 4.1 pints (2.35 litre)
5-speed (plug at rear) .... 4.8 pints (2.70 litre)
5-speed (plug at front - up to 1985) .... 6.2 pints (3.50 litre)
5-speed (plug at front - from 1985) .... 5.3 pints (3.00 litre)
Note: *All capacities 0.4 pint (0.2 litres) less at oil change*

Final drive unit

Ratios (4-speed):
  B14:
    Up to 1982 .... 3.91:1
    1982 and 1983 .... 3.82:1
    From 1984 .... 3.64:1
  B19:
    Up to 1982 .... 3.64:1
    1982 and 1983 .... 3.45:1
    From 1984 .... 3.36:1
Ratios (5-speed):
  B14 from 1983 .... 3.82:1
  B172 from 1986 .... 3.64:1
  B19A:
    1982 and 1983 .... 3.45:1
    From 1984 .... 3.36:1
  B19E:
    Hatchback 3.64:1
    Saloon 3.36:1
  B200K 3.27:1
  B200KO 3.45:1
  B200EO 3.64:1
  B200E:
    Hatchback 3.64:1
    Saloon 3.45:1
Oil capacity:
  B14:
    Up to 1982 .... 2.6 pints (1.45 litre)
    From 1982 .... 2.4 pints (1.35 litre)
  B172 .... 2.4 pints (1.36 litre)
  B19 and B200:
    4-speed .... 2.6 pints (1.50 litre)
    5-speed .... 2.4 pints (1.35 litre)
Oil type .... Hypoid gear oil, viscosity SAE 90, to API GL5

Torque wrench settings

	lbf ft	Nm
Gearbox		
Front casing bolts	31	42
Gearbox-to-final drive bolts	31	42
Gearbox cover bolts	15	20
Level and drain plugs:		
Hexagon-headed bolt	26	35
Socket-headed bolt	24	33
Front casing-to-crossmember bolts (up to 1981)	19	26
Fifth gearwheel bolt	30	41
Drive flange to gearbox (B19 and B200)	51	72
Propeller shaft clamp bolts:		
B14 and B172	27	37
B19 and B200	25	34
Front crossmember-to-subframe nuts	34	47
Output shaft bearing housing bolts (5-speed)	15	20
Gear lever locking bolt	7	10
Reaction rod-to-torque tube bolt	6	8
Torque tube-to-clutch housing bolt	35	47
Torque tube-to-gearbox bolt	53	72
Fifth gear self-locking nut	96	130
Final drive unit		
Level and drain plugs	31	42
Rear cover bolts	6	8
Driveshafts:		
Socket-headed bolt	29	40
Flanged head bolt	36	49

6

Part A: Automatic transmission

1 General description

The transmission is of automatic continuously variable type. The drive is taken from the propeller shaft to the two primary pulleys, via two drivebelts to the two secondary pulleys, then through a single reduction gear and differential unit to the rear wheels (photo).

The reduction ratio produced by a drivebelt running between two pulleys depends on the ratio of the pulley diameters. Changing the pulleys' diameters changes the reduction ratio and this is the basic principle employed in the continuously variable transmission (CVT). The CVT consists of two separate units connected by drivebelts. The primary unit comprises an input pinion shaft which is in constant mesh with the two bevel gears. Forward or reverse gear is provided by engaging a sliding collar in either one of these bevel gears; as the collar is splined to the cross-shaft, the drive is transmitted to the primary pulleys at either side of the transmission, and so to the secondary pulleys. The secondary unit comprises a reduction gear train, a differential, and driveshaft flanges.

On the primary pulleys the inner discs are fixed and the outer ones may be moved in and out to vary the effective diameter of the pulley. On the secondary pulleys the outer discs are fixed and the inner ones can move inwards against the tension of an internal spring. As the primary pulley expands, the drivebelt is pulled deeper into the secondary pulley against the spring loading; as the primary pulley contracts the belt relaxes its tension and the spring pushes the discs together and the effective diameter of the pulley increases. The expansion and contraction of the primary pulley which results in the variations in the gear ratio is caused by:

1) *Centrifugal weights operating inside the disc, which push the sliding discs towards the fiexd inner discs as the engine speed increases*
2) *Vacuum to the inner chambers, which counteracts the action of the centrifugal weights*
3) *Vacuum to the outer chambers, which augments the action of the centrifugal weights to provide an overdrive effect*

An electromagnetic four-way vacuum valve controls the application of the vacuum from the inlet manifold to the primary sliding disc chambers (photo). When acceleration is required, the action of the centrifugal weights is counteracted, and the transmission reduction is increased to provide good acceleration. When the throttle is at a cruising position, vacuum is channelled to the outer

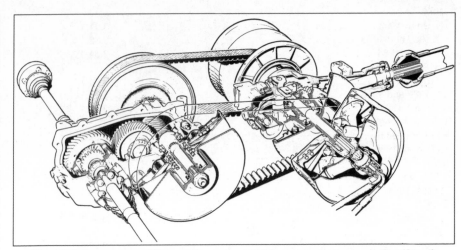

Fig. 6.1 Cutaway view of the continuously variable automatic transmission (Sec 1)

chambers, which assist the centrifugal weights and provide an overdrive condition. The vacuum is maintained at a constant level by a regular valve (photo).

The transmission 'change-up' function is achieved by a solenoid mounted in the four-way valve, which on pre-1978 models is energised via a microswitch actuated by a cam on the carburettor. An earth switch (fitted to the throttle cable where it passes through the bulkhead on pre-1978 models), earths the 'change-up' solenoid when transmission 'kickdown' is required. A 'change-down'

solenoid is also incorporated in the four-way valve, so that the transmission will change down under braking. On pre-1978 models, the brake light switch energises the solenoid. This solenoid also operates the low-ratio 'hold' facility.

Models from 1978 are equipped with an electric vacuum control unit (Fig. 6.2). On these models, the carburettor-mounted microswitch is deleted, as the electronic control unit actuates the 'change-up' solenoid directly. The throttle cable earth switch is connected to a relay in the electronic control

1.1 The continuously variable automatic transmission

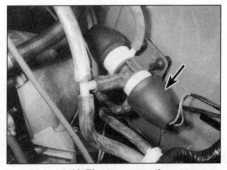

1.4A Electromagnetic four-way vacuum valve

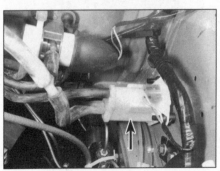

1.4B Vacuum regulator valve

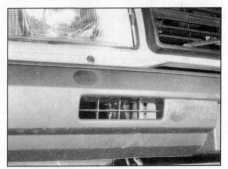

1.8 Transmission cooling air inlet in front bumper

Fig. 6.2 Vacuum control unit fitted to models from 1978 (Sec 1)

Fig. 6.3 Transmission guard panels (Sec 3)

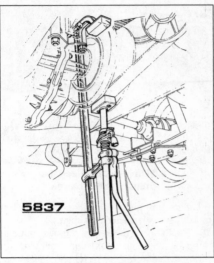

Fig. 6.4 Using tool No 5837 to separate the secondary pulley halves (Sec 3)

unit, and when kickdown is required, the relay earths the 'change-up' solenoid and energises the 'change-down' solenoid. The 'change-down' solenoid is also linked to a hydraulic switch on the brake master cylinder, to sense the braking effort applied. Depending on the amount of effort applied, and also on the engine speed when the brakes are applied (determined by a tachometric relay in the electronic control unit), the transmission change-down effect is increased or decreased. The low-ratio 'hold' facility is also controlled by a relay in the electronic control unit on post-1978 models, which energises the 'change-down' solenoid.

In addition to the characteristic already described, road conditions will automatically alter the position of the drivebelts. Increased resistance when ascending a hill will tension the drivebelts causing them to run deeper in the primary pulleys, thus providing greater overall reduction. On the overrun the converse will apply. A low ratio hold is provided whereby vacuum is continuously channelled to the inner sliding disc chambers.

The transmission is cooled by an airflow system through grilles at the front of the car (photo); the guard panels also serve to direct the air over the transmission. Because of this, the transmission should never be operated for long periods with the car stationary.

When the brakes are applied on models up to 1978, the stop-light circuit activates the vacuum control valve to supply vacuum to the primary sliding disc inner chambers. At the same time the outer chambers are connected to atmospheric pressure. This action causes the sliding discs to move outwards quickly, and the transmission is therefore changed immediately to a low ratio ready for starting off again. On models from 1978, the system functions in a similar way, but under normal braking will only occur at engine speeds below 1750 rpm. Under heavy braking, the high pressure switch on the master cylinder operates the system as on earlier models.

The selector lever is provided with park (P), reverse (R), neutral (N), and drive (D) positions. With the lever in position (P), the reverse drivegear in the primary transmission is engaged and the forward gear is also mechanically locked. The engine should not

be run at fast speeds with the lever in position P otherwise the clutch or transmission may be damaged. Starting the engine is only possible with the selector lever in position P or N.

2 Routine maintenance - automatic transmission

At the intervals laid down in the Routine Maintenance Section at the beginning of this manual, carry out the following operations:

Lubrication

1 Check oil level.
2 Renew the oil in both the primary and secondary units.

Drivebelts (Section 3)

3 Inspect the drivebelts and check the pulley gaps.

General

4 Check for oil leaks.
5 Check the vacuum microswitch.

3 Transmission drivebelts - removal, refitting and adjustment

1 Place the car over an inspection pit, or alternatively jack up the rear and support it adequately on axle stands.
2 Unscrew and remove the retaining screws and lower the guard panel from the car.

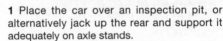

3.3A Vacuum hoses to the primary transmission unit

3 Carefully pull the vacuum hoses from both sides of the primary transmission unit (photo); the hoses are of different diameters and it is therefore not possible to refit them incorrectly (photo).
4 To simplify the next operation it is advisable to obtain a special clamping tool from a tool agent, or to construct a similar tool (see Fig. 6.4). Clamp the drivebelt so that the secondary pulley halves are forced apart, then insert a 1 in (25 mm) spacer between the halves to keep them apart. If a tool is not available, pull the lower section of the drivebelt downwards so that the secondary pulley halves move apart.
5 Loosen the four secondary unit mounting nuts, and adjustment bracket nuts, and slide the secondary unit forwards. Unscrew the mounting nuts to the ends of the bolts.
6 Pull the drivebelts on both sides into the primary (front) pulley halves (photo).
7 Remove the drivebelts from the rear pulleys, then from the front pulleys.
8 Examine the drivebelts for deterioration, cracks and loss of toothed segments, and if evident, renew both drivebelts. Renewal of one drivebelt is not possible because of the difference in length between new and worn belts.

6

3.3B Showing the different diameters of the primary transmission vacuum hoses

3.6 Drivebelt between the primary pulley halves

3.12A Drivebelt adjustment nuts

3.12B Checking the drivebelt tension adjustment

9 Clean the pulley surfaces with a cloth moistened with methylated spirit.

10 Refitting is a reversal of removal, but care must be taken to avoid contaminating the pulley surfaces with oil or foreign matter, and the drivebelts must be tensioned as follows.

11 Turn either the rear wheels or transmission pulleys until the drivebelts have settled at the top of the secondary pulleys.

12 Turn the adjustment nuts until the drivebelts are tensioned, and the gap between the inner and outer rear pulleys on both sides is as given in the Specifications (photos). Measure the gap at the centre of the pulleys with a feeler blade or length of metal of suitable thickness. The transmission pulleys should be turned several times and the final adjustment checked after the retaining nuts and adjustment locknut have been tightened.

13 The difference between left and right-hand pulley gaps should not exceed 0.04 in (1.0 mm), but if it does, the belt should be changed side-to-side and the adjustment made again. The belts must be renewed if correct adjustment cannot be obtained.

14 After fitting new drivebelts the adjustment should be checked again after 3000 miles (5000 km) have been completed.

4 Primary transmission unit - removal and refitting

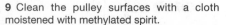

1 Jack up the rear of the car and support it adequately on axle stands. Allow plenty of

Fig. 6.5 Secondary transmission unit adjustment (1 and 2) and mounting nut (3 to 6) locations (Sec 5)

room for manoeuvring the transmission unit from under the car; the use of a ramp or pit is preferable.

2 Remove the screws and withdraw the transmission guard panel.

3 Unhook the front exhaust mounting rubber, then remove the screws and withdraw the transmission outer guard panel.

4 Remove the drivebelts as described in Section 3.

5 Spray the clutch and pinion shafts with penetrating oil, then push the propeller shaft to the rear as far as it will go and detach it from the clutch shaft. Slide it forwards, remove it from the transmission pinion shaft, and rest it on the exhaust heat shield.

6 Remove the clip and clevis pin securing the selector rod to the selector lever.

7 Disconnect the reversing light switch wires.

8 Support the primary transmission unit with a trolley jack.

9 Unscrew the retaining bolts and adjusting locknut, and withdraw the adjustment bracket.

10 Remove the rubber cover from the front of the primary unit.

11 Unscrew the remaining mounting nuts and lower the primary unit to the ground.

12 Refitting is a reversal of removal but note the following additional points:

a) Grease the pinion shaft splines sparingly before fitting the propeller shaft

b) Adjust the drivebelts as described in Section 3

5.9 Refilling the secondary transmission unit with oil

5 Secondary transmission unit - removal and refitting

1 Jack up the rear of the car and support it adequately on axle stands. Allow plenty of room for manoeuvring the transmission unit from under the car; the use of a ramp or pit is preferable.

2 Remove the screws and withdraw the transmission guard panel.

3 Unhook the front exhaust mounting rubber, then remove the screws and withdraw the transmission outer guard panel.

4 Remove the drivebelts (see Section 3).

5 Remove the drain plug and drain the oil into a suitable container.

6 Mark the driveshaft inner couplings in relation to the transmission drive flanges, then unscrew and remove the retaining bolts and plates. An Allen key will be required to do this.

7 Detach the driveshafts from the transmission unit and tie them to the handbrake cables. At the same time remove the flange gaskets.

8 Support the secondary transmission unit with a trolley jack, then unscrew and remove the retaining nuts and adjustment nuts, then lower the transmission unit to the ground; the help of an assistant is desirable in order to prevent the unit slipping from the trolley jack. Extract the rubber bushes from the transmission case mounting holes and renew them if they show signs of deterioration.

9 Refitting is a reversal of removal, but the following additional joints should be noted:

a) Fit new gaskets to the driveshaft flanges

b) Renew all self-locking nuts and tighten all nuts and bolts to the specified torque wrench settings

c) Thoroughly clean the drive pulley surfaces with methylated spirit

d) Refill the secondary transmission to the bottom of the filler plug aperture with the correct grade of oil; the filler plug is located forward of the drain plug (photo)

e) Adjust the drivebelt tension as described in Section 3

f) Make sure that the driveshaft is clean and free of any foreign matter which could contaminate the drive pulleys

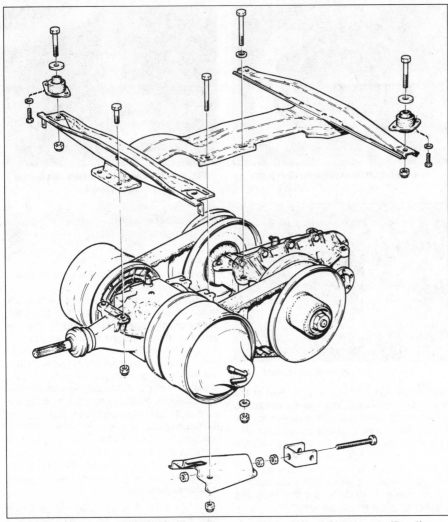

Fig. 6.6 Automatic transmission mounting and adjustment components (Sec 6)

a) *Make sure that the handbrake cable lies beneath the front crossmember before tightening the mounting nuts*
b) *Fit new gaskets to the driveshaft flanges*
c) *Renew all self-locking nuts and tighten them to the specified torque wrench settings*
d) *Clean the driveshafts of any grease or foreign matter which could contaminate the drive pulleys*

7 Transmission units - overhaul

Overhauling a transmission unit is a difficult and involved job for the DIY home mechanic. In addition to dismantling and reassembling many small parts, clearances must be precisely measured and, if necessary, changed by selecting shims and spacers. Internal transmission components are also often difficult to obtain, and in many instances, are extremely expensive. Because of this, if the transmission develops a fault or becomes noisy, the best course of action is to have the unit overhauled by a specialist repairer, or to obtain an exchange reconditioned unit.

Nevertheless, it is not impossible for the more experienced mechanic to overhaul the transmission, provided the special tools are available, and that the job is done in a deliberate step-by-step manner so that nothing is overlooked.

The tools necessary for an overhaul may include internal and external circlip pliers, bearing pullers, a slide hammer, a set of pin punches, a dial test indicator, and possibly a hydraulic press. In addition, a large, sturdy workbench and a vice will be required.

During dismantling of the transmission, make careful notes of how each component is fitted, to make reassembly easier and accurate.

Before dismantling the transmission, it will help if you have some idea which area is malfunctioning. Certain problems can be closely related to specific areas in the transmission, which can make component examination and replacement easier.

6 Primary and secondary transmission units - removal and refitting as one assembly

1 If repairs are required on both the primary and secondary transmission units, they can be removed together as a complete assembly.
2 Follow the instructions given in Section 4, paragraphs 1 to 7 omitting paragraph 4.
3 Remove the secondary unit drain plug and drain the oil into a suitable container.
4 Mark the driveshaft inner couplings in relation to the transmission drive flanges, then unscrew and remove the retaining bolts and plates using an Allen key.
5 Detach the driveshafts from the transmission unit and tie them to the handbrake cables. At the same time remove the flange gaskets.
6 Support the transmission units with two trolley jacks and suitable lengths of wood. Disconnect the handbrake cable mountings (photo).

7 Unscrew and remove the transmission frame mounting nuts.
8 Carefully lower the front trolley jack, then move the assembly forwards and lower the rear of the frame clear of the handbrake cables. Finally lower the transmission to the ground.
9 Refitting is a reversal of removal, but the following additional points should be noted:

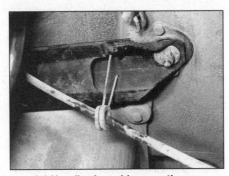

6.6 Handbrake cable mounting on transmission frame

8 Driveshaft - removal, inspection and refitting

1 Jack up the rear of the car and support it on axle stands. Chock the front wheels.
2 Remove the screws and withdraw the transmission central and outer guard panels (photo).
3 Mark the drive flange, axleshaft flange and driveshaft in relation to each other, then, using an Allen key, unscrew the inner and outer flange bolts and remove the plates.
4 Withdraw the driveshaft, together with the

6

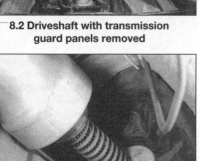

8.2 Driveshaft with transmission guard panels removed

8.4 Halfshaft homokinetic (CV) joint

Fig. 6.7 Removing the driveshaft flange bolts (Sec 8)

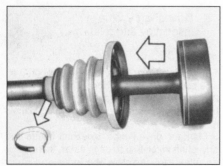

9.5 Rear of propeller shaft and tension spring

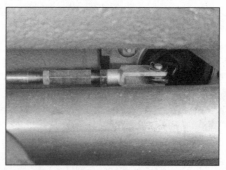

10.3 Selector rod and lever joint

gaskets, from the car (photo). **Note**: *On early manual gearbox models the drive flanges on the final drive unit incorporate machined recesses in order to accommodate gaskets, however, on later models, there are no recesses or gaskets.*

5 Using circlip pliers, extract the circlip from the driveshaft groove.

6 Remove the clip from the small diameter of the rubber bellows and slide the bellows along the shaft.

7 Support the inner race of the joint and press or drive out the shaft; the rubber bellows can now be removed from the shaft, together with the protection cap.

8 If necessary, the homokinetic (CV) joint may be dismantled by turning the inner race diagonally to the outer race and removing the balls. Clean the components in paraffin, and when dry examine the balls and races for wear and pitting; if evident a new joint should be obtained. If the components are serviceable,

reassemble the joint using a reversal of the dismantling procedure, but make sure that the recess in the outer race and the spline run-out on the inner race face the same way, also ensure that the assembled position of the inner and outer races is as shown in Fig. 6.10.

9 The remaining reassembly and refitting of the halfshaft is a reversal of the dismantling and removal procedure, but the following additional points should be noted:

a) *Pack the joints with lithium based grease*
b) *Fit new gaskets to the joint and flange faces. Glue them in position if necessary*
c) *Tighten the flange bolts to the specified torque wrench setting*
d) *Wipe away any excess grease or foreign matter which could contaminate the transmission pulleys*
e) *On B19 and B200 engine models the driveshaft flange bolt threads must be coated with locking fluid before tightening to the specified torque*

9 Propeller shaft - removal and refitting

1 Jack up the front and rear of the car and support it on axle stands.

2 Remove the screws and withdraw the transmission central and outer guard panels.

3 Remove the screws and withdraw the heat shield located above the exhaust silencer.

4 Spray the clutch and pinion shafts with penetrating oil then push the propeller shaft to the rear as far as it will go and detach it from the clutch shaft. If difficulty is experienced obtain tool No 5948 or construct a similar tool to lever the propeller shaft rearwards.

5 Slide the shaft forwards, remove it from the transmission pinion shaft, and withdraw it from the car (photo).

6 Refitting is a reversal of removal, but lightly grease the splines and ensure that the spring is located correctly.

10 Selector lever - removal and refitting

1 Jack up the front and rear of the car and support it on axle stands.

2 Remove the propeller shaft (see Section 9).

3 Remove the clip and clevis pin, and disconnect the fork from the bottom of the selector lever (photo).

4 Similarly disconnect the selector rod from the primary transmission lever, and remove it.

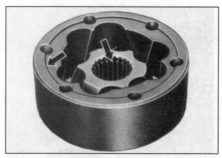

Fig. 6.9 Driveshaft joint outer race recess and inner race spline run-out location - arrowed (Sec 8)

Fig. 6.8 Removing the bellows from a driveshaft joint (Sec 8)

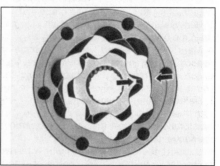

Fig. 6.10 Driveshaft joint race positioning (Sec 8)

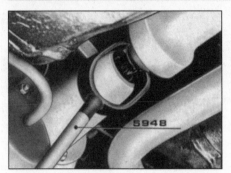

Fig. 6.11 Propeller shaft removal tool (Sec 9)

5 Prise the tray from the front of the console.

6 Disconnect the battery negative lead, then prise the two switches from the console and disconnect the wires after noting their location.

7 Move the selector lever to position R, then unscrew and remove the retaining screws and withdraw the console; the screws are located beneath the plastic covers.

Models up to 1978

8 Detach the contact holder and sliding contact.

9 Disconnect the illumination supply wire, then unbolt the selector lever and gate.

10 Prise the cover from the top of the lever and disconnect the wire.

11 Detach the detent button and remove the spring and centring block.

12 Using a soft metal drift, drive the pin from the selector lever handle after removing the retaining spring, then withdraw the knob.

13 Unscrew and remove the retaining screws and withdraw the selector scale and dust cover.

14 Remove the selector lever housing and detach the earth cable and illumination fitting.

15 Prise out the clip then remove the selector gate and return spring.

16 Drive out the spring pin, remove the stop bracket and remove the pullrod after disconnecting the cable.

17 Check the selector lever grommet and selector rod bushes for deterioration and renew them if necessary.

Models from 1978 to 1983

18 Prise the upper part of the selector knob free using a knife.

19 Depress the white ring and remove the detent button, then remove the white ring and spring.

20 Withdraw the lower part of the selector knob.

21 Remove the screws and withdraw the surround (photo).

22 Remove the screws and withdraw the selector lever scale. Remove the illumination lamp and fitting (photos).

23 Unscrew the bolt and remove the flat spring.

24 Remove the pivot pin and withdraw the selector lever from the gate housing.

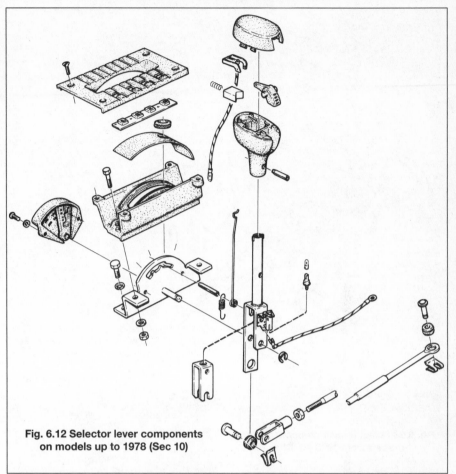

Fig. 6.12 Selector lever components on models up to 1978 (Sec 10)

10.21 Removing the selector lever surround

10.22A Removing the selector lever scale

10.22B Selector lever scale showing illumination bulb (arrowed)

10.22C Removing the selector lever illumination bulb

6

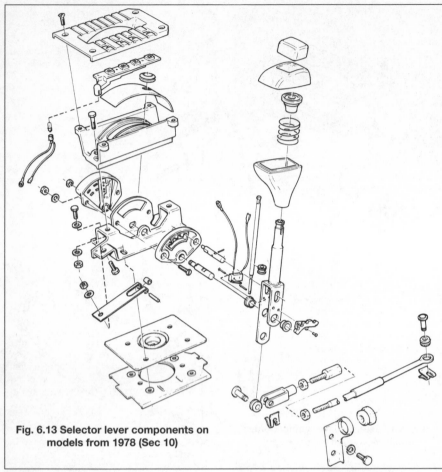

Fig. 6.13 Selector lever components on models from 1978 (Sec 10)

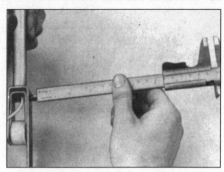

Fig. 6.14 Checking the selector lever spring pin protrusion (Sec 10)

All models

44 Refitting is a reversal of removal but the following points should be noted:

a) *Adjust the length of the selector rod so that with the selector lever and primary transmission lever in the neutral position, the clevis pin can be inserted without moving the levers. Tighten the locknuts when the adjustment is completed*

b) *Refit the propeller shaft (see Section 9)*

Models up to 1978

c) *The spring pin must protrude from the selector lever 0.16 ± 0.012 in (4.0 ± 0.3 mm) plus the thickness of the selector gate*

Models from 1978

d) *The micro switch operating pin must allow the pushrod to rotate*

e) *The pivot pin recess must face the pushrod*

f) *Attach the knob halves to each other using suitable glue*

Models from 1983

g) *Check the setting of the gear selector mechanism as follows: With the engine at idle, move the selector lever from N to D several times then repeat the operation slowly, releasing the detent knob as soon as the lever has cleared the N position. Keep moving the lever towards the D position, but stop as soon as the gears in the primary unit are heard to engage. If the detent knob only springs up after further movement towards D the setting is correct. If the detent knob has already sprung up, readjust the length of the selector control rod and recheck the setting*

11 Vacuum control microswitch models up to 1978 - adjustment

1 Start the engine and allow it to reach the normal operating temperature, then adjust the idling speed as described in Chapter 3.

2 Using a T-connection and additional hose, connect a vacuum gauge into the primary transmission outer (overdrive) chamber supply hose between the control valve and the transmission (photo).

25 Remove the selector gate. Remove the bushes and grommet from the selector lever.

26 Extract the pin from the pushrod, and the locking pin from the shaft.

27 Withdraw the pushrod and shaft.

28 Drill out the rivets and remove the microswitch.

Models from 1983

29 During 1983 the gear selector mechanism was modified to improve gear selection. The modification includes an audible and visual signal when a selection is not properly engaged, improved tolerances, and an extra drive position indicator to the right of the selector lever.

30 This modification can be fitted to all models from 1978, although it is best fitted by your Volvo dealer on models up to 1983.

31 The procedure given here describes the modification to models from 1983 as well as describing the removal and refitting of the selector lever on later models.

32 Disconnect the battery negative lead.

33 Remove the propeller shaft as described in Section 9.

34 Disconnect the fork from the bottom of the selector lever.

35 Remove the selector scale panel from around the selector lever.

36 Remove the three bolts, and fourth bolt and leaf spring securing the gear selector mechanism to the transmission tunnel, disconnect the electrical leads and remove the mechanism.

37 To refit the modified selector mechanism, first remove the tunnel console side panel at the left of the centre console.

38 Remove the selector scale panel from the new assembly and fit the selector mechanism to the tunnel using the three bolts and tightening them finger tight only. **Note:** *Never release or reposition the leaf spring of the gear selector mechanism.*

39 Tighten the fourth bolt, then tighten the other three bolts.

40 Connect the plug and connector for the indicator light.

41 Fit the warning buzzer and relay to a suitable position behind the centre console, remove the right-hand lower console panel and run the wiring from the selector lever to the buzzer and relay and connect them up. (**Note:** *A bracket and clips are supplied with the modification kit for fitting of the buzzer and relay.*)

42 Fit the lamp into the new selector scale panel, connect the wiring and fit the panel to the tunnel console.

43 Refit the console side panels, connect up the selector lever to the control rod and adjust the selector rod as described in paragraph 44.

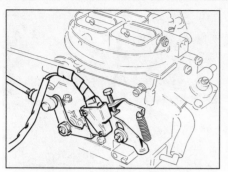

Fig. 6.15 Vacuum control microswitch fitted to models up to 1978 (Sec 11)

11.2 Checking transmission vacuum control switch adjustment with a vacuum gauge

3 Apply the handbrake and move the selector lever to N, then connect up an engine revolution counter (tachometer).
4 Unscrew the adjustment bolt fully, and pull back the microswitch after loosening the locking screw.
5 Start the engine and increase its speed to 2650 rpm.
6 Tighten the adjustment screw until the vacuum gauge returns to zero, then tighten the locking screw.
7 The microswitch is now adjusted, but check its operation by gradually increasing the engine speed to 2650 rpm, at which time the vacuum gauge should start indicating.
8 Switch off the engine and remove the tachometer and vacuum gauge.

Part B: Manual transmission

12 General description

The manual gearbox is of either 4-speed (designated M45R) or 5-speed (designated M47R). Both have synchromesh on all forward gears. The gearbox is bolted directly to the final drive casing, both of which are bolted to crossmembers attached to the underbody.

Gearchange is by means of a floor-mounted gear lever, connected to the gearbox by a control rod.

On B14 and B172 models, the engine and gearbox are connected by the propeller shaft.

On B19 and B200 models, the propeller shaft is encased in a torque tube to reduce vibration and torsional movement and ensure more accurate gear changing. While the four and five-speed gearboxes fitted to all models are basically the same, the casings vary in order to fit the propeller shaft or torque tube as necessary.

The final drive unit is the same in all models; that fitted to the B19 and B200 being a heavy duty version, and from 1982 this version is used in the other models as well.

Note: *Socket-headed or Allen type bolts are used extensively in the construction of the gearbox and final drive unit, and a set of good Allen keys or hexagonal bit sockets are required to carry out servicing work.*

13 Routine maintenance - manual gearbox

At the intervals laid down in the Routine Maintenance Section at the beginning of this manual, carry out the following operations:

Lubrication

1 Check the level of oil in the gearbox, and refill if necessary using the recommended oil (see paragraph 2 below).
2 Fill the gearbox with the recommended oil until the oil level reaches the bottom of the filler hole. Pour the oil in slowly to allow the oil to penetrate to all parts of the gearbox (this is especially important on 5-speed models) then wait at least 1 minute for the oil to settle. Refill if necessary and refit the filler plug (photo).

General

3 Inspect the propeller shaft for damage or distortion, bearings for wear and the rubber bellows for splits, holes etc.
4 Check the gearbox and final drive unit for oil leakage. If leakage is evident, check the oil level and top up as necessary, following the same general principles as for the gearbox (photo).
Note: *Depending on model type the final drive*

6

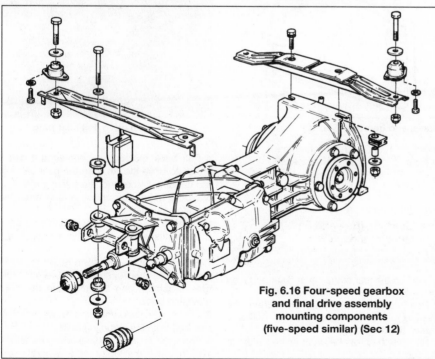

Fig. 6.16 Four-speed gearbox and final drive assembly mounting components (five-speed similar) (Sec 12)

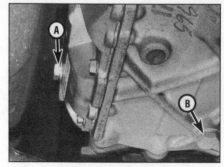

13.2 The gearbox filler (A) and drain (B) plugs

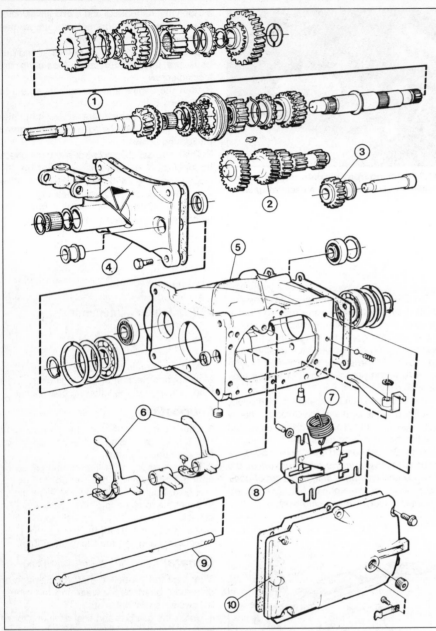

Fig. 6.17 Exploded view of the four-speed gearbox (Sec 12)

1 Input shaft	5 Main casing	8 Selector plate
2 Countershaft	6 Selector forks	9 Selector shaft
3 Reverse idler gear	7 Spring	10 Cover
4 Front cover		

Fig. 6.18 Gearbox drain and filler plugs (alternative positions) (Sec 13)

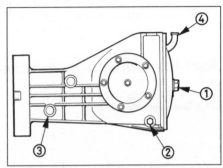

Fig. 6.19 Final drive drain and filler plugs (Sec 13)

1 Filler plug
2 Drain plug
3 Inspection plug (to be discarded - see text)
4 Breather pipe

13.4 Final drive unit filler plug

unit may or may not have a drain plug, but in either case there is no requirement to renew the oil at any prescribed interval. Also depending on model type there may or may not be a plug fitted near the front flange of the final drive unit. The purpose of this plug was to enable oil leakage past the final drive unit or gearbox oil seals to be detected. As the plug has to be removed in order to do this, the manufacturers now recommend that the plug is permanently removed in order that any leakage may be seen as soon as it occurs, and remedial action taken.

14 Gearbox (B14 and B172) - removal and refitting

1 Jack up the rear of the car and support it on axle stands. Chock the front wheels.
2 Remove the drain plug and drain the gearbox oil into a suitable container. Refit and tighten the drain plug.
3 Remove the propeller shaft as described in Section 17.

4 Pull back the rubber bellows and use a punch to drive the pin from the gear selector rod balljoint. Disconnect the selector rod.
5 Where necessary unbolt and remove the vibration damper.
6 Remove the clip and clevis pin and detach the stabiliser rod from the front of the gearbox.
7 Support the weight of the gearbox with a trolley jack, then unscrew and remove the nuts, washers, and bushes from the front mounting bolts.
8 Lower the jack until the front cover is released from the mounting bolts.
9 Clean the gearbox-to-final drive joint area.
10 Unscrew the bolts and separate the

Fig. 6.20 Gearbox-to-final drive coupling sleeve - arrowed (Sec 14)

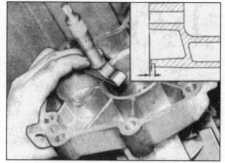

Fig. 6.21 Final drive bearing shim calculation using a micrometer (Sec 14)

gearbox from the final drive. Lower the jack and remove the gearbox from under the car. Take care not to lose the mainshaft and countershaft shims.

11 Remove the gasket from the final drive casing, and slide the coupling sleeve from the gearbox mainshaft.

12 Before refitting the gearbox to the final drive, the countershaft and mainshaft shim thicknesses must be calculated as follows.

13 Place the gearbox on the bench with the mainshaft uppermost.

14 Press the countershaft outer race firmly into contact with the rollers and measure the distance from the casing to the race using a micrometer.

15 Add to the dimension obtained in paragraph 14 0.010 in (0.25 mm) for the gasket thickness, and deduct 0.002 in (0.06 mm) for the countershaft endfloat. The resulting dimension is the thickness of the shim to be fitted against the countershaft outer race. For ease of calculation, add 0.007 in (0.19 mm) to the dimension obtained in paragraph 14.

Example:

Measured depth	0.047 in (1.20 mm)
Add	0.007 in (0.19 mm)
Shim thickness	0.054 in (1.39 mm)

16 Using a micrometer, measure the distance from the mainshaft bearing outer race to the casing.

17 Again using a micrometer, measure the distance from the final drive contact face to the bottom of the bearing recess (see Fig. 6.21). Note that the bearing seat upper edge is lower than the contact face.

18 Add to the dimension obtained in paragraph 17 0.010 in (0.25 mm) for the gasket thickness, and deduct the dimension obtained in paragraph 16. Deduct a further 0.004 in (0.10 mm) for the mainshaft endfloat. The resulting dimension is the thickness of the shim to be fitted in the final drive bearing recess.

Example:

Paragraph 17 depth	0.213 in (5.40 mm)
Gasket thickness	+ 0.010 in (0.25 mm)
	0.223 in (5.65 mm)
Paragraph 16 size	- 0.188 in (4.78 mm)
	0.035 in (0.87 mm)
Mainshaft endfloat	-0.004 in (0.10 mm)
Shim thickness	0.031 in (0.77 mm)

19 The remaining refitting procedure is a

reversal of removal, but the following points should be noted:

a) *Clean the gearbox and final drive contact faces and always use a new gasket*
b) *Retain the shims with grease while the gearbox is being fitted to the final drive unit*
c) *The gearbox-to-final drive upper and lower centre bolts are longer than the others*
d) *Fill the gearbox with the correct quantity of oil*

15 Gearbox and final drive (B14 and B172) - removal and refitting

1 Follow the instructions given in Section 14, paragraph 1 to 6.

2 Mark the driveshaft inner couplings and drive flanges in relation to each other, then unscrew and remove the retaining bolts and plates. An Allen key may be required to do this (photo).

3 Detach the driveshafts and tie them to the handbrake cables. Remove the flange gaskets.

4 Support the weight of the gearbox and final drive assembly with a trolley jack.

5 Unscrew and remove the nuts, washers and bushes from the front mounting bolts.

6 Unclip the handbrake cable mountings from the rear transmission crossmember and unscrew the crossmember mounting nuts.

7 Lower the jack until the handbrake cables can be positioned over the rear crossmember.

8 Lower the gearbox and final drive to the ground and withdraw the assembly from under the car.

15.2 Driveshaft flange on the final drive unit

9 Clean the gearbox-to-final drive joint area.

10 Unscrew the bolts and separate the gearbox from the final drive. Take care not to lose the mainshaft and countershaft shims.

11 Remove the gasket from the final drive casing and slide the coupling sleeve from the gearbox mainshaft.

12 Before fitting the gearbox to the final drive, select the correct countershaft and mainshaft shims with reference to Section 14, paragraphs 13 to 18.

13 Refitting is a reversal of removal, but note the points given in Section 14, paragraph 19 in addition to the following points:

a) *Fit new gaskets to the driveshaft flanges (if fitted)*
b) *Check and, if necessary, top up the oil level in the final drive*

16 Manual gearbox - overhaul

Overhauling a manual transmission unit is a difficult and involved job for the DIY home mechanic. In addition to dismantling and reassembling many small parts, clearances must be precisely measured and, if necessary, changed by selecting shims and spacers. Internal transmission components are also often difficult to obtain, and in many instances, are extremely expensive. Because of this, if the transmission develops a fault or becomes noisy, the best course of action is to have the unit overhauled by a specialist repairer, or to obtain an exchange reconditioned unit.

Nevertheless, it is not impossible for the more experienced mechanic to overhaul the transmission, provided the special tools are available, and that the job is done in a deliberate step-by-step manner so that nothing is overlooked.

The tools necessary for an overhaul may include internal and external circlip pliers, bearing pullers, a slide hammer, a set of pin punches, a dial test indicator, and possibly a hydraulic press. In addition, a large, sturdy workbench and a vice will be required.

During dismantling of the transmission, make careful notes of how each component is fitted, to make reassembly easier and accurate.

Before dismantling the transmission, it will help if you have some idea which area is malfunctioning. Certain problems can be closely related to specific areas in the gearbox, which can make component examination and replacement easier.

17 Propeller shaft - removal and refitting (B14 and B172 models)

1 Jack up the front and rear of the car and support it on axle stands.

2 Remove the screws and withdraw the heat shield located above the exhaust silencer.

6

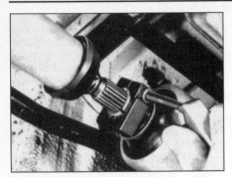

Fig. 6.22 Unscrewing a propeller shaft clamp bolt (Sec 17)

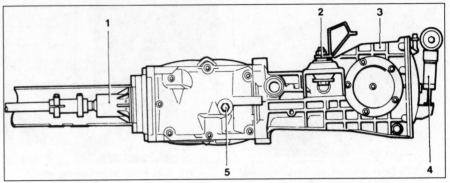

Fig. 6.23 Diagram of the B19 and B200 models four-speed transmission (Sec 18)

1 Torque tube and front gearbox casing
2 Mountings and crossmembers
3 Final drive unit

4 Shock absorber
  (discontinued - see text)
5 Filler/level plug

3 With the gear lever in neutral, turn the propeller shaft so that the front clamp socket bolt is visible. Fully loosen the bolt to release the clamp from the clutch using an Allen key.

4 Similarly, fully loosen the rear clamp socket bolt.

5 Slide the propeller shaft to the rear as far as it will go. If difficulty is experienced, obtain tool No. 5948 (see Fig. 6.11) or construct a similar tool to lever the propeller shaft rearwards.

6 Loosen the transmission front crossmember-to-body mounting nuts as far as possible without removing them.

7 Disconnect the propeller shaft from the clutch shaft, then slide it from the gearbox input shaft and withdraw it from the car.

8 To refit the propeller shaft, first slide it fully onto the clutch shaft.

9 Engage the propeller shaft with the gearbox input shaft, then tighten the crossmember mounting nuts to the specified torque.

10 Push the propeller shaft fully forwards so that it abuts the circlip on the clutch shaft.

11 Tighten both clamp socket bolts.

12 Refit the exhaust heat shield and lower the car to the ground.

18 Gearbox and final drive (B19 and B200 models) - removal and refitting

1 Jack up the rear of the car and support on axle stands. Chock the front wheels.

2 Remove the heat shield below the fuel tank.

3 Disconnect the gearchange rod at the gearbox and unbolt the gearchange from the middle of the torque tube.

18.10 Speed sensor on the final drive unit

4 Unclip the handbrake cable from the right-hand fuel tank.

5 Where fitted, disconnect the shock absorber at the rear of the final drive unit from the underbody.

6 Unhook the rear mounting rubbers and lower the rear of the exhaust system.

7 Unbolt the driveshafts from the final drive unit and tie them to one side.

8 Remove the plugs from the rear of the torque tube, then unscrew the propeller shaft clamp coupling bolt using an Allen key. If the bolt is not aligned with the access hole, remove the front engine splash guard and turn the engine on the crankshaft centre bolt as necessary.

9 Support the gearbox and final drive unit with a trolley jack then unbolt the side mountings.

10 Lower the assembly and, where applicable, disconnect the wiring from the speed sensor (photo).

11 Remove the rear torque tube bolts, pull the assembly from the torque tube and withdraw it from the car.

12 Refitting is a reversal of removal, but check the oil levels and top up if necessary.

19 Torque tube (B19 and B200) - removal and refitting

1 Remove the gearbox and final drive unit, as described in Section 18.

2 Remove the exhaust U-bolt mounting from the rear of the torque tube.

3 Disconnect the exhaust system at the end

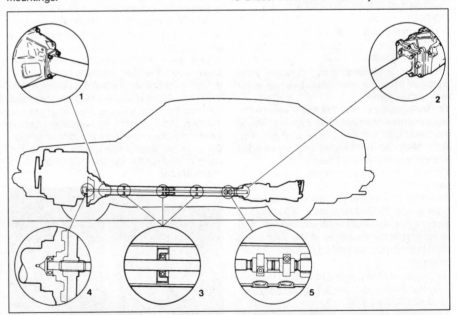

Fig. 6.24 Diagram of the torque tube fitted to B19 and B200 models (Sec 19)

1 Torque tube front connection
2 Torque tube rear connection
3 Propeller shaft bearings

4 Spigot bearing in the crankshaft
5 Clamp coupling

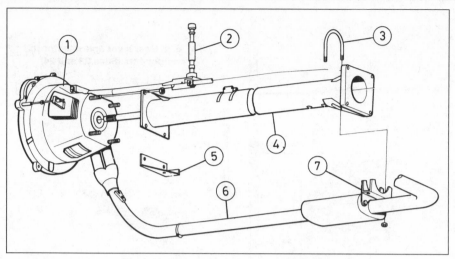

Fig. 6.25 Torque tube components (Sec 19)

1 Clutch housing
2 Gearchange mechanism
3 Exhaust mounting U-bolt
4 Torque tube
5 Front exhaust mounting bracket
6 Exhaust
7 Rear exhaust mounting bracket

of the front downpipe and remove it from the car. Also unbolt the downpipe from the front bracket.

4 Unscrew the nuts securing the torque tube to the clutch housing and remove the exhaust bracket (photo).

5 Withdraw the torque tube and propeller shaft from the clutch housing.

6 Refitting is a reversal of removal.

20 Gearbox cover gasket (B19 and B200) - renewal

1 Jack up the rear of the car and support it on axle stands. Chock the front wheels.

2 Unscrew the drain plug and drain the oil into a suitable container. Refit and tighten the plug.

3 Remove the heat shield from beneath the fuel tank.

4 Unclip the handbrake cable from the right-hand fuel tank.

5 Unhook the rear mounting rubbers and lower the rear of the exhaust system.

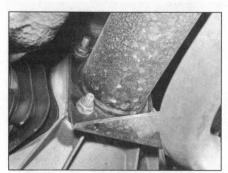

19.4 Torque tube-to-clutch housing nuts

6 Where fitted, disconnect the shock absorber at the rear of the final drive unit from the underbody.

7 Support the gearbox and final drive unit with a trolley jack then unbolt the side mountings.

8 Lower the assembly enough to provide access to the gearbox cover, then unbolt the cover and remove the gasket.

9 Clean the mating faces and locate the new gasket using a little grease to hold it in place. The remaining refitting procedure is a reversal of removal. Finally fill the gearbox with the specified quantity of oil.

21 Gearbox front casing (B19 and B200) - removal and refitting

1 Jack up the rear of the car and support it on axle stands. Chock the front wheels.

2 Unscrew the drain plug and drain the gearbox oil into a suitable container. Refit and tighten the plug.

3 Remove the gearbox and final drive unit, as described in Section 18.

4 Unbolt the front casing from the gearbox and remove all traces of the gasket.

5 If a new front casing is being fitted remove the shim from the gearbox input shaft.

6 From the casing remove the nylon bush and grommet for the gearchange rod, and remove the O-ring and oil seal.

7 To renew the needle bearing, first remove the circlip and use an extractor tool to pull out the bearing, then remove the remaining circlip. Lubricate the new bearing with grease then fit the inner circlip and drive in the bearing using a soft metal drift. Fit the outer circlip.

8 Drive in the new oil seal using a block of wood.

9 Locate a new torque tube O-ring in the groove, and fit the grommet and nylon bush.

10 If a new front casing is being fitted, determine the thickness of the shim then fit it over the input shaft.

11 Fit the front casing to the gearbox, with a new gasket, and tighten the bolts.

12 Refit the gearbox and final drive unit using a reversal of the removal procedure, then finally fill the gearbox with the specified quantity of oil.

6

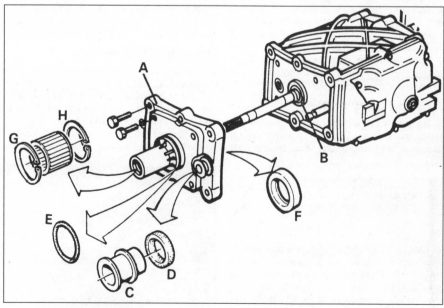

Fig. 6.26 Gearbox front casing components (B19 and B200 models) (Sec 21)

A Front casing
B Shim
C Nylon bush
D Rubber grommet
E O-ring
F Oil seal
G Circlip (front)
H Circlip (rear)

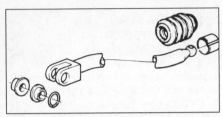

Fig. 6.27 Selector rod components (Sec 23)

22 Driveshaft - removal, inspection and refitting

The procedure is identical to that described in Section 8, but paragraphs 2 and 9d should be omitted.

23 Gear selector rod - removal and refitting

B14 and B172 models

1 Remove the propeller shaft as described in Section 17.
2 Using an Allen key, unscrew the lockbolt from the bottom of the gear lever.
3 Drive the selector rod pivot pin from the gear lever and disconnect the selector rod.
4 Pull back the rubber bellows from the rear of the selector rod, then use a punch to drive the pin from the balljoint. Withdraw the selector rod.
5 Remove the bushes and bellows and check all components for wear and damage, renewing them as necessary.
6 Fit the bushes and bellows to the selector rod, locating the O-ring between the left-hand bush and the rod fork. Smear the bushes and balljoint surfaces with graphite grease.
7 Refitting is a reversal of removal, but apply a liquid locking agent to the threads of the pivot pin lockbolt before tightening it.

B19 and B200 models

8 The procedure is similar to that described in paragraphs 1 to 7, but the transmission assembly and torque tube must be removed first.

24 Gear lever - removal and refitting

1 The gear lever consists of two sections held together by a dowel pin. The top section can be removed separately for repairs to the reverse gear detent mechanism by removing the leather gaiter and tapping out the pin (support the gear lever with a reaction bar during this operation to prevent damage to the synchroniser ring).
2 To remove the complete gear lever on

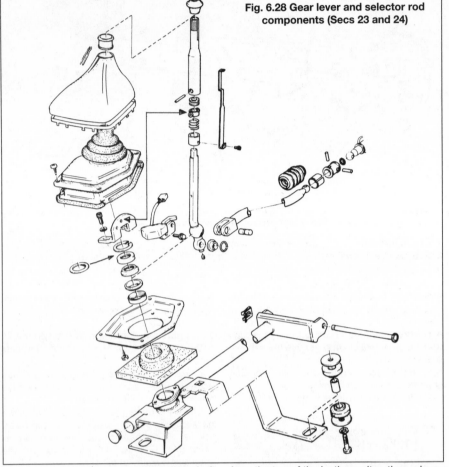

Fig. 6.28 Gear lever and selector rod components (Secs 23 and 24)

B14 and B172 models the propeller shaft must first be removed, and on B19 and B200 models the complete torque tube and gearbox assembly also have to be removed.

B14 and B172 models

3 With the propeller shaft removed (see Section 17), remove the lockbolt from the bottom of the gear lever using an Allen key, then drive out the selector rod pivot pin to disconnect the selector rod.
4 Disconnect the battery negative terminal.
5 Working inside the car, disconnect the clip

from the top of the leather gaiter, then release the plate holding the leather gaiter to the tunnel gaiter. The plate is secured by a variety of methods depending on model and year, but is either clipped in or held by screws.
6 Lift the leather gaiter and plate off the gear lever.
7 The rubber gaiter can now be removed in similar fashion to the leather gaiter.
8 Remove the screws securing the reversing light switch and, where fitted, the change-up indicator microswitch (photo), and set them to one side.

Fig. 6.29 Disconnecting the selector rod (Sec 23)

24.8 Reverse lamp switch (A) and gear position indicator switch (B)

9 Using an Allen key, remove the bolt from the detent bracket and remove the bracket.

10 Prise out the lock washer and the spacer (if fitted) and withdraw the gear lever.

11 Dismantle the gear lever by gently tapping off the knob, remove the screw and withdraw the reverse gear detent, rubber bush and boot.

12 Drive out the dowel pin and remove the shaft and bush, pullrod, spring and sleeve.

13 Reassembly and refitting is a reversal of removal with the following points

a) Lubricate the gear lever ball with grease

b) Before fully tightening the detent screws, select first gear and adjust the position of the detent bracket so that the gap between it and the gear lever is between 0.020 and 0.059 in (0.5 and 1.5 mm), tighten the screws and check that the gap isthe same with second gear selected

c) Refit the reverse light switch and change-up indicator switch (refer to Chapter 10)

B19 and B200 models

14 Start as described in paragraphs 2 and 4 to 9 above, then proceed as follows:

15 Extract the circlip from the pin at the front of the gearchange support rod, and pull the pin out approximately 0.4 in (10.0 mm).

16 Lift the front of the support rod then withdraw the gearchange lever from under the car.

17 Refit in the reverse order, referring to the notes in paragraph 13.

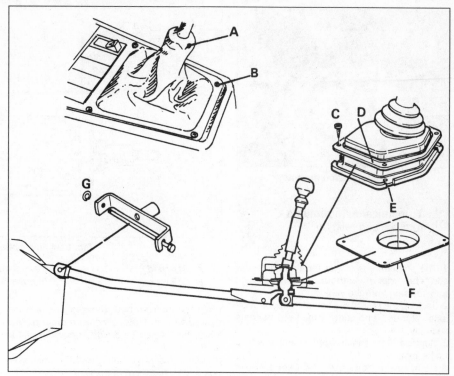

Fig. 6.30 Components of the gear lever and selector rod on B19 and B200 models (Secs 23 and 24)

A Clip	C Screw	E Rubber gaiter	G Support rod front
B Screw	D Surround	F Lower rubber cover	mounting

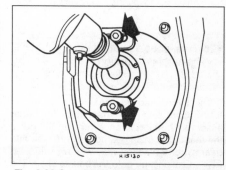

Fig. 6.32 Gear lever detent bracket screws (Sec 24)

Fig. 6.31 Gear lever gaiter components from 1983 (Sec 24)

1 Leather gaiter and surround	3 Rubber gaiter	5 Baseplate
2 Surround	4 Reverse lamp switch	6 Sealing rubber

Fig. 6.33 Checking the gear lever detent adjustment (Sec 24)

6

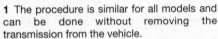

25.4 Transmission mounting

25 Transmission mountings - removal and refitting

1 The procedure is similar for all models and can be done without removing the transmission from the vehicle.
2 Jack up the rear of the car and support it on axle stands, chocking the front wheels securely.
3 Support the transmission assembly with a trolley jack.
4 Remove the bolts from the centre of the rubber mountings (photo).
5 Gently lower the transmission assembly on the trolley jack sufficiently to allow the rubber mountings to be removed from the cross-members.
6 Fit new rubber mountings and refit the transmission following a reverse of this procedure.

26 Five-speed gearbox - general description

The five-speed gearbox is similar to the four-speed unit but has the fifth gear assembly housed in an extension bolted to the rear of the main gearbox. In 1986 the fifth gear synchronisation ring was repositioned from the mainshaft onto the countershaft. The final drive unit used with the five-speed gearbox is shorter and more compact than on the four-speed. It should be noted that, where a five-speed gearbox is fitted to a B14 engined model, the final drive unit cannot be removed separately. The following sections deal only with the five-speed gearbox where it differs from the four-speed, the general procedures for dismantling and reassembly being the same.

27 Final drive unit - removal and refitting

B14 - four-speed models

1 Engage neutral gear, clean the joint between the gearbox and final drive unit, then

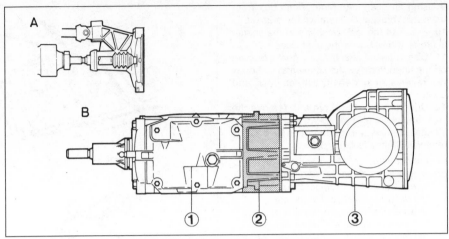

Fig. 6.34 Five-speed gearbox (Sec 26)

A B14 model
B B19 model

1 Main gearbox
2 5th gear extension

3 Modified final drive unit

drain the oil from both the gearbox and the final drive unit. **Note:** *Where no drain plug is fitted, the oil can be drained once the unit is on the bench.*
2 Detach the driveshafts from the final drive unit and tie them out of the way (Section 22).
3 Support the gearbox on an axle stand, then remove the nuts from the rear crossmember, and slightly lower the final drive.
4 Unhook the clips from the handbrake cables and position the cables on top of the crossmember.
5 Remove the bolts from the final drive-to-gearbox flange and remove the final drive unit, taking careful note of the shims for the output and intermediate shaft, and the rubber boot.

B19 - four-speed models

6 Proceed as in paragraphs 1 to 3 above, then remove the shock absorber (if fitted). This shock absorber is no longer used and its bracket and the shock absorber should be removed and discarded.
7 Remove the bolts from the crossmember and lower the unit slightly to allow enough room to remove the retaining bolts between the gearbox and final drive unit flange.
8 Remove the final drive unit by pulling it to the rear and turning it to one side, taking note of the shims between the output shafts and intermediate shaft, and the rubber boot.

B14 - five-speed models

9 It is not possible to remove the final drive unit separately on these models. The complete gearbox/final drive unit must be removed, as described in Section 15.

B19 - five-speed models

10 The procedure is as described for four-speed models, but as from 1984 the rear suspension leaf springs must be detached from the shackles in order to lower the rear axle sufficiently to give enough room to remove the final drive unit.

B172 models

11 The procedure is as described for B14 models.

B200 models

12 The procedure is as described for B19 models.

28 Final drive flange and oil seal - removal and refitting

1 Jack up the rear of the car and support it on axle stands. Chock the front wheels.
2 Mark the driveshaft inner coupling and drive flange in relation to each other, then unscrew and remove the retaining bolts and plates. An Allen key will be required to do this.
3 Detach the driveshaft and tie it up out of the way. Remove the flange gasket.
4 Place a drip tray beneath the drive flanges.
5 Temporarily refit two adjacent bolts to the drive flange and use a lever between the bolts to hold the drive flange stationary. Unscrew the retaining bolt and withdraw the drive flange (photos).
6 Using a screwdriver, prise the oil seal from the side bearing cover.

28.5A Showing drive flange retaining bolt on final drive

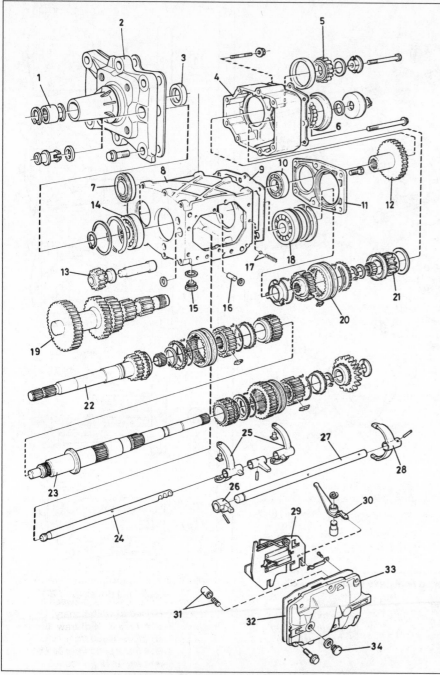

Fig. 6.35 Exploded view of an early five-speed gearbox (Sec 26)

1 Needle bearing	14 Input shaft bearing	25 Selector forks
2 Front cover	15 Drain plug	26 Selector dogs
3 Oil seal	16 Dowel	27 Selector shaft (5th)
4 5th gear extension	17 Detent ball and spring	28 Selector fork
5 Countershaft bearing	18 Mainshaft bearing	29 Selector plate
6 Mainshaft bearing	19 Countershaft	30 Reverse selector lever
7 Countershaft bearing	20 5th synchro unit	31 Hold-down spring and
8 Gearbox casing	21 5th gear	bush
9 Gasket	22 Input shaft	32 Gasket
10 Countershaft bearing	23 Mainshaft	33 Cover
11 Bearing retainer	24 Selector shaft (1st/2nd and	34 Filler/level plug
12 5th gear	3rd/4th)	
13 Reverse idler gear		

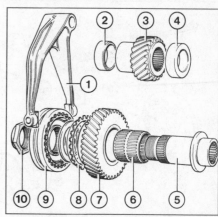

Fig. 6.36 Exploded view of components of the modified 5th gear (Sec 26)

1 Shift fork	6 Needle bearing
2 Spacer sleeve	7 5th gear
3 5th gear	8 Synchroniser ring
4 Spacer sleeve	9 Baulk ring
5 Countershaft	10 Locknut
extension	

28.5B Removing the drive flange

28.7 Installing drive flange oil seal

7 Wipe clean the oil seal recess, then tap in the new seal using a metal tube of suitable size (photo).

8 Lubricate the oil seals with oil, then fit the drive flange and tighten the retaining bolt to the specified torque.

9 Reconnect the driveshaft, together with a new gasket, and tighten the retaining bolts to the specified torque.

10 Lower the car to the ground, then remove the filler/level plug and if necessary top up the oil level. Refit and tighten the plug.

6

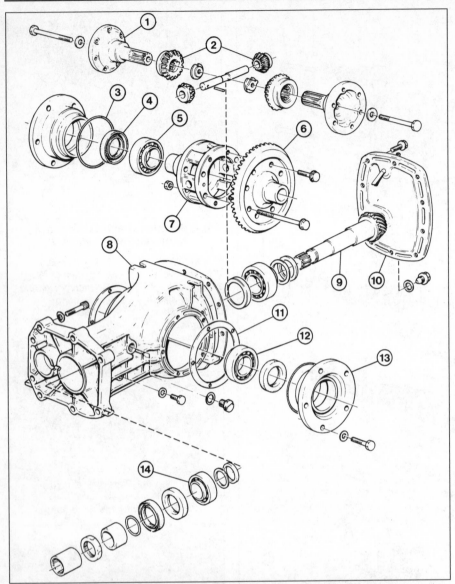

Fig. 6.37 Exploded view of the four-speed final drive (Secs 27 and 28)

1 Drive flange	6 Crownwheel	11 Gasket
2 Differential gears	7 Differential unit	12 Bearing
3 O-ring	8 Casing	13 Bearing retainer
4 Oil seal	9 Pinion shaft	14 Pinion bearing
5 Bearing	10 Rear cover	

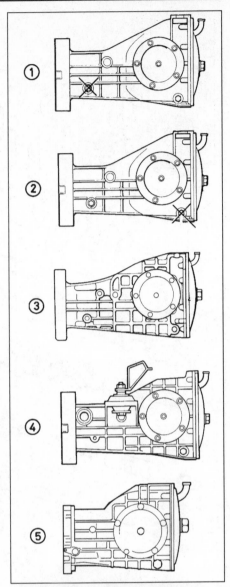

Fig. 6.38 Distinguishing features of the various final drives (Sec 27)

1 B14 up to 1978
2 B14 1979 to 1981
3 B14 four-speed from 1982
4 B19 four-speed from 1981
5 B14 and B 19 five-speed

29 Final drive rear cover gasket - renewal

1 Jack up the rear of the car and support it on axle stands. Chock the front wheels.
2 Place a drip tray beneath the rear cover.
3 Unscrew the bolts and remove the final drive rear cover and gasket (photos).
4 When all the oil has drained, wipe clean the mating faces of the cover and final drive. Then refit the rear cover, together with a new gasket, and tighten the bolts in diagonal sequence to the specified torque.
5 Lower the car to the ground, then remove the filler/level plug and refill the final drive with oil to the bottom of the plug aperture. Refit and tighten the plug.

30 Final drive pinion shaft oil seals - renewal

1 Remove the final drive unit, as described in Section 27.
2 Using a screwdriver, prise the seals from the housing, being careful not to damage the bore of the housing. **Note:** *There are two seals fitted shoulder to shoulder.*
3 Grease both the bearing surface and the lips of the seals, then fit the first seal open side facing inward, using a suitable sized mandrel to tap it into the housing so that it is just below the rim of the housing.
4 Fit the second seal against the first, open side facing outward and tap it into the housing using the mandrel until it is recessed in the housing by approximately 0.04 in (1.0 mm).
5 Refit the final drive unit to the gearbox as described in Section 30.

Fig. 6.39 Removing a drive flange oil seal
(Sec 28)

29.3A Removing final drive rear cover

29.3B View of differential unit with rear
cover removed

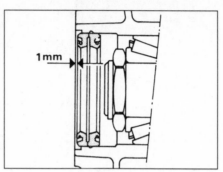

Fig. 6.40 Correct fitting of the five-speed
gearbox pinion shaft oil seals (Sec 30)

Fault finding - automatic transmission

Lack of drive
- [ ] Broken drivebelts
- [ ] Drivebelts out of adjustment or contaminated with oil
- [ ] Selector rod disconnected or selector mechanism faulty

Excessive vibration and whine
- [ ] Drivebelts out of adjustment
- [ ] Old, congealed oil in primary sliding discs
- [ ] Worn bearings or gear teeth
- [ ] Worn drivebelts
- [ ] Worn propeller shaft splines

Engine overrevs - transmission fails to change up correctly
- [ ] Vacuum hoses broken or blocked
- [ ] Vacuum control valve or microswitch faulty
- [ ] Primary sliding disc diaphragm broken or not sealing

Low ratio hold inoperative
- [ ] Vacuum control valve faulty
- [ ] Low ratio switch faulty
- [ ] Electronic vacuum control faulty

Fault finding - manual transmission

Gearbox noisy
- [ ] Input shaft bearings worn
- [ ] Countershaft bearings worn
- [ ] Mainshaft or spigot bearings worn
- [ ] Worn or chipped gear teeth

Ineffective synchromesh
- [ ] Worn synchro units and baulk rings

Jumps out of gear
- [ ] Worn detent ball and spring
- [ ] Worn synchro units and baulk rings
- [ ] Worn selector mechanism

Difficulty engaging gears
- [ ] Clutch not releasing fully
- [ ] Worn selector mechanism

Final drive noisy
- [ ] Lack of oil
- [ ] Worn bearings or gear teeth

6

Chapter 7
Braking system

Contents

Degrees of difficulty

Easy, suitable for novice with little experience	Fairly easy, suitable for beginner with some experience	Fairly difficult, suitable for competent DIY mechanic	Difficult, suitable for experienced DIY mechanic	Very difficult, suitable for expert DIY or professional

Specifications

System type .... Four wheel hydraulic, discs at front, self-adjusting drums at rear, dual circuit. Mechanical handbrake to rear wheels

Hydraulic fluid
Type/specification .... Hydraulic fluid to DOT 4

Front brakes

	Models up to 1980	Models from 1980
Discs:		
Diameter	9.16 in (232.7 mm)	9.41 in (239.0 mm)
Thickness (new)	0.39 in (9.85 mm)	0.51 in (12.85 mm)
Minimum thickness after resurfacing	0.36 in (9.1 mm)	0.46 in (11.8 mm)
Maximum run-out	0.006 in (0.15 mm)	0.006 in (0.15 mm)
Disc pads:		
Thickness (new)	0.38 in (9.7 mm)	0.56 in (14.3 mm)
Minimum thickness	0.08 in (2.0 mm)	0.08 in (2.0 mm)

Rear brakes (B14 and B172)
Drums:
Diameter (new) .... 8.00 in (203.2 mm)
Maximum diameter after resurfacing .... 8.04 in (204.2 mm)
Shoe linings:
Thickness (new) .... 0.18 in (4.5 mm)
Minimum thickness .... 0.08 in (2.0 mm)

Rear brakes (B19 and B200)
Drums:
Diameter (new) .... 9.00 in (228.6 mm)
Maximum diameter after resurfacing .... 9.04 in (229.6 mm)
Shoe linings:
Thickness (new) .... 0.20 in (5.0 mm)
Minimum thickness .... 0.04 in (1.0 mm)

Master cylinder
Type .... Tandem, with fluid level warning switch. Hydraulic stop-light switch fitted up to chassis number 321597. As from 1978 models, automatic transmission control switch fitted to CVT models

7

Servo unit

Type:

B14:	
Up to chassis No 451742	Girling 385V
From chassis No 451743	Bendix 7.5 in
From 1985	Isovac 9.0 in
B172	Isovac 9.0 in
B19:	
Up to 1985	Bendix 9.0 in
From 1985	Isovac 9.0 in
B200	Isovac 9.0 in

Handbrake

Lever adjustment:

B14 and B172	3 to 4 notches
B19 and B200	5 to 7 notches

Torque wrench settings

	lbf ft	Nm
Caliper bolts (models up to 1980)	49	67
Caliper housing bolts (models from 1980)	86	117
Disc-to-hub bolts	35	47
Caliper locating pin bolts (models from 1980)	24	33
Disc guard bolts	15	21
Servo unit nuts	18	24
Master cylinder nuts:		
Models up to 1980	17	23
Models from 1980	10	14
Wheel cylinder nuts:		
B14 and B172	4	6
B19 and B200	6	8
Pedal pivot bolt	15	21
Brake line unions	8	11
Bleed screws	7	10

1 General description

The four wheel braking system is of dual circuit hydraulic type, with discs at the front and self-adjusting drum brakes at the rear. A vacuum servo unit is fitted as standard equipment. The handbrake is mechanically operated on the rear wheels only.

The front brake calipers on models up to 1980 are of the fixed type, having two opposed pistons in each caliper. As from 1980, single piston sliding calipers are fitted.

A pressure regulating valve is installed in the hydraulic circuit to prevent the rear wheels locking in advance of the front wheels during heavy braking.

As from 1978 the master cylinder on automatic transmission versions is provided with a high pressure switch which operates the transmission low ratio hold during excessive braking.

The self-adjusting brakes on B19 models are slightly different to those fitted to earlier models and, as from 1983, the handbrake cable system on all models was modified to ease adjustment.

In 1986 the front brake discs were modified and cooling slots introduced into the brake disc guard. These new discs and disc guards may be fitted to older models, but the older type without cooling slots must never be fitted to models with steel wheels because of the danger of overheating.

As from 1986, all brake pads and drum linings fitted as original equipment are asbestos free.

2 Routine maintenance

At the intervals laid down in the Routine Maintenance Section at the beginning of this manual, carry out the following operations:

Hydraulic fluid

1 Remove the fluid reservoir cap and check the fluid level, topping-up as necessary. Inspect the brake system for leaks if frequent topping-up is necessary.
2 Renew the fluid at suitable intervals (Section 13).

Servo unit (Sections 17 to 20)

3 Check the servo for operation.
4 Renew the air filter.

Handbrake (Section 14)

5 Check the handbrake for correct adjustment.

Friction linings (Sections 3 and 4)

6 Inspect the disc pads and shoes for wear.

General inspection (Sections 11 and 12)

7 Inspect all brake hoses and pipelines for corrosion, chafing damage, leaks and security.

3 Disc pads - inspection and renewal

1 Jack up the front of the car, support it on axle stands, and remove the roadwheels.
2 Working at each side in turn, turn the steering wheel so that the caliper aperture is facing outwards.
3 Measure each disc pad lining thickness and compare it with the minimum thickness given in the Specifications.
4 If any lining is worn to below the minimum thickness, renew the front disc pads as a set.

Models up to 1980

5 Extract the spring clips from the retaining pins, then pull the pins from the caliper using a suitable drift if necessary.
6 Remove the two disc pads, using pliers if difficulty is encountered due to the backing plates being rusted.

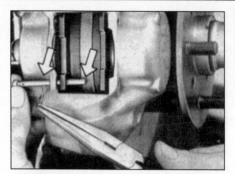
Fig. 7.1 Removing the disc pad retaining clips and pins on models up to 1980 (Sec 3)

3.7 Removing the lower caliper locating bolt (models from 1980)

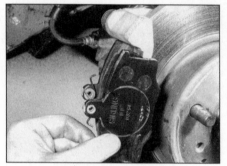
3.8 Removing a disc pad (models from 1980)

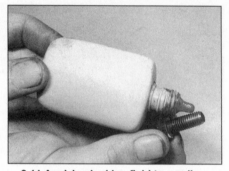
3.11 Applying locking fluid to a caliper locating bolt (models from 1980)

Models from 1980

7 Using an open-ended spanner, unscrew the lower caliper locating bolt (photo).

8 Swivel the caliper upwards from the disc pads, then slide each disc pad from the mounting bracket (photo).

All models

9 Brush away dust or dirt from the caliper recesses, being careful not to inhale any, then use a flat piece of wood to press the piston(s) into the caliper to accommodate the new pads. While doing this, check that the brake fluid in the master cylinder reservoir does not overflow- syphon some out if necessary.

Models from 1980

10 Check the caliper guide pins for wear and smooth movement, and the rubber boots for splits. Renew the boots if necessary, and lubricate the pins with a little grease.

All models

11 Fit the new disc pads using a reversal of the removal procedure. On models from 1980 use thread locking compound on the caliper locating bolts. Give the footbrake pedal several hard applications to bring the pads to their correct positions. Check and, if necessary, top up the brake fluid level.

---

4 Rear brake shoes - inspection and renewal

B14 and B172 models

1 Jack up the rear of the car and support it adequately on axle stands.

2 Mark the roadwheel in relation to the wheel studs, then remove it.

3 Fully release the handbrake lever.

4 Using a wooden or soft-head mallet, tap the brake drum from the hub and wheel studs. If difficulty is experienced as a result of worn brake drums, loosen the handbrake adjustment at the handbrake lever (see Section 14), then using a screwdriver, lever the handbrake operating lever away from the backplate and pull the nylon stop from the

Fig. 7.2 Removing the rear brake nylon stop in order to withdraw a worn brake drum (Sec 4)

rubber boot of the lever. On release of the lever, the brake shoes will retract enough to allow the brake drums to be removed.

5 Brush away any accumulated dust (taking care not to inhale any) and inspect the linings; if they are worn down to within 0.04 in (1 mm) of the rivets or if the total thickness is under 0.08 in (2 mm), renew the shoes as a complete set. If the linings are in good condition, clean the interior of the brake drum and refit it.

6 Where the shoes must be renewed, obtain new or reconditioned units.

7 Note the location of the return and retaining springs to ensure correct refitting.

8 Remove both shoe steady posts. To do this, grip the dished washer with a pair of pliers, depress it and rotate it through 90°, then release it and withdraw the washer and spring from the T-shaped post.

9 Using a screwdriver or adjustable spanner, prise the two shoes from the lower anchor block and unhook the lower return spring (photo).

10 Prise the front shoe from the groove in the wheel cylinder and detach it from the self-adjusting mechanism quadrant. Unhook the upper return spring from the trailing shoe and withdraw the leading shoe forwards.

11 Unhook the remaining return spring from the trailing shoe and withdraw the shoes rearwards.

12 Clean the brake backplate and check the wheel cylinders for leaks; if evident, renew or overhaul the wheel cylinder as necessary.

13 Do not touch the brake pedal while the shoes are removed.

14 Check the self-adjusting mechanism for free movement and lubricate it sparingly, being careful to wipe any excess oil away. Smear a little brake grease on the ends of the shoe webs which will contact the wheel cylinder and anchor block. Place the self-adjusting mechanism in its start position.

15 Refitting the brake shoes is a reversal of the removal procedure but the following additional points should be noted:

a) *The arrows marked on new shoes should point upwards towards the wheel cylinder*

b) *Make sure that all the springs are fitted correctly; in particular check that the*

7

4.9 Rear brake shoes and lower anchor block

4.15 Fitted rear brake shoes

4.17A Rear brake auto adjuster spring and carrier (B19 models)

4.17B Top and bottom return spring locations on the rear brake (B19 models)

steady spring T-posts are at right angles to the slots in the dished washer (photo)
c) Refit the handbrake lever nylon stop as necessary
d) Refit the brake drum and wheel, then depress the footbrake several times to operate the self-adjusting mechanism, and adjust the handbrake as described in Section 14

16 Lower the car to the ground.

B19 and B200 models

17 The procedure is similar to that for B14 and B172 models; referring to the relevant Figures (Figs, 7.4, 7.5 and 7.6) and photos.

4.17C The auto adjuster rod on B19 models (arrowed)

4.17D Handbrake cable location on B19 models (arrowed)

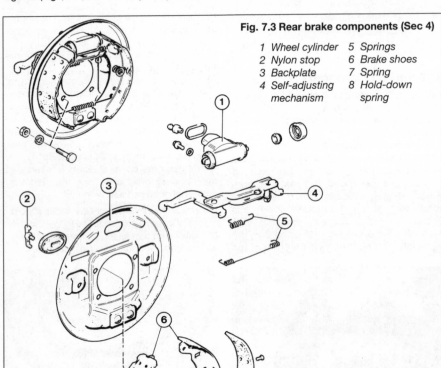

Fig. 7.3 Rear brake components (Sec 4)

1 Wheel cylinder
2 Nylon stop
3 Backplate
4 Self-adjusting mechanism
5 Springs
6 Brake shoes
7 Spring
8 Hold-down spring

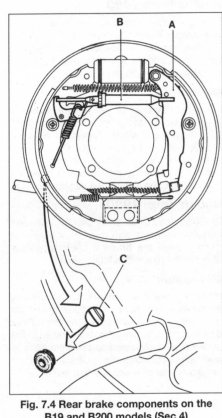

Fig. 7.4 Rear brake components on the B19 and B200 models (Sec 4)

A Handbrake lever
B Automatic adjuster pushrod
C Brake shoe lining inspection hole

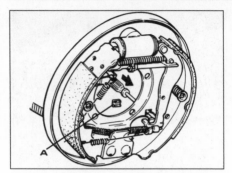

Fig. 7.5 Method of releasing brake shoes to remove the brake drum (Sec 4)
A Plastic plug

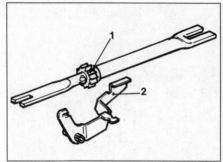

Fig. 7.6 Rear brake auto adjuster pushrod (1) and spring carrier (2) (Sec 4)

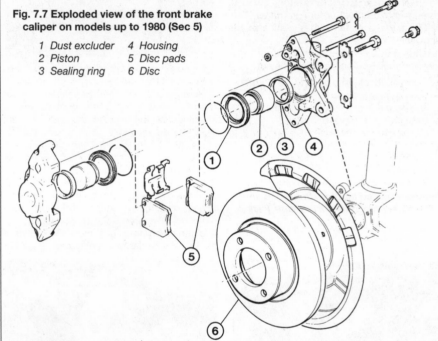

Fig. 7.7 Exploded view of the front brake caliper on models up to 1980 (Sec 5)

1 Dust excluder	4 Housing
2 Piston	5 Disc pads
3 Sealing ring	6 Disc

Models from 1980

12 Slide the caliper and pin from the mounting bracket.

13 Unscrew the caliper from the hose, discard the brake fluid, and seal the aperture with masking tape to prevent the ingress of foreign matter.

14 Unscrew the bolt and remove the upper locating pin from the caliper.

15 Place the caliper in a soft-jawed vice after cleaning the external surfaces with methylated spirit.

16 Pull the piston from the caliper with the fingers, or alternatively use a tyre pump connected to the inlet aperture to force the piston out.

17 Remove the dust excluder, then prise out the sealing ring using a plastic or copper needle.

All models

18 Clean the piston(s) and caliper bore(s) with methylated spirit and inspect the surfaces for scoring, rust and bright wear areas; if evident the complete caliper must be renewed.

19 If the components are in good condition, discard the seal(s) and obtain a repair kit.

20 Install the new seal(s) using the fingers only to manipulate it (them) into the grooves.

21 Dip the piston(s) in clean hydraulic fluid and insert it (them) squarely into the cylinder bore(s).

22 Where supplied with the repair kit, apply the special grease to the inside surfaces of the dust excluder.

23 Install the dust excluder(s) and, where fitted, the spring retainers. On models from

5 Disc caliper - removal, servicing and refitting

1 Jack up the front of the car and support it on axle stands. Remove the roadwheel.

2 Remove the disc pads (see Section 3).

3 Remove the cap from the master cylinder reservoir and place a piece of polythene sheeting over the opening, then refit the cap. This will prevent excessive loss of hydraulic fluid during subsequent operations. Alternatively, use a brake pipe compressor to pinch the flexible hose leading to the caliper.

4 Loosen the brake hose union at the caliper a quarter of a turn.

Models up to 1980

5 Unscrew and remove the two caliper retaining bolts after bending back the locktabs, but do not allow the caliper to hang by the hydraulic hose.

6 Unscrew the caliper from the hose and seal the aperture with masking tape to prevent the ingress of foreign matter.

7 Place the caliper in a soft-jaw vice.

8 Clean the external surfaces of the caliper with methylated spirit. On no account loosen the nuts that secure the two halves of the caliper body together.

9 Extract the spring retaining rings and dust excluders from the ends of the caliper pistons.

10 Using two screwdrivers as levers, and taking care not to scratch the pistons, prise the pistons from the caliper body. Mark each piston in relation to its respective bore. An alternative method of removing the pistons is by using a tyre pump connected to the inlet aperture with the bleed nipple closed; wrap the caliper in rag and restrain one piston while the other piston is being removed, then seal the piston aperture and remove the remaining piston.

11 Using a plastic or copper needle, prise the sealing rings from the caliper bores.

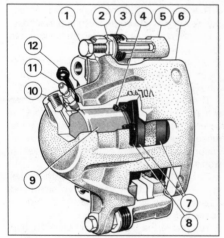

Fig 7.8 Cutaway view of the front caliper on models from 1980 (Sec 5)

1 Caliper locating bolt	6 Caliper body
2 Guide pin	7 Brake pads
3 Rubber boot	8 Dust excluder
4 Sealing ring	9 Piston
5 Caliper mounting bracket	10 Brake hose union
	11 Bleed nipple
	12 Dust cover

7

Fig. 7.9 Using a brake pipe compressor to prevent loss of fluid when unscrewing the caliper union - arrowed (Sec 5)

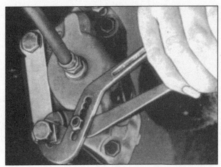

Fig. 7.10 Bending the caliper mounting bolt lockplate on models up to 1980 (Sec 5)

5.23 Dust excluder correctly fitted to the caliper and piston (models from 1980)

1980, make sure that the dust excluder is located correctly in the piston groove (photo).
24 Refitting the caliper is now a reversal of removal, but the following additional points should be noted:

a) *Tighten all bolts and unions to the correct specified torque. On models up to 1980, lock the bolts by bending the lockplate - on models from 1930, use a liquid locking agent to lock the bolts*

b) *When fitted, the brake hose must not be twisted. New hoses have a white line to help align the hose visually*

c) *After removing the plastic sheeting from the master cylinder or the brake hose clamp, bleed the hydraulic system as described in Section 13*

6 Brake disc - examination, removal and refitting

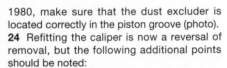

1 Remove the caliper as described in Section 5, but do not disconnect the brake hose. Suspend the caliper with a length of wire from the coil spring.
2 On models from 1980, unbolt the caliper mounting bracket from the suspension strut (photos).
3 The disc should now be examined for deep scoring or grooving (light scoring is normal). If severe, the disc should be removed and either renewed or ground within limits (see Specifications) by a suitably equipped engineering works.
4 Check the disc for run-out with a dial gauge, or alternatively with a fixed stand and a feeler gauge by taking readings at various points around the disc.
5 To remove the disc, first withdraw the hub assembly as described in Chapter 8.
6 Unscrew and remove the four bolts securing the disc to the hub. To do this, fit the hub to a wheel and tighten the wheel nuts. Place the wheel flat on the ground and loosen the four bolts; an Allen key will be required (photo).
7 Use a wooden or soft-head mallet to carefully remove the disc from the hub.
8 Clean the disc guard plate (photo), and if

the original disc is being refitted, clean it thoroughly of any rust or foreign matter. The contact surface of the hub should also be thoroughly cleaned.
9 Refitting is a reversal of removal, but the following additional points should be noted:

a) *Tighten the retaining bolts to the correct specified torque wrench setting*

b) *Refit and adjust the hub bearings as described in Chapter 8*

c) *Check that the disc run-out is within limits. If it is not, it may be possible to correct it by moving the disc half a turn on the hub*

d) *To prevent the car pulling to one side it is recommended that both front discs are renewed or reground at the same time*

6.2A Removing the caliper mounting bracket bolts (models from 1980)

6.6 Using an Allen key to unscrew the brake disc-to-hub bolts

7 Wheel cylinder - removal, servicing and refitting

1 Remove the rear brake shoes as described in Section 4.
2 Remove the cap from the master cylinder reservoir and place a piece of polythene sheeting over the opening, then refit the cap. This will prevent loss of hydraulic fluid in subsequent operations. Alternatively, use a brake pipe compressor to pinch the flexible hose to the wheel cylinder.
3 Place a small container beneath the wheel cylinder and extract the dust excluders and two pistons, noting from which side they were removed, then remove the interior spring.
4 Using methylated spirit, clean the interior of the wheel cylinder thoroughly and check the

6.2B Removing the caliper mounting bracket (models from 1980)

6.8 Tightening the brake disc guard bolts

Fig. 7.11 Dismantling the rear wheel cylinder (Sec 7)

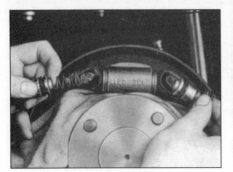

Fig. 7.12 Removing the rear wheel cylinder gasket (Sec 7)

bore surfaces for scoring or bright wear areas. Similarly clean the pistons and check them for wear.

5 If the components are in good condition, discard the rubber seals and obtain new ones in the form of a repair kit. Install the new seals using the fingers only to manipulate them into position. Fit the spring then dip the pistons in clean fluid and insert them into the cylinder. Fit the dust excluders and spring clips.

6 If the components are excessively worn, the wheel cylinder must be renewed. To remove it, unscrew the hydraulic supply lines (or supply line and bleed nipple), then unscrew and remove the retaining bolts and withdraw the wheel cylinder and gasket from the backplate.

7 Refitting is a reversal of removal, but the following additional points should be noted:

a) *Fit a new gasket between the wheel cylinder and backplate*

b) *Tighten the bolts and unions to the correct torque*

c) *After refitting the brake shoes, as described in Section 4, remove the plastic sheeting from the master cylinder and bleed the hydraulic system (Section 13).*

8 Brake drum - inspection and renovation

When the drums are removed, they should be examined for deterioration and cracking.

After high mileage the drums may become slightly oval internally and may also be excessively scored. If this is evident the drums should be renewed or surface ground within limits (see Specifications).

9 Master cylinder - removal, servicing and refitting

1 The tandem type master cylinder is mounted on the front of the servo unit (photos). First, disconnect the battery negative lead.

2 On right-hand drive cars, remove the air cleaner (Chapter 3); on left-hand drive cars remove the spare wheel.

3 Where fitted, disconnect the wiring from the stop-light switch located on the master cylinder. Disconnect the wiring from the brake fluid level warning switch (photo).

9.1A Master cylinder and servo unit location (early models)

9.1B Later 9 inch servo and master cylinder

9.3 Disconnecting the brake fluid warning switch (1981 model)

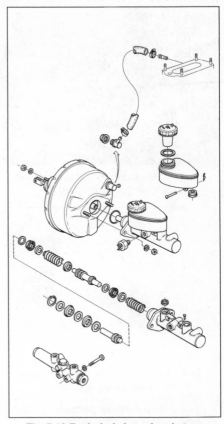

Fig. 7.13 Exploded view of early type brake master cylinder and servo unit (Secs 9 and 17)

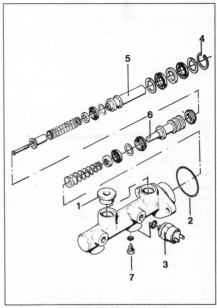

Fig. 7.14 Exploded view of the master cylinder fitted to models from chassis number 451743 (Sec 9)

1 Seal	4 Circlip
2 O-ring	5 Primary piston
3 High pressure switch (CVT models only)	6 Secondary piston
	7 Stop screw

7

Fig. 7.15 Removing the master cylinder retaining pin clips (Sec 9)

Fig. 7.16 Removing the master cylinder stop pin (Sec 9)

10.1A Upper view of the pressure-conscious reducing valve (arrowed) - early type

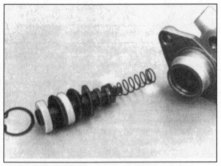

Fig. 7.17 Master cylinder primary piston components (Sec 9)

Fig. 7.18 Master cylinder secondary piston components (Sec 9)

10.1B Lower view of the pressure-conscious reducing valve (arrowed) - early type

4 Place a small container beneath the master cylinder, and if possible syphon the brake fluid from the reservoir.

5 Unscrew the unions and pull the hydraulic lines clear of the master cylinder. Plug the cylinder apertures and pipe ends to prevent the ingress of foreign matter.

6 Unscrew the retaining nuts and withdraw the master cylinder from the front of the servo unit. Empty and discard the hydraulic fluid from the reservoir.

7 Clamp the master cylinder in a soft-jawed vice and remove the reservoir by extracting the locking clips and withdrawing the two retaining pins.

8 Remove the master cylinder-to-servo sealing ring.

9 Prise the reservoir seals from the two ports.

10 Unscrew and remove the stop-light switch and washer where fitted.

11 Depress the primary piston and extract the stop pin from the front port with a pair of long-nosed pliers.

12 With the primary piston still depressed, use circlip pliers to extract the circlip from the mouth of the cylinder bore.

13 Extract the primary and secondary pistons together with the springs, noting the exact order of removal. Tap the end of the cylinder on a block of wood if any of the components are difficult to remove.

14 Clean all the components in methylated spirit and allow them to dry, then examine the piston and cylinder bore surfaces for scoring or bright wear areas. Where these are evident the master cylinder must be renewed.

15 If the components are in good order, discard the seals and obtain a repair kit.

16 Install the new seals using the fingers only to manipulate them into position. Make sure that the sealing lips are facing the correct way.

17 Lubricate the internal components of the master cylinder with the paste supplied with the repair kit, or alternatively dip them in clean hydraulic fluid, then assemble them to the bore of the master cylinder using a reversal of the removal procedure.

18 Depress the primary piston in order to fit the stop pin and circlip.

19 Refitting the master cylinder is a reversal of removal, but it will then be necessary to top up the hydraulic fluid and bleed the system as described in Section 13.

10 Pressure-conscious reducing valve - description, removal and refitting

1 This unit is located on the left-hand side of the engine compartment (photos) and contains two plungers. A spring tensioner plunger is included in the rear braking circuit and effectively limits the braking effort that can be applied to the rear wheels. The device ensures that under extreme braking the greatest percentage of braking effort is applied to the front wheels, and rear wheel locking is prevented.

2 If the front brake circuit should fail, a pressure differential sensing plunger will

10.1C Later type pressure-conscious reducing valve (arrowed)

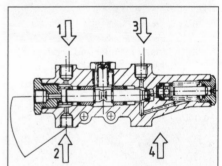

Fig. 7.19 Cross-section diagram of the brake pressure-conscious reducing valve (Sec 10)

1 Front circuit entry port
2 Front circuit exit port
3 Rear circuit entry port
4 Rear circuit exit port

operate, opening a bypass orifice so that the rear brake pressure reducing valve becomes inoperative.

3 The valve cannot be repaired and, in the event of a fault developing, must be renewed complete.

4 Removal of the valve is simply a matter of disconnecting the hydraulic lines.

5 Refitting is a reversal of removal, but it will be necessary to bleed the hydraulic system as described in Section 13.

11 Flexible hoses - inspection, removal and refitting

1 The flexible hydraulic hoses should be inspected regularly for deterioration and damage. If they are swollen or chafed they must be renewed.

2 To remove a hose, first place some polythene sheeting beneath the reservoir filler cap to prevent excessive loss of hydraulic fluid.

3 Unscrew the rigid line union while holding the flexible hose union stationary (photo).

4 Remove the spring clip and withdraw the flexible hose, then unscrew the union at the other end of the hose.

5 Refitting is a reversal of removal, but make sure that the hose is not twisted when the front wheels are in the straight-ahead position. The hose must not foul any part of the body or wheel. It will be necessary to bleed the hydraulic system as described in Section 13.

12 Rigid brake lines - inspection, removal and refitting

1 Regularly clean the rigid pipelines and inspect them for signs of corrosion or damage caused by flying stones.

2 Examine the securing clips and adjust them as necessary to prevent the pipes from vibrating which could cause chafing.

3 Check that the pipes are not touching any adjacent components and bend them away if necessary.

11.3 Front brake flexible hose-to-rigid line connection (arrowed)

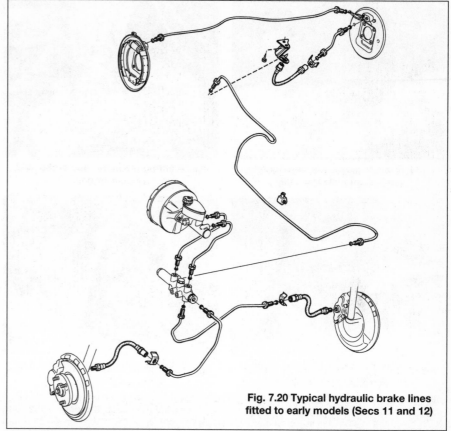

Fig. 7.20 Typical hydraulic brake lines fitted to early models (Secs 11 and 12)

4 If the pipes are corroded badly, they must be renewed. Unscrew the unions from each end of the pipe, using a split ring spanner if possible (photo).

5 Fit the new pipes, making sure that bends are kept to a minimum. Bleed the hydraulic system as described in Section 13 after tightening the unions to the correct specified torque wrench setting.

13 Hydraulic system - bleeding

1 If any of the hydraulic components in the braking system have been removed or disconnected, or if the fluid level in the master

12.4 Right-hand rear brake rigid line-to-flexible hose connection

cylinder has been allowed to fall appreciably, it is inevitable that air will have been introduced into the system. The removal of all this air from the hydraulic system is essential if the brakes are to function correctly, and the process of removing it is known as bleeding.

2 There are a number of one-man, do-it-yourself, brake bleeding kits currently available from motor accessory shops. It is recommended that one of these kits should be used wherever possible, as they greatly simplify the bleeding operation and also reduce the risk of expelled air and fluid being drawn back into the system.

3 If one of these kits is not available, then it will be necessary to gather together a clean jar and a suitable length of clear plastic tubing which is a tight fit over the bleed screw, and also to engage the help of an assistant.

4 Before commencing the bleeding operation, check that all rigid pipes and flexible hoses are in good condition and that all hydraulic unions are tight.

 Take great care not to allow hydraulic fluid to come into contact with the vehicle paintwork, otherwise the finish will be seriously damaged. **Wash off any spilled fluid immediately with cold water.**

5 If hydraulic fluid has been lost from the master cylinder due to a leak in the system, ensure that the cause is traced and rectified

7

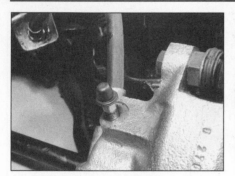

13.6 Front brake caliper bleed screw location (models from 1980)

13.7A Fitting the automatic brake fluid dispenser cap

13.7B Fitting the automatic brake fluid dispenser

13.8A One man brake bleeding kit tube connected to the front caliper

13.8B Using a one man brake bleed kit

before proceeding further or a serious malfunction of the braking system may occur.

6 To bleed the system, clean the area around the bleed screw at the wheel cylinder or caliper to be bled and remove the rubber cap (photo). If the hydraulic system has only been partially disconnected and suitable precautions were taken to prevent further loss of fluid, it should only be necessary to bleed that part of the system. However, if the entire system is to be bled, start at the rear wheel to which is fitted the single bleed screw for bleeding the rear brakes (right-hand side for early models, left-hand side for later models).

7 Remove the master cylinder filler cap and top up the reservoir. Periodically check the fluid level during the bleeding operation and top up as necessary. If available, fit an automatic brake fluid dispenser to the reservoir (photos); remove the air cleaner first, if necessary, to provide adequate access.

8 If a one-man brake bleeding kit is being used, connect the outlet tube to the bleed screw and then open the screw half a turn (photo). If possible position the unit so that it can be viewed from the car, then depress the brake pedal to the floor and slowly release it (photo). The one-way valve in the kit will prevent expelled air from returning to the system at the end of each stroke. Repeat this operation until clean hydraulic fluid, free from air bubbles, can be seen coming through the tube. Now tighten the bleed screw and remove the outlet tube. Refit the rubber cap.

9 If a one-man brake bleeding kit is not available, connect one end of the plastic tubing to the bleed screw and immerse the

other end in a jar containing sufficient clean hydraulic fluid to keep the end of the tube submerged. Open the bleed screw half a turn and have your assistant depress the brake pedal to the floor and then slowly release it. Tighten the bleed screw at the end of each downstroke to prevent expelled air and fluid from being drawn back into the system. Repeat this operation until clean hydraulic fluid, free from air bubbles, can be seen coming through the tube. Now tighten the bleed screw and remove the plastic tube. Refit the rubber cap.

10 If the entire system is being bled, the procedures described above should now be repeated at the left-hand front wheel and

right-hand front wheel. Do not forget to recheck the fluid level in the master cylinder at regular intervals and top up as necessary.

11 When completed, recheck the fluid level in the master cylinder, top up if necessary and refit the cap. Check the "feel" of the brake pedal which should be firm and free from any 'sponginess' which would indicate air still present in the system.

12 Discard any expelled hydraulic fluid as it is likely to be contaminated with moisture, air and dirt which makes it unsuitable for further use.

14 Handbrake - adjustment

1 Before adjusting the handbrake, make sure that the rear brake shoes are fully adjusted by depressing the footbrake pedal several times. This will operate the self-adjusting mechanism.

2 Raise the rear of the car and support it securely on axle stands.

3 On B14 models up to 1982 the adjusting nut is inside the car at the rear of the handbrake. On late B14 models and on B172 models the adjuster is on the top of the gearbox, or primary unit on automatic

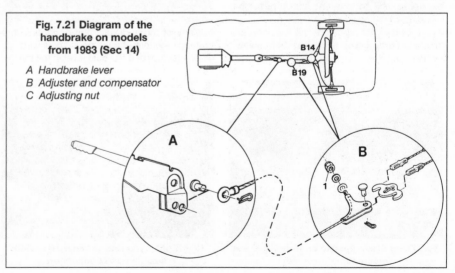

Fig. 7.21 Diagram of the handbrake on models from 1983 (Sec 14)

A Handbrake lever
B Adjuster and compensator
C Adjusting nut

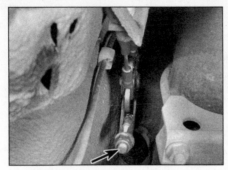

14.3 Handbrake cable adjusting nut on a B19 model

15.9 Rear handbrake cable components and brake operating arm

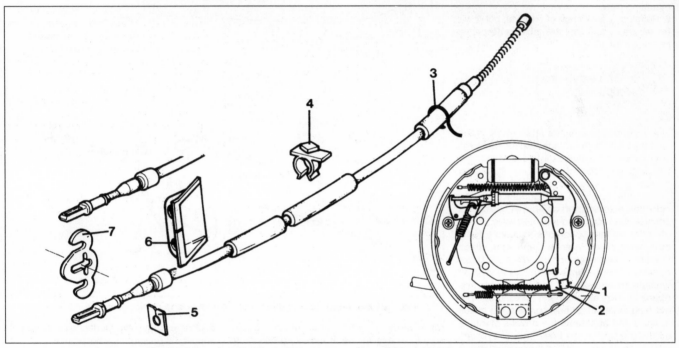

Fig. 7.22 Rear handbrake cable components on B19 and B200 models (Sec 15)

1 Cable end	3 Support clip (wire)	5 Retaining clip	7 Compensator
2 Lever	4 Support clip (plastic)	6 Mounting bracket	

versions. On B19 models the adjuster is between the exhaust pipe and the propeller shaft (photo).

4 Turn the adjuster until it is impossible to turn the rear wheels with the handbrake pulled up 3 to 4 notches on B14 and B172 models and 5 to 7 notches on B19 and B200.

5 After adjustment, securely tighten the locknut on the adjuster and lower the vehicle to the ground.

15 Handbrake cables - removal and refitting

1 Jack up the rear of the car and support it adequately on axle stands.

2 Fully release the handbrake lever and pull back the rubber grommet, then detach the cable from the lever.

3 Working beneath the car, disconnect the front cable from the equaliser. On automatic transmission models it will first be necessary to remove the transmission covers.

4 Withdraw the front cable under the car.

5 To remove a rear handbrake cable, fully release the handbrake lever and loosen the adjuster nut on the front cable.

6 Working under the car, detach the cable from the equaliser.

7 Prise out the front outer cable retaining clip.

8 Spring the cable suspension hook from the bracket, then remove the relevant roadwheel.

9 Prise the cable clamp from the De Dion axle bracket and unhook the cable end from the operating arm (photo). The cable can now be withdrawn from the car.

10 Refitting is a reversal of removal, but it will be necessary to adjust the handbrake as described in Section 14.

11 Note that on models from 1983 the handbrake lever has two holes for the cable. The front hole is for B19 and B200 models and the rear for B14 and B172 models.

7

Fig. 7.23 Removing the handbrake cable suspension hook (Sec 15)

16 Handbrake lever - removal and refitting

1 Move the left-hand seat fully forwards.
2 Refer to Chapter 9 and remove those parts of the tunnel console necessary to gain access to the handbrake lever.
3 Unscrew the cable locknut and adjusting nut and remove the cable.
4 Disconnect the wiring to the handbrake warning switch.
5 Unscrew and remove the handbrake lever retaining bolts, and lift the assembly from the mounting plate.
6 Refitting is a reversal of removal, but it will be necessary to adjust the cable as described in Section 14.

17 Vacuum servo unit - description

A vacuum servo unit is fitted to the brake hydraulic circuit to provide assistance to the driver when the brake pedal is depressed. The unit is fitted between the pedal and the master cylinder and is attached to the bulkhead.

The unit operates by vacuum from the induction manifold and comprises basically a booster diaphragm and a control valve.

Under normal conditions vacuum affects both sides of the internal diaphragm, which therefore remains stationary. When the brake pedal is depressed, the internal valve cuts off vacuum to one side of the diaphragm and opens it to atmospheric pressure. The resulting inrush of air pushes the servo piston forward and augments the driver's pressure on the pushrod to the brake master cylinder. A non-return valve retains the vacuum in the servo if the engine cuts out or is switched off. The servo will then provide assistance for two or three applications of the brakes before it is exhausted; this will be apparent because of the sudden increase in pedal pressure required.

The air entering the unit passes through a small air filter, and the only service operations that should be carried out on the servo unit are to renew the non-return valve (Section 20) and the air filter (Section 19).

Should the unit fail, the braking system will still be operating, but extra effort will be required at the foot pedal.

18 Vacuum servo unit - testing, removal and refitting

1 To test the unit, first depress the brake pedal several times to exhaust the vacuum within the unit, then, with the pedal depressed, start the engine. If the servo unit is functioning correctly the pedal will be forced

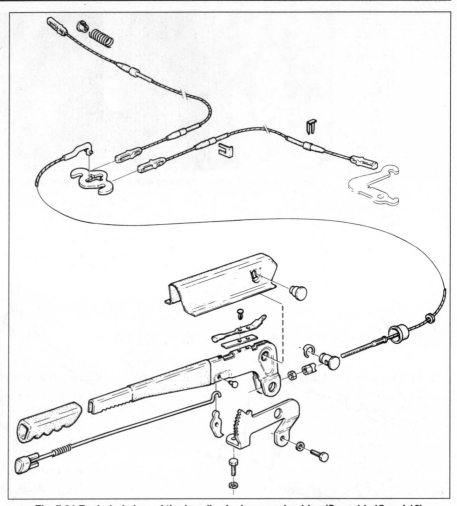

Fig. 7.24 Exploded view of the handbrake lever and cables (Secs 14, 15 and 16)

downwards a little, thus providing the additional assistance. If the servo ceases to function immediately the engine is switched off, the non-return valve is faulty.
2 To remove the vacuum servo unit, first remove the master cylinder as described in Section 9.
3 Working inside the car, disconnect the servo pushrod from the brake pedal by extracting the split pin and removing the clevis pin (photo).
4 Disconnect the vacuum hose.

18.3 Brake pedal and servo pushrod connection (arrowed)

5 Unscrew the servo mounting nuts and bolts and lift the unit from the car.
6 Refitting is a reversal of removal, but it will be necessary to bleed the hydraulic system as described in Section 13.

19 Vacuum servo unit air filter - renewal

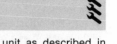

1 Remove the servo unit as described in Section 18.
2 Pull back the dust cover and prise the end cover out with a screwdriver.
3 Extract the filter elements and discard them.
4 Fitting the new elements is a reversal of removal.

20 Vacuum servo unit non-return valve - renewal

1 Remove the vacuum hose from the non-return valve (photo).

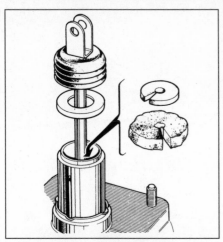

Fig. 7.25 Vacuum servo filter location (Sec 19)

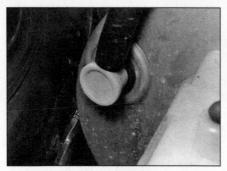

20.1 Vacuum servo non-return valve

2 Lever the valve from its seating grommet using the blade of a screwdriver. Remove the grommet from the servo housing.
3 Refitting is a reversal of removal. A little rubber grease or brake fluid should be used to ease the valve into the grommet.

20.4 Check valve (white side faces servo)

4 On late models there is also an additional check valve in the vacuum hose. Note that the white side of the check valve faces the servo unit (photo).

Fault finding - braking system

Excessive pedal travel before brakes operate

- ☐ Brake fluid level too low
- ☐ Leaking caliper or wheel cylinder
- ☐ Leaking master cylinder (bubbles in reservoir)
- ☐ Fractured hose or brake line
- ☐ Loose brake system unions
- ☐ Brake shoes excessively worn
- ☐ Faulty master cylinder seals

Brake pedal feels springy

- ☐ New linings not yet bedded-in
- ☐ Brake discs or drums badly worn or cracked
- ☐ Master cylinder securing nuts and bolts loose

Brake pedal feels spongy

- ☐ Caliper or wheel cylinder leaking
- ☐ Leaking master cylinder (bubbles in reservoir)
- ☐ Fractured hose or brake line
- ☐ Loose brake system unions
- ☐ Air in hydraulic system

Excessive effort required to stop car

- ☐ Faulty vacuum servo unit
- ☐ Badly worn pad or shoe linings
- ☐ New linings not yet bedded-in
- ☐ Incorrect linings fitted (too hard)
- ☐ Oil or fluid contaminated linings

Brakes uneven and pulling to one side

- ☐ Tyre pressures unequal and incorrect
- ☐ Incorrect linings or contaminated with oil or fluid
- ☐ Suspension or steering joints loose
- ☐ Loose caliper
- ☐ Brake discs or drums badly worn or cracked

Brakes bind or drag

- ☐ Seized caliper or wheel cylinder
- ☐ Air in system
- ☐ Seized handbrake cables
- ☐ Handbrake over-adjusted

7

Chapter 8
Suspension and steering

For modifications, and information applicable to later models, see supplement at end of manual

Contents

Degrees of difficulty

Easy, suitable for novice with little experience	**Fairly easy,** suitable for beginner with some experience	**Fairly difficult,** suitable for competent DIY mechanic 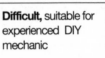
Difficult, suitable for experienced DIY mechanic	**Very difficult,** suitable for expert DIY or professional	

Specifications

Front suspension

Type	MacPherson struts consisting of coil springs and integral telescopic shock absorbers, anti-roll bar
Wheel alignment settings:	
Camber:	
B14	+30' ± 30'
All other models	-30' ± 30'
Castor:	
B172	7° 30' ± 30'
All other models	7° 35' ± 45'
King pin inclination:	
B172	9° 35' ± 30'
All other models	9° 30' ± 30'
Toe-in (all models)	0.16 ± 0.04 in (4.0 ± 1.0 mm)

Rear suspension

Type	De Dion axle, frictionless parabolic leaf springs, telescopic shock absorbers
Wheel alignment settings:	
Camber	-2° ± 30'
Toe-in	0 ± 0.12 in (0 ±3.0 mm)

Steering

Type	Rack and pinion, collapsible steering column
Number of turns (lock-to-lock):	
B14	4.13
All other models	4.40
Pinion shaft bearing endfloat/preload:	
B14 up to March 1981	0.002 in (0.04 mm) endfloat to 0.003 in (0.07 mm) preload
All other models	0.004 in (0.10 mm) endfloat - maximum
Pinion shaft turning torque	1.1 lbf ft (1.5 Nm) - maximum
Housing lubrication:	
Up to chassis No 398385	100 cc of Tivela compound
From chassis No 398386	50 cc of Alvania R1

Note: *For servicing purposes use Volvo grease 1161001. Volvo grease and Tivela compound should never be mixed and a housing previously filled with Tivela should be thoroughly cleaned out before using the Volvo grease.*

8

Wheels and tyres

Roadwheels:
Type .... Pressed steel or alloy
Size .... 4 1/2 J x 13, 5J x 13, 5 1/2 J x 13 (alloy) or 5 1/2 J x 14 (alloy)
Tyre sizes:
4 1/2 J x 13 .... 155 SR 13 or 155 D 13 (special spare for certain markets)
5J x 13 .... 155 SR 13, 175/70 SR 13 or 175/70 R 13T
5 1/2 J x 13 .... 175/70 R 13T
5 1/2 J x 14 .... 185/60 HR 14
*Wheels of this size are not fully interchangeable between model years. Consult your Volvo dealer
Tyre pressures (cold):
Front .... 27 lbf/in² (1.9 kgf/cm²)
Rear (normal load) .... 30 lbf/in² (2.1 kgf/cm²)
Rear (heavy load) .... 34 lbf/in² (2.4 kgf/cm²)
Special spare .... 35 lbf/in² (2.5 kgf/cm²)

Torque wrench settings

	lbf ft	Nm
Front suspension and steering		
Steering housing bolts	16	22
Steering wheel nut	41	55
Thrust block cover bolts	16	22
Steering rod balljoints at steering housing	52	70
Steering swivel balljoints	41	55
Shock absorber nut	89	120
Strut upper bolts	16	22
Track rod end nuts	41	55
Radius arm to suspension arm	44	60
Vibration damper clamp bolt	16	22
Front hub nut	Refer to Section 9	
Rear suspension		
Spring bolt nuts	38	52
Spring anchor plate nuts	38	52
Shock absorber nuts	16	22
Axleshaft nuts	181	245
Bearing housing, brake backplate bolts	38	52
Roadwheels		
Roadwheel nuts	85	115

1 General description

The independent front suspension is of the MacPherson strut type incorporating coil springs. The shock absorbers are integral within the suspension struts, and on late models are of the replaceable cartridge type. An anti-roll bar is fitted and, on 1986 models, it is attached to the suspension struts by link rods and balljoints.

The rear suspension uses a De Dion axle with leaf springs and double-acting telescopic shock absorbers.

Steering is by rack and pinion which is mounted forward of the front wheels. A collapsible steering column is fitted to all models.

2 Routine maintenance

At the intervals given in the Routine Maintenance Section at the beginning of this manual, carry out the following operations:

Tyres (Section 24)

Check the tyre pressures (cold) including the spare. Check all tyres for excessive wear, cuts, bulges (not forgetting the inner side walls) and tread depth.

General

Inspect the front and rear suspension components and the steering system components for wear and damage. Check all balljoints and mounting bushes; using a lever to detect wear. Inspect all rubber covers and gaiters for integrity, and shock absorbers and steering rack for leaks. Check also the condition of all rubber mounting blocks. Check for excessive play in the steering system.

3 Front coil spring - removal and refitting

1 Open the bonnet and loosen the upper suspension nut one or two turns.
2 Loosen the three upper strut retaining bolts, but do not remove them (photos).

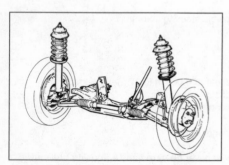

Fig. 8.1 The front suspension (Sec 1)

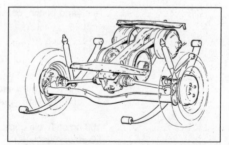

Fig. 8.2 The rear suspension (automatic transmission shown) (Sec 1)

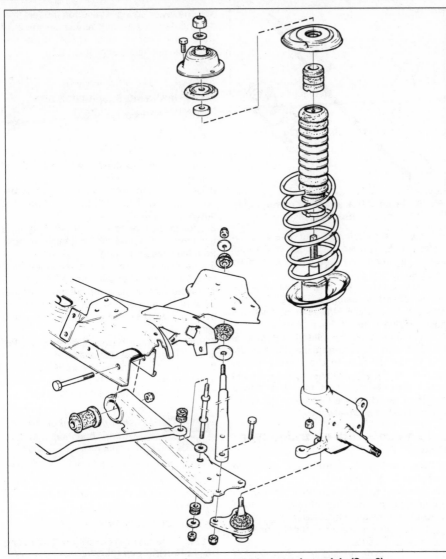

Fig. 8.3 Front suspension components on early models (Sec 3)

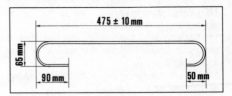

Fig. 8.4 Strut restraining hook dimensions (Sec 3)

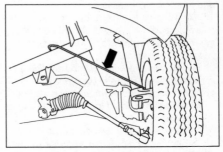

Fig. 8.5 Strut hook in position - arrowed (Sec 3)

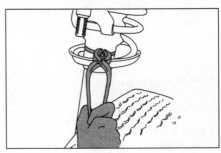

Fig. 8.6 Tightening the protector clamps (Sec 3)

3 Jack up the front of the car and support it adequately on axle stands.

4 Extract the split pin from the track rod end and remove the nut. Using a balljoint remover, separate the track rod end from the steering arm.

5 Where the left-hand spring is being removed, disconnect the speedometer cable by pulling it out of the rubber bush.

6 Loosen the radius arm rear nut one or two turns, then unscrew and remove the anti-roll bar retaining nut from the lower suspension arm.

7 Make up a steel wire hook out of 0.24 in (6 mm) diameter wire to the dimensions shown in Fig. 8.4. Hook it around the lower part of the strut and the engine bearer; this will prevent damage to the brake hoses and steering balljoints.

8 Support the strut with a trolley jack, then unscrew and remove the upper strut retaining bolts. Lower the jack and at the same time guide the strut down until it can be moved outside the front wing.

9 Obtain coil spring compressors from a tool agent or garage, and fit the two sections of the coil spring opposite each other and with four coils between the hooks (photo).

8

3.2A Loosening the front suspension strut upper retaining bolts on a B14 model

3.2B Front suspension upper mounting on a B172 model

3.9 Using coil spring compressors on the front suspension coil spring

10 Compress the spring, then unscrew and remove the shock absorber retaining nut.
11 Loosen the clips retaining the rubber protector and withdraw the mounting, seal and bearing.
12 Lift off the spring cover, protector, spring and rubber pad.
13 Remove the spring compressor from the spring.
14 Examine the rubber protector for damage and renew it as necessary.
15 Refitting is a reversal of removal but the following additional points should be noted:
a) *Install the rubber stops with their flat sides uppermost*
b) *When new protector clamps are fitted, use a pair of pliers to tighten them*
c) *If the original upper mounting bolts are used again, a liquid locking agent must be applied*
d) *Where necessary remove the left-hand wheel cap and hub cap and relocate the speedometer drive cable*
e) *Tighten all nuts to the correct torque wrench setting, but delay tightening the shock absorber retaining nut until the weight of the car is on the wheels*
f) *Install new split pins where necessary*

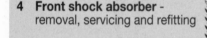

4 Front shock absorber - removal, servicing and refitting

Early models without cartridge type insert

1 Remove the coil spring as described in Section 3, paragraphs 1 to 12 inclusive.
2 Using the special tool (Volvo tool No 5862) unscrew and remove the shock absorber retaining nut. On the right-hand side it will be necessary to support the strut with a length of wood inserted between the lower end of the strut and the wheel rim.
3 Withdraw the seal and holder.
4 Slowly withdraw the piston rod and inner tube, and then remove the fluid from the tube with a syringe.
5 Thoroughly clean the interior of the tube with lint-free cloth saturated with methylated spirit.

6.4A Remove the split pin . . .

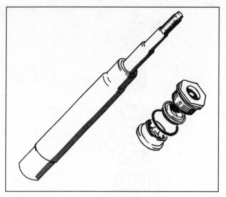

Fig. 8.7 Front shock absorber components (Sec 4)

6 Clean the piston rod and check it for distortion; if it is more than 0.004 in (0.1 mm) out of alignment or if it is worn, it must be renewed.
7 Obtain a repair kit, and reassemble the shock absorber using a reversal of the removal procedure. Fill the inner tube with the fluid supplied in the kit.
8 Make sure that the piston rod seal is installed with the spring facing downwards, and tighten all nuts to the correct torque wrench setting. When tightening the left-hand shock absorber, support the strut with a length of wood inserted between the lower end of the strut and the wheel.

Late models with cartridge type insert

9 Carry out the instructions given in paragraphs 1 to 3 above.
10 Remove the shock absorber cartridge as a complete unit from the strut casing, then clean out the inside of the casing.
11 Obtain and fit the new shock absorber cartridge to the strut.
12 The remaining procedure is a reversal of removal.

General

13 The cartridge type inserts may be fitted to the earlier type struts.
14 Shock absorbers should always be changed in pairs (ie both front or both rear changed together).

6.4B . . . and unscrew the steering swivel balljoint nut

15 The lower spring retainer on models from 1980 is located 10 mm higher on the strut than on earlier models. These struts are, therefore, not interchangeable.

5 Front lower suspension arm - removal and refitting

1 Jack up the front of the car and support it adequately on axle stands. Remove the guard shield.
2 Unscrew and remove the anti-roll bar retaining nut and withdraw it from the suspension arm.
3 Loosen the rear radius arm retaining nut a few turns and remove the front retaining bolts from the suspension arm.
4 Unscrew and remove the remaining bolt from the outer end of the suspension arm.
5 Unscrew and remove the nut from the inner pivot of the suspension arm and remove the bolt; the suspension arm can now be lowered and withdrawn.
6 Prise the rubber bush which separates the anti-roll bar from the suspension arm.
7 Examine the pivot bush and, if it requires renewing, press it from the arm using suitable diameter washers, tubing and a long bolt.

> **HAYNES HINT** *To assist the fitting of the new rubber bush, dip it in brake fluid or soapy water.*

8 Refitting is a reversal of removal, but delay final tightening of the nuts until the weight of the car is on the wheels.

6 Steering swivel balljoint - removal and refitting

1 Jack up the front of the car and support it adequately on axle stands placed beneath the body.
2 When working on the left-hand balljoint it will be necessary to remove the speedometer cable by pulling it from its rubber bush.
3 Unscrew and remove the two nuts and bolts securing the balljoint to the suspension arm.
4 Extract the split pin and unscrew and remove the castellated nut from the balljoint (photos).
5 Using a balljoint remover, separate the balljoint and withdraw it from the strut. Should there not be enough room to accommodate the tool in use, it will be necessary to obtain the special tool (Volvo No 5866); disconnecting the track rod may also help accommodate the remover (photos).
6 Refitting is a reversal of removal, but delay tightening the nuts to the correct torque

6.5A Using a balljoint remover to separate the steering swivel balljoint from the steering swivel

6.5B Steering swivel balljoint and lower suspension arm

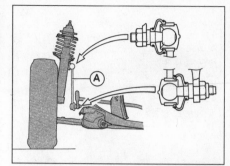

Fig. 8.8 Link rod (A) connecting the anti-roll bar to the suspension strut on models from 1986 (Sec 7)

wrench setting until the weight of the car is on the wheels. When refitting the left-hand unit, remove the wheel cap and hub cap in order to relocate the speedometer cable. Use new split pins where necessary.

7 Front anti-roll bar - removal and refitting

Models up to 1986

1 Jack up the front of the car and support it adequately on axle stands. Remove the guard shields.
2 Unscrew the front mounting bolts and remove the clamps (photo).
3 Unscrew the nuts and washers from each end of the bar while holding the links with a pair of grips.
4 Withdraw the anti-roll bar from the car. As the arms of the bar are cranked, mark each side to facilitate refitting.
5 Remove all bushes from the bar and renew them if they show any signs of wear or deterioration. Where necessary lubricate the bushes with soapy water to facilitate refitting.
6 Refitting is a reversal of removal, but tighten the front mounting bolts before the link nuts.

Models from 1986

7 On late models the anti-roll bar is connected directly to the shock absorber strut

by link rods attached to the strut and anti-roll bar by balljoints.
8 The anti-roll bar can be removed by undoing the balljoint nuts on both sides, but at time of writing no details were available of how the balljoint on the strut casing can be released.

8 Front radius arm - removal and refitting

1 Jack up the front of the car and support it adequately on axle stands.
2 Unscrew and remove the rear mounting nut, washer, and rubber bush, then unscrew and remove the bolts securing the radius arm to the lower suspension arm and withdraw the radius arm (photo).
3 Examine the rubber bushes for wear and deterioration and renew them as necessary.
4 Refitting is a reversal of removal, but the following additional points should be noted:
a) Renew all self-locking nuts
b) The large washer and large rubber bush must be located on the radius arm before fitting it to the rear support (see Fig. 8.9)
c) Tighten all nuts to the correct torque wrench setting with the weight of the car on the wheels.

7.2 Anti-roll bar front mounting

9 Front hub bearings and seal - removal and refitting

1 Jack up the front of the car, remove the roadwheel, and support the car adequately with axle stands.
2 Using a screwdriver, carefully tap the grease cap from the centre of the hub (photo); the left-hand cap contains the speedometer drive cable.
3 Remove the brake caliper (and mounting bracket on models from 1981) as described in Chapter 7, and suspend it with wire out of the way.
4 Unscrew and remove the hub nut and withdraw the hub assembly, taking care to

8

8.2 Right-hand radius arm and suspension components

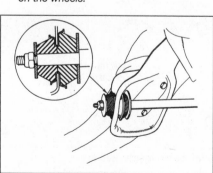

Fig. 8.9 Front radius arm rear mounting (Sec 8)

9.2 Removing the front hub grease cap

9.4A Removing the front hub thrust washer

9.4B Removing the front hub outer bearing

9.5 Removing the front hub bearing oil seal

collect the outer bearing and washer as the hub is removed from the stub axle (photos).

5 Prise the oil seal from the inner end of the hub (photo), then remove the inner bearing.

6 Using a soft metal drift, drive both outer tracks from the hub (photo).

7 Check the wheel bearings for wear by spinning them with the fingers. If they sound noisy or are rough-running, or have grooves or chips in the rollers they must be renewed.

8 Clean the hub of all grease with paraffin, and wipe dry with a lint-free cloth.

9 Pack fresh wheel bearing grease into the hub until it is one third full, then pack grease into the wheel bearings.

10 Drive in the outer wheel bearing followed by the inner wheel bearing track, using a suitable diameter tube. Ensure that they enter squarely. Place the roller races in their respective tracks (photo).

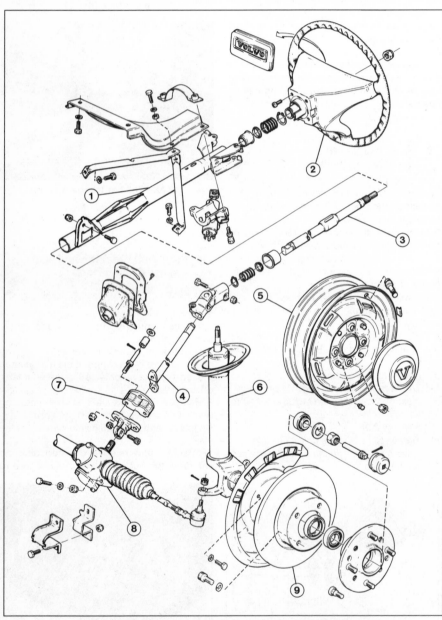

Fig. 8.10 Front hub and steering components (Sec 9)

1 Outer column	4 Steering shaft	7 Vibration damper
2 Steering wheel	5 Roadwheel	8 Steering gear
3 Inner column	6 Suspension strut	9 Brake disc

9.6 Using a drift (arrowed) to drive out the inner bearing outer track

9.10 Installing an inner bearing in the front hub

9.11 Installing the front hub bearing oil seal

9.13A Adjusting the front hub bearings

9.13B Locking the front hub nut

11 Clean the oil seal location, then carefully tap it into position with the sealing lip facing into the hub (photo).

12 The remaining procedure is a reversal of removal, on completion adjusting the bearing as follows:

13 Tighten the hub nut to 38 lbf ft (52 Nm), then loosen the nut by 90 degrees (equivalent to 1 1/2 flats) then lock the nut by staking the locking collar to the axleshaft (photos).

14 Before fitting the grease cap, pack it with fresh grease.

10 Rear spring - removal and refitting

1 Jack up the rear of the car and support it adequately on axle stands placed beneath the body. To facilitate the removal procedure, it is advisable to arrange the height of the supports so that the wheels are just touching the ground.

2 Loosen the rear upper shackle nut one or two turns (photo).

3 Unscrew and remove the front and rear nuts from the spring eye mounting bolts.

4 Unscrew and remove the spring anchor plate retaining nuts and bolts (photo).

5 Jack up the spring a little to enable the anchor plate to be moved to one side and remove the plastic locking plates.

6 Drive out the spring eye bolts and lower the spring to the ground.

7 Refitting is a reversal of removal, but the following points should be noted:

a) Grease the plastic locking plates before assembly

b) Where the part number is stamped on the lower side of the spring, this must be facing towards the front

c) Before tightening the nuts to the correct torque wrench setting, the full weight of the car plus a 110 lb (50 kg) weight in the luggage compartment should be on the wheels

d) The radius arm mounting nuts should be loosened and retightened to settle the mountings, and at the same time the eccentric bolts at the rear of the radius arms should be adjusted so that they are central within the radius arm bushes

Note: On models from 1984 the rear end of the leaf spring has been modified, resulting in the leaf spring being lower, but this does not affect the servicing procedure given above (photo).

11 Rear spring bushes - removal and refitting

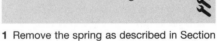

1 Remove the spring as described in Section 10.

2 Using a long bolt, tubing and spacers, press the bushes from the spring and shackle.

3 Before installing the new bushes, lubricate them with soapy water or petroleum jelly.

4 The remaining refitting procedure is a reversal of removal, referring to Section 10 as necessary.

12 Rear radius arm - removal and refitting

1 Jack up the rear of the car and support it adequately on axle stands.

2 Unscrew and remove the two mounting nuts, noting that the rear bolt is eccentric. Note the location of any shims fitted to the rear bolt.

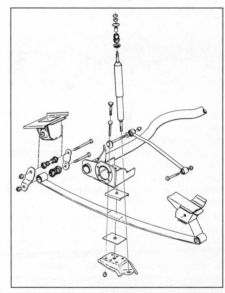

Fig. 8.11 Rear suspension components (Sec 10)

8

10.2 A rear spring rear shackle

10.4 Rear spring anchor plate

10.8 Curved section on the rear spring fitted to models from 1984

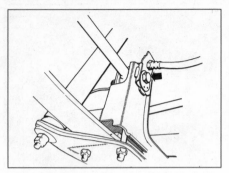

Fig. 8.12 Rear radius arm eccentric bolt location - arrowed (Sec 12)

3 Withdraw the radius arm.
4 Using a long bolt, tubing and spacers, press the bushes from the arm.
5 Lubricate the new bushes with soapy water or petroleum jelly and press them into the radius arm.
6 Refitting is a reversal of removal, but the nuts should only be tightened to their correct torque wrench setting when the full weight of the car plus 110 lb (50 kg) weight in the luggage compartment is on the wheels. Before tightening the rear bolt, adjust it so that it is central within the radius arm bush.

13 De Dion axle - removal and refitting

1 Jack up the rear of the car and support it adequately with axle stands placed beneath the body.
2 Remove the rear wheels.
3 Using a brake hose clamp, pinch the right-hand brake hose and unscrew the brake line union. Alternatively, remove the brake fluid reservoir cap and tighten it down onto a sheet of polythene.
4 Detach the two driveshafts from their outer flanges by unscrewing and removing the retaining bolts. An Allen key will be required and the flanges should be marked in relation to each other to ensure correct refitting.
5 Use welding wire or string to suspend the driveshafts out of the way.
6 Remove the brake drums and shoes as described in Chapter 7.

14.2C Rear shock absorber mounting on a 360 GLE model

7 Remove the outer short axleshafts as described in Section 15.
8 Disconnect the handbrake cable from the brake backplates.
9 Disconnect the brake lines from the axle but not from the wheel cylinders.
10 Unscrew and remove the backplate retaining bolts and withdraw the backplates.
11 Unscrew and remove the eccentric retaining bolts from the radius arm mountings.
12 Unscrew and remove the nuts and bolts and swivel the anchor plates to one side.
13 Remove the spring plastic locking plates.
14 Withdraw the De Dion axle from the car.
15 Refitting is a reversal of removal, but the following additional points should be noted:
a) *Grease the plastic locking plates before assembly*
b) *Fit new gaskets to the driveshaft flanges*
c) *Refer to Section 15 and Chapter 7 as necessary*
d) *Tighten the nuts to the correct torque wrench setting only when the full weight of the car plus a 110 lb (50 kg) weight in the luggage compartment is on the wheels*
e) *Bleed the brake hydraulic system (see Chapter 7)*

14 Rear shock absorber - removal and refitting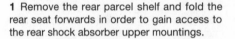

1 Remove the rear parcel shelf and fold the rear seat forwards in order to gain access to the rear shock absorber upper mountings.

14.4 Rear shock absorber and lower mounting

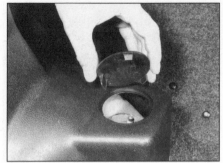

14.2A Removing the access cover to a rear shock absorber upper mounting

2 Withdraw the cover, then unscrew and remove the two mounting nuts and washer (photos).
3 Jack up the rear of the car and support it adequately on axle stands.
4 Unscrew and remove the lower mounting nut(s) and withdraw the shock absorber, bushes and washers (photo).
5 To test the shock absorber for service-ability, grip the lower mounting in a soft-jaw vice with the shock absorber vertical. Fully extend and retract the unit ten or twelve times; the unit should give an even resistance when extending with somewhat less resistance when retracting. Any jerkiness or lack of resistance indicates that the unit is faulty and should be renewed.
6 Examine the mounting rubbers and renew them as necessary.
7 Refitting is a reversal of removal. Tighten the mounting nuts to the correct torque wrench setting.

15 Rear hub bearings and seal - removal and refitting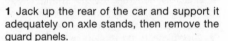

1 Jack up the rear of the car and support it adequately on axle stands, then remove the guard panels.
2 Remove the wheel, then remove the brake drum (see Chapter 7).
3 Unscrew and remove the driveshaft flange retaining bolts after marking the flanges in relation to each other, then suspend the

14.2B Rear shock absorber upper mounting nut (arrowed)

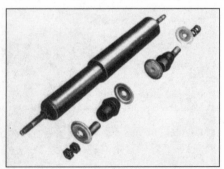

Fig. 8.13 Rear shock absorber components (Sec 14)

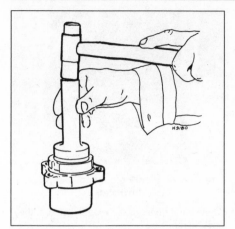

Fig. 8.14 Installing rear hub oil seals (Sec 15)

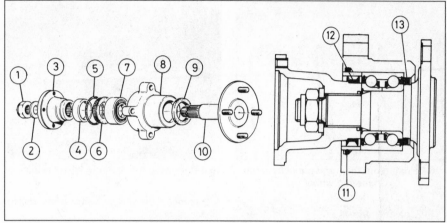

Fig. 8.15 Rear hub and bearing fitted to B19 and B200 models up to 1986 (Sec 15)

1 Self-locking nut	5 O-ring	9 Oil seal	12 Drive flange oil
2 Washer	6 Oil seal	10 Axleshaft	seal
3 Drive flange	7 Bearing	11 O-ring	13 Axleshaft oil seal
4 Spacer	8 Housing		

driveshaft outer end with wire or string so that it is out of the way.

4 Unscrew and remove the flange nut; to do this, temporarily refit the wheel and use this to restrain the shaft while the nut is being loosened.

5 Using a two or three-legged puller, withdraw the drive flange from the shaft.

6 Drive the shaft out of the bearings from the inside using a soft metal drift.

7 Unscrew and remove the four backplate retaining bolts, move the backplate forwards and withdraw the bearing housing; detach the brake line from the axle if necessary.

B14 models up to 1986

8 Using a screwdriver, extract the inner and outer oil seals.

9 Heat the bearing housing with a blowlamp, and then immediately drive the bearings out from either side with a soft metal drift.

10 Clean the housing with paraffin and wash all grease from the bearings. Examine the bearings for wear by spinning them and attempting to rock them laterally. Any worn or damaged bearings must be renewed.

11 Refitting is a reversal of removal, but the following additional points should be noted:
a) Pack the bearings with a lithium based grease
b) Install the oil seals with their sealing lips facing inwards towards the bearings
c) Apply a liquid locking agent to the inner threads of the driveshaft
d) Tighten all nuts to the correct torque wrench setting

B19 and B200 models up to 1986

12 Using a soft metal drift, drive the bearing and spacer from the housing and remove the O-ring.

13 Using a suitable puller draw the bearing inner race from the axleshaft.

14 Clean all components in paraffin and wipe dry. Check them for wear and renew them as necessary.

15 Grease the bearing location in the housing, then locate the new bearing on the inner side of the housing with the part number facing outwards. Drive the bearing into the housing using a metal tube on the outer track.

16 Locate the O-ring in the groove then press in the spacer.

17 Fit the bearing housing and backplate to the axle and tighten the bolts to the specified torque. Secure the hydraulic brake line to the axle.

18 Press new oil seals on the axleshaft and drive flange and lightly grease their outer lips.

19 Apply locking fluid to the inner splines of the drive flange and locate the flange in the housing. Insert the axleshaft, then firmly support the flange and housing while driving in the shaft with a wooden or soft metal mallet. If available use Volvo counterhold tool 5947.

20 Fit the washer and a new nut, and tighten the nut to the specified torque while holding the shaft stationary.

21 Refit the brake drum, driveshaft and wheel then lower the car to the ground.

B172 and all models from 1986

22 The modified bearing is similar to that fitted to B19/200 models but with improved sealing arrangement. Dismantle the bearing as follows:

23 Proceed as described in paragraphs 1 to 7 above.

24 Remove the bearing cup from the drive flange. It may be necessary to obtain Volvo special tools 5433 and 5434 to do this.

25 Remove the circlip from the bearing housing, then press the bearing from the housing using a suitable press.

26 Clean all parts with a suitable solvent, then inspect them for wear; renewing any which show signs of wear.

27 Apply a lithium based grease to the bearing seats, locate the bearing with the centring collar on the outside and, using a suitable drift, press the bearing into the housing.

28 Refit the circlip, then fit the housing to the brake backplate.

29 Coat the axleshaft with a lithium based grease and insert it as far as possible into the bearing housing. Do not use excessive force or the bearing may be damaged.

30 Apply a high strength sealing and locking compound, such as Loctite 270 to the splines of the drive flange, fit the flange to the axleshaft and use a new self-locking nut; tightening it to the specified torque (see Specifications). **Note:** *Allow the locking compound to fully harden before using the car.*

31 The remaining procedure is a reversal of removal.

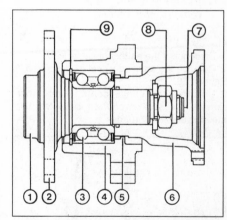

Fig. 8.16 Rear hub and bearing fitted to models from 1986 (Sec 15)

1 Centring collar	6 Drive flange
2 Wheel flange	7 Axleshaft
3 Angular contact bearing	8 Locknut and washer
4 Bearing housing	9 Circlip
5 Labyrinth gland	

8

16.2 Prising out the motif panel from the steering wheel

16.3 Removing the steering wheel retaining nut

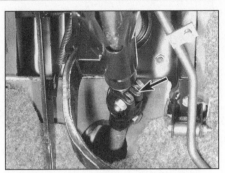

18.3 Lower steering column clamp bolt (arrowed)

16 Steering wheel - removal and refitting

1 Set the front roadwheels in the straight-ahead position.
2 Prise the motif from the centre of the steering wheel (photo).
3 Using a socket and extension bar, unscrew and remove the steering wheel retaining nut (and washer when fitted) (photo).
4 Mark the relative position of the wheel to the steering shaft by dot punching the end faces.
5 Using both hands, pull the steering wheel from the shaft; if necessary use the palms of the hands to knock the steering wheel free, but do not use excessive force or the collapsible steering column may be deformed, or injury may result as the wheel is suddenly released.
6 Refitting is a reversal of removal. Tighten the retaining nut to the correct torque wrench setting.

17 Ignition/steering lock - removal and refitting

1 Disconnect the battery negative lead.
2 Remove the steering wheel as described in Section 16.
3 Unscrew the choke control knob, then remove the screws and withdraw the two steering column shrouds.

4 Disconnect the ignition switch wires, noting their location.
5 Using a 0.35 in (9 mm) drill, drill through the steering lock retaining bolts, then remove the lock and extract the bolts with a pair of pliers.
6 Refitting is a reversal of removal, but the new retaining bolts should only be tightened finger tight until it is established that the lock functions correctly. After checking the lock, tighten the bolts until their heads shear off.

18 Steering column - removal, servicing and refitting

1 Remove the ignition/steering lock as described in Section 17.
2 Unscrew the retaining screws and remove the direction indicator and windscreen wiper switches from the steering column, letting them hang to one side.
3 Unscrew and remove the lower clamp bolt and column mounting bolt and withdraw the steering column from the car (photo).
4 Carefully clamp the steering column in a vice and, using a two-legged puller, press the shaft through the column a little way so that the circlip at the other end can be removed. At the same time remove the spring and seat.
5 Extract the circlip, spring and seat from the upper end of the column.
6 Heat each end of the column with a blowlamp and remove the bearings using the steering shaft as a puller.
7 Clean all components with paraffin and

examine the bearings for wear; if evident, they must be renewed.
8 Refitting is a reversal of removal, but the following additional points should be noted:
a) *Drive the bearings into the column until they are flush with the end of the column*
b) *Refer to Section 17 when refitting the ignition/steering lock*

19 Steering shaft vibration damper - removal and refitting

1 Jack up the front of the car and support it adequately with axle stands.
2 Set the front wheels to the straight-ahead position.
3 Remove the guard panels from under the engine.
4 Unscrew and remove the bolts securing the steering shaft to the lower steering flange.
5 Unscrew and remove the clamp bolt and withdraw the flange and vibration damper.
6 Mount the damper in a vice and unscrew the two flange nuts; the flange and damper can now be removed.
7 Refitting is a reversal of removal, but the following additional points should be noted:
a) *Make sure that the flange stud washers are retained by a split pin in good order*
b) *Tighten the steering shaft bolts before the clamp bolt*

20 Steering gear - removal and refitting

1 Jack up the front of the car and support it adequately on axle stands.
2 Set the front wheel to the straight-ahead position and remove the engine guard panels where fitted.
3 Extract the split pins from the two track rod ends and unscrew the castellated nuts.
4 Using a balljoint remover, separate the track rod ends from the steering arms.
5 Mark the position of the lower steering shaft in relation to the vibration damper, then unscrew and remove the two retaining bolts.
6 Unscrew and remove the steering gear

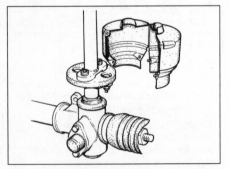

Fig. 8.17 Vibration damper on B19 and late B14 models

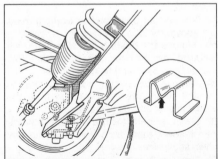

Fig. 8.18 Location of the steering gear right-hand clamp seat (Sec 20)

20.6 View of steering gear from front

retaining nuts and lower the steering gear from the car (photo).

7 Refitting is a reversal of removal, but the following additional points should be noted:

a) *Renew all self-locking nuts and split pins*

b) *Before installing the steering gear, turn the pinion clockwise as far as possible, then two turns anti-clockwise*

c) *The inner right-hand clamp seat has a deep curve on one edge; this edge must face the wheel*

d) *Tighten the steering gear retaining nuts before the steering shaft bolts*

e) *Adjust the wheel alignment as described in Section 23*

21 Steering gear - overhaul

Note: *There are four different types of rack-and-pinion steering gear fitted, according to model and year of manufacture. They are all basically the same, but servicing and adjustment procedures are different. These procedures are described in the following paragraphs where they differ from the original steering gear. Special tools and gauges are needed to accurately adjust the steering gear, and where these are not available it is recommended that overhaul of the steering gear be left to your Volvo dealer.*

B14 models up to March 1981 up to chassis No 593524)

1 Clean the exterior of the steering gear with paraffin and wipe dry (removal is described in Section 20).

2 Mount the steering gear in a vice and turn the pinion fully clockwise.

3 Mark the housing directly below the damper flange clamp split to facilitate refitting, then unscrew and remove the clamp bolt and withdraw the vibration damper and flange.

4 Check the steering rod inner balljoints for excessive play and note where this is evident.

5 Loosen the locknuts, then unscrew the track rod ends from the steering rods, noting how many turns are required to remove them.

6 Loosen the clips and remove the rubber bellows from the housing and steering rods.

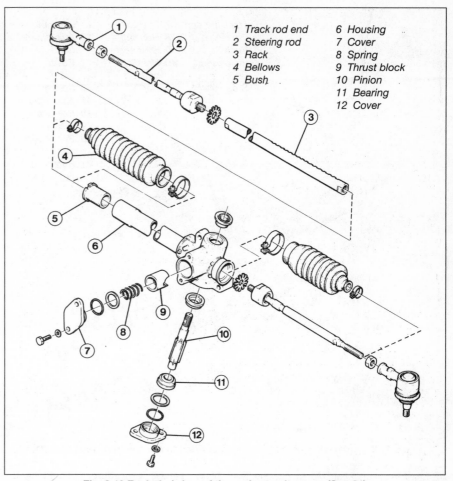

1 Track rod end
2 Steering rod
3 Rack
4 Bellows
5 Bush
6 Housing
7 Cover
8 Spring
9 Thrust block
10 Pinion
11 Bearing
12 Cover

Fig. 8.19 Exploded view of the early steering gear (Sec 21)

7 Using a screwdriver, prise the locktabs from the steering rod inner ends, then, using an open-ended spanner to stop the rack turning, unscrew the rods from the rack.

8 Unscrew and remove the bolts and withdraw the thrust block cover, springs, shims and thrust block.

9 Unscrew and remove the retaining bolts and withdraw the pinion cover, bearing cup and shims. Tap the pinion if necessary to release the cup.

10 Remove the rack from the steering gear.

11 Withdraw the pinion and seal then, using a soft metal drift, drive out the pinion bearing outer race.

12 Depress the two locking pins and extract the rack locating bush with a pair of pliers.

13 Thoroughly clean all components with paraffin and wipe dry with a lint-free cloth. Examine all components for damage and excessive wear, and renew them as necessary. Obtain all new seals for the steering gear.

14 Before starting reassembly, grease all moving parts and surfaces with a lithium based grease.

15 Using suitable diameter tubing, drive the inner bearing race onto the pinion shaft, then similarly drive the outer race of the upper

pinion bearing into the steering gear housing.

16 Fit the rack locating bush so that the two locking pins engage in the housing recess.

17 Install the pinion and bearings and drive in the outer race of the lower bearing.

18 Insert the rack into the housing from the pinion end until it protrudes 2.8 in (71 mm) from the opposite end.

19 Fit the pinion cover and tighten the retaining bolts. Check the rack protrusion is still the same.

20 With the pinion uppermost, lightly tap the shaft to settle the bearings, then measure the endfloat with a dial gauge.

21 Remove the pinion cover and fit suitable shims which will keep the pinion shaft bearing endfloat/preload within the specified tolerance.

22 Refit the cover with a new O-ring.

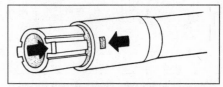

Fig. 8.20 Fitting bush locating pins into the recess (Sec 21)

8

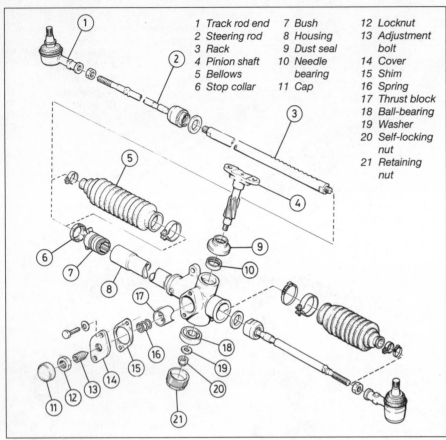

1 Track rod end
2 Steering rod
3 Rack
4 Pinion shaft
5 Bellows
6 Stop collar
7 Bush
8 Housing
9 Dust seal
10 Needle bearing
11 Cap
12 Locknut
13 Adjustment bolt
14 Cover
15 Shim
16 Spring
17 Thrust block
18 Ball-bearing
19 Washer
20 Self-locking nut
21 Retaining nut

Fig. 8.21 Exploded view of the steering gear fitted to models from 1981 (Sec 21)

21.33 Steering gear housing on models from 1981

32 Temporarily remove the thrust block cover, spring, shim and block and fill the cavity with a lithium based grease, then press the thrust block into position and refit the shim, spring and cover.

All models from March 1981 to 1985

33 The main difference from the earlier steering gear is that the pinion upper roller bearing is replaced by a needle bearing and the pinion cover is replaced by a cap nut arrangement (photo).

34 The shim adjustment procedure for the earlier steering gear described in paragraph 21 is not applicable, and the thrust block adjustment is carried out as follows:

35 With the steering gear installed in the car, turn the steering wheel to the straight-ahead position.

36 Remove the protective cap from the thrust block adjusting nut, slacken the locknut and unscrew the adjusting bolt.

37 Fit Volvo special tool 5098 to a torque wrench and tighten the adjusting bolt to 0.96 lbf ft (1.3 Nm) then, using the special tool as a guide, slacken the nut by 40 degrees.

38 Tighten the locknut and refit the protective cap. If resultant road testing reveals that the steering is unsatisfactory, the steering gear must be removed from the car as described in Section 20 and the same procedure repeated, but with the steering rack centred at the point

23 Fit the pinion seal. Up to chassis No 384506 the seal is retained by a clamping ring which should be pressed down firmly.

24 Fit the thrust block, and use a micrometer to measure the distance from the block to the housing face whilst keeping the block firmly in contact with the rack. Similarly measure the distance from the cover inside face to the outer contact face.

25 Select shims which will allow a clearance of 0.008 ± 0.003 in (0.20 ± 0.08 mm) between the cover and the block.

26 Install the shim, spring, O-ring and cover and tighten the retaining bolts evenly.

27 Using a torque wrench, turn the rack from the extreme left to the extreme right and check that the torque does not exceed 1.1 lbf ft (1.5 Nm) at any point. If it does repeat the

block setting procedure. Should it be impossible to obtain the correct torque or the rack moves unevenly with the thrust block removed, the rack is distorted and must be renewed.

28 Tighten the steering rods into position using two open-ended spanners and lock them by bending the tabs onto the rack and balljoints.

29 Refit the two bellows and tighten the clips, making sure that the right-hand bellows locates over the locking pins.

30 Install the track rod ends to their original positions and tighten the locknuts.

31 Position the flange on the pinion shaft in alignment with the previously made mark, but leave the clamp nut loose until the steering gear is installed in the car.

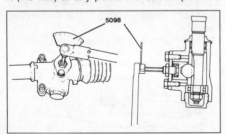

Fig. 8.22 Later type steering gear thrust block adjustment using Volvo special tool 5098 (Sec 21)

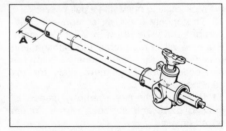

Fig. 8.23 Rack and pinion alignment (Sec 21)

A = 2.87 in (73 mm)

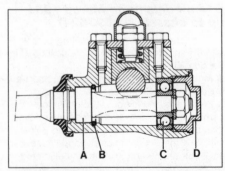

Fig. 8.24 Sectional view of the steering gear housing fitted to models from 1985 (Sec 21)

A Needle bearing
B Circlip
C Ball-bearing
D Retaining nut

22.1 Track rod end location (arrowed)

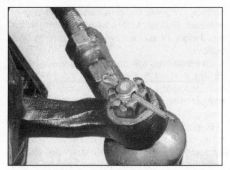

22.3A Remove the split pin . . .

22.3B . . . and the track rod end nut

of most resistance, which can be found by using a torque meter on the pinion shaft.

39 When refitting the pinion shaft the flange must be aligned with the steering gear and the rack centralised, as shown in Fig. 8.23.

All models from 1985

40 The modified steering gear fitted to all models during the course of 1985 can be recognised by the three recesses in the bottom of the housing for staking the pinion retaining nut.

41 Internally, the roller and needle bearings are secured and located by circlip.

42 The components of these new steering assemblies are not supplied separately and if any major part becomes defective the complete rack and pinion assembly must be renewed. Similarly, the older type steering gear fitted to early models can only be replaced by the complete new assembly.

43 The steering gear can be removed as described in Section 20, and overhaul of the gear is as described for the earlier versions with the following differences:

44 With the rack and pinion removed from the housing, tap out the roller bearing using a drift.

45 Remove the circlip, then use a puller to remove the needle bearing from the bottom of the housing.

46 Coat the bearing seats with a lithium based grease before fitting the bearings, which is a reversal of removal, using a drift to tap them home in the housing.

47 Fit the rack and pinion as described for earlier versions then, using the special tools

22.4 Using a balljoint remover to separate a track rod end balljoint from the steering swivel

described in paragraph 37, adjust the thrust block clearance as follows:

48 Set the steering rack to the straight-ahead position and tighten the thrust block adjusting nut to 0.74 lbf ft (1.0 Nm), then slacken the bolt by 40 degrees. Tighten the locknut and fit the cap.

49 Check the torque required to turn the pinion shaft which should be between 0.44 and 1.26 lbf ft (0.6 to 1.7 Nm).

50 Fit a new locking nut, tighten it to 27 lbf ft (37 Nm) and deform the collar into the three recesses in the housing. **Note**: *Some early 1985 models may be found with the old type of locknut. This should be discarded and a new type fitted.*

22 Track rod end balljoints - testing and renewal

1 Periodically check the condition of the track rod end balljoints (photo). If there is any free movement in a vertical direction when the track rod is moved up and down, the balljoint must be renewed.

2 To remove the balljoint, first jack up the front of the car and support it on axle stands. Remove the roadwheel.

3 Extract the split pin and unscrew the retaining nut (photos).

4 Using a balljoint remover, separate the balljoint from the steering arm (photo).

5 Loosen the locknut and unscrew the track rod end, noting the number of turns required to remove it.

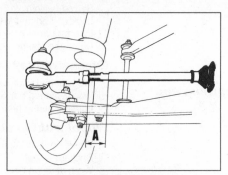

Fig. 8.25 Track rod end checking dimension (A) (Sec 22)

6 Fit the new track rod end to the same position as the old one and tighten the locknut. The distance from the locknut to the shoulder on the track rod (Fig. 8.25) must not vary more than 0.08 in (2 mm) on either side.

7 Insert the balljoint into the steering arm, tighten the nut, and fit a new split pin.

8 Lower the car to the ground then adjust the wheel alignment as described in Section 23.

23 Steering angles and front wheel alignment

1 Accurate front wheel alignment is essential for good steering and even tyre wear.

2 Before making any check, note that wear in the steering balljoints, incorrect tyre pressures, worn or incorrectly adjusted front wheel bearings, loose suspension mountings and buckled wheels can give incorrect readings.

3 There are four factors to consider:

Camber is the angle at which the front wheels are set from the vertical when viewed from the front; when the top of the wheel tilts outwards it is said to have positive camber.

Castor is the angle at which the steering axis is set from the vertical when viewed from the side of the car; when the top of the axis tilts towards the rear of the car it is said to have positive castor.

Kingpin inclination is the angle between the vertical and an imaginary line down the steering axis when viewed from the front.

Toe-in is the amount by which the distance between the front inside edges of the front wheels is less than the distance between the rear inside edges of the front wheels measured at hub height.

4 Accurate checking of the steering angles is only possible with specialised equipment and is therefore best left to a competent garage. Neither camber nor castor angles are adjustable, and if shown to be incorrect the steering and suspension components and mountings must be checked for damage or distortion. The same applies to kingpin inclination.

5 To adjust the toe-in, first place the car on level ground with the front wheels in the straight-ahead position.

8

6 Make up a gauge which can be adjusted between the inner or outer wheel rims at hub height.

7 Adjust the gauge between the rear of the rims of the front wheels and mark the contact points with chalk on the tyres.

8 Remove the gauge and roll the car forwards so that the chalk marks are now at the front.

9 Place the gauge between the front of the rims of the front wheels by the chalk marks; the resulting gap should equal the toe-in setting (see Specifications).

10 If adjustment is required, loosen the track rod end locknuts and bellows outer clip where necessary.

11 Turn the track rods equal amounts on either side until the adjustment is correct, then tighten the locknuts. The position of the track rod ends on the track rods must not vary more than 0.08 in (2 mm) when compared side for side.

24 Wheels and tyres - general care and maintenance

Wheels and tyres should give no real problems in use provided that a close eye is kept on them with regard to excessive wear or damage. To this end, the following points should be noted.

Ensure that tyre pressures are checked regularly and maintained correctly. Checking should be carried out with the tyres cold and not immediately after the vehicle has been in use. If the pressures are checked with the tyres hot, an apparently high reading will be obtained owing to heat expansion. Under no circumstances should an attempt be made to reduce the pressures to the quoted cold reading in this instance, or effective underinflation will result.

Underinflation will cause overheating of the tyre owing to excessive flexing of the casing, and the tread will not sit correctly on the road surface. This will cause a consequent loss of adhesion and excessive wear, not to mention the danger of sudden tyre failure due to heat build-up.

Overinflation will cause rapid wear of the centre part of the tyre tread coupled with reduced adhesion, harsher ride, and the danger of shock damage occurring in the tyre casing.

Regularly check the tyres for damage in the form of cuts or bulges especially in the sidewalls. Remove any nails or stones embedded in the tread before they penetrate the tyre to cause deflation. If removal of a nail *does* reveal that the tyre has been punctured, refit the nail so that its point of penetration is marked. Then immediately change the wheel and have the tyre repaired by a tyre dealer. Do *not* drive on a tyre in such a condition. In many cases a puncture can be simply repaired by the use of an inner tube of the correct size and type. If in any doubt as to the possible consequences of any damage found, consult your local tyre dealer for advice.

Periodically remove the wheels and clean any dirt or mud from the inside and outside surfaces. Examine the wheel rims for signs of rusting, corrosion or other damage. Light alloy wheels are easily damaged by 'kerbing' whilst parking, and similarly steel wheels may become dented or buckled. Renewal of the wheel is very often the only course of remedial action possible.

The balance of each wheel and tyre assembly should be maintained to avoid excessive wear, not only to the tyres but also to the steering and suspension components. Wheel imbalance is normally signified by vibration through the vehicle's bodyshell, although in many cases it is particularly noticeable through the steering wheel. Conversely, it should be noted that wear or damage in suspension or steering components may cause excessive tyre wear. Out-of-round or out-of-true tyres, damaged wheels and wheel bearing wear/maladjustment also fall into this category. Balancing will not usually cure vibration caused by such wear.

Wheel balancing may be carried out with the wheel either on or off the vehicle. If balanced on the vehicle, ensure that the wheel-to-hub relationship is marked in some way prior to subsequent wheel removal so that it may be refitted in its original position.

General tyre wear is influenced to a large degree by driving style harsh - braking and acceleration or fast cornering will all produce more rapid tyre wear. Interchanging of tyres may result in more even wear, but this should only be carried out where there is no mix of tyre types on the vehicle. However, it is worth bearing in mind that if this is completely effective, the added expense of replacing a complete set of tyres simultaneously is incurred, which may prove financially restrictive for many owners.

Front tyres may wear unevenly as a result of wheel misalignment. The front wheels should always be correctly aligned according to the settings specified by the vehicle manufacturer.

Legal restrictions apply to the mixing of tyre types on a vehicle. Basically this means that a vehicle must not have tyres of differing construction on the same axle. Although it is not recommended to mix tyre types between front axle and rear axle, the only legally permissible combination is crossply at the front and radial at the rear. When mixing radial ply tyres, textile braced radials must always go on the front axle with steel braced radials at the rear. An obvious disadvantage of such mixing is the necessity to carry two spare tyres to avoid contravening the law in the event of a puncture.

In the UK, the Motor Vehicles Construction and Use Regulations apply to many aspects of tyre fitting and usage. It is suggested that a copy of these regulations is obtained from your local police if in doubt as to the current legal requirements with regard to tyre condition, minimum tread depth, etc.

Fault finding - suspension and steering

Car pulls to one side

☐ Uneven tyre pressures
☐ Suspension geometry incorrect
☐ Brakes binding
☐ Shock absorber weak
☐ Incorrect front wheel alignment
☐ Incorrectly adjusted or worn wheel bearings
☐ Worn suspension balljoints

Excessive pitching and rolling on corners and during braking

☐ Faulty shock absorber
☐ Weak or broken spring

Excessive tyre wear

☐ Incorrect tyre pressures
☐ Incorrect front wheel alignment
☐ Wheels out-of-balance

Heavy or stiff steering

☐ Low tyre pressures
☐ Seized balljoint
☐ Lack of lubricant in steering gear
☐ Incorrect front wheel alignment
☐ Damaged steering column

Excessive play in steering

☐ Worn or maladjusted steering gear
☐ Worn steering balljoint
☐ Loose steering gear mounting bolts

Wheel wobble and vibration

☐ Wheels out-of-balance
☐ Buckled wheel
☐ Worn steering balljoints
☐ Faulty shock absorber
☐ Faulty tyre

Chapter 9
Bodywork and fittings

For modifications, and information applicable to later models, see Supplement at end of manual

Contents

Degrees of difficulty

Easy, suitable for novice with little experience	**Fairly easy,** suitable for beginner with some experience	**Fairly difficult,** suitable for competent DIY mechanic	**Difficult,** suitable for experienced DIY mechanic	**Very difficult,** suitable for expert DIY or professional

1 General description

The main bodyshell and underframe is of all-steel unitary construction and incorporates many safety features. The passenger compartment is in the form of a safety cage, and impact energy on collision is absorbed by the front and rear body panels, the passenger compartment remaining intact. Impact protection bars are also built into the side doors at waist level.

The front wings and front panel are bolted to the main bodyframe, and renewal of these items is therefore straightforward.

The B19 model was introduced in 1981, and the existing B14 models also received an update in the same year.

In 1982 the front end was modified, including a new bonnet, grille and front wings. In 1983 a redesigned facia panel was fitted, and the Saloon version was introduced.

In 1984 the side window quarterlights were discontinued in favour of a one-piece window, and the ventilation ducts were moved from the C-pillars to the openings at the bottom of the luggage area.

1986 saw the introduction of the B172 models which, along with the existing range of models, received various facelifting changes.

2 Maintenance -
bodywork and underframe

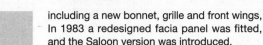

The general condition of a vehicle's bodywork is the one thing that significantly affects its value. Maintenance is easy, but needs to be regular. Neglect, particularly after minor damage, can lead quickly to further deterioration and costly repair bills. It is important also to keep watch on those parts of the vehicle not immediately visible, for instance the underside, inside all the wheel arches, and the lower part of the engine compartment.

The basic maintenance routine for the bodywork is washing - preferably with a lot of water, from a hose. This will remove all the loose solids which may have stuck to the vehicle. It is important to flush these off in such a way as to prevent grit from scratching the finish. The wheel arches and underframe need washing in the same way, to remove any accumulated mud, which will retain moisture and tend to encourage rust. Paradoxically enough, the best time to clean the underframe and wheel arches is in wet weather, when the mud is thoroughly wet and soft. In very wet weather, the underframe is usually cleaned of

9

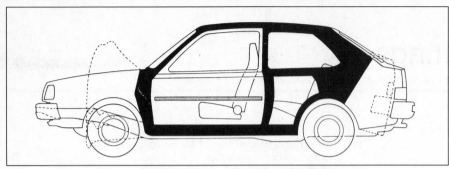

Fig. 9.1 Body safety cage construction (Sec 1)

large accumulations automatically, and this is a good time for inspection.

Periodically, except on vehicles with a wax-based underbody protective coating, it is a good idea to have the whole of the underframe of the vehicle steam-cleaned, engine compartment included, so that a thorough inspection can be carried out to see what minor repairs and renovations are necessary. Steam-cleaning is available at many garages, and is necessary for the removal of the accumulation of oily grime, which sometimes is allowed to become thick in certain areas. If steam-cleaning facilities are not available, there are some excellent grease solvents available which can be brush-applied; the dirt can then be simply hosed off. Note that these methods should not be used on vehicles with wax-based underbody protective coating, or the coating will be removed. Such vehicles should be inspected annually, preferably just prior to Winter, when the underbody should be washed down, and any damage to the wax coating repaired. Ideally, a completely fresh coat should be applied. It would also be worth considering the use of such wax-based protection for injection into door panels, sills, box sections, etc, as an additional safeguard against rust damage, where such protection is not provided by the vehicle manufacturer.

After washing paintwork, wipe off with a chamois leather to give an unspotted clear finish. A coat of clear protective wax polish will give added protection against chemical pollutants in the air. If the paintwork sheen has dulled or oxidised, use a cleaner/polisher combination to restore the brilliance of the shine. This requires a little effort, but such

dulling is usually caused because regular washing has been neglected. Care needs to be taken with metallic paintwork, as special non-abrasive cleaner/polisher is required to avoid damage to the finish. Always check that the door and ventilator opening drain holes and pipes are completely clear, so that water can be drained out (photos). Brightwork should be treated in the same way as paintwork. Windscreens and windows can be kept clear of the smeary film which often appears, by the use of proprietary glass cleaner. Never use any form of wax or other body or chromium polish on glass.

3 Maintenance - upholstery and carpets

Mats and carpets should be brushed or vacuum-cleaned regularly, to keep them free of grit. If they are badly stained, remove them from the vehicle for scrubbing or sponging, and make quite sure they are dry before refitting. Seats and interior trim panels can be kept clean by wiping with a damp cloth. If they do become stained (which can be more apparent on light-coloured upholstery), use a little liquid detergent and a soft nail brush to scour the grime out of the grain of the material. Do not forget to keep the headlining clean in the same way as the upholstery. When using liquid cleaners inside the vehicle, do not over-wet the surfaces being cleaned. Excessive damp could get into the seams and padded interior, causing stains, offensive odours or even rot.

4 Minor body damage - repair

Note: *For more detailed information about bodywork repair, Haynes Publishing produce a book by Lindsay Porter called 'The Car Bodywork Repair Manual'. This incorporates information on such aspects as rust treatment, painting and glass-fibre repairs, as well as details on more ambitious repairs involving welding and panel beating.*

Repairs of minor scratches in bodywork

If the scratch is very superficial, and does not penetrate to the metal of the bodywork, repair is very simple. Lightly rub the area of the scratch with a paintwork renovator, or a very fine cutting paste, to remove loose paint from the scratch, and to clear the surrounding bodywork of wax polish. Rinse the area with clean water.

Apply touch-up paint to the scratch using a fine paint brush; continue to apply fine layers of paint until the surface of the paint in the scratch is level with the surrounding paintwork. Allow the new paint at least two weeks to harden, then blend it into the surrounding paintwork by rubbing the scratch area with a paintwork renovator or a very fine cutting paste. Finally, apply wax polish.

Where the scratch has penetrated right through to the metal of the bodywork, causing the metal to rust, a different repair technique is required. Remove any loose rust from the bottom of the scratch with a penknife, then apply rust-inhibiting paint to prevent the formation of rust in the future. Using a rubber or nylon applicator, fill the scratch with bodystopper paste. If required, this paste can be mixed with cellulose thinners to provide a very thin paste which is ideal for filling narrow scratches. Before the stopper-paste in the scratch hardens, wrap a piece of smooth cotton rag around the top of a finger. Dip the finger in cellulose thinners, and quickly sweep it across the surface of the stopper-paste in the scratch; this will ensure that the surface of the stopper-paste is slightly hollowed. The scratch can now be painted over as described earlier in this Section.

Repairs of dents in bodywork

When deep denting of the vehicle's bodywork has taken place, the first task is to pull the dent out, until the affected bodywork almost attains its original shape. There is little point in trying to restore the original shape

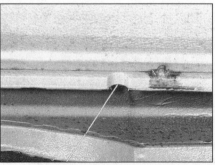

2.4A Door drain hole location

2.4B Body drain hole location

completely, as the metal in the damaged area will have stretched on impact, and cannot be reshaped fully to its original contour. It is better to bring the level of the dent up to a point which is about 3 mm below the level of the surrounding bodywork. In cases where the dent is very shallow anyway, it is not worth trying to pull it out at all. If the underside of the dent is accessible, it can be hammered out gently from behind, using a mallet with a wooden or plastic head. Whilst doing this, hold a suitable block of wood firmly against the outside of the panel, to absorb the impact from the hammer blows and thus prevent a large area of the bodywork from being 'belled-out'.

Should the dent be in a section of the bodywork which has a double skin, or some other factor making it inaccessible from behind, a different technique is called for. Drill several small holes through the metal inside the area - particularly in the deeper section. Then screw long self-tapping screws into the holes, just sufficiently for them to gain a good purchase in the metal. Now the dent can be pulled out by pulling on the protruding heads of the screws with a pair of pliers.

The next stage of the repair is the removal of the paint from the damaged area, and from an inch or so of the surrounding 'sound' bodywork. This is accomplished most easily by using a wire brush or abrasive pad on a power drill, although it can be done just as effectively by hand, using sheets of abrasive paper. To complete the preparation for filling, score the surface of the bare metal with a screwdriver or the tang of a file, or alternatively, drill small holes in the affected area. This will provide a really good 'key' for the filler paste.

To complete the repair, see the Section on filling and respraying.

Repairs of rust holes or gashes in bodywork

Remove all paint from the affected area, and from an inch or so of the surrounding 'sound' bodywork, using an abrasive pad or a wire brush on a power drill. If these are not available, a few sheets of abrasive paper will do the job most effectively. With the paint removed, you will be able to judge the severity of the corrosion, and therefore decide whether to renew the whole panel (if this is possible) or to repair the affected area. New body panels are not as expensive as most people think, and it is often quicker and more satisfactory to fit a new panel than to attempt to repair large areas of corrosion.

Remove all fittings from the affected area, except those which will act as a guide to the original shape of the damaged bodywork (eg headlight shells, etc). Then, using tin snips or a hacksaw blade, remove all loose metal and any other metal badly affected by corrosion. Hammer the edges of the hole inwards, in order to create a slight depression for the filler paste.

Wire-brush the affected area to remove the powdery rust from the surface of the remaining metal. Paint the affected area with rust-inhibiting paint, if the back of the rusted area is accessible, treat this also.

Before filling can take place, it will be necessary to block the hole in some way. This can be achieved by the use of aluminium or plastic mesh, or aluminium tape.

Aluminium or plastic mesh, or glass-fibre matting, is probably the best material to use for a large hole. Cut a piece to the approximate size and shape of the hole to be filled, then position it in the hole so that its edges are below the level of the surrounding bodywork. It can be retained in position by several blobs of filler paste around its periphery.

Aluminium tape should be used for small or very narrow holes. Pull a piece off the roll, trim it to the approximate size and shape required, then pull off the backing paper (if used) and stick the tape over the hole; it can be overlapped if the thickness of one piece is insufficient. Burnish down the edges of the tape with the handle of a screwdriver or similar, to ensure that the tape is securely attached to the metal underneath.

Bodywork repairs - filling and respraying

Before using this Section, see the Sections on dent, deep scratch, rust holes and gash repairs.

Many types of bodyfiller are available, but generally speaking, those proprietary kits which contain a tin of filler paste and a tube of resin hardener are best for this type of repair. A wide, flexible plastic or nylon applicator will be found invaluable for imparting a smooth and well-contoured finish to the surface of the filler.

Mix up a little filler on a clean piece of card or board - measure the hardener carefully (follow the maker's instructions on the pack), otherwise the filler will set too rapidly or too slowly. Using the applicator, apply the filler paste to the prepared area; draw the applicator across the surface of the filler to achieve the correct contour and to level the surface. As soon as a contour that approximates to the correct one is achieved, stop working the paste - if you carry on too long, the paste will become sticky and begin to 'pick-up' on the applicator. Continue to add thin layers of filler paste at 20-minute intervals, until the level of the filler is just proud of the surrounding bodywork.

Once the filler has hardened, the excess can be removed using a metal plane or file. From then on, progressively-finer grades of abrasive paper should be used, starting with a 40-grade production paper, and finishing with a 400-grade wet-and-dry paper. Always wrap the abrasive paper around a flat rubber, cork, or wooden block - otherwise the surface of the filler will not be completely flat. During the smoothing of the filler surface, the wet-and-

dry paper should be periodically rinsed in water. This will ensure that a very smooth finish is imparted to the filler at the final stage.

At this stage, the 'dent' should be surrounded by a ring of bare metal, which in turn should be encircled by the finely 'feathered' edge of the good paintwork. Rinse the repair area with clean water, until all of the dust produced by the rubbing-down operation has gone.

Spray the whole area with a light coat of primer - this will show up any imperfections in the surface of the filler. Repair these imperfections with fresh filler paste or bodystopper, and once more smooth the surface with abrasive paper. Repeat this spray-and-repair procedure until you are satisfied that the surface of the filler, and the feathered edge of the paintwork, are perfect. Clean the repair area with clean water, and allow to dry fully.

HAYNES HiNT *If bodystopper is used, it can be mixed with cellulose thinners to form a really thin paste which is ideal for filling small holes.*

The repair area is now ready for final spraying. Paint spraying must be carried out in a warm, dry, windless and dust-free atmosphere. This condition can be created artificially if you have access to a large indoor working area, but if you are forced to work in the open, you will have to pick your day very carefully. If you are working indoors, dousing the floor in the work area with water will help to settle the dust which would otherwise be in the atmosphere. If the repair area is confined to one body panel, mask off the surrounding panels; this will help to minimise the effects of a slight mis-match in paint colours. Bodywork fittings (eg chrome strips, door handles, etc) will also need to be masked off. Use genuine masking tape, and several thicknesses of newspaper, for the masking operations.

Before commencing to spray, agitate the aerosol can thoroughly, then spray a test area (an old tin, or similar) until the technique is mastered. Cover the repair area with a thick coat of primer; the thickness should be built up using several thin layers of paint, rather than one thick one. Using 400-grade wet-and-dry paper, rub down the surface of the primer until it is really smooth. While doing this, the work area should be thoroughly doused with water, and the wet-and-dry paper periodically rinsed in water. Allow to dry before spraying on more paint.

Spray on the top coat, again building up the thickness by using several thin layers of paint. Start spraying at one edge of the repair area, and then, using a side-to-side motion, work until the whole repair area and about 2 inches of the surrounding original paintwork is covered. Remove all masking material 10 to 15 minutes after spraying on the final coat of paint.

Allow the new paint at least two weeks to

9

harden, then, using a paintwork renovator, or a very fine cutting paste, blend the edges of the paint into the existing paintwork. Finally, apply wax polish.

Plastic components

With the use of more and more plastic body components by the vehicle manufacturers (eg bumpers, spoilers, and in some cases major body panels), rectification of more serious damage to such items has become a matter of either entrusting repair work to a specialist in this field, or renewing complete components. Repair of such damage by the DIY owner is not really feasible, owing to the cost of the equipment and materials required for effecting such repairs. The basic technique involves making a groove along the line of the crack in the plastic, using a rotary burr in a power drill. The damaged part is then welded back together, using a hot-air gun to heat up and fuse a plastic filler rod into the groove. Any excess plastic is then removed, and the area rubbed down to a smooth finish. It is important that a filler rod of the correct plastic is used, as body components can be made of a variety of different types (eg polycarbonate, ABS, polypropylene).

Damage of a less serious nature (abrasions, minor cracks, etc) can be repaired by the DIY owner using a two-part epoxy filler repair material. Once mixed in equal proportions, this is used in similar fashion to the bodywork filler used on metal panels. The filler is usually cured in twenty to thirty minutes, ready for sanding and painting.

If the owner is renewing a complete component himself, or if he has repaired it with epoxy filler, he will be left with the problem of finding a suitable paint for finishing which is compatible with the type of plastic used. At one time, the use of a universal paint was not possible, owing to the complex range of plastics encountered in body component applications. Standard paints, generally speaking, will not bond to plastic or rubber satisfactorily. However, it is now possible to obtain a plastic body parts finishing kit which consists of a pre-primer treatment, a primer and coloured top coat. Full instructions are normally supplied with a kit, but basically, the method of use is to first apply the pre-primer to the component concerned, and allow it to dry for up to 30 minutes. Then the primer is applied, and left to dry for about an hour before finally applying the special-coloured top coat. The result is a correctly-coloured component, where the paint will flex with the plastic or rubber, a property that standard paint does not normally possess.

5 Major body damage - repair

Where serious damage has occurred or large areas need renewal due to neglect, it means that completely new sections or panels will need welding in, and this is best left to professionals. If the damage is due to impact, it will also be necessary to completely check the alignment of the bodyshell structure. Due to the principle of construction, the strength and shape of the whole car can be affected by damage to one part. In such instances the services of a Volvo agent with specialist checking jigs are essential. If a body is left misaligned, it is first of all dangerous as the car will not handle properly, and secondly, uneven stresses will be imposed on the steering, engine and transmission, causing abnormal wear or complete failure. Tyre wear may also be excessive.

6 Maintenance - hinges and locks

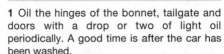

1 Oil the hinges of the bonnet, tailgate and doors with a drop or two of light oil periodically. A good time is after the car has been washed.
2 Oil the bonnet release catch pivot pin and the bonnet location roller pivots.
3 Do not over-lubricate door latches and strikers.

7 Doors - tracing rattles and their rectification

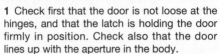

1 Check first that the door is not loose at the hinges, and that the latch is holding the door firmly in position. Check also that the door lines up with the aperture in the body.
2 If the hinges are loose or the door is out of alignment it will be necessary to renew the hinge pins or hinges; renewal of the pins is straightforward, but as the hinges are welded in position, renewal of the hinges is best left to a suitably equipped garage.
3 If the latch is holding the door properly, it should hold the door tightly when fully latched and the door should line up with the body. If it is out of alignment it needs adjustment. If loose, some part of the lock mechanism must be worn out and require renewal.
4 Other rattles from the door would be caused by wear or looseness in the window winder, the glass channels and sill strips or the door interior latch release mechanism.

8 Front wings and front panel - removal and refitting

1 The front wings and front panel are bolted to the main bodyframe, and it is therefore a simple matter for the home mechanic to renew either of these items.
2 Refer to Fig. 9.2 for the location of the retaining bolts, and to chapter 10 for the removal of the headlamps and (on later models) the side repeater lamps.
3 Refitting is a reversal of removal, but renew any mastic sealing compound, and apply a protective coating to the under surface. The outer surface can be resprayed to match the body colour.

9 Windscreen glass - removal and refitting

1 Removal and refitting of the windscreen is best left to specialist firms, the procedure given here being for those intrepid enough to attempt the task themselves.
2 Due to design changes over the years there are different procedures for different models, the methods given here covering most applications.
3 On all models remove the windscreen wiper arms and the interior rear view mirror.
4 Also on all models remove the A-pillar panels and the windscreen header panel.

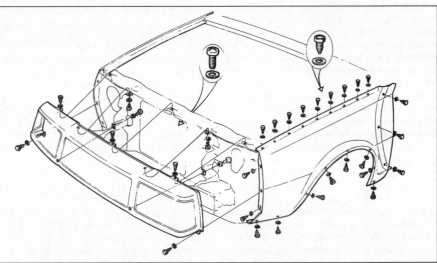

Fig. 9.2 Front wing and front panel retaining screw locations on early models (later type similar) (Sec 8)

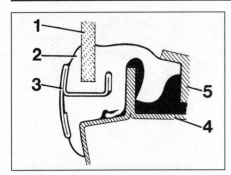

Fig. 9.3 Cross-section of windscreen weatherstrip (Sec 9)

1 Windscreen   *4 Body*
2 Weatherstrip   *5 Facia*
3 Ornamental moulding

5 On models up to 1978, release the facia panel and pull it forwards slightly.
6 On models built from 1979 remove the defroster panel and the windscreen weatherstrip supports.
7 On models built from 1983 remove the cover panels from under the facia panel to gain access to the weatherstrip supports and remove them.
8 On all models release the weatherstrip from the windscreen frame by working around its perimeter with a screwdriver blade.
9 With an assistant, apply steady pressure to the inside of the windscreen using the feet, and press the windscreen out of the frame, complete with weatherstrip and trim moulding.
10 Before refitting the windscreen, thoroughly clean the windscreen, weatherstrip and trim moulding with methylated spirit.
11 Fit the weatherstrip and trim moulding to the windscreen, using washing up liquid as a lubricant.
12 Place a length of strong cord into the weatherstrip channel right round its perimeter and overlapping in the centre.
13 Offer the windscreen up to the frame, placing the ends of the cord inside the vehicle.
14 Apply pressure to the outside of the windscreen and at the same time pull on the cord so that the inner lip of the seal is pulled over the frame edge.
15 Gently tap around the edge of the screen and weatherstrip using a rubber mallet to settle the seal in the frame.
16 Refit the weatherstrip supports, facia

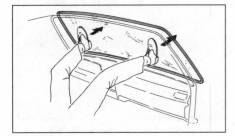

Fig. 9.6 Removing the windscreen (Sec 9)

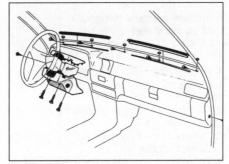

Fig. 9.4 Early facia panel retaining screws (Sec 9)

panel, trim panels and windscreen wiper arms.
17 When refitting a windscreen with a metal trim moulding, apply sealant between the windscreen and weatherstrip, and between the weatherstrip and window frame, using a sealant gun.

10 Windscreen header panel - removal and refitting

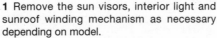

1 Remove the sun visors, interior light and sunroof winding mechanism as necessary depending on model.
2 On models up to 1978, pull the top part of the door sealing strip away from the door frame, remove the top screws from the A-panel and pull the header panel down from the roof.
3 On models from 1979, remove the retaining screws from the header panel and pull it free from the roof.
4 Refitting is a reversal of removal.

11 A-panels - removal and refitting

1 The A-panels are those interior trim panels which cover the two roof support pillars either side of the windscreen.
2 To remove the A-panels, remove the sun visor if necessary and remove the screws securing the panel to the pillar.
3 Refitting is a reversal of removal.

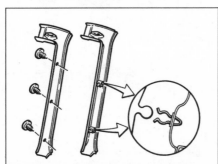

Fig. 9.7 A-panel assembly (Sec 11)

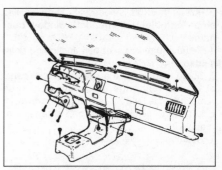

Fig. 9.5 Later type facia panel retaining screws (Sec 9)

12 B-panels - removal and refitting

1 The B-panels are those interior trim panels which cover the centre roof support pillars.
2 If fitted remove the hinged side window, complete with hinges.
3 Remove the seat belt anchorages at top and bottom points as necessary.
4 Remove the panel securing screws.
5 Pull the door sealing strip away from the frame as necessary.
6 Remove the panel by pulling it out of the sill at the bottom first.
7 Refit in the reverse order.

13 C-panels - removal and refitting

1 The C-panels are those interior panels which cover the rear roof support pillars.
2 Disconnect the wiring from the tailgate strut (if necessary).

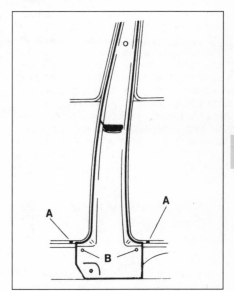

Fig. 9.8 B-panel assembly (Sec 12)

A Sill moulding screws   *B Panel screws*

9

3 Pull as much as is necessary of the sealing strip from the tailgate and window/door frame.
4 Remove the rear seat belt anchorage point if fitted.
5 Some models have a separate small panel at the top rear edge which should also be removed - it is held by self-tapping screws.
6 Lift the C-pillar upward and sideways to remove it.
7 Refitting is a reversal of removal.

14 Side window (fixed) - removal and refitting

1 Have an assistant support the outside of the window, then place two wads of cloth on the inside of the window and use the feet to push the glass from the aperture.
2 Remove the trim moulding and bridge piece.
3 Remove the weatherstrip from the window.
4 To refit, fit the weatherstrip, trim mouldings, and bridge piece to the window.
5 Using the method described in Section 9, refit the window into the body aperture. There is no need to seal the weatherstrip.

15 Side window (hinged) - removal and refitting

1 Remove the cross-head screws securing the hinges and stay to the side window, and lift the window from the car.
2 Remove the rubber grommets and nuts from the window.
3 To remove the hinges, release the caps and unscrew the bolts.
4 To remove the stay on models up to chassis number 426261 first remove the C-panel (Section 13). On models from chassis number 426262 remove the plug from the C-panel. On all models remove the Allen screws and withdraw the stay.
5 Refitting is a reversal of removal.

16 Rear window (Hatchback and Saloon) - removal and refitting

1 The procedure is similar to that for windscreen removal (Section 9) with the following pointers:

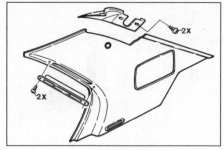

Fig. 9.9 C-panel assembly (Sec 13)

2 Disconnect the rear screen heater and remove the parcel shelf.
3 The remarks concerning sealant when refitting a window with a metal trim moulding apply also to the rear window.
4 From 1986, the rear window is bonded in position, and removal and fitting should be left to a specialist firm or your Volvo dealer.

17 Front door window - removal and refitting

Models up to 1984

1 Remove the door trim panel as described in Section 22, and the door panel support bracket if fitted.
2 Remove the plastic plugs from the door, and remove the moistureproof sheet and access panels where fitted (photos).

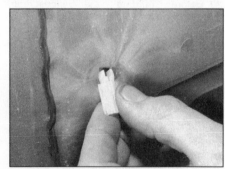

17.2A Removing a plastic plug from the door prior to removing the moistureproof sheet

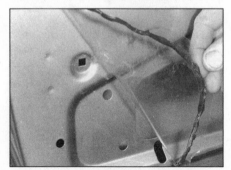

17.2B Peeling back the moistureproof sheet

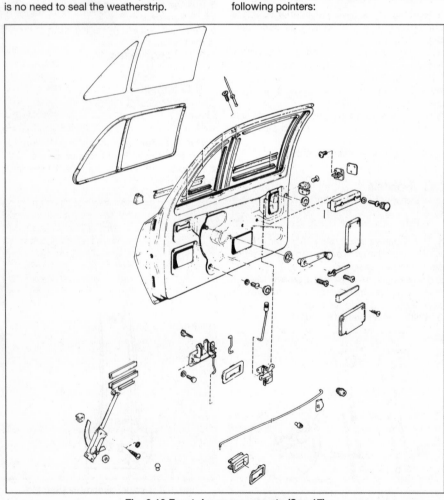

Fig. 9.10 Front door components (Sec 17)

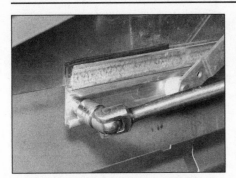

17.9A Removing a lift channel bolt . . .

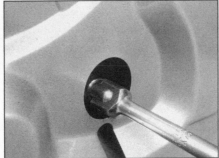

17.9B . . . the other one being accessible through the hole

17.10 Lifting out the window

3 Wind the window fully down.

4 On models with a quarterlight, remove the bolts securing the window channel to the door (on some models a rivet is used at the top end and this will have to be drilled out).

5 Prise the remote control latch assembly from the door.

6 Remove the trim moulding from the window channel, press the channel down and then up and out of the door.

7 Wind the window up until the winding mechanism is horizontal, slide the arm from the lift channel and remove the window.

Models from 1984

8 On these models carry out operations 1 and 2 above.

9 Position the window so that the lift channel bolts can be undone (photos).

10 Undo the nuts and then pull the lift mechanism from the window and lift channel, and lift the window up and out of the door to the outside and at an angle (photo).

All models

11 If the lift channel is to be transferred to a new window, measure the distance from the front edge of the window to the leading edge of the lift channel and fit the channel to the new window in same position.

12 Refitting is a reversal of removal but leave the screws in the lift channel loose until the window is refitted, then wind the window up

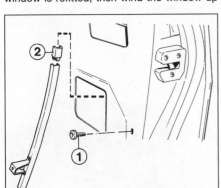

Fig. 9.11 Front door window channel assembly (Sec 20)

1 Bolt   2 U-clamp

to centralise the glass in the door channels and then tighten the screws. **Note:** *It is important that the moistureproof sheet is refitted intact, and sealed around its edges to prevent moisture ingress to the inside of the trim panel.*

18 Front door quarterlight - removal and refitting
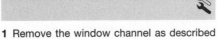

1 Remove the window channel as described in Section 17, paragraphs 1 to 4.

2 Remove the rubber strip and pull out the quarterlight.

3 Refitting is a reversal of removal, but apply some soapy water to the rubber strip to facilitate fitting the window channel. Delay tightening the window channel screws until the window has been operated several times.

19 Rear door window and quarterlight - removal and refitting

The procedure is similar to that described in Sections 17 and 18 but the quarterlight weatherstrip is fitted around the glass.

20 Window channel (models from 1983) - removal and refitting

Note: *Refers to models with no quarterlight*

1 Remove the door trim panel as described in Section 22 and remove the moistureproof sheet.

2 Remove the screw from the lower end of the channel.

3 Pull the weatherstrip from the channel and then remove the channel through the bottom opening.

4 Should the U clamp at the top end of the channel remain in the door, remove it from the door and refit it to the channel.

5 Refitting is a reversal of removal, but when pushing the channel upward into place a

'click' should be heard from the U-clamp indicating that it is properly in position. It is important that the moistureproof sheet is refitted intact, and sealed around its edges.

21 Door - removal and refitting

1 Open the door and disconnect the check arm (photo). To do this on the front door, remove the clevis pin using a suitable metal drift from beneath the pin. On the rear door unscrew the two bolts at the door end.

2 Where door mounted speakers, central locking or electric windows are fitted, remove the door trim panel and disconnect the necessary leads, feeding them through the hole in the door.

3 Remove the plastic plugs from the hinges, where fitted, and drive out the lower hinge pin followed by the upper hinge pin. The lower hinge pin must be tapped up through the hinge; the upper pin down through the hinge.

4 Lift the door away from the car.

5 If a new door is being fitted, the window, regulator, door lock and handles must be transferred to the new door by referring to the applicable Sections of this Chapter (photo)

6 Refitting is a reversal of removal, but it will be necessary to adjust the striker plate (photo). Loosen the striker plate retaining screws, and adjust the plate so that its upper edge is horizontal, and so that when the door is shut it is neither lifted up nor pressed down

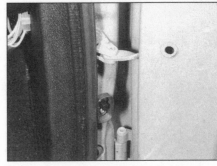

21.1 Front door check arm and lower hinge

9

21.5 Removing the interior remote door handle

21.6 Front door striker plate

22.2A Remove the plastic cover . . .

22.2B . . . and window handle screw (early models)

to engage the striker. Check that the lock engages its second position when the door is fully shut and that the door panel aligns with the rear wing panel or rear door as applicable.

22 Door trim panel - removal and refitting

1 Fully close the window and note the position of the window winder handle, so that it can be refitted in the same position.
2 Prise out the plastic panel from the handle (if fitted) and remove the handle securing screw (photos).
3 On early models remove the screws and

withdraw the armrest. On some models these are covered by plastic plugs which should be prised out. Where the armrest incorporates a grab handle, turn the armrest through 90 degrees to disengage the upper mounting (photos).
4 On 1986 models the armrest is integral with the door trim moulding.
5 Slide the interior door remote control handle trim moulding to the rear to remove it (photo). If fitted, remove the intermediate moulding.
6 On 1986 models remove the retaining screws (photos) and then (on all models) using a wide-bladed screwdriver, prise the trim panel and fasteners away from the door (photo).

22.2C Remove the plastic cover . . .

22.2D . . . and window handle screw (late models)

22.3A Remove the plug . . .

22.3B . . . screws . . .

22.3C . . . and armrest (345 model shown)

22.5 Slide the interior door handle to the rear to remove it

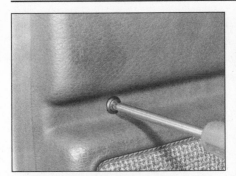

22.6A Removing a screw from the door interior trim panel

22.6B On some models there is a screw in the door pull recess

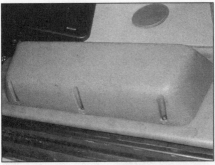

22.6C The lower screws are under the door pocket

7 Disconnect the leads to the door mounted speakers (photo), central locking solenoids and electric window lift motors where this equipment is fitted.
8 Refitting is a reversal of removal.

23 Door lock - removal and refitting (all models)

1 Remove the door panel as described in Section 22.
2 On models up to 1983, remove the rear panel from the access hole. On later models remove the protective cover from inside the door (if fitted) (photo).
3 Disconnect the rods from the door lock.
4 Remove the door lock retaining screws and remove the lock (photo).
5 Refitting is a reversal of removal.

24 Door outside handle - removing and refitting

1 Remove the trim panel as described in Section 22.
2 Remove the rear cover plate from the door.

Models up to 1983 (front door)

3 Disconnect the control rods at the lock.

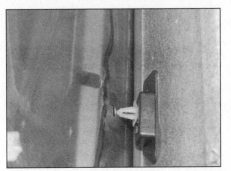

22.6D Door trim panel retaining plastic plug

4 Remove the nut or bolt and remove the handle (photo).
5 Remove the rubber sealing ring.

Models up to 1983 (rear door)

6 On the right-hand door only, depress the lower guide.
7 Extract the pullrod from the guides and disconnect the lower rod from the locking rod lever after removing the circlip.
8 Unscrew the retaining bolt and withdraw the handle sufficiently to unclip the pullrod.

Models from 1983 (front door)

9 Remove the window channel (Section 20).
10 Remove the handle retaining bolt.
11 On 4/5 door models remove the protective cover.
12 Pull the control rods from the handle mechanism and withdraw the handle in the open position.

22.7 Disconnect the radio speaker

Models from 1983 (rear door)

13 The procedure is similar to that for models up to 1983.

All models

14 Refitting is a reversal of removal.

25 Door lock cylinder - removal and refitting

1 Remove the door outside handle as described in Section 24.
2 The door lock cylinder can be removed from the handle assembly by knocking out the lock pin with a punch and removing the lockplate and spring.
3 Refit the cylinder in the reverse order, but insert the key in the lock first, which will ensure the trip levers in the lock are correctly positioned.

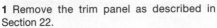

23.2 Removing the rear access cover plate

23.4 Front door lock retaining screw location

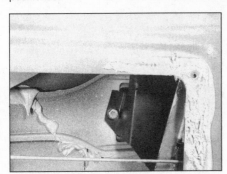

24.4 Front door outside handle retaining bolt location

9

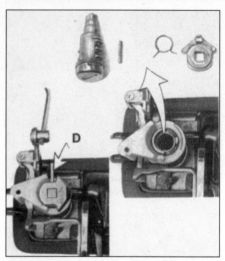

Fig. 9.12 Door lock cylinder removal (Sec 25)

D Lock pin

26 Window winder mechanism - removal and refitting

For electric windows see Section 28
1 Remove the trim panel as described in Section 22.

Front door - models up to 1983

Three-door variants

2 Fully lower the window.
3 Remove the middle access panel by removing the two screws and lifting the panel from the lower edge of the aperture.
4 As from chassis number 388532 remove the front access panel as well.
5 Remove the four screws securing the winder mechanism to the door.
6 On models with a chassis number before 388532 slide the lift arm from the window channel and withdraw the mechanism through the aperture while swivelling the lift arm forwards.
7 As from chassis number 388532 slide the lift arm from the window channel (photo), then refit the handle and turn it fully anti-clockwise. Withdraw the mechanism through the front opening in the door.
8 Refitting is a reversal of removal.

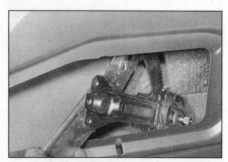

26.18A Removing the window winder mechanism from the door (models from 1983)

26.7 Front door window lift arm and channel

Five-door variants

9 Remove the rear and middle access panels.
10 Unscrew the two window channel retaining bolts; access to the lower bolt is gained by prising out the plug.
11 Fully raise the window and support it with a block of wood.
12 Remove the four screws securing the winder mechanism to the door (photo).
13 Using a screwdriver, move the lower end of the window channel backwards, then detach the mechanism from the door and slide it from the window channel.
14 Withdraw the mechanism through the rear opening in the door.
15 Refitting is a reversal of removal.

Front door - 1983 models

16 Remove the retaining screws from the winder mechanism and the window channel (see Section 17).
17 Wind the mechanism towards the closed position until the mechanism turns freely, and then press the mechanism out of the lift channel.
18 To remove the mechanism from the door it must be wound to the half open position and pulled out of the front opening in the door (photos).
19 Refitting is a reversal of removal, but ensure that the arm is located on the correct side of the window channel when inserting the mechanism into the door.
20 Wind the mechanism to the open position until the threaded holes line up so that the screws can be fitted and tightened.

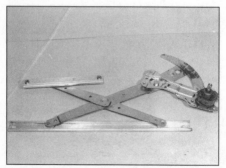

26.18B View of the window winder mechanism (models from 1983)

26.12 Front door window winder and retaining screws

Front door - models from 1984

21 Remove the window as described in Section 17.
22 On three-door models, wind the window mechanism to the half way position, and on other models towards the closed position until the mechanism turns freely.
23 Remove the two screws from the window channel bracket and the screws from the widow winding mechanism, then remove the mechanism from the door via the rear opening.
24 Refitting is a reversal of removal.

Rear door - all models

25 Remove the lower access panel.
26 Remove the four screws securing the winder mechanism to the door.
27 Support the window and slide the lift arm from the window channel. Fully raise the window and support it with a block of wood.
28 Withdraw the mechanism through the lower access opening.
29 Refitting is a reversal of removal.

27 Tailgate - removal and refitting

1 Open the tailgate and disconnect the wiring from the struts.
2 Have an assistant support the tailgate, then pull out the clips and detach the struts from the balljoints (photo).

27.2 Tailgate strut balljoint and retaining clip

27.5A Tailgate buffer

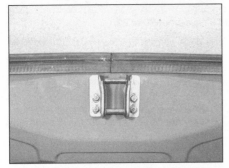

27.5B Tailgate striker plate as fitted to early models

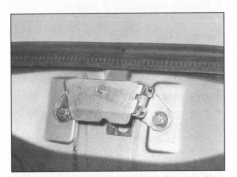

27.5C Tailgate striker plate as fitted to late models

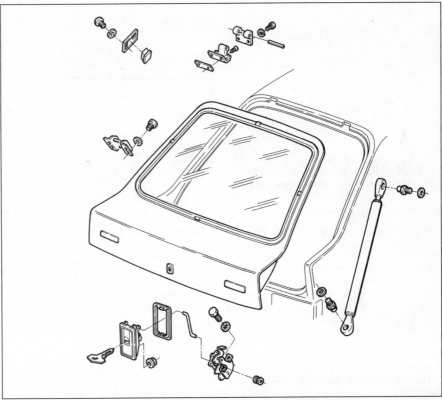

Fig. 9.13 Tailgate components (Sec 27)

3 Pull the rear edge of the headlining from the retaining strip, or prise out the covers to gain access to the hinge bolts.

4 Unscrew the hinge bolts and withdraw the tailgate.

5 Refitting is a reversal of removal, but check that the tailgate aligns with the body when shut. Adjustment of the top of the tailgate is made possible by loosening the hinge bolts.

Slotted buffers are provided for adjustment of the bottom of the tailgate (photo). Check that the tailgate is held firmly shut without any free play, and if necessary adjust the position of the striker plate (photos).

28 Electrically operated window motor and mechanism - removal and refitting

1 Remove the window as described in Section 17.

2 Position the window lift mechanism as shown in Fig. 9.14 (this is dependent on the door panel openings).

3 Disconnect the electric leads to the servo motor.

4 Remove the screws from the window lift channel and the servo motor and remove the complete assembly from the door via the lower opening (photos).

28.4A Door motor for electrically operated windows

28.4B Spring for electrically operated windows

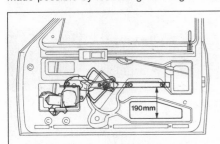 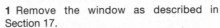 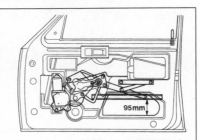

Fig. 9.14 Lift mechanism position according to door panel openings (Sec 28)

9

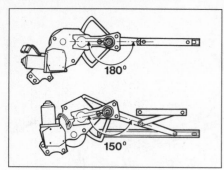

Fig. 9.15 Lift mechanism position for refitting according to door panel opening (Sec 28)

See also Fig. 9.14

5 To separate the motor from the lift mechanism remove the three bolts. **Note:** *On three-door models one of these bolts is a countersunk Allen bolt, and because of the limited space this Allen bolt should never be replaced by a normal hexagon-headed bolt.*
6 Refitting is a reversal of removal; setting the lift mechanism as shown in Fig. 9.15.
7 For details of operating switches see Chapter 10.

29 Central door locking system

General description

1 This system is fitted to some models and enables all doors (except the boot/tailgate) to

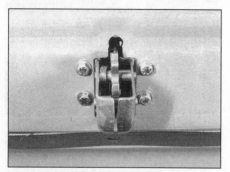

30.3A Tailgate lock on early models

30.3B Rear view of the tailgate handle

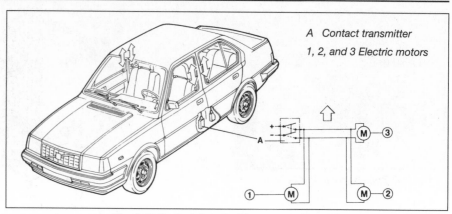

A Contact transmitter

1, 2, and 3 Electric motors

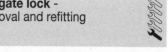

Fig. 9.16 Central door locking system (Sec 29)

be locked in conjunction with the driver's door.
2 The driver's door incorporates a contact transmitter which, on operation of the driver's door lock, activates electric motors in the other doors which in turn are linked to the door lock mechanism.

Contact transmitter - removal and refitting

3 Remove the door trim panel from the driver's door as described in Section 22.
4 Remove the two screws securing the transmitter to the door, then unhook the control rod and disconnect the electric leads before removing the transmitter.
5 Refit in the reverse order.

Central door locking motors - removal and refitting

6 Remove the door trim panel(s), as described in Section 22.
7 Unhook the control rod from under the door lock button and, on the driver's door, from the transmitter.
8 Remove the two screws securing the motor bracket to the door, remove the motor and disconnect the electric leads.
9 Refitting is a reversal of removal, but if new motors are being fitted, transfer the bracket from the old motor to the new before fitting.

General

10 For details of operating switches see Chapter 10.

30.3C Tailgate lock on late models

30 Tailgate lock - removal and refitting

1 Detach the cover from the tailgate interior.
2 Disconnect and remove the handle and lock connecting rod.
3 Unscrew and remove the retaining bolts, and withdraw the lock. If necessary the handle may be removed by unscrewing the retaining nut (photos).
4 Refitting is a reversal of removal.

31 Bonnet - removal and refitting

Early models

1 Fully open the bonnet and mark the position of the hinges on the bonnet.
2 While an assistant supports the bonnet, prise the retaining clip and washer from the left-hand hinge pin.
3 Where the windscreen washer jets are fitted to the bonnet, disconnect the plastic tubing.
4 Detach the stay from the front crossmember.
5 Unscrew the hinge bolts from the right-hand hinge and withdraw the bonnet to the left (photo). If necessary, prise out the clip and remove the right-hand hinge from the lever, then remove the left-hand hinge from the bonnet.

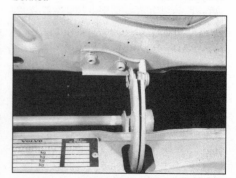

31.5 Bonnet right-hand hinge on early models

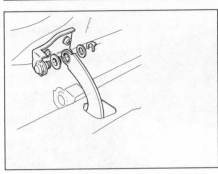

Fig. 9.17 Bonnet hinge components on early models (Sec 31)

31.6A Bonnet rear locking bracket

31.6B Bonnet roller bracket

6 Refitting is a reversal of removal, but check that the bonnet aligns with the body when shut, and that the gaps on opposite edges are equal. Fore-and-aft alignment is provided at the hinges, front height at the bonnet lock (after removal of the grille), rear height at the rear locking brackets, front lateral adjustment at the bonnet catch, and rear lateral adjustment at the roller brackets (photos).

Late models

7 On models which have a modified hinge and torsion bar assembly, the procedure is similar to that for early models, but the front grille must be removed to gain access to the hinge retaining bolts (photos). Do not forget to disconnect the earth wire.

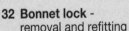

32 Bonnet lock - removal and refitting

Early models

1 Remove the grille and open the bonnet.
2 Unhook the two return springs from the centre of the hinge bar (if fitted) (photo).
3 Unscrew the lock retaining screws, then pull the cable clip from the body crossmember (photos).
4 Withdraw the lock, unhook the cable, and remove the clip.
5 Remove the spare wheel and release the cable from the clips in the engine compartment.

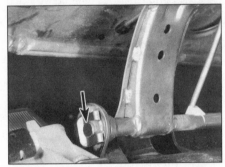

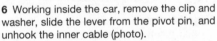
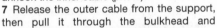

31.7A Hinge bar retaining clip on late models (arrowed)

6 Working inside the car, remove the clip and washer, slide the lever from the pivot pin, and unhook the inner cable (photo).
7 Release the outer cable from the support, then pull it through the bulkhead and

31.7B Removing the hinge retaining bolts on late models

withdraw it from the engine compartment. Remove the grommet.
8 Refitting is a reversal of removal, but if necessary adjust the outer cable at the release lever.

31.7C Left-hand hinge assembly and earthing wire

32.2 Bonnet hinge bar and spring on early models

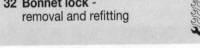

32.3A Bonnet lock retaining bolts on early models . . .

32.3B . . . and on late models

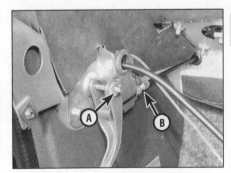

32.6 Bonnet release lever in the car
A Retaining clip   B Adjusting point

9

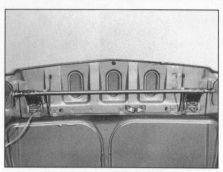

32.9 View of the modified bonnet hinge bar and torsion springs (bonnet removed)

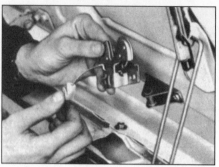

Fig. 9.18 Removing the bonnet lock (Sec 32)

33.2A Removing the front grille centre screws

Late models

9 On later models with the modified hinge bar incorporating torsion springs (photo) ignore the reference to removing the springs.

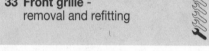

33 Front grille - removal and refitting

Early models

1 On early models turn the quick release clips located on the side of the grille through 90 degrees to release them from the slotted brackets.
2 Remove the two screws from the centre of the grille and withdraw the grille from the front panel (photos).
3 When refitting the grille, make sure the two buffers are installed as these provide a

clearance of 0.06 in (1.5 mm) between the grille and front panel.

Late models

4 On later models, open the bonnet and release the two quick release clips at the top of the grille and undo the central clip (photos).
5 The grille can now be removed by lifting it out of the front panel.
6 When refitting, ensure the lower locating dowels engage in the holes in the front panel (photo).

34 Bumpers - removal and refitting

Front bumper

1 Where fitted, refer to Chapter 10 and disconnect the headlamp washer tube and remove the wiper arm.

2 Disconnect the side repeater lights where these are fitted into the bumper, again referring to Chapter 10.
3 Remove the plastic panels at the front of the bumper covering the retaining bolts (these vary depending upon model) (photos).
4 Undo and remove the bolts (photo), then slide the bumper forward off the side retaining brackets (only on wrap around type bumpers) and lift the bumper away.
5 If required, the mouldings and side-members can be removed from the main bumper by unclipping them or removing the bolts.
6 Refitting is a reversal of removal.

Rear bumper

7 The procedure is similar to that for the front bumper; disconnecting the rear number plate light(s) on applicable models, and removing the bolts from the bumper mounting brackets accessible from under the car.

33.2B Removing the grille

33.4A Quick release fasteners secure the later type grille . . .

33.4B . . . with a screw at the centre

33.6 Lower locating dowel

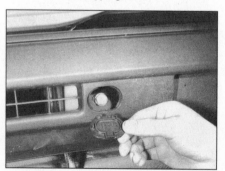

34.3A Removing a bumper bolt cover on early models . . .

34.3B . . . and on later models

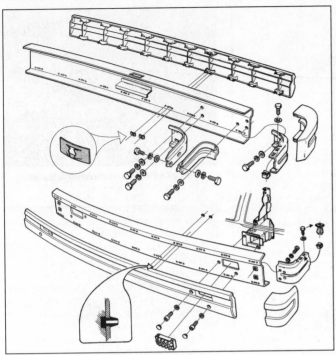

Fig. 9.19 Front and rear bumper components for models up to 1981 (Sec 34)

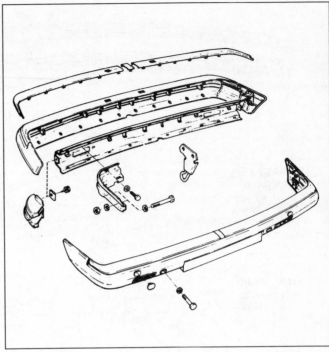

Fig. 9.20 Front and rear bumper components for models from 1981 to 1985 (Sec 34)

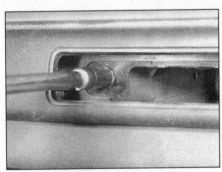

34.4 Removing a bumper bolt

35 Facia panel -
removal and refitting

1 Disconnect the battery negative lead.
2 Remove the steering wheel (see Chapter 8).
3 Unscrew and remove the choke control knob and steering column shrouds.
4 Unscrew and remove the retaining screws and withdraw the direction indicator and wiper switch stalks (not models from 1983).

Models up to 1979

5 Disconnect the ignition switch wiring plug and the choke cable wire.
6 Detach the ashtray, then unscrew and remove the retaining bolts and withdraw the compartment below the heater control levers.
7 Disconnect all wiring and plugs from the facia panel, noting their locations.
8 Disconnect the cable from the rear of the speedometer head.

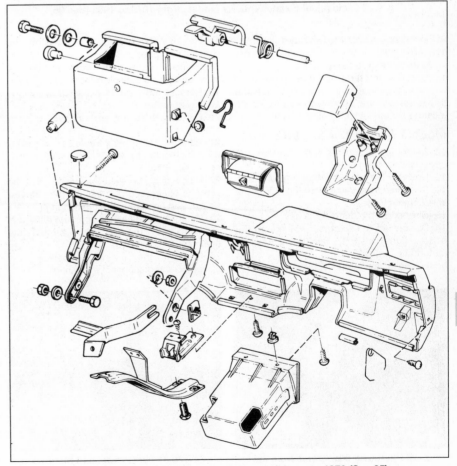

Fig. 9.21 Facia panel components for models up to 1979 (Sec 35)

9

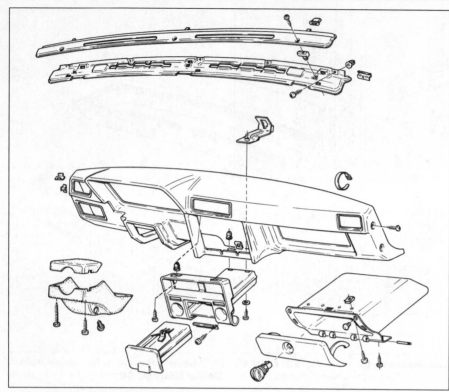

Fig. 9.22 Facia panel components for models from 1979 to 1983 (Sec 35)

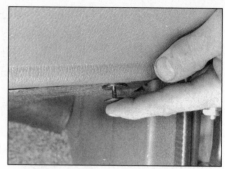

35.27A Facia lower panel retainer

35.27B Component parts of the retainer

9 Pull the hoses from the two outer air vents.

10 Using a screwdriver, prise the defroster vents from the facia panel.

11 Unscrew and remove the retaining screw and withdraw the facia panel; note that the upper screws are fitted with covers which must be prised out with a screwdriver.

Models from 1979 to 1983

12 Remove the screws and withdraw the upper (windscreen) panel.

13 Unscrew the left-hand retaining screws.

14 Disconnect the cable from the rear of the speedometer head.

15 Disconnect the defroster hoses.

16 Disconnect the electrical wiring from the brake light switch, kickdown switch (automatic transmission), ignition switch, horns, choke, and interior lighting.

17 Remove the screws and withdraw the console side panels.

18 Remove the radio compartment (4 screws), and the console support (4 screws).

19 Remove the central facia screw below the ashtray aperture.

20 Pull out the ashtray and remove the lower bracket.

21 Remove the upper screws and withdraw the switch panel by depressing the lugs in the ashtray opening.

22 Disconnect the electrical wiring from the ashtray illumination, cigar lighter, heater switch, and heater panel illumination.

23 Remove the glovebox light, turn it through 90°, and push the light back through the opening.

24 Remove the screws, withdraw the glovebox, and disconnect the wiring.

25 Disconnect the multi-plug connectors to the console switches, and all the remaining wiring to the facia panel.

26 Unscrew the right-hand retaining screws, then slightly raise the facia panel and withdraw it from the car.

Models from 1983

27 Remove the panels from under the facia (photos).

28 Refer to Chapter 10 and remove the instrument panel.

29 Remove the screws from the instrument panel surround and move the surround to one side (photo).

30 Reach up behind the facia panel and disconnect the side vent hoses.

31 Remove the bolts from each end of the facia (photo).

32 Remove the two screws from under the centre section of the facia (photo).

35.29 Removing the screws from the instrument panel surround

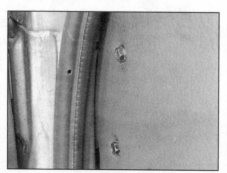

35.31 Facia panel end bolts

35.32 Removing the screws from under the centre section

35.33 Removing the screws from inside the radio aperture (arrowed)

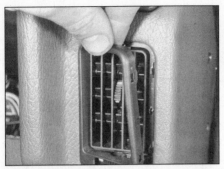

35.38 Side vent grilles clip in place

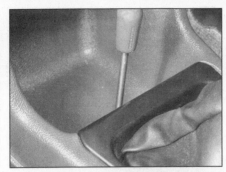

36.1A Removing a screw from a 1986 model transmission tunnel . . .

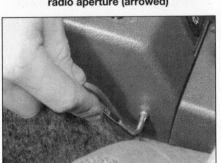

36.1B . . . and from the side

36.2A Gear lever cover plate and leather gaiter clip in place

36.2B Rear compartment air distribution ducts (arrowed)

33 Remove the radio/tape player (if fitted), or the blanking panel, and remove the two screws from the front sides of the aperture (photo).
34 Disconnect the wiring loom from under the facia.
35 Refer to Chapter 10 and remove the glovebox lamp. Where fitted also disconnect the ignition switch lamp.
36 Refer to Section 36 and remove the transmission tunnel console.
37 Ease the facia panel forward, taking care not to damage the
steering column stalk switches, disconnect the glove boxlamp negative terminal, and remove the facia from the car.
38 The two side vent grilles are held in place by plastic clips (photo).

All models

39 Refitting is a reversal of removal, but make sure that no electrical wires are trapped between the facia and bulkhead.

36 Transmission tunnel console - removing and refitting

1 There are a variety of transmission tunnel consoles fitted depending on model, but removal is straightforward referring to Figs. 9.23 and 9.24 for screw locations (photos).
2 The gear lever cover and switch panel should be removed first and, on some models, the rear compartment air distribution ducts need to be released and removed with the console (photos).
3 The screws are sometimes hidden under plastic plugs, which should be prised out, or under the ashtray (photo).
4 Lift the console carefully and then disconnect any wiring, which again will vary according to model and equipment levels.
5 Refitting is a reversal of removal.
6 The facia support bracket fitted to later

36.3 Removing a retaining screw from inside the tunnel console

models (photos) can be fitted to earlier models as a modification, but slots will have to be cut in the console as shown in Fig. 9.25.

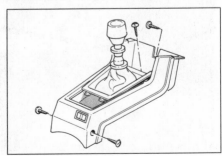

Fig. 9.23 Early type transmission tunnel console (Sec 36)

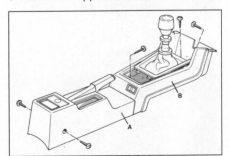

Fig. 9.24 Later type transmission tunnel console (Sec 36)

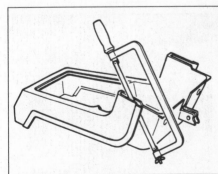

Fig. 9.25 Cutting slots in the tunnel console (Sec 36)

9

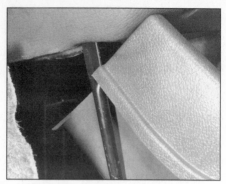

36.6A Facia support bracket under the tunnel console (console partly withdrawn)

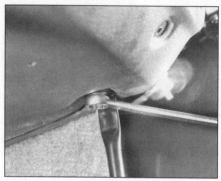

36.6B Removing a facia support bracket bolt

36.6C Support bracket lower screws

37.2A Remove the ashtray . . .

37.2B . . . and screws . . .

37 Rear ashtray - removal and refitting

1 Prise the ashtray from the housing (photo).
2 Remove the four screws and withdraw the ashtray housing (photos).
3 Refitting is a reversal of removal.

38 Boot lid (Saloon version) - removing and refitting

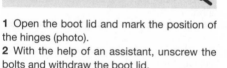

1 Open the boot lid and mark the position of the hinges (photo).
2 With the help of an assistant, unscrew the bolts and withdraw the boot lid.
3 Refitting is a reversal of removal. If necessary adjust the position of the boot lid on the hinges so that it is central and level with the surrounding bodywork. Adjust the striker so that the latch engages correctly and the boot lid is held firmly against the weatherseal (photos).
4 The tension in the boot lid balance spring can be adjusted by hooking the spring into the desired hole in the rear fillet panel.

37.2C . . . and remove the housing

38.1 Boot lid hinge on a 360 GLE model

38.3A Boot lid striker plate on the same model . . .

38.3B . . . and the boot lid lock

39.1 Removing a screw from an early type door mirror

39.3 Interior handle retaining screw

39.4A Prise off the trim panel . . .

39.4B . . . remove the screws . . .

39 Front door mirrors - removal and refitting

Non-remote control

1 Remove the two screws securing the mirror base to the door and remove the mirror (photo).
2 The glass can be removed from the mirror assembly by prising out the plastic moulding strip from around the glass using a small screwdriver, starting at the narrow end.

Remote control type

3 Remove the screw from the interior control handle and remove the handle (photo).
4 Prise off the trim panel and then remove the three screws securing the mirror to the door, holding the mirror to prevent it falling, and then remove the mirror assembly from the door (photos).
5 To remove the glass, pivot the glass inward at its outer edge so that a wide-bladed screwdriver can be inserted through the slot in the inner edge, and used to prise the glass off the balljoint pivot.
6 Coat the balljoint with vaseline, slide a new glass over the remote control rod end, and press it firmly back on to the balljoint.

All mirrors

7 Refitting of both types of mirror to the door is a reversal of removal.

39.4C . . . and remove the mirror

40 Sunroof - removal, refitting and adjustment

1 Move the sunroof to the ventilating position, then pull the leaf springs from the clamps on both sides.

2 Remove the lining from the front of the sunroof and slide it to the rear with the sun roof half open.
3 Unscrew the front bolts and close the sunroof.
4 Loosen the cable guide block locknuts, remove the retaining pins, and withdraw the sunroof.

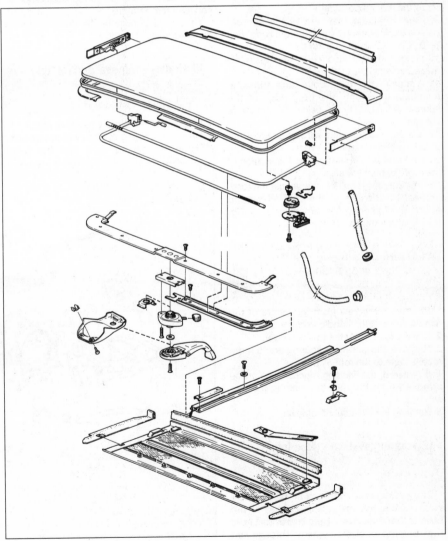

Fig. 9.26 Sunroof components (Sec 40)

9

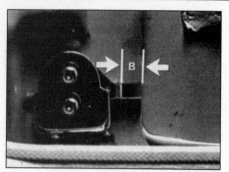

Fig. 9.27 Sunroof setting dimension B (Sec 40)

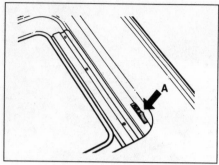

Fig. 9.28 Sunroof run-on lugs (A) (Sec 40)

5 To refit the sunroof, place it in position and tighten the front bolts finger tight. Note that dimension B in Fig. 9.27 should be 0.47 in (12 mm).
6 Fit the rear retaining pins in the lower grooves and tighten the locknuts.
7 Before fitting the lining and leaf spring, adjust the sunroof as follows.
8 Position the run-on lugs (A in Fig. 9.28) as far to the rear as possible.
9 Check that the rear end of the sunroof begins to lift as soon as the sunroof is opened by 0.20 to 0.31 in (5 to 8 mm).
10 If not, move the lugs forward to obtain this measurement.
11 Loosen the front bolts and turn the adjusting rings until the front edge of the sunroof is 0.04 in (1 mm) below the surface of the roof.
12 Loosen the link plate screws and turn the small ratchets until the rear edge of the sunroof is 0.04 in (1 mm) above the surface of the roof. Tighten the screws.
13 With the front bolts loose, adjust the fore-and-aft positioning of the roof within the aperture by altering the dimension B in Fig. 9.27. Tighten the bolts.

41 Sunroof handle - removal and refitting

1 Remove the screw from the centre of the handle and pull the handle from the shaft.
2 Pull the knob from the position lever.
3 Remove the screws securing the handle recess plate to the roof.
4 If required, the winding mechanism can be removed from the roof by undoing the two screws.
5 Refitting is a reversal of removal.

42 Heating system - description

The system is of the fresh air type, the air entering through the grilles located at the base of the windscreen. Heat is provided from the engine cooling system through an adjustable water flow valve.

Levers on the instrument panel control the temperature and the adjustment of the air deflectors for interior heating or screen demisting or defrosting.

Air is drawn over the heater matrix by an electric fan which can be set to different speeds.

The temperature control valve is fitted with a thermostat which keeps the car interior at a constant temperature.

Later models have heater ducts to the rear compartment.

43 Heater - removal and refitting

1 Disconnect the battery negative lead.
2 Drain the cooling system with reference to Chapter 2, making sure that the heater temperature controls are set to maximum heat and that the bleed nipple on the air unit is loosened.
3 Disconnect the supply and return hoses in the engine compartment.

Models up to 1977

4 Unscrew and remove the retaining bolts and withdraw the small compartment below the control levers.
5 Disconnect the wiring and remove the transmission tunnel console switches.
6 Prise out the console retaining bolt covers, remove the bolts and withdraw the console.
7 Remove the heater bracket from below the control levers.
8 Reach under the facia panel and detach the speedometer cable, then remove the speedometer.
9 Prise out the defroster vents and remove the ashtray.
10 Disconnect the hoses from the vents and heater, press out the locking clamps, and remove the vents.
11 Disconnect the heater control panel wires and remove the lamp.
12 Detach the two rods from the control levers.
13 Release the heater control cable while bending the facia outwards, lower the rear of the panel and withdraw the control panel.
14 Disconnect the throttle cable wire at the pedal.
15 Disconnect the bleed hose from the top of the heater unit, and the water hoses from the bottom of the unit.

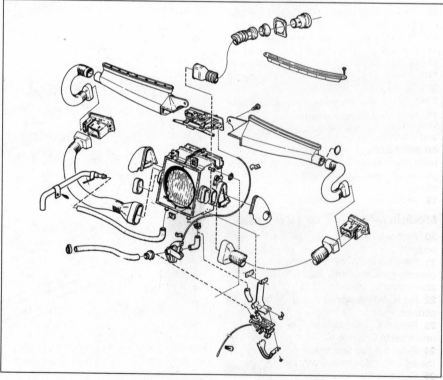

Fig. 9.29 Early heater components (Sec 43)

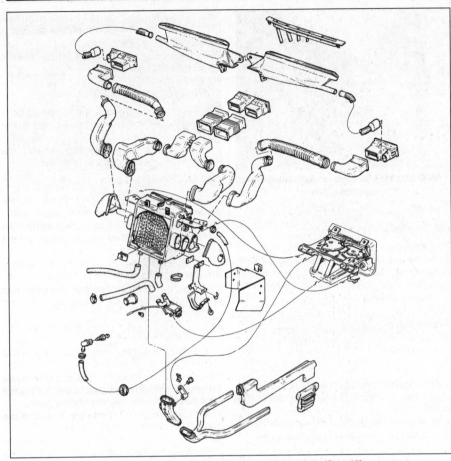

Fig. 9.30 Heater components for late models (Sec 43)

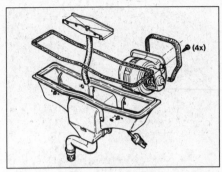

Fig. 9.31 Heater air inlet components for models from 1981 (Sec 43)

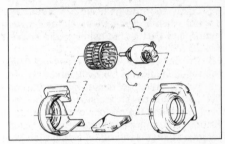

Fig. 9.32 Radial fan motor fitted to models from 1981 (Sec 43)

16 Unscrew and remove the lower heater retaining bolts, and disconnect the motor connecting plug.
17 Working in the engine compartment, disconnect the bleed hose and return hose from the air inlet chamber. Turn the nipple a quarter of a turn and pull it from the inlet chamber.
18 Lift the cover from the air inlet chamber, unscrew and remove the four retaining bolts and withdraw the air inlet chamber. Note that on some early models, the upper retaining bolts are fitted from inside, and access is then gained by removing the facia instruments and clock.
19 Withdraw the heater unit from the car.

Models late 1977 to 1978

20 Remove the air inlet unit cross-head screws.
21 Remove the oddments tray, prise out the console switches, and disconnect the wiring after noting its location.
22 Remove the screws and withdraw the console.
23 Remove the instrument panel with reference to Chapter 10.
24 Prise out the two defrosters and remove the ashtray, clock and glovebox.
25 Remove the screw(s) and withdraw the heater housing bracket.

26 Disconnect the flexible air hoses from the heater.
27 Unscrew the central bolt and remove the side ducts from the heater.
28 Remove the clamp and disconnect the bleed hose.
29 Disconnect the wiring from the heater control panel, remove the pullrods, then withdraw the panel from the facia and allow it to hang from the control cable.
30 Disconnect the hoses from the heater radiator.
31 Working through the ashtray opening, unscrew the top bolt.
32 Disconnect the multi-plug connector.
33 Unscrew the bottom bolts and withdraw the heater downwards.

Models from 1978 to 1983

34 Remove the air inlet unit cross-head screws.
35 Remove the facia panel with reference to Section 35.
36 Disconnect the flexible air hoses from the heater.
37 On 1979 models, prise out the two top defrosters.
38 On all models remove the centre bolt if fitted, then remove the heater side ducts.
39 Remove the clamp and disconnect the bleed hose.
40 Disconnect the heater wiring multi-plug.

41 Unscrew the upper cross-head retaining screws.
42 Withdraw the heater from the car. On 1979 models lift the housing out of the branch pipe.

Models from 1983 to 1986

43 Remove the facia panel and centre console, as described in Section 35.
44 Disconnect the heater hoses in the engine compartment.
45 Disconnect the control cables and rods.
46 Disconnect the air ducts from the heater.
47 Unscrew the mounting bolts, two inside the car and two in the engine compartment, then withdraw the heater to one side.

Models from 1986

48 To remove the air inlet ducting in the engine compartment, remove the two screws securing the unit to the engine bulkhead and the single screw from the lower securing point inside the vehicle (photo).

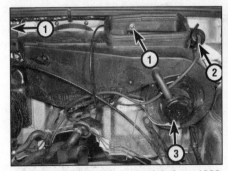

43.48 Air inlet ducting on models from 1986
1 Retaining screws 3 Electrical connections
2 Vacuum hose

44.4 Pull off the air distribution ducts

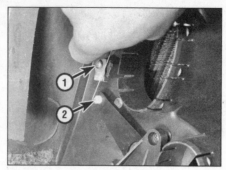

44.5 Disconnecting the air distribution flap control cable

1 Clamp   *2 Cable hook*

45.3A Corrugated panel securing screw (arrowed)

49 Disconnect the hose from the vacuum control valve and the wiring to the blower motor, and then lift the unit from the engine compartment.

50 The blower motor can be removed from the air inlet ducting without removing the ducting as described above, by undoing the five securing screws, disconnecting the earth lead and lifting the motor from the ducting. **Note:** *On B14 models, if the motor is being removed with the inlet duct in situ then the screenwash reservoir must first be removed.*

51 To remove the impeller from the motor, ease it from the shaft using two levers either side, then remove the stop plate from the shaft.

52 There may be small balance weights fitted to the impellor and these should be left in place.

53 Further dismantling of the air inlet ducting is straightforward.

45.3B Removing the corrugated panel

All models

54 Refitting is reversal of removal, and refill the cooling system with reference to Chapter 2. However, there is no need to bleed the system on late models as the heater matrix has been modified.

44 Heater matrix (models from 1986) - removal and refitting

1 The aluminium heater matrix is contained within the air distributor ducting inside the vehicle.

2 To remove the matrix, first remove the air inlet ducting in the engine compartment as described in Section 43.

3 Drain the cooling system (Chapter 2).

4 Remove the foam rubber insert from the bottom of the heater matrix and disconnect the heater hoses, being prepared for some spillage of coolant, and remove the air distribution ducts. These simply pull off (photo).

5 Disconnect the distribution flap control cable and the cable to the control valve by loosening the clamp screw and unhooking the cable (photo).

6 Remove the four screws securing the matrix to the bulkhead and then manoeuvre the heater unit from the vehicle.

7 The heater matrix can be removed from the air distribution duct by cutting the sealing ring and removing the steel and plastic clips to

separate the two halves. **Note:** *Aluminium matrices which will not be refilled within 48 hours should be flushed out with clean water and then dried, if possible using compressed air.*

8 Refitting is a reversal of removal; on completion fill the cooling system as described in Chapter 2.

45 Heater control panel (models from 1986) - removal and refitting

1 Remove the left-hand panel from under the facia and the tunnel console side panels.

2 Remove the radio/tape player or blanking plate from centre console (refer to Chapter 10).

3 Remove the two screws from inside the radio aperture and withdraw the corrugated panel (photos).

4 Remove the two screws holding the heater control panel to the side brackets (photo) and pull the panel forwards.

5 Disconnect the lighting, blower motor switch and air conditioning switch (if fitted) at their connectors (photo).

6 Slacken the clips on the control cable clamps and unhook the outer cables and the inner cables from the control levers.

7 Disconnect the vacuum hose from the recirculation switch and then remove the heater control panel from the centre console (photo).

8 The control levers and switches are clipped into the control panel and removal is self-

45.4 Heater control panel screw (arrowed)

45.5 Removing the switch prior to disconnecting the leads

45.7 Removing the heater control panel from the centre section console

45.8 Control knobs prise off

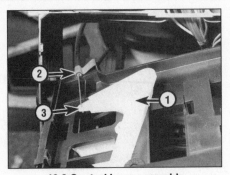

46.2 Control lever assembly

1 Lever   2 Clamp   3 Cable hook

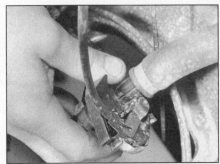

46.6 Water cock with spring clip fitting

evident, after having prised off the control knobs (photo).

9 Refitting is a reversal of removal but refer to the next Section for details of control cable fitting and adjustment.

46 Heater control cables (models from 1986) - fitting and adjustment

1 The control cables should be fitted to the control lever end first.

2 Hook the inner cable onto the control lever, press the outer cable toward the lever against its stop and then tighten the clamp (photo).

3 Move the control levers fully to the left.

4 Take the heater control valve cable and feed it through the bulkhead into the engine compartment.

5 Hook the inner cable into the outermost hole in the heater control valve lever.

6 Pull the outer cable taut, close the heater control valve (move the lever away from the cable clamp), and then tighten the screw in the cable clamp (early type), or fit the spring clip (later type) (photo).

7 Hook the inner cable of the air shutter flap to the air shutter lever and move the shutter to the closed position.

8 Pull the outer cable taut and tighten the clamp (photo).

9 Check that both the heater control valve and air shutter flap operate over their full range.

47 Ventilation system - general

1 Stale air from the inside of the vehicle is drawn outside by natural air movement via air extractor vents in the C-pillar on earlier Hatchback models and on Saloon versions.

2 On later Hatchback models (from 1984) the vents in the C-pillar have been discontinued and the air is drawn out through openings at the bottom of each side of the luggage compartment. This system is also used additionally on Saloon models, there being vent holes along the rear edge of the parcel shelf.

3 It is possible to have the air extractor vents fitted to those models which do not have them as standard, but consult your Volvo dealer for details.

4 The fresh air vents in the facia panel and the centre section panel above the heater controls are held in place by plastic clips.

5 To remove the vents, the clips must be depressed (photo) as the vent is withdrawn. On refitting, the clips will snap back into place.

48 Recirculation vacuum control valve (models from 1986) - removal and refitting

1 Models with the new heating and ventilation system produced since 1986 have a facility

known as recirculation, whereby all ingress of outside air can be blocked and the interior air only used on a recirculation basis.

2 The system is controlled by a vacuum operated valve mounted on the right-hand side of the air inlet unit in the engine compartment which is connected by tube to the recirculation control knob and the inlet manifold (photo).

3 Normally the valve remains in the open position and the flap in the air inlet duct is also open.

4 On selecting 'recirculation', the vacuum valve operates under the vacuum force from the inlet manifold and closes the flap in the air intake duct closing off the supply of outside air. The engine must be running for the system to operate, although a non-return valve situated in the vacuum hose between the inlet manifold and the valve will prevent the flap from opening should the engine subsequently be turned off, provided that 'recirculation' is still selected.

5 Should the system fail, check the vacuum hoses for leaks and if these are serviceable then renew the vacuum valve as follows:

6 Disconnect the vacuum hoses from the valve, and remove the clip and two screws holding the valve to the air inlet ducting.

7 Disconnect the lever to the flap in the air inlet duct and remove the valve.

8 Fit a new valve in the reverse order of removal.

9 When renewing the non-return valve fitted in the vacuum hose from the engine, the

46.8 Tightening the outer cable clamp

47.5 Depress the clips to remove the fresh air vents

48.2 Recirculation vacuum control valve

9

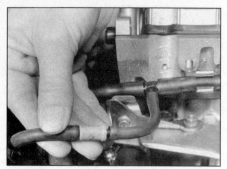

48.9 Non-return valve arrow faces recirculation valve

49.1A Front seat belt inertia reel anchor bolt . . .

49.1B Rear seat belt anchor point under the seat squab

arrow on the non-return valve should face toward the recirculation valve (photo).

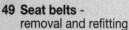

49 Seat belts - removal and refitting

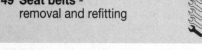

1 All the seat anchorage points are similar, being held to strong points in the frame by single bolts (photos).
2 To remove the anchor bolts, first remove as much of the trim panelling or carpeting as is necessary to gain access. The front inertia reel is under panelling in the sill (photo), and the rear behind the side panel in the luggage area (photo).
3 On later Hatchback models, the webbing is looped around a bar bolted to the sill, to improve access to the rear seats (photo).
4 Some of the rear seat belt anchorages are

under the rear seat squab, which should be removed as described in Section 50.
5 Refitting is a reversal of removal.

50 Seats - removal and refitting

Front

1 To remove the front seats, remove the four bolts securing the seat runners to the floorpan (photo) and lift out the complete seat assembly (if the seats are electrically heated, first disconnect the leads).
2 Refit in the reverse order.

Rear - Hatchback

3 The squab is either secured to the floor by hinges, or a slot and tongue arrangement. In either case to remove the squab, hinge the

squab forward and remove the hinge pin, or simply lift the seat to disengage the tongues from the slots.
4 To remove the backrest, first remove the metal panel at the base of the seat back in the luggage area, release the latches and pull the seat forwards, then undo the screws holding the lower hinges (photo).
5 Refit in the reverse order.

Rear - Saloon

6 From inside the luggage area, remove the ten bolts securing the backrest to the frame (if head restraints are fitted, there are 18 bolts) and then, from inside the car, remove the two bolts from the left and right-hand wheel arch brackets.
7 Lift the backrest from the car.
8 The seat squab is held to the floorpan in much the same way as on Hatchback models.
9 Refit in the reverse order.

51 Spoilers (rear mounted) - removal and refitting

1 The rear spoiler is bolted to the tailgate, the bolts being accessible through holes on the inner side of the tailgate.
2 If a spoiler is removed for any reason, all traces of adhesive must be removed from both the spoiler and tailgate before refitting, and double-sided tape applied to the contact surface of the spoiler.
3 A template is supplied with new spoilers for drilling the holes in the tailgate.

49.2A Removing an inertia reel seat belt anchor bolt

49.2B Rear inertia seat belt reel under the side panel

49.3 Rear retaining bolt on seat belt bar

50.1 Seat runner retaining bolt

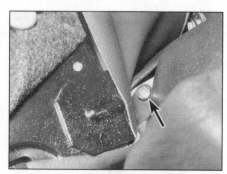

50.4 Seat back lower hinge retaining screw - arrowed (Hatchback)

Chapter 10
Electrical system

For modifications, and information applicable to later models, see Supplement at end of manual

Contents

Degrees of difficulty

Easy, suitable for novice with little experience		**Fairly easy,** suitable for beginner with some experience		**Fairly difficult,** suitable for competent DIY mechanic		**Difficult,** suitable for experienced DIY mechanic		**Very difficult,** suitable for expert DIY or professional

Specifications

System type .... 12 volt, negative earth

Battery
Capacity:
B14	36 Ah
B172	36 Ah
B19A up to 1982	55 Ah
B19A from 1983	45 Ah
B19E	55 Ah
B200E	55 Ah
B200K	45 Ah

Alternator
Type:
	Output	
B14	Ducellier	36 amp
B14 up to chassis No 379887	SEV Marchal	50 amp
B14 from chassis No 379888	Paris-Rhone A 13R 222	50 amp
	Paris-Rhone A 13N 64	50 amp
B172	Paris-Rhone A 13N 89	50 amp
B19 and B200	Bosch	55 amp

Minimum brush length:
B14 and B172	0.31 in (8.0 mm)
B19 and B200	0.20 in (5.0 mm)

10

Starter motor

Type:
B14	Ducellier or Paris-Rhone
B172	Paris-Rhone
B19	Hitachi
B200	Bosch

Armature endfloat:
B14 Ducellier	0.020 in (0.50 mm)
B14 Paris-Rhone	0.008 to 0.043 in (0.21 to 1.10 mm)
B172	0.031 in (0.80 mm)
B19	0.001 to 0.004 in (0.03 to 0.10 mm)
B200	0.004 to 0.012 in (0.10 to 0.30 mm)

Minimum brush length:
B14 Ducellier	0.31 in (8.0 mm)
B14 Paris-Rhone	0.35 in (9.0 mm)
B172	0.08 in (2.0 mm)
B19	0.43 in (11.0 mm)
B200	0.33 in (8.5 mm)

Windscreen and rear screen/window wipers

Wiper blades	Champion X4503 (18 in)
Wiper arms	Champion CCA 5

Bulbs

	Wattage
Headlamp (standard)	45/40
Headlamp (halogen)	60/55
Front foglamp	55
Parking lamps	4
Direction indicators:	
Front and rear	21
Side	5
Tail lamp	10
Tail/brake lamp	5/21
Rear foglamp	21
Reversing lamp	21
Number plate light:	
Up to 1980	10
From 1981	5
Interior lighting	5
Glovebox lamp	3
Ignition switch lamp	3
Instrument lighting	1.2
Switch lighting	1 (24V)
Luggage compartment lamp	3
Selector lamp (automatic transmission)	1 (24V)
Warning and indicator lamps	1.2
Heater control panel lamp:	
Up to 1978	2
From 1979	1.2
Lighting switch illumination	1.2
Cigar lighter illumination	1.2
Torch key	1.2 (1.5V)
Ashtray illumination	1.2
Search -find illumination in switches	1.2
Clock illumination	1.2
Low gear warning lamp	1.2

Fuses and relays (typical, early models)

Fuse no:	Rating	Circuits protected
1	8A	Direction indicators
2	8A	Heated rear window, wipers, low ratio hold and rear foglamp switches
3	8A	Voltmeter, voltage regulator, heater blower and instrument panel warning lamps
4	8A	Windscreen wiper motor, stop -lights and declutching

Fuse

no:	Rating		Circuits protected
5	8A	....	Selector lever and headlamp wash/wipe mechanism
6	8A	....	LH headlamp dipped beam
7	8A	....	RH headlamp dipped beam
8	8A	....	LH headlamp main beam and warning lamp
9	8A	....	RH headlamp main beam
10	8A	....	LH parking light and LH tail light
11	8A	....	RH parking light and RH tail light
12	16A	....	Headlamp flasher and hazard warning lamps
13	8A	....	Clock, radio and luggage compartment light
14	8A	....	Cigar lighter, instrument lights and courtesy light
15	16A	....	Heated rear window
16	8A	....	Horns

Relay

		Circuits supplied
A	....	Direction indicators
B	....	Hazard warning system
C	....	Horns
D	....	Headlamps
E	....	Vehicle lighting
F	....	Start inhibitor
G	....	Heated rear window
H	....	Headlamp wash/wipe

Fuses (typical, late models)

Fuse

no:	Rating		Circuits protected
1	8A	....	RH headlamp dipped beam and rear foglamps (some markets)
2	8A	....	LH headlamp dipped beam
3	8A	....	LH headlamp main beam and warning lamp
4	8A	....	RH headlamp main beam
5	8A	....	LH parking light and instrument lights
6	8A	....	RH parking light
7	8A	....	Direction indicators and cigar lighter (some markets)
8	8A	....	Fuel cut -off relay, declutching mechanism and vacuum control unit
9	8A/25A		Instrument panel warning lights, headlamp wipers (park) and electric windows
10	8A	....	Heated driver's seat, reversing lights, idle solenoid and start inhibitor relay
11	16A	....	Horn and engine cooling fan
12	25A	....	Heater blower, stop -lights and radio
13	8A	....	Hazard warning
14	16A	....	Courtesy light, luggage compartment light, glovebox light, ignition switch lighting, central locking system, cigar lighter and clock
15	8A	....	LH tail light and number plate lights
16	8A	....	RH tail light
17	8A	....	Spare
18	16A	....	Heated rear window
19	16A	....	Heater blower switch
20	8A	....	Wiper motor, washer pump and headlamp wash/wipe

Additional fuses:

Behind the glovebox 8A	....	Rear foglamps
Auxiliary fusebox 2 x 8A	....	Fuel pump and foglamps

Torque wrench settings

All nuts and bolts oiled

	lbf ft	Nm
Alternator mounting bolts:		
Ducellier	Not specified	
SEV Marchal	Not specified	
Paris-Rhone:		
A 13R 222	3.9	5.3
A 13N 64 and A 13N 89	4.6	6.3
Bosch	3.0	4.0
Alternator pulley nut:		
Ducellier and Bosch	30	40
SEV Marchal and Paris-Rhone	33	45

10

1 General description

The electrical system is of 12 volt negative earth type. The battery is charged by a belt-driven alternator. On early models, a remote type voltage regulator is located on the right-hand side of the engine compartment by the battery, but on later models (1979 on) the regulator is incorporated into the alternator.

Although repair procedures are fully described in this Chapter, in view of the long life of the major electrical components, it is recommended that consideration be given to exchanging the relevant unit for a factory reconditioned assembly when a fault does develop.

2 Routine maintenance

At the intervals specified in the Routine Maintenance Section at the beginning of this manual, carry out the following servicing operations:

Battery (Section 4)

1 Check electrolyte level, and keep the battery and tray clean and dry.
2 Check the terminals for corrosion and security, and the case for cracks.
3 Check the specific gravity of the electrolyte in each cell.

Alternator (Section 7)

4 Keep the unit clean and dry.
5 Check the electrical connections for security.
6 Check the drivebelt(s) for tension.

Wiper (Sections 27, 32 and 33)

7 Check the operation of all wash/wipe systems.

General

8 Check the operation of all lights, horn(s) and other electrical circuits.

3.1 Battery and clamp

3 Battery - removal and refitting

1 The battery is located at the front of the engine compartment, on the right-hand side (photo).
2 Disconnect the lead from the negative (-) terminal followed by the positive (+) terminal. On some later models, access to the positive terminal is gained by lifting the plastic cover (photo).
3 Remove the battery clamp and lift the battery from its mounting platform, taking care not to spill any electrolyte on the bodywork.
4 Refitting is a reversal of removal, but make sure that the polarity is correct before connecting the leads, and do not overtighten the clamp bolts. Refit the earth lead last.

4 Battery - maintenance

1 Carry out the regular maintenance described in the Routine Maintenance Section at the front of the manual.
2 Clean the top of the battery, removing all dirt and moisture.
3 As well as keeping the terminals clean and covered with petroleum jelly, the top of the battery, and especially the top of the cells, should be kept clean and dry. This helps prevent corrosion and ensures that the battery does not become partially discharged by leakage through dampness and dirt.
4 Regularly remove the battery and inspect the battery securing bolts, the battery clamp plate, tray, and battery leads for corrosion (white fluffy deposits on the metal which are brittle to touch). If any corrosion is found, clean off the deposits with ammonia and paint over the clean metal with an anti-rust/anti-acid paint.
5 At the same time inspect the battery case for cracks. Cracks are frequently caused to the top of the battery case by pouring in distilled water in the middle of winter *after* instead of *before* a run. This gives the water

3.2 Lifting plastic cover on positive terminal (late models)

no chance to mix with the electrolyte and so the former freezes and splits the battery case.
6 If topping-up the battery becomes excessive and the case has been inspected for cracks that could cause leakage, but none are found, the battery is being overcharged and the voltage regulator will have to be checked.
7 With the battery on the bench, measure the specific gravity with a hydrometer to determine the state of charge and condition of the electrolyte. There should be very little variation between the different cells, and if a variation in excess of 0.025 is present it will be due to either:
a) Loss of electrolyte from the battery, sometimes caused by spillage or a leak, resulting in a drop in the specific gravity of the electrolyte when the deficiency was replaced with distilled water instead of fresh electrolyte
b) An internal short circuit caused by buckling of the plates or a similar malady, pointing to the likelihood of total battery failure in the near future
8 The specific gravity of the electrolyte for fully charged conditions, at the electrolyte temperature indicated, is listed in Table A. The specific gravity of a fully discharged battery at different temperatures of the electrolyte is given in Table B.

Table A
Specific gravity - battery fully charged
1.268 at 100°F or 38°C electrolyte temperature
1.272 at 90°F or 32°C electrolyte temperature
1.276 at 80°F or 27°C electrolyte temperature
1.280 at 70°F or 21°C electrolyte temperature
1.284 at 60°F or 16°C electrolyte temperature
1.288 at 50°F or 10°C electrolyte temperature
1.292 at 40°F or 4°C electrolyte temperature
1.296 at 30°F or -1°C electrolyte temperature

Table B
Specific gravity - battery fully discharged
1.098 at 100°F or 38°C electrolyte temperature
1.102 at 90°F or 32°C electrolyte temperature
1.106 at 80°F or 27°C electrolyte temperature
1.110 at 70°F or 21°C electrolyte temperature
1.114 at 60°F or 16°C electrolyte temperature
1.118 at 50°F or 10°C electrolyte temperature
1.122 at 40°F or 4°C electrolyte temperature
1.126 at 30°F or -1°C electrolyte temperature

5 Battery - electrolyte replenishment

1 If the battery is in a fully charged state and one of the cells maintains a specific gravity reading which is 0.025 or more lower than the others, and a check has been made with a voltmeter for short circuits, then it is likely that electrolyte has been lost from the cell which shows the low reading.
2 Top up the cell with a solution of 1 part sulphuric acid to 2.5 parts of water. If the cell is already fully topped up, draw some electrolyte out of it with a pipette.

8.2 Alternator and pivot bolt (arrowed) on early models

8.8 Rear view of a late Bosch alternator on B19/B200 models

8.11 Front view of the alternator and drive belts on a B19/B200 engine

3 When mixing the sulphuric acid and water *never add water to sulphuric acid* - always pour acid slowly into the water in a glass container. *If water is added to sulphuric acid it will explode.*

4 Continue to top up the cell with the freshly made electrolyte, and then recharge the battery and check the hydrometer readings.

6 Battery - charging
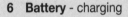

1 In winter time when heavy demand is placed upon the battery, such as when starting from cold, and much electrical equipment is continually in use, it is a good idea to occasionally have the battery fully charged from an external source.

2 Disconnect the battery leads (earth lead first) and connect the charger following the manufacturer's instructions. Charge the battery at the rate of 3.5 to 4 amps. Continue to charge the battery at this rate until no further rise in specific gravity is noted over a four hour period.

3 Alternatively, a trickle charger charging at the rate of 1.5 amps can be safely used overnight.

4 Specially rapid boost charges which are claimed to restore the power of the battery in 1 to 2 hours are most dangerous, as they can cause serious damage to the battery plates through overheating.

7 Alternator - maintenance and special precautions
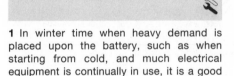

1 Periodically wipe away any dirt or grease which has accumulated on the outside of the unit, and check the security of the leads.

2 At the intervals specified in the Routine Maintenance Section at the beginning of this manual, check the tension of the drivebelt, and adjust if necessary, as described in Chapter 2.

3 Take extreme care when making electrical circuit connections on the car, otherwise damage may occur to the alternator. Always

make sure that the battery leads are connected to the correct terminals. Before using electric-arc welding equipment to repair any part of the car, disconnect the battery leads and the alternator output lead. Disconnect the battery leads before using a mains charger. Never run the alternator with the output lead disconnected. When using jumper leads from another battery, always match the correct polarity.

8 Alternator - removal and refitting

B14 models

1 Remove the spare wheel, then disconnect the battery negative terminal.

2 Loosen the alternator mounting and adjustment bolts, and swivel the unit in towards the engine (photo).

3 Remove the drivebelt from the pulley.

4 Unscrew and remove the terminal nuts and disconnect the supply wires, noting their locations.

5 Remove the mounting and adjustment bolts and withdraw the alternator from the engine compartment.

6 Refitting is a reversal of removal, but adjust the drivebelt as described in Chapter 2.

B19 and B200 models

7 Disconnect the battery negative lead and the air inlet preheating hose.

8 Disconnect the wiring from the rear of the

8.15 Disconnecting the multi-plug, and the other connections (arrowed) on a B172 model

alternator and remove the nut from the harness clip, where fitted (photo).

9 Jack up the front of the car and support it on axle stands. Apply the handbrake.

10 Remove the engine splash guard.

11 Loosen the pivot and adjustment bolts, swivel the alternator towards the engine, and remove both drivebelts (photo).

12 Remove the bolts and withdraw the alternator from the car.

13 Refitting is a reversal of removal, but tension the drivebelts as described in Chapter 2.

B172 models

14 Disconnect the battery negative lead.

15 Disconnect electrical leads and multi-plug on the rear of the alternator (photo), not forgetting the earth lead.

16 Slacken the alternator pivot bolt, then loosen the adjusting bolt. Swivel the unit in towards the engine and remove the drivebelt.

17 Remove the bolt securing the adjuster to the alternator, and the pivot bolt (photo), and remove the alternator.

18 Refit in the reverse order to removal and tension the drivebelt with reference to Chapter 2.

9 Alternator - dismantling, servicing and reassembly

1 Remove the alternator as described in Section 8 and clean the unit with a fuel-moistened cloth.

8.17 Alternator pivot bolt on B172 models

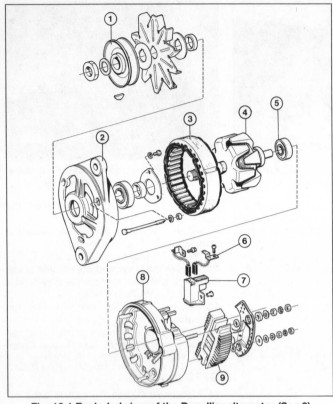

Fig. 10.1 Exploded view of the Ducellier alternator (Sec 9)

1 Pulley	4 Rotor	7 Brush holder
2 End bracket	5 Bearing	8 End bracket
3 Stator	6 Brushes	9 Diode holder

Fig. 10.2 Exploded view of the Paris-Rhone alternator (Sec 9)

1 Pulley	4 Rotor	6 Diode and brush
2 End bracket	5 End bracket	holder
3 Stator		7 Cover

B14 models

Note: *This sub-section describes the procedure for the Ducellier alternator. However, the procedure for Paris-Rhone and SEV Marchal alternators is similar, but it will be necessary to refer to Figs. 10.2 and 10.3.*

2 Remove the screws and withdraw the brush holder.

3 Mark the end housings and stator in relation to each other, then unscrew the nuts on the three through-bolts. Remove the washers and through-bolts.

4 Using two screwdrivers in the special recesses, prise the slip ring end housing and stator from the drive end housing. Do not damage the stator windings.

5 Grip the rotor in a soft-jawed vice and unscrew the pulley nut.

6 Withdraw the pulley, fan and key.

7 Drive the rotor from the drive end housing with a wooden mallet.

8 Unbolt the retaining plate from the drive end housing and drive out the bearing.

9 Remove the bearing from the slip ring end of the rotor using a suitable puller.

10 If necessary, unscrew the nuts and remove the cover from the slip ring end housing. Note the location of the washers.

11 Inspect the brushes for free movement and renew them if they have worn below their minimum specified length.

12 Clean the components in petrol or white spirit and thoroughly dry them, but do not dip the rotor or stator windings in the fuel; wipe them off with a fuel moistened lint-free cloth.

13 Examine the surfaces of the slip rings; if they are deeply scored have them machined on a lathe.

14 To accurately test the rotor and stator windings requires the use of specialised instruments, but a simple check can be made with a 12 volt battery, test lamp and leads. To test the rotor for insulation, connect the negative lead to the rotor shaft and connect the positive lead to each slip ring in turn. The test lamp will not glow if the insulation is in good order. To test the rotor windings for open circuit, connect each lead to separate slip rings; the test lamp will glow if the circuit is not broken.

15 Check the bearings for excessive wear and renew them if necessary.

16 Reassembly is a reversal of dismantling, but the following additional points should be noted:

a) *Make sure that the brushes are free to move in their holders, and if necessary use a fine file to smooth out any irregularities on the sides of the brushes*

b) *Use suitable diameter tubing to drive the bearings into position*

c) *Tighten the pulley nut to the correct specified torque wrench setting*

B19 and B200 models

17 On early Bosch alternators the voltage regulator is mounted separately in the engine compartment, but on later models it is an integral part of the alternator.

18 Dismantling should be restricted to removing the brushes which on later models form part of the voltage regulator. To do this, disconnect the wiring on early models. Remove the two screws and withdraw the brushes.

19 Check the brushes for wear and renew them if necessary. Check the slip rings with reference to paragraph 13.

20 Refitting is a reversal of removal.

B172 models

21 Remove the yellow cable from its terminal and then remove the guard cap (photo).

22 Disconnect the lead from the diode carrier (photo).

23 Remove the two bolts securing the voltage regulator to the alternator and withdraw the regulator (photos). The alternator brushes in the regulator can now be checked for length (see Specifications).

24 Any further dismantling and testing of the alternator should be left to an auto-electrician.

25 To remove the pulley wheel from the alternator, use a ring spanner on the retaining nut, and an Allen key inserted in the driveshaft to prevent it turning (photo).

26 Reassembly is a reversal of removal.

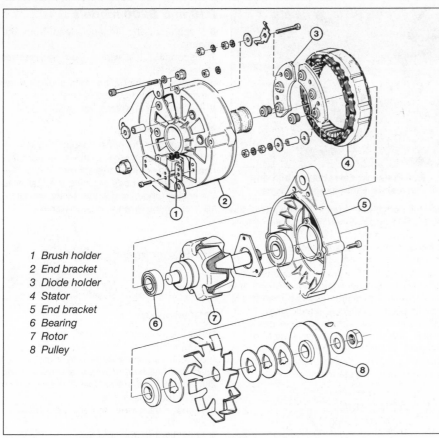

1 Brush holder
2 End bracket
3 Diode holder
4 Stator
5 End bracket
6 Bearing
7 Rotor
8 Pulley

Fig. 10.3 Exploded view of the SEV Marchal alternator (Sec 9)

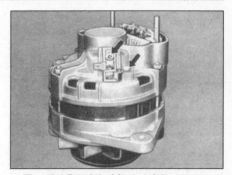

Fig. 10.4 Brush holder retaining screw locations - arrowed (Sec 9)

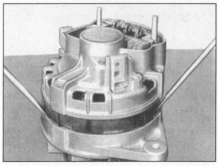

Fig. 10.5 Removing the alternator stator and slip ring end housing (Sec 9)

Fig. 10.6 Unscrewing the alternator pulley nut (Sec 9)

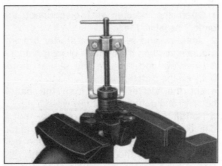

Fig. 10.7 Removing the bearing from the alternator rotor shaft (Sec 9)

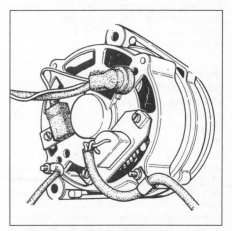

Fig. 10.8 Rear view of the early Bosch alternator (Sec 9)

9.21 Removing the guard from the back of the Paris-Rhone alternator on B172 models

9.22 Disconnecting the diode carrier

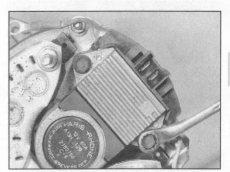

9.23A Removing the voltage regulator

10

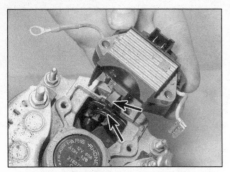

9.23B Location of the brushes (arrowed)

9.25 Pulley wheel retaining bolt and driveshaft with hexagonal recess

10 Starter motor - description

The starter motor is of the pre-engaged type and has two brushes operating on a commutator located on the front of the armature.

A solenoid, mounted on the starter motor drive end housing, engages the pinion with the flywheel ring gear when the ignition key is turned to the start position, through the medium of an engagement fork. As the solenoid reaches the end of its stroke, internal contacts energise the starter motor and the flywheel is rotated. The drive pinion incorporates a one-way roller clutch to prevent damage to the starter motor when the engine fires.

11 Starter motor - testing in the car

1 If the starter motor fails to operate, first check the condition of the battery by switching on the headlamps. If they glow brightly, then gradually dim after a few seconds, the battery is in an uncharged condition.

2 If the battery is in good condition, check the terminal connections for security. Also check that the earth lead is making good contact with the bodyframe. Check the security of the main cable and solenoid cable connections on the starter motor.

3 If the starter motor still fails to turn, check that the solenoid is being energised. To do this, connect a 12 volt test lamp and leads between the solenoid-to-motor terminal and earth. When the ignition key is turned to the starting position the lamp should glow. If not, either the supply circuit is open due to a broken wire or a faulty ignition switch, or the solenoid is defective. If the solenoid is supplying current to the starter motor, the fault must be in the starter motor.

12 Starter motor - removal and refitting

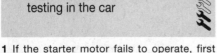

B14 models

1 Open the bonnet and disconnect the battery negative terminal.

2 Unscrew and remove the starter bracket mounting bolt on the cylinder block (photos).

3 Unscrew and remove the starter motor bolts on the clutch housing.

4 Lift the starter motor from the clutch housing and detach the supply wires.

5 Refitting is a reversal of removal, but if difficulty is experienced in locating the upper mounting bolt, bend wire around the bolt head, insert it in the hole, then pull the wire free. Always tighten the main mounting bolts before the bracket bolt.

B19 and B200 models

6 Disconnect the negative lead from the battery.

7 Disconnect the wiring from the starter motor (photo).

8 Unscrew the mounting bolts and withdraw the starter motor from the engine.

9 Refitting is a reversal of removal.

B172 models

10 Disconnect the battery negative lead.

11 Disconnect the three electrical connections on the starter (photo).

12 Remove the bolts securing the starter to the engine (photo) and withdraw the starter.

13 Refit in the reverse order to removal.

13 Starter motor - overhaul

B14 models

Note: *The procedure given here is specific to the Ducellier starter motor fitted up to 1981. From then, a Paris-Rhone starter motor was used, the overhaul of which is similar to the Ducellier but using the Specifications which relate to the Paris-Rhone.*

1 Remove the starter motor as described in Section 12.

2 Unscrew the solenoid switch terminal nut and detach the motor cable.

3 Using a suitable diameter soft metal drift, drive the fork hinge pin from the end housing.

4 Unscrew and remove the starter motor commutator end cover retaining nuts, and the four solenoid switch retaining nuts.

5 Withdraw the end housing from the starter motor and solenoid switch, then lift the solenoid switch and fork assembly from the starter motor housing.

6 Prise the starter motor commutator end cover from the starter motor and push the armature from the motor housing until the brushes are visible.

7 Lift the tension springs and pull the carbon brushes from their holders.

8 Remove the housing and field windings

12.2 Starter motor mounting bracket on early models (note the solenoid mounted on the top)

12.11 Starter motor electrical connections on B172 models

12.12 Removing the retaining bolts from B172 starter

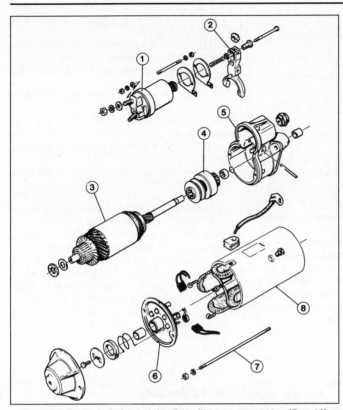

Fig. 10.9 Exploded view of the Ducellier starter motor (Sec 13)

1 Solenoid	4 One-way drive	6 Brush holder
2 Fork	pinion	7 Bolt
3 Armature	5 Housing	8 Yoke housing

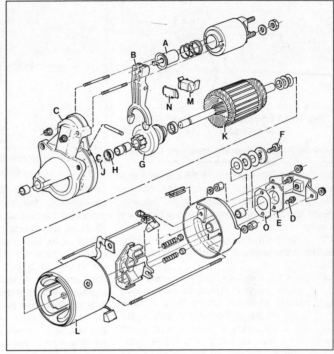

Fig. 10.10 Exploded view of the Paris-Rhone starter motor fitted to B14 models (Sec 13)

A Armature	E Cap	K Armature (motor)
(solenoid)	F Bolt	L Yoke
B Fork	G Pinion	M Rubber seal
C Front end shield	H Stop collar	N Plate
D Screws	J Circlip	O Cap

from the armature, then mount the armature in a soft-jaw vice.

9 Unscrew and remove the retaining bolt and withdraw the brush holder from the end of the armature, together with the washers and spring.

10 Clean all components with petrol, but do not dip the armature or field windings in the fuel; use a fuel moistened lint-free cloth to wipe them clean.

11 Inspect the components for wear or damage and renew them as necessary. If the

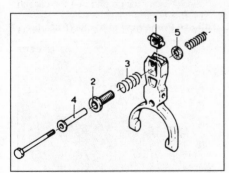

Fig. 10.11 Starter motor engagement fork assembly (Sec 13)

1 Nut	4 Plastic tube
2 Adjusting sleeve	5 Fibre washer
3 Spring	

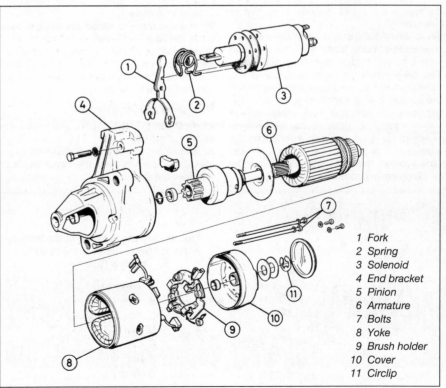

1 Fork
2 Spring
3 Solenoid
4 End bracket
5 Pinion
6 Armature
7 Bolts
8 Yoke
9 Brush holder
10 Cover
11 Circlip

Fig. 10.12 Exploded view of the Hitachi starter motor (Sec 13)

10

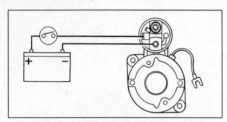

Fig. 10.13 Energising the Hitachi starter motor solenoid . . . (Sec 13)

brushes are less than the minimum specified length they must be renewed.

12 Examine the surface of the commutator for scoring and pitting; if slight this can be removed with fine glasspaper. In extreme cases the commutator must be machined on a lathe.

13 Using a suitable width hacksaw blade, undercut the segment insulation to a depth of 0.02 in (0.5 mm).

14 Check the armature bushes for wear, and if necessary, press in new ones using a vice and suitable diameter tubing. Bear in mind that if too many components have to be renewed, it will probably be more economical to obtain a reconditioned or good second-hand starter motor. When installing the commutator end bush, the inside edge of the bush must be flush with the inside edge of the brush holder bore. New bushes should be soaked in SAE 80 oil for half an hour prior to fitting them.

15 Check the teeth of the pinion for wear, and renew the drive if necessary by extracting the circlip from the end of the shaft. Lubricate the splines with a little graphite grease before reassembly.

16 If the armature and field windings are suspected of being faulty, they can be tested with a 12 volt battery, test lamp and leads. Test the armature for insulation by connecting the negative lead to the armature shaft and the positive lead to each segment in turn. The test lamp will not glow if the insulation is in good order. The windings can be similarly checked for open circuit by connecting the leads to opposite segments of the commutator: the test lamp will glow if the windings are in good order.

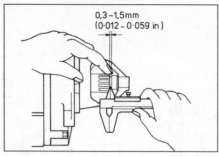

Fig. 10.14 . . . to check the pinion clearance (Sec 13)

17 Reassembly is basically a reversal of dismantling, but the following essential procedures should be noted.

18 With the armature assembled to the starter motor housing, the distance from the edge of the housing to the further edge of the pinion should be between 2.30 and 2.35 in (58.4 and 59.6 mm). If not, shims must be fitted at the commutator end of the armature until the dimension is correct.

19 Move the pinion drive to the engaged position and check that the distance in paragraph 18 is now between 2.74 and 2.81 in (69.5 and 71.5 mm).

20 With the complete starter motor assembled, check the fork for correct function. To do this, press in the bolt at the end of the solenoid switch as far as possible, and check that the distance from the pinion stop to the nearest pinion edge is between 0.002 and 0.059 in (0.05 and 1.50 mm). If not, adjust the bolt outer sleeve until the dimension is correct.

21 If adjustment is made impossible by a faulty fork, it must be renewed as necessary; refer to Fig. 10.11 for the correct location of the components. Note that where a fibre washer is fitted, the plastic sleeve is not required and *vice-versa*.

B19 and B200 models

22 First remove the starter and clean the exterior of the unit.

23 Disconnect the field coil cable from the solenoid, then unscrew the two bolts and withdraw the solenoid.

24 Prise off the dust cap and remove the circlip and shims.

25 Unscrew the bolts and screws, and withdraw the cover and brush holder while disconnecting the positive brushes from their guides.

26 Separate the yoke, armature and fork from the end bracket.

27 Using a metal tube drive back the stop collar and extract the circlip. Remove the collar, pinion and support bearing from the armature.

28 Clean all the components and check them as described for B14 models.

29 Before reassembly, fill both of the armature bearings with oil and squeeze with the thumb and index finger until the oil permeates the bushes. Also grease the pinion, armature shaft, fork and solenoid pullrod.

30 Reassembly is a reversal of the dismantling procedure. If necessary use a puller to position the collar over the circlip. Check the pinion setting by energising the solenoid, as shown in Fig. 10.13 then press the pinion to the rear and use vernier calipers to measure the distance between the pinion and the stop collar. If the distance is not as shown in Fig. 10.14 select and fit a different shim between the solenoid and the end bracket.

B172 models

31 The overhaul procedure is very similar to that given for B14 models, using the related specifications. An exploded view of the starter motor appears in Fig. 10.15 (photos).

13.31A Front view of the B172 starter

13.31B Rear view of the B172 starter

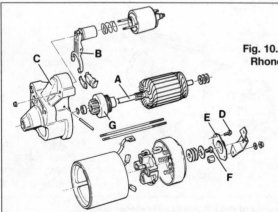

Fig. 10.15 Exploded view of the Paris-Rhone starter motor fitted to B172 models (Sec 13)

A Armature
B Fork
C Front end shield
D Bolt
E Cap
F Bolt
G Pinion

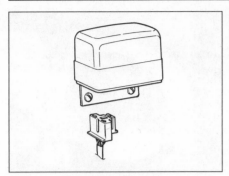

Fig. 10.16 Voltage regulator for the early Bosch alternator (Sec 14)

14 Voltage regulator - general

On most models the voltage regulator is integral with the alternator, but on the Bosch alternator fitted to early B19 models it is mounted separately in the engine compartment.

If the voltage regulator is found to be defective, it should be renewed as a unit, no repairs being possible.

15 Fuses and relays - general

1 The fusebox on all models is located in the engine bay on the right-hand bulkhead (photo). On models equipped with fuel injection there is an auxiliary fusebox located by the battery (photo). On some models this auxiliary fusebox also houses fuses for the front foglamps.
2 The number of fuses and the circuits protected differs from model to model and with the level of equipment fitted.
3 Always renew a fuse with one of the same rating and, if a fuse blows frequently, then the source of the problem should be sought. Usually this is the result of a short circuit, which may be caused by broken or chafed wiring.
4 The fusebox also houses the relays. Relays are designed to use a small current to direct a

16.2 Removing the headlamp rear cover

15.1A Fusebox and relay location on late models

A Headlamp relay   *B Spare*
C Starter inhibitor
D Heater blower motor, wash/wipe system
  and heated rear window

larger current to the relevant consumer. Thus the control switches in the facia use only small current to remotely control the larger current needed by consumers.
5 There are other relays in the electrical system, controlling various circuits. These are generally mounted behind or under the facia (photo), or in the engine bay.

16 Lighting system - bulb renewal

Headlamps

1 Open the bonnet and remove the spare wheel if the left-hand bulb is to be renewed.
2 Turn the lamp cover anti-clockwise to release it and remove the cover (photo).
3 Pull the multi-plug terminal from the connector (photo).
4 With standard bulbs, prise up the two retaining spring clips and withdraw the bulb, taking care not to touch the glass.
5 Where halogen bulbs are fitted, on early models press down the two projections and turn the retaining clip anti-clockwise, remove the clip and withdraw the bulbs without touching the glass.
6 On late models with halogen bulbs, unhook the spring clips and withdraw the bulb (photo). Do not touch the glass.

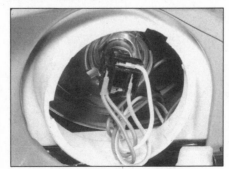

16.3 Headlamp bulb multi-plug

15.1B Auxiliary fusebox location

15.5 Additional relay location under the facia (facia removed for clarity)

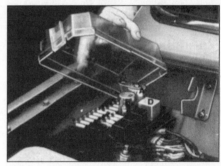

Fig. 10.17 Fusebox on early models (Sec 15)

A Direction indicator unit
B Hazard warning unit
C Horn relay
D Main beam relay
E Lighting relay
F Starter inhibitor (automatic transmission)
G Heated rear window relay

10

16.6 The headlamp bulb retaining clip (late models)

16.7A The headlamp bulb retaining plate on models from 1982

16.7B Headlamp bulb being removed from the holder on models from 1982

16.9 Removing a front parking lamp bulb on early models

7 On models from 1982, depress and twist the retaining plate anti-clockwise and remove it before removing the bulb, which is a bayonet fit in the holder (photos).

16.10 Parking lamp bulb location in the headlamp bulb retaining plate on late models

Front parking lamp

8 The front parking lamp is part of the headlamp unit.

9 On early models the bulb holder is a push-fit in the headlamp unit, and the bulb a bayonet fix in the holder (photo).

10 On late models the parking light holder is part of the headlamp bulb holder (photo). Follow the procedure for removal of the headlamp bulb to gain access to the parking light. The bulb is a bayonet fix in the holder.

Front direction indicator lamps

11 The procedure is similar on all models. Push the bulb holder in and turn it anti-clockwise to release the bulb holder. The bulb is a bayonet fix in the holder (photo).

Side repeater lamp

12 On models where the lamp is fitted on the

front wing, remove the screw and pull the unit away from the wing. Pull the bulb holder from the unit. The bulb is a bayonet fix in the holder (photo).

13 On late models, where the lamp is mounted in the bumper, the procedure is similar; the lamp unit being prised out of the bumper (photos).

Front foglamps

14 Remove the rear cover on the foglamp unit (photo), unclip and remove the holder, then remove the bulb (photo). On refitting ensure that the location cut-out is correctly aligned.

Rear lamp cluster

15 All the bulbs in the rear lamp cluster can be changed after removal of the plastic cover in the luggage area (photos).

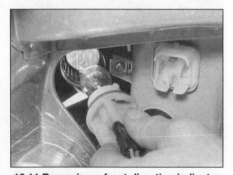

16.11 Removing a front direction indicator lamp bulb from inside the engine bay

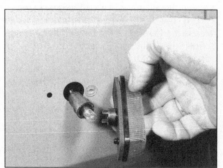

16.12 Removing a side repeater lamp bulb from the front wing

16.13A Prising out the side repeater lamp from the bumper

16.13B Removing the bulb and bulb holder from the lens unit

16.14A Front foglamp bulb access plate removed

16.14B Removing the front foglamp bulb

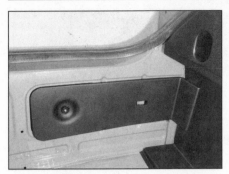

16.15A Rear lamp cluster inner cover . . .

16.15B . . . removed

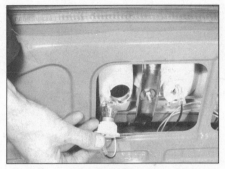

16.16 Removing a bulb from the rear lamp cluster

16 Pull out the bulb holder (photo), and twist the bulb from the holder.

Rear number plate light

17 On early models the number plate light is housed in the bumper moulding. Prise the unit from the bumper then pull the bulb holder from the unit. The bulb is a bayonet fix in the holder (photo).

18 Push the unit firmly back into the bumper on refitting.

19 On late models, the number plate lamp is part of the rear lamp cluster already described.

Interior lamps

20 The interior lamps consist of the following: courtesy lamp, ignition switch lamp, glovebox lamp and luggage compartment (boot) lamp.

21 All are basically the same, the bulb being reached by prising out the cover (photos).

17 Headlamps, front indicator lamps and front foglamps - removal and refitting

Headlamp - models up to 1982

1 Open the bonnet and remove the spare wheel and spare wheel bracket. Disconnect the battery negative terminal.

2 Unscrew and remove the inner front panel retaining screws, gaining access through the spare wheel bracket aperture and air filter aperture; turn the air supply pipe to one side to do this.

3 Unscrew and remove the three upper retaining screws (photo).

4 Remove the front grille as described in Chapter 9 then unscrew and remove the two upper retaining screws from within the grille aperture.

16.17 Removing a rear number plate lamp bulb holder from the bumper

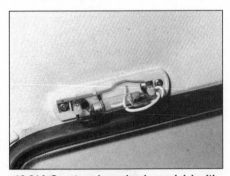

16.21A Courtesy lamp (early models) with cover removed

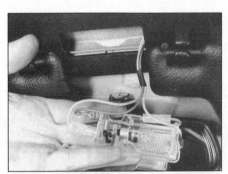

16.21B Removing the courtesy lamp (late models)

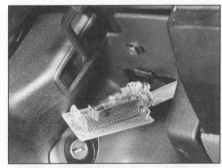

16.21C Removing the ignition switch lamp bulb

16.21D Removing the luggage compartment lamp (late models)

16.21E Glovebox lamp removed from its housing

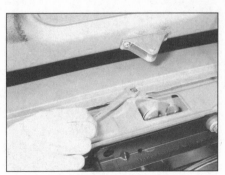

17.3 Removing the front panel upper retaining screws

10

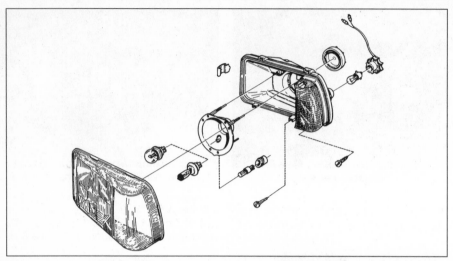

Fig. 10.18 Early type headlamp components (Sec 17)

5 Unscrew and remove the two side retaining screws located just above the bumper.
6 Remove the headlamp, parking, and direction indicator bulbs as described in Section 16, and disconnect the lighting multi-plug (photo).
7 Withdraw the front panel a little way from the body, then disconnect the wiring from the horn.
8 Completely withdraw the front panel (photo).
9 Unscrew and remove the four retaining screws and lift the headlamp unit from the front panel (photo).

10 If necessary, the headlamp may be dismantled by prising away the spring clamps and removing the glass cover. Unscrew and remove the two retaining screws and withdraw the direction indicator glass (photos).
11 Refitting is a reversal of removal.

Headlamp - models from 1982

12 Disconnect the headlamp washer tube and the electrical connections to the headlamp, direction indicator lamp and the headlamp wiper motor (photo).

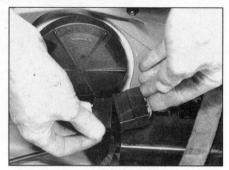

17.6 Disconnecting the lighting multi-plug

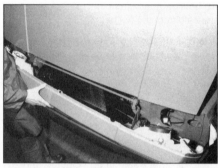

17.8 Removing the front panel, complete with headlamps (early models)

13 Refer to Section 31 and remove the headlamp wiper arm.
14 Refer to Chapter 9 and remove the bumper.
15 Remove the four screws securing the

17.9 Removing a headlamp unit from the front panel

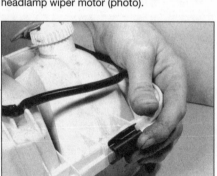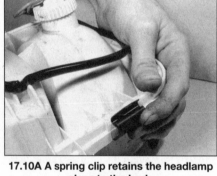

17.10A A spring clip retains the headlamp glass to the body

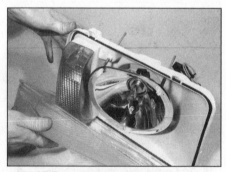

17.10B Removing headlamp glass cover

17.10C Headlamp glass reflector

17.10D Removing the direction indicator lens

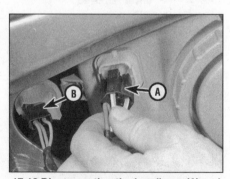

17.12 Disconnecting the headlamp (A) and indicator lamp (B) direction/wiring connections

17.15 Removing a headlamp retaining screw

17.17A Direction indicator lamp retaining screw (arrowed)

17.17B Removing the direction indicator lamp

headlamp unit and lift the headlamp out (photo).

16 Refer to Section 31 and remove the wiper motor from the headlamp unit.

17 The direction indicator lamp can be removed from the headlamp unit by removing the self-tapping screw (photos). The direction indicator lamp is a sealed unit and should be renewed as a complete unit if defective.

18 The lens can be separated from the headlamp back unit by prising off the securing clips (photo).

19 Refitting is a reversal of removal, but the headlamp aim should be adjusted as described in Section 18.

Foglamps

20 The front foglamps are housed in the front spoiler.

21 Remove the screws securing the foglamp unit to the spoiler, disconnect the electrical lead and remove the unit.

22 Refit in the reverse order.

23 The foglamp beam can be adjusted in similar fashion to that described for the headlamps in Section 18, using the adjuster knobs (photo).

18 Headlamps - alignment

1 It is recommended that headlamp alignment is carried out by your dealer using modern beam setting equipment. However, in an emergency, the following procedure will provide an acceptable light pattern.

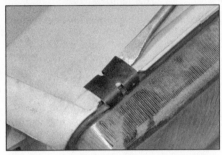

17.18 Prising off a headlamp lens retaining clip

2 Position the car on a level surface with tyres correctly inflated, about 33 feet (10 metres) in front of a vertical surface such as a wall or garage door. Make sure that the car is at right angles to the surface.

3 Measure the distance from ground level to the centre of the headlamps (do not include the direction indicator lens), then draw a horizontal chalk line on the vertical surface 4 in (100 mm) lower than the dimension obtained.

4 Mark the line at each side at a point where the distance between the headlamp centres is projected onto the vertical surface, then mark a further point midway between these two marks.

5 Switch on dipped headlamps and observe whether the light pattern is as given in Fig. 10.19. It will help if each headlamp is checked separately while shielding the remaining one.

6 Vertical adjustment is made by screwing the lower screw (on rear of headlamp) in or

17.23 Front foglamp adjuster (arrowedl)

out; horizontal adjustment is made by screwing one of the upper screws in or out, then screwing the remaining screw in the opposite direction by an equal amount (photo). It will be observed that the first horizontal adjustment must be half of the total adjustment. Access to the adjustment screws is gained from the engine compartment.

7 On late models, knurled adjusting knobs are provided in place of the screws (photo).

18.6 Headlamp adjuster screw on early models . . .

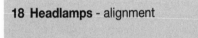

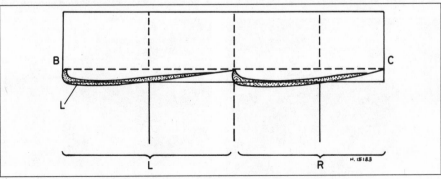

Fig. 10.19 Headlamp beam setting diagram (Sec 18)

B - C Height of headlamp centres   *L Line drawn 4 in (100 mm) below B - C*

18.7 . . . and the knob on late models

19.1 Removing the interior cover panel from the rear lamp cluster

19.2 Removing a securing nut from the rear lamp cluster

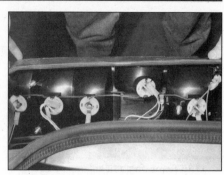

19.3 Removing the rear lamp cluster

19 Rear lamp cluster - removal and refitting

1 Remove the interior cover panel (photo).
2 Remove the nuts securing the unit to the frame (photo).
3 Lift the unit away from the body and disconnect the leads to the bulb (photo).
4 The unit is complete in itself and if defective (ie broken or cracked lens) should be renewed as a whole.
5 Refit in the reverse order.

20 Direction indicator/hazard flasher system - description

As from late 1979 models, a combined direction indicator/hazard flasher unit is fitted

20.1 Direction indicator/hazard warning flasher unit (arrowed) located behind the instrument panel (removed)

behind the instrument panel and is mounted on the dashboard (photo). On all previous models, separate units are located in the fusebox.
Failure of either system may be due to blown bulbs, disconnected wiring, a blown fuse, faulty switch contacts or corroded bulb contacts. If these are in order, renew the flasher unit. To do this on models up to 1979, simply pull the relevant unit from the fusebox and insert the new unit. On later models, remove the instrument panel with reference to Section 25 then disconnect the wiring plug and remove the unit. Fitting the new unit is a reversal of removal.

21 Ignition/steering lock switch - removal and refitting

The procedure is covered in Chapter 8 as it involves work on the steering column.

22 Steering column mounted stalk switches - removal and refitting

1 Disconnect the battery negative lead.
2 Refer to Chapter 8 and remove the steering wheel.
3 Unscrew and remove the choke control knob.
4 Remove the steering column shrouds.
5 The two switches are mounted on a central plastic collar which is fitted on to the steering

22.5A Removing the screw from the collar

22.5B Lifting the switch assembly from the steering column

column. Remove the screw on the underside (photo) and the complete unit can be withdrawn after disconnecting the leads (photo).
6 Each switch is held in the central collar by two screws. Remove these screws to detach the switches.
7 Refitting is a reversal of removal.

23 Facia panel switches - removal and refitting

1 Three types of switch are fitted: rocker type, 'push-push' type, and turn type.
2 Before removing a switch, the battery negative lead must be disconnected.
3 On the rocker type switch, prise the switch out from the facia panel, then disconnect the supply wires after noting their location.
4 On the 'push-push' type switch, pull the multi-plug connections from the rear of the switch and press the switch out from the facia panel.
5 Where a turn type lighting switch is fitted, pull off the knob to expose the retaining nut. Remove the complete switch panel, if applicable, or gain access to the rear of the switch from below the instrument panel. Disconnect the wires, noting their location if necessary. Undo the nut and remove the switch.
6 Refitting is a reversal of removal, but make sure that the switch is fully entered in the facia panel.
7 Some switches are illuminated and the bulb

23.7A Removing a facia panel switch

23.7B Pulling out the illumination bulb

25.3 Removing an instrument panel retaining screw

25.4 Tilting the instrument panel forward

can be renewed after removing the switch and pulling out the bulb holder. The bulb is a push-fit in the holder (photos). In the case of the main lighting switch located immediately to the right of the instrument panel, access to the illumination bulb can be gained from below the panel.

8 Refit in the reverse order.

24 Speedometer cable - removal and refitting

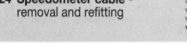

1 Disconnect the battery negative lead.
2 Reach up behind the instrument panel and disconnect the speedometer cable by depressing the plastic clip. On late models the cable is held by a bayonet type connector which is twisted to release it.
3 Jack up the left-hand front of the car, support it on axle stands and remove the left-hand front wheel.
4 Remove the cable connection to the suspension strut, then withdraw the speedometer cable from the engine compartment.
5 If necessary, tap off the left-hand hub grease cap, remove the split pin, and withdraw the speedometer cable driving pin.
6 Clean the bore in the steering swivel and the rubber bush of the speedometer cable.
7 When refitting the cable, which is a reversal of removal, lubricate the rubber bush with a water/soap solution.

Note: *If alloy wheels are being fitted to a vehicle previously equipped with steel wheels, a shorter speedometer cable should be fitted to avoid fouling the wheel.*

25 Instrument panel - removal and refitting

1 Disconnect the battery negative lead.
2 Reach behind the instrument panel and disconnect the speedometer cable (see Section 24).
3 Remove the screws from the top edge of the instrument panel (photo).
4 Tilt the panel forward from the top edge sufficiently to disconnect the multi-plugs, taking note of their location (photo).
5 Where fitted, on early models, disconnect the reset button cable from the back of the clock (photo).
6 Withdraw the instrument panel from the facia.
7 Although the instrument panel has changed over the years, they are all still basically the same. The warning lamp bulbs and instrument bulbs can all be changed by removing

their holders and pulling out the bulbs (photos).
8 The individual instruments are held by screws or nuts (photos), but if they are malfunctioning, we recommend that an auto-electrician carry out the repair.
9 Refitting is a reversal of removal.

25.5 Instrument panel multi-plug and clock reset button

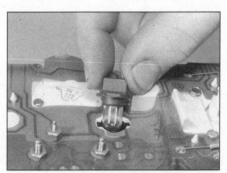
25.7A Instrument bulb holder

25.7B Removing a bulb from the holder

25.7C Warning lamp bulb and holder being removed

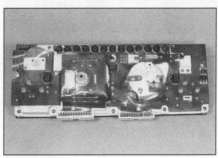
25.8A Rear view of the instrument panel

25.8B Close-up of the printed circuitry, speedometer connection (later type) and instrument securing nuts (arrowed)

10

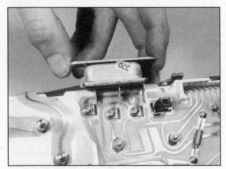

26.2 Removing the voltage stabilizer from the rear of the instrument panel on early models

26 Temperature and fuel gauges - testing, removal and refitting

1 If the temperature and fuel gauges are faulty, first check the voltage stabilizer, as this component is largely responsible for the correct functioning of the gauges.
2 Remove the instrument panel and locate the voltage stabilizer on the rear of the panel (photo). With a voltmeter connected between the *I* and *E* terminals of the stabilizer, the voltage should oscillate between 0 and 5 volts. If this is not the case, the voltage stabilizer is faulty and must be renewed.
3 If the fuel gauge is still faulty, remove the fuel tank unit (see Chapter 3) and connect an ohmmeter between the terminal and base; with the float in the empty position the resistance should be 250 ohms, and with it in the full position the resistance should be 19 ohms.
4 If the float operates correctly, trace the wiring to the fuel gauge and warning lamp terminals on the rear of the instrument panel. If the wiring is good, renew the gauge by withdrawing the rear of the instrument panel. To do this, unscrew and remove the eight retaining screws.
5 If the temperature gauge is still faulty, check the temperature sender resistance with the engine at operating temperature; this should be between 35 and 45 ohms. If an ohmmeter is not available, obtain a new

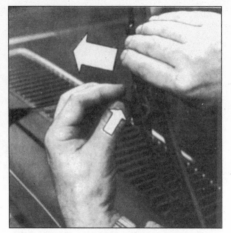

Fig. 10.20 Removing a wiper blade with a hook type fitting (Sec 27)

sender and observe whether the fault is corrected.
6 If the sender appears to be in good order, trace the wiring to the temperature gauge terminals on the rear of the instrument panel. If the wiring is good, unscrew and remove the eight retaining screws, withdraw the cover, and renew the gauge.
7 Refitting is a reversal of removal.

27 Wiper blades - renewal

1 The wiper blades should be renewed whenever they no longer clean the windscreen effectively.
2 On the spindle type fitting, depress the clip on the wiper arm and withdraw the blade complete with the spindle (photo).
3 On the hook type fitting, depress the clip on the wiper arm and slide out the blade.
4 The headlamp wiper blade is a push-fit in the plastic fork at the end of the wiper arm (photo).
5 Ease the blade assembly from the plastic fork using a lever. Ensure the longest end of the replacement blade points away from the arm on refitting.
6 Refitting is a reversal of removal.

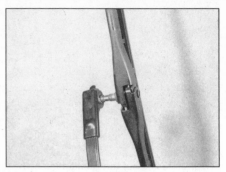

27.2 Removing a wiper blade - spindle type fitting

28 Wiper linkage - removal and refitting

1 Disconnect the battery negative lead.
2 Remove the windscreen wiper blades as described in Section 27.
3 Lift the wiper arm covers and unscrew the retaining nuts (photo). Prise the wiper arms from the spindles using a wide-bladed screwdriver.
4 Unscrew and remove the retaining nuts and spacers from the two spindles.
5 Working inside the car, mark the position of the connecting rod adjustment, and the position of the motor crank relative to the motor spindle (photo).
6 Unscrew and remove the retaining nuts and withdraw the crank and short connecting rod from the motor spindle.
7 Detach the left-hand defroster and defroster hose, then remove the ashtray.
8 Remove the left-hand air supply pipe from the heater unit after releasing the central press stud.
9 Unscrew and remove the spindle flange retaining screws.
10 Lower the wiper linkage and remove it from beneath the facia panel.
11 Refitting is a reversal of removal, but the following additional points should be noted:
a) *Align the previously made marks before tightening the connecting rod nuts*

27.4 Headlamp wiper blade plastic fork

28.3 Windscreen wiper arm retaining nut location

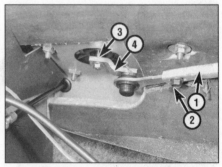

28.5 Wiper linkage inside the car (facia panel removed for clarity)

| 1 Link arm | 3 Motor drive spindle |
| 2 Adjusting bolt | 4 Connecting link |

29.3A Windscreen wiper motor location (early model)

29.3B Late type windscreen wiper motor

b) Lubricate the spindles with a few drops of engine oil
c) If necessary, adjust the position of the wiper blades so that they are parallel to the lower edge of the windscreen when parked. To do this, loosen the connecting rod nuts and adjust the length of the connecting rod accordingly.

29 Windscreen wiper motor - removal and refitting

1 Disconnect the battery negative lead.
2 Unscrew the nut and remove the crank from the motor spindle.
3 Disconnect the supply wires, then unscrew the mounting bolts and withdraw the wiper motor from the car (photos).
4 Refitting is a reversal of removal.

30 Windscreen wiper motor - overhaul

1 Remove the wiper motor as described in Section 29.
2 Unscrew and remove the gearwheel cover retaining screws and lift the cover away.
3 Extract the circlip and withdraw the gearwheel and washers from the housing; on some models the circlip is omitted.
4 Unscrew and remove the retaining nuts and remove the gearwheel housing from the armature, together with the brushes.

5 Lift out the armature.
6 Inspect all components for wear, and clean them with petrol. If the armature commutator is worn, light scoring may be removed with fine glasspaper. Renew the carbon brushes if they are excessively worn; this will necessitate unsoldering the leads, and on some models removing the three rubber suspension pins to release the brush carrier.
7 If the motor bearings, gearwheel, or wormwheel are worn it will probably be more economical to obtain a reconditioned or good second-hand unit.
8 Reassembly is a reversal of dismantling, but the following additional points should be noted:
a) Grease the gearwheel and wormwheel surfaces sparingly
b) On Femsá units, adjust the armature endfloat by turning the adjustment screw which locates on the ball-bearing
c) On all but Femsa units, adjust the gearwheel endfloat by loosening the locknut and turning the adjustment screw clockwise as far as possible. Then loosen the screw a quarter of a turn and tighten the locknut; where a locknut is not fitted,

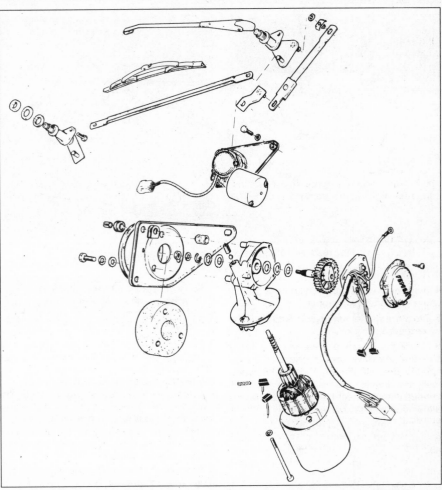

Fig. 10.21 Exploded view of the Femsa type windscreen wiper motor (Sec 30)

retain the screw by application of a liquid locking agent

31 Headlamp wiper motor - removal and refitting

1 Disconnect the battery negative lead.
2 Disconnect the washer tubing then lift the cover, unscrew the nut and remove the wiper arm from the spindle (photo).

31.2 Removing the nut from the headlamp wiper arm

10

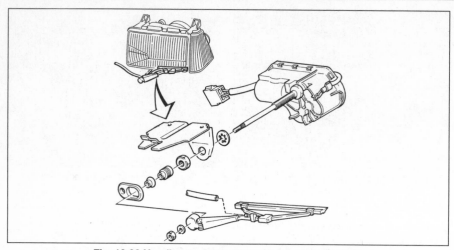

Fig. 10.22 Headlamp wiper motor components (Sec 31)

3 Remove the front panel.

4 Remove the dust cap then unscrew the nut and remove the spacer (photo).

5 Disconnect the wiring and withdraw the wiper motor.

6 Refitting is a reversal of removal, but make sure that the wave washer is located on the spindle and fill the dust cap with water resistant grease. Before refitting the arm, temporarily reconnect the battery so that the motor returns to the parked position.

7 In the parked position, the wiper arm should be approximately 0.39 in (10 mm) above the lower edge of the headlamp. If not, reposition the arm on the motor spindle splines.

32 Rear screen wiper blade and motor - removal and refitting

1 Disconnect the battery negative lead.

2 Removal of the wiper blade and the wiper arm is the same as described for the windscreen blades in Sections 27 and 28.

3 Open the rear hatch and remove the plastic cover panel on the inside of the hatch by depressing the clips (photo).

4 Disconnect the leads to the motor and remove the two screws securing the motor support bracket (photo).

5 Remove the two bolts and separate the motor from the bracket.

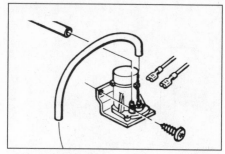

Fig. 10.23 Washer pump for B14 models (Sec 33)

6 If the motor is faulty, it should be renewed.

7 Refitting is a reversal of removal.

33 Windscreen washer system - maintenance

1 Periodically check the pipe connections and check the security of the wiring to the electric pump (photo).

2 The fluid in the washer reservoir should be kept topped up at the routine weekly checks. It is recommended that a cleaning solvent is added to the water to aid the cleaning action and reduce the chance of freezing during winter conditions. Never use engine coolant antifreeze.

3 The washer jets can be adjusted as required by inserting a pin and moving them to the desired angle.

4 On early models the pump(s) are separate from the reservoir, but on late models they are fitted in the reservoir (photo).

31.4 Removing the nut securing the motor to the bracket

32.3 Retaining clips on the rear wiper motor cover (arrowed)

32.4 Rear wiper motor assembly

*1 Electrical leads   2 Bracket securing screws
3 Motor-to-bracket bolts*

33.1 Location of washer pump on early models

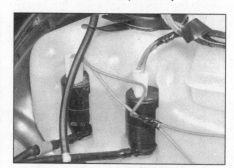

33.4 Later type washer pumps

33.8 Arrow on non-return valves should face toward washers

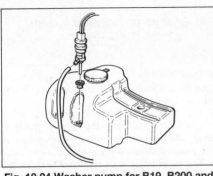

Fig. 10.24 Washer pump for B19, B200 and B172 models (Sec 33)

5 To remove a pump, disconnect the electrical leads and washer tubing.
6 On early models remove the self-tapping screws. On late models the pumps are a push-fit in the reservoir.
7 Refitting is a reversal of removal.
8 Any non-return valves (photo) in the tubing should be fitted with the arrow pointing toward the washers.

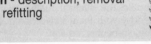

34 Horn - description, removal and refitting

1 Early models are equipped with twin horns producing a high and low combined note. As from 1981 a single horn is fitted (photo).
2 A relay is fitted between the fusebox and horn(s) to protect the switch contacts.
3 To remove the horn(s) first disconnect the battery negative lead, then remove the radiator grille with reference to Chapter 9.
4 Disconnect the supply wires (photo) and unbolt the bracket from the body. Withdraw the horn.
5 Refitting is a reversal of removal.

35 Horn control - removal and refitting

1 Disconnect the battery negative lead.
2 Prise out the pushbutton pads using a small screwdriver.

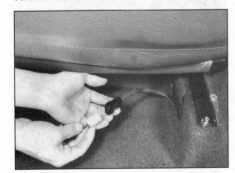

36.1A Seat belt warning system multi-plug connector

34.1 Horn location seen with radiator grille removed

1 Electrical leads   2 Mounting bracket bolt

3 Remove the steering wheel, as described in Chapter 8.
4 Depress the lugs on the horn slip ring and remove the slip ring.
5 Unplug the connectors and press the sliding contacts from the top of the steering column.
6 Refit in the reverse order.

36 Seat belt warning system - description

Late models are equipped with a seat belt warning lamp system to remind the driver and/or passenger to fasten the seat belt. The system operates by a pressure switch in the seat and contacts in the seat belt buckle

Fig. 10.25 Depress the lugs (arrowed) to remove the horn slip ring from the steering wheel (Sec 35)

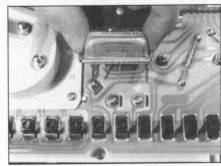

36.1B Removing the seat belt flasher unit from the rear of the instrument panel

34.4 Disconnecting the horn leads

(photos). When the ignition is switched on, the warning light flashes if either front seat is occupied without the seat belt fastened.

37 Seat heating pads - general

1 Some models are equipped with seat heating pads in the driver's seat and, on some models, in the front passenger seat as well.
2 The electrical connections for these pads are under the seat (photo), and should be disconnected when removing a seat, and reconnected on refitting the seat.
3 Repair and testing of the seat is best left to your Volvo dealer.

Fig. 10.26 Disconnect the wiring (arrowed) when removing the horn sliding contacts (Sec 35)

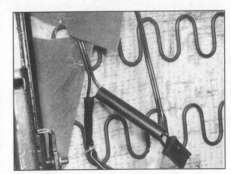

37.2 Seat heating pad electrical connections

10

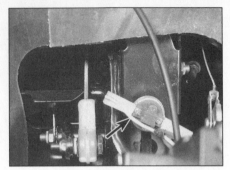

38.1 Brake light switch (arrowed)

38 Brake light switch - removal, refitting and adjustment

1 As from chassis number 321597 the brake light switch is located on the brake pedal bracket, above the brake pedal (photo).
2 To remove the switch, disconnect the electrical leads, undo the locknut and lift the switch from the bracket.
3 Refit in the reverse order, and adjust the switch so that the brake lights come on when the pedal is depressed by 0.6 in (15 mm).
Note: *Prior to the above chassis number the brake light switch was hydraulically operated and was mounted in the brake master cylinder. No adjustment of this switch is necessary but when fitting, all air should be bled from behind the switch by pressing down on the brake pedal as the switch is finally tightened*

39 Reversing light switch - removing, refitting and adjustment

1 The reversing light switch is mounted in the tunnel console at the bottom of the gear lever.
2 To remove the switch, gain access to the bottom of the gear lever by removing the tunnel console (Chapter 9). On automatic transmission models from 1979, just release the switch panel from the console, then release the selector scale and turn it through 90°.
3 Remove the two screws or nuts which retain the switch. On automatic transmission

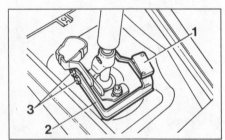

Fig. 10.27 Change-up indicator microswitch at base of gear lever (Sec 41)

1 Microswitch   2 Bracket   3 Bolts

40.2 Removing the electrically operated window switches

models release the retaining clip as well. Disconnect the wires from the switch or at the adjacent connector, making notes if necessary for refitting.
4 Refit in the reverse order, and adjust the switch so that the reversing lights come on when reverse gear is selected and go off when the gear lever is returned to neutral.

40 Electrically operated window switches - removal and refitting

1 The electrically operated window switches are housed in the tunnel console by the handbrake lever.
2 To remove the switches, disconnect the battery negative lead, prise out the switch panel (photo), and disconnect the wiring plugs.
3 Refit in the reverse order.

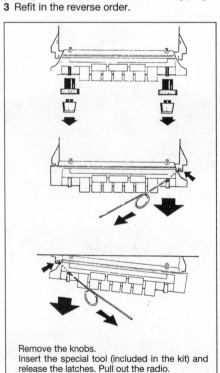

Remove the knobs.
Insert the special tool (included in the kit) and release the latches. Pull out the radio.

Fig. 10.28 Removing the standard fit radio (Sec 42)

41 Change-up indicator system - general description

1 The change-up indicator system is operated electronically through the Renix ignition control unit.
2 The control unit is connected to a microswitch situated at the base of the gear lever, and also senses changes in vacuum in the vacuum advance system.
3 The information thus received enables the control unit to send 'change-up' signals to the indicator in the instrument panel at the correct moment.
4 The microswitch at the base of the gear lever is riveted to a bracket which is bolted to the transmission tunnel.
5 To renew the microswitch, disconnect the leads, remove the bolts from the bracket and transfer the unit to a vice.
6 Use a 3 mm drill to remove the rivet heads and then remove the microswitch.
7 Fit a new microswitch and rivet it back on to the bracket.
8 The remaining procedure is a reversal of removal.
9 Should the system malfunction, have it tested by your local Volvo dealer as special test equipment is required.

42 Standard fit radio/tape player - removal and refitting

1 The standard fit radio supplied by Volvo is housed in the centre console.
2 To remove the radio, pull off the control knobs then, using the special hook tool (supplied with the radio) inserted as shown in Fig. 10.28, release the clips, first from one side and then the other, and pull the radio forward (photos).
3 Disconnect the aerial and electrical lead and remove the radio.
4 On refitting, connect the aerial and lead, then push the radio back into the aperture until the clips spring back into place.
5 Refit the control knobs.

42.2A Using a wire hook to release the radio clips

43 Door mounted speakers - removal and refitting

1 Remove the three securing screws from the speaker surround and pull the speaker away from the door panel sufficiently to disconnect the electrical leads (photo).

2 Refit in the reverse order.

Note: *There is no need to remove the door panel to remove the speaker as is shown in the photo. This is shown for clarity and as part of the door panel removal procedure.*

42.2B Withdrawing the radio

43.1 Disconnecting the door-mounted speaker leads

Fault finding - electrical system

Starter motor fails to turn engine; no voltage at starter motor

☐ Battery discharged
☐ Battery defective internally
☐ Battery terminal leads loose or earth lead not securely attached to body
☐ Loose or broken connections in starter motor circuit
☐ Starter motor switch or solenoid faulty

Starter motor fails to turn engine; voltage at starter motor

☐ Starter motor pinion jammed in mesh with flywheel ring gear
☐ Starter brushes badly worn, sticking or brush wires loose
☐ Commutator dirty, worn or burnt
☐ Starter motor armature faulty
☐ Field coils earthed

Starter motor turns engine very slowly

☐ Battery in discharged condition
☐ Starter brushes badly worn, sticking or brush wires loose
☐ Loose wires in starter motor circuit

Starter motor operates without turning engine

☐ Pinion or flywheel ring gear teeth broken or worn

Starter motor noisy or rough engagement

☐ Pinion or flywheel ring gear teeth broken or worn
☐ Starter motor retaining bolts loose

Battery will not hold charge

☐ Battery defective internally
☐ Electrolyte level too low or electrolyte too weak due to leakage
☐ Plate separators no longer fully effective
☐ Battery plates severely sulphated
☐ Drivebelt slipping
☐ Battery terminal connections loose or corroded
☐ Alternator not charging properly
☐ Short in lighting circuit causing continual battery drain
☐ Regulator unit not working correctly

Ignition light fails to go out

☐ Drivebelt loose and slipping, or broken
☐ Alternator brushes worn or sticking
☐ Brush springs weak or broken
☐ Faulty regulator
☐ Alternator internal fault

Instrument readings increase with engine speed

☐ Voltage stabilizer faulty

Fuel or temperature gauge gives no reading

☐ Wiring to gauges disconnected
☐ Fuel gauge tank unit faulty
☐ Temperature gauge transmitter faulty
☐ Gauges faulty

Fuel or temperature gauge registers full all the time

☐ Fuel gauge tank unit faulty
☐ Temperature gauge transmitter faulty
☐ Wiring to gauges earthed
☐ Gauges faulty

Horn fails to operate

☐ Blown fuse
☐ Cable connection loose or broken
☐ Horn incorrectly adjusted
☐ Internal fault
☐ Horn relay faulty

Horn operates all the time

☐ Horn push contacts stuck
☐ Short in horn circuit

Lights fail to come on

☐ If engine not running, battery discharged
☐ Light bulb filament burnt out or bulbs broken
☐ Wire connections loose, disconnected or broken
☐ Light switch shorting or otherwise faulty

Lights give poor illumination

☐ Lamp glasses dirty
☐ Reflectors tarnished or dirty
☐ Lamps out of adjustment

Lights work erratically

☐ Battery terminals or earth connections loose
☐ Faulty light switch

Wipers fail to operate

☐ Blown fuse
☐ Wire connections loose, disconnected or broken
☐ Brushes or armature worn

Wipers operate very slowly

☐ Commutator dirty or worn
☐ Linkage restriction
☐ Seized armature
☐ Worn brushes

10

Notes

Chapter 11 Supplement:
Revisions and information on later models

Contents

Degrees of difficulty

| Easy, suitable for novice with little experience | | Fairly easy, suitable for beginner with some experience | | Fairly difficult, suitable for competent DIY mechanic | | Difficult, suitable for experienced DIY mechanic | | Very difficult, suitable for expert DIY or professional | |

1 Introduction

This Supplement contains information which is additional to, or a revision of, the material contained in the preceding ten Chapters of this manual. To use the Supplement to its best advantage, it is recommended that it is referred to before the main Chapters of this manual.

Since the manual was first written the Volvo 340 and 360 range has undergone few significant changes or revisions apart from the introduction of catalytic converters on some models.

Some of the following information is based on the model (or production) year of a car; this is not necessarily the same as the date of registration. If the model year is not known, any Volvo dealer will have the information required to identify exactly when a particular vehicle was built, using the details recorded on its vehicle identification plate.

2 Specifications

The Specifications given below are revisions of, or supplementary to, those at the beginning of the preceding Chapters. Models with B 14.4E-D, B172K-D or B200F engines are the same as the earlier 1.4, 1.7 or 2.0 litre models except where noted.

Fuel and exhaust systems

Fuel octane rating

B14.4E, B172K, B200K	96 RON leaded, 95 RON unleaded
B14.4E-D, B172K-D	95 RON unleaded **only**
B200E - without catalytic converter	92 RON leaded, 91 RON unleaded
B200E - with catalytic converter, B200F	91 RON unleaded **only**
CO level at idle speed B200F	0.4 to 0.8%

Torque wrench setting	lbf ft	Nm
Oxygen (Lambda) sensor	37	50

Suspension and steering

Power-assisted steering

Number of turns lock-to-lock	3.1
Fluid type	ATF type A, suffix A

Torque wrench settings	lbf ft	Nm
Steering gear mounting nuts and screws	15	21
Steering column lower universal joint pinch-bolt and nut	15	21
Track rod end balljoint self-locking nut	41	55
System hose unions:		
At pump	19	26
At steering gear	26	35
Pump mounting bolts and adjuster locknut	15	21

3 Routine Maintenance

Models from 1989

General

1 A slightly revised maintenance schedule has been introduced for all models from 1989. As previously, it assumes an average annual mileage of 12 000 miles (20 000 km) and consists of a Minor and a Major Service. Servicing is to be carried out at the specified time intervals or sooner, at the specified mileage interval, if the car covers a higher than average mileage.

2 The Minor Service is to be carried out every six months or 6000 miles/10 000 km, whichever occurs first.

3 The Major Service is to be carried out annually or 12 000 miles/20 000 km, whichever occurs first.

4 Essential points to note are as follows:

Alternator/water pump drivebelt - B172 models

5 The drivebelt should be checked at the **first** Minor Service (six months or 6000 miles/10 000 km), but then it does not require rechecking until the **second** Major Service (2 years or 24 000 miles/40 000 km).

6 At the **fourth** Major Service (4 years or 48 000 miles/80 000 km), the belt must be renewed as a matter of course, regardless of its apparent condition.

7 The cycle is then repeated so that the belt must then be checked at the first Minor Service after renewal (54 months or 54 000 miles/90 000 km), at the second Major Service after renewal (6 years or 72 000 miles/120 000 km) and renewed at the fourth Major Service after renewal (8 years or 96 000 miles/160 000 km).

CO level and idle speed - B200F models

8 These must be checked at every Major Service; however, as noted in Section 5 of this Chapter, this is a task for a Volvo dealer only.

Spark plug renewal - all models

9 The spark plugs should be renewed irrespective of their apparent condition, at every Major Service. As noted in Chapter 4, there is no need for cleaning and/or regapping between these intervals.

Pulley gap and drivebelt check - models with automatic transmission

10 This check is now to be carried out at every Major Service.

Centrifugal clutch plate check - models with automatic transmission

11 This check is to be made at every second Major Service (2 years or 24 000 miles/40 000 km); refer to Chapter 5, Section 2.

Transmission oil level checks - all models

12 At every Minor Service check the complete transmission (primary and secondary units, or gearbox and final drive, as applicable) for signs of oil/fluid leakage, check the oil/fluid levels and top up if necessary, as described in the relevant Sections of Chapter 6.

13 If any leaks are found they must be rectified as soon as possible.

14 Note that oil change recommendations remain the same; while the oil in the automatic transmission primary and secondary units must be changed every **second** Major Service (2 years or 24 000 miles/40 000 km), there is no specified change interval for the manual transmission oil or fluid.

Propeller shaft check - all models

15 This check is now made at every **second** Major Service (2 years or 24 000 miles/40 000 km).

Braking system vacuum servo unit check and air filter renewal - all models

16 Owners should note that while neither of these tasks is included in the revised schedule, the operation of the braking system should be checked at regular intervals; this will naturally include the servo unit check described in Chapter 7, Section 18.

Power-assisted steering - where fitted

17 **At every Minor Service, check the fluid level and look for signs of fluid leaks from any part of the system; refer to Section 6 of this Chapter.**

18 At every Major Service, check the condition of the pump drivebelt, renewing it if necessary, then check its tension and adjust it if required. Refer to Section 6 of this Chapter.

Alternator check - all models

19 Owners should note that while the check of the alternator cleanliness and security is no longer included in the revised schedule, the condition of the unit, its connections and mountings, should be checked as a matter of course during the drivebelt checks.

Washer/wiper check - all models

20 Owners should note that while this check is only called up in the schedule at every Major Service, the windscreen, rear window and headlamp washers and wipers should be checked regularly (ie weekly, or before any long journey) to ensure that the car complies with legal requirements in these respects.

21 Check that the washer reservoir is full (with clean water, or in winter particularly, water and a screenwash antifreeze additive), that the washer jets are clear and accurately aimed and that the wiper blades sweep the glass cleanly and without leaving smears. Renew the blades whenever they are found to be no longer effective.

4 Engine

B14.4E-D and B172K-D engines

1 Fitted to the corresponding 340 1.4 and 1.7 litre models from 1989, these engines are equipped with the revised carburettor settings and equipment necessary for their catalytic converters. Apart from this, as far as can be ascertained at the time of writing, there are no differences from the engines, components and systems described in the main Chapters of this manual.

B200F engine

2 Fitted (where applicable) to some 360 models from 1987, this engine, as far as can be ascertained at the time of writing, differs from the B200E unit described in the main Chapters of this manual only in the fitting of the oxygen (Lambda) sensor and catalytic converter.

5 Fuel and exhaust systems

CO level and idle speed adjustment - B14.4E-D, B172K-D and B200E models

Note: *If the CO level reading is incorrect (or if any other symptom is encountered which causes you to suspect the presence of a fault) always check that the air cleaner element is clean, that the spark plugs are in good condition and correctly gapped, that the engine breather and vacuum hoses are clear and undamaged, that there are no leaks in the air intake trunking, the carburettor/throttle body or the manifolds and that the throttle cable is correctly adjusted (Chapter 3). If the engine is running very roughly, check the valve clearances and compression pressures (Chapter 1). Check also that all wiring is in good condition, with securely-fastened connectors, that the fuel filter has been renewed at the recommended intervals and that the exhaust system is entirely free of air leaks which might upset the operation of the catalytic converter.*

1 The procedure is essentially as described in the relevant Sections of Chapter 3, noting the following points.

2 The check requires the use of equipment such as an exhaust gas analyser which puts it beyond the capabilities of most home mechanics; for most owners the simplest answer will be to have this work carried out by a Volvo dealer. For those who have access to such equipment, proceed as follows.

3 When checking the CO level on B14.4E-D and B172K-D engined models, use an exhaust gas analyser connected to the

measuring point ahead of the catalytic converter (unscrew the sealing plug to insert the analyser probe). The check must be made with the electric cooling fan disconnected and within 3 minutes of the opening of the cooling system thermostat. If readings cannot be taken within this time, increase engine speed briefly to 1500 rpm to clear any fuel droplets from the manifold and to allow colder fuel to enter the carburettor.

4 When checking the CO level on B200E engined models, use an exhaust gas analyser connected to the measuring point ahead of the catalytic converter (unscrew the sealing plug to insert the analyser probe) and within 5 minutes of the opening of the cooling system thermostat.

5 On all models, if the CO level is too high but the engine appears to function normally in all other respects (starting, smoothness of running when warming-up, fuel economy and performance), one possible cause is that the engine oil is contaminated with petrol (usually as a result of extensive stop-start, low-speed driving) and so the re-circulated crank-case fumes are affecting the meter reading. If this is suspected, it is worth checking by disconnecting the crankcase breather hose from the intake and capping the union so that excess air cannot enter and weaken the mixture. The CO level can be expected to drop slightly as a result of this, but if the drop is considerable, it indicates that the oil is contaminated and that it and the oil filter must be changed as soon as possible. Do not forget to reconnect the breather system on completion of the check.

Bosch LU-Jetronic injection system - B200F models

Description

6 This system is essentially the same as that described in Chapter 3, with the addition of closed-loop mixture control to cater for the three-way regulated catalytic converter.

7 The oxygen (Lambda) sensor screwed into the exhaust downpipe provides the ECU with constant feedback which enables it to continuously adjust the mixture closed-loop control to provide the best possible conditions for the catalytic converter to operate.

8 Until the sensor is fully warmed-up it gives no feedback so the ECU uses pre-programmed values (open-loop control) to determine the correct injector pulse width. When the sensor reaches its normal operating temperature, the tip (which is sensitive to oxygen) sends the ECU a varying voltage depending on the amount of oxygen in the exhaust gases; if the intake air/fuel mixture is too rich, the exhaust gases are low in oxygen so the sensor sends a low-voltage signal, the voltage rising as the mixture weakens and the amount of oxygen rises in the exhaust gases. Peak conversion efficiency of all major

pollutants occurs if the intake air/fuel mixture is maintained at the chemically-correct ratio for the complete combustion of petrol of 14.7 parts (by weight) of air to 1 part of fuel (the 'stoichiometric' ratio). The sensor output voltage alters in a large step at this point, the ECU using the signal change as a reference point and correcting accordingly the intake air/fuel mixture by altering the fuel injector pulse width.

CO level and idle speed - checking and adjustment

Note: *Refer first to the note at the beginning of this Section.*

9 The check requires the use of equipment such as a good-quality, carefully-calibrated exhaust gas analyser which puts it beyond the capabilities of most home mechanics. Note also that the operation of the fuel injection system with closed-loop mixture control should mean that the CO level will never require adjustment unless a fault arises in the system. For most owners the simplest answer will be to have this work carried out by a Volvo dealer. For those who have access to the equipment required, as well as the skill and experience to use it effectively, proceed as follows.

10 The check must be made using the analyser connected to the measuring point ahead of the catalytic converter (unscrew the sealing plug to insert the analyser probe) and within 5 minutes of the opening of the cooling system thermostat. If readings cannot be taken within this time, increase engine speed briefly to 1500 rpm to clear any fuel droplets from the manifold and to allow colder fuel to enter the system.

11 First check, and adjust if necessary, the idle speed as described in Chapter 3.

12 Disconnect the oxygen (Lambda) sensor wiring and take a CO level reading, working as quickly as possible while ensuring that an accurate result is obtained. If the CO level is high but the engine appears to function normally in all other respects (starting, smoothness of running when warming-up, fuel economy and performance) bear in mind the possibility of petrol-contaminated engine oil (see paragraph 5 above) and recheck the CO level with the crankcase breather hose disconnected, as described.

13 If adjustment is required, proceed as described in Chapter 3, Section 34.

14 When the setting is correct, reconnect the oxygen (Lambda) sensor and recheck the idle speed and CO level.

Oxygen (Lambda) sensor - removal and refitting

15 The sensor is screwed into the exhaust downpipe, upstream of the catalytic converter. When handling the sensor, note that it is fragile; take care not to drop it and do not allow it to contact fuel or silicone substances.

16 Start the engine and run it until it reaches normal operating temperature, then switch off

and disconnect the battery. If access is required from below, jack up the front of the car and support it securely on axle stands, then unbolt the splash guard(s) as necessary from the underside of the engine compartment to gain access to the exhaust system from beneath.

17 Trace the wiring from the sensor itself to the connector, release it from any clips or ties and disconnect the wiring before unscrewing the sensor.

18 Using a suitable spanner and wearing heavy gloves to protect your hands from the hot exhaust system and sensor, unscrew the sensor and withdraw it.

19 On refitting, apply anti-seize compound (Volvo recommend 'Never-Seez', available under Part No 1161 035-9) to the threads of the sensor.

20 The sensor must be tightened to the specified torque wrench setting; this will require the use of either a deep socket, slotted to allow for the sensor wiring, or of an open-ended spanner and a spring balance. To tighten a fastener or component to a torque value using an open-ended spanner hook a spring balance to the spanner's outer end and apply the desired force by pulling the spring balance. Since a torque setting of 37 lbf ft is a turning force of 37 lb applied at a distance of 1 ft from the fastener/component's centre, it is easy to calculate that a force of 37 x 2 (ie 74 lb) must be applied if the spanner is only 6 inches long; if the spanner is longer, the applied force can be reduced proportionally.

Catalytic converters - general information and precautions

21 The exhaust gases of any internal combustion engine (however efficient or well-tuned) which burns petrol consist largely (approximately 99%) of nitrogen (N_2), carbon dioxide (CO_2), oxygen (O_2), other inert gases, and water vapour (H_2O). The remaining 1% is made up of the noxious materials which are currently seen (CO_2 apart) as the major polluters of the environment; carbon monoxide (CO), unburned hydrocarbons (HC), oxides of nitrogen (NOx) and some solid matter, including a small lead content.

22 Left to themselves, most of these pollutants are thought eventually to break down naturally (CO and NOx, for example, break down in the upper atmosphere to release CO_2) having first caused ground-level environmental problems, but the massive increase world-wide in the use of motor cars and the current popular concern for the environment has caused the introduction of legislation in most countries, in varying stages of severity, to combat the problem.

23 The device most commonly used to clean up car exhausts is the catalytic converter. It is fitted into the car's exhaust system and uses precious metals (platinum and palladium or rhodium) as catalysts to speed up the reaction between the pollutants and the oxygen in the car's exhaust gases, CO and HC being

11

oxidised to form H_2O and CO_2 and (in the three-way type of catalytic converter) NOx being reduced to N_2. **Note**: *The catalytic converter is not a filter in the physical sense; its function is to promote a chemical reaction, but it is not itself affected by that reaction.*

24 The converter consists of an element (or 'substrate') of ceramic honeycomb coated with a combination of precious metals in such a way as to produce a vast surface area over which the exhaust gases must flow; the whole being mounted in a stainless-steel box. A simple 'oxidation' (or 'two-way') catalytic converter can deal with CO and HC only, while a 'reduction' (or 'three-way') catalytic converter can deal with CO, HC and NOx. Three-way catalytic converters are further sub-divided into open-loop (or 'uncontrolled') converters which can remove 50 to 70% of pollutants and closed-loop (also known as 'controlled' or 'regulated') converters which can remove over 90% of pollutants.

25 The converters fitted to B14.4E-D, B172K-D and B200E engines are of the three-way open-loop type, while those fitted to B200F engines are of the three-way closed-loop type.

26 The catalytic converter is a reliable and simple device which needs no maintenance in itself, but there are some facts of which an owner should be aware if the converter is to function properly for its full service life.

a) *DO NOT use leaded petrol in a car equipped with a catalytic converter - the lead will coat the precious metals, reducing their converting efficiency and will eventually destroy the converter. Opinions vary as to how much leaded fuel is necessary to affect the converter's performance and whether it can recover even if only unleaded petrol is used afterwards; the best course of action is, therefore, to assume the worst and to ensure that NO leaded petrol is used at any time.*

b) *Always keep the ignition and fuel systems well-maintained in accordance with the manufacturer's schedule (Routine Maintenance and Section 3 of this Chapter) - particularly, ensure that the air cleaner filter element, the fuel filter(s) and the spark plugs are renewed at the correct interval - if the intake air/fuel mixture is allowed to become too rich due to neglect, the unburned surplus will enter and burn in the catalytic converter, overheating the element and eventually destroying the converter.*

c) *If the engine develops a misfire, do not drive the car at all (or at least as little as possible) until the fault is cured - the misfire will allow unburned fuel to enter the converter, which will result in its overheating, as noted above.*

d) *DO NOT push- or tow-start the car - this will soak the catalytic converter in unburned fuel causing it to overheat when the engine does start -see (b) above.*

e) *DO NOT switch off the ignition at high engine speeds - if the ignition is switched off at anything above idle speed, unburned fuel will enter the (very hot) catalytic converter, with the possible risk of its igniting on the element and damaging the converter.*

f) *DO NOT use fuel or engine oil additives - these may contain substances harmful to the catalytic converter.*

g) *DO NOT continue to use the car if the engine burns oil to the extent of leaving a visible trail of blue smoke - the unburned-carbon deposits will clog the converter passages and reduce its efficiency; in severe cases the element will overheat.*

h) *Remember that the catalytic converter operates at very high temperatures - hence the heat shields on the car's underbody - and the casing will become hot enough to ignite combustible materials which brush against it. DO NOT, therefore, park the car in dry undergrowth, over long grass or piles of dead leaves.*

i) *Remember that the catalytic converter is FRAGILE - do not strike it with tools during servicing work, take great care when working on the exhaust system, ensure that the converter is well clear of any jacks or other lifting gear used to raise the car and do not drive the car over rough ground, road humps, etc., in such a way as to 'ground' the exhaust system.*

j) *In some cases, particularly when the car is new and/or is used for stop/start driving, a sulphurous smell (like that of rotten eggs) may be noticed from the exhaust. This is common to many catalytic converter-equipped cars and seems to be due to the small amount of sulphur found in some petrols reacting with hydrogen in the exhaust to produce hydrogen sulphide (H_2S) gas; while this gas is toxic, it is not produced in sufficient amounts to be a problem. Once the car has covered a few thousand miles the problem should disappear - in the mean-while a change of driving style or of the brand of petrol used may effect a solution.*

k) *The catalytic converter used on a well-maintained and well-driven car, should last for between 50 000 and 100 000 miles - from this point on, careful checks should be made at all specified service intervals of the CO level to ensure that the converter is still operating efficiently, if the converter is no longer effective it must be renewed.*

Catalytic converter - removal and refitting

27 Note that the only test of the catalytic converter's effectiveness is to check the level of CO in the exhaust gas, comparing the level in front of the converter with that at the tailpipe; if there is no significant decrease, the

fault must lie in the converter, which must be renewed.

28 To remove the catalytic converter, undo the nuts securing the front and rear ends, then prise away the rear part of the system until the converter can be withdrawn, collect any gaskets fitted.

29 On refitting, carefully clean the mating surfaces, fit new gaskets (where applicable) and tighten the nuts securely. If the converter is marked with an arrow, this indicates direction of flow, the unit must be fitted with the arrow pointing to the rear of the car.

Recommended fuel - all models

30 All 340 and 360 models built up to model year 1986 must use leaded petrol; this now means using four-star, irrespective of the originally-recommended octane rating.

31 All 340 and 360 models built from model year 1987, but not fitted with catalytic converters, may use either unleaded or leaded petrol as desired. No adjustment (ie to the ignition timing) is required to allow any of these models to use unleaded petrol.

32 All cars equipped with catalytic converters must use only unleaded petrol; the nearest equivalent to the octane rating recommended is the Premium grade unleaded petrol most often found on sale in UK filling stations. Note that no adjustment is required to allow these to run on unleaded petrol and that Super/Superplus grade unleaded petrol may also be used if wished, with no ill-effects save that on the driver's wallet.

33 Note that some B200-engined models may use 91 RON Regular or Normal grade unleaded petrol not yet available in the UK. If you are taking such a vehicle abroad, seek the advice of a Volvo dealer or of one of the motoring organisations to ensure that you are aware of the grades of petrol that you are likely to encounter and be sure that you are aware of the different (and sometimes confusingly contradictory) names used for these grades, compared with the UK terms with which you are familiar.

6 Suspension and steering

Steering gear rubber bellows (all models) - renewal

1 Remove the track rod end balljoint and locknut (Chapter 8, Section 22) and cut, remove or release (as applicable) the bellows outer clip.

2 Similarly release the bellows inner clip and slide the bellows off the steering gear.

3 Check the bellows for any signs of splits, tears or perishing; renew it if any such damage is found or if it is not a tight fit on the steering gear or track rod. The clips should be renewed if they are found to be damaged or if they no longer fasten correctly.

4 Thoroughly clean the track rod and the steering gear housing, using fine abrasive paper to polish off any corrosion, burrs or sharp edges which might damage the new bellows sealing lips on installation.

5 On refitting, grease the bellows lips and slide it on, then fasten the first clip to secure it and replace any lost lubricant.

6 Settle the bellows evenly on the track rod and fasten the remaining clip.

7 Refit the track rod end balljoint and locknut as described in Chapter 8.

8 When checking the steering's operation, ensure that the bellows does not snag or bulge at any point in the steering gear travel; if necessary, slacken the clip(s) and reposition the bellows, then fasten the clip(s).

Power-assisted steering

Fluid level check

9 The (black plastic) power steering fluid reservoir is located on the left-hand side of the engine compartment.

10 With the car on level ground and the engine stopped and cold, first use a clean rag to wipe the filler cap and the surrounding area to prevent any foreign matter from entering the reservoir. Unscrew the filler cap and use clean, lint-free rag to wipe clean the dipstick. Refit the dipstick, screwing it fully home to ensure an accurate check, then remove it again. The level of fluid in the reservoir must be between the dipstick 'MIN' and 'MAX' marks (shown, in some cases, by a cross-hatched area). It is preferable for the level to be up to the 'MAX' mark, however it must never be allowed to drop below the 'MIN' mark.

11 If topping up is required, pour in the specified type of fluid until the level is up to the 'MAX' mark. Be careful not to introduce dirt into the system, and do not overfill. Frequent topping-up indicates a leak which should be investigated. Refit the filler cap on completion.

12 Check the fluid hoses for chafing or deterioration and the pipe and hose unions for fluid leaks. Also check for signs of fluid leakage under pressure from the steering gear rubber bellows which would indicate failed fluid seals within the steering gear.

Bleeding the system

13 This will only be required if any part of the system has been disconnected, or if the level

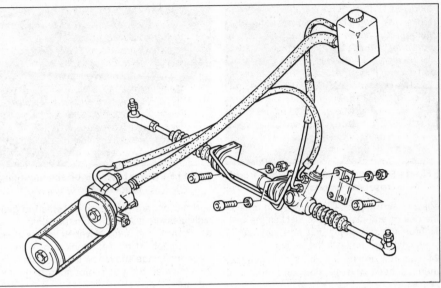

Fig. 11.1 Power-assisted steering system components (Sec 6)

has been allowed to fall so low that air has entered.

14 Remove the fluid reservoir filler cap and top up the fluid level to the 'MAX' mark using only the specified fluid.

15 With the engine stopped, slowly move the steering from lock-to-lock several times to purge out the internal air, then top up the level in the fluid reservoir. Repeat as necessary until the fluid level no longer falls.

16 Repeat this procedure with the engine running (at no more than idle speed) and again top up the level.

17 Take the car for a test drive, checking for correct operation of the steering and listening for any unusual noises; if air is present pronounced clicking or buzzing noises may be heard. On returning, stop the engine and allow it to cool completely, then recheck the fluid level and top up if required.

18 After refilling the system following a repair to the pump or steering gear, the fluid may initially contain lots of minute air bubbles which will cause the fluid to take on a milky appearance. Before continuing to bleed the system, wait for several minutes to allow the air to disperse.

Pump drivebelt check, adjustment and renewal

19 Unbolt the splash guard(s) from the underside of the engine compartment to gain access to the pump from beneath.

20 With the engine switched off, inspect the full length of the drive-belt for cracks and deterioration, turning the engine so that the belt can be inspected thoroughly. Twist the belt between the pulleys so that both sides can be viewed. Also check for fraying, and glazing which gives the belt a shiny appearance. Check the pulleys for nicks, cracks, distortion and corrosion.

21 To renew the drivebelt, slacken the belt tension as described below, then slip the belt off the pulleys. Fit the new belt and adjust it as described.

22 The tension of the drivebelt is checked by pushing on it with a finger midway between the pulleys on the longest run and checking the deflection, which should be between 0.2 and 0.4 in (5 and 10 mm).

23 If adjustment is necessary, loosen the pump mounting bolt and adjuster locknut (items B and A in Fig. 11.4), then turn the

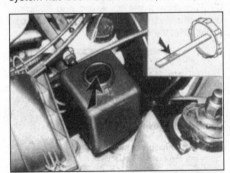

Fig. 11.2 Checking the power-assisted steering system fluid level - dipstick 'MAX' and 'MIN' marks shown by cross-hatched area arrowed (Sec 6)

Fig. 11.3 Power-assisted steering pump seen from below - drivebelt tension checking point and adjuster screw arrowed (Sec 6)

Fig. 11.4 Power-assisted steering pump mountings and adjuster components (Sec 6)

A Adjuster locknut   B Mounting bolt
C Adjuster screw

11

Fig. 11.5 Disconnecting fluid hoses from reservoir unions (Sec 6)

Fig. 11.6 Prising reservoir off the mounting bracket (Sec 6)

Fig. 11.7 Disconnecting fluid hoses from pump unions (Sec 6)

A Reservoir-to-pump feed hose
B Pump-to-steering gear high-pressure hose

adjuster screw (item C) clockwise to tension the belt or anti-clockwise to slacken the belt. Tighten the mounting bolt and locknut on completion and recheck the setting.

24 Run the engine for about five minutes, then recheck the tension and adjust if necessary.

Fluid reservoir - removal and refitting

25 Cut, remove or release (as applicable) the clips and disconnect the fluid hoses from the reservoir unions; allow the fluid to drain into a suitable container.

26 Prise the reservoir off its mounting bracket; the bracket can be unbolted if required.

27 Refitting is the reverse of the removal procedure, using new clips, if required. Fill the reservoir with clean fluid of the specified type and bleed any trapped air from the system with reference to paragraphs 14 to 18 of this Section.

Pump - removal and refitting

28 Unbolt the splash guard(s) from the underside of the engine compartment to gain access to the pump from beneath. Disconnect the air intake ducting if the extra working space is required.

29 Using brake hose clamps, clamp both hoses leading from the pump and place a suitable container under the pump to catch any escaping fluid.

30 Cut, remove or release (as applicable) the clip and disconnect the reservoir-to-pump feed hose from the pump union; allow the fluid to drain into the container. Unscrew its union

and disconnect the pump-to-steering gear high-pressure fluid hose from the pump.

31 Remove the pump drivebelt as described in paragraph 21 above; check it for signs of wear or damage and renew it if necessary.

32 Unfasten the pump mounting bolts and withdraw it.

33 Refitting is a reversal of the removal procedure, but note the following additional points.

a) *Tighten the mounting bolts gradually so that there are no uneven forces in the brackets or pump.*

b) *Tighten all nuts and bolts to the specified torque wrench settings.*

c) *Tension the drivebelt with reference to paragraphs 22 to 24 of this Section.*

d) *Check the high-pressure hose union sealing washer (where fitted) and if necessary renew. Use a new feed hose clip if required.*

e) *Bleed any trapped air from the system with reference to paragraphs 14 to 18 in this Section.*

Pump - overhaul

34 Overhaul of the pump is not recommended even if the parts are available. Obtain a new or reconditioned unit from a Volvo dealer or other specialist.

Steering gear - removal and refitting

35 Place the steering wheel in the straight-ahead position and engage the steering lock.

36 Jack up the front of the car and support it

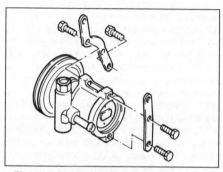

Fig. 11.8 Power-assisted steering pump mounting bracket details (Sec 6)

securely on axle stands, then unbolt the splash guard(s) from the underside of the engine compartment to gain access to the steering gear from beneath.

37 Remove the heat shield (A in Fig. 11.9) from around the steering column lower universal joint, then the heat shield (B in Fig. 11.9) from above the steering gear rubber bellows.

38 Unscrew and remove the pinch-bolt and nut securing the steering column lower universal joint to the steering gear pinion shaft. Check if there are any alignment marks on the pinion shaft and steering gear housing, and if necessary make them to indicate the straight-ahead position.

39 Disconnect the track rod end balljoints from the suspension strut steering arms (Chapter 8, Section 22).

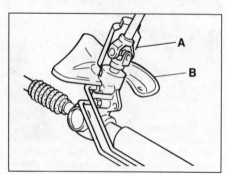

Fig. 11.9 Remove heat shields A and B when removing steering gear (Sec 6)

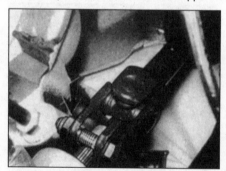

Fig. 11.10 Remove pinch-bolt and nut (arrowed) securing steering column lower universal joint to steering gear pinion shaft (Sec 6)

Fig. 11.11 Disconnect fluid hoses (unions arrowed) from steering gear (Sec 6)

Fig. 11.12 Undo mounting screws and nuts (arrows) to release steering gear (Sec 61)

1 Heat shield *2 Spacer*

40 Using brake hose clamps, clamp both hoses leading from the steering gear and place a suitable container under the unions to catch any escaping fluid. Note their connections carefully, or label the pump-to-steering gear high-pressure hose (upper union) and the steering gear-to-reservoir return hose to ensure correct reconnection.

41 Unscrew the unions and release the hoses. Plug the hoses and the steering gear unions to prevent the entry of dust and dirt.

42 With reference to Fig. 11.12, unscrew and remove the (socket-headed) screws and nuts securing the steering gear to the engine rear mounting, withdraw the heat shield (1) and the spacer (2), then turn the left-hand roadwheel as far as possible to full left lock.

43 Pivot the steering gear forwards, separating the pinion shaft from the steering column universal joint, then manoeuvre the steering gear out of the car to the left.

44 Refitting is a reversal of the removal procedure, noting the following points:

a) *If a new steering gear is being fitted, transfer the mounting plate and clamp assembly from the old unit; position the clamp approximately on the housing and tighten only the upper clamp screw to its specified torque wrench setting. Leave the lower screw finger-tight until the clamp has been correctly located when the steering gear is installed.*

b) *Determine the steering gear's straight-ahead position by disconnecting the rubber bellows from one end, then turning the pinion fully to the right. Measure the distance from the steering gear housing to the end of the rack, then move the rack to the half-way position. Mark the pinion shaft and housing in relation to each other. Reconnect the rubber bellows.*

c) *Do not forget to locate the heat shield and spacer as the steering gear is installed, and ensure that both are in the straight-ahead position before engaging the steering gear pinion shaft in the steering column universal joint.*

d) *Tighten all nuts, bolts and screws to their specified torque wrench settings.*

e) *Note that the pump-to-steering gear*

high-pressure hose is connected to the steering gear upper union.

f) *Check, if fitted, the hose union sealing washers and if necessary renew. Tighten the unions securely, to their specified torque wrench settings if possible.*

g) *Bleed any trapped air from the system with reference to paragraphs 14 to 18 of this Section.*

h) *Check, and if necessary adjust, the front wheel alignment (Chapter 8).*

Steering gear - overhaul

45 As with the pump, overhaul of the steering gear is not recommended for the home mechanic. Obtain a new or reconditioned unit from a Volvo dealer or other specialist.

Track rod end balljoints - general

46 The track rod end balljoints are secured to the suspension strut steering arms by self-locking nuts; these **must** be renewed whenever they are disturbed and must be tightened to the specified torque wrench setting.

7 Bodywork and fittings

Bumpers - removal and refitting

1 The bumpers fitted to models from 1986 are slightly modified. Refer to Fig. 11.13 for details. If the rear bumper is to be repaired, it is best to unbolt the complete bumper assembly from the car's body and then to dismantle it as required.

Electrically heated/operated front door mirrors

2 Later models may be fitted with exterior rear view mirrors, the glasses of which incorporate heating elements, and which may be remote-controlled by means of an electric motor mounted in each mirror and a switch mounted on the transmission tunnel console.

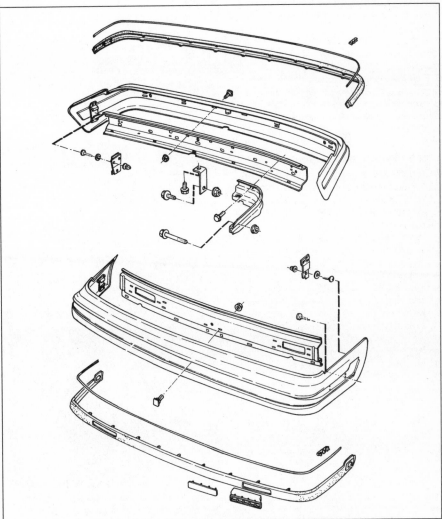

Fig. 11.13 Front and rear bumper components for models from 1986 (Sec 7)

11

Mirror assembly - removal and refitting

3 Remove the door trim panel (Chapter 9) and peel back the moisture-proof sheet as necessary to reach and disconnect the mirror wiring lead.

4 The remainder of the procedure is as described in Chapter 9.

Mirror glass - removal and refitting

5 Using a length of plastic, prise out the mirror glass at one side so that it snaps out of the plastic holder.

6 Disconnect the heater wiring from the glass.

7 On electrically-operated mirrors, the electric motors may be removed by unscrewing the mounting screws.

8 Refitting is a reversal of the removal procedure, but lightly grease the plastic holder to help the mirror to enter it; if the glass is marked to show which way up it is to be fitted, ensure that these instructions are followed.

8 Electrical system

Electrically heated front door mirrors

1 Later models may be fitted with exterior rear view mirrors, the glasses of which incorporate heating elements. These elements are part of the heated rear window circuit and are thus controlled by the heated rear window switch and relay (Chapter 10).

2 Refer to Section 7 of this Chapter for details of removal and refitting of the mirror assembly and of the mirror glass.

Electrically operated front door mirrors

3 Later models may be fitted with exterior rear view mirrors which can be remote-controlled by means of an electric motor mounted in each mirror and a switch mounted on the transmission tunnel console.

4 The circuit consists of the two switches and the motor assemblies and is fed, via the ignition switch and ignition switch relay, through fuse No 9.

Mirror switches - removal and refitting

5 Proceed as described in Chapter 10, Section 40.

Mirror motor - removal and refitting

6 Remove the mirror glass (Section 7).

7 Unscrew the mounting screws and withdraw the motor, disconnecting the wiring. If the motor cannot be separated from its wiring, the door trim panel will have to be removed (Chapter 9) so that the mirror assembly wiring lead can be disconnected.

8 Refitting is the reverse of the removal procedure; if the motor is marked to show which way up it is to be fitted, ensure that these instructions are followed.

Key to wiring diagram for early 343 models

1.0	Battery	C2	Temperature gauge	C38	Lamp for heater controls illumination
2.0	Fusebox	C3	Fuel gauge	C39	Lamp for main/dipped beam switch illumination
2.1	Direction indicator	C4	Coolant temperature warning light		
2.2	Hazard warning installation	C5	Fuel reserve light	C40	Lamp for parking lights switch illumination
2.3	Horn relay	C6	Left direction indicator warning light		
2.4	Main beam/dipped beam relay	C7	Parking light warning light	C41	Lamp for heated rear window switch illumination
2.5	Vehicle lighting relay	C8	Handbrake warning light		
2.6	Interlock (start inhibitor) relay	C9	Oil pressure warning light	C42	Lamp for rear fog lamp switch illumination
2.7	Heated rear window relay (DL)	C10	Brake fluid level warning light		
2.8	Headlamp wash/wipe installation relay (Nordic)	C11	Choke warning light	C43	Lamp for cigar lighter illumination
		C12	Seat belt warning light	C44	Lamp for clock illumination (DL)
A1	Headlamp main beam/dipped beam	C13	Hazard warning light	C45	Radio (optional)
A2	Parking light	C14	Main beam warning light	D1	Selector lever switch
A3	Direction indicator	C15	Rear foglamp warning light	D2	Low ratio hold switch
A4	Headlamp main beam/dipped beam	C16	Low ratio hold warning light	D3	Switch for hazard warning installation
A5	Parking lights	C17	Heated rear window warning light	D4	Seat belt contact (left front)
A6	Direction indicator	C18	Right direction indicator warning light	D5	Seat belt contact (right front)
A7	Horn (high-tone)	C19	Switch for main beam/dipped beam	D6	Seat cushion contact (rear seat)
A8	Horn (low-tone)	C20	Switch for parking lights	D7	Handbrake switch
A9	Headlamp wiper motor (Nordic)	C21	Switch for heater rear window	D8	Selector scale switch
B1	Voltage regulator	C22	Switch for rear foglamp	E1	Heated rear window
B2	Water pump	C23	Courtesy light door switch (left)	E2	Boot light switch
B3	Microswitch	C24	Courtesy light, car interior	E3	Boot light
B4	Four-way valve	C25	Choke	E4	Direction indicator
B5	Starter motor	C26	Direction indicator switch	E5	Tail light/brake light
B6	Coolant temperature sender/switch	C27	Ignition switch	E6	Tail light
B7	Declutching valve	C28	Windscreen wiper switch	E7	Rear foglamp
B8	Brake light switch	C29	Kickdown switch	E8	Reversing light
B9	Brake fluid level float	C30	Clock	E9	Float
B10	Ignition coil	C31	Blower	E10	Number plate light
B11	Oil pressure sender	C32	Blower rheostat	E11	Reversing light
B12	Alternator	C33	Cigar lighter	E12	Rear foglamp
B13	Three-way valve (Sweden)	C34	Switch for glove compartment light	E13	Tail light
B14	Pilot jet (Sweden)	C35	Light for glove compartment	E14	Tail light/brake light
B15	Windscreen wiper motor	C36	Direction indicator	E15	Direction indicator
C1	Voltmeter	C37	Lamp for instrument lighting	E16	Courtesy light door switch (right)

Colour code

G	Grey	GE	Yellow	LBR	Light brown	RS	Pink
DBL	Dark blue	GR/GE	Green/Yellow	LGR	Light green	W	White
DBR	Dark brown	L	Lilac	OR	Orange	ZW	Black
DGR	Dark green	LBL	Light blue	R	Red		

12

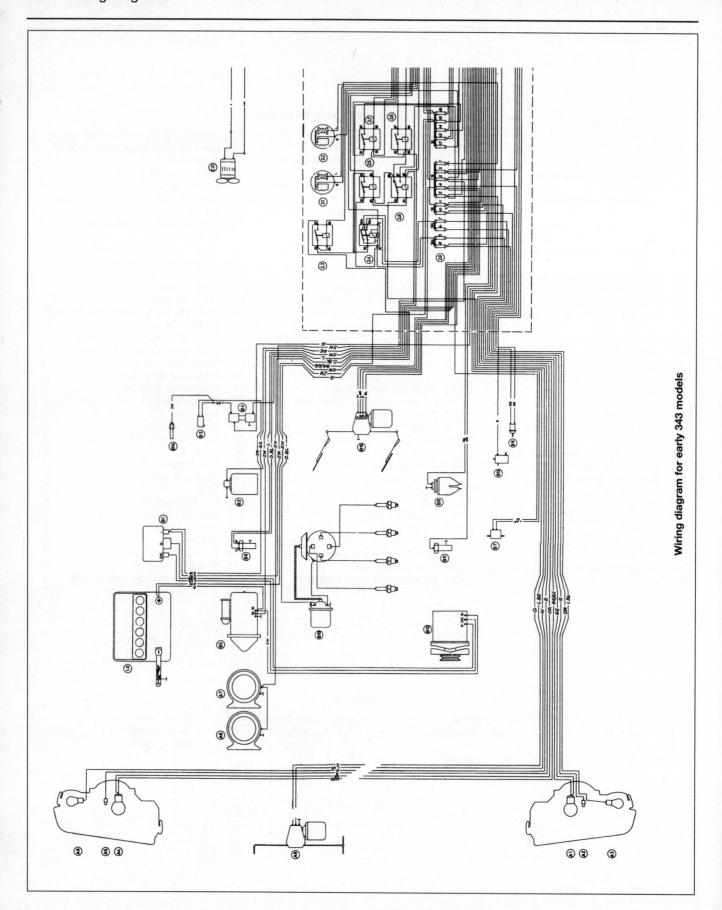

Wiring diagram for early 343 models

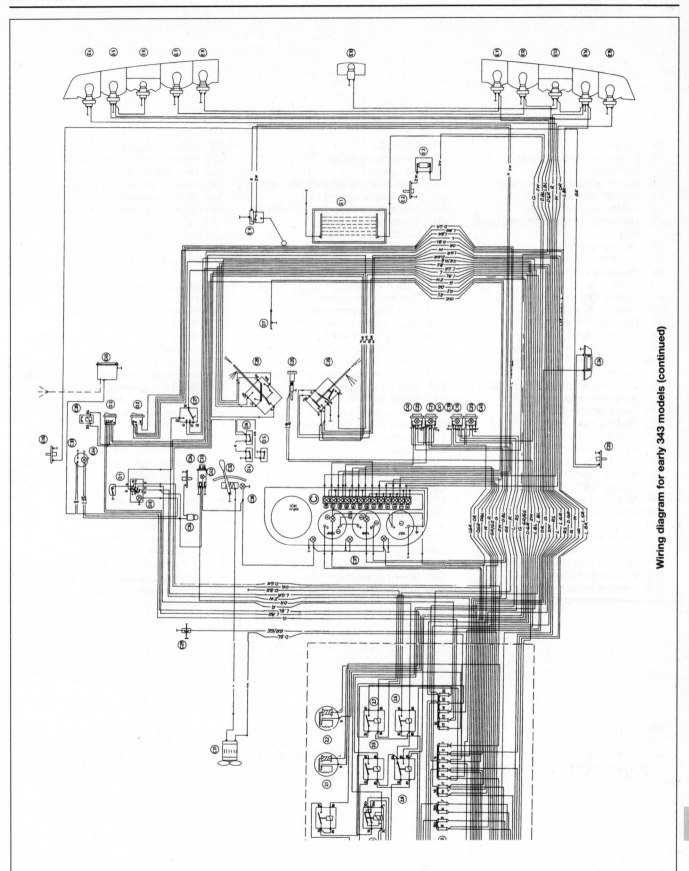

Wiring diagram for early 343 models (continued)

12

Key to wiring diagram for 1979 models

1.0	Battery	C1	Clock (DL)	C37	Instrument lighting
2.0	Central fuse and relay box	C2	Temperature gauge	C38	Blower switch illumination
2.3	Horn relay	C3	Fuel gauge	C39	Horn switch (DL)
2.4	Main beam/dipped beam relay	C4	Coolant temperature warning light	C40	Heater controls illumination
2.6	Start inhibitor relay (CVT)	C5	Fuel reserve warning light	C41	Blower resistance
2.7	Heated rear window relay	C6	Direction indicator warning light (left)	C43	Cigar lighter illumination
A1	Headlamp main beam/dipped beam (left)	C7	Charge warning light	C44	Lighting switch illumination
A2	Parking light (left)	C8	Handbrake warning light	C45	Radio (optional)
A3	Direction indicator (left)	C9	Choke warning light	C46	Brake light switch
A4	Headlamp main beam/dipped beam (right)	C10	Oil pressure warning light	C47	Intermittent wiper relay
A5	Parking light (right)	C11	Brake fluid level warning light	D1	Selector lever switches (CVT)
A6	Direction indicator (right)	C12	Hazard warning light	D2	Low gear hold switch (CVT)
A7	Horn (high-tone)	C13	Seat belt warning light	D3	Hazard warning switch
A8	Horn (low-tone)	C14	Main beam warning light	D4	Seat belt contact (front passenger)
A9	Headlamp wiper motor (Nordic) (left)	C15	Rear foglamp warning light	D5	Seat belt contact (driver)
A10	Headlamp wiper motor (Nordic) (right)	C16	Low gear hold warning light (CVT)	D6	Seat cushion contact front passenger
B2	Washer pump	C17	Heated rear window warning light	D7	Handbrake switch
B3	CVT vacuum control unit (including tachometer relay)	C18	Direction indicator warning light (right)	D8	Selector scale illumination (CVT)
B4	Four-way valve (CVT)	C19	Lighting reminder buzzer (Nordic)	D9	Seat heating element and thermostat
B5	Starter motor	C20	Vehicle lighting switch	D10	Seat heating element
B6	Coolant temperature transmitter/switch	C21	Switch for heated rear window	D11	Reversing light switch (MT)
B7	Declutching servo (CT)	C22	Rear foglamp switch	E1	Heated rear window
B8	Hydraulic switch on brake master cylinder (CVT)	C23	Courtesy light door switch (left)	E2	Boot light switch
B9	Brake fluid level float	C24	Courtesy light	E3	Boot light
B10	Ignition coil	C25	Choke	E4	Direction indicator (right)
B11	Oil pressure transmitter/switch	C26	Direction indicator switch	E5	Tail/brake light (right)
B12	Alternator and voltage regulator	C27	Ignition switch	E6	Tail light (right)
B13	Three-way (Sweden)	C28	Windscreen wash/wipe switch	E7	Rear foglamp (right)
B14	Electrical pilot jet	C29	Kickdown switch (CVT)	E8	Reversing light (right)
B15	Windscreen wiper motor	C30	Parking light warning light	E9	Fuel tank float
B16	Direction repeater lamp (left)	C31	Blower motor	E10	Number plate light
B17	Direction repeater lamp (right)	C32	Blower switch	E11	Reversing light (left)
		C33	Cigar lighter	E12	Rear foglamp (left)
		C34	Switch for glove compartment light	E13	Tail light (left)
		C35	Glove compartment light	E14	Tail/brake light (left)
		C36	Combined direction/hazard flasher unit	E15	Direction indicator (left)
				E16	Courtesy light door switch (right)

Colour code

dBl	Light blue	Gr	Grey	lGn	Light green	SB	Black
dBr	Light brown	L	Lilac	Or	Orange	W	White
dGn	Light green	lBl	Light blue	P	Pink	Y	Yellow
Gn/Y	Green/yellow	lBr	Light brown	R	Red		

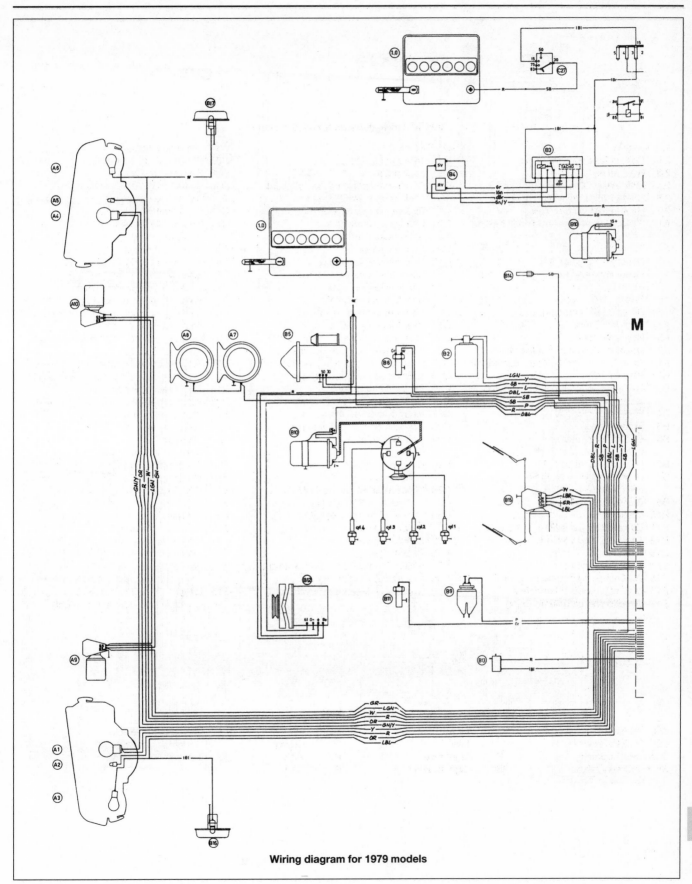

Wiring diagram for 1979 models

M

12

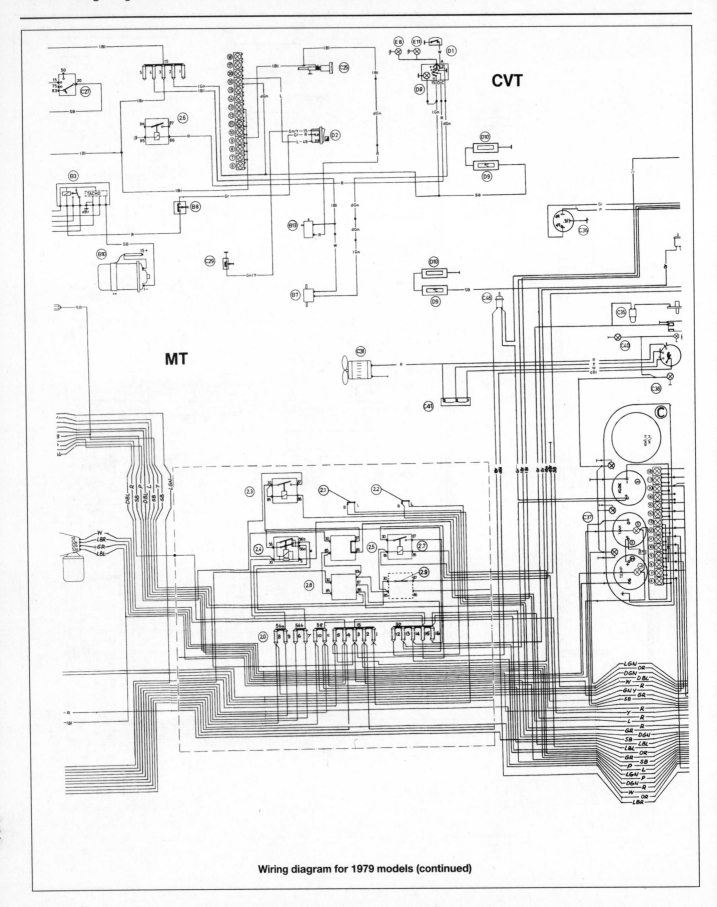

CVT

MT

Wiring diagram for 1979 models (continued)

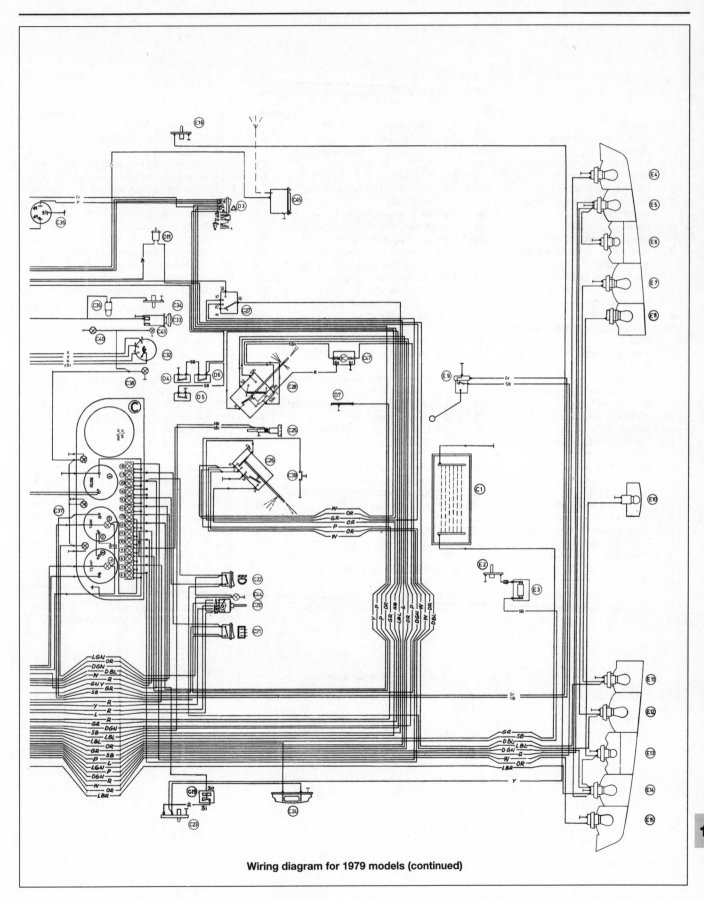

Wiring diagram for 1979 models (continued)

Key to wiring diagram for 1980 models

		Location
1.0	Battery	3c
2.1	Central fuse and relay box	7h
2.3	Horn relay	5h
2.4	Main beam/dipped beam relay	6h
2.6	Start inhibitor relay (CVT)	1g
2.7	Heated rear window relay	6i
A1	Headlight main beam/dipped beam (left)	8a
A2	Parking light (left)	8a
A3	Direction indicator (left)	9a
A4	Headlight main beam/dipped beam (right)	3a
A5	Parking light (right)	3a
A6	Direction indicator (right)	2a
A7	Horn (high-tone)	4c
A8	Horn (low-tone)	4b
A9	Headlamp wiper motor (Nordic) (left)	7a
A10	Headlamp wiper motor (Nordic) (right)	4a
B2	Washer pump	4e
B3	CVT vacuum control unit (including tachometer relay)	2f
B4	Four-way valve (CVT)	2e
B5	Starter motor	4c
B6	Coolant temperature transmitter/switch	4d
B7	Declutching servo (CVT)	3h
B8	Hydraulic switch on brake master cylinder (CVT)	2g
B9	Brake fluid level float	7e
B10	Ignition coil	5c
B11	Oil pressure transmitter/switch	7d
B12	Alternator and voltage regulator	7c
B13	Three-way valve (Sweden)	7e
B14	Electrical pilot jet	3f
B15	Windscreen wiper motor	6g
B16	Direction repeater lamp (left)	9b
B17	Direction repeater lamp (right)	2b
C1	Clock (DL)	5m

		Location
C2	Temperature gauge	6m
C3	Fuel gauge	6m
C4	Coolant temperature warning light	6m
C5	Fuel reserve warning light	6m
C6	Direction indicator warning light (left)	6m
C7	Charge warning light	6m
C8	Handbrake warning light	6m
C9	Choke warning light	6m
C10	Oil pressure warning light	6m
C11	Brake fluid level warning light	6m
C12	Hazard warning light	6m
C13	Seat belt warning light	6m
C14	Main beam warning light	5m
C15	Rear foglamp warning light	5m
C16	Low gear hold warning light (CVT)	5m
C17	Heated rear window warning light	5m
C18	Direction indicator warning light (right)	5m
C19	Lighting reminder buzzer (Nordic)	8m
C20	Vehicle lighting switch	6n
C21	Switch for heated rear window	7n
C22	Rear foglamp switch	6n
C23	Courtesy light door switch (left)	9m
C24	Courtesy light	8o
C25	Choke	5n
C26	Direction indicator switch	5n
C27	Ignition switch	3n
C28	Windscreen wash/wipe switch	4n
C29	Kickdown switch (CVT)	3h
C30	Parking light warning light	5m
C31	Blower motor	4i
C32	Blower switch	4m
C33	Cigar lighter	4m
C34	Switch for glove compartment light	3m
C35	Glove compartment light	3m
C36	Combined direction/hazard flasher unit	3k

		Location
C37	Instrument lighting	5k
C38	Blower switch illumination	4m
C39	Horn switch	5o
C40	Heater controls illumination	4m
C41	Blower resistances	4j
C43	Cigar lighter illumination	4m
C44	Lighting switch illumination	6n
C45	Radio (optional)	2n
C46	Brake light switch	3j
C47	Intermittent wiper relay	4o
D1	Selector lever switches (CVT)	1j
D2	Low gear hold switch (CVT)	2i
D3	Hazard warning switch	2n
D4	Seat belt contact (front passenger)	4m
D5	Seat belt contact (driver)	4m
D6	Seat cushion contact (front passenger)	4n
D7	Handbrake switch	4o
D8	Selector scale (CVT)	1j
D9	Seat heating element and thermostat	3j
D10	Seat heating element	3j
D11	Reversing lights switch (MT)	3m
E1	Heated rear window	5p
E2	Boot light switch	6q
E3	Boot light	6q
E4	Direction indicator (right)	2r
E5	Tail/brake light (right)	2r
E6	Tail/light (right)	3r
E7	Rear foglamp (right)	3r
E8	Reversing light (right)	3r
E9	Fuel tank float	4p
E10	Number plate light	5r
E11	Reversing light (left)	7r
E12	Rear foglamp (left)	7r
E13	Tail light (left)	8r
E14	Tail/brake light (left)	8r
E14	Direction indicator (left)	8r
E16	Courtesy light door switch (right)	2m

Colour code

dBl	Dark blue	Gr	Grey	lGn	Light green	SB	Black
dBr	Dark brown	L	Lilac	Or	Orange	W	White
dGn	Dark green	lBl	Light blue	P	Pink	Y	Yellow
Gn/Y	Green/yellow	lbr	Light brown	R	Red		

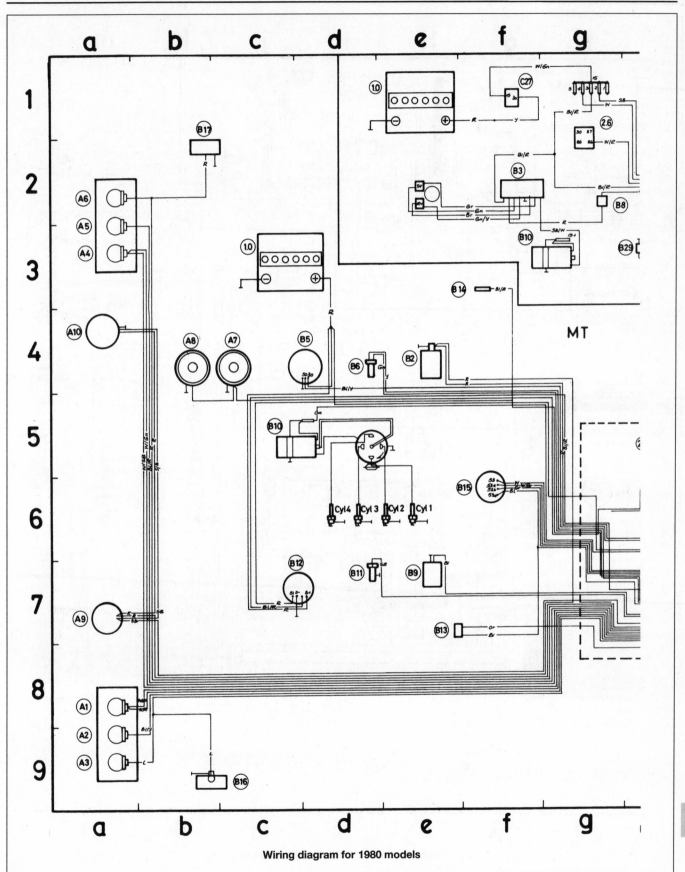

Wiring diagram for 1980 models

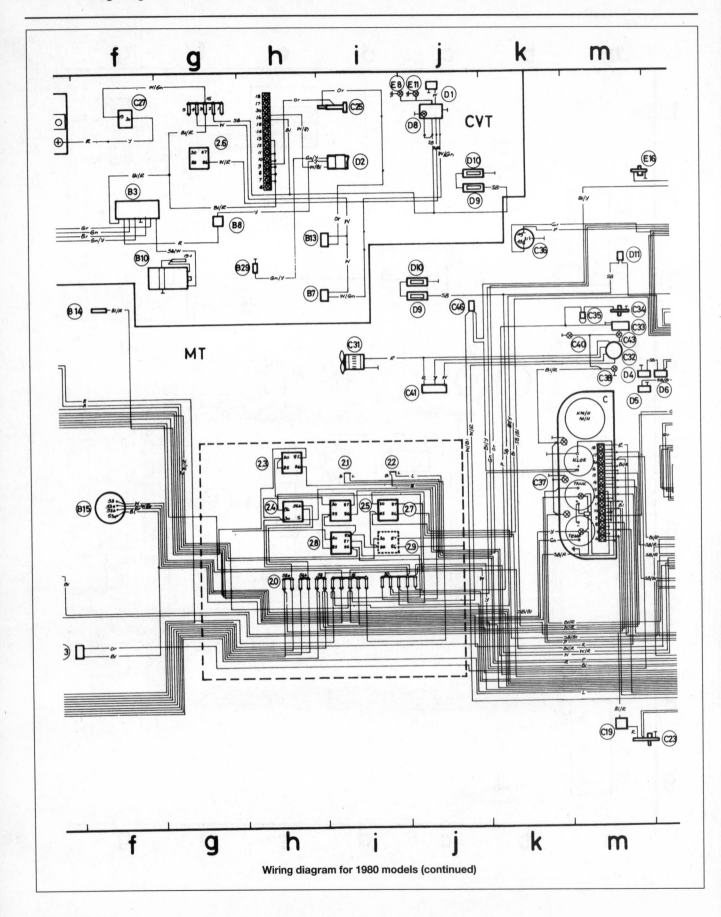

Wiring diagram for 1980 models (continued)

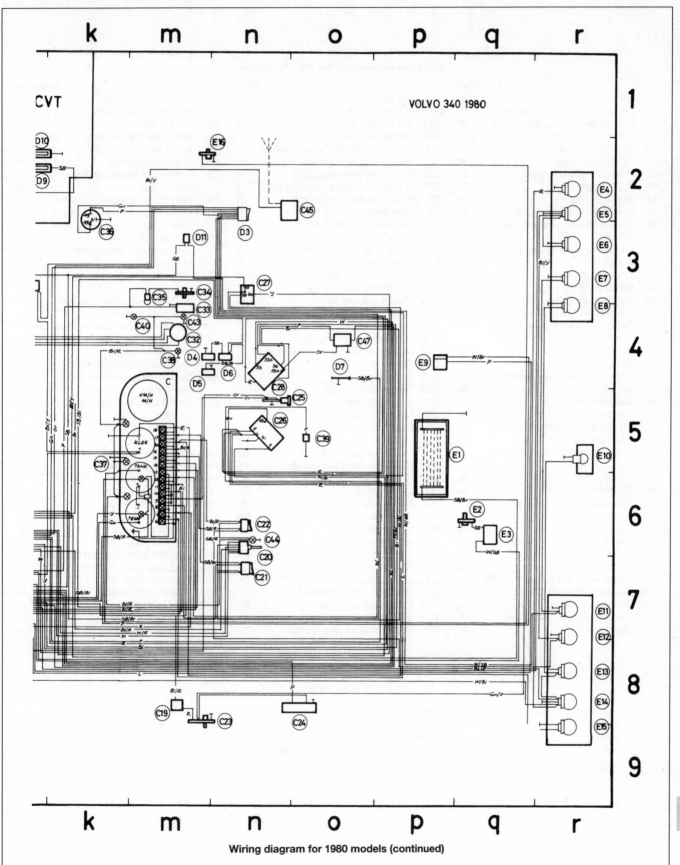

Wiring diagram for 1980 models (continued)

Ket to wiring diagram for 1981 B14 models

		Location				Location				Location
1.0	Battery	1b	B18	Not applicable			D17	Rear foglamp switch		9m
2.1	Central junction box/fuse box	2h	B19	Not applicable			E1	Heater blower motor		5g
2.1	Main beam/dipped beam relay	4f	B20	Not applicable			E2	Blower resistance		5h
2.2	(Connecting strip)	4g	B21	Not applicable			E3	Intermittent wiper relay		6h
2.3	Start inhibitor relay (CVT)	4h	C1	Direction indicator lamp (right)	7i		E4	Kickdown switch, CVT		6h
2.4	"X" contact relay	4i	C2	Heated rear window warning light	7i		E5	Brake light switch		7h
A1	Direction indicator (right)	2a	C3	Parking light warning light	7i		E6	Combined direction/hazard		
A2	Parking light (right)	2a	C4	Low gear hold warning light (CVT)	7i			flasher unit		9h
A3	Headlight (right)	2a	C5	Rear foglamp warning light	7i		E7	Relays, radial blower switch		5h
A4	Horn (high-tone) (not L, DL)	3b	C6	Main beam warning light	7i		F1	Interior light switch (right door)		1m
A5	Headlamp wiper motor (right)		C7	Seat belt warning light	7i		F2	Interior light switch (left door)		9m
	(Nordic)	3a	C8	Hazard warning light	7i		F3	Interior light fitting		5o
A6	Headlamp wiper motor (left)		C9	Brake fluid level warning light	7i		G1	Seat cushion contact (front		
	(Nordic)	7a	C10	Oil pressure warning light	7i			passenger)		3o
A7	Horn (low-tone)	7b	C11	Choke warning light	8i		G2	(CVT) Selector lever panel switch		
A8	Headlamp (left)	8a	C12	Handbrake warning light	8i			and lamp		3n
A9	Parking light (left)	8a	C13	Charge warning light	8i		G2	(MT) Reversing lights switch		3n
A10	Direction indicator (left)	9a	C14	Direction indicator lamp (left)	8i		G3	Low gear hold switch (CVT)		4n
B1	Direction repeater lamp (right)	2d	C15	Lamps, instrument lighting	6i		G4	Seat belt contact (front passenger)		5o
B2	Screen and headlamp washer		C16	Fuel reserve warning light	7i		G5	Hazard warning switch		5n
	pump	3d	C17	Coolant temperature warning light	8i		G6	Handbrake switch		5o
B2	Not applicable		C18	Clock	7i		G7	Seat belt contact (driver)		6o
B3	Coolant temperature sensor/		C19	Fuel gauge	7i		G8	Seat heating elements and		
	switch	4d	C20	Temperature gauge	8i			thermostat		6o
B3	Not applicable		C21	Not applicable			G9	Declutching servo switch (CVT)		4n
B4	Electrical pilot jet	4d	C22	Not applicable			H1	Direction indicator light (rear right)		2q
B5	Oil pressure sensor/switch	5d	D1	Switch for glove compartment			H2	Tail/brake light (right)		2q
B6	Four-way valve (CVT)	5g		light	3m		H3	Tail light (right)		2q
B7	Alternator and voltage regulator	6b	D2	Glove compartment light	3m		H4	Rear foglamp (right)		3q
B7	Not applicable		D3	Heater controls illumination	5m		H5	Reversing light (right)		3q
B8	Distributor	6c	D4	Cigar lighter illumination	5m		H6	Number plate light (right)		5r
B9	Brake fluid level float	6e	D5	Cigar lighter	5m		H7	Number plate light (left)		5r
B10	CVT vacuum control unit		D6	Radio (optional)	5n		H8	Reversing light (left)		7q
	(including		D7	Blower switch illumination	5m		H9	Rear foglamp (left)		8q
	tachometer relay)	6g	D8	Blower switch	5m		H10	Tail light (left)		8q
B11	Hydraulic switch, brake master		D9	Ignition switch	6m		H11	Tail/brake light (left)		9q
	cylinder (CVT)	7e	D10	Windscreen wash/wipe switch	6m		H12	Direction indicator light (rear left)		9q
B12	Ignition coil	7g	D11	Choke	7m		H13	Boot light		2p
B13	Three-way valve (Sweden 1980)	7c	D12	Horn switch	7o		H14	Fuel tank float		4p
B14	Declutching servo (CVT)	7d	D13	Direction indicator switch	7m		H15	Heated rear window		5p
B15	Windscreen wiper motor	8g	D14	Vehicle lighting switch	8m		H16	Boot light switch		8p
B16	Direction repeater lamp (left)	9d	D15	Vehicle lighting switch illumination	9m		H17	Tailgate stay (left)		2p
B17	Starter motor	4c	D16	Rear window heater switch	9m		H18	Tailgate stay (right)		8p

Colour code

dBl	Dark blue		lBl	Light blue		Gr	Grey		SB	Black
dBr	Dark brown		lBr	Light brown		Or	Orange		W	White
dGn	Dark green		lGn	Light green		P	Pink		Y	Yellow
L	Lilac		Gn/Y	Green/yellow		R	Red			

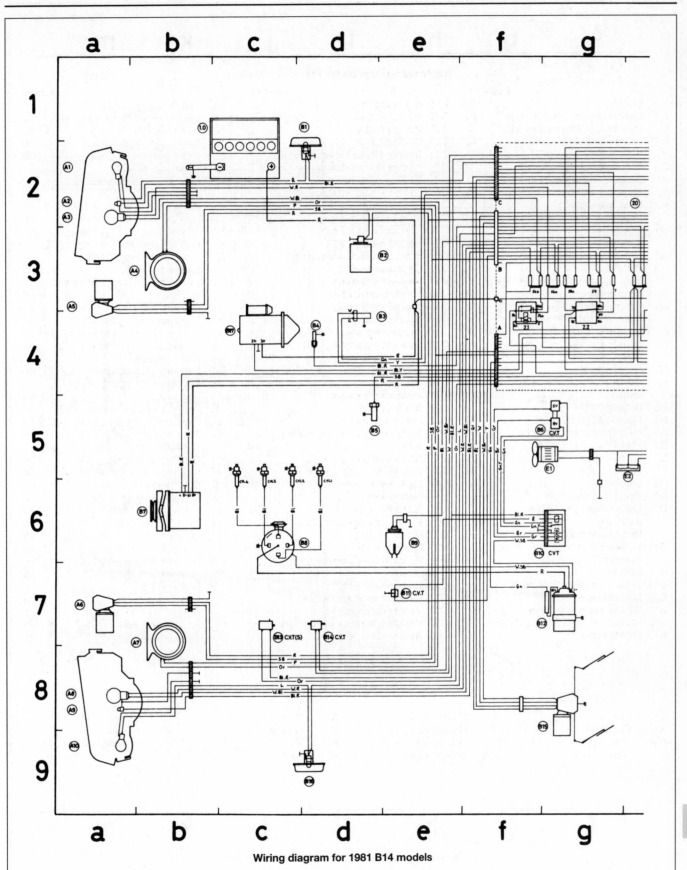

Wiring diagram for 1981 B14 models

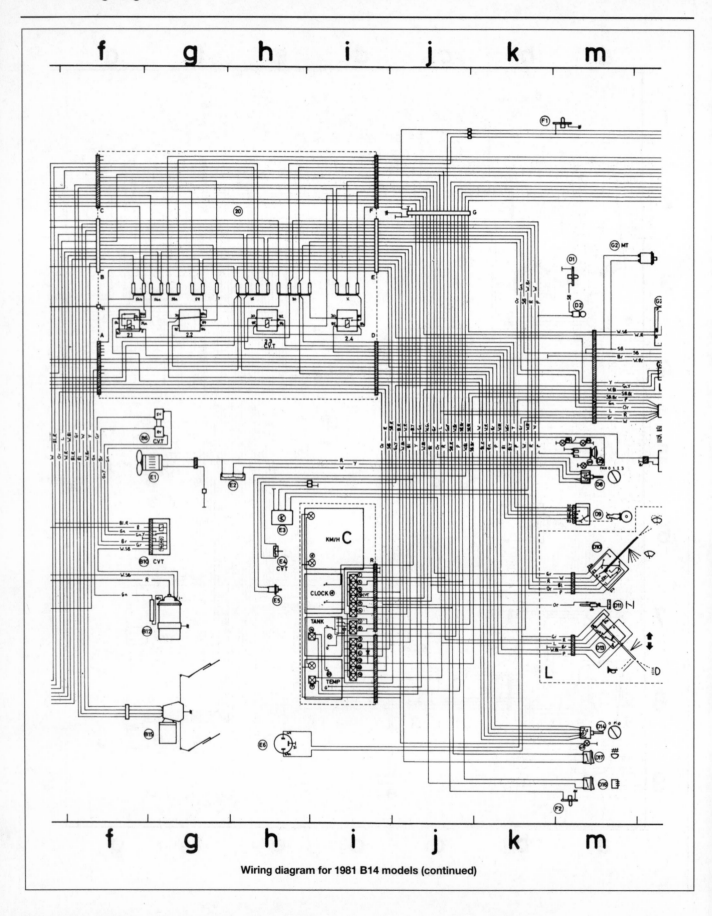

Wiring diagram for 1981 B14 models (continued)

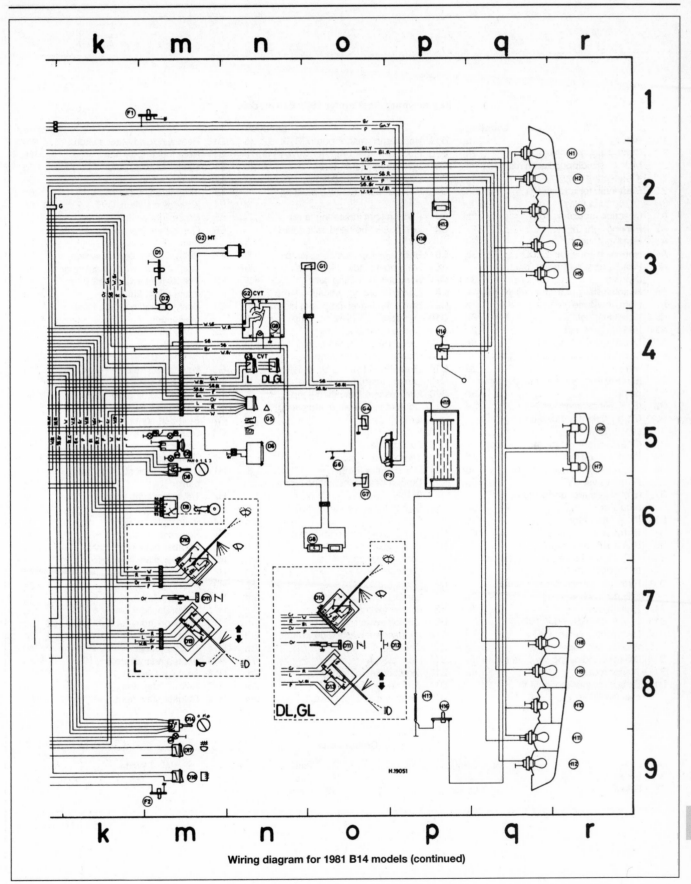

Wiring diagram for 1981 B14 models (continued)

H.19051

Key to wiring diagram for 1981 B19 models

		Location
1.0	Battery	1b
2.1	Central junction box/fuse box	2h
2.1	Main beam/dipped beam relay	4f
2.2	(Connecting strip)	4g
2.3	Start inhibitor relay (CVT)	4h
2.4	"X" contact relay	4i
A1	Direction indicator, right	2a
A2	Parking light, right	2a
A3	Headlight, right	2a
A4	Horn high-tone (not L, DL)	3b
A5	Headlamp wiper motor, right (Nordic)	3a
A6	Headlamp wiper motor, left (Nordic)	7a
A7	Horn, low-tone	7b
A8	Headlamp, left	8a
A9	Parking light, left	8a
A10	Direction indicator, left	9a
B1	Direction indicating lamp, right wing	2d
B2	(B14) Screen and headlamp washer pump	3d
B2	(B19) Windscreen washer pump	3d
B3	(B14) Coolant temperature sensor/switch	4d
B3	(B19) Coolant temperature sensor	4d
B4	Electrical pilot jet	4d
B5	Oil pressure sensor/switch	5d
B6	4-way valve, CVT	5g
B7	(B14) Alternator and voltage regulator	6b
B7	(B19) Alternator	4b
B8	Distributor	6c
B9	Brake fluid level float	6e
B10	CVT vacuum control unit (including tachometric relay)	6g
B11	Hydraulic switch, brake master cylinder CVT	7e
B12	Ignition coil	7g
B13	3-way valve (Sweden 1980)	7c
B14	Declutching servo, CVT	7d
B15	Windscreen wiper motor	8g
B16	Direction indicating lamp, left wing	9d
B17	Starter motor	4c
B18	Ballast resistor (on ignition coil) (B19)	7f

		Location
B19	Headlamp washer pump (B19)	3d
B20	Float chamber breather valve (B19)	7e
B21	Voltage regulator (B19)	2c
C1	Direction indicating lamp, right	7i
C2	Heated rear window indicating lamp	7i
C3	Parking light indicating lamp	7i
C4	Low "gear" hold indicating lamp, CVT	7i
C5	Rear foglamp indicating lamp	7i
C6	Main beam indicating lamp	7i
C7	Seat belt indicating lamp	7i
C8	Hazard warning indicating lamp	7i
C9	Brake fluid level indicating lamp	7i
C10	Oil pressure indicating lamp	7i
C11	Choke indicating lamp	8i
C12	Handbrake indicating lamp	8i
C13	Charge indicating lamp	8i
C14	Direction indicating lamp, left	8i
C15	Lamps, instrument lighting	6i
C16	Fuel/reserve indicating lamp	7i
C17	Coolant temperature indicating lamp	8i
C18	Clock	7i
C19	Fuel gauge	7i
C20	Temperature gauge	8i
C21	Rev counter (B19)	8i
C22	Dipped beams indicating lamp (B19)	7i
D1	Switch for glove compartment light	3m
D2	Lamp, glove compartment light	3m
D3	Lamp, heater controls	5m
D4	Lamp, cigar lighter	5m
D5	Cigar lighter	5m
D6	Radio (optional)	5n
D7	Lamp, blower switch	5m
D8	Blower switch	5m
D9	Ignition switch	6m
D10	Windscreen wash/wipe switch	6m
D11	Choke	7m
D12	Horn switch	7o
D13	Direction indicator switch	7m
D14	Vehicle lighting switch	8m
D15	Lamp, vehicle light switch	9m

		Location
D16	Rear window heater switch	9m
D17	Rear foglamp switch	9m
E1	Heater blower motor	5g
E2	Blower resistances	5h
E3	Intermittent wiper relay	6h
E4	Kickdown switch, CVT	6h
E5	Brake light switch	7h
E6	Combined direction/hazard flasher unit	9h
E7	Relays, radial blower switch	5h
F1	Interior light switch, right door	1m
F2	Interior light switch, left door	9m
F3	Interior light fitting	5o
G1	Seat cushion contact, front passenger	3o
G2	(CVT) Selector lever panel switch and lamp	3n
G2	(MT) Reversing light switch	3n
G3	Low "gear" hold switch, CVT	4n
G4	Seat belt contact, front passenger	5o
G5	Hazard warning switch	5o
G6	Handbrake switch	5o
G7	Seat belt contact, driver	6o
G8	Seat heating elements and thermostat	6o
G9	Declutching servo switch, CVT	4n
H1	Direction indicator light (rear), right	2q
H2	Tail/brake light, right	2q
H3	Tail light, right	2q
H4	Rear foglamp, right	3q
H5	Reversing light, right	3q
H6	Number plate light, right	5r
H7	Number plate light, left	5r
H8	Reversing light, left	7q
H9	Rear foglamp, left	8q
H10	Tail light, left	8q
H11	Tail/brake light, left	9q
H12	Direction indicator light (rear), left	9q
H13	Boot light lamp	2p
H14	Fuel tank float	4p
H15	Heated rear window	5p
H16	Boot light switch	8p
H17	Tailgate stay, left	8p
H18	Tailgate stay, right	8p

Colour code

Bl	Blue	Gr	Grey	P	Pink	W	White
Br	Brown	L	Lilac	R	Red	Y	Yellow
Gn	Green	Or	Orange	SB	Black		

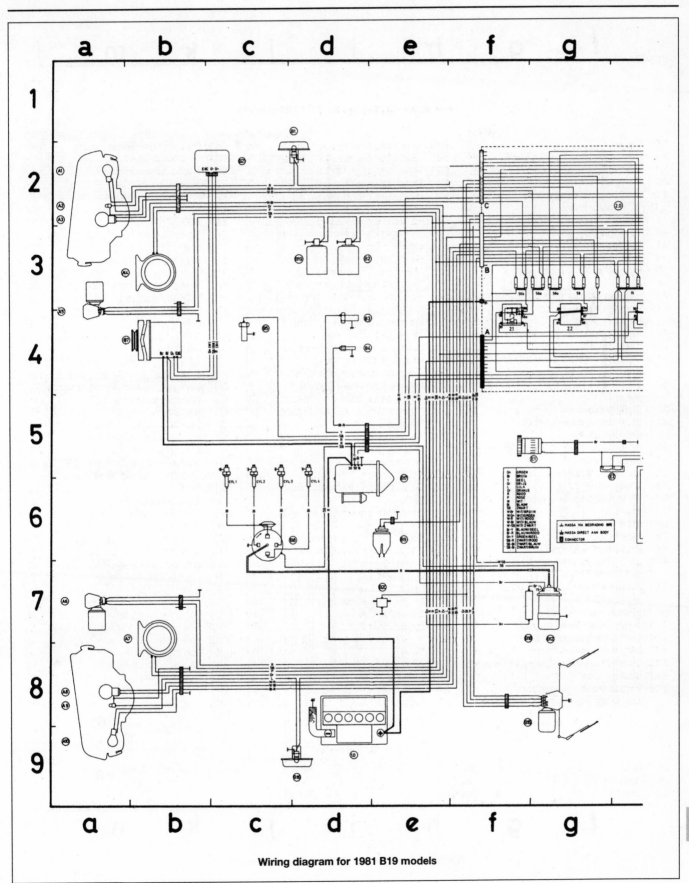

Wiring diagram for 1981 B19 models

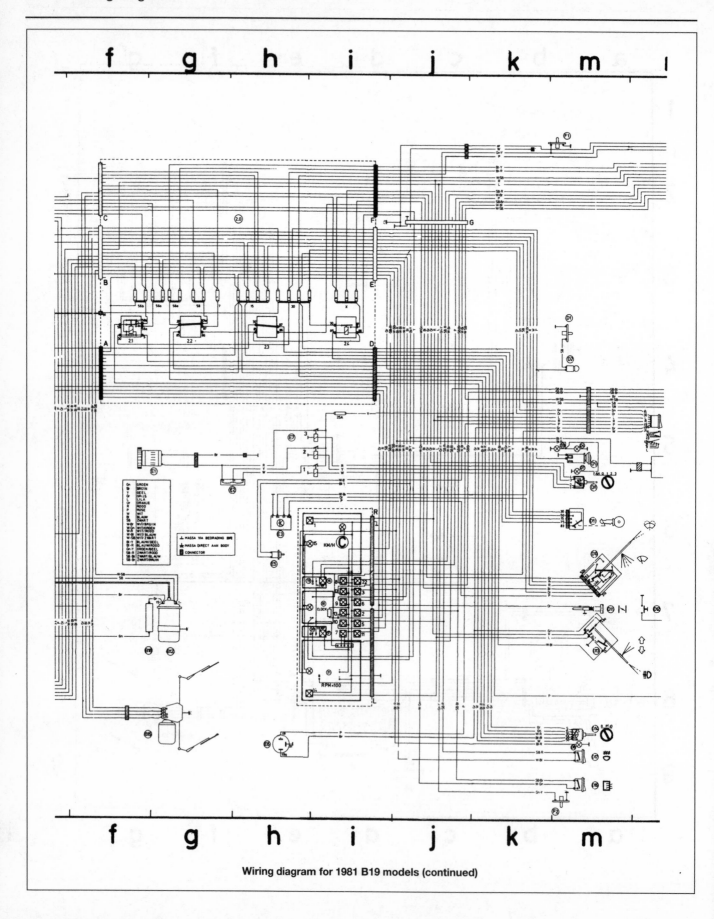

Wiring diagram for 1981 B19 models (continued)

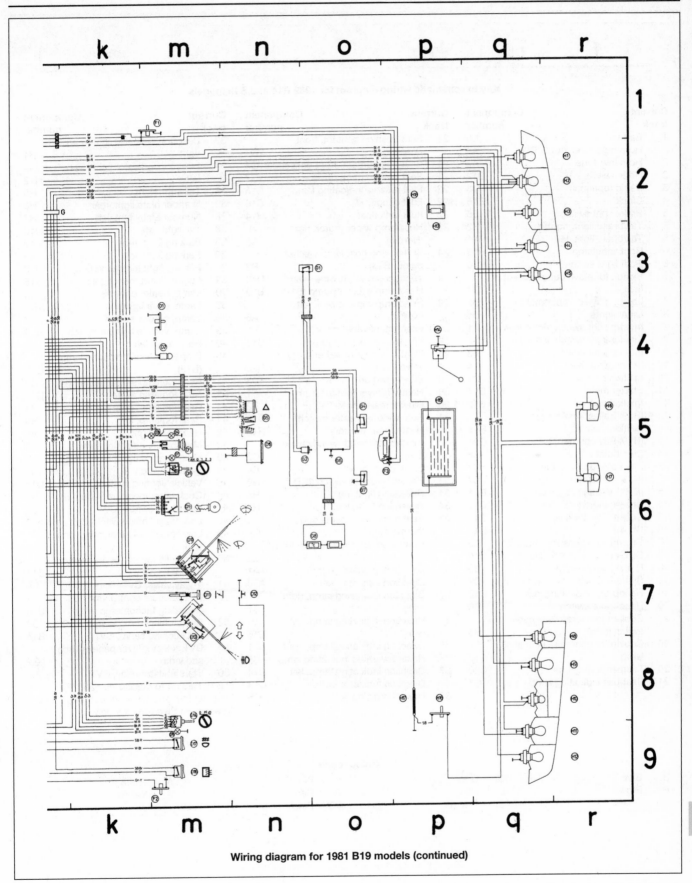

Wiring diagram for 1981 B19 models (continued)

Key to schematic wiring diagram for 1982 B14 and B19 models

Current track		Component number	Current track		Component number	Current track		Component number
1	Battery	1.0	21	Seat cushion contact, front passenger	G1	37	Direction indicator light (rear), right	H1
2	Horn high-tone (not L, DL)	A4	21	Seat belt contact, front passenger	G4	37	Direction indicator light (rear), left	H12
2	Horn low-tone	A7	21	Seat belt contact, driver	G7	38	Tail light, right	H3
2	Horn switch	D12	22	Fuel reserve indicating lamp	C16	38	Number plate light, rear	H6
3	Radio (optional)	D6	22	Fuel gauge	C19	38	Number plate light, left	H7
4	Clock	C18	22	Fuel tank float	H14	38	Tail light, left	H10
5	Brake light switch	E5	23	Headlamp wiper motor, right (Nordic)	A5	39	Parking light, rear	A2
5	Tail/brake light, right	H2	24	Screen and headlamp washer pump (B14)	B2	39	Parking light, left	A9
5	Tail/brake light, left	H11	24	Windscreen wash/wipe switch	D10	39	Parking light indicating lamp	C3
6	Boot light lamp	H13	25	Headlamp washer pump (B19)	B19	39	Lamps, instrument lighting	C15
6	Boot light switch	H16	26	Headlamp wiper motor, left (Nordic)	A6	39	Lamp, heater controls	D3
7	Switch for glove compartment light	D1	27	Intermittent wiper relay	E3	39	Lamp, cigar lighter	D4
7	Lamp, glove compartment	D2	28	Windscreen wiper motor	B15	39	Lamp, blower switch	D7
8	Cigar lighter	D5	29	Float chamber breather valve (B19)	B20	39	Lamp, vehicle lighting switch	D15
9	Interior light switch, right door	F1	30	Blower switch	D8	40	Headlamp, left	A8
9	Interior light switch, left door	F2	30	Heater blower motor	E1	40	Dipped beams indicating lamp (B19)	C22
9	Interior light fitting	F3	30	Blower resistances	E2	41	Rear foglamp indicating lamp	C5
10	"X" contact relay	2.4	31	Rear window heater switch	D16	41	Rear foglamp switch	D17
10	Ignition switch	D9	31	Heated rear window	H15	41	Rear foglamp, right	H4
11	Starter motor	B17	32	Heated rear window indicating lamp	C2	41	Rear foglamp, left	H9
12	Ignition coil	B12	33	Electrical pilot jet	B4	42	Headlight, right	A3
12	(B19) Ballast resistor (on ignition coil)	B18	34	Reversing lights switch (MT)	G2	42	Main beam indicating lamp	C6
13	(B19) Rev counter	C21	34	Reversing light, right	H5	43	Main beam/dipped beam relay	2.1
14	Distributor	B8	34	Reversing light, left	H8	44	Ignition switch	D9
15	Alternator and voltage regulator	B7	35	Seat heating elements and thermostat	G8	45	Vehicle lighting switch	D14
15	(B19* Alternator	B7	36	Combined direction/hazard flasher unit	E6	46	Coolant temperature sensor (B19)	B3
15	(B19*) Voltage regulator	B21	37	Direction indicator, right	A1	47	Kickdown switch, CVT	E4
15	Charge indicating lamp	C13	37	Direction indicator, left	A10	48	Low "gear" hold switch, CVT	G3
16	Choke indicating lamp	C11	37	Direction indicating lamp, right wing	B1	49	Low "gear" hold indicating lamp, CVT	C4
16	Choke	D11	37	Direction indicating lamp, left wing	B16	50	Hydraulic switch, brake master cylinder, CVT	B11
17	Oil pressure sensor/switch	B5	37	Direction indicating lamp, right	C1	51	4-way valve, CVT	B6
17	Oil pressure indicating lamp	C10	37	Hazard warning indicating lamp	C8	52	CVT vacuum control unit (including tachometric relay)	B10
18	Brake fluid level float	B9	37	Direction indicating lamp, left	C14	53	Declutching servo switch, CVT	G9
18	Brake fluid level indicating lamp	C9	37	Direction indicator switch	D13	54	Declutching servo, CVT	B14
19	Handbrake indicating lamp	C12	37	Hazard warning switch	G5	55	CVT selector lever panel switch and lamp	G2
19	Handbrake switch	G6				56	Start inhibitor relay, CVT	2.3
20	Coolant temperature sensor/switch (B14)	B3						
20	Coolant temperature indicating lamp	C17						
20	Temperature gauge	C20						
21	Seat belt indicating lamp	C7						

*B19 cars up to chassis no 629517

The wiring shown with a broken line is present on Swedish cars only

Colour code

Bl	Blue	Gr	Grey	P	Pink	W	White
Br	Brown	L	Lilac	R	Red	Y	Yellow
Gn	Green	Or	Orange	SB	Black		

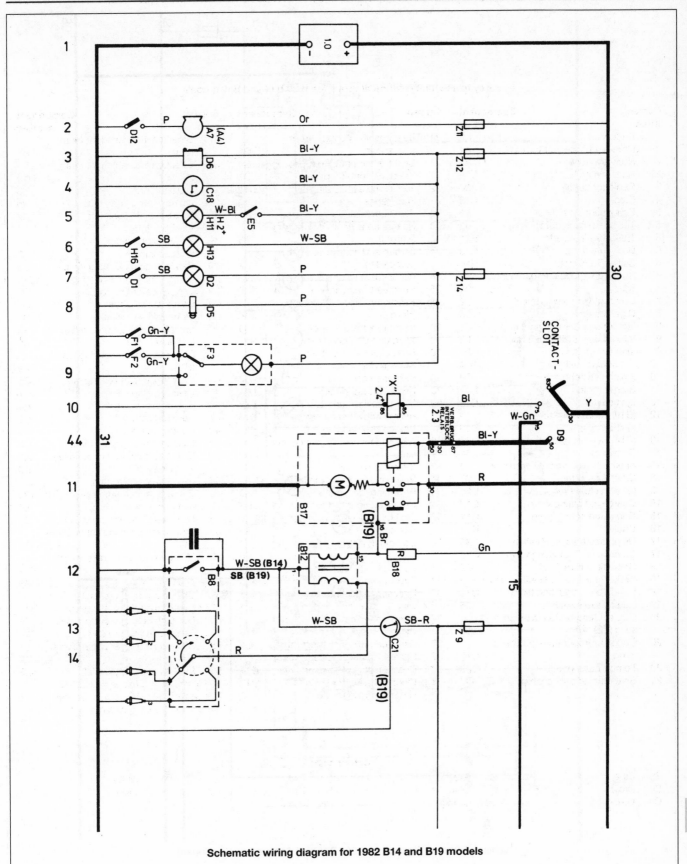

Schematic wiring diagram for 1982 B14 and B19 models

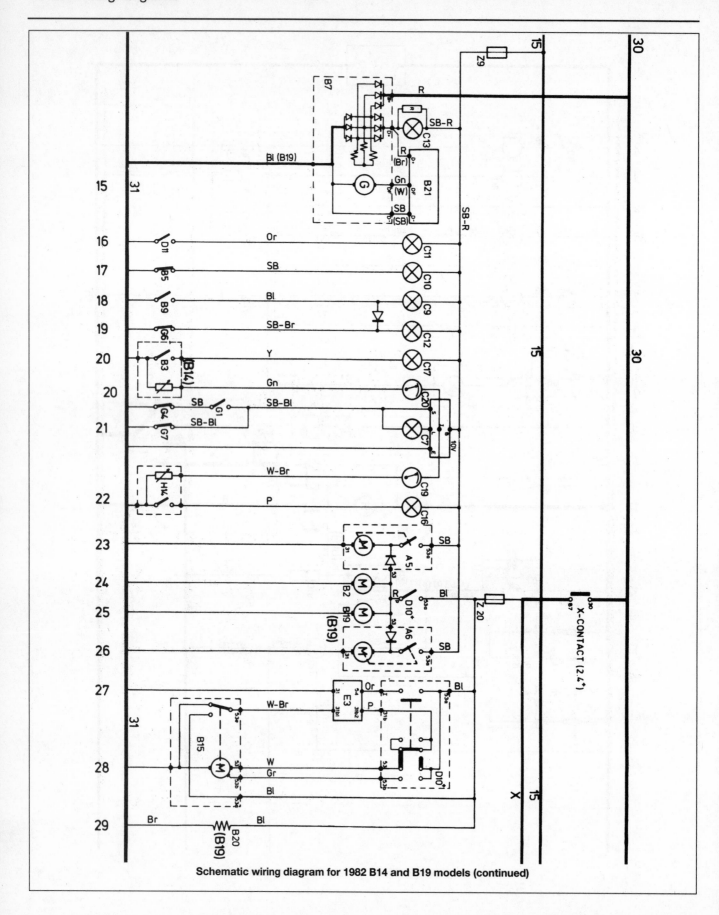

Schematic wiring diagram for 1982 B14 and B19 models (continued)

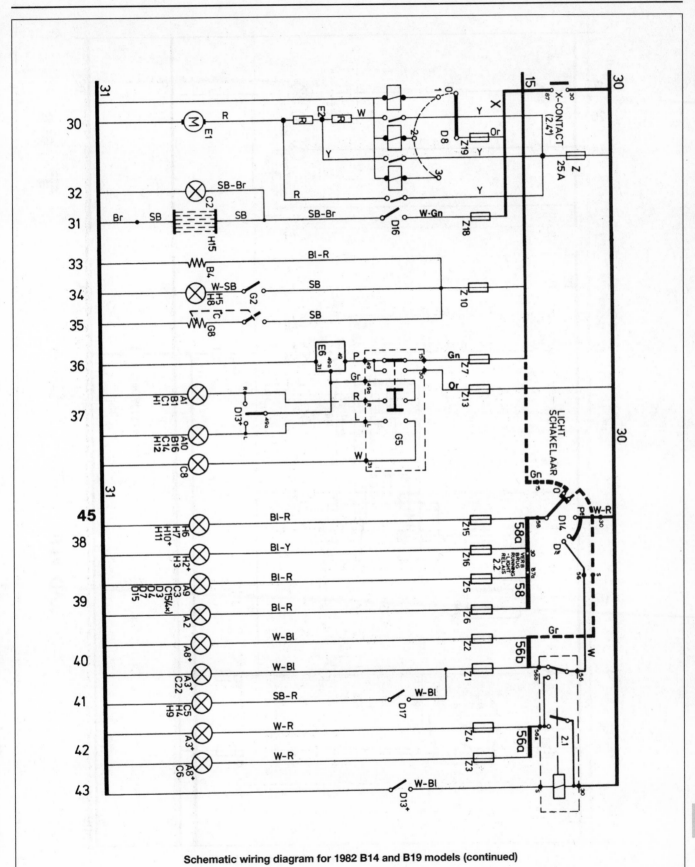

Schematic wiring diagram for 1982 B14 and B19 models (continued)

12

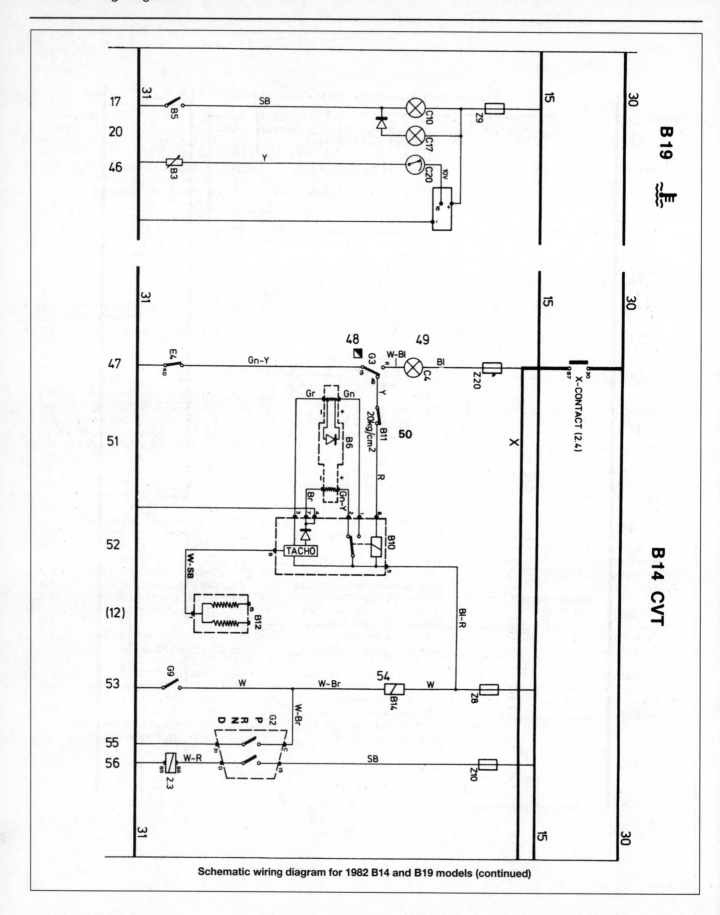

Schematic wiring diagram for 1982 B14 and B19 models (continued)

Key to all wiring diagrams for 1983 B14 and B19 models

Current track		Component number
1	Battery	1.0
2	Horn	A7
2	Horn switch	D12
3	Radio connection	D6
4	Cigar lighter	D5
5	Clock	(D21) C18
6	Brake light switch	E5
6	Tail/brake light, right	H2
6	Tail/brake light, left	H11
7	Boot light lamp	H13
7	Boot light switch	H16
8	Switch for glove compartment light	D1
8	Lamp, glove compartment	D2
9	Interior light switch, right door	F1
9	Interior light switch, left door	F2
9	Interior light fitting	F3
9	Lamp, ignition switch light	D22
10	Ignition switch	D9
10	"X" contact relay	2.4
11	Starter motor	B17
12	Ignition coil	B12
12	Ballast resistor (on ignition coil)	B19A B18
13	Rev counter (360)	C21
14	Distributor	B8
15	Alternator and voltage regulator	B7
15	Battery charge indicating lamp	C13
16	Choke indicating lamp	C11
16	Choke	D11
17	Oil pressure sensor/switch	B5
17	Oil pressure indicating lamp	C10
18	Brake fluid level float	B9
18	Brake fluid level indicating lamp	C9
19	Handbrake indicating lamp	C12
19	Handbrake switch	G6
20	Fuel reserve indicating lamp	C16
20	Fuel gauge	C19
20	Fuel tank float	H14
21	Coolant temperature sensor	B3
21	Coolant temperature indicating lamp	C17
21	Temperature gauge	C20
22	Seat belt indicating lamp	C7
22	Seat cushion contact, front passenger	G1
22	Seat belt contact, driver	G7
23	Instrument panel with Multi-function Unit	C7
24	Headlamp wiper motor, right (Nordic)	A5
24	Headlamp wiper motor, left (Nordic)	A6
25	Screen washer pump	B2
25	Windscreen wash/wiper switch	D10
26	Headlamp washer pump (Nordic)	B19
27	Intermittent wiper relay	E3
28	Windscreen wiper motor	B15
29	Float chamber breather valve (B19A)	B20
30	Blower switch	D8
30	Heater blower motor	E1
30	Blower resistances	E2
31	Relay, heater blower motor	E7
32	Rear window heater switch	D16
32	Heated rear window	H15
32	Heated rear window indicating lamp	C2
33	Electrical pilot jet	B4
34	(MT) Reversing lights switch	G2
34	Reversing light, right	H5
34	Reversing light, left	H8
35	Seat heating elements and thermostat	G8
36	Combined direction/hazard flasher unit	E6
37	Direction indicator, right	A1
37	Direction indicator, left	A10
37	Direction indicating lamp, right wing	B1
37	Direction indicating lamp, left wing	B16
37	Direction indicating lamp, right	C1
37	Hazard warning indicating lamp	C8
37	Direction indicating lamp, left	C14
37	Direction indicator switch	D13
37	Hazard warning switch	D19
37	Direction indicator light (rear), right	H1
37	Direction indicator light (rear), left	H12
38	Vehicle lighting switch	D14
39	Tail light, right	H3
39	Number plate light, right	H6
39	Number plate light, left	H7
39	Tail light, left	H10
40	Parking light, left	A9
40	Parking light indicating lamp	C3
40	Lamps, instrument lighting	C15
40	Dimmer switch, instrument lighting	D18
40	Lamp, ashtray lighting	D3
40	Lamp, cigar lighter	D4
40	Lamp, heater controls lighting	D7
40	Lamp, vehicle lighting switch	D15
40	Lamps, illumination switches	D16, D17, D18
41	Parking light, right	A2
42	Headlamp, left, dipped beam	A8
42	Headlight, right, dipped beam	A3
42	Rear foglamp indicating lamp	C5
42	Rear foglamp switch	D17
42	Rear foglamp, right	H4
42	Rear foglamp, left	H9
43	Headlamp, left, main beam	A8
43	Headlamp, right, main beam	A3
43	Main beam indicating lamp	C6
43	Main beam/dipped beam relay	2.1
44	Electronic control unit, LE-Jetronic	J1
45	Control relay, LE-Jetronic	J12
46	Fuel pump, LE-Jetronic	J14
47	Kickdown switch, CVT	E4
48	Low "gear" hold switch, CVT	G3
49	Low "gear" hold indicating lamp, CVT	G3
50	Hydraulic switch, brake master cyl., CVT	B11
51	4-Way valve, CVT	B6
52	CVT vacuum control unit (including tachometric relay)	B10
53	Declutching servo switch, CVT	G9
54	Declutching servo, CVT	B14
55	CVT selector lever panel switch and lamp	G2
56	Start inhibitor relay, CVT	2.3
57	Foglamps (GLT)	-
58	Foglamp relay (GLT)	-
59	Foglamp switch (GLT)	G10
60	Ignition switching unit, B19E	B23
61	Hall pulse transmitter, ignition B19E	B23

The wiring shown with a broken line is present on Swedish cars only

Colour code

Bl	Blue	Gr	Grey	P	Pink	W	White
Br	Brown	L	Lilac	R	Red	Y	Yellow
Gn	Green	Or	Orange	SB	Black		

12

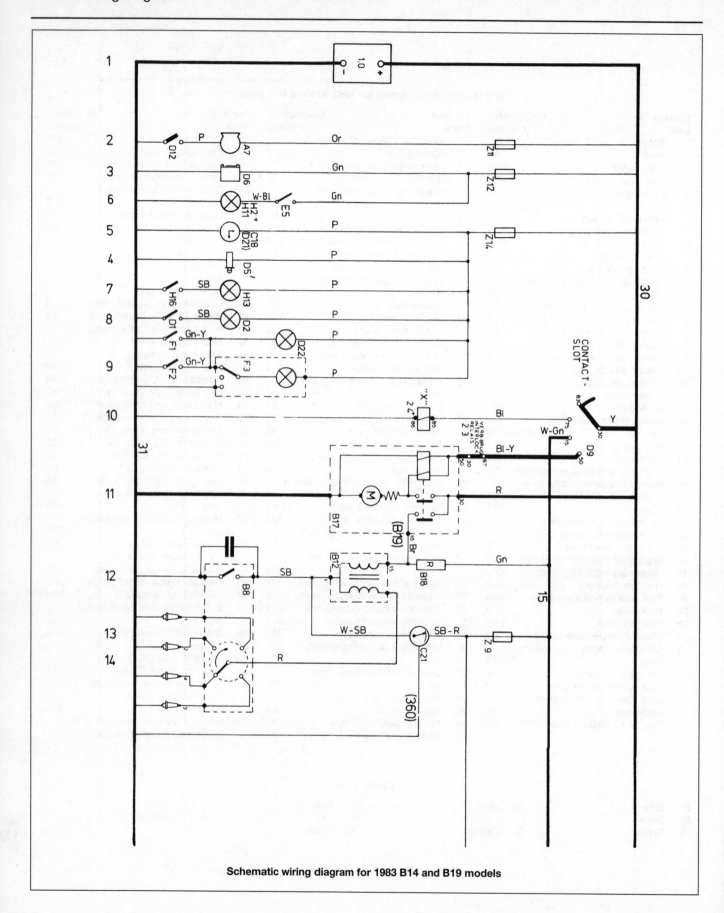

Schematic wiring diagram for 1983 B14 and B19 models

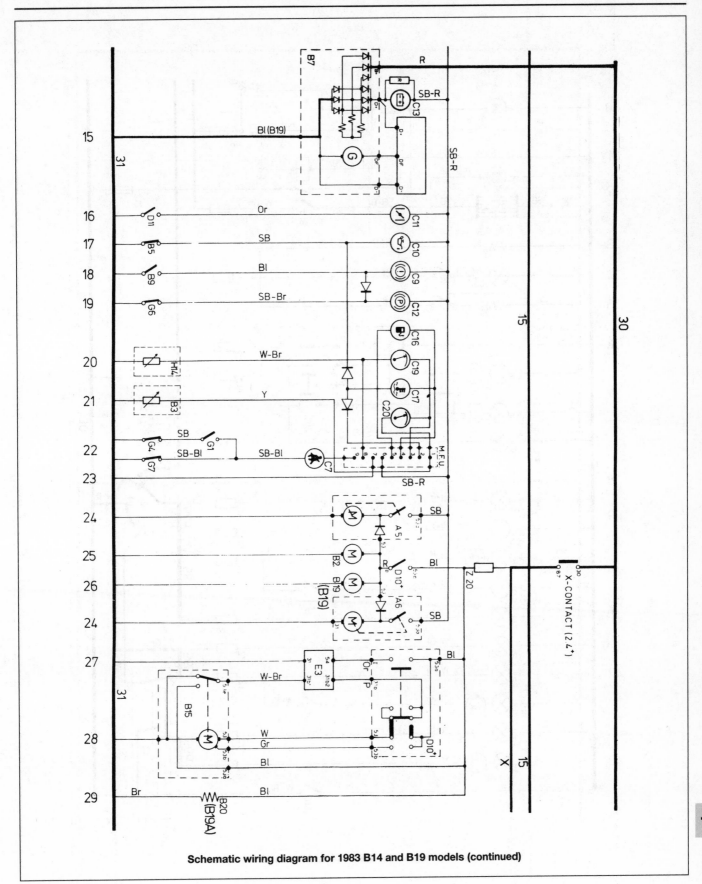

Schematic wiring diagram for 1983 B14 and B19 models (continued)

12

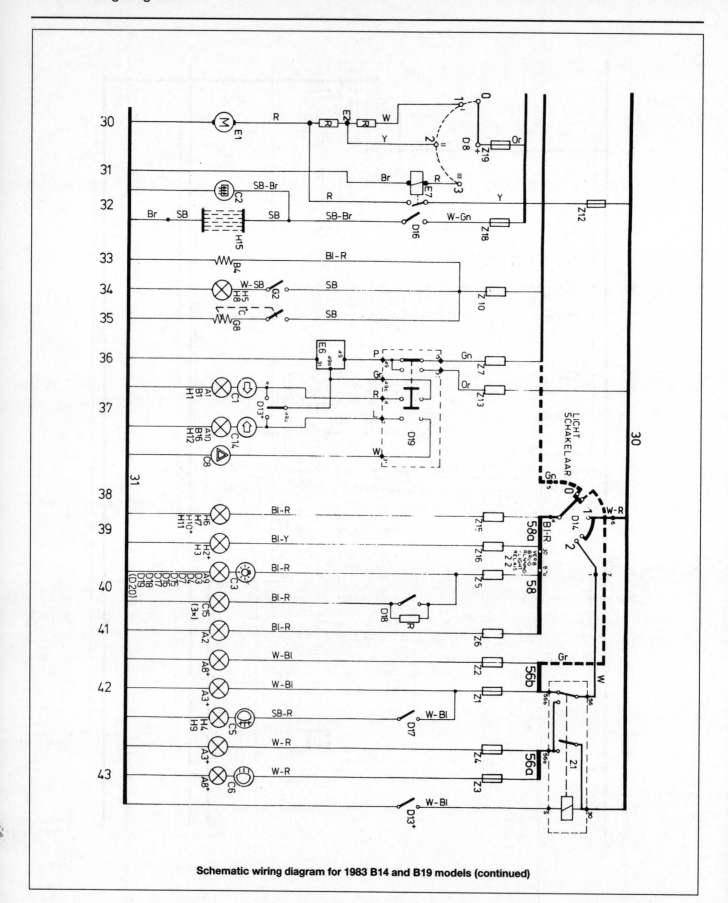

Schematic wiring diagram for 1983 B14 and B19 models (continued)

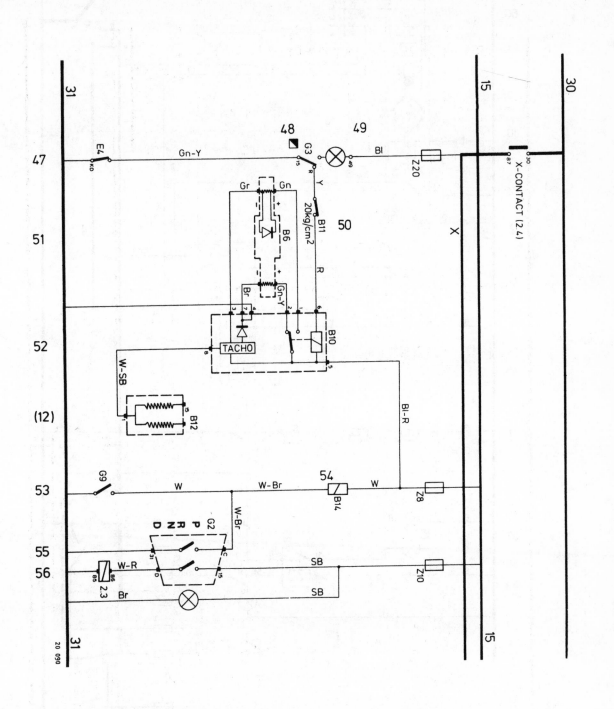

CVT supplement for schematic wiring diagram for 1983 B14 and B19 models

12

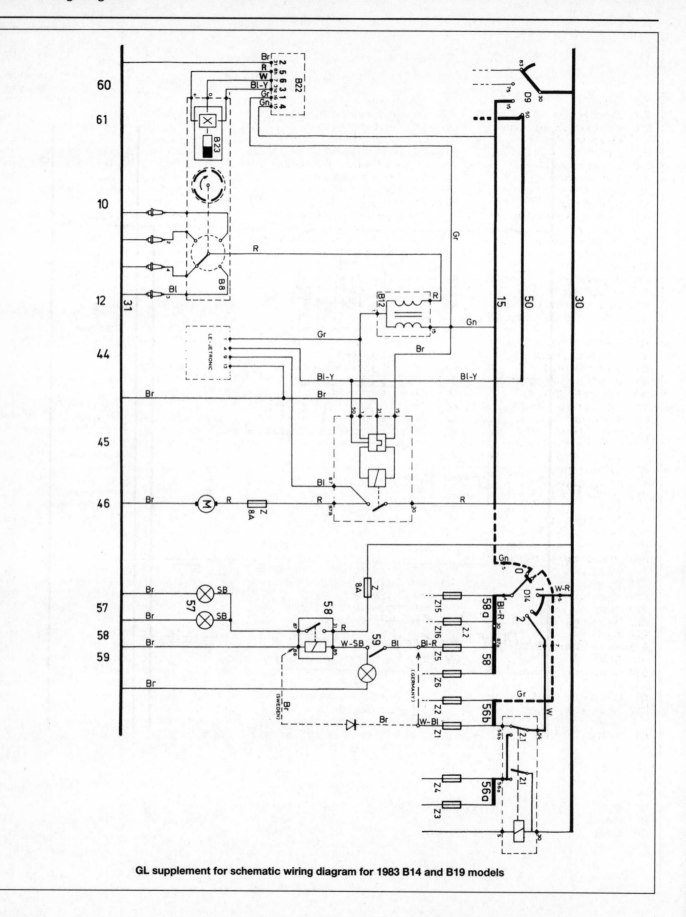

GL supplement for schematic wiring diagram for 1983 B14 and B19 models

Key to all wiring diagrams for 1984 models

		Location (B14 only)
1.0	Battery	1b
2.0	Central junction box/fusebox	2h
2.1	Main beam/dipped beam relay	4f
2.2	(Connecting strip)	4g
2.3	Start inhibitor relay, CVT	4h
2.4	X contact relay	4i
A1	Direction indicator, right	2a
A2	Sidelight, right	2a
A3	Headlight, right	2a
A5	Headlamp wiper motor, right (Nordic)	3a
A6	Headlamp wiper motor, left (Nordic)	7a
A7	Horn	7b
A8	Headlight, left	8a
A9	Sidelight, left	8a
A10	Direction indicator, left	9a
B1	Direction indicating lamp, right wing	2d
B2	Windscreen washer pump	3d
B3	Coolant temperature sensor	4d
B4	Electrical pilot jet	4d
B5	Oil pressure sensor/switch	5d
B6	4-way valve, CVT	5g
B7	Alternator and voltage regulator	6b
B8	Distributor	6c
B9	Brake fluid level float	6e
B10	CVT vacuum control unit (including tachometric relay)	6g
B11	Hydraulic switch, brake master cylinder CVT	7e
B12	Electronic ignition (ignition coil, B19E)	7g
B13	Air temperature sensor	7c
B14	Declutching servo, CVT	7d
B15	Windscreen wiper motor	8g
B16	Direction indicating lamp, left wing	9d
B17	Starter motor	4c
B19	Headlamp washer pump	3d
B20	Cooling fan (radiator) B14	5a
B21	Switch, cooling fan B14	5b
B22	Ignition switching unit, B19E	7q
B23	Hall-pulse transmitter, ignition B19E	7m
B24	Engine revs sensor, electronic ignition	7f
C1	Direction indicating lamp, right	6i
C2	Heated rear window indicating lamp	7i
C3	Sidelight indicating lamp	7i

		Location (B14 only)
C5	Rear foglamp indicating lamp	7i
C6	Main beam indicating lamp	7i
C7	Seat belt indicating lamp	7i
C8	Hazard warning indicating lamp	7i
C9	Brake fluid level indicating lamp	7i
C10	Oil pressure indicating lamp	7i
C11	Choke indicating lamp	7i
C12	Handbrake indicating lamp	7i
C13	Charge indicating lamp	7i
C14	Direction indicating lamp, left	7i
C15	Lamps, instrument lighting	7i
C16	Fuel reserve indicating lamp	8i
C17	Coolant temperature indicating lamp	6i
C18	Clock	7i
C19	Fuel gauge	8i
C20	Temperature gauge	6i
C21	Rev counter (optional)	7i
C22	Air temperature gauge (optional)	6i
D1	Switch for glove compartment light	3m
D2	Lamp, glove compartment	3m
D3	Lamp, ashtray lighting	5m
D4	Lamp, cigar lighter	5m
D5	Cigar lighter	5m
D6	Radio (optional)	5n
D7	Lamp, heater controls lighting	5m
D8	Blower switch	5m
D9	Ignition switch	6m
D10	Windscreen wash/wipe switch	6m
D11	Choke	7m
D12	Horn switch	7n
D13	Direction indicator switch	7m
D14	Vehicle lighting switch	8m
D15	Lamp, vehicle lighting switch	9m
D16	Illuminated switch, heated rear window	9m
D17	Illuminated switch, rear foglamps	9m
D18	Dimming switch (illuminated) instrument lighting	8m
D19	Hazard warning switch (illuminated)	5n
D20	Lamp, console clock lighting	5n
D21	Console clock (optional)	6n
D22	Lamp, ignition switch lighting	6m
E1	Heater blower motor	5g
E2	Blower resistances	6h
E3	Intermittent wiper relay (L, DL)	6h
E4	Kickdown switch, CVT	6h
E5	Brake light switch	7h
E6	Combined direction/hazard flasher unit	9h

		Location (B14 only)
E7	Relay, blower motor speed 3	5i
E8	Ignition switch relay	6m
E9	Intermittent wash/wiper relay (GL,-S,-E,-T)	6h
F1	Interior light switch, right door	1m
F2	Interior light switch, left door	9m
F3	Interior light fitting	5p
F4	Switch, central locking system (driver's door)	8o
F5	Motor, central locking system, left-hand rear door	8p
F6	Motor, central locking system, right-hand front door*	2n
F7	Motor, central locking system, right-hand rear door	2o
F8	Powered window switch, right door	7o
F9	Powered window switch, left door	7o
F10	Powered window motor, left door	7o
F11	Powered window motor, right door	3o
G1	Seat cushion contact, front passenger	3o
G2	(CVT) switch and lighting, selector lever panel	3n
G2	(MT) reversing lights switch	3n
G3	Low "gear" hold switch, CVT	4n
G4	Seat belt contact, front passenger	5o
G6	Handbrake switch	5o
G7	Seat belt contact, driver	6o
G8	Seat heating elements and thermostat	6o
G9	Declutching servo switch, CVT	4n
H1	Direction indicator light (rear), right	2q
H2	Tail/brake light, right	2q
H3	Tail light, right	2q
H4	Rear foglamp, right	3q
H5	Reversing light, right	3q
H6	Number plate light, right	5r
H7	Number plate light, left	5r
H8	Reversing light, left	8q
H9	Rear foglamp, left	8q
H10	Tail light, left	8q
H11	Tail/brake light, left	9q
H12	Direction indicator light (rear), left	9q
H13	Boot light lamp	2p
H14	Fuel tank float	4p
H15	Heated rear window	5p
H16	Boot light switch	2q
RHD cars: left-hand front door		

Colour code

Bl	Blue	Gr	Grey	P	Pink	W	White
Br	Brown	L	Lilac	R	Red	Y	Yellow
Gn	Green	Or	Orange	SB	Black		

12

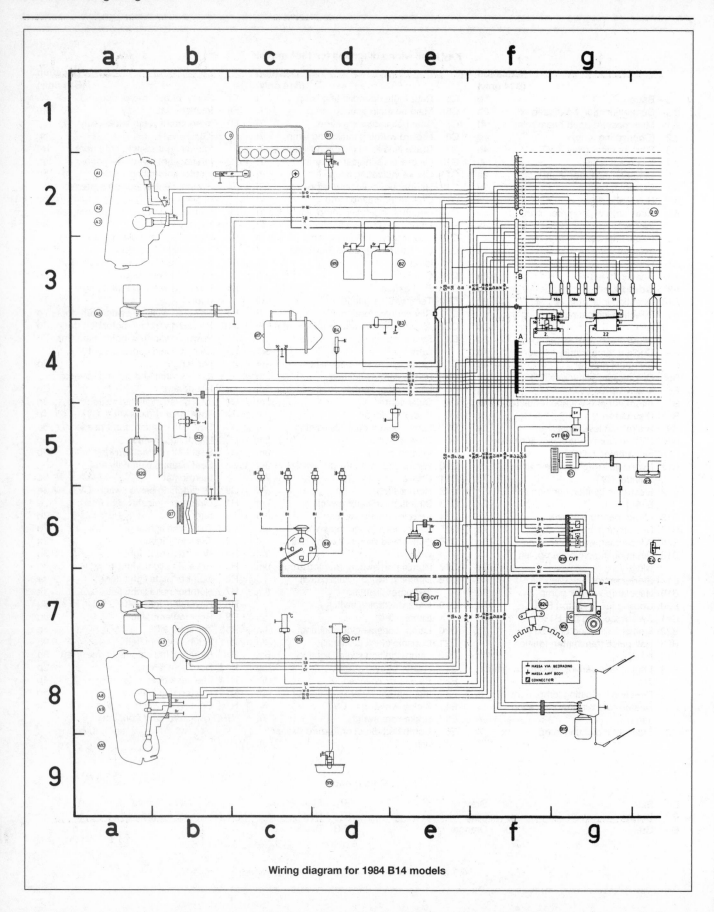

Wiring diagram for 1984 B14 models

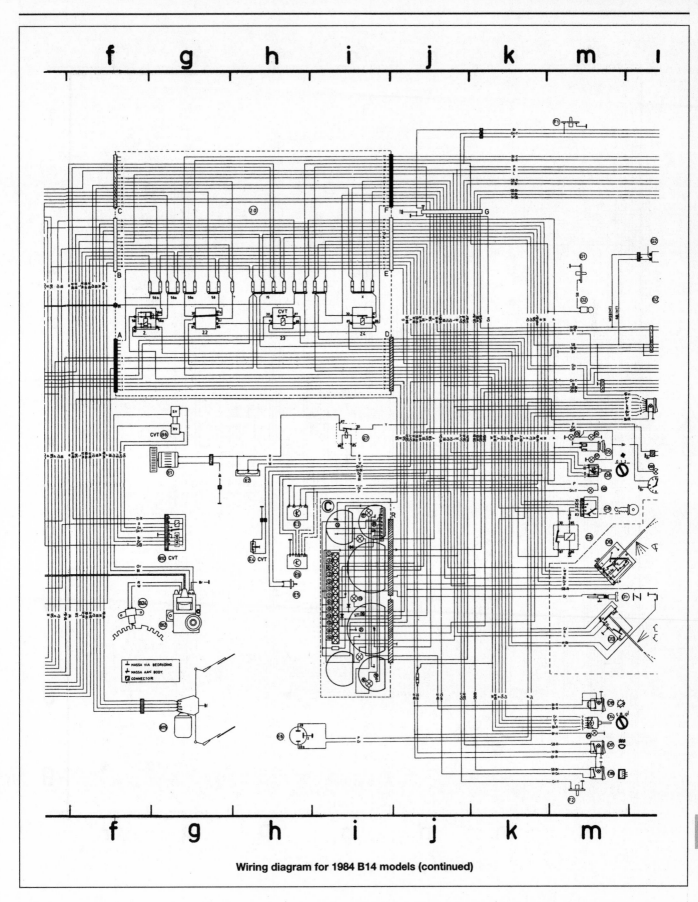

Wiring diagram for 1984 B14 models (continued)

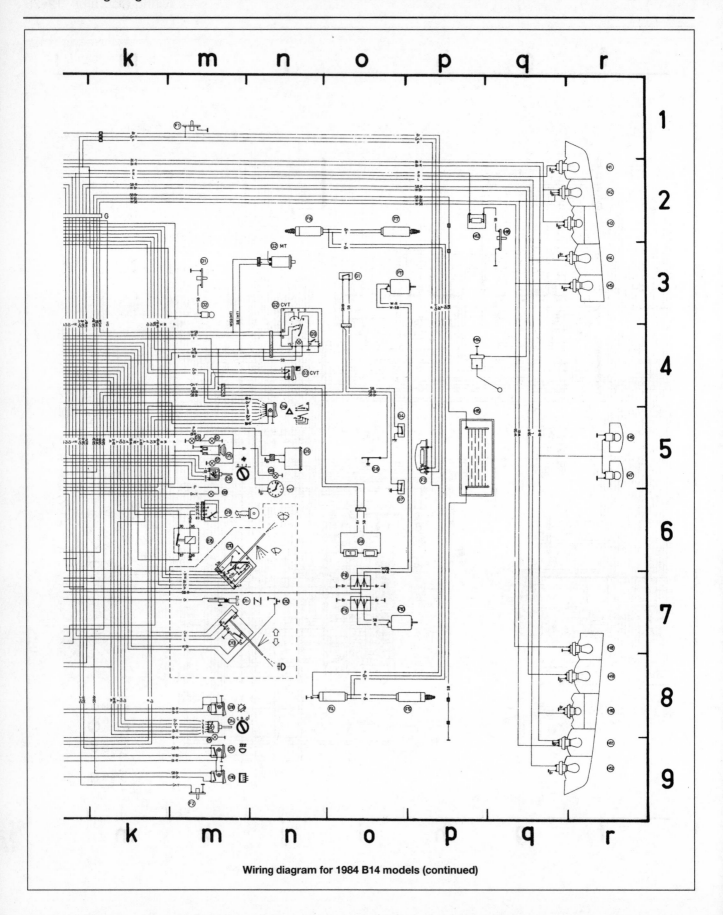

Wiring diagram for 1984 B14 models (continued)

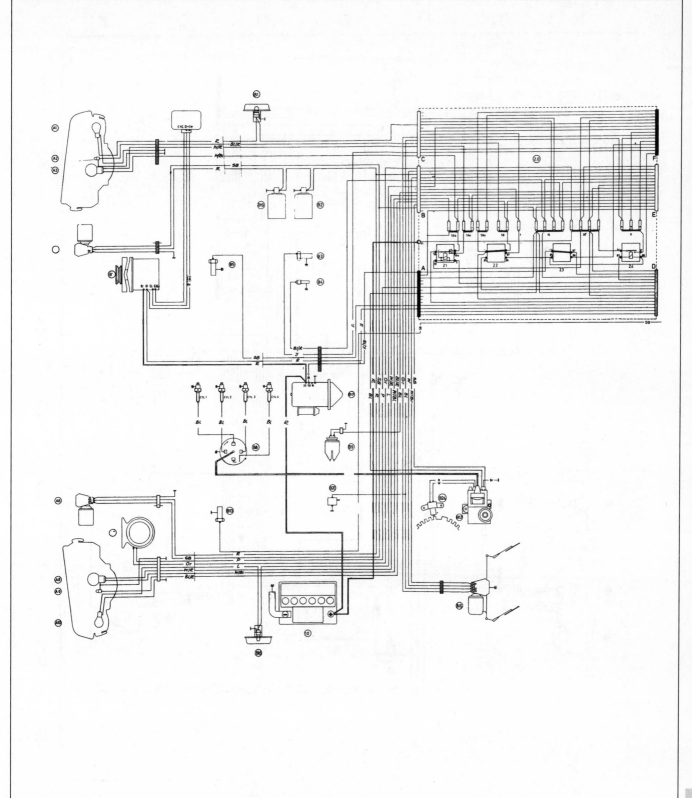

Wiring diagram for 1984 B19A models

Use as supplement to 1984 B14 diagram

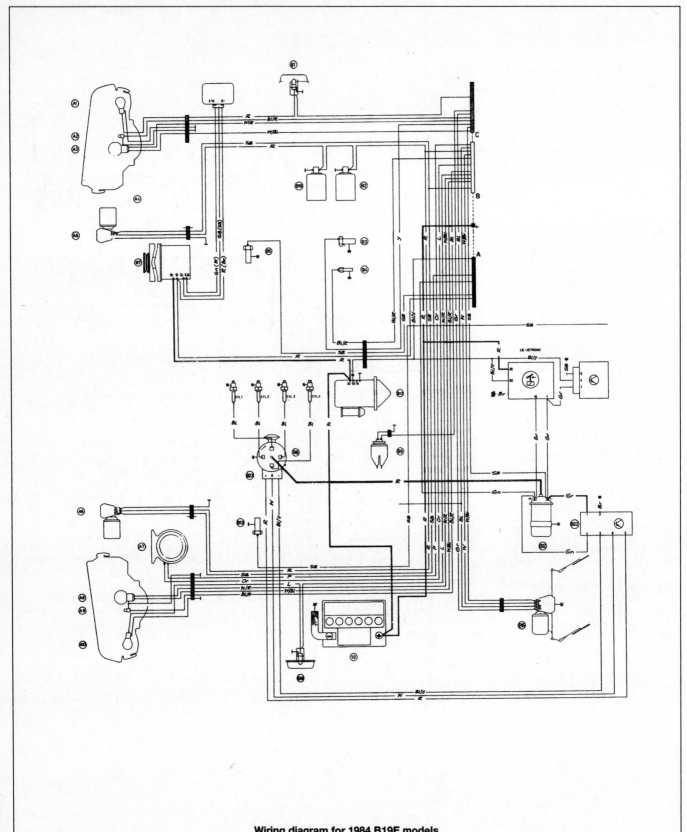

Wiring diagram for 1984 B19E models

Use as supplement to 1984 B14 diagram

Key to all wiring diagrams for 1985 models

		Location (B14 only)
1.0	Battery	1c
2.0	Central junction box/fuse box	2h
2.1	Main beam/dipped beam relay	4f
2.2	(bridge)	4g
2.3	Start inhibitor relay, AT	4h
2.4	"X"-contact relay	4f
A1	Direction indicator light, right	2a
A2	Parking light, right	2a
A3	Headlight, right	2a
A5	Headlamp wiper motor, right (Nordic)	3a
A6	Headlamp wiper motor, left (Nordic)	7a
A7	Horn	7b
A8	Headlight, left	8a
A9	Parking light, left	8a
A10	Direction indicator light, left	9a
B1	Direction indicator light, right wing	2d
B2	Windscreen washer pump	3d
B3	Coolant temperature sensor	4d
B4	Carburettor pilot jet (and preheating B200K)	4d
B5	Oil pressure sensor	5e
B6	Four-way valve, AT	5g
B7	Alternator and voltage regulator	6b
B8	Distributor	6c
B9	Brake fluid level float	6e
B10	AT vacuum control unit (including tachometric relay)	6g
B11	Hydraulic switch, brake master cylinder, AT	7e
B12	Electronic ignition	7g
B13	Air temperature sensor	7c
B14	Declutching servo, AT	7d

		Location (B14 only)
B15	Windscreen wiper motor	8g
B16	Direction indicator light, left wing	9d
B17	Starter motor	4c
B19	Headlamp washer pump	3d
B20	Cooling fan (radiator), B14	5a
B21	Switch, cooling fan B14	5b
B24	Engine revs sensor, electronic ignition	7f
C1	Direction indicator lamp, right	6i
C2	Heated rear window indicator lamp	7i
C3	Parking light indicator lamp	6i
C5	Rear fog lamp indicator lamp	7i
C6	Main beam indicator lamp	7i
C7	Seat belt indicator lamp	7i
C8	Hazard warning indicator lamp	7i
C9	Brake fluid level indicator lamp	7i
C10	Oil pressure indicator lamp	7i
C11	Choke indicator lamp (carburettor engines)	7i
C12	Handbrake indicator lamp	7i
C13	Charge indicator lamp	7i
C14	Direction indicator lamp, left	7i
C15	Lamps, instrument lighting	7i
C16	Fuel reserve indicator lamp (LED)	8i
C17	Coolant temperature indicator lamp (LED)	6i
C18	Clock, instrument panel	7i
C19	Fuel gauge	8i
C20	Engine, temperature gauge	6i
C21	Rev counter	7i
C22	Air temperature gauge	6i
C23	Lamp, gearchange indicator (LED)	8i
D1	Switch for glove compartment light	3m

		Location (B14 only)
D2	Lamp, glove compartment	3m
D3	Lamp, ashtray	5m
D4	Lamp, cigar lighter	5m
D5	Cigar lighter	5m
D6	Radio (optional)	5n
D7	Lamp, heater controls lighting	5m
D8	Blower switch	5m
D9	Ignition switch	6m
D10	Windscreen wash/wipe switch	6m
D11	Choke switch	7m
D12	Horn switch	7n
D13	Direction indicator switch	7m
D14	Lighting switch	8m
D15	Lamp, lighting switch	8m
D16	Illuminated switch, heated rear window	9m
D17	Illuminated switch, rear foglamp(s)	9m
D18	Dimming switch (illuminated) instrument lighting	8m
D19	Hazard warning switch (illuminated)	5n
D20	Lamp, console clock lighting	5n
D21	Console clock (optional)	6n
D22	Lamp, ignition switch lighting	6m
E1	Heater blower motor	5g
E2	Blower resistances	5h
E3	Intermittent wiper relay (DL)	6h
E4	Kickdown switch, AT	6h
E5	Brake light switch	7h
E6	Combined direction/hazard flasher unit	9h
E7	Relay, blower motor speed 3	5i
E8	Ignition switch relay	6m

12

Key to all wiring diagrams for 1985 models (continued)

		Location (B14 only)			Location (B14 only)			Location (B14 only)
E9	Intermittent wash/wipe relay (GL, -S, -E, -T)	6h	F12	Interior light switch, RH rear door	1n	H2	Tail/brake light, right	2q
E10	Main lighting relay	7m	F13	Interior light switch, LH rear door	9n	H3	Tail light, right	2q
E11	Rear foglamp relay	8m	F14	RH rear interior light	1o	H4	Rear foglamp, right	3q
E12	Delay relay, interior lights (GLE, GLT)	3m	F15	LH rear interior light	9o	H5	Reversing light, right	3q
F1	Interior light switch, right door	1m	G1	Seat cushion contact, front passenger	3o	H6	Number plate light, right	5r
F2	Interior light switch, left door	9m	G2	(AT) Switch and lighting, selector lever panel 3n		H7	Number plate light, left	5r
F3	Interior light, front	5p				H8	Reversing light, left	7q
F4	Switch, central locking system (driver's door)	8n	G2	(MT) Reversing light switch	3n	H9	Rear foglamp, left	8q
F5	Motor, central locking system, LH rear door	8o	G3	Low "gear" hold switch, AT	4n	H10	Tail light, left	8q
			G4	Seat belt contact, front passenger	5o	H11	Tail/brake light, left	9q
F6	Motor, central locking system, RH front door*	2n	G5	Top gear switch, gear change indicator	8i	H12	Direction indicator light (rear), left	9q
F7	Motor, central locking system, RH rear door	2o	G6	Handbrake switch	5o	H13	Boot light lamp	2p
F8	Power window switch, right door	7o	G7	Seat belt contact, driver	6o	H14	Fuel tank float	4p
F9	Power window switch, left door	7o	G8	Seat heating elements and thermostat	6o	H15	Heated rear window	5p
F10	Power window motor, left door	7o	G9	Declutching servo switch, AT	4n	H16	Boot light switch	2q
F11	Power window motor, right door	3o	H1	Direction indicator light (rear), right	2q	J1	Electronic control unit, LE-Jetronic	5r
						J12	Control relay, LE-Jetronic	5q

RHD cars: Left-hand front door

Colour code

Bl	Blue	Or	Orange	W	White
Bl-R	Blue/red	P	Pink	W-Bl	White/blue
Bl-Y	Blue/yellow	R	Red	W-Br	White/brown
Br	Brown	SB	Black	W-Gn	White/green
Gn-Y	Green/yellow	SB-BL	Black/blue	W-R	White/red
Gr	Grey	SB-Br	Black/brown	W-SB	White/black
L	Lilac	SB-R	Black/red	Y	Yellow

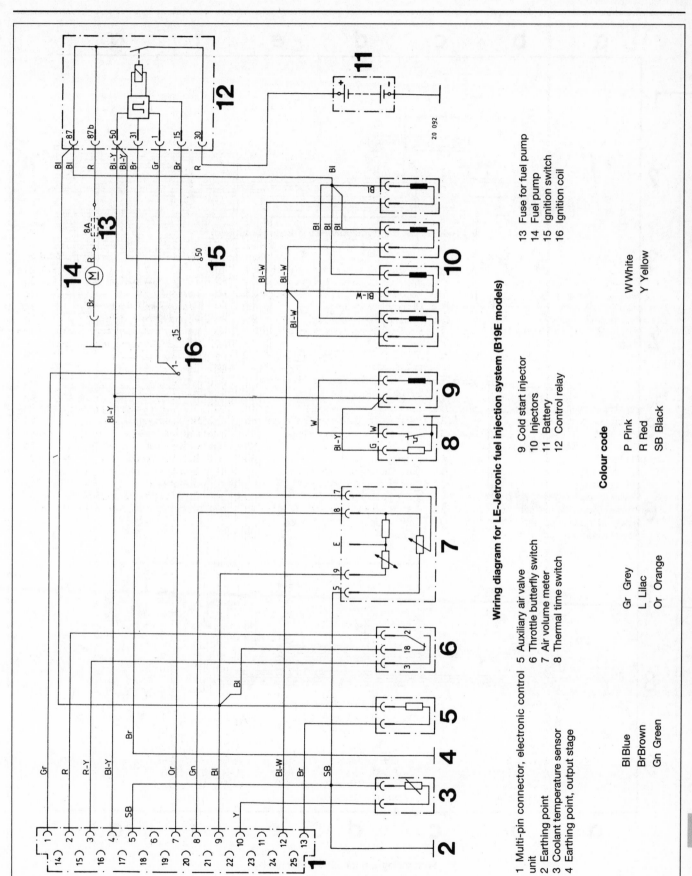

20 092

Wiring diagram for LE-Jetronic fuel injection system (B19E models)

1 Multi-pin connector, electronic control unit
2 Earthing point
3 Coolant temperature sensor
4 Earthing point, output stage
5 Auxiliary air valve
6 Throttle butterfly switch
7 Air volume meter
8 Thermal time switch
9 Cold start injector
10 Injectors
11 Battery
12 Control relay
13 Fuse for fuel pump
14 Fuel pump
15 Ignition switch
16 Ignition coil

Colour code

Bl Blue	Gr Grey	P Pink	W White
Br Brown	L Lilac	R Red	Y Yellow
Gn Green	Or Orange	SB Black	

12

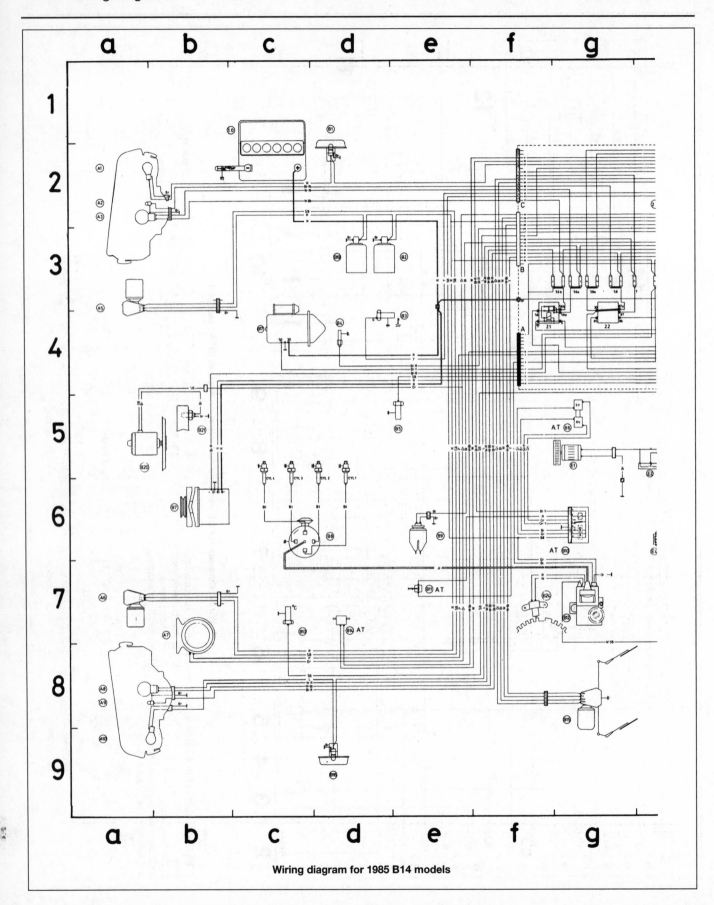

Wiring diagram for 1985 B14 models

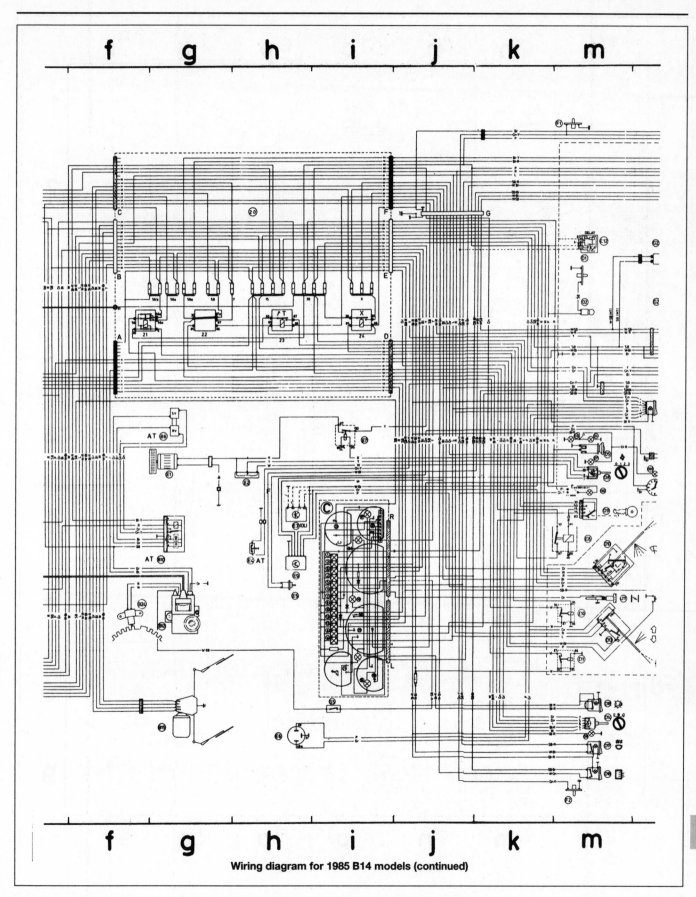

Wiring diagram for 1985 B14 models (continued)

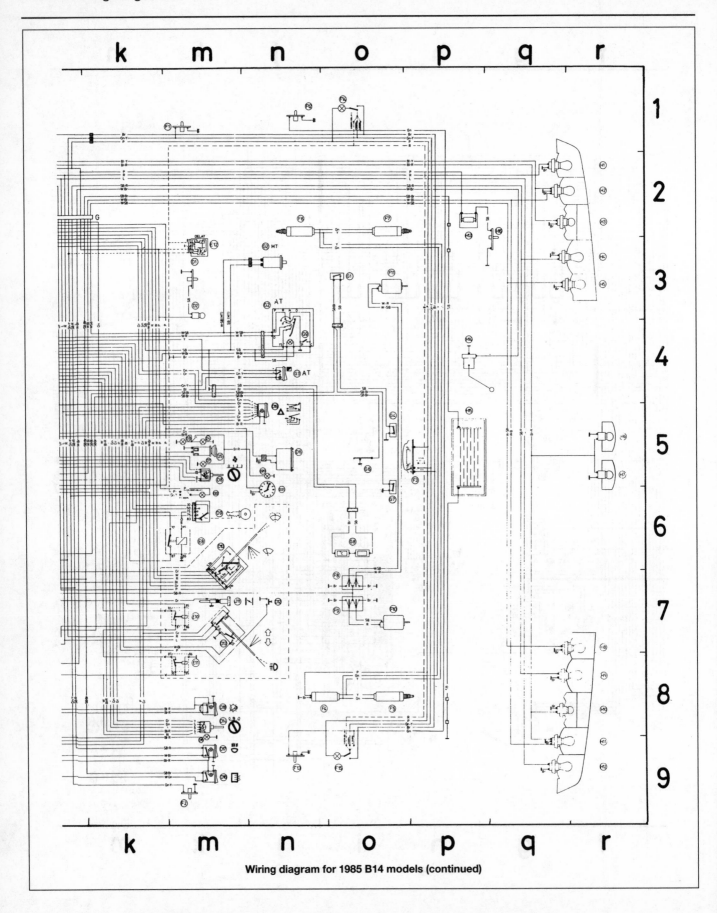

Wiring diagram for 1985 B14 models (continued)

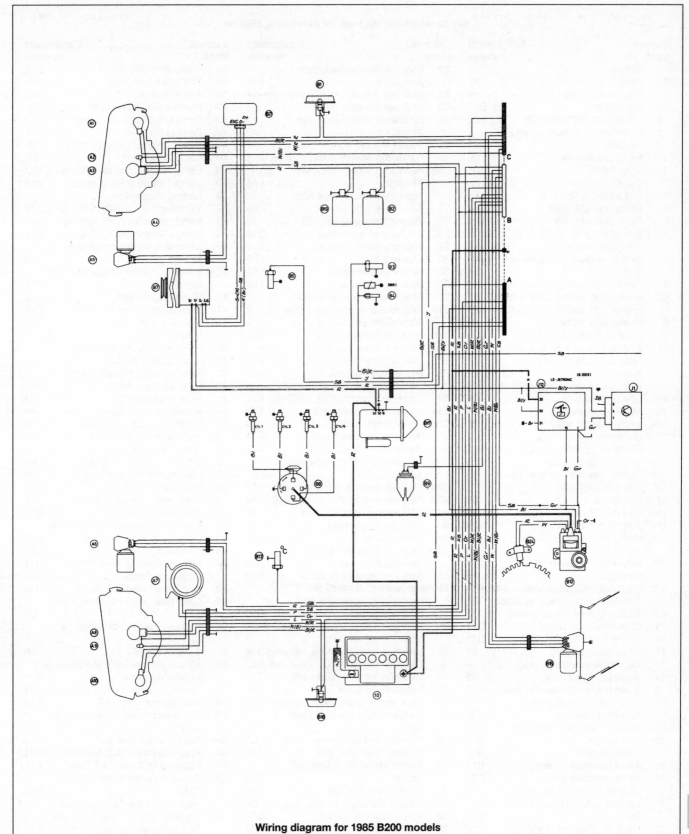

Wiring diagram for 1985 B200 models

Use as supplement to 1985 B14 diagram

Key to schematic diagram for all models, 1986-on

Current track		Component number
1	Battery	1.0
2	Horn	A7
2	Second horn (360)	A4
2	Horn switch	D12
2a	Cooling fan, radiator (340)	B20
2a	Thermostatic switch, cooling fan (340)	B21
3	Radio connection	D6
4	Cigar lighter	D5
5	Clock	C18, (D21)
6	Brake light switch	E5
6	Tail/brake light, right	H2
6	Tail/brake light, left	H11
7	Boot light lamp	H13
7	Boot light switch	H16
8	Switch for glove compartment light	D1
8	Lamp, glove compartment	D2
9	Interior light switch, right door	F1
9	Interior light switch, left door	F2
9	Interior light fitting	F3
9	Lamp, ignition switch light	D22
9a	Switch, central locking system	F4
9a	Motors, central locking system	F5, F6, F7
9c	Interior light delay relay (B200E)	E12
10	Ignition switch	D9
10	"X" contact relay	2.4
10a	Ignition switch relay	E8
11	Starter motor	B17
12	Electronic ignition system	B12
12a	Gearchange indicator	C23
12a	Switch, gearchange indicator	G5
13	Rev counter (360)	C21
14	Distributor	B8
14a	Fuel cut-off relay	B28
14a	Throttle butterfly switch	B29
14b	Carburettor pilot jet, B14E, B200KE	B4
14c	Powered window rocker switches	F8, F9
14c	Powered window motors	F10, F11
15	Alternator and voltage regulator	B7
15	Battery charge indicator lamp	C13
16	Choke indicator lamp	C11
16	Choke switch	D11
17	Oil pressure switch	B5
17	Oil pressure indicator lamp	C10
18	Brake fluid level float	B9
18	Brake fluid level indicator lamp	C9
19	Handbrake indicator lamp	C12
19	Handbrake switch	G6
20	Fuel reserve indicator lamp	C16
20	Fuel gauge	C19
20	Fuel tank float	H14
21	Air temperature sensor	B13
21	Air temperature gauge	C22
22	Coolant temperature sensor	B3
22	Coolant temperature indicator lamp	C17
22	Coolant temperature gauge	C20
23	Seat belt indicator lamp	C7

Current track		Component number
23	Seat cushion contact, front passenger	G1
23	Seat belt contact, front passenger	G4
23	Seat belt contact, driver	G7
24	Headlamp wiper motor, right (Nordic)	A5
25	Screen washer pump	B2
26	Headlamp washer pump (Nordic)	B19
26a	Headlamp wiper motor, left (Nordic)	A6
27	Intermittent wash/wipe relay (GL, -S, -E, -T)	E9
28	Intermittent wiper relay (DL)	E3
29	Windscreen wash/wipe switch	D10
29	Windscreen wiper motor	B15
30	Blower switch	D8
30	Heater blower motor	E1
30	Blower resistances	E2
31	Relay, heater blower switch	E7
31a	Heated rear window (and door mirrors) indicator lamp	C2
31a	Door mirror heater, left	F16
31a	Door mirror heater, right	F17
32	Rear window heater switch	D16
32	Heated rear window	H15
33	Carburettor pilot jet, B200KS/KO	B4
33	Carburettor preheating, B200KE	B27
33a	Power mirror motor, left	F18
33a	Power mirror motor, right	F19
33a	Power mirror switch, left	G14
33a	Power mirror switch, right	G15
33b	Rear window wash/wipe switch (GB)	G16*
33b	Rear window wiper motor (GB)	H17
33b	Rear window washer pump (GB)	B30
34	(MT) Reversing lights switch	G2
34	Reversing light, right	H5
34	Reversing light, left	H8
35	Seat heating elements and thermostat, driver	G8
35	Seat heating switch, driver	G12
35a	Seat heating elements and thermostat, passenger	G11
35a	Seat heater switch, passenger	G13
36	Combined direction/hazard flasher unit	E6
37	Direction indicator lamp, left wing	B16
37	Direction indicator light (rear), left	H12
37	Direction indicator lamp, left	C14
37	Direction indicator, right	A1
37	Direction indicator lamp, right wing	B1
37	Direction indicator light (rear), right	H1
37	Direction indicator lamp, right	C1
37	Direction indicator, left	A10
37	Switch, direction indicators/flasher	D13
37	Hazard warning switch	D19
37	Hazard warning indicator lamp	C8
38	Vehicle lighting switch	D14
39	Number plate light, left	H7
39	Tail light, left	H10

Current track		Component number
39	Tail/brake light, left	H11
39	Tail/brake light, right	H2
39	Tail light, right	H3
39	Number plate light, right	H6
40	Parking light indicator lamp	C3
40	Parking light, left	A9
40	Lamp, ashtray lighting	D3
40	Lamp, cigar lighter	D4
40	Lamp, heater controls lighting	D7
40	Lamp, vehicle lighting switch	D15
40	Lamps, illumination switches	D16, D17, D18, D19
40	Lamp, (console) clock lighting	D20
40	Lamps, instrument lighting	C15
40	Dimmer rheostat, instrument lighting	D18
40a	Resistor, instrument lighting (340 basic)	D23
41	Parking light, right	A2
41a	Main vehicle lighting relay	E10
41a	Rear foglamp relay	E11
41a	Ignition switch	D9
42	Fuse, rear foglamps (not CH)	E13
42	Rear foglamp switch	D17
42	Rear foglamp indicator lamp	C5
42	Rear foglamp, right	H4
42	Rear foglamp, left	H9
42	Headlamp, left, dipped beam	A8
42	Headlamp, right, dipped beam	A3
43	Main beam/dipped beam relay	2.1
43	Headlamp, left, main beam	A8
43	Headlamp, right, main beam	A3
43	Main beam indicator lamp	C6
43	Main beam switch	D13
43	Main beam indicator lamp	C6
43	Main beam flash switch	D13
44	Electronic control unit, LE-Jetronic	J1
45	Control relay, LE-Jetronic	J12
46	Fuel pump, LE-Jetronic	J14
46	Fuse, fuel pump, LE-Jetronic	J13
47	Kickdown switch	E4
48	Low "gear" hold switch, AT	G3
49	Low "gear" hold indicating lamp, AT	G3
50	Hydraulic switch, brake master cyl., AT	B11
51	4-Way valve, AT	B6
52	AT vacuum control unit (including tachmetric relay)	B10
53	Declutching servo switch, AT	G9
54	Declutching servo, AT	B14
55	AT selector level panel switch and lamp	G2
56	Start inhibitor relay, AT	2.3
57	Fuse, foglamps GLT, 360 GLE	B31
57	Foglamp GLT, 360 GLE, left	A11
58	Foglamp power relay GLT, 360 GLE	B32
58	Foglamp switch GLT, 360 GLE	G10
58	Foglamp control relay GLT, 360 GLE (not Germany and Austria)	E14
58	Foglamp GLT, 360 GLE, right	A12

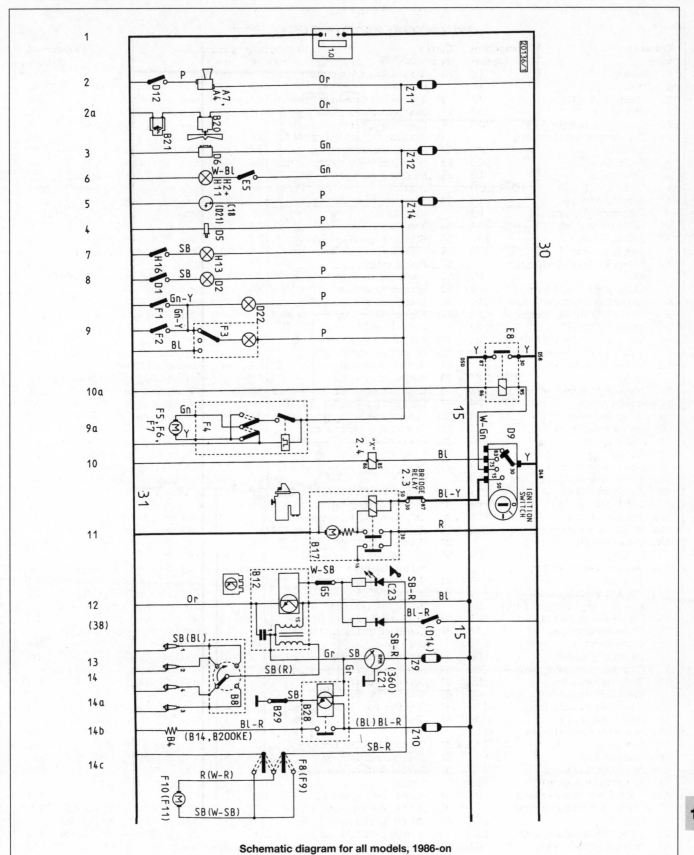

Schematic diagram for all models, 1986-on

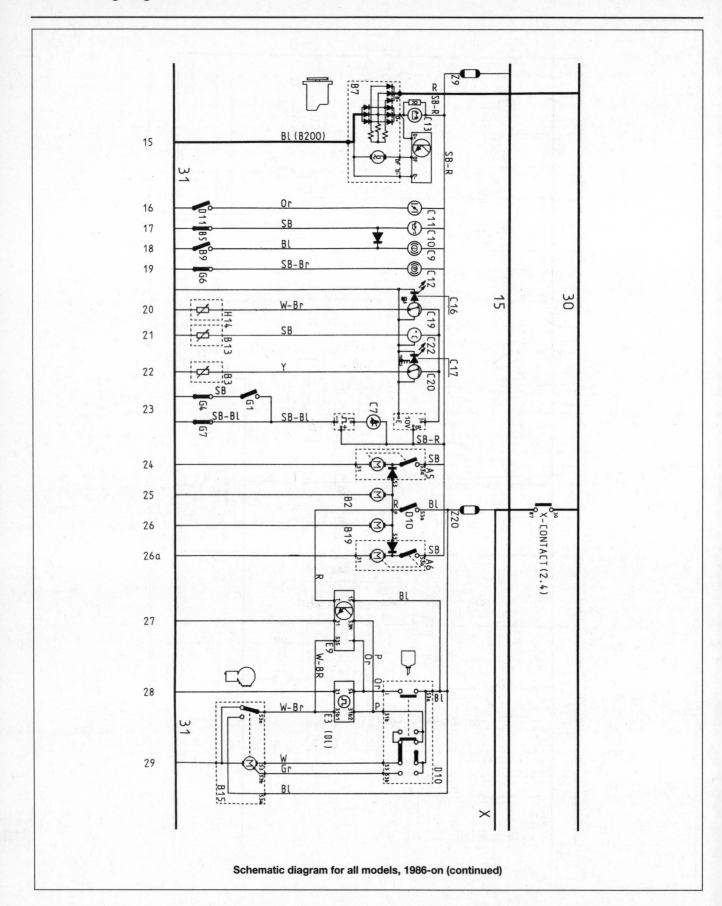

Schematic diagram for all models, 1986-on (continued)

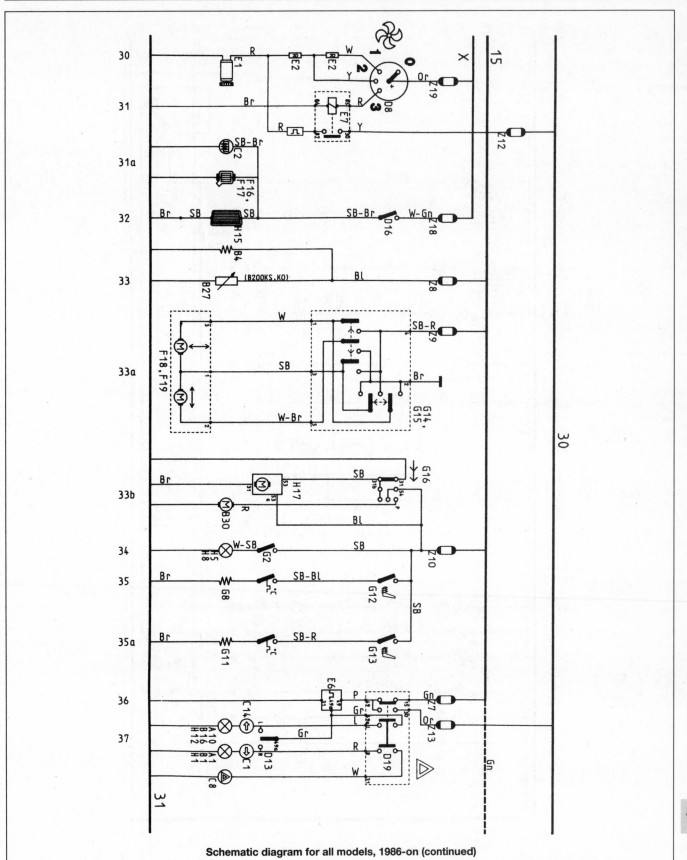

Schematic diagram for all models, 1986-on (continued)

12

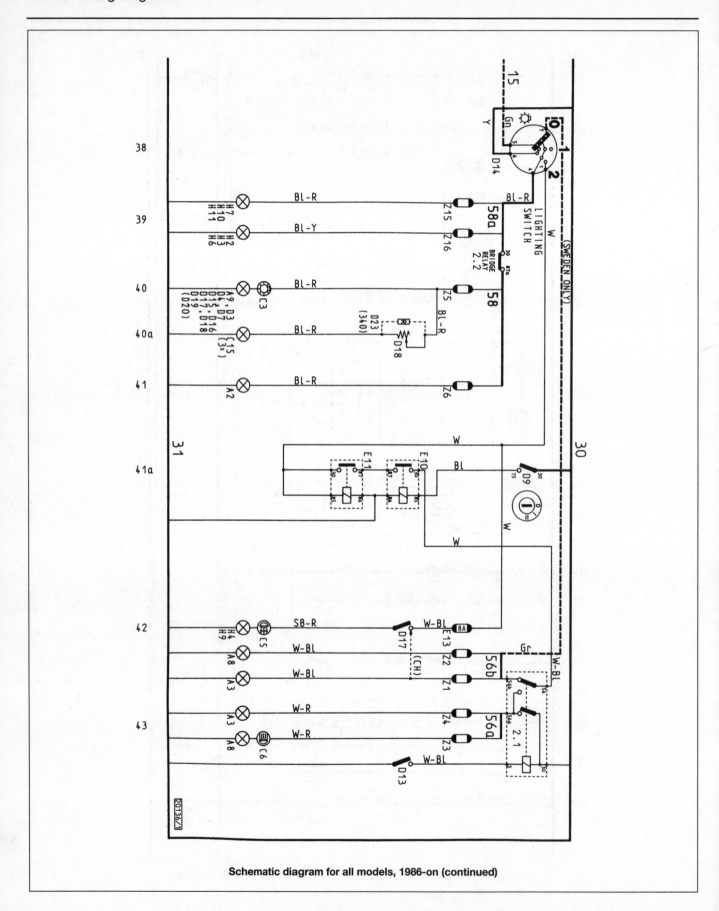

Schematic diagram for all models, 1986-on (continued)

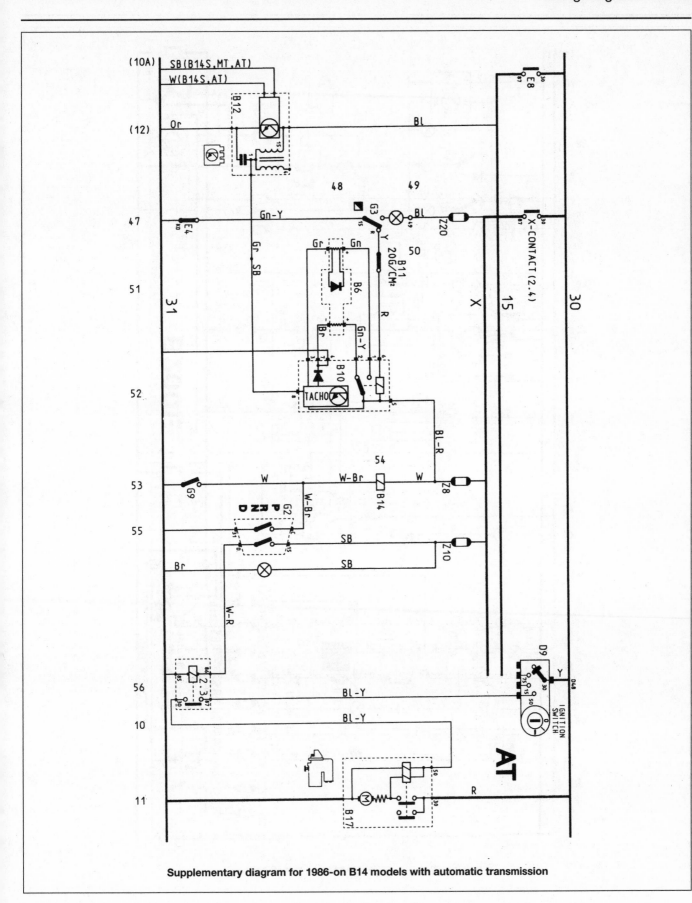

Supplementary diagram for 1986-on B14 models with automatic transmission

12

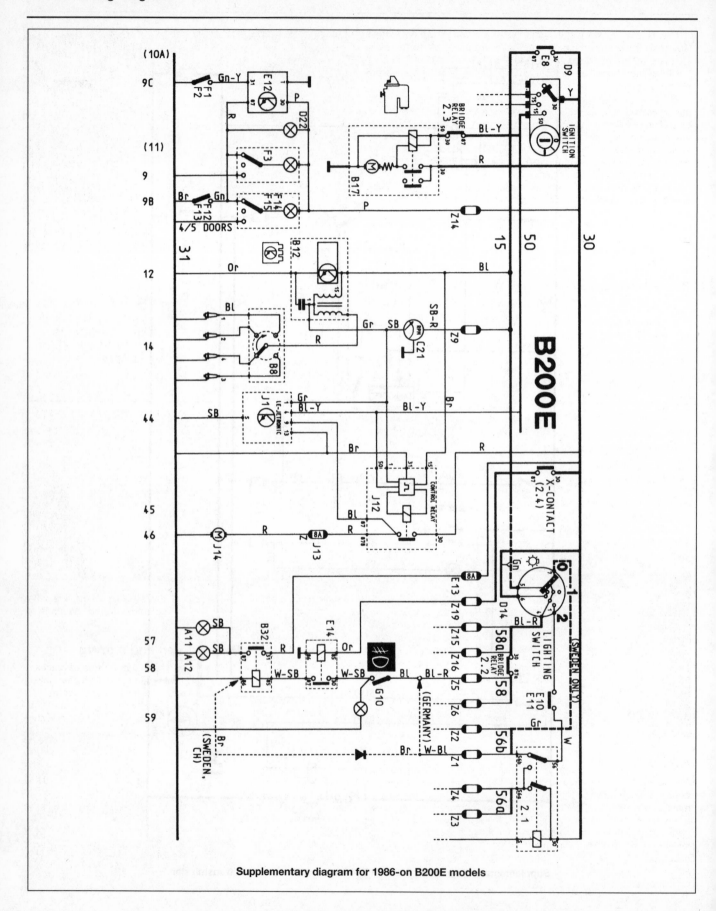

Supplementary diagram for 1986-on B200E models

This is a guide to getting your vehicle through the MOT test. Obviously it will not be possible to examine the vehicle to the same standard as the professional MOT tester. However, working through the following checks will enable you to identify any problem areas before submitting the vehicle for the test.

Where a testable component is in borderline condition, the tester has discretion in deciding whether to pass or fail it. The basis of such discretion is whether the tester would be happy for a close relative or friend to use the vehicle with the component in that condition. If the vehicle presented is clean and evidently well cared for, the tester may be more inclined to pass a borderline component than if the vehicle is scruffy and apparently neglected.

It has only been possible to summarise the test requirements here, based on the regulations in force at the time of printing. Test standards are becoming increasingly stringent, although there are some exemptions for older vehicles. For full details obtain a copy of the Haynes publication Pass the MOT! (available from stockists of Haynes manuals).

An assistant will be needed to help carry out some of these checks.

The checks have been sub-divided into four categories, as follows:

1 Checks carried out **FROM THE DRIVER'S SEAT**

2 Checks carried out **WITH THE VEHICLE ON THE GROUND**

3 Checks carried out **WITH THE VEHICLE RAISED AND THE WHEELS FREE TO TURN**

4 Checks carried out on **YOUR VEHICLE'S EXHAUST EMISSION SYSTEM**

---

1 Checks carried out **FROM THE DRIVER'S SEAT**

Handbrake

☐ Test the operation of the handbrake. Excessive travel (too many clicks) indicates incorrect brake or cable adjustment.

☐ Check that the handbrake cannot be released by tapping the lever sideways. Check the security of the lever mountings.

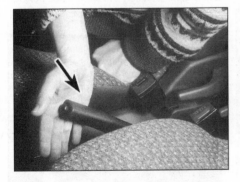

Footbrake

☐ Depress the brake pedal and check that it does not creep down to the floor, indicating a master cylinder fault. Release the pedal, wait a few seconds, then depress it again. If the pedal travels nearly to the floor before firm resistance is felt, brake adjustment or repair is necessary. If the pedal feels spongy, there is air in the hydraulic system which must be removed by bleeding.

☐ Check that the brake pedal is secure and in good condition. Check also for signs of fluid leaks on the pedal, floor or carpets, which would indicate failed seals in the brake master cylinder.

☐ Check the servo unit (when applicable) by operating the brake pedal several times, then keeping the pedal depressed and starting the engine. As the engine starts, the pedal will move down slightly. If not, the vacuum hose or the servo itself may be faulty.

Steering wheel and column

☐ Examine the steering wheel for fractures or looseness of the hub, spokes or rim.

☐ Move the steering wheel from side to side and then up and down. Check that the steering wheel is not loose on the column, indicating wear or a loose retaining nut. Continue moving the steering wheel as before, but also turn it slightly from left to right.

☐ Check that the steering wheel is not loose on the column, and that there is no abnormal

movement of the steering wheel, indicating wear in the column support bearings or couplings.

Windscreen and mirrors

☐ The windscreen must be free of cracks or other significant damage within the driver's field of view. (Small stone chips are acceptable.) Rear view mirrors must be secure, intact, and capable of being adjusted.

290mm

Seat belts and seats

Note: *The following checks are applicable to all seat belts, front and rear.*

☐ Examine the webbing of all the belts (including rear belts if fitted) for cuts, serious fraying or deterioration. Fasten and unfasten each belt to check the buckles. If applicable, check the retracting mechanism. Check the security of all seat belt mountings accessible from inside the vehicle.

☐ The front seats themselves must be securely attached and the backrests must lock in the upright position.

Doors

☐ Both front doors must be able to be opened and closed from outside and inside, and must latch securely when closed.

2 Checks carried out WITH THE VEHICLE ON THE GROUND

Vehicle identification

☐ Number plates must be in good condition, secure and legible, with letters and numbers correctly spaced – spacing at (A) should be twice that at (B).

☐ The VIN plate and/or homologation plate must be legible.

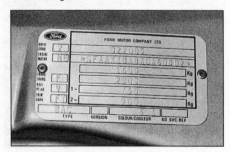

Electrical equipment

☐ Switch on the ignition and check the operation of the horn.

☐ Check the windscreen washers and wipers, examining the wiper blades; renew damaged or perished blades. Also check the operation of the stop-lights.

☐ Check the operation of the sidelights and number plate lights. The lenses and reflectors must be secure, clean and undamaged.

☐ Check the operation and alignment of the headlights. The headlight reflectors must not be tarnished and the lenses must be undamaged.

☐ Switch on the ignition and check the operation of the direction indicators (including the instrument panel tell-tale) and the hazard warning lights. Operation of the sidelights and stop-lights must not affect the indicators - if it does, the cause is usually a bad earth at the rear light cluster.

☐ Check the operation of the rear foglight(s), including the warning light on the instrument panel or in the switch.

Footbrake

☐ Examine the master cylinder, brake pipes and servo unit for leaks, loose mountings, corrosion or other damage.

☐ The fluid reservoir must be secure and the fluid level must be between the upper (**A**) and lower (**B**) markings.

☐ Inspect both front brake flexible hoses for cracks or deterioration of the rubber. Turn the steering from lock to lock, and ensure that the hoses do not contact the wheel, tyre, or any part of the steering or suspension mechanism. With the brake pedal firmly depressed, check the hoses for bulges or leaks under pressure.

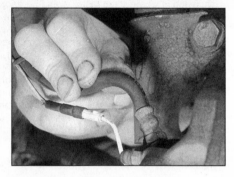

Steering and suspension

☐ Have your assistant turn the steering wheel from side to side slightly, up to the point where the steering gear just begins to transmit this movement to the roadwheels. Check for excessive free play between the steering wheel and the steering gear, indicating wear or insecurity of the steering column joints, the column-to-steering gear coupling, or the steering gear itself.

☐ Have your assistant turn the steering wheel more vigorously in each direction, so that the roadwheels just begin to turn. As this is done, examine all the steering joints, linkages, fittings and attachments. Renew any component that shows signs of wear or damage. On vehicles with power steering, check the security and condition of the steering pump, drivebelt and hoses.

☐ Check that the vehicle is standing level, and at approximately the correct ride height.

Shock absorbers

☐ Depress each corner of the vehicle in turn, then release it. The vehicle should rise and then settle in its normal position. If the vehicle continues to rise and fall, the shock absorber is defective. A shock absorber which has seized will also cause the vehicle to fail.

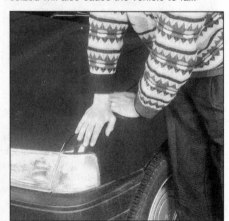

Exhaust system

☐ Start the engine. With your assistant holding a rag over the tailpipe, check the entire system for leaks. Repair or renew leaking sections.

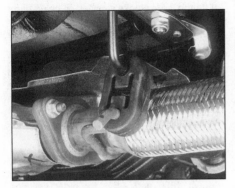

3 Checks carried out **WITH THE VEHICLE RAISED AND THE WHEELS FREE TO TURN**

Jack up the front and rear of the vehicle, and securely support it on axle stands. Position the stands clear of the suspension assemblies. Ensure that the wheels are clear of the ground and that the steering can be turned from lock to lock.

Steering mechanism

☐ Have your assistant turn the steering from lock to lock. Check that the steering turns smoothly, and that no part of the steering mechanism, including a wheel or tyre, fouls any brake hose or pipe or any part of the body structure.

☐ Examine the steering rack rubber gaiters for damage or insecurity of the retaining clips. If power steering is fitted, check for signs of damage or leakage of the fluid hoses, pipes or connections. Also check for excessive stiffness or binding of the steering, a missing split pin or locking device, or severe corrosion of the body structure within 30 cm of any steering component attachment point.

Front and rear suspension and wheel bearings

☐ Starting at the front right-hand side, grasp the roadwheel at the 3 o'clock and 9 o'clock positions and shake it vigorously. Check for free play or insecurity at the wheel bearings, suspension balljoints, or suspension mountings, pivots and attachments.

☐ Now grasp the wheel at the 12 o'clock and 6 o'clock positions and repeat the previous inspection. Spin the wheel, and check for roughness or tightness of the front wheel bearing.

☐ If excess free play is suspected at a component pivot point, this can be confirmed by using a large screwdriver or similar tool and levering between the mounting and the component attachment. This will confirm whether the wear is in the pivot bush, its retaining bolt, or in the mounting itself (the bolt holes can often become elongated).

☐ Carry out all the above checks at the other front wheel, and then at both rear wheels.

Springs and shock absorbers

☐ Examine the suspension struts (when applicable) for serious fluid leakage, corrosion, or damage to the casing. Also check the security of the mounting points.

☐ If coil springs are fitted, check that the spring ends locate in their seats, and that the spring is not corroded, cracked or broken.

☐ If leaf springs are fitted, check that all leaves are intact, that the axle is securely attached to each spring, and that there is no deterioration of the spring eye mountings, bushes, and shackles.

☐ The same general checks apply to vehicles fitted with other suspension types, such as torsion bars, hydraulic displacer units, etc. Ensure that all mountings and attachments are secure, that there are no signs of excessive wear, corrosion or damage, and (on hydraulic types) that there are no fluid leaks or damaged pipes.

☐ Inspect the shock absorbers for signs of serious fluid leakage. Check for wear of the mounting bushes or attachments, or damage to the body of the unit.

Driveshafts (fwd vehicles only)

☐ Rotate each front wheel in turn and inspect the constant velocity joint gaiters for splits or damage. Also check that each driveshaft is straight and undamaged.

Braking system

☐ If possible without dismantling, check brake pad wear and disc condition. Ensure that the friction lining material has not worn excessively, (A) and that the discs are not fractured, pitted, scored or badly worn (B).

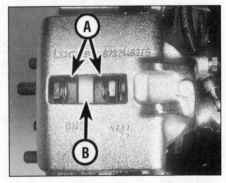

☐ Examine all the rigid brake pipes underneath the vehicle, and the flexible hose(s) at the rear. Look for corrosion, chafing or insecurity of the pipes, and for signs of bulging under pressure, chafing, splits or deterioration of the flexible hoses.

☐ Look for signs of fluid leaks at the brake calipers or on the brake backplates. Repair or renew leaking components.

☐ Slowly spin each wheel, while your assistant depresses and releases the footbrake. Ensure that each brake is operating and does not bind when the pedal is released.

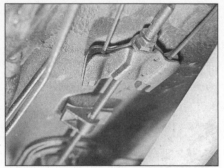

☐ Examine the handbrake mechanism, checking for frayed or broken cables, excessive corrosion, or wear or insecurity of the linkage. Check that the mechanism works on each relevant wheel, and releases fully, without binding.

☐ It is not possible to test brake efficiency without special equipment, but a road test can be carried out later to check that the vehicle pulls up in a straight line.

Fuel and exhaust systems

☐ Inspect the fuel tank (including the filler cap), fuel pipes, hoses and unions. All components must be secure and free from leaks.

☐ Examine the exhaust system over its entire length, checking for any damaged, broken or missing mountings, security of the retaining clamps and rust or corrosion.

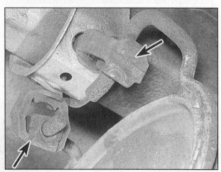

Wheels and tyres

☐ Examine the sidewalls and tread area of each tyre in turn. Check for cuts, tears, lumps, bulges, separation of the tread, and exposure of the ply or cord due to wear or damage. Check that the tyre bead is correctly seated on the wheel rim, that the valve is sound and

properly seated, and that the wheel is not distorted or damaged.

☐ Check that the tyres are of the correct size for the vehicle, that they are of the same size and type on each axle, and that the pressures are correct.

☐ Check the tyre tread depth. The legal minimum at the time of writing is 1.6 mm over at least three-quarters of the tread width. Abnormal tread wear may indicate incorrect front wheel alignment.

Body corrosion

☐ Check the condition of the entire vehicle structure for signs of corrosion in load-bearing areas. (These include chassis box sections, side sills, cross-members, pillars, and all suspension, steering, braking system and seat belt mountings and anchorages.) Any corrosion which has seriously reduced the thickness of a load-bearing area is likely to cause the vehicle to fail. In this case professional repairs are likely to be needed.

☐ Damage or corrosion which causes sharp or otherwise dangerous edges to be exposed will also cause the vehicle to fail.

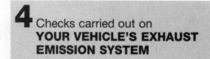

4 Checks carried out on **YOUR VEHICLE'S EXHAUST EMISSION SYSTEM**

Petrol models

☐ Have the engine at normal operating temperature, and make sure that it is in good tune (ignition system in good order, air filter element clean, etc).

☐ Before any measurements are carried out, raise the engine speed to around 2500 rpm, and hold it at this speed for 20 seconds. Allow

the engine speed to return to idle, and watch for smoke emissions from the exhaust tailpipe. If the idle speed is obviously much too high, or if dense blue or clearly-visible black smoke comes from the tailpipe for more than 5 seconds, the vehicle will fail. As a rule of thumb, blue smoke signifies oil being burnt (engine wear) while black smoke signifies unburnt fuel (dirty air cleaner element, or other carburettor or fuel system fault).

☐ An exhaust gas analyser capable of measuring carbon monoxide (CO) and hydrocarbons (HC) is now needed. If such an instrument cannot be hired or borrowed, a local garage may agree to perform the check for a small fee.

CO emissions (mixture)

☐ At the time of writing, the maximum CO level at idle is 3.5% for vehicles first used after August 1986 and 4.5% for older vehicles. From January 1996 a much tighter limit (around 0.5%) applies to catalyst-equipped vehicles first used from August 1992. If the CO level cannot be reduced far enough to pass the test (and the fuel and ignition systems are otherwise in good condition) then the carburettor is badly worn, or there is some problem in the fuel injection system or catalytic converter (as applicable).

HC emissions

☐ With the CO emissions within limits, HC emissions must be no more than 1200 ppm (parts per million). If the vehicle fails this test at idle, it can be re-tested at around 2000 rpm; if the HC level is then 1200 ppm or less, this counts as a pass.

☐ Excessive HC emissions can be caused by oil being burnt, but they are more likely to be due to unburnt fuel.

Diesel models

☐ The only emission test applicable to Diesel engines is the measuring of exhaust smoke density. The test involves accelerating the engine several times to its maximum unloaded speed.

Note: *It is of the utmost importance that the engine timing belt is in good condition before the test is carried out.*

☐ Excessive smoke can be caused by a dirty air cleaner element. Otherwise, professional advice may be needed to find the cause.

Introduction

A selection of good tools is a fundamental requirement for anyone contemplating the maintenance and repair of a motor vehicle. For the owner who does not possess any, their purchase will prove a considerable expense, offsetting some of the savings made by doing-it-yourself. However, provided that the tools purchased meet the relevant national safety standards and are of good quality, they will last for many years and prove an extremely worthwhile investment.

To help the average owner to decide which tools are needed to carry out the various tasks detailed in this manual, we have compiled three lists of tools under the following headings: *Maintenance and minor repair, Repair and overhaul,* and *Special.* Newcomers to practical mechanics should start off with the *Maintenance and minor repair* tool kit, and confine themselves to the simpler jobs around the vehicle. Then, as confidence and experience grow, more difficult tasks can be undertaken, with extra tools being purchased as, and when, they are needed. In this way, a *Maintenance and minor repair* tool kit can be built up into a *Repair and overhaul* tool kit over a considerable period of time, without any major cash outlays. The experienced do-it-yourselfer will have a tool kit good enough for most repair and overhaul procedures, and will add tools from the *Special* category when it is felt that the expense is justified by the amount of use to which these tools will be put.

Maintenance and minor repair tool kit

The tools given in this list should be considered as a minimum requirement if routine maintenance, servicing and minor repair operations are to be undertaken. We recommend the purchase of combination spanners (ring one end, open-ended the other); although more expensive than open-ended ones, they do give the advantages of both types of spanner.

- [ ] *Combination spanners: 8, 9, 10, 11, 12, 13, 14, 15, 16, 17, 19, 21, 22, 24 & 26 mm*
- [ ] *Adjustable spanner - 35 mm jaw (approx)*
- [ ] *Engine sump/gearbox drain plug key*
- [ ] *Set of feeler gauges*
- [ ] *Spark plug spanner (with rubber insert)*
- [ ] *Spark plug gap adjustment tool*
- [ ] *Brake bleed nipple spanner*
- [ ] *Brake adjuster spanner*
- [ ] *Screwdrivers: Flat blade and cross blade – approx 100 mm long x 6 mm dia*
- [ ] *Combination pliers*
- [ ] *Hacksaw (junior)*
- [ ] *Tyre pump*
- [ ] *Tyre pressure gauge*
- [ ] *Grease gun*
- [ ] *Oil can*
- [ ] *Oil filter removal tool*
- [ ] *Fine emery cloth*
- [ ] *Wire brush (small)*
- [ ] *Funnel (medium size)*

Repair and overhaul tool kit

These tools are virtually essential for anyone undertaking any major repairs to a motor vehicle, and are additional to those given in the *Maintenance and minor repair* list. Included in this list is a comprehensive set of sockets. Although these are expensive, they will be found invaluable as they are so versatile - particularly if various drives are included in the set. We recommend the half-inch square-drive type, as this can be used with most proprietary torque wrenches. If you cannot afford a socket set, even bought piecemeal, then inexpensive tubular box spanners are a useful alternative.

The tools in this list will occasionally need to be supplemented by tools from the *Special* list:

- [ ] *Sockets (or box spanners) to cover range in previous list*
- [ ] *Reversible ratchet drive (for use with sockets) (see illustration)*
- [ ] *Extension piece, 250 mm (for use with sockets)*
- [ ] *Universal joint (for use with sockets)*
- [ ] *Torque wrench (for use with sockets)*
- [ ] *Self-locking grips*
- [ ] *Ball pein hammer*
- [ ] *Soft-faced mallet (plastic/aluminium or rubber)*
- [ ] *Screwdrivers:*
  Flat blade - long & sturdy, short (chubby), and narrow (electrician's) types
  Cross blade - Long & sturdy, and short (chubby) types
- [ ] *Pliers:*
  Long-nosed
  Side cutters (electrician's)
  Circlip (internal and external)
- [ ] *Cold chisel - 25 mm*
- [ ] *Scriber*
- [ ] *Scraper*
- [ ] *Centre-punch*
- [ ] *Pin punch*
- [ ] *Hacksaw*
- [ ] *Brake hose clamp*
- [ ] *Brake bleeding kit*
- [ ] *Selection of twist drills*
- [ ] *Steel rule/straight-edge*
- [ ] *Allen keys (inc. splined/Torx type) (see illustrations)*
- [ ] *Selection of files*
- [ ] *Wire brush*
- [ ] *Axle stands*
- [ ] *Jack (strong trolley or hydraulic type)*
- [ ] *Light with extension lead*

Special tools

The tools in this list are those which are not used regularly, are expensive to buy, or which need to be used in accordance with their manufacturers' instructions. Unless relatively difficult mechanical jobs are undertaken frequently, it will not be economic to buy many of these tools. Where this is the case, you could consider clubbing together with friends (or joining a motorists' club) to make a joint purchase, or borrowing the tools against a deposit from a local garage or tool hire specialist. It is worth noting that many of the larger DIY superstores now carry a large range of special tools for hire at modest rates.

The following list contains only those tools and instruments freely available to the public, and not those special tools produced by the vehicle manufacturer specifically for its dealer network. You will find occasional references to these manufacturers' special tools in the text of this manual. Generally, an alternative method of doing the job without the vehicle manufacturers' special tool is given. However, sometimes there is no alternative to using them. Where this is the case and the relevant tool cannot be bought or borrowed, you will have to entrust the work to a franchised garage.

- [ ] *Valve spring compressor (see illustration)*
- [ ] *Valve grinding tool*
- [ ] *Piston ring compressor (see illustration)*
- [ ] *Piston ring removal/installation tool (see illustration)*
- [ ] *Cylinder bore hone (see illustration)*
- [ ] *Balljoint separator*
- [ ] *Coil spring compressors (where applicable)*
- [ ] *Two/three-legged hub and bearing puller (see illustration)*

Sockets and reversible ratchet drive

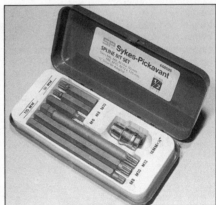

Spline bit set

Tools and Working Facilities

Spline key set

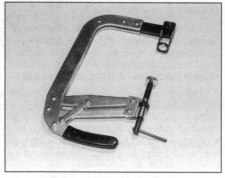

Valve spring compressor

Piston ring compressor

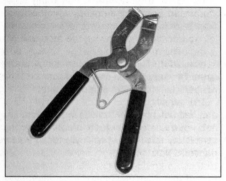

Piston ring removal/installation tool

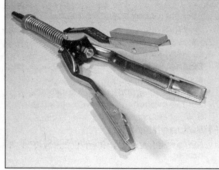

Cylinder bore hone

Three-legged hub and bearing puller

Micrometer set

Vernier calipers

Dial test indicator and magnetic stand

Compression testing gauge

Clutch plate alignment set

Brake shoe steady spring cup removal tool

- ☐ Impact screwdriver
- ☐ Micrometer and/or vernier calipers **(see illustrations)**
- ☐ Dial gauge **(see illustration)**
- ☐ Universal electrical multi-meter
- ☐ Cylinder compression gauge **(see illustration)**
- ☐ Clutch plate alignment set **(see illustration)**
- ☐ Brake shoe steady spring cup removal tool **(see illustration)**
- ☐ Bush and bearing removal/installation set **(see illustration)**
- ☐ Stud extractors **(see illustration)**
- ☐ Tap and die set **(see illustration)**
- ☐ Lifting tackle
- ☐ Trolley jack

Buying tools

For practically all tools, a tool factor is the best source, since he will have a very comprehensive range compared with the average garage or accessory shop. Having said that, accessory shops often offer excellent quality tools at discount prices, so it pays to shop around.

Remember, you don't have to buy the most expensive items on the shelf, but it is always advisable to steer clear of the very cheap tools. There are plenty of good tools around at reasonable prices, but always aim to purchase items which meet the relevant national safety standards. If in doubt, ask the proprietor or manager of the shop for advice before making a purchase.

Care and maintenance of tools

Having purchased a reasonable tool kit, it is necessary to keep the tools in a clean and serviceable condition. After use, always wipe off any dirt, grease and metal particles using a clean, dry cloth, before putting the tools away. Never leave them lying around after they have been used. A simple tool rack on the garage or workshop wall for items such as screwdrivers and pliers is a good idea. Store all normal spanners and sockets in a metal box. Any measuring instruments, gauges, meters, etc, must be carefully stored where they cannot be damaged or become rusty.

Take a little care when tools are used. Hammer heads inevitably become marked, and screwdrivers lose the keen edge on their blades from time to time. A little timely attention with emery cloth or a file will soon restore items like this to a good serviceable finish.

Working facilities

Not to be forgotten when discussing tools is the workshop itself. If anything more than routine maintenance is to be carried out, some form of suitable working area becomes essential.

It is appreciated that many an owner-mechanic is forced by circumstances to remove an engine or similar item without the benefit of a garage or workshop. Having done this, any repairs should always be done under the cover of a roof.

Wherever possible, any dismantling should be done on a clean, flat workbench or table at a suitable working height.

Any workbench needs a vice; one with a jaw opening of 100 mm is suitable for most jobs. As mentioned previously, some clean dry storage space is also required for tools, as well as for any lubricants, cleaning fluids, touch-up paints and so on, which become necessary.

Another item which may be required, and which has a much more general usage, is an electric drill with a chuck capacity of at least 8 mm. This, together with a good range of twist drills, is virtually essential for fitting accessories.

Last, but not least, always keep a supply of old newspapers and clean, lint-free rags available, and try to keep any working area as clean as possible.

Bush and bearing removal/installation set

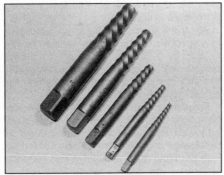
Stud extractor set

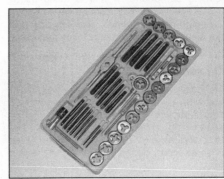
Tap and die set

Whenever servicing, repair or overhaul work is carried out on the car or its components, it is necessary to observe the following procedures and instructions. This will assist in carrying out the operation efficiently and to a professional standard of workmanship.

Joint mating faces and gaskets

When separating components at their mating faces, never insert screwdrivers or similar implements into the joint between the faces in order to prise them apart. This can cause severe damage which results in oil leaks, coolant leaks, etc upon reassembly. Separation is usually achieved by tapping along the joint with a soft-faced hammer in order to break the seal. However, note that this method may not be suitable where dowels are used for component location.

Where a gasket is used between the mating faces of two components, ensure that it is renewed on reassembly, and fit it dry unless otherwise stated in the repair procedure. Make sure that the mating faces are clean and dry, with all traces of old gasket removed. When cleaning a joint face, use a tool which is not likely to score or damage the face, and remove any burrs or nicks with an oilstone or fine file.

Make sure that tapped holes are cleaned with a pipe cleaner, and keep them free of jointing compound, if this is being used, unless specifically instructed otherwise.

Ensure that all orifices, channels or pipes are clear, and blow through them, preferably using compressed air.

Oil seals

Oil seals can be removed by levering them out with a wide flat-bladed screwdriver or similar implement. Alternatively, a number of self-tapping screws may be screwed into the seal, and these used as a purchase for pliers or some similar device in order to pull the seal free.

Whenever an oil seal is removed from its working location, either individually or as part of an assembly, it should be renewed.

The very fine sealing lip of the seal is easily damaged, and will not seal if the surface it contacts is not completely clean and free from scratches, nicks or grooves.

Protect the lips of the seal from any surface which may damage them in the course of fitting. Use tape or a conical sleeve where possible. Lubricate the seal lips with oil before fitting and, on dual-lipped seals, fill the space between the lips with grease.

Unless otherwise stated, oil seals must be fitted with their sealing lips toward the lubricant to be sealed.

Use a tubular drift or block of wood of the appropriate size to install the seal and, if the seal housing is shouldered, drive the seal down to the shoulder. If the seal housing is unshouldered, the seal should be fitted with its face flush with the housing top face (unless otherwise instructed).

Screw threads and fastenings

Seized nuts, bolts and screws are quite a common occurrence where corrosion has set in, and the use of penetrating oil or releasing fluid will often overcome this problem if the offending item is soaked for a while before attempting to release it. The use of an impact driver may also provide a means of releasing such stubborn fastening devices, when used in conjunction with the appropriate screwdriver bit or socket. If none of these methods works, it may be necessary to resort to the careful application of heat, or the use of a hacksaw or nut splitter device.

Studs are usually removed by locking two nuts together on the threaded part, and then using a spanner on the lower nut to unscrew the stud. Studs or bolts which have broken off below the surface of the component in which they are mounted can sometimes be removed using a proprietary stud extractor. Always ensure that a blind tapped hole is completely free from oil, grease, water or other fluid before installing the bolt or stud. Failure to do this could cause the housing to crack due to the hydraulic action of the bolt or stud as it is screwed in.

When tightening a castellated nut to accept a split pin, tighten the nut to the specified torque, where applicable, and then tighten further to the next split pin hole. Never slacken the nut to align the split pin hole, unless stated in the repair procedure.

When checking or retightening a nut or bolt to a specified torque setting, slacken the nut or bolt by a quarter of a turn, and then retighten to the specified setting. However, this should not be attempted where angular tightening has been used.

For some screw fastenings, notably cylinder head bolts or nuts, torque wrench settings are no longer specified for the latter stages of tightening, "angle-tightening" being called up instead. Typically, a fairly low torque wrench setting will be applied to the bolts/nuts in the correct sequence, followed by one or more stages of tightening through specified angles.

Locknuts, locktabs and washers

Any fastening which will rotate against a component or housing in the course of tightening should always have a washer between it and the relevant component or housing.

Spring or split washers should always be renewed when they are used to lock a critical component such as a big-end bearing retaining bolt or nut. Locktabs which are folded over to retain a nut or bolt should always be renewed.

Self-locking nuts can be re-used in non-critical areas, providing resistance can be felt when the locking portion passes over the bolt or stud thread. However, it should be noted that self-locking stiffnuts tend to lose their

effectiveness after long periods of use, and in such cases should be renewed as a matter of course.

Split pins must always be replaced with new ones of the correct size for the hole.

When thread-locking compound is found on the threads of a fastener which is to be re-used, it should be cleaned off with a wire brush and solvent, and fresh compound applied on reassembly.

Special tools

Some repair procedures in this manual entail the use of special tools such as a press, two or three-legged pullers, spring compressors, etc. Wherever possible, suitable readily-available alternatives to the manufacturer's special tools are described, and are shown in use. Unless you are highly-skilled and have a thorough understanding of the procedures described, never attempt to bypass the use of any special tool when the procedure described specifies its use. Not only is there a very great risk of personal injury, but expensive damage could be caused to the components involved.

Environmental considerations

When disposing of used engine oil, brake fluid, antifreeze, etc, give due consideration to any detrimental environmental effects. Do not, for instance, pour any of the above liquids down drains into the general sewage system, or onto the ground to soak away. Many local council refuse tips provide a facility for waste oil disposal, as do some garages. If none of these facilities are available, consult your local Environmental Health Department for further advice.

With the universal tightening-up of legislation regarding the emission of environmentally-harmful substances from motor vehicles, most current vehicles have tamperproof devices fitted to the main adjustment points of the fuel system. These devices are primarily designed to prevent unqualified persons from adjusting the fuel/air mixture, with the chance of a consequent increase in toxic emissions. If such devices are encountered during servicing or overhaul, they should, wherever possible, be renewed or refitted in accordance with the vehicle manufacturer's requirements or current legislation.

OIL CARE

FOLLOW THE CODE

OIL BANK LINE
0800 66 33 66

Note: It is antisocial and illegal to dump oil down the drain. To find the location of your local oil recycling bank, call this number free.

Introduction

The vehicle owner who does his or her own maintenance according to the recommended schedules should not have to use this section of the manual very often. Modern component reliability is such that, provided those items subject to wear or deterioration are inspected or renewed at the specified intervals, sudden failure is comparatively rare. Faults do not usually just happen as a result of sudden failure, but develop over a period of time. Major mechanical failures in particular are usually preceded by characteristic symptoms over hundreds or even thousands of miles. Those components which do occasionally fail without warning are often small and easily carried in the vehicle.

With any fault finding, the first step is to decide where to begin investigations. Sometimes this is obvious, but on other occasions a little detective work will be necessary. The owner who makes half a dozen haphazard adjustments or replacements may be successful in curing a fault (or its symptoms), but he will be none the wiser if the fault recurs and he may well have spent more time and money than was necessary. A calm and logical approach will be found to be more satisfactory in the long run. Always take into account any warning signs or abnormalities that may have been noticed in the period preceding the fault – power loss, high or low gauge readings, unusual noises or smells, etc – and remember that failure of components such as fuses or spark plugs may only be pointers to some underlying fault.

The pages which follow here are intended to help in cases of failure to start or breakdown on the road. There is also a Fault Diagnosis Section at the end of each Chapter which should be consulted if the preliminary checks prove unfruitful. Whatever the fault, certain basic principles apply. These are as follows:

Verify the fault. This is simply a matter of being sure that you know what the symptoms are before starting work. This is particularly important if you are investigating a fault for someone else who may not have described it very accurately.

Don't overlook the obvious. For example, if the vehicle won't start, is there petrol in the tank? (Don't take anyone else's word on this particular point, and don't trust the fuel gauge either!) If an electrical fault is indicated, look for loose or broken wires before digging out the test gear.

Cure the disease, not the symptom. Substituting a flat battery with a fully charged one will get you off the hard shoulder, but if the underlying cause is not attended to,the new battery will go the same way. Similarly, changing oil-fouled spark plugs for a new set will get you moving again, but remember that the reason for the fouling (if it wasn't simply an incorrect grade of plug) will have to be established and corrected.

Don't take anything for granted. Particularly, don't forget that a 'new' component may itself be defective (especially if it's been rattling round in the boot for months), and don't leave components out of a fault diagnosis sequence just because they are new or recently fitted. When you do finally diagnose a difficult fault, you'll probably realise that all the evidence was there from the start.

Electrical faults

Electrical faults can be more puzzling than straightforward mechanical failures, but they are no less susceptible to logical analysis if the basic principles of operation are understood. Vehicle electrical wiring exists in extremely unfavourable conditions – heat, vibration and chemical attack and the first things to look for are loose or corroded connections and broken or chafed wires, especially where the wires pass through holes in the bodywork or are subject to vibration.

All metal-bodied vehicles in current production have one pole of the battery 'earthed', ie connected to the vehicle bodywork, and in nearly all modern vehicles it is the negative (–) terminal. The various electrical components – motors, bulb holders, etc – are also connected to earth, either by means of a lead or directly by their mountings. Electric current flows through the component and then back to the battery via the bodywork. If the component mounting is loose or corroded, or if a good path back to the battery is not available, the circuit will be incomplete and malfunction will result. The engine and/or gearbox are also earthed by means of flexible metal straps to the body or subframe; if these straps are loose or missing, starter motor, generator and ignition trouble may result.

Assuming the earth return to be satisfactory, electrical faults will be due either to component malfunction or to defects in the current supply. Individual components are dealt with in Chapter 9. If supply wires are broken or cracked internally this results in an open-circuit, and the easiest way to check for this is to bypass the suspect wire temporarily with a length of wire having a crocodile clip or suitable connector at each end. Alternatively, a 12V test lamp can be used to verify the presence of supply voltage at various points along the wire and the break can be thus isolated.

If a bare portion of a live wire touches the bodywork or other earthed metal part, the electricity will take the low-resistance path thus formed back to the battery: this is known as a short-circuit. Hopefully a short-circuit will blow a fuse, but otherwise it may cause burning of the insulation (and possibly further short-circuits) or even a fire. This is why it is inadvisable to bypass persistently blowing fuses with silver foil or wire.

Spares and tool kit

Most vehicles are supplied only with sufficient tools for wheel changing; the *Maintenance and minor repair* tool kit detailed in *Tools and working facilities,* with the addition of a hammer, is probably sufficient for those repairs that most motorists would consider attempting at the roadside. In addition a few items which can be fitted without too much trouble in the event of a breakdown should be carried. Experience and available space will modify the list below, but the following may save having to call on professional assistance:

- ☐ Spark plugs, clean and correctly gapped
- ☐ HT lead and plug cap – long enough to reach the plug furthest from the distributor
- ☐ Distributor rotor, condenser and contact breaker points (where applicable)

- ☐ Drivebelt(s) — emergency type may suffice
- ☐ Spare fuses
- ☐ Set of principal light bulbs
- ☐ Tin of radiator sealer and hose bandage
- ☐ Exhaust bandage
- ☐ Roll of insulating tape
- ☐ Length of soft iron wire
- ☐ Length of electrical flex
- ☐ Torch or inspection lamp (can double as test lamp)
- ☐ Battery jump leads
- ☐ Tow-rope
- ☐ Ignition waterproofing aerosol
- ☐ Litre of engine oil
- ☐ Sealed can of hydraulic fluid
- ☐ Emergency windscreen
- ☐ Wormdrive clips
- ☐ Tube of filler paste

If spare fuel is carried, a can designed for the purpose should be used to minimise risks of leakage and collision damage. A first aid kit and a warning triangle, whilst not at present compulsory in the UK, are obviously sensible items to carry in addition to the above. When touring abroad it may be advisable to carry additional spares which, even if you cannot fit them yourself, could save having to wait while parts are obtained. The items below may be worth considering:

- ☐ Clutch and throttle cables
- ☐ Cylinder head gasket
- ☐ Alternator brushes
- ☐ Tyre valve core

One of the motoring organisations will be able to advise on availability of fuel, etc, in foreign countries.

Engine will not start

Engine fails to turn when starter operated

- ☐ Flat battery (recharge use jump leads or push start)
- ☐ Battery terminals loose or corroded
- ☐ Battery earth to body defective
- ☐ Engine earth strap loose or broken
- ☐ Starter motor (or solenoid) wiring loose or broken
- ☐ Automatic transmission selector in wrong position, or inhibitor switch faulty
- ☐ Ignition/starter switch faulty
- ☐ Major mechanical failure (seizure)
- ☐ Starter or solenoid internal fault (see Chapter 12)
- ☐ Faulty stop-start system (where fitted)

Starter motor turns engine slowly

- ☐ Partially discharged battery (recharge, use jump leads, or push start)
- ☐ Battery terminals loose or corroded
- ☐ Battery earth to body defective

- ☐ Engine earth strap loose
- ☐ Starter motor (or solenoid) wiring loose
- ☐ Starter motor internal fault (see Chapter 9)

Starter motor spins without turning engine

- ☐ Flywheel gear teeth damaged or worn
- ☐ Starter motor mounting bolts loose

Engine turns normally but fails to start

- ☐ Damp or dirty HT leads and distributor cap (crank engine and check for spark)
- ☐ No fuel in tank (check for delivery at carburettor)

- ☐ Excessive choke (hot engine) or insufficient choke (cold engine)
- ☐ Fouled or incorrectly gapped spark plugs (remove, clean and regap)
- ☐ Other ignition system fault (see Chapter 4)
- ☐ Other fuel system fault (see Chapter 3)
- ☐ Poor compression (see Chapter 1)
- ☐ Major mechanical failure (eg camshaft drive)

Engine fires but will not run

- ☐ Insufficient choke (cold engine)
- ☐ Air leaks at carburettor or inlet manifold
- ☐ Fuel starvation (see Chapter 3)
- ☐ Ballast resistor defective, or other ignition fault (see Chapter 4)

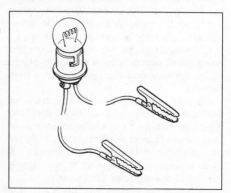

A simple test lamp is useful for checking electrical faults

Carrying a few spares may save you a long walk!

Engine cuts out and will not restart

Engine cuts out suddenly – ignition fault

- [ ] Loose or disconnected LT wires
- [ ] Wet HT leads or distributor cap (after traversing water splash)
- [ ] Coil failure (check for spark)
- [ ] Other ignition fault (see Chapter 4)

Engine misfires before cutting out – fuel fault

- [ ] Fuel tank empty
- [ ] Fuel pump defective or filter blocked (check for delivery)

Check for spark using insulated pliers and metal rod in lead extension

Checking carburettor fuel hose for delivery while cranking the engine

- [ ] Fuel tank filler vent blocked (suction will be evident on releasing cap)
- [ ] Carburettor needle valve sticking
- [ ] Carburettor jets blocked (fuel contaminated)
- [ ] Other fuel system fault (see Chapter 3)

Engine cuts out – other causes

- [ ] Serious overheating
- [ ] Major mechanical failure (eg camshaft drive)

Engine overheats

Ignition (no-charge) warning light illuminated

- [ ] Slack or broken drivebelt — retension or renew (Chapter 9)

Ignition warning light not illuminated

- [ ] Coolant loss due to internal or external leakage (see Chapter 2)
- [ ] Thermostat defective
- [ ] Low oil level
- [ ] Brakes binding
- [ ] Radiator clogged externally or internally
- [ ] Electric cooling fan not operating correctly
- [ ] Engine waterways clogged
- [ ] Ignition timing incorrect or automatic advance malfunctioning
- [ ] Mixture too weak

Note: *Do not add cold water to an overheated engine or damage may result*

Low engine oil pressure

Note: *Low oil pressure in a high-mileage engine at tickover is not necessarily a cause for concern. Sudden pressure loss at speed is far more significant. In any event check the gauge or warning light sender before condemning the engine.*

Gauge reads low or warning light illuminated with engine running

- [ ] Oil level low or incorrect grade
- [ ] Defective gauge or sender unit
- [ ] Wire to sender unit earthed
- [ ] Engine overheating
- [ ] Oil filter clogged or bypass valve defective
- [ ] Oil pressure relief valve defective
- [ ] Oil pick-up strainer clogged
- [ ] Oil pump worn or mountings loose
- [ ] Worn main or big-end bearings

Engine noises

Pre-ignition (pinking) on acceleration

- [ ] Incorrect grade of fuel
- [ ] Ignition timing incorrect
- [ ] Distributor faulty or worn
- [ ] Worn or maladjusted carburettor
- [ ] Excessive carbon build-up in engine

Whistling or wheezing noises

- [ ] Leaking vacuum hose
- [ ] Leaking carburettor or manifold gasket
- [ ] Blowing head gasket

Tapping or rattling

- [ ] Incorrect valve clearances (where applicable)
- [ ] Worn valve gear
- [ ] Worn timing chain or belt
- [ ] Broken piston ring (ticking noise)

Knocking or thumping

- [ ] Unintentional mechanical contact (eg fan blades)
- [ ] Worn drivebelt
- [ ] Peripheral component fault (generator, water pump, etc)
- [ ] Worn big-end bearings (regular heavy knocking, perhaps less under load)
- [ ] Worn main bearings (rumbling and knocking, perhaps worsening under load)
- [ ] Piston slap (most noticeable when cold)

Conversion Factors

Length (distance)

Inches (in)	25.4	=	Millimetres (mm)	x 0.0394	=	Inches (in)
Feet (ft)	0.305	=	Metres (m)	x 3.281	=	Feet (ft)
Miles	1.609	=	Kilometres (km)	x 0.621	=	Miles

Volume (capacity)

Cubic inches (cu in; in³)	x 16.387	=	Cubic centimetres (cc; cm³)	x 0.061	=	Cubic inches (cu in; in³)
Imperial pints (Imp pt)	x 0.568	=	Litres (l)	x 1.76	=	Imperial pints (Imp pt)
Imperial quarts (Imp qt)	x 1.137	=	Litres (l)	x 0.88	=	Imperial quarts (Imp qt)
Imperial quarts (Imp qt)	x 1.201	=	US quarts (US qt)	x 0.833	=	Imperial quarts (Imp qt)
US quarts (US qt)	x 0.946	=	Litres (l)	x 1.057	=	US quarts (US qt)
Imperial gallons (Imp gal)	x 4.546	=	Litres (l)	x 0.22	=	Imperial gallons (Imp gal)
Imperial gallons (Imp gal)	x 1.201	=	US gallons (US gal)	x 0.833	=	Imperial gallons (Imp gal)
US gallons (US gal)	x 3.785	=	Litres (l)	x 0.264	=	US gallons (US gal)

Mass (weight)

Ounces (oz)	x 28.35	=	Grams (g)	x 0.035	=	Ounces (oz)
Pounds (lb)	x 0.454	=	Kilograms (kg)	x 2.205	=	Pounds (lb)

Force

Ounces-force (ozf; oz)	x 0.278	=	Newtons (N)	x 3.6	=	Ounces-force (ozf; oz)
Pounds-force (lbf; lb)	x 4.448	=	Newtons (N)	x 0.225	=	Pounds-force (lbf; lb)
Newtons (N)	x 0.1	=	Kilograms-force (kgf; kg)	x 9.81	=	Newtons (N)

Pressure

Pounds-force per square inch (psi; lbf/in²; lb/in²)	x 0.070	=	Kilograms-force per square centimetre (kgf/cm²; kg/cm²)	x 14.223	=	Pounds-force per square inch (psi; lbf/in²; lb/in²)
Pounds-force per square inch (psi; lbf/in²; lb/in²)	x 0.068	=	Atmospheres (atm)	x 14.696	=	Pounds-force per square inch (psi; lbf/in²; lb/in²)
Pounds-force per square inch (psi; lbf/in²; lb/in²)	x 0.069	=	Bars	x 14.5	=	Pounds-force per square inch (psi; lbf/in²; lb/in²)
Pounds-force per square inch (psi; lbf/in²; lb/in²)	x 6.895	=	Kilopascals (kPa)	x 0.145	=	Pounds-force per square inch (psi; lbf/in²; lb/in²)
Kilopascals (kPa)	x 0.01	=	Kilograms-force per square centimetre (kgf/cm²; kg/cm²)	x 98.1	=	Kilopascals (kPa)
Millibar (mbar)	x 100	=	Pascals (Pa)	x 0.01	=	Millibar (mbar)
Millibar (mbar)	x 0.0145	=	Pounds-force per square inch (psi; lbf/in²; lb/in²)	x 68.947	=	Millibar (mbar)
Millibar (mbar)	x 0.75	=	Millimetres of mercury (mmHg)	x 1.333	=	Millibar (mbar)
Millibar (mbar)	x 0.401	=	Inches of water (inH₂O)	x 2.491	=	Millibar (mbar)
Millimetres of mercury (mmHg)	x 0.535	=	Inches of water (inH₂O)	x 1.868	=	Millimetres of mercury (mmHg)
Inches of water (inH₂O)	x 0.036	=	Pounds-force per square inch (psi; lbf/in²; lb/in²)	x 27.68	=	Inches of water (inH₂O)

Torque (moment of force)

Pounds-force inches (lbf in; lb in)	x 1.152	=	Kilograms-force centimetre (kgf cm; kg cm)	x 0.868	=	Pounds-force inches (lbf in; lb in)
Pounds-force inches (lbf in; lb in)	x 0.113	=	Newton metres (Nm)	x 8.85	=	Pounds-force inches (lbf in; lb in)
Pounds-force inches (lbf in; lb in)	x 0.083	=	Pounds-force feet (lbf ft; lb ft)	x 12	=	Pounds-force inches (lbf in; lb in)
Pounds-force feet (lbf ft; lb ft)	x 0.138	=	Kilograms-force metres (kgf m; kg m)	x 7.233	=	Pounds-force feet (lbf ft; lb ft)
Pounds-force feet (lbf ft; lb ft)	x 1.356	=	Newton metres (Nm)	x 0.738	=	Pounds-force feet (lbf ft; lb ft)
Newton metres (Nm)	x 0.102	=	Kilograms-force metres (kgf m; kg m)	x 9.804	=	Newton metres (Nm)

Power

Horsepower (hp)	x 745.7	=	Watts (W)	x 0.0013	=	Horsepower (hp)

Velocity (speed)

Miles per hour (miles/hr; mph)	x 1.609	=	Kilometres per hour (km/hr; kph)	x 0.621	=	Miles per hour (miles/hr; mph)

Fuel consumption*

Miles per gallon (mpg)	x 0.354	=	Kilometres per litre (km/l)	x 2.825	=	Miles per gallon (mpg)

* It is common practice to convert from miles per gallon (mpg) to litres/100 kilometres (l/100km), where mpg x l/100 km = 282

Temperature

Degrees Fahrenheit = (°C x 1.8) + 32   Degrees Celsius (Degrees Centigrade; °C) = (°F - 32) x 0.56

Buying spare parts

Spare parts are available from many sources, for example: Volvo garages, other garages and accessory shops, and motor factors. Our advice regarding spare part sources is as follows.

Officially appointed Volvo garages - This is the best source of parts which are peculiar to your car and otherwise not generally available (eg complete cylinder heads, transmission components, badges, interior trim, etc). It is also the only place at which you should buy parts if your vehicle is still under warranty - use of non-Volvo components may invalidate the warranty. To be sure of obtaining the correct parts it will always be necessary to give the storeman your car's vehicle identification number, and if possible, to take the 'old' part along for positive identification. Remember that many parts are available on a factory exchange scheme - any parts returned should always be clean! It obviously makes good sense to go straight to the specialists on your car for

this type of part for they are best equipped to supply you.

Other garages and accessory shops - These are often very good places to buy materials and components needed for the maintenance of your car (eg oil filters, spark plugs, bulbs, drivebelts, oils and greases, touch-up paint, filler paste, etc). They also sell general accessories, usually have convenient opening hours, charge lower prices and can often be found not far from home.

Motor factors - Good factors will stock all of the more important components which wear out relatively quickly (eg clutch components, pistons, valves, exhaust systems, brake cylinders/pipes/hoses/ seals/shoes and pads, etc). Motor factors will often provide new or reconditioned components on a part exchange basis - this can save a considerable amount of money.

Vehicle identification numbers

Although many individual parts, and in

some cases sub-assemblies, fit a number of different models, it is dangerous to assume that just because they look the same, they are the same. Differences are not always easy to detect except by serial numbers. Make sure, therefore, that the appropriate identity number for the model or sub-assembly is known and quoted when a spare part is ordered.

The engine number on B14 models is located on a metal plate fixed to the left-hand side of the cylinder block above the oil filter. On B19 and B200 models it is punched in the cylinder block above the distributor and on B172 models, next to the oil dipstick.

The chassis number is stamped on the right-hand side of the bulkhead, behind the fusebox in the engine compartment.

The vehicle identification plate is located within the engine compartment on the front crossmember.

The servicing data plate is located under the driver's side door lock.

Engine number location

Vehicle identification plate location

A

ABS (Anti-lock brake system) A system, usually electronically controlled, that senses incipient wheel lockup during braking and relieves hydraulic pressure at wheels that are about to skid.

Air bag An inflatable bag hidden in the steering wheel (driver's side) or the dash or glovebox (passenger side). In a head-on collision, the bags inflate, preventing the driver and front passenger from being thrown forward into the steering wheel or windscreen.

Air cleaner A metal or plastic housing, containing a filter element, which removes dust and dirt from the air being drawn into the engine.

Air filter element The actual filter in an air cleaner system, usually manufactured from pleated paper and requiring renewal at regular intervals.

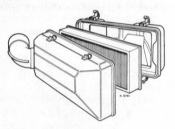

Air filter

Allen key A hexagonal wrench which fits into a recessed hexagonal hole.

Alligator clip A long-nosed spring-loaded metal clip with meshing teeth. Used to make temporary electrical connections.

Alternator A component in the electrical system which converts mechanical energy from a drivebelt into electrical energy to charge the battery and to operate the starting system, ignition system and electrical accessories.

Alternator (exploded view)

Ampere (amp) A unit of measurement for the flow of electric current. One amp is the amount of current produced by one volt acting through a resistance of one ohm.

Anaerobic sealer A substance used to prevent bolts and screws from loosening. Anaerobic means that it does not require oxygen for activation. The Loctite brand is widely used.

Antifreeze A substance (usually ethylene glycol) mixed with water, and added to a vehicle's cooling system, to prevent freezing of the coolant in winter. Antifreeze also contains chemicals to inhibit corrosion and the formation of rust and other deposits that

would tend to clog the radiator and coolant passages and reduce cooling efficiency.

Anti-seize compound A coating that reduces the risk of seizing on fasteners that are subjected to high temperatures, such as exhaust manifold bolts and nuts.

Anti-seize compound

Asbestos A natural fibrous mineral with great heat resistance, commonly used in the composition of brake friction materials. Asbestos is a health hazard and the dust created by brake systems should never be inhaled or ingested.

Axle A shaft on which a wheel revolves, or which revolves with a wheel. Also, a solid beam that connects the two wheels at one end of the vehicle. An axle which also transmits power to the wheels is known as a live axle.

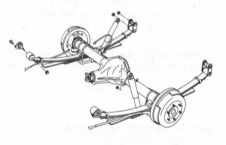

Axle assembly

Axleshaft A single rotating shaft, on either side of the differential, which delivers power from the final drive assembly to the drive wheels. Also called a driveshaft or a halfshaft.

B

Ball bearing An anti-friction bearing consisting of a hardened inner and outer race with hardened steel balls between two races.

Bearing

Bearing The curved surface on a shaft or in a bore, or the part assembled into either, that permits relative motion between them with minimum wear and friction.

Big-end bearing The bearing in the end of the connecting rod that's attached to the crankshaft.

Bleed nipple A valve on a brake wheel cylinder, caliper or other hydraulic component that is opened to purge the hydraulic system of air. Also called a bleed screw.

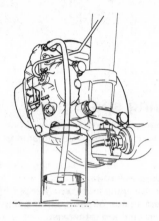

Brake bleeding

Brake bleeding Procedure for removing air from lines of a hydraulic brake system.

Brake disc The component of a disc brake that rotates with the wheels.

Brake drum The component of a drum brake that rotates with the wheels.

Brake linings The friction material which contacts the brake disc or drum to retard the vehicle's speed. The linings are bonded or riveted to the brake pads or shoes.

Brake pads The replaceable friction pads that pinch the brake disc when the brakes are applied. Brake pads consist of a friction material bonded or riveted to a rigid backing plate.

Brake shoe The crescent-shaped carrier to which the brake linings are mounted and which forces the lining against the rotating drum during braking.

Braking systems For more information on braking systems, consult the *Haynes Automotive Brake Manual*.

Breaker bar A long socket wrench handle providing greater leverage.

Bulkhead The insulated partition between the engine and the passenger compartment.

C

Caliper The non-rotating part of a disc-brake assembly that straddles the disc and carries the brake pads. The caliper also contains the hydraulic components that cause the pads to pinch the disc when the brakes are applied. A caliper is also a measuring tool that can be set to measure inside or outside dimensions of an object.

Camshaft A rotating shaft on which a series of cam lobes operate the valve mechanisms. The camshaft may be driven by gears, by sprockets and chain or by sprockets and a belt.

Canister A container in an evaporative emission control system; contains activated charcoal granules to trap vapours from the fuel system.

Canister

Carburettor A device which mixes fuel with air in the proper proportions to provide a desired power output from a spark ignition internal combustion engine.

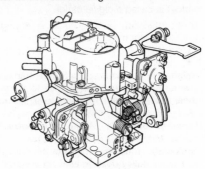

Carburettor

Castellated Resembling the parapets along the top of a castle wall. For example, a castellated balljoint stud nut.

Castellated nut

Castor In wheel alignment, the backward or forward tilt of the steering axis. Castor is positive when the steering axis is inclined rearward at the top.

Catalytic converter A silencer-like device in the exhaust system which converts certain pollutants in the exhaust gases into less harmful substances.

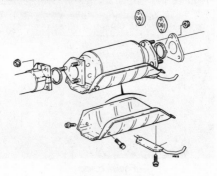

Catalytic converter

Circlip A ring-shaped clip used to prevent endwise movement of cylindrical parts and shafts. An internal circlip is installed in a groove in a housing; an external circlip fits into a groove on the outside of a cylindrical piece such as a shaft.

Clearance The amount of space between two parts. For example, between a piston and a cylinder, between a bearing and a journal, etc.

Coil spring A spiral of elastic steel found in various sizes throughout a vehicle, for example as a springing medium in the suspension and in the valve train.

Compression Reduction in volume, and increase in pressure and temperature, of a gas, caused by squeezing it into a smaller space.

Compression ratio The relationship between cylinder volume when the piston is at top dead centre and cylinder volume when the piston is at bottom dead centre.

Constant velocity (CV) joint A type of universal joint that cancels out vibrations caused by driving power being transmitted through an angle.

Core plug A disc or cup-shaped metal device inserted in a hole in a casting through which core was removed when the casting was formed. Also known as a freeze plug or expansion plug.

Crankcase The lower part of the engine block in which the crankshaft rotates.

Crankshaft The main rotating member, or shaft, running the length of the crankcase, with offset "throws" to which the connecting rods are attached.

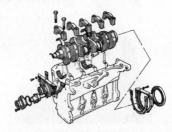

Crankshaft assembly

Crocodile clip See Alligator clip

D

Diagnostic code Code numbers obtained by accessing the diagnostic mode of an engine management computer. This code can be used to determine the area in the system where a malfunction may be located.

Disc brake A brake design incorporating a rotating disc onto which brake pads are squeezed. The resulting friction converts the energy of a moving vehicle into heat.

Double-overhead cam (DOHC) An engine that uses two overhead camshafts, usually one for the intake valves and one for the exhaust valves.

Drivebelt(s) The belt(s) used to drive accessories such as the alternator, water pump, power steering pump, air conditioning compressor, etc. off the crankshaft pulley.

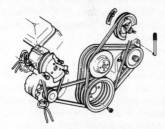

Accessory drivebelts

Driveshaft Any shaft used to transmit motion. Commonly used when referring to the axleshafts on a front wheel drive vehicle.

Driveshaft

Drum brake A type of brake using a drum-shaped metal cylinder attached to the inner surface of the wheel. When the brake pedal is pressed, curved brake shoes with friction linings press against the inside of the drum to slow or stop the vehicle.

Drum brake assembly

E

EGR valve A valve used to introduce exhaust gases into the intake air stream.

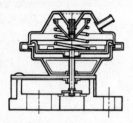

EGR valve

Electronic control unit (ECU) A computer which controls (for instance) ignition and fuel injection systems, or an anti-lock braking system. For more information refer to the *Haynes Automotive Electrical and Electronic Systems Manual*.

Electronic Fuel Injection (EFI) A computer controlled fuel system that distributes fuel through an injector located in each intake port of the engine.

Emergency brake A braking system, independent of the main hydraulic system, that can be used to slow or stop the vehicle if the primary brakes fail, or to hold the vehicle stationary even though the brake pedal isn't depressed. It usually consists of a hand lever that actuates either front or rear brakes mechanically through a series of cables and linkages. Also known as a handbrake or parking brake.

Endfloat The amount of lengthwise movement between two parts. As applied to a crankshaft, the distance that the crankshaft can move forward and back in the cylinder block.

Engine management system (EMS) A computer controlled system which manages the fuel injection and the ignition systems in an integrated fashion.

Exhaust manifold A part with several passages through which exhaust gases leave the engine combustion chambers and enter the exhaust pipe.

Exhaust manifold

F

Fan clutch A viscous (fluid) drive coupling device which permits variable engine fan speeds in relation to engine speeds.

Feeler blade A thin strip or blade of hardened steel, ground to an exact thickness, used to check or measure clearances between parts.

Feeler blade

Firing order The order in which the engine cylinders fire, or deliver their power strokes, beginning with the number one cylinder.

Flywheel A heavy spinning wheel in which energy is absorbed and stored by means of momentum. On cars, the flywheel is attached to the crankshaft to smooth out firing impulses.

Free play The amount of travel before any action takes place. The "looseness" in a linkage, or an assembly of parts, between the initial application of force and actual movement. For example, the distance the brake pedal moves before the pistons in the master cylinder are actuated.

Fuse An electrical device which protects a circuit against accidental overload. The typical fuse contains a soft piece of metal which is calibrated to melt at a predetermined current flow (expressed as amps) and break the circuit.

Fusible link A circuit protection device consisting of a conductor surrounded by heat-resistant insulation. The conductor is smaller than the wire it protects, so it acts as the weakest link in the circuit. Unlike a blown fuse, a failed fusible link must frequently be cut from the wire for replacement.

G

Gap The distance the spark must travel in jumping from the centre electrode to the side

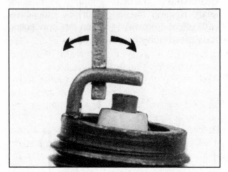

Adjusting spark plug gap

electrode in a spark plug. Also refers to the spacing between the points in a contact breaker assembly in a conventional points-type ignition, or to the distance between the reluctor or rotor and the pickup coil in an electronic ignition.

Gasket Any thin, soft material - usually cork, cardboard, asbestos or soft metal - installed between two metal surfaces to ensure a good seal. For instance, the cylinder head gasket seals the joint between the block and the cylinder head.

Gasket

Gauge An instrument panel display used to monitor engine conditions. A gauge with a movable pointer on a dial or a fixed scale is an analogue gauge. A gauge with a numerical readout is called a digital gauge.

H

Halfshaft A rotating shaft that transmits power from the final drive unit to a drive wheel, usually when referring to a live rear axle.

Harmonic balancer A device designed to reduce torsion or twisting vibration in the crankshaft. May be incorporated in the crankshaft pulley. Also known as a vibration damper.

Hone An abrasive tool for correcting small irregularities or differences in diameter in an engine cylinder, brake cylinder, etc.

Hydraulic tappet A tappet that utilises hydraulic pressure from the engine's lubrication system to maintain zero clearance (constant contact with both camshaft and valve stem). Automatically adjusts to variation in valve stem length. Hydraulic tappets also reduce valve noise.

I

Ignition timing The moment at which the spark plug fires, usually expressed in the number of crankshaft degrees before the piston reaches the top of its stroke.

Inlet manifold A tube or housing with passages through which flows the air-fuel mixture (carburettor vehicles and vehicles with throttle body injection) or air only (port fuel-injected vehicles) to the port openings in the cylinder head.

J

Jump start Starting the engine of a vehicle with a discharged or weak battery by attaching jump leads from the weak battery to a charged or helper battery.

L

Load Sensing Proportioning Valve (LSPV) A brake hydraulic system control valve that works like a proportioning valve, but also takes into consideration the amount of weight carried by the rear axle.

Locknut A nut used to lock an adjustment nut, or other threaded component, in place. For example, a locknut is employed to keep the adjusting nut on the rocker arm in position.

Lockwasher A form of washer designed to prevent an attaching nut from working loose.

M

MacPherson strut A type of front suspension system devised by Earle MacPherson at Ford of England. In its original form, a simple lateral link with the anti-roll bar creates the lower control arm. A long strut - an integral coil spring and shock absorber - is mounted between the body and the steering knuckle. Many modern so-called MacPherson strut systems use a conventional lower A-arm and don't rely on the anti-roll bar for location.

Multimeter An electrical test instrument with the capability to measure voltage, current and resistance.

N

NOx Oxides of Nitrogen. A common toxic pollutant emitted by petrol and diesel engines at higher temperatures.

O

Ohm The unit of electrical resistance. One volt applied to a resistance of one ohm will produce a current of one amp.

Ohmmeter An instrument for measuring electrical resistance.

O-ring A type of sealing ring made of a special rubber-like material; in use, the O-ring is compressed into a groove to provide the sealing action.

O-ring

Overhead cam (ohc) engine An engine with the camshaft(s) located on top of the cylinder head(s).

Overhead valve (ohv) engine An engine with the valves located in the cylinder head, but with the camshaft located in the engine block.

Oxygen sensor A device installed in the engine exhaust manifold, which senses the oxygen content in the exhaust and converts this information into an electric current. Also called a Lambda sensor.

P

Phillips screw A type of screw head having a cross instead of a slot for a corresponding type of screwdriver.

Plastigage A thin strip of plastic thread, available in different sizes, used for measuring clearances. For example, a strip of Plastigage is laid across a bearing journal. The parts are assembled and dismantled; the width of the crushed strip indicates the clearance between journal and bearing.

Plastigage

Propeller shaft The long hollow tube with universal joints at both ends that carries power from the transmission to the differential on front-engined rear wheel drive vehicles.

Proportioning valve A hydraulic control valve which limits the amount of pressure to the rear brakes during panic stops to prevent wheel lock-up.

R

Rack-and-pinion steering A steering system with a pinion gear on the end of the steering shaft that mates with a rack (think of a geared wheel opened up and laid flat). When the steering wheel is turned, the pinion turns, moving the rack to the left or right. This movement is transmitted through the track rods to the steering arms at the wheels.

Radiator A liquid-to-air heat transfer device designed to reduce the temperature of the coolant in an internal combustion engine cooling system.

Refrigerant Any substance used as a heat transfer agent in an air-conditioning system. R-12 has been the principle refrigerant for many years; recently, however, manufacturers have begun using R-134a, a non-CFC substance that is considered less harmful to the ozone in the upper atmosphere.

Rocker arm A lever arm that rocks on a shaft or pivots on a stud. In an overhead valve engine, the rocker arm converts the upward movement of the pushrod into a downward movement to open a valve.

Rotor In a distributor, the rotating device inside the cap that connects the centre electrode and the outer terminals as it turns, distributing the high voltage from the coil secondary winding to the proper spark plug. Also, that part of an alternator which rotates inside the stator. Also, the rotating assembly of a turbocharger, including the compressor wheel, shaft and turbine wheel.

Runout The amount of wobble (in-and-out movement) of a gear or wheel as it's rotated. The amount a shaft rotates "out-of-true." The out-of-round condition of a rotating part.

S

Sealant A liquid or paste used to prevent leakage at a joint. Sometimes used in conjunction with a gasket.

Sealed beam lamp An older headlight design which integrates the reflector, lens and filaments into a hermetically-sealed one-piece unit. When a filament burns out or the lens cracks, the entire unit is simply replaced.

Serpentine drivebelt A single, long, wide accessory drivebelt that's used on some newer vehicles to drive all the accessories, instead of a series of smaller, shorter belts. Serpentine drivebelts are usually tensioned by an automatic tensioner.

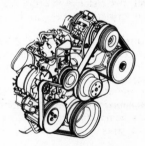

Serpentine drivebelt

Shim Thin spacer, commonly used to adjust the clearance or relative positions between two parts. For example, shims inserted into or under bucket tappets control valve clearances. Clearance is adjusted by changing the thickness of the shim.

Slide hammer A special puller that screws into or hooks onto a component such as a shaft or bearing; a heavy sliding handle on the shaft bottoms against the end of the shaft to knock the component free.

Sprocket A tooth or projection on the periphery of a wheel, shaped to engage with a chain or drivebelt. Commonly used to refer to the sprocket wheel itself.

Starter inhibitor switch On vehicles with an

automatic transmission, a switch that prevents starting if the vehicle is not in Neutral or Park.

Strut See MacPherson strut.

T

Tappet A cylindrical component which transmits motion from the cam to the valve stem, either directly or via a pushrod and rocker arm. Also called a cam follower.

Thermostat A heat-controlled valve that regulates the flow of coolant between the cylinder block and the radiator, so maintaining optimum engine operating temperature. A thermostat is also used in some air cleaners in which the temperature is regulated.

Thrust bearing The bearing in the clutch assembly that is moved in to the release levers by clutch pedal action to disengage the clutch. Also referred to as a release bearing.

Timing belt A toothed belt which drives the camshaft. Serious engine damage may result if it breaks in service.

Timing chain A chain which drives the camshaft.

Toe-in The amount the front wheels are closer together at the front than at the rear. On rear wheel drive vehicles, a slight amount of toe-in is usually specified to keep the front wheels running parallel on the road by offsetting other forces that tend to spread the wheels apart.

Toe-out The amount the front wheels are closer together at the rear than at the front. On front wheel drive vehicles, a slight amount of toe-out is usually specified.

Tools For full information on choosing and using tools, refer to the *Haynes Automotive Tools Manual.*

Tracer A stripe of a second colour applied to a wire insulator to distinguish that wire from another one with the same colour insulator.

Tune-up A process of accurate and careful adjustments and parts replacement to obtain the best possible engine performance.

Turbocharger A centrifugal device, driven by exhaust gases, that pressurises the intake air. Normally used to increase the power output from a given engine displacement, but can also be used primarily to reduce exhaust emissions (as on VW's "Umwelt" Diesel engine).

U

Universal joint or U-joint A double-pivoted connection for transmitting power from a driving to a driven shaft through an angle. A U-joint consists of two Y-shaped yokes and a cross-shaped member called the spider.

V

Valve A device through which the flow of liquid, gas, vacuum, or loose material in bulk may be started, stopped, or regulated by a movable part that opens, shuts, or partially obstructs one or more ports or passageways. A valve is also the movable part of such a device.

Valve clearance The clearance between the valve tip (the end of the valve stem) and the rocker arm or tappet. The valve clearance is measured when the valve is closed.

Vernier caliper A precision measuring instrument that measures inside and outside dimensions. Not quite as accurate as a micrometer, but more convenient.

Viscosity The thickness of a liquid or its resistance to flow.

Volt A unit for expressing electrical "pressure" in a circuit. One volt that will produce a current of one ampere through a resistance of one ohm.

W

Welding Various processes used to join metal items by heating the areas to be joined to a molten state and fusing them together. For more information refer to the *Haynes Automotive Welding Manual.*

Wiring diagram A drawing portraying the components and wires in a vehicle's electrical system, using standardised symbols. For more information refer to the *Haynes Automotive Electrical and Electronic Systems Manual.*

Note: *References throughout this index relate to Chapter•page number*

Haynes Manuals – The Complete List

Title	Book No.
ALFA ROMEO	
Alfa Romeo Alfasud/Sprint (74 - 88)	0292
Alfa Romeo Alfetta (73 - 87)	0531
AUDI	
Audi 80 (72 - Feb 79)	0207
Audi 80, 90 (79 - Oct 86) & Coupe (81 - Nov 88)	0605
Audi 80, 90 (Oct 86 - 90) & Coupe (Nov 88 - 90)	1491
Audi 100 (Oct 76 - Oct 82)	0428
Audi 100 (Oct 82 - 90) & 200 (Feb 84 - Oct 89)	0907
AUSTIN	
Austin Ambassador (82 - 84)	0871
Austin/MG Maestro 1.3 & 1.6 (83 - 95)	0922
Austin Maxi (69 - 81)	0052
Austin/MG Metro (80 - May 90)	0718
Austin Montego 1.3 & 1.6 (84 - 94)	1066
Austin/MG Montego 2.0 (84 - 95)	1067
Mini (59 - 69)	0527
Mini (69 - Oct 96)	0646
Austin/Rover 2.0 litre Diesel Engine (86 - 93)	1857
BEDFORD	
Bedford CF (69 - 87)	0163
Bedford Rascal (86 - 93)	3015
BL	
BL Princess & BLMC 18-22 (75 - 82)	0286
BMW	
BMW 316, 320 & 320i (4-cyl) (75 - Feb 83)	0276
BMW 320, 320i, 323i & 325i (6-cyl) (Oct 77 - Sept 87)	0815
BMW 3-Series (Apr 91 - 96)	3210
BMW 3-Series (sohc) (83 - 91)	1948
BMW 520i & 525e (Oct 81 - June 88)	1560
BMW 525, 528 & 528i (73 - Sept 81)	0632
BMW 5-Series (sohc) (81 - 93)	1948
BMW 1500, 1502, 1600, 1602, 2000 & 2002 (59 - 77)	0240
CITROEN	
Citroen 2CV, Ami & Dyane (67 - 90)	0196
Citroen AX Petrol & Diesel (87 - 94)	3014
Citroen BX (83 - 94)	0908
Citroen CX (75 - 88)	0528
Citroen Visa (79 - 88)	0620
Citroen Xantia Petrol & Diesel (93 - Oct 95)	3082
Citroen ZX Diesel (91 - 93)	1922
Citroen ZX Petrol (91 - 94)	1881
Citroen 1.7 & 1.9 litre Diesel Engine (84 - 96)	1379
COLT	
Colt 1200, 1250 & 1400 (79 - May 84)	0600
DAIMLER	
Daimler Sovereign (68 - Oct 86)	0242
Daimler Double Six (72 - 88)	0478
DATSUN (see also **Nissan**)	
Datsun 120Y (73 - Aug 78)	0228
Datsun 1300, 1400 & 1600 (69 - Aug 72)	0123
Datsun Cherry (71 - 76)	0195
Datsun Pick-up (75 - 78)	0277
Datsun Sunny (Aug 78 - May 82)	0525
Datsun Violet (78 - 82)	0430

Title	Book No.
FIAT	
Fiat 126 (73 - 87)	0305
Fiat 127 (71 - 83)	0193
Fiat 500 (57 - 73)	0090
Fiat 850 (64 - 81)	0038
Fiat Panda (81 - 95)	0793
Fiat Punto (94 - 96)	3251
Fiat Regata (84 - 88)	1167
Fiat Strada (79 - 88)	0479
Fiat Tipo (88 - 91)	1625
Fiat Uno (83 - 95)	0923
Fiat X1/9 (74 - 89)	0273
FORD	
Ford Capri II (& III) 1.6 & 2.0 (74 - 87)	0283
Ford Capri II (& III) 2.8 & 3.0 (74 - 87)	1309
Ford Cortina Mk IV (& V) 1.6 & 2.0 (76 - 83)	0343
Ford Cortina Mk IV (& V) 2.3 V6 (77 - 83)	0426
Ford Escort (75 - Aug 80)	0280
Ford Escort (Sept 80 - Sept 90)	0686
Ford Escort (Sept 90 - 97)	1737
Ford Escort Mk II Mexico, RS 1600 & RS 2000 (75 - 80)	0735
Ford Fiesta (inc. XR2) (76 - Aug 83)	0334
Ford Fiesta (inc. XR2) (Aug 83 - Feb 89)	1030
Ford Fiesta (Feb 89 - Oct 95)	1595
Ford Granada (Sept 77 - Feb 85)	0481
Ford Granada (Mar 85 - 94)	1245
Ford Mondeo 4-cyl (93 - 96)	1923
Ford Orion (83 - Sept 90)	1009
Ford Orion (Sept 90 - 93)	1737
Ford Sierra 1.3, 1.6, 1.8 & 2.0 (82 - 93)	0903
Ford Sierra 2.3, 2.8 & 2.9 (82 - 91)	0904
Ford Scorpio (Mar 85 - 94)	1245
Ford Transit Petrol (Mk 1) (65 - Feb 78)	0377
Ford Transit Petrol (Mk 2) (78 - Jan 86)	0719
Ford Transit Petrol (Mk 3) (Feb 86 - 89)	1468
Ford Transit Diesel (Feb 86 - 95)	3019
Ford 1.6 & 1.8 litre Diesel Engine (84 - 96)	1172
Ford 2.1, 2.3 & 2.5 litre Diesel Engine (77 - 90)	1606
FREIGHT ROVER	
Freight Rover Sherpa (74 - 87)	0463
HILLMAN	
Hillman Avenger (70 - 82)	0037
Hillman Minx & Husky (56 - 66)	0009
HONDA	
Honda Accord (76 - Feb 84)	0351
Honda Accord (Feb 84 - Oct 85)	1177
Honda Civic 1300 (80 - 81)	0633
Honda Civic (Feb 84 - Oct 87)	1226
Honda Civic (Nov 91 - 96)	3199
HYUNDAI	
Hyundai Pony (85 - 94)	3398
JAGUAR	
Jaguar E Type (61 - 72)	0140
Jaguar MkI & II, 240 & 340 (55 - 69)	0098
Jaguar XJ6, XJ & Sovereign (68 - Oct 86)	0242
Jaguar XJ6 & Sovereign (Oct 86 - Sept 94)	3261
Jaguar XJ12, XJS & Sovereign (72 - 88)	0478

Title	Book No.
JEEP	
Jeep Cherokee Petrol (93 - 96)	1943
LADA	
Lada 1200, 1300, 1500 & 1600 (74 - 91)	0413
Lada Samara (87 - 91)	1610
LAND ROVER	
Land Rover 90, 110 & Defender Diesel (83 - 95)	3017
Land Rover Discovery Diesel (89 - 95)	3016
Land Rover Series IIA & III Diesel (58 - 85)	0529
Land Rover Series II, IIA & III Petrol (58 - 85)	0314
MAZDA	
Mazda 323 fwd (Mar 81 - Oct 89)	1608
Mazda 626 fwd (May 83 - Sept 87)	0929
Mazda B-1600, B-1800 & B-2000 Pick-up (72 - 88)	0267
MERCEDES-BENZ	
Mercedes-Benz 190 & 190E (83 - 87)	0928
Mercedes-Benz 200, 240, 300 Diesel (Oct 76 - 85)	1114
Mercedes-Benz 250 & 280 (68 - 72)	0346
Mercedes-Benz 250 & 280 (123 Series) (Oct 76 - 84)	0677
Mercedes-Benz 124 Series (85 - Aug 93)	3253
MG	
MGB (62 - 80)	0111
MG Maestro 1.3 & 1.6 (83 - 95)	0922
MG Metro (80 - May 90)	0718
MG Midget & AH Sprite (58 - 80)	0265
MG Montego 2.0 (84 - 95)	1067
MITSUBISHI	
Mitsubishi 1200, 1250 & 1400 (79 - May 84)	0600
Mitsubishi Shogun & L200 Pick-Ups (83 - 94)	1944
MORRIS	
Morris Ital 1.3 (80 - 84)	0705
Morris Marina 1700 (78 - 80)	0526
Morris Marina 1.8 (71 - 78)	0074
Morris Minor 1000 (56 - 71)	0024
NISSAN (See also Datsun)	
Nissan Bluebird 160B & 180B rwd (May 80 - May 84)	0957
Nissan Bluebird fwd (May 84 - Mar 86)	1223
Nissan Bluebird (T12 & T72) (Mar 86 - 90)	1473
Nissan Cherry (N12) (Sept 82 - 86)	1031
Nissan Micra (K10) (83 - Jan 93)	0931
Nissan Micra (93 - 96)	3254
Nissan Primera (90 - Oct 96)	1851
Nissan Stanza (82 - 86)	0824
Nissan Sunny (B11) (May 82 - Oct 86)	0895
Nissan Sunny (Oct 86 - Mar 91)	1378
Nissan Sunny (Apr 91 - 95)	3219
OPEL	
Opel Ascona & Manta (B Series) (Sept 75 - 88)	0316
Opel Ascona (81 - 88)	3215
Opel Astra (Oct 91 - 96)	3156
Opel Corsa (83 - Mar 93)	3160
Opel Corsa (Mar 93 - 94)	3159
Opel Kadett (Nov 79 - Oct 84)	0634
Opel Kadett (Oct 84 - Oct 91)	3196
Opel Omega & Senator (86 - 94)	3157

Title	Book No.
Opel Rekord (Feb 78 - Oct 86)	0543
Opel Vectra (88 - Oct 95)	3158
PEUGEOT	
Peugeot 106 Petrol & Diesel (91 - June 96)	1882
Peugeot 205 (83 - 95)	0932
Peugeot 305 (78 - 89)	0538
Peugeot 306 Petrol & Diesel (93 - 95)	3073
Peugeot 309 (86 - 93)	1266
Peugeot 405 Petrol (88 - 96)	1559
Peugeot 405 Diesel (88 - 96)	3198
Peugeot 406 Petrol & Diesel (96 - 97)	3394
Peugeot 505 (79 - 89)	0762
Peugeot 1.7 & 1.9 litre Diesel Engines (82 - 96)	0950
Peugeot 2.0, 2.1, 2.3 & 2.5 litre Diesel Engines (74 - 90)	1607
PORSCHE	
Porsche 911 (65 - 85)	0264
Porsche 924 & 924 Turbo (76 - 85)	0397
PROTON	
Proton (89 - 97)	3255
RANGE ROVER	
Range Rover V8 (70 - Oct 92)	0606
RELIANT	
Reliant Robin & Kitten (73 - 83)	0436
RENAULT	
Renault 5 (72 - Feb 85)	0141
Renault 5 (Feb 85 - 96)	1219
Renault 9 & 11 (82 - 89)	0822
Renault 12 (70 - 80)	0097
Renault 15 & 17 (72 - 79)	0763
Renault 18 (79 - 86)	0598
Renault 19 Petrol (89 - 94)	1646
Renault 19 Diesel (89 - 95)	1946
Renault 21 (86 - 94)	1397
Renault 25 (84 - 86)	1228
Renault Clio Petrol (91 - 93)	1853
Renault Clio Diesel (91 - June 96)	3031
Renault Espace (85 - 96)	3197
Renault Fuego (80 - 86)	0764
Renault Laguna (94 - 96)	3252
ROVER	
Rover 111 & 114 (95 - 96)	1711
Rover 213 & 216 (84 - 89)	1116
Rover 214 & 414 (Oct 89 - 92)	1689
Rover 216 & 416 (Oct 89 - 92)	1830
Rover 618, 620 & 623 (93 - 97)	3257
Rover 820, 825 & 827 (86 - 95)	1380
Rover 2000, 2300 & 2600 (77 - 87)	0468
Rover 3500 (76 - 87)	0365
Rover Metro (May 90 - 94)	1711
SAAB	
Saab 90, 99 & 900 (79 - Oct 93)	0765
Saab 9000 (4-cyl) (85 - 95)	1686
SEAT	
Seat Ibiza & Malaga (85 - 92)	1609
SIMCA	
Simca 1100 & 1204 (67 - 79)	0088
Simca 1301 & 1501 (63 - 76)	0199

Title	Book No.
SKODA	
Skoda Estelle 105, 120, 130 & 136 (77 - 89)	0604
Skoda Favorit (89 - 92)	1801
SUBARU	
Subaru 1600 (77 - Oct 79)	0237
Subaru 1600 & 1800 (Nov 79 - 90)	0995
SUZUKI	
Suzuki SJ Series, Samurai & Vitara (82 - 97)	1942
Suzuki Supercarry (86 - Oct 94)	3015
TALBOT	
Talbot Alpine, Solara, Minx & Rapier (75 - 86)	0337
Talbot Horizon (78 - 86)	0473
Talbot Samba (82 - 86)	0823
TOYOTA	
Toyota Carina E (May 92 - 97)	3256
Toyota Celica (Feb 82 - Sept 85)	1135
Toyota Corolla (fwd) (Sept 83 - Sept 87)	1024
Toyota Corolla (rwd) (80 - 85)	0683
Toyota Corolla (Sept 87 - 92)	1683
Toyota Corolla (Aug 92 - 97)	3259
Toyota Hi-Ace & Hi-Lux (69 - Oct 83)	0304
Toyota Starlet (78 - Jan 85)	0462
TRIUMPH	
Triumph Acclaim (81 - 84)	0792
Triumph Herald (59 - 71)	0010
Triumph Spitfire (62 - 81)	0113
Triumph Stag (70 - 78)	0441
Triumph TR7 (75 - 82)	0322
VAUXHALL	
Vauxhall Astra (80 - Oct 84)	0635
Vauxhall Astra & Belmont (Oct 84 - Oct 91)	1136
Vauxhall Astra (Oct 91 - 96)	1832
Vauxhall Carlton (Oct 78 - Oct 86)	0480
Vauxhall Carlton (Nov 86 - 94)	1469
Vauxhall Cavalier 1300 (77 - July 81)	0461
Vauxhall Cavalier 1600, 1900 & 2000 (75 - July 81)	0315
Vauxhall Cavalier (81 - Oct 88)	0812
Vauxhall Cavalier (Oct 88 - Oct 95)	1570
Vauxhall Chevette (75 - 84)	0285
Vauxhall Corsa (Mar 93 - 94)	1985
Vauxhall Nova (83 - 93)	0909
Vauxhall Rascal (86 - 93)	3015
Vauxhall Senator (Sept 87 - 94)	1469
Vauxhall Viva HB Series (ohv) (66 - 70)	0026
Vauxhall Viva & Firenza (ohc) (68 - 73)	0093
Vauxhall/Opel 1.5, 1.6 & 1.7 litre Diesel Engines (82 - 96)	1222
VOLKSWAGEN	
VW Beetle 1200 (54 - 77)	0036
VW Beetle 1300 & 1500 (65 - 75)	0039
VW Beetle 1302 & 1302S (70 - 72)	0110
VW Beetle 1303, 1303S & GT (72 - 75)	0159
VW Golf Mk 1 1.1 & 1.3 (74 - Feb 84)	0716
VW Golf Mk 1 1.5, 1.6 & 1.8 (74 - 85)	0726
VW Golf Mk 1 Diesel (78 - Feb 84)	0451
VW Golf Mk 2 (Mar 84 - Feb 92)	1081
VW Golf Mk 3 Petrol & Diesel (Feb 92 - 96)	3097

Title	Book No.
VW Jetta Mk 1 1.1 & 1.3 (80 - June 84)	0716
VW Jetta Mk 1 1.5, 1.6 & 1.8 (80 - June 84)	0726
VW Jetta Mk 1 Diesel (81 - June 84)	0451
VW Jetta Mk 2 (July 84 - 92)	1081
VW LT vans & light trucks (76 - 87)	0637
VW Passat (Sept 81 - May 88)	0814
VW Passat (May 88 - 91)	1647
VW Polo & Derby (76 - Jan 82)	0335
VW Polo (82 - Oct 90)	0813
VW Polo (Nov 90 - Aug 94)	3245
VW Santana (Sept 82 - 85)	0814
VW Scirocco Mk 1 1.5, 1.6 & 1.8 (74 - 82)	0726
VW Scirocco (82 - 90)	1224
VW Transporter 1600 (68 - 79)	0082
VW Transporter 1700, 1800 & 2000 (72 - 79)	0226
VW Transporter with air-cooled engine (79 - 82)	0638
VW Type 3 (63 - 73)	0084
VW Vento Petrol & Diesel (Feb 92 - 96)	3097
VOLVO	
Volvo 66 & 343, Daf 55 & 66 (68 - 79)	0293
Volvo 142, 144 & 145 (66 - 74)	0129
Volvo 240 Series (74 - 93)	0270
Volvo 262, 264 & 260/265 (75 - 85)	0400
Volvo 340, 343, 345 & 360 (76 - 91)	0715
Volvo 440, 460 & 480 (87 - 92)	1691
Volvo 740 & 760 (82 - 91)	1258
Volvo 850 (92 - 96)	3260
Volvo 940 (90 - 96)	3249
YUGO/ZASTAVA	
Yugo/Zastava (81 - 90)	1453

TECH BOOKS	
Automotive Brake Manual	3050
Carburettor Manual	3288
Diesel Engine Service Guide	3286
Automotive Electrical & Electronic Systems	3049
Automotive Engine Management and Fuel Injection Manual	3344
In-Car Entertainment Manual	3363
Automotive Tools Manual	3052
Automotive Welding Manual	3053

CAR BOOKS	
Automotive Fuel Injection Systems	9755
Car Bodywork Repair Manual	9864
Caravan Manual (2nd Edition)	9894
Haynes Technical Data Book (88 - 97)	1997
How to Keep Your Car Alive	9868
Japanese Vehicle Carburettors	1786
Small Engine Repair Manual	1755
SU Carburettors	0299
Weber Carburettors (to 79)	0393

C6684.CL04.04/97

Preserving Our Motoring Heritage

< The Model J Duesenberg Derham Tourster. Only eight of these magnificent cars were ever built – this is the only example to be found outside the United States of America

Almost every car you've ever loved, loathed or desired is gathered under one roof at the Haynes Motor Museum. Over 300 immaculately presented cars and motorbikes represent every aspect of our motoring heritage, from elegant reminders of bygone days, such as the superb Model J Duesenberg to curiosities like the bug-eyed BMW Isetta. There are also many old friends and flames. Perhaps you remember the 1959 Ford Popular that you did your courting in? The magnificent 'Red Collection' is a spectacle of classic sports cars including AC, Alfa Romeo, Austin Healey, Ferrari, Lamborghini, Maserati, MG, Riley, Porsche and Triumph.

A Perfect Day Out

Each and every vehicle at the Haynes Motor Museum has played its part in the history and culture of Motoring. Today, they make a wonderful spectacle and a great day out for all the family. Bring the kids, bring Mum and Dad, but above all bring your camera to capture those golden memories for ever. You will also find an impressive array of motoring memorabilia, a comfortable 70 seat video cinema and one of the most extensive transport book shops in Britain. The Pit Stop Cafe serves everything from a cup of tea to wholesome, home-made meals or, if you prefer, you can enjoy the large picnic area nestled in the beautiful rural surroundings of Somerset.

> John Haynes O.B.E., Founder and Chairman of the museum at the wheel of a Haynes Light 12.

< Graham Hill's Lola Cosworth Formula 1 car next to a 1934 Riley Sports.

The Museum is situated on the A359 Yeovil to Frome road at Sparkford, just off the A303 in Somerset. It is about 40 miles south of Bristol, and 25 minutes drive from the M5 intersection at Taunton.

Open 9.30am - 5.30pm (10.00am - 4.00pm Winter) 7 days a week, *except Christmas Day, Boxing Day and New Years Day*

Special rates available for schools, coach parties and outings Charitable Trust No. 292048